MOSIOATUNYA, OR VICTORIA FALLS) AND OF THE
HICH THE RIVER ESCAPES.

BIRD'S-EYE VIEW OF THE GREAT CATARACTS OF THE ZAMBESI (CALLE
ZIGZAG CHASM BELOW THE FALLS THROUGH W

NARRATIVE

OF AN

EXPEDITION TO THE ZAMBESI

AND ITS TRIBUTARIES;

AND OF THE DISCOVERY OF THE LAKES SHIRWA
AND NYASSA.

1858—1864.

By DAVID and CHARLES LIVINGSTONE.

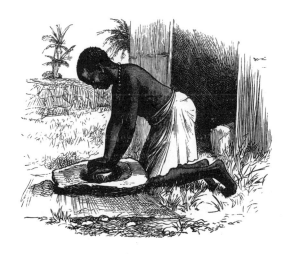

WITH MAP AND ILLUSTRATIONS.

LONDON:

JOHN MURRAY, ALBEMARLE STREET.

1865.

The right of Translation is reserved.

JOHNSON REPRINT CORPORATION

New York • London

1971

Library of Congress Catalog Card Number: 72-148595

Landmarks in Anthropology, a series of reprints in cultural anthropology
General Editor: Weston La Barre

First reprinting 1971, Johnson Reprint Corporation

Johnson Reprint Corporation
111 Fifth Avenue
New York, N.Y. 10003, U.S.A.

Johnson Reprint Company Ltd.
Berkeley Square House
London, W1X6BA, England

Printed in the U.S.A.

TO

THE RIGHT HON. LORD PALMERSTON,

K.G., G.C.B.

My Lord,

I beg leave to dedicate this Volume to your Lordship, as a tribute justly due to the great Statesman who has ever had at heart the amelioration of the African race; and as a token of admiration of the beneficial effects of that policy which he has so long laboured to establish on the West Coast of Africa; and which, in improving that region, has most forcibly shown the need of some similar system on the opposite side of the Continent.

DAVID LIVINGSTONE.

PREFACE.

——◆◇◆——

IT has been my object in this work to give as clear an account as I was able of tracts of country previously unexplored, with their river systems, natural productions, and capabilities; and to bring before my countrymen, and all others interested in the cause of humanity, the misery entailed by the slave-trade in its inland phases; a subject on which I and my companions are the first who have had any opportunities of forming a judgment. The eight years spent in Africa, since my last work was published, have not, I fear, improved my power of writing English; but I hope that, whatever my descriptions want in clearness, or literary skill, may in a measure be compensated by the novelty of the scenes described, and the additional information afforded on that curse of Africa, and that shame, even now, in the 19th century, of an European nation,—the slave-trade.

I took the "Lady Nyassa" to Bombay for the express purpose of selling her, and might without any difficulty have done so; but with the thought of parting with her arose, more strongly than ever, the feeling of disinclination to abandon the East Coast of Africa to the Portuguese and slave-trading, and I determined to run home and consult my friends before I allowed the little vessel to pass from my hands. After, therefore, having put two Ajawa lads to school under the eminent Missionary the Rev. Dr. Wilson, and having provided satisfactorily for the native crew, I started homewards with the three white sailors, and reached London July 20th,

b

1864. Mr. and Mrs. Webb, my much-loved friends, wrote
to Bombay inviting me, in the event of my coming to England, to make Newstead Abbey my headquarters, and on
my arrival renewed their invitation: and though, when
I accepted it, I had no intention of remaining so long
with my kind-hearted generous friends, I stayed with them
until April, 1865, and under their roof transcribed from my
own and my brother's journal the whole of this present book.
It is with heartfelt gratitude I would record their unwearied
kindness. My acquaintance with Mr. Webb began in Africa,
where he was a daring and successful hunter, and his continued friendship is most valuable, because he has seen
missionary work, and he would not accord his respect and
esteem to me had he not believed that I, and my brethren
also, were to be looked on as honest men earnestly trying
to do our duty.

The Government have supported the proposal of the Royal
Geographical Society made by my friend Sir Roderick Murchison, and have united with that body to aid me in another
attempt to open Africa to civilizing influences, and a valued
private friend has given a thousand pounds for the same object.
I propose to go inland, north of the territory which the Portuguese in Europe claim, and endeavour to commence that
system on the East which has been so eminently successful
on the West Coast; a system combining the repressive efforts
of H.M. cruisers with lawful trade and Christian Missions—
the moral and material results of which have been so gratifying. I hope to ascend the Rovuma, or some other river
North of Cape Delgado, and, in addition to my other work,
shall strive, by passing along the Northern end of Lake
Nyassa and round the Southern end of Lake Tanganyika, to
ascertain the watershed of that part of Africa. In so doing,
I have no wish to unsettle what with so much toil and danger

was accomplished by Speke and Grant, but rather to confirm their illustrious discoveries.

I have to acknowledge the obliging readiness of Lord Russell in lending me the drawings taken by the artist who was in the first instance attached to the Expedition. These sketches, with photographs by Charles Livingstone and Dr. Kirk, have materially assisted in the illustrations. I would also very sincerely thank my friends Professor Owen and Mr. Oswell for many valuable hints and other aid in the preparation of this volume.

Newstead Abbey,
  April 16, 1865.

POSTSCRIPT TO PREFACE.

The credit which I was fain to award to the Lisbon statesmen for a sincere desire to put an end to the slave-trade, is, I regret to find, totally undeserved. They have employed one Mons. Lacerda, to try to extinguish the facts adduced by me before the meeting of the " British Association for the Advancement of Science," at Bath, by a series of papers in the Portuguese Official Journal ; and their Minister for Foreign Affairs has since devoted some of the funds of his Government to the translation and circulation of Mons. Lacerda's articles in the form of an English tract. Nothing is more conspicuous in this official document than the extreme ignorance displayed of the geography of the country of which they pretend that they possess not only the knowledge, but also the dominion. A vague rumour, cited by some old author, about two marshes below Murchison's Cataracts, is considered conclusive evidence that the ancient inhabitants of Senna, a village on the Zambesi, found no difficulty in navigating the Shire to Lake Nyassa up what modern travellers find to be an ascent of 1200 feet in 35 miles of latitude. A broad shallow lake, with a strong current, which Senhor Candido declared he had visited N.W. of Tette, is assumed to be the narrow deep Lake Nyassa, without current, and about N.N.E. of the same point. Great offence is also taken because the discovery of the main sources of the Nile has been ascribed to Speke and Grant, instead of to Ptolemy and F. Lobo.

But the main object of the Portuguese Government is not geographical. It is to bolster up that pretence to power which has been the only obstacle to the establishment of lawful commerce and friendly relations with the native inhabitants of Eastern Africa. The following work contains abundant confirmation of all that was advanced by me at the Bath meeting of the British Association; and I may here add that it is this unwarranted assumption of power over 1360 miles of coast—from English River to Cape Delgado, where the Portuguese have in fact little real authority —which perpetuates the barbarism of the inhabitants. The Portuguese interdict all foreign commerce, except at a very few points where they have established custom-houses, and even at these, by an exaggerated and obstructive tariff and differential duties, they completely shut out the natives from any trade, except that in slaves.

Looking from South to North, let us glance at the enormous seaboard which the Portuguese in Europe endeavour to make us believe belongs to them. Delagoa Bay has a small fort called Lorenzo Marques, but nothing beyond the walls. At Inhambane they hold a small strip of land by sufferance of the natives. Sofala is in ruins, and from Quillimane northwards for 690 miles, they have only one small stockade, protected by an armed launch in the mouth of the River Angoxa to prevent foreign vessels from trading there. Then at Mosambique they have the little island on which the fort stands, and a strip about three miles long on the mainland, on which they have a few farms, which are protected from hostility only by paying the natives an annual tribute, which they call "having the blacks in their pay." The settlement has long been declining in trade and importance. It is garrisoned by a few hundred sickly soldiers shut up in the fort, and even with a small coral island near can hardly be called secure. On the island of Oibo, or Iboe, an immense number of slaves are collected, but there is little trade of any kind. At Pomba Bay a small fort was made, but it is very doubtful whether it still exists; the attempt to form a settlement there having entirely failed. They pay tribute to the Zulus, for the lands they cultivate on the right bank of the Zambesi; and the general effect of the pretence to power and obstruction to commerce, is to drive the independent native chiefs to the Arab dhow slave-trade, as the only one open to them.

It is well known to the English Government, from reliable documents at the Admiralty and Foreign Office, that no longer ago than November, 1864, two months after my speech was delivered at Bath, when the punishment of the perpetrators of an outrage on the crew of the cutter of H.M.S. "Lyra," near a river 45 miles S.W. of Mosambique, was demanded by H.M.S. "Wasp," at Mosambique, the present Governor-General declared that he had no power over the natives there. They have never been subdued, and being a fine energetic race, would readily enter into commercial treaties with foreigners, were it not for the false assertion of power by which the Portuguese, with the tacit consent of

European Governments, shut them out from commerce and every civilizing influence.

This Portuguese pretence to dominion is the curse of the negro race on the East Coast of Africa, and it would soon fall to the ground, were it not for the moral support it derives from the respect paid to it by our own flag. The Emperor Napoleon III. disregarded it in the case of the "Charles et Georges," while only by the aid of English sailors has the Government of Mosambique, on more than one occasion, been saved from being overturned. Our squadron on the East Coast costs over 70,000*l.* a year, and, by our acquiescence in the sham sovereignty of the Portuguese, we effect only a partial suppression of the slave-trade, and none of the commercial benefits which have followed direct dealing with the natives on the West Coast. A new law for the abolition of slavery has been proposed by the King of Portugal; but it inspires me with no confidence, as no means have ever been taken to put similar enactments already passed into execution, and we can only view this as a new bid for still further acquiescence in a system which perpetuates barbarism. Mons. Lacerda has unwittingly shown, by his eager advocacy, that the real sentiments of his employers are decidedly pro-slavery. The great fact that the Americans have rid themselves of the incubus of slavery, and will probably not tolerate the continuance of the murderous slave-trade by the Portuguese nation, has done more to elicit their king's recent speech than the opinions of his ministry.

CONTENTS.

CHAPTER VI.

CHAPTER VII.

CHAPTER VIII.

CHAPTER IX.

CHAPTER X.

CHAPTER XI.

CHAPTER XII.

CHAPTER XIII.

CHAPTER XIV.

CHAPTER XV.

CHAPTER XVI.

CHAPTER XVII.

CHAPTER XVIII.

CHAPTER XIX.

CHAPTER XX.

CHAPTER XXI.

CHAPTER XXII.

CHAPTER XXIII.

CHAPTER XXIV.

CHAPTER XXV.

CHAPTER XXVI.

CHAPTER XXVII.

CHAPTER XXVIII.

CHAPTER XXIX.

LIST OF ILLUSTRATIONS.

THE

ZAMBESI AND ITS TRIBUTARIES.

INTRODUCTION.

WHEN first I determined on publishing the narrative of
my 'Missionary Travels,' I had a great misgiving as to
whether the criticism my endeavours might provoke would
be friendly or the reverse, more particularly as I felt that I
had then been so long a sojourner in the wilderness, as to be
quite a stranger to the British public.   But I am now in this,
my second essay at authorship, cheered by the conviction that
very many readers, who are personally unknown to me, will
receive this narrative with the kindly consideration and
allowances of friends; and that many more, under the
genial influences of an innate love of liberty, and of a
desire to see the same social and religious blessings they
themselves enjoy, disseminated throughout the world, will
sympathize with me in the efforts by which I have striven,

B

however imperfectly, to elevate the position and character of our fellow-men in Africa. This knowledge makes me doubly anxious to render my narrative acceptable to all my readers ; but, in the absence of any excellence in literary composition, the natural consequence of my pursuits, I have to offer only a simple account of a mission which, with respect to the objects proposed to be thereby accomplished, formed a noble contrast to some of the earlier expeditions to Eastern Africa. I believe that the information it will give, respecting the people visited and the countries traversed, will not be materially gainsaid by any future commonplace traveller like myself, who may be blest with fair health and a gleam of sunshine in his breast. This account is written in the earnest hope that it may contribute to that information which will yet cause the great and fertile continent of Africa to be no longer kept wantonly sealed, but made available as the scene of European enterprise, and will enable its people to take a place among the nations of the earth, thus securing the happiness and prosperity of tribes now sunk in barbarism or debased by slavery ; and, above all, I cherish the hope that it may lead to the introduction of the blessings of the Gospel.

The first expedition sent to East Africa, after the Portuguese had worked a passage round the Cape, was instituted under the auspices of the Government of Portugal, for the purpose, it is believed, of discovering the land of Ophir, made mention of in Holy Scripture as the country whence King Solomon obtained sandal-wood, ivory, apes, peacocks, and gold. The terms used by the Jews to express the first four articles had, according to Max Müller, no existence in the Hebrew language, but were words imported into it from the Sanscrit. It is curious then, that the search was not directed to the Coast of India,—more particularly as Sanscrit was known on the Malabar Coast,—and there also peacocks and sandal-wood are met with in abundance. The Portuguese, like some others of more modern times, were led to believe that Sofalla, because sometimes pronounced Zophar by the Arabs, from being the lowest or most southerly port they visited, was identical with the Ophir alluded to in Sacred History.

Eastern Africa had been occupied from the most remote times by traders from India and the Red Sea. Vasco da Gama, in 1497-8, found them firmly established at Mosambique, and, after reaching India, he turned with longing eyes from Calicut towards Sofalla, and actually visited it in 1502. As the Scriptural Ophir, it was expected to be the most lucrative of all the Portuguese stations; and, under the impression that an important settlement could be established there, the Portuguese conquered, at great loss of both men and money, the district in which the gold-washings were situated; but, in the absence of all proper machinery, a vast amount of labour returned so small an amount of gain, that they abandoned them in disgust.

The next expedition, consisting of three ships and a thousand men, mostly gentlemen volunteers, left Lisbon in 1569 for the conquest of the gold mines or washings of the Chief of Monomotapa, west of Tette, and of those in Manica, still further west, but in a more southerly direction; and also to find a route to the west coast. In this last object they failed; and to this day it has been accomplished by only one European, and that an Englishman. The expedition was commanded by Francisco Barreto, and abundantly supplied with horses, asses, camels, and provisions. Ascending the Zambesi as far as Senna, they found many Arab and other traders already settled there, who received the strangers with great hospitality. The horses, however,

having passed through a district abounding with tsetse, an
insect whose bite is fatal to domestic animals, soon showed
the emaciation peculiar to the poison; and Senna being
notoriously unhealthy, the sickness of both men and horses
aroused Barreto's suspicion that poison had been administered by the inhabitants, most of whom, consequently, he
put to the sword or blew away from his guns. Marching
beyond Senna with a party five hundred and sixty strong, he
and his men suffered terribly from hunger and thirst, and,
after being repeatedly assaulted by a large body of natives,
the expedition was compelled to return without ever reaching
the gold-mines which Barreto so eagerly sought.

Previous to this, however, devoted Roman Catholic missionaries had penetrated where an army could not go; for
Senhor Bordalo, in his excellent Historical Essays, mentions
that the Jesuit father Gonçalo da Silveira had already
suffered martyrdom by command of the Chief of Monomotapa.
Indeed, missionaries of that body of Christians established
themselves in a vast number of places in Eastern Africa, as
the ruins of mission stations still testify; but, not having succeeded in meeting with any reliable history of the labours of
these good men, it is painful for me to be unable to contradict
the calumnies which Portuguese writers still heap on their
memory. So far as the impression left on the native mind
goes, it is decidedly favourable to their zeal and piety; while
the writers referred to roundly assert that the missionaries
engaged in the slave-trade; which is probably as false as the
more modern scandals occasionally retailed against their
Protestant brethren. Philanthropists sometimes err in accepting the mere gossip of coast villages as facts, when
asserting the atrocities of our countrymen abroad; while
others, pretending to regard all philanthropy as weakness,

yet practising that silliest of all hypocrisies, the endeavour to appear worse than they are, accept and publish the mere brandy-and-water twaddle of immoral traders, against a body of men who, as a whole, are an honour to human kind. In modern missionary literature, now widely spread, we have a record which will probably outlive all misrepresentation; and it is much to be regretted that there is no available Catholic literature of the same nature, and that none of the translations which may have been made into the native tongues can now be consulted. We cannot believe that these good men would risk their lives for the unholy gains which, even were they lawful, by the rules of their order they could not enjoy; but it would be extremely interesting to all their successors to know exactly what were the real causes of their failure in perpetuating the faith.

In order that the following narrative may be clearly under-stood, it is necessary to call to mind some things which took place previous to the Zambesi Expedition being sent out. Most geographers are aware that, before the discovery of Lake Ngami and the well watered country in which the Makololo dwell, the idea prevailed that a large part of the interior of Africa consisted of sandy deserts, into which rivers ran and were lost. During my journey in 1852-6, from sea to sea, across the south intertropical part of the continent, it was found to be a well watered country, with large tracts of fine fertile soil covered with forest, and beautiful grassy valleys, occupied by a considerable population; and one of the most wonderful waterfalls in the world was brought to light. The peculiar form of the continent was then ascertained to be an elevated plateau, somewhat depressed in the centre, and with fissures in the sides by which the rivers escaped to the sea; and this great fact in physical geography can never be referred to without calling to mind the remarkable hypothesis by which the distinguished President of the Royal Geographical Society (Sir Roderick I. Murchison) clearly indicated this peculiarity, before it was verified by actual observation of the altitudes of the country and by the courses of the rivers. New light was thrown on other portions of the continent by the famous travels of Dr. Barth, by the researches of the Church of England Missionaries Krapf, Erkhardt, and Rebman, by the persevering efforts of Dr. Baikie, the last martyr to the climate and English enterprise, by the journey of Francis Galton, and by the most interesting discoveries of Lakes Tanganyika and Victoria Nyanza by Captain Burton, and by Captain Speke, whose untimely end we all so deeply deplore. Then followed the researches of Van der Decken, Thornton, and others; and last of all the grand discovery of the main source of the Nile, which every Englishman must feel an honest pride in knowing was accomplished by our gallant countrymen, Speke and Grant. The fabulous torrid zone, of parched and burning sand, was now proved to be a well watered region resembling North America in its fresh-water lakes, and India in its hot humid lowlands, jungles, ghauts, and cool highland plains.

In our exploration the chief object in view was not to discover objects of nine days' wonder, to gaze and be gazed at by barbarians; but to note the climate, the natural productions, the local diseases, the natives and their relation to the rest of the world; all which were observed with that peculiar interest which, as regards the future, the first white man cannot but feel in a continent whose history is only just beginning. When proceeding to the West Coast, in order to find a path to the sea by which lawful commerce might be introduced to aid missionary operations, it was quite striking to observe, several hundreds of miles from the ocean, the very decided influence of that which is known as Lord Palmerston's policy. Piracy had been abolished, and the slave-trade so far suppressed, that it was spoken of by Portuguese, who had themselves been slave-traders, as a thing of the past. Lawful commerce had increased from an annual total of 20,000l. in ivory and gold-dust, to between two and three millions, of which one million was in palm oil to our own country. Over twenty Missions had been established, with schools, in which more than twelve thousand pupils were taught. Life and property were rendered secure on the Coast, and comparative peace imparted to millions of people in the interior, and all this at a time when, by the speeches of influential men in England, the world was given to understand that the English cruisers had done nothing but aggravate the evils of the slave-trade. It is so reasonable to expect that self-interest would induce the slave-trader to do his utmost to preserve the lives by which he makes his gains, that men yielded ready credence to the plausible theory; but the atrocious waste of human life was just as great when the slave-trade was legal; it always has been, and must be, marked by the want of foresight characteristic of the murderer. Every one wonders why he, who has taken another's life, did not take this, that, or the other precaution to avoid detection; and every one may well wonder why slave-traders have always, by over-crowding and all its evils, acted so much in direct opposition to their own interests, but it is the fatality of the murderer; the loss of life from this cause, simply baffles exaggeration.

On this subject the opinion of the Rev. J. L. Wilson, a most intelligent American Missionary, who has written by

far the ablest work on the West Coast that has yet appeared,
is worth a host. He declares that the efforts of the English
Government are worthy of all praise. Had it not been for
the cruisers, and especially those of England, Africa would
still have been inaccessible to missionary labour; "and it is
devoutly to be hoped," he adds, " that these noble and disinterested measures may not be relaxed until the foul demon
be driven away from the earth." The slave-trade is the
greatest obstacle in existence to civilization and commercial
progress; and as the English are the most philanthropic
people in the world, and will probably always have the
largest commercial stake in the African continent, the policy
for its suppression in every possible way shows thorough
wisdom and foresight.

When, in pursuit of the same object, the East Coast was
afterwards reached, it was found sealed up. Although praiseworthy efforts had been made by Her Majesty's cruisers,
yet in consequence of foreigners being debarred from
entering the country, neither traders nor missionaries had
established themselves. The trade was still only in a
little ivory, gold-dust, and slaves, just as it was on the West
Coast, before Lord Palmerston's policy came into operation
there. It was, however, subsequently discovered that the
Portuguese Government professed itself willing, nay anxious,
to let the country be opened to the influences of civilization
and lawful commerce—indeed it could scarcely be otherwise,
seeing that not a grain of benefit ever accrued to Portugal by
shutting it up;—and the Zambesi, a large river, promised
to be a fine inlet to the highlands and interior generally;
the natives were agricultural, and all fond of trading; the
soil was fertile—indigo, cotton, tobacco, sugar-cane, and other
articles of value, were already either cultivated or growing

wild. It seemed, therefore, that if this region could be opened to lawful commerce and Christian Missions, it would have the effect of aiding or supplementing our cruisers in the same way as had been done by the missionaries and traders on the West Coast, and that an inestimable service would be thereby rendered to Africa and Europe.

The main object of the Zambesi Expedition, as our instructions from Her Majesty's Government explicitly stated, was to extend the knowledge already attained of the geography and mineral and agricultural resources of Eastern and Central Africa—to improve our acquaintance with the inhabitants, and to endeavour to engage them to apply themselves to industrial pursuits and to the cultivation of their lands, with a view to the production of raw material to be exported to England in return for British manufactures; and it was hoped, that, by encouraging the natives to occupy themselves in the development of the resources of the country, a considerable advance might be made towards the extinction of the slave-trade, as they would not be long in discovering that the former would eventually be a more certain source of profit than the latter. The Expedition was sent in accordance with the settled policy of the English Government; and the Earl of Clarendon, being then at the head of the Foreign Office, the Mission was organized under his immediate care. When a change of Government ensued, we experienced the same generous countenance and sympathy from the Earl of Malmesbury, as we had previously received from Lord Clarendon; and, on the accession of Earl Russell to the high office he has so long filled, we were always favoured with equally ready attention and the same prompt assistance. Thus the conviction was produced that our work embodied the principles, not of any one party, but of the hearts of the statesmen and of the people of England generally. The Expedition owes great obligations to the Lords of the Admiralty for their unvarying readiness to render us every assistance in their power; and to the warm-hearted and ever-obliging hydrographer to the Admiralty, the late Admiral Washington, as a subordinate, but most effective agent, our heartfelt gratitude is also due; and we must ever thankfully acknowledge that our efficiency was mainly due to the kind services of Admirals Sir Frederick Grey, Sir Baldwin Walker, and all the naval officers serving under them on the East Coast. Nor must I omit to record our obligations to Mr. Skead, R.N. The Luawe was carefully sounded and surveyed by this officer, whose skilful and zealous labours, both on that river, and afterwards on the Lower Zambesi, were deserving of all praise.

In speaking of what has been done by the Expedition, it should always be understood that Dr. Kirk, Mr. Charles Livingstone, Mr. R. Thornton, and others composed it. In using the plural number they are meant, and I wish to bear testimony to the untiring zeal, energy, courage, and perseverance with which my companions laboured; undaunted by difficulties, dangers, or hard fare. It is my firm belief that, were their services required in any other capacity, they might be implicitly relied on to perform their duty like men. The reason why Dr. Kirk's name does not appear on the title-page of this narrative is, because it is hoped that he may give an account of the botany and natural history of the Expedition in a separate work from his own pen. He collected above four thousand species of plants, specimens of most of the valuable woods, of the different native manufactures, of the articles of food, and of the different kinds of cotton from every spot we visited, and a great variety of birds and insects; besides making meteorological observations, and affording, as our instructions required, medical assistance to the natives in every case where he could be of any use.

Charles Livingstone was also fully occupied in his duties in following out the general objects of our mission, in encouraging the culture of cotton, in making many magnetic and meteorological observations, in photographing so long as the materials would serve, and in collecting a large number of birds, insects, and other objects of interest. The collections, being Government property, have been forwarded to the British Museum, and to the Royal Botanic Gardens at Kew; and, should Dr. Kirk undertake their description, three or four years will be required for the purpose.

Though collections were made, it was always distinctly understood that, however desirable these and our explorations might be, " Her Majesty's Government attached more importance to the moral influence that might be exerted on the minds of the natives by a well regulated and orderly household of Europeans setting an example of consistent moral conduct to all who might witness it; treating the people with kindness, and relieving their wants, teaching them to make experiments in agriculture, explaining to them the more simple arts, imparting to them religious instruction as far as they are capable of receiving it, and inculcating peace and good will to each other."

It would be tiresome to enumerate in detail all the little acts which were performed by us while following out our instructions. As a rule, whenever the steamer stopped to take in wood, or for any other purpose, Dr. Kirk and Charles Livingstone went ashore to their duties: one of our party, who it was intended should navigate the vessel and lay down the geographical positions, having failed to answer the expectations formed of him, these duties fell chiefly to my share. They involved a considerable amount of night work, in which I was always cheerfully aided by my companions, and the results were regularly communicated to our warm and ever-ready friend, Sir Thomas Maclear of the Royal Observatory, Cape of Good Hope. While this work was going through the press, we were favoured with the longitudes of several stations determined from observed occultations of stars by the moon, and from eclipses and reappearances of Jupiter's satellites, by Mr. Mann, the able Assistant to the Cape Astronomer Royal; the lunars are still in the hands of Mr. G. W. H. Maclear of the same Observatory. In addition to these, the altitudes, variation of the compass, latitudes and longitudes, as calculated on the spot, appear in the map by Mr. Arrowsmith, and it is hoped may not differ much from the results of the same data in abler hands. The office of "skipper," which, rather than let the Expedition come to a stand, I undertook, required no great ability in one "not too old to learn:" it saved a salary, and, what was much more valuable than gold, saved the Expedition from the drawback of any one thinking that he was indispensable to its further progress. The office required attention to the vessel both at rest and in motion. It also involved considerable exposure to the sun; and to my regret kept me from much anticipated intercourse with the natives, and the formation of full vocabularies of their dialects.

I may add that all wearisome repetitions are as much as possible avoided in the narrative; and, our movements and operations having previously been given in a series of despatches, the attempt is now made to give as fairly as possible just what would most strike any person of ordinary intelligence in passing through the country. For the sake of the freshness which usually attaches to first impressions, the Journal of Charles Livingstone has been incorporated in the narrative; and many remarks made by the natives, which he put down at the moment of translation, will convey to others the same ideas as they did to ourselves. Some are no doubt trivial; but it is by the little acts and words of every-day life that character is truly and best known. And doubtless many will prefer to draw their own conclusions from them rather than to be schooled by us.

CHAPTER I.

THE Expedition left England on the 10th of March, 1858, in Her Majesty's Colonial Steamer " Pearl," commanded by Captain Duncan ; and, after enjoying the generous hospitality of our friends at Cape Town, with the obliging attentions of Sir George Grey, and receiving on board Mr. Francis Skead, R.N., as surveyor, we reached the East Coast in the following May.

Our first object was to explore the Zambesi, its mouths and tributaries, with a view to their being used as highways for commerce and Christianity to pass into the vast interior of Africa. When we came within five or six miles of the land, the yellowish-green tinge of the sea in soundings was suddenly succeeded by muddy water with wrack, as of a river in flood. The two colours did not intermingle, but the line of contact was as sharply defined as when the ocean meets the land. It was observed that under the wrack—consisting of reeds, sticks, and leaves,—and even under floating cuttlefish bones and Portuguese "men-of-war" (Physalia), numbers of small fish screen themselves from the eyes of birds of prey, and from the rays of the torrid sun.

The coast is low and covered with mangrove swamps, among which are sandy patches clothed with grass, creeping plants, and stunted palms. The land trends nearly east and west, without any notable feature to guide the navigator, and it is difficult to make out the river's mouth; but the water shoals gradually, and each fathom of lessening depth marks about a mile.

We entered the River Luawe first, because its entrance is so smooth and deep, that the "Pearl," drawing 9 feet 7 inches, went in without a boat sounding ahead. A small steam launch having been brought out from England in three sections on the deck of the "Pearl" was hoisted out and screwed together at the anchorage, and with her aid the exploration was commenced. She was called the "Ma Robert," after Mrs. Livingstone, to whom the natives, according to their custom, gave the name Ma (mother) of her eldest son. The harbour is deep, but shut in by mangrove swamps; and though the water a few miles up is fresh, it is only a tidal river; for, after ascending some seventy miles, it was found to end in marshes blocked up with reeds and succulent aquatic plants. As the Luawe had been called " West Luabo," it was supposed to be a branch of the Zambesi, the main stream of which is called "Luabo," or "East Luabo." The "Ma Robert" and "Pearl" then went to what proved to be a real mouth of the river we sought.

The Zambesi pours its water into the ocean by four mouths, namely, the Milambe, which is the most westerly the Kongone, the Luabo, and the Timbwe (or Muselo).

When the river is in flood, a natural canal running parallel with the coast, and winding very much among the swamps, forms a secret way for conveying slaves from Quillimane to the bays Massangano and Nameara, or to the Zambesi itself. The Kwakwa, or river of Quillimane, some sixty miles distant from the mouths of the Zambesi, has long been represented as the principal entrance to the Zambesi, in order, as the Portuguese now maintain, that the English cruisers might be induced to watch the false mouth, while slaves were quietly shipped from the true one ; and strange to say this error has lately been propagated by a map issued by the colonial minister of Portugal.*

---

* Stranger still, the Portuguese official paper, "Annaes do Conselho Ultramarinho" for 1864 shamelessly asserts that "in that harbour (Kongone), which Dr. Livingstone says he discovered, many vessels with slaves have taken refuge from the persecutions of English cruisers." This (shall we admit?) was known to the Portuguese Government! Would any other gentleman in Europe construct a map such as that mentioned in the text, and send it to the English Government as showing the *true* mouth of the Zambesi ? We did not think of printing the following letter from one Portuguese official to another in Africa, till we saw the poor swagger of the Lisbon official paper, evidently intended for other statesmen in Europe. The editor of a Cape paper says—

"Chevalier Duprat has, by the same opportunity, received a communication from the Portuguese governor of Tette, of which the following is a translation :

'Sir,—When in the middle of last year, was delivered to me by the hands of Dr. Livingstone, the letters with which your Excellency honoured me, under date of April of that same year, I was at that moment involved in war with the Kafirs of the district of Senna. After this, other works, affairs and ailing health, prevented me from immediately addressing to your Excellency my thanks for the kind expressions with which I have been honoured by you. Your Excellency recommended to me the illustrious Dr. Livingstone. My relations with this gentleman are so sympathetic that I can never omit rendering him the services which he requires, and which are within my reach. Still, my wishes are subordinate to my powers, both as an individual and as an authority. I am aware how profitable to geographical knowledge and science are the explorations of the Doctor, as well as to the prosperity of this country,— as rich as neglected. I sincerely hope it will be in my power to help him as I could wish. Nevertheless, I assure your Excellency that I will serve him as far as lies in my power. It is said that our Government is about to es-

After the examination of three branches by the able and energetic surveyor, Francis Skead, R.N., the Kongone was found to be the best entrance. The immense amount of sand brought down by the Zambesi has in the course of ages formed a sort of promontory, against which the long swell of the Indian Ocean, beating during the prevailing winds, has formed bars, which, acting against the waters of the delta, may have led to their exit sideways. The Kongone is one of these lateral branches, and the safest; inasmuch as the bar has nearly two fathoms on it at low water, and the rise at spring tides is from twelve to fourteen feet. The bar is narrow, the passage nearly straight, and, were it buoyed and a beacon placed on Pearl Island, would always be safe to a steamer. When the wind is from the east or north, the bar is smooth; if from the south and south-east, it has a heavy break on it, and is not to be attempted in boats. A strong current setting to the east when the tide is flowing, and to the west when ebbing, may drag a boat or ship into the breakers. If one is doubtful of his longitude and runs east, he will soon see the land at Timbwe disappear away to the north; and coming

---

tablish a post at the bar of Luabo; and from there to carry on direct navigation to this district. Should this take place, great advantages will result to this country, and to Livingstone's great glory, because he was the first who passed over from the sea by this way of communication. I thank your Excellency for the newspapers with which you furnished me. I appreciate them as articles which very seldom appear here. Your Excellency also obliged me with some seeds; but, unfortunately, I was at Mosambique, and having planted them this year, they produced little; I fear they were already old. My capability for service is very limited, but if your Excellency thinks that I can be of any use, I shall be most gratified.

'I have, &c.,

'Tito A. d'A. Sicard,
        Governor of Tette.

'*Tette, July* 9, 1859.'

"These letters were brought to Natal by H.M.'s brig 'Persian,' which had called there from Mosambique for supplies, and were put on board the 'Waldensian,' as she steamed out."

C

west again, he can easily make out East Luabo from its great
size; and Kongone follows seven miles west. East Luabo has
a good but long bar, and not to be attempted unless the wind
be north-east or east. It has sometimes been called "Barra
Catrina," and was used in the embarkations of slaves. This
may have been the "River of Good Signs," of Vasco da
Gama, as the mouth is more easily seen from the seaward
than any other; but the absence of the pillar dedicated by
that navigator to "St. Raphael," leaves the matter in doubt.
No Portuguese live within eighty miles of any mouth of the
Zambesi. The names given by the natives refer more to
the land on each side than to the streams; thus, one side
of the Kongone is Nyamisenga, the other Nyangalule; and
Kongone, the name of a fish, is applied to one side of the
natural canal which leads into the Zambesi proper, or Cuama,
and gives the port its value.

When a native of the temperate north first lands in the
tropics, his feelings and emotions resemble in some respects
those which the First Man may have had on his entrance
into the Garden of Eden. He has set foot in a new world,
another state of existence is before him; everything he sees,
every sound that falls upon the ear, has all the freshness and
charm of novelty. The trees and the plants are new, the
flowers and the fruits, the beasts, the birds, and the insects
are curious and strange; the very sky itself is new, glowing
with colours, or sparkling with constellations, never seen in
northern climes.

The Kongone is five miles east of the Milambe, or western
branch, and seven miles west from East Luabo, which again is
five miles from the Timbwe. We saw but few natives, and
these, by escaping from their canoes into the mangrove
thickets the moment they caught sight of us, gave unmis-

PANDANUS OR SCREW PALM, COVERED WITH CLIMBING PLANTS, NEAR THE
KONGONE CANAL OF THE ZAMBESI.

takeable indications that they had no very favourable opinion of white men. They were probably fugitives from Portuguese slavery. In the grassy glades buffaloes, warthogs, and three kinds of antelope were abundant, and the latter easily obtained. A few hours' hunting usually provided venison enough for a score of men for several days.

On proceeding up the Kongone branch it was found that, by keeping well in the bends, which the current had worn deep, shoals were easily avoided. The first twenty miles are straight and deep; then a small and rather tortuous natural canal leads off to the right, and, after about five miles, during which the paddles almost touch the floating grass of the sides, ends in the broad Zambesi. The rest of the Kongone branch comes out of the main stream considerably higher up as the outgoing branch called Doto.

The first twenty miles of the Kongone are enclosed in mangrove jungle; some of the trees are ornamented with orchilla weed, which appears never to have been gathered. Huge ferns, palm bushes, and occasionally wild date-palms peer out in the forest, which consists of different species of mangroves; the bunches of bright yellow, though scarcely edible fruit, contrasting prettily with the graceful green leaves. In some spots the Milola, an umbrageous hibiscus, with large yellowish flowers, grows in masses along the bank. Its bark is made into cordage, and is especially valuable for the manufacture of ropes attached to harpoons for killing the hippopotamus. The Pandanus or screw-palm, from which sugar-bags are made in the Mauritius, also appears, and on coming out of the canal into the Zambesi many are so tall as in the distance to remind us of the steeples of our native land, and make us relish the remark of an old sailor, " that but one thing was wanting to

c 2

complete the picture, and that was 'a grog-shop near the church.'" We find also a few guava and lime-trees growing wild, but the natives claim the crops. The dark woods resound with the lively and exultant song of the kinghunter (*Halcyon striolata*), as he sits perched on high among the trees. As the steamer moves on through the winding channel, a pretty little heron or bright kingfisher darts out in alarm from the edge of the bank, flies on ahead a short distance, and settles quietly down to be again frightened off in a few seconds as we approach. The magnificent fishhawk (*Halietus vocifer*) sits on the top of a mangrove-tree, digesting his morning meal of fresh fish, and is clearly unwilling to stir until the imminence of the danger compels him at last to spread his great wings for flight. The glossy ibis, acute of ear to a remarkable degree, hears from afar the unwonted sound of the paddles, and, springing from the mud where his family has been quietly feasting, is off, screaming out his loud, harsh, and defiant Ha! ha! ha! long before the danger is near.

The mangroves are now left behind and are succeeded by vast level plains of rich dark soil, covered with gigantic grasses, so tall that they tower over one's head, and render hunting impossible. Beginning in July the grass is burned off every year after it has become dry. These fires prevent the growth of any great amount of timber, as only a few trees from among the more hardy kinds, such as the Borassus-palm and lignum-vitæ, can live through the sea of fire, which annually roars across the plains.

Several native huts now peep out from the bananas and cocoa-palms on the right bank; they stand on piles a few feet above the low damp ground, and their owners enter them by means of ladders. The soil is wonderfully rich, and the gardens are really excellent. Rice is cultivated largely;

sweet potatoes, pumpkins, tomatoes, cabbages, onions (sha-
lots), peas, a little cotton, and sugar-cane are also raised.
It is said that English potatoes, when planted at Quillimane
on soil resembling this, in the course of two years become
in taste like sweet potatoes (*convolvulus batatas*), and are like
our potato frosted. The whole of the fertile region extending
from the Kongone canal to beyond Mazaro, some eighty
miles in length, and fifty in breadth, is admirably adapted for
the growth of sugar-cane; and were it in the hands of our
friends at the Cape, would supply all Europe with sugar.
The remarkably few people seen appeared to be tolerably
well fed, but there was a shivering dearth of clothing
among them ; all were blacks, and nearly all Portuguese " colonos" or serfs. They manifested no fear of
white men, and stood in groups on the bank gazing
in astonishment at the steamers, especially at the " Pearl,"
which accompanied us thus far up the river. One old
man who came on board remarked that never before had
he seen any vessel so large as the " Pearl," it was like a
village, " Was it made out of one tree?" All were eager
traders, and soon came off to the ship in light swift canoes
with every kind of fruit and food they possessed; a few
brought honey and beeswax, which are found in quantities in
the mangrove forests. As the ships steamed off, many
anxious sellers ran along the bank, holding up fowls, baskets
of rice and meal, and shouting " Malonda, Malonda," " things
for sale," while others followed in canoes, which they sent
through the water with great velocity by means of short
broad-bladed paddles.

The *deep* channel, or Qwete as the canoe-men call it,
of the Zambesi is winding, and narrow when contrasted with the great breadth of the river itself. The

river bottom appears to be a succession of immense sub-merged sandbanks, having, when the stream is low, from one to four feet of water on them. The main channel runs for some distance between the sandbank and the river's bank, with a depth in the dry season varying from five to fifteen feet, and a current of nearly two knots an hour. It then turns and flows along the lower edge of the sandbank in a diagonal direction across the river, and continues this process, winding from bank to bank repeatedly during the day's sail, making expert navigators on the ocean feel help-lessly at sea on the river. On these crossings the channel is shallowest. It is in general pretty clearly defined. In calm weather there is a peculiar boiling up of its water from some action below. With a light breeze the Qwete assumes a characteristic ripple, and when the wind freshens and blows up the river, as it usually does from May to November, the waves on it are larger than those of other parts of the river, and a line of small breakers marks the edge of the shoal-bank above.

Finding the "Pearl's" draught too great for that part of the river near the island of Simbo, where the branch called the Doto is given off to the Kongone on the right bank, and another named Chinde departs to the secret canal already mentioned on the left, the goods belonging to the expedition were taken out of her, and placed on one of the grassy islands about forty miles from the bar. The "Pearl" then left us, and we had to part with our good friends Duncan and Skead; the former for Ceylon, the latter to return to his duties as Government Surveyor at the Cape.

Of those who eventually did the work of the expedition the majority took a sober common-sense view of the enterprise

in which we were engaged. Some remained on Expedition
Island from the 18th June until the 13th August, while the
launch and pinnace were carrying the goods up to Shupanga
and Senna. The country was in a state of war, our luggage
was in danger, and several of our party were exposed to
disease from inactivity in the malaria of the Delta. Here
some had their first introduction to African life, and African
fever. Those alone were safe who were actively employed
with the vessels, and of course, remembering the perilous'
position of their fellows, they strained every nerve to finish
the work and take them away. This was the time, too, for
the feeble-minded to make a demand for their Sundays of
rest and full meal-hours, which even our crew of twelve
Kroomen, though tampered with, had more sense and good-
feeling than to endorse. It is a pity that some people cannot
see that the true and honest discharge of the common duties
of every-day life is Divine Service.

The weather was delightful, with only an occasional shower
or cold foggy morning. Those who remained on the island
made the most of their time, taking meteorological and
magnetical observations, and botanizing, so far as the dried
vegetation would allow. No one seemed to place much
reliance on the "official report" of two naval commanders,
who now, after about a fortnight's experience in the Zambesi,
solemnly declared it to be "more like an inland-sea than a
river, with a climate like that of Italy, and infinitely more
healthy than any river on the West Coast:" but, by the
leader's advice, each began to examine and to record his
observations for himself, and did not take even his chief's
previous experience as infallible.

Large columns of smoke rose daily from different points
of the horizon, showing that the natives were burning off the

immense crops of tall grass, here a nuisance, however valuable elsewhere. A white cloud was often observed to rest on the head of the column, as if a current of hot damp air was sent up by the heat of the flames and its moisture was condensed at the top. Rain did not follow, though theorists have imagined that in such cases it ought.

Large game, buffaloes, and zebras, were abundant abreast the island, but no men could be seen. On the mainland, over on the right bank of the river, we were amused by the eccentric gyrations and evolutions of flocks of small seed-eating birds, who in their flight wheeled into compact columns with such military precision as to give us the impression that they must be guided by a leader, and all directed by the same signal. Several other kinds of small birds now go in flocks, and among others the large Senegal swallow. The presence of this bird, being clearly in a state of migration from the north, while the common swallow of the country, and the brown kite are away beyond the equator, leads to the conjecture that there may be a double migration, namely, of birds from torrid climates to the more temperate, as this now is, as well as from severe winters to sunny regions; but this could not be verified by such birds of passage as ourselves.

On reaching Mazaro, the mouth of a narrow creek which in floods communicates with the Quillimane river, we found that the Portuguese were at war with a half-caste named Mariano *alias* Matakenya, from whom they had generally fled, and who, having built a stockade near the mouth of the Shire, owned all the country between that river and Mazaro. Mariano was best known by his native name Mata-kenya, which in their tongue means "trembling," or quivering as trees do in a storm. He was a keen slave-hunter, and kept a large number of men, well armed with muskets. It is an entire mistake to suppose that the slave-trade is one of buying and selling alone ; or that engagements can be made with labourers in Africa as they are in India ; Mariano, like other Portuguese, had no labour to spare. He had been in the habit of sending out armed parties on slave hunting-forays among the helpless tribes to the north-east, and carrying down the kidnapped victims in chains to Quillimane, where they were sold by his brother-in-law Cruz Coimbra, and shipped as "Free emigrants" to the French island of Bourbon. So long as his robberies and murders were restricted to the natives at a distance, the authorities did not interfere ; but his men, trained to deeds of violence and bloodshed in their slave forays, naturally began to practise on the people nearer at hand, though belonging to the Portuguese, and even in the village of Senna, under the guns of the fort. A gentleman of the highest standing told us that, while at dinner with his family, it was no uncommon event for a slave to rush into the room pursued by one of Mariano's men with spear in hand to murder him.

The atrocities of this villain, aptly termed by the late governor of Quillimane a "notorious robber and murderer," became at length intolerable. All the Portuguese spoke of him as a rare monster of inhumanity. It is unaccountable why half-castes, such as he, are so much more cruel than the Portuguese, but such is undoubtedly the case.

It was asserted that one of his favourite modes of creating an impression in the country, and making his name dreaded, was to spear his captives with his own hands. On one occasion he is reported to have thus killed forty poor wretches placed in a row before him. We did not at first credit these statements, and thought that they were merely exaggerations of the incensed Portuguese, who naturally enough were exasperated with him for stopping their trade, and harbouring their runaway slaves; but we learned afterwards from the natives, that the accounts given us by the Portuguese had not exceeded the truth; and that Mariano was quite as great a ruffian as they had described him. One expects slave-owners to treat their human chattels as well as men do other animals of value, but the slave-trade seems always to engender an unreasoning ferocity, if not bloodthirstiness.

War was declared against Mariano, and a force sent to take him; he resisted for a time; but seeing that he was likely to get the worst of it, and knowing that the Portuguese governors have small salaries, and are therefore "disposed to be reasonable," he went down to Quillimane to "arrange" with the Governor, as it is termed here; but Colonel da Silva put him in prison, and then sent him for trial to Mosambique. When we came into the country, his people were fighting under his brother Bonga. The war had lasted six months and stopped all trade on the river during that period. On the 15th June we first came into contact with the "rebels." They appeared as a crowd of well-armed and fantastically-dressed people under the trees at Mazaro. On explaining that we were English, some at once came on board and called to those on shore to lay aside their arms. On landing among them we saw that many had the branded marks of slaves on their chests, but they warmly approved our objects, and knew well the distinctive character of our nation on the slave question. The shout at our departure contrasted strongly with the suspicious questioning on our approach. Henceforth we were recognised as friends by both parties.

At a later period we were taking in wood within a mile of

the scene of action, but a dense fog prevented our hearing the noise of a battle at Mazaro; and on arriving there, immediately after, many natives and Portuguese appeared on the bank.

Dr. Livingstone, landing to salute some of his old friends among the latter, found himself in the sickening smell, and among the mutilated bodies of the slain; he was requested to take the Governor, who was very ill of fever, across to Shupanga, and just as he gave his assent, the rebels renewed the fight, and the balls began to whistle about in all directions. After trying in vain to get some one to assist the Governor down to the steamer, and unwilling to leave him in such danger, as the officer sent to bring our Kroomen did not appear, he went into the hut, and dragged along his Excellency to the ship. He was a very tall man, and as he swayed hither and thither from weakness, weighing down Dr. Livingstone, it must have appeared like one drunken man helping another. Some of the Portuguese white soldiers stood fighting with great bravery against the enemy in front, while a few were coolly shooting at their own slaves for fleeing into the river behind. The rebels soon retired, and the Portuguese escaped to a sandbank in the Zambesi, and thence to an island opposite Shupanga, where they lay for some weeks, looking at the rebels on the mainland opposite. This state of inactivity on the part of the Portuguese could not well be helped, as they had expended all their ammunition and were waiting anxiously for supplies; hoping, no doubt, sincerely that the enemy might not hear that their powder had failed. Luckily their hopes were not disappointed; the rebels waited until a supply came, and were then repulsed after three-and-a-half hours' hard fighting. Two months afterwards Mariano's stockade was burned, the garrison having fled in a panic; and as Bonga declared that he did not wish to fight with this Governor, with whom he had no quarrel, the war soon came to an end. His Excellency meanwhile, being a disciple of Raspail, had taken nothing for the fever but a little camphor, and after he was taken to Shupanga became comatose. More potent remedies were administered to him, to his intense disgust, and he soon recovered. The Colonel in attendance, whom he never afterwards forgave, encouraged the treatment. " Give what is right; never mind him; he is very (*muito*) impertinent:" and all night long, with every draught of water the Colonel gave a quantity of quinine: the consequence was, next morning the patient was cinchonized and better. The sketch opposite represents the scene of action, and is interesting in an historical point of view, because the opening in which a large old canoe, with a hole in its bottom, is seen lying on its side, is the mouth of the creek Mutu, which in 1861 appeared in a map published by the Portuguese " Minister of Marine and the Colonies " as that through which the chief portion of the Zambesi, here about a mile wide, flowed to Quillimane. In reality this creek, eight or ten yards wide, is filled with grass, and its bed is six feet or more above the level of the Zambesi. The side of the creek opposite to the canoe is seen in the right of the picture, and sloping down from the bed to one of the dead bodies, may be marked the successive heights at which the water of the main stream stood from flood time in March to its medium height in June.

For sixty or seventy miles before reaching Mazaro, the scenery is tame and uninteresting. On either hand is a dreary uninhabited expanse, of the same level grassy plains, with merely a few trees to relieve the painful monotony.

VIEW OF MAZARO.—FIGHT OF PORTUGUESE AND REBELS IN THE DISTANCE.

The round green top of the stately palm-tree looks at a distance, when its grey trunk cannot be seen, as though hung in mid-air.   Many flocks of busy sandmartins, which here, and as far south as the Orange River, do not migrate, have perforated the banks two or three feet horizontally, in order to place their nests at the ends, and are now chasing on restless wing the myriads of tropical insects.   The broad river has many low islands, on which are seen various kinds of waterfowl, such as geese, spoonbills, herons, and flamingoes. Repulsive crocodiles, as with open jaws they sleep and bask in the sun on the low banks, soon catch the sound of the revolving paddles and glide quietly into the stream.   The hippopotamus, having selected some still reach of the river to spend the day, rises from the bottom, where he has been enjoying his morning bath after the labours of the night on shore, blows a puff of spray out of his nostrils, shakes the water out of his ears, puts his enormous snout up straight and yawns, sounding a loud alarm to the rest of the herd, with notes as of a monster bassoon.

As we approach Mazaro the scenery improves.   We see the well-wooded Shupanga ridge stretching to the left, and in front blue hills rise dimly far in the distance.   There is no trade whatever on the Zambesi below Mazaro.   All the merchandise of Senna and Tette is brought to that point in large canoes, and thence carried six miles across the country on men's heads to be reshipped on a small stream that flows into the Kwakwa, or Quillimane river, which is entirely distinct from the Zambesi.   Only on rare occasions and during the highest floods can canoes pass from the Zambesi to the Quillimane river through the narrow natural canal *Mutu.*   The natives of Maruru or the country around Mazaro, the word Mazaro meaning the "mouth of the creek"

Mutu, have a bad name among the Portuguese; they are
said to be expert thieves, and the merchants sometimes
suffer from their adroitness while the goods are in transit
from one river to the other. In general they are trained
canoe-men, and man many of the canoes that ply thence
to Senna and Tette; their pay is small, and, not trusting
the traders, they must always have it before they start.
Africans being prone to assign plausible reasons for their
conduct, like white men in more enlightened lands, it is
possible they may be goodhumouredly giving their reason
for insisting on being invariably paid in advance in the
words of their favourite canoe-song, " Uachingere, Uachingere
Kale," "You cheated me of old;" or, "Thou art slippery,
slippery truly."

The Landeens or Zulus are lords of the right bank of the
Zambesi; and the Portuguese, by paying this fighting tribe a
pretty heavy annual tribute, practically admit this. Regularly
every year come the Zulus in force to Senna and Shupanga
for their accustomed tribute. The few wealthy merchants of
Senna groan under the burden, for it falls chiefly on them.
They submit to pay annually 200 pieces of cloth, of sixteen
yards each, besides beads and brass wire, knowing that
refusal involves war, which might end in the loss of all they
possess. The Zulus appear to keep as sharp a look-out on
the Senna and Shupanga people as ever landlord did on
tenant; the more they cultivate, the more tribute they
have to pay. On asking some of them why they did not
endeavour to raise certain highly profitable products, we were
answered, "What's the use of our cultivating any more than
we do? the Landeens would only come down on us for more
tribute."

In the forests of Shupanga the Mokundu-kundu tree

DANCE OF LANDEENS, OR ZULUS, ARRIVED AT SHUPANGA TO LIFT THE ANNUAL TRIBUTE
OF THE PORTUGUESE.

THE GRAVE OF MRS. LIVINGSTONE UNDER THE BAOBAB TREE, NEAR TO SHUPANGA HOUSE.

abounds; its bright yellow wood makes good boat-masts, and yields a strong bitter medicine for fever; the Gunda-tree attains to an immense size; its timber is hard, rather cross-grained, with masses of silica deposited in its substance; the large canoes, capable of carrying three or four tons, are made of its wood. For permission to cut these trees, a Portuguese gentleman of Quillimane was paying the Zulus, in 1858, two hundred dollars a year, and his successor now pays three hundred.

At Shupanga, a one-storied stone house stands on the prettiest site on the river. In front a sloping lawn, with a fine mango orchard at its southern end, leads down to the broad Zambesi, whose green islands repose on the sunny bosom of the tranquil waters. Beyond, northwards, lie vast fields and forests of palms and tropical trees, with the massive mountain of Morambala towering amidst the white clouds; and further away more distant hills appear in the blue horizon. This beautifully situated house possesses a melancholy interest from having been associated in a most mournful manner with the history of two English expeditions. Here, in 1826, poor Kirkpatrick, of Captain Owen's Surveying Expedition, died of fever; and here, in 1862, died, of the same fatal disease, the beloved wife of Dr. Livingstone. A hundred yards east of the house, under a large Baobab-tree, far from their native land, both are buried.

The Shupanga-house was the head-quarters of the Governor during the Mariano war. He told us that the province of Mosambique costs the Home Government between 5000l. and 6000l. annually, and East Africa yields no reward in return to the mother country. We met there several other influential Portuguese. All seemed friendly, and expressed their willingness to assist the expedition in every way in their power;

and better still, Colonel Nunes and Major Sicard put their
good-will into action, by cutting wood for the steamer and
sending men to help in unloading. It was observable that not
one of them knew anything about the Kongone Mouth; all
thought that we had come in by the "Barra Catrina," or East
Luabo.* Dr. Kirk remained here a few weeks; and, besides
exploring a small lake twenty miles to the south-west, had the
sole medical care of the sick and wounded soldiers, for which
valuable services he received the thanks of the Portuguese
Government. We wooded up at this place with African ebony
or black wood, and lignum vitæ; the latter tree attains an
immense size, sometimes as much as four feet in diameter;
our engineer, knowing what ebony and lignum vitæ cost at
home, said it made his heart sore to burn woods so valuable.
Though botanically different, they are extremely alike; the
black wood as grown in some districts is superior, and
the lignum vitæ inferior in quality, to these timbers brought
from other countries. Caoutchouc, or India-rubber, is found
in abundance inland from Shupanga-house, and calumba-root
is plentiful in the district; indigo, in quantities, propagates
itself close to the banks of the river, and was probably at some
time cultivated, for manufactured indigo was once exported.
The India-rubber is made into balls for a game resembling
"fives," and calumba-root is said to be used as a mordant
for certain colours, but not as a dye itself.

---

* The reason of their want of knowledge—in which, notwithstanding the tone subsequently assumed in official papers, the Government at Lisbon unquestionably shared—was probably, as we conjecture, its recent formation. During the period of our acquaintance with the Kongone, about eighty yards were washed away on one side and deposited on the other. A navigable channel by Nyangalule was quite filled up, and Pearl Island nearly all washed away. As nothing whatever is done to preserve the channel, it will soon be as shallow as the Milambe, and entirely useless for navigation.

We started for Tette on the 17th August, 1858; the navigation was rather difficult, the Zambesi from Shupanga to Senna being wide and full of islands; our black pilot, John Scissors, a serf, sometimes took the wrong channel and ran us aground. Nothing abashed, he would exclaim in an aggrieved tone, "This is not the path, it is back yonder." "Then why didn't you go yonder at first?" growled out our Kroomen, who had the work of getting the vessel off. When they spoke roughly to poor Scissors, the weak cringing slave-spirit came forth in, "Those men scold me so, I am ready to run away." This mode of finishing up an engagement is not at all uncommon on the Zambesi; several cases occurred, when we were on the river, of hired crews decamping with most of the goods in their charge. If the trader cannot redress his own wrongs, he has to endure them. The Landeens will not surrender a fugitive slave, even to his master. One belonging to Mr. Azevedo fled, and was, as a great favour only, returned after a present of much more than his value.

Our steamer's badly-constructed furnaces consumed a frightful amount of wood. Fires were lighted at two in the morning, but steam was seldom up before six. A great deal of time was lost in wood-cutting. The large heavy-laden country canoes could nearly keep up with us, and the small ones shot ahead, and the paddlers looked back in wonder and pity at the slow puffing "Asthmatic." For us, steam was no labour-saving power; boats, or canoes even, would have done for the expedition all that *it* did, with half the toil and expense.

We landed to wood at Shamoara, just below the confluence of the Shire. Its quartz hills are covered with trees and gigantic grasses; the buaze, a small forest-tree, grows abundantly; it is a species of polygala; its beautiful clusters

D

of sweet-scented pinkish flowers perfume the air with a rich fragrance; its seeds produce a fine drying oil, and the bark of the smaller branches yields a fibre finer and stronger than flax; with which the natives make their nets for fishing. Bonga, the brother of the rebel Mariano, and now at the head of the revolted natives, with some of his principal men came to see us, and were perfectly friendly, though told of our having carried the sick Governor across to Shupanga, and of our having cured him of fever. On our acquainting Bonga with the object of the expedition, he remarked that we should suffer no hindrance from his people in our good work. He sent us a present of rice, two sheep, and a quantity of fire-wood. He never tried to make any use of us in the strife; the other side showed less confidence, by carefully cross-questioning our pilot whether we had sold any powder to the enemy. We managed, however, to keep on good terms with both rebels and Portuguese.

Being unable to take the steamer up the shoal channel along which Senna stands, we anchored at Nyaruka, a small hamlet of blacks, six miles below, and walked up to Senna next morning. The narrow winding footpath, along which we had to march in Indian file, lay through gardens and patches of wood, the loftiest trees being thorny acacias. The sky was cloudy, the air cool and pleasant, and the little birds, in the gladness of their hearts, poured forth sweet strange songs, which, though equal to those of the singing birds at home on a spring morning, yet seemed, somehow, as if in a foreign tongue. We met many natives on the road. Most of the men were armed with spears, bows and arrows, or old Tower muskets; the women had short-handled iron hoes, and were going to work in the gardens;

THE MA-ROBERT IN THE ZAMBESI ABOVE SENNA, WITH THE SADDLE-SHAPED HILL KEVRAMISA
IN THE DISTANCE.

they stepped aside to let us pass, and saluted us politely, the men bowing and scraping, and the women, even with heavy loads on their heads, curtseying—a curtsey from bare legs is startling!

Senna is built on a low plain, on the right bank of the Zambesi, with some pretty detached hills in the back-ground; it is surrounded by a stockade of living trees to protect its inhabitants from their troublesome and rebellious neighbours. It contains a few large houses, some ruins of others, and a weatherbeaten cross, where once stood a church; a mound shows the site of an ancient monastery, and a mud fort by the river is so dilapidated, that cows were grazing peacefully over its prostrate walls. This grieves not the villagers, for its black garrison was wont to keep within doors when the foe came near, leaving the merchants to settle the strife as best they could; and they therefore consider that the decay of the fort has not caused them to be any more helpless than they were before.

The few Senna merchants, having little or no trade in the village, send parties of trusted slaves into the interior to hunt for, and purchase ivory. It is a dull place, and very conducive to sleep. One is sure to take fever in Senna on the second day, if by chance one escapes it on the first day of a sojourn there; but no place is entirely bad. Senna has one re-deeming feature: it is the native village of the large-hearted and hospitable Senhor H. A. Ferrão. The benevolence of this gentleman is unbounded. The poor black stranger passing through the town goes to him almost as a matter of course for food, and is never sent away hungry. In times of famine the starving natives are fed by his generosity; hundreds of his own people he never sees except on these occasions; and the only benefit derived from being their

D 2

master is, that they lean on him as a patriarchal chief, and he has the satisfaction of settling their differences, and of saving their lives in seasons of drought and scarcity. His father, a man of superior attainments, was formerly the Portuguese governor of Senna, and acquired a vast tract of rich country to the southward, called Chiringoma, in a most honourable manner; but the Government ordered it to be split up, and reserved two leagues only for the heir, apportioning the rest in free grants to emigrants; the reason assigned for the robbery, was that "It would never do for a subject to possess more land than the crown of Portugal." The Landeens soon followed, took possession of the whole, and spoiled the spoilers.

Senhor Ferrão received us with his usual kindness, and gave us a bountiful breakfast. During the day the principal men of the place called, and were unanimously of opinion that the free natives would willingly cultivate large quantities of cotton, could they find purchasers. They had in former times exported largely both cotton and cloth to Manica and even to Brazil. "On their own soil," they declared, "the natives are willing to labour and trade, provided only they can do so to advantage: when it is for their interest, blacks work very hard." We often remarked subsequently that this was the opinion of men of energy; and that all settlers of activity, enterprise, and sober habits had become rich, while those who were much addicted to lying on their backs smoking invariably complained of the laziness of the negroes, and were poor, proud, and despicable. We dined with another very honourable Portuguese, Major Tito A. d'A. Sicard, who quoted the common remark that Dr. Livingstone's discovery of the Kongone Bar had ruined Quillimane; for the Government had proposed to abandon that fever-haunted locality, and to found a new town at the mouth of the Kongone. It was not then known

LANDEENS, OR ZULUS, WHO LIFT TRIBUTE OF THE PORTUGUESE AT SENNA, EXHIBITING WAR EXERCISES.

that householders in the old village preferred to resign all offices rather than remove. The Major had a great desire to assist Dr. Livingstone in his enterprise; and said that when the war was past he would at once take up his goods to Tette in canoes; and this he afterwards most generously did. While returning to Nyaruka, we heard a bird like a nightingale pouring forth its sweet melody in the stillness of the evening.

A picturesque range of lofty hills commences on the left bank opposite Senna, and runs in a northerly direction, nearly parallel with the river. Here we first fell in with that fine antelope, the koodoo (*Antelope strepsiceros*). Some miles above Senna is the island of Pita, with a considerable native population, which appeared to be well off for food. A half-caste, claiming to be the headman, came on board, and gave us a few ears of green maize as a "seguati." This is not an ordinary present, but a very small gift, which is to win back to the donor at least twice its value. When a stingy native has a tough little fowl, or a few ears of Indian corn, the value of which is hardly appreciable,—as a dozen of their best fowls only cost two yards of cloth (once threepence a yard), and a basket of maize but half a yard,—he forms it into a "seguati," his heart overflowing with that gratitude once described as a lively sense of favours to come, and is rather disappointed if he does not get twice the value in return. We soon learned to dislike "seguati" from common people, but it was in vain to say to the shrewd African, "Sell it; we will buy it." "Oh, no, sir; it is a seguati; it is not for sale," was the invariable reply. As it is understood to be a compliment, we always submitted to this customary politeness from headmen. To have done otherwise would have seemed to ourselves like ungracious manners from the rich and exalted to the poor and lowly. When private persons attempted it, we declined.

Beyond Pita lies the little island Nyamotobsi, where we met a small fugitive tribe of hippopotamus hunters, who had been driven by war from their own island in front. All were busy at work; some were making gigantic baskets for grain, the men plaiting from the inside. With the civility so common among them the chief ordered a mat to be spread for us under a shed, and then showed us the weapon with which they kill the hippopotamus; it is a short iron harpoon inserted in the end of a long pole, but being intended to unship, it is made fast to a strong cord of milola, or hibiscus, bark, which is wound closely round the entire length of the shaft, and secured at its opposite end. Two men in a swift canoe steal quietly down on the sleeping animal. The bowman dashes the harpoon into the unconscious victim, while the quick steersman sweeps the light craft back with his broad paddle; the force of the blow separates the harpoon from its corded handle, which, appearing on the surface, sometimes with an inflated bladder attached, guides the hunters

to where the wounded beast hides below until they despatch it.

These hippopotamus hunters form a separate people, called
Akombwi, or Mapodzo, and rarely—the women it is said never
—intermarry with any other tribe.   The reason for their keeping aloof from certain of the natives on the Zambesi is obvious
enough, some having as great an abhorrence of hippopotamus
meat as Mahomedans have of swine's flesh.   Our pilot, Scissors,
was one of this class; he would not even cook his food in a pot
which had contained hippopotamus meat, preferring to go
hungry till he could find another; and yet he traded eagerly
in the animal's tusks, and ate with great relish the flesh of
the foul-feeding marabout.   These hunters go out frequently
on long expeditions, taking in their canoes their wives and
children, cooking-pots, and sleeping-mats.   When they reach
a good game district, they erect temporary huts on the bank,
and there dry the meat they have killed.   They are rather a
comely-looking race, with very black smooth skins, and never
disfigure themselves with the frightful ornaments of some of
the other tribes.   The chief declined to sell a harpoon, because
they could not now get the milola bark from the coast on
account of Mariano's war.   He expressed some doubts about
our being children of the same Almighty Father, remarking
that "they could not become white, let them wash ever so
much."   We made him a present of a bit of cloth, and he
very generously gave us in return some fine fresh fish and
Indian corn.

The heat of the weather steadily increases during this month
(August), and foggy mornings are now rare.   A strong breeze
ending in a gale blows up stream every night.   It came in the
afternoon a few weeks ago, then later, and at present its arrival is near midnight; it makes our frail cabin-doors fly open

before it, but continues only for a short time, and is succeeded by a dead calm. Game becomes more abundant; near our wooding-places we see herds of zebras, both Burchell's and the mountain variety, pallahs (*Antelope melampus*), waterbuck, and wild hogs, with the spoor of buffaloes and elephants.

Shiramba Dembe, on the right bank, is deserted; a few old iron guns show where a rebel stockade once stood; near the river above this, stands a magnificent Baobab hollowed out into a good-sized hut, with bark inside as well as without. The old oaks in Sherwood Forest, when hollow, have the inside dead or rotten; but the Baobab, though stripped of its bark outside, and hollowed to a cavity inside, has the power of exuding new bark from its substance to both the outer and inner surfaces; so, a hut made like that in the oak called the "Forest Queen," in Sherwood, would soon all be lined with bark.

The portions of the river called Shigogo and Shipanga are bordered by a low level expanse of marshy country, with occasional clumps of palm-trees and a few thorny acacias. The river itself spreads out to a width of from three to four miles, with many islands, among which it is difficult to navigate, except when the river is in flood. In front, a range of high hills from the north-east crosses and compresses it into a deep narrow channel, called the Lupata Gorge. The Portuguese thought the steamer would not stem the current here; but as it was not more than about three knots, and as there was a strong breeze in our favour, steam and sails got her through with ease. Heavy-laden canoes take two days to go up this pass. A current sweeps round the little rocky promontories Chifura and Kangomba, forming whirlpools and eddies dangerous for the clumsy craft, which are dragged past with long ropes.

The paddlers place meal on these rocks as an offering to the turbulent deities, which they believe preside over spots fatal to many a large canoe. We were slily told that native Portuguese take off their hats to these river gods, and pass in solemn silence; when safely beyond the promontories, they fire muskets, and, as we ought to do, give the canoe-men grog. From the spoor of buffaloes and elephants it appears that these animals frequent Lupata in considerable numbers, and — we have often observed the association—the tsetse fly is common. A horse for the Governor of Tette was sent in a canoe from Quillimane; and, lest it should be wrecked on the Chifura and Kangomba rocks, it was put on shore and sent in the daytime through the pass. It was of course bitten by the tsetse, and died soon after; it was thought that the *air* of Tette had not agreed with it. The currents above Lupata are stronger than those below; the country becomes more picturesque and hilly, and there is a larger population. Within a few miles of Tette are numerous ruins of stone houses, which were destroyed some years ago by hostile natives. On our approaching the village, crowds of people, chiefly blacks, appeared on the beach gazing in astonishment at the steamer, and, by the motions of their arms, demonstrating to others further off the manner in which the paddles revolved.

CHAPTER II.

Meet Makololo at Tette — Murder of six of them by Bonga, the son of Nyaude — Ravages of smallpox — Makololo supported not according to public orders, but by the private bounty of Major Sicard — Convict class called "Incorrigibles" — Superstitions about mangoes, coffee, and rain-making — Securing slaves by means of domestic ties — Case of voluntary slavery — Cruel nature of half-castes — Native love of trade — Native medical profession — Elephant and crocodile schools of medicine — Dice doctors and their use as detective police — Senna and indigo plants — Coal, gold, and iron — Ascent to Kebrabasa Rapids — Black glaze on rocks — Tribe of Badèma — A traveller's tale — The river Luia — Hippopotamus flesh — Difficult travelling — Curative sleep — Sunstroke — Morumbwa Cataract — Kebrabasa surveyed from end to end.

THE ship anchored in the stream, off Tette, on the 8th September, 1858, and Dr. Livingstone went ashore in the boat. No sooner did the Makololo* recognise him, than they rushed to the water's edge, and manifested great joy at seeing him again. Some were hastening to embrace him, but others cried out, " Don't touch him, you will spoil his new clothes." The five headmen came on board and listened in quiet sadness to the story of poor Sekwebu, who died at the Mauritius on his way to England. " Men die in any country," they observed, and then told us that thirty of their own number had died of smallpox, having been bewitched by the people of Tette, who envied them because, during the first year, none of their party had died. Six of their young men, becoming

---

* Makololo, Manganja, Ajawa, Batoka, Matebele, Babisa, Bawe, &c. &c., are all plural nouns ; Ma, Ba, A, being plural prefixes which the Arabs change into Wa, as Wanyassa, the people of Nyassa, or Manganja, Wabisa, who call themselves Babisa, and sometimes Avisa. It has not been deemed necessary to add s to words already plural.

tired of cutting firewood for a meagre pittance, proposed to go and dance for gain before some of the neighbouring Chiefs. "Don't go," said the others, "we don't know the people of this country;" but the young men set out and visited an independent half-caste Chief, a few miles to the north, named Chisaka, who some years ago burned all the Portuguese villas on the north bank of the river; afterwards the young men went to Bonga, son of another half-caste Chief, who bade defiance to the Tette authorities, and had a stockade at the confluence of the Zambesi and Luenya, a few miles below that village.* Asking the Makololo whence they came, Bonga rejoined, "Why do you come from my enemy to me? You have brought witchcraft medicine to kill me." In vain they protested that they did not belong to the country; they were strangers, and had come from afar with an Englishman. The superstitious savage put them all to death. "We do not grieve," said their companions, "for the thirty victims of the smallpox, who were taken away by Morimo (God); but our hearts are sore for the six youths who were murdered by Bonga." Any hope of obtaining justice on the murderer was out of the question. Bonga once caught a captain of the Portuguese army, and forced him to perform the menial labour of pounding maize in a wooden mortar. No punishment followed on this outrage. The Government of Lisbon has since given Bonga the honorary title of Captain, by way of coaxing him to own their authority; but he still holds his stockade.

One of the headmen remarked "that they had some pigs;

---

* This is not that Bonga, brother of Mariano, who was carrying on war in another quarter: the word means a "tiger-cat;" and this was the son of Nyaude, who, when the whole force of Tette was mustered at the Luenya, was sent up the opposite bank by his father, and burned all the village, save the church and fort.

they wished they had been oxen, but they were only pigs."
"Would the Doctor eat pig?" "Why do you ask?" rejoined
another; "if he won't, his people will." When parting
they remarked, "We shall sleep to-night." The use of
the Residencia or Government-house was kindly given us
by Major Tito A. d'A. Sicard; it is a stone house of one
story, thatched with grass, its windows of cloth, and the floors
of clay. The Makololo carried up our goods, the minstrel
of the party, called Singeleka, followed jingling his native
bells, and chanting an energetic song extemporised for the
occasion. Some readers may remember that when Dr. Livingstone was in England, it was commonly reported that the Portuguese Government had sent out orders to have the Makololo
supported at the public expense until he returned to take them
back to their own country. This generous sympathy on the
part of the Ministers in Lisbon gratified many English philanthropists, and, relieving the Doctor's mind from anxiety, gave
him time to prepare his journal for the press before setting out
again to his work. When our own Government promises to
perform any thing, no one in his senses ever doubts their word
of honour; and for this reason the English people and the
English Government naturally err by giving too ready credit
to the assurances of Governments, whose moral tone is pitched
much lower than their own. The Makololo never heard of the
order from Portugal, and the Portuguese authorities at Tette
were in profound ignorance of its existence. The pay of the
officials, in fact, was several years in arrear, and for His Most
Faithful Majesty's Government to pretend to order them to
feed a hundred men out of their own private means looked a
little like the not unusual kind of benevolence of being generous
with other people's property. The poor fellows had to go
far to cut wood, and then hawk it round the village to buy a

little food. They received no aid from the Mosambique Government; but Major Sicard did assist them most generously at his own cost, and also gave them land and hoes to raise some food for themselves.

Tette stands on a succession of low sandstone ridges on the right bank of the Zambesi, which is here nearly a thousand yards wide (960 yards). Shallow ravines, running parallel with the river, form the streets, the houses being built on the ridges. The whole surface of the streets, except narrow footpaths, were overrun with self-sown indigo, and tons of it might have been collected. In fact indigo, senna, and stramonium, with a species of cassia, form the weeds of the place, which are annually hoed off and burned. A wall of stone and mud surrounds the village, and the native population live in huts outside. The fort and the church, near the river, are the strongholds; the natives having a salutary dread of the guns of the one, and a superstitious fear of the unknown power of the other. The number of white inhabitants is small, and rather select, many of them having been considerably sent out of Portugal " for their country's good." The military element preponderates in society; the convict and " incorrigible " class of soldiers, receiving very little pay, depend in great measure on the produce of the gardens of their black wives ; the moral condition of the resulting population may be imagined. Even the officers seldom receive their pay from Government; but, being of an enterprising spirit, they contrive to support themselves by marrying the daughters or widows of wealthy merchants; and trade in ivory by means of the slaves, of whom they thus become the masters.

Droughts are of frequent occurrence at Tette, and the crops suffer severely. This may arise partly from the position of the town between the ranges of hills north and south, which appear to have a strong attraction for the rain-clouds. It is often seen to rain on these hills when not a drop falls at Tette. Our first season was one of drought. Thrice had the women planted their gardens in vain, the seed, after just vegetating, was killed by the intense dry heat. A fourth planting shared the same hard fate, and then some of the knowing ones discovered the cause of the clouds being frightened away: our unlucky rain-gauge in the garden. We got a bad name through that same rain-gauge, and were regarded by many as a species of evil omen. The Makololo in turn blamed the people of Tette for drought: "A number of witches live here, who won't let it rain." Africans in general are sufficiently superstitious, but those of Tette are in this particular pre-eminent above their fellows. Coming from many different tribes, all the rays of the separate superstitions converge into a focus at Tette, and burn out common sense from the minds of the mixed breed. They believe that many evil spirits live in the air, the earth, and the water. These invisible malicious beings are thought to inflict much suffering on the human race; but, as they have a weakness for beer and a craving for food, they may be propitiated from time to time by offerings of meat and drink. The serpent is an object of worship, and hideous little images are hung in the huts of the sick and dying. The uncontaminated Africans believe that Morungo, the Great Spirit who formed all things, lives above the stars; but they never pray to him, and know nothing of their relation to him, or of his interest in them. The spirits of their departed ancestors are all good, according to their ideas, and on special occasions aid them in their enterprises. When a man has his hair cut, he is careful to burn it, or bury it secretly, lest, falling into the hands of one who has an evil eye, or is a witch, it should be used as a charm to afflict him with headache.   They believe, too, that they will live after the death of the body, but do not know anything of the state of the Barimo (gods, or departed spirits).

The mango-tree grows luxuriantly above Lupata, and furnishes a grateful shade.   Its delicious fruit is superior to that on the coast.   For weeks the natives who have charge of the mangoes live entirely on the fruit, and, as some trees bear in November and some in March, while the main crop comes between, fruit in abundance may easily be obtained during four months of the year; but no native can be induced to plant a mango.   A wide-spread superstition has become riveted in the native mind, that if any one plants this tree he will soon die.   The Makololo, like other natives, were very fond of the fruit; but when told to take up some mango-stones, on their return, and plant them in their own country—they too having become deeply imbued with the belief that it was a suicidal act to do so—replied "they did not wish to die too soon."   There is also a superstition even among the native Portuguese of Tette that if a man plants coffee he will never afterwards be happy: they drink it, however, and seem the happier for it.

During the drought of 1858 a neighbouring chief got up a performance, with divers ceremonies and incantations, to bring rain, but it would not come.   The Goanese padre of Tette, to satisfy his compatriots, appointed a procession and prayers in honour of Saint Antonio for the same purpose.   The first attempt did not answer, but on the second occasion, arranged to come off after the new-moon appeared, a grand procession in the saint's honour ended in so much rain that the roof of the Residencia gave way: Saint Antonio's image was decorated the following week with a golden coronal, worth 22*l.*, for sending the long-delayed and much-needed rain. We never looked with disdain on the rites or ceremonies of any church; but, on witnessing the acts of worship on this occasion, so great was the irreverence manifested,—the kneeling worshippers laughing and joking between the responses, not even ceasing their grins when uttering "Ora pro nobis,"—that we could not help believing that if, like the natives, they have faith in rain-making, they have faith in nothing else.

Most of the trees shed their leaves in May, the beginning of winter, and remain bare until the rains come in November; several kinds are in the curious habit of anticipating, as it were, the rains by instinct; and in the beginning of October, when the dry season has reached its driest point and there is not a drop of dew, they begin to generate buds, and in a few days put forth fresh and various-hued foliage, and sometimes beautiful blossoms. In a somewhat similar manner, the trees in the Arctic regions are said to anticipate the coming spring, and display fresh green leaves, when the ground is hard frozen, to a depth greater than that to which roots ever penetrate.

The Portuguese of Tette have many slaves, with all the usual vices of their class, as theft, lying, and impurity. As a general rule the real Portuguese are tolerably humane masters and rarely treat a slave cruelly; this may be due as much to natural kindness of heart as to a fear of losing the slaves by their running away. When they purchase an adult slave they buy at the same time, if possible, all his relations along with him. They thus contrive to secure him to his new home by domestic ties. Running away then would be to forsake all who hold a place in his heart, for the mere chance of acquiring a freedom, which would probably be forfeited on his entrance into the first native village, for the Chief might, without compunction, again sell him into slavery.

A rather singular case of voluntary slavery came to our knowledge: a free black, an intelligent active young fellow, called Chibanti, who had been our pilot on the river, told us that he had sold himself into slavery. On asking why he had done this, he replied that he was all alone in the world, had neither father nor mother, nor any one else to give him water when sick, or food when hungry; so he sold himself to Major Sicard, a notoriously kind master, whose slaves had little to do, and plenty to eat. "And how much did you get for yourself?" we asked. "Three thirty-yard pieces of cotton cloth," he replied; "and I forthwith bought a man, a woman, and child, who cost me two of the pieces, and I had one piece left." This, at all events, showed a cool and calculating spirit; he afterwards bought more slaves, and in two years owned a sufficient number to man one of the large canoes. His master subsequently employed him in carrying ivory to Quillimane, and gave him cloth to hire mariners for the voyage; he took his own slaves, of course, and thus drove a thriving business; and was fully convinced that he had made a good speculation by the sale of himself, for had he been sick his master must have supported him. Occasionally some of the free blacks become slaves voluntarily by going through the simple but significant ceremony of breaking a spear in the presence of their future master. A Portuguese officer, since dead, persuaded one of the Makololo to remain in Tette, instead of returning to his own country, and tried also to induce him to break a spear before him, and thus

E

acknowledge himself his slave, but the man was too shrewd
for this; he was a great elephant doctor, who accompanied
the hunters, told them when to attack the huge beast, and
gave them medicine to ensure success. Unlike the real
Portuguese, many of the half-castes are merciless slaveholders;
their brutal treatment of the wretched slaves is notorious.
What a humane native of Portugal once said of them is
appropriate if not true : " God made white men, and God
made black men, but the devil made half-castes."

The officers and merchants send parties of slaves under
faithful headmen to hunt elephants and to trade in ivory,
providing them with a certain quantity of cloth, beads, &c., and
requiring so much ivory in return. These slaves think that
they have made a good thing of it, when they kill an elephant near a village, as the natives give them beer and meal
in exchange for some of the elephant's meat, and over every
tusk that is bought there is expended a vast amount of
time, talk, and beer. Most of the Africans are natural-born
traders, they love trade more for the sake of trading than for
what they make by it. An intelligent gentleman of Tette
told us that native traders often come to him with a tusk for
sale, consider the price he offers, demand more, talk over it,
retire to consult about it, and at length go away without
selling it; next day they try another merchant, talk, consider,
get puzzled and go off as on the previous day, and continue
this course daily until they have perhaps seen every merchant
in the village, and then at last end by selling the precious
tusk to some one for even less than the first merchant had
offered. Their love of dawdling in the transaction arises
from the self-importance conferred on them by their being
the object of the wheedling and coaxing of eager merchants,
a feeling to which even the love of gain is subordinate.

The native medical profession is reasonably well represented. In addition to the regular practitioners, who are a
really useful class, and know something of their profession,
and the nature and power of certain medicines, there are others
who devote their talents to some speciality. The elephant
doctor prepares a medicine which is considered indispensable
to the hunters when attacking that noble and sagacious
beast; no hunter is willing to venture out before investing
in this precious nostrum. The crocodile doctor sells a charm
which is believed to possess the singular virtue of protecting
its owner from crocodiles. Unwittingly we offended the
crocodile school of medicine while at Tette, by shooting one
of these huge reptiles as it lay basking in the sun on a
sandbank; the doctors came to the Makololo in wrath, cla-
mouring to know why the white man had shot their crocodile.

A shark's hook was baited one evening with a dog,
of which the crocodile is said to be particularly fond;
but the doctors removed the bait, on the principle
that the more crocodiles the more demand for medicine,
or perhaps because they preferred to eat the dog themselves. Many of the natives of this quarter are known,
as in the South Seas, to eat the dog without paying any
attention to its feeding. The dice doctor or diviner is
an important member of the community, being consulted by
Portuguese and natives alike. Part of his business is that of
a detective, it being his duty to discover thieves. When goods
are stolen, he goes and looks at the place, casts his dice, and
waits a few days, and then, for a consideration, tells who is the
thief: he is generally correct, for he trusts not to his dice
alone; he has confidential agents all over the village, by whose
inquiries and information he is enabled to detect the culprit.
Since the introduction of muskets, gun-doctors have sprung

E 2

up, and they sell the medicine which professes to make good marksmen; others are rain doctors, &c. &c. The various schools deal in little charms, which are hung round the purchaser's neck to avert evil : some of them contain the medicine, others increase its power.

Indigo, about three or four feet high, grows in great luxuriance in the streets of Tette, and so does the Senna plant. The leaves are undistinguishable from those imported in England. We set the Makololo to collect specimens, but the natives objected to their doing so, though they themselves never make use of them. A small amount of first-rate cotton is cultivated by the native population for the manufacture of a coarse cloth. In former times the Portuguese collected it at a cheap rate, and made use of it instead of the calico now imported, to exchange for the Manica gold dust. A neighbouring tribe raises the sugar-cane, and makes a little sugar; but they use most primitive wooden rollers, and having no skill in mixing lime with the extracted juice, the product is of course of very inferior quality. Plenty of magnetic iron-ore is found near Tette, and coal also to any amount; a single cliff-seam measuring twenty-five feet in thickness. It was found to burn well in the steamer on the first trial. The ash showed a large quantity of shaly refuse; but, suspecting that this was from the coal near the surface having been exposed to the weather for ages, we drove a shaft of some thirty feet, and the mineral was found to improve the further we went in. Gold is washed for in the beds of rivers, within a couple of days of Tette. The natives are fully aware of its value, but seldom search for it, and never dig deeper than four or five feet. They dread lest the falling in of the sand of the river's bed should bury them. In former times, when traders went with hundreds of slaves to the washings,

VIEW OF A PORTION OF KEBRABASA RAPIDS.

the produce was considerable. It is now insignificant. The gold-producing lands have always been in the hands of independent tribes.   Deep cuttings near the sources of the gold-yielding streams seem never to have been tried here, as in California and Australia, nor has any machinery been used save common wooden basins for washing.

Our curiosity had been so much excited by the reports we had heard of the Kebrabasa rapids, that we resolved to make a short examination of them, and seized the opportunity of the Zambesi being unusually low, to endeavour to ascertain their character while uncovered by the water.   We reached them on the 9th of November.   The country, between Tette and Panda Mokua, where navigation ends, is well wooded and hilly on both banks.   Panda Mokua is a hill two miles below the rapids, capped with dolomite containing copper ore.

Conspicuous among the trees, for its gigantic size, and bark coloured exactly like Egyptian syenite, is the burly Baobab. It often makes the other trees of the forest look like mere bushes in comparison.   A hollow one, already mentioned, is 74 feet in circumference, another was 84, and some have been found on the West Coast which measure 100 feet.   Their great size induced some to imagine that they afforded evidence that the flood of Noah never took place.   On careful examination of many hundreds in the forests, and some which had sprung up in the floors of old stone houses, the number of concentric rings convince us that even the very largest specimens of this remarkably soft-wooded tree are not 500 years old.   The lofty range of Kebrabasa, consisting chiefly of conical hills, covered with scraggy trees, crosses the Zambesi, and confines it within a narrow, rough, and rocky dell of about a quarter of a mile in breadth; over this, which may be called the flood-bed of the river, large masses of rock are huddled in indescribable confusion. The drawing, for the use of which, and of others, our thanks are due to Lord Russell, conveys but a faint idea of the scene, inasmuch as the hills which confine the river do not appear in the sketch. The chief rock is syenite, some portions of which have a beautiful blue tinge like *lapis lazuli* diffused through them; others are grey. Blocks of granite also abound, of a pinkish tinge; and these with metamorphic rocks, contorted, twisted, and thrown into every conceivable position, afford a picture of dislocation or unconformability which would gladden a geological lecturer's heart; but at high flood this rough channel is all smoothed over, and it then conforms well with the river below it, which is half a mile wide. In the dry season the stream runs at the bottom of a narrow and deep groove, whose sides are polished and fluted by the boiling action of the water in flood, like the rims of ancient Eastern wells by the draw-ropes. The breadth of the groove is often not more than from forty to sixty yards, and it has some sharp turnings, double channels, and little cataracts in it. As we steamed up, the masts of the " Ma Robert," though some thirty feet high, did not reach the level of the flood-channel above, and the man in the chains sung out, "No bottom at ten fathoms." Huge pot-holes, as large as draw-wells, had been worn in the sides, and were so deep that in some instances, when protected from the sun by over-hanging boulders, the water in them was quite cool. Some of these holes had been worn right through, and only the side next the rock remained; while the sides of the groove of the flood-channel were polished as smooth as if they had gone through the granite-mills of Aberdeen. The pressure of the water must be enormous to produce this polish. It had wedged round pebbles into chinks and crannies of the rocks so firmly that, though they looked quite loose, they could not be moved except with a hammer. The mighty power of the water here seen gave us an idea of what is going on in thousands of cataracts in the world. All the information we had been able to obtain from our Portuguese friends amounted to this, that some three or four detached rocks jutted out of the river in Kebrabasa, which, though dangerous to the cumbersome native canoes, could be easily passed by a steamer, and that if one or two of these obstructions were blasted away with gunpowder, no difficulty would hereafter be experienced. After we had painfully explored seven or eight miles of the rapid, we returned to the vessel satisfied that much greater labour was requisite for the mere examination of the cataracts than our friends supposed necessary to remove them; we therefore went down the river for fresh supplies, and made preparation for a more serious survey of this region.

The steamer having returned from the bar, we set out on the 22nd of November to examine the rapids of Kebrabasa.* We reached the foot of the hills again, late in the afternoon of the 24th, and anchored in the stream. Canoe-men never sleep on the river, but always spend the night on shore. The natives on the right bank, in the country called Shidima, who are Banyai, and even at this short distance from Tette, independent, and accustomed to lord it over Portuguese traders, wondered what could be our object in remaining afloat, and were naturally suspicious at our departing from the universal custom.

---

* The word as pronounced by the natives is Kaora-basa, "finish or break the service." The Portuguese word Kebra (quebra) means the same thing, and refers to the break which occurs in the labour of toiling up thus far in heavy canoes and then carrying the luggage hence overland to Chicova.

They hailed us from the bank in the evening with "Why don't you come and sleep on shore like other people?"

The answer they received from our Makololo, who now felt as independent as the Banyai, was, "We are held to the bottom with iron; you may see we are not like your Bazungu."

This hint, a little amplified, saved us from the usual exactions. It is pleasant to give a present, but that pleasure the Banyai usually deny to strangers by making it a fine, and demanding it in such a supercilious way, that only a sorely-cowed trader could bear it. They often refuse to touch what is offered—throw it down and leave it—sneer at the trader's slaves, and refuse a passage until the tribute is raised to the utmost extent of his means.

Leaving the steamer next morning, we proceeded on foot, accompanied by a native Portuguese and his men and a dozen Makololo, who carried our baggage. The morning was pleasant, the hills on our right furnished for a time a delightful shade; but before long the path grew frightfully rough, and the hills no longer shielded us from the blazing sun. Scarcely a vestige of a track was now visible; and, indeed, had not our guide assured us to the contrary, we should have been innocent of even the suspicion of a way along the patches of soft yielding sand, and on the great rocks over which we so painfully clambered. These rocks have a singular appearance, from being dislocated and twisted in every direction, and covered with a thin black glaze, as if highly polished and coated with lamp-black varnish. This seems to have been deposited while the river was in flood, for it covers only those rocks which lie between the highest water-mark and a line about four feet above the lowest. Travellers who have visited the rapids of the Orinoco and the Congo say that the rocks there have a similar appearance, and it is attributed to some deposit from the water, formed only when the current is strong. This may account for it in part here, as it prevails only where the narrow river is confined between masses of rock, backed by high hills, and where the current in floods is known to be the strongest; and it does not exist where the rocks are only on one side, with a sandy beach opposite, and a broad expanse of river between. The hot rocks burnt the thick soles of our men's feet, and sorely fatigued ourselves. Our first day's march did not exceed four miles in a straight line, and that we found more than enough to be pleasant.

A few inhabitants, of the tribe called Badèma, were seen living in the valleys. They cultivate small quantities of maize, tobacco, and cotton in the available hollows, and the holcus sorghum, or as they call it "mapira", on the steep slopes of their mountains. Fish are caught in the river with casting nets. Zebras, antelopes, and other animals are taken by driving them into ravines, strong nets made of baobab-bark being stretched across the narrow outlets.

The state of insecurity in which the Badèma tribe live is indicated by the habit of hiding their provisions in the hills, and keeping only a small quantity in their huts; they strip a particular species of tree of its bitter bark, to which both mice and monkeys are known to have an antipathy, and, turning the bark inside out, sew it into cylindrical vessels for their grain, and bury them in holes and in crags on the wooded hill-sides. By this means, should a marauding party plunder their huts, they save a supply of corn. They "could give us no information, and they had no food; Chisaka's men had robbed them a few weeks before."

"Never mind," said our native Portuguese, "they will sell you plenty when you return, they are afraid of you now, as yet they do not know who you are." We slept under trees in the open air, and suffered no inconvenience from either mosquitoes or dew: and no prowling wild beast troubled us; though one evening, while we were here, a native sitting with some others on the opposite bank was killed by a leopard.

One of the Tette slaves, who wished to be considered a great traveller, gave us, as we sat by our evening fire, an interesting account of a strange race of men whom he had seen in the interior; they were only three feet high, and had horns growing out of their heads; they lived in a large town, and had plenty of food. The Makololo pooh-poohed this story, and roundly told the narrator that he was telling a downright lie. "*We* come from the interior," cried out a tall fellow, measuring some six feet four, "are *we* dwarfs? have *we* horns on our heads?" and thus they laughed the fellow to scorn. But he still stoutly maintained that he had seen these little people, and had actually been in their town; thus making himself the hero of the traditional story, which before and since the time of Herodotus has, with curious persistency, clung to the native mind. The mere fact that such absurd notions are permanent, even in the entire absence of literature, invests the religious ideas of these people also with importance, as fragments of the wreck of a primitive faith floating down the stream of time.

We waded across the rapid Luia, which took us up to the waist, and was about forty yards wide. The water was discoloured at the time, and we were not without apprehension that a crocodile might chance to fancy a white man for dinner. Next day one of the men crawled over the black rocks to within ten yards of a sleeping hippopotamus, and shot him through the brain. The weather being warm, the body floated in a few hours, and some of us had our first trial of hippo-

potamus flesh. It is a coarse-grained meat, something between pork and beef,—pretty good food when one is hungry
and can get nothing better. When we reached the foot of
the mountain named Chipereziwa, whose perpendicular rocky
sides are clothed with many-coloured lichens, our Portuguese
companion informed us there were no more obstructions
to navigation, the river being all smooth above; he had
hunted there and knew it well. Supposing that the object
of our trip was accomplished we turned back; but two
natives, who came to our camp at night, assured us that
a cataract, called Morumbwa, did still exist in front. Drs.
Livingstone and Kirk then decided to go forward with
three Makololo and settle the question for themselves.
It was as tough a bit of travel as they ever had in Africa,
and after some painful marching the Badèma guides refused
to go further; "the Banyai," they said, "would be angry
if they showed white men the country; and there was
besides no practicable approach to the spot, neither elephant, nor hippopotamus, nor even a crocodile could reach
the cataract." The slopes of the mountains on each side of
the river, now not 300 yards wide, and without the flattish
flood-channel and groove, were more than 3000 feet from
the sky-line down, and were covered either with dense
thornbush, or huge black boulders; this deep trough-like
shape caused the sun's rays to converge as into a focus,
making the surface so hot that the soles of the feet of
the Makololo became blistered. Around, and up and down,
the party clambered among these heated blocks, at a
pace not exceeding a mile an hour; the strain upon the
muscles in jumping from crag to boulder, and wriggling
round projections, took an enormous deal out of them, and
they were often glad to cower in the shadow formed by

one rock overhanging and resting on another; the shelter induced the peculiarly strong and overpowering inclination to sleep, which too much sun sometimes causes. This sleep is curative of what may be incipient sunstroke: in its first gentle touches, it caused the dream to flit over the boiling brain, that they had become lunatics and had been sworn in as members of the Alpine club; and then it became so heavy that it made them feel as if a portion of existence had been cut out from their lives. The sun is excessively hot, and feels sharp in Africa; but, probably from the greater dryness of the atmosphere, we never heard of a single case of sunstroke, so common in India. The Makololo told Dr. Livingstone they "always thought he had a heart, but now they believed he had none," and tried to persuade Dr. Kirk to return, on the ground that it must be evident that, in attempting to go where no living foot could tread, his leader had given unmistakeable signs of having gone mad. All their efforts of persuasion, however, were lost upon Dr. Kirk, as he had not yet learned their language, and his leader knowing his companion to be equally anxious with himself to solve the problem of the navigableness of Kebrabasa, was not at pains to enlighten him. At one part a bare mountain spur barred the way, and had to be surmounted by a perilous and circuitous route, along which the crags were so hot that it was scarcely possible for the hand to hold on long enough to ensure safety in the passage; and had the foremost of the party lost his hold, he would have hurled all behind him into the river at the foot of the promontory; yet in this wild hot region, as they descended again to the river, they met a fisherman casting his hand-net into the boiling eddies, and he pointed out the cataract of Morumbwa; within an hour they were trying to measure it from an overhanging rock, at a height of about one hundred feet. When you stand facing the cataract, on the north bank, you see that it is situated in a sudden bend of the river, which is flowing in a short curve; the river above it is jammed between two mountains in a channel with perpendicular sides, and less than fifty yards wide; one or two masses of rock jut out, and then there is a sloping fall of perhaps twenty feet in a distance of thirty yards. It would stop all navigation, except during the highest floods; the rocks showed that the water then rises upwards of eighty feet perpendicularly.

Still keeping the position facing the cataract, on its right side rises Mount Morumbwa from 2000 to 3000 feet high, which gives the name to the spot. On the left of the cataract stands a noticeable mountain which may be called onion-shaped, for it is partly conical, and a large concave flake has peeled off, as granite often does, and left a broad, smooth convex face as if it were an enormous bulb. These two mountains extend their bases northwards about half a mile, and the river in that distance, still very narrow, is smooth, with a few detached rocks standing out from its bed. They climbed as high up the base of Mount Morumbwa, which touches the cataract, as they required. The rocks were all waterworn and smooth, with huge pot-holes, even at 100 feet above low water. When at a later period they climbed up the north-western base of this same mountain, the familiar face of the onion-shaped one opposite was at once recognised; one point of view on the talus of Mount Morumbwa was not more that 700 or 800 yards distant from the other, and they then completed the survey of Kebrabasa from end to end.

They did not attempt to return by the way they came, but scaled the slope of the mountain on the north. It took them three hours' hard labour in cutting their way up through the dense thornbush which covered the ascent. The face of the slope was often about an angle of 70°, yet their guide Shokumbenla, whose hard, horny soles, resembling those of elephants, showed that he was accustomed to this rough and hot work, carried a pot of water for them nearly all the way up. They slept that night at a well in a tufaceous rock on the N.W. of Chipereziwa, and never was sleep more sweet.

WOMEN WITH WATER-POTS, LISTENING TO THE MUSIC OF THE MARIMBA, SANSA, AND PAN'S PIPES.

CHAPTER III.

Return from Kebrabasa — Native musicians and their instruments — Ignorance
at Tette — Changes produced by rain after hot season — Christmas in tropical dress — Opinions modified by early associations in Northern climes —
The seasons at Tette — Cotton-seed not needed — African fever — Quinine
not a preventive of — The best precaution and remedy — "Warburgh's
drops" — Expedition turns from Kebrabasa towards River Shire in January,
1859 — Reported barrier to navigation — First intercourse with unknown
people — Navigation of Shire — Progress prevented by Murchison's cataracts
— Return to Tette — Second trip up the Shire in March, 1859 — Chibisa —
Nyanja Mukulu — Maniac guides — Discover Lake Shirwa on 18th April,
1859 — Mountains — Return to vessel — Severe case of fever — Return to
Tette 23rd June — Vessel found to be built of unstable materials — At Kongone in August.

A BAND of native musicians came to our camp one evening,
on our own way down, and treated us with their wild and not
unpleasant music on the Marimba, an instrument formed of
bars of hard wood of varying breadth and thickness, laid
on different-sized hollow calabashes, and tuned to give the
notes; a few pieces of cloth pleased them, and they
passed on.

As our companion had told us, the people were perfectly
willing to sell us provisions on our way back. When we arrived at Tette the Commandant informed us that, shortly after
we had left, the river rose a foot and became turbid; and on
seeing this, a native Portuguese came to him with a grave
countenance, and said, "That Englishman is doing something
to the river." This, we regret to say, is a fair sample of the
ignorance and superstition common to the native-born, and,
unfortunately, sometimes shared in even by men reared

in Portugal.   While we were at Tette, a Captain of Infantry was sent prisoner to Mosambique, for administering the Muave, or ordeal, and for putting the suspected person to death on that evidence alone.

At the end of the hot season everything is dry and dusty ; the atmosphere is loaded with blue haze, and very sultry. After the rains begin, the face of the country changes with surprising rapidity for the better.   Though we have not the moist hothouse-like atmosphere of the west coast, fresh green herbage quickly springs up over the hills and dales, so lately parched and brown.   The air becomes cleared of the smoky-looking haze, and one sees to great distances with ease ; the landscape is bathed in a perfect flood of light, and a delightful sense of freshness is given from everything in the morning before the glare of noon overpowers the eye.   On asking one of the Bechuanas once, what he understood by the word used for " holiness " (boitsépho) ? he answered, " When copious showers have descended during the night, and all the earth and leaves and cattle are washed clean, and the sun rising shows a drop of dew on every blade of grass, and the air breathes fresh, that is holiness."   The young foliage of several trees, more especially on the highlands, comes out brown, pale red, or pink, like the hues of autumnal leaves in England ; and as the leaves increase in size they change to a pleasant fresh light green ; bright white, scarlet, pink, and yellow flowers are everywhere ; and some few of dark crimson, like those of the kigelia, give warmth of colouring to Nature's garden.   Many trees, such as the scarlet erythrina, attract the eye by the beauty of their blossoms.   The white, full bloom of the baobab, coming at times before the rains, and the small and delicate flowers of other trees, grouped into rich clusters, deck the forest.   Myriads of wild bees are

busy from morning till night.   Some of the acacias possess a
peculiar attraction for one species of beetle; while the palm
allures others to congregate on its ample leaves.   Insects of
all sorts are now in full force; brilliant butterflies flit from
flower to flower, and, with the charming little sun-birds,
which represent the humming-birds of America and the
West Indies, never seem to tire.   Multitudes of ants are
hard at work hunting for food, or bearing it home in
triumph.   The winter birds of passage, such as the yellow
wagtail and blue drongo shrikes, have all gone, and other
kinds have come; the brown kite with his piping like a
boatswain's whistle, the spotted cuckoo with a call like
" pula," and the roller and horn-bill with their loud high
notes, are occasionally distinctly heard, though generally
this harsher music is half drowned in the volume of sweet
sounds poured forth from many a throbbing throat, which
makes an African Christmas seem like an English May.
Some birds of the weaver kind have laid aside their winter
garments of a sober brown, and appear in a gay summer dress
of scarlet and jet black; others have passed from green to
bright yellow with patches like black velvet.   The brisk little
cock whydah-bird with a pink bill, after assuming his summer
garb of black and white, has graceful plumes attached to his
new coat; his finery, as some believe, is to please at least
seven hen birds with which he is said to live.   Birds of
song are not entirely confined to villages; but they have
in Africa so often been observed to *congregate* around villages,
as to produce the impression that song and beauty may have
been intended to please the ear and eye of man, for it is
only when we approach the haunts of men that we know
that the time of the singing of birds is come.   We once
thought that the little creatures were attracted to man only

F

by grain and water, till we saw deserted villages, the people all swept off by slavery, with grain standing by running streams, but no birds. A red-throated black weaver-bird comes in flocks a little later, wearing a long train of magnificent plumes, which seem to be greatly in his way when working for his dinner among the long grass. A goatsucker or night jar (*Cometornis vexillarius*), only ten inches long from head to tail, also attracts the eye in November by a couple of feathers twenty-six inches long in the middle of each wing, the ninth and tenth from the outside. They give a slow wavy motion to the wings, and evidently retard his flight, for at other times he flies so quick that no boy could hit him with a stone. The natives can kill a hare by throwing a club, and make good running shots, but no one ever struck a night jar in common dress, though in the evening twilight they settle close to one's feet. What may be the object of the flight of the male bird being retarded we cannot tell. The males alone possess these feathers, and only for a time.

It appears strange to have Christmas come in such a cheerful bright season as this; one can hardly recognise it in summer dress, with singing birds, springing corn, and flowery plains, instead of in the winter robes of bygone days, when the keen bracing air, and ground clad in a mantle of snow, made the cozy fireside meeting-place of families doubly comfortable. The associations of early days spent in a Northern clime dispose us to view other lands with rather contracted notions, and, like the Esquimaux who were brought to Europe, to look cheerlessly at this sunny portion of our fair world, which is unhealthy only because the exuberant fertility with which the Maker has endowed it to yield abundant food for man and beast, is allowed to run

to waste. In reference to it, and its inhabitants, it was
long ago remarked, that in Africa everything was contrary;
"wool grows on the heads of men, and hair on the backs of
sheep." In feeble imitation of this dogma let us add, that the
men often wear their hair long, the women scarcely ever.
Where there are cattle, the women till the land, plant the
corn, and build the huts. The men stay at home to sew, spin,
weave, and talk, and milk the cows. The men seem to pay
a dowry for their wives instead of getting one with them.
The mountaineers of Europe are reckoned hospitable, generous, and brave. Those of this part of Africa are feeble,
spiritless, and cowardly, even when contrasted with their
own countrymen on the plains. Some Europeans aver that
Africans and themselves are descended from monkeys. Some
Africans believe that souls at death pass into the bodies of
apes. Most writers believe the blacks to be savages, nearly
all blacks believe the whites to be cannibals. The nursery
hobgoblin of the one is black, of the other white. Without
going further on with these unwise comparisons, we must
smile at the heaps of nonsense which have been written
about the negro intellect. When for greater effect we employ broken English, and use silly phrases as if translations of remarks, which, ten to one, were never made,
we have unconsciously caricatured ourselves and not the
negroes; for it is a curious fact that Europeans almost
invariably begin to speak with natives by adding the letters
e and *o* to their words " Give*e* me corn*o*, me give*e* you biscuit*o*," or " Look*o*, look*o*, me want*e* beer*o* much*e*." Our
sailors began thus, though they had never seen blacks
before. It seemed an innate idea that they could thus suit
English to a people who all speak a beautiful language,
and have no vulgar *patois*. Owing to the difference of

idiom, very few Europeans acquire an accurate knowledge
of African tongues unless they begin to learn when young.
A complaint as to the poverty of the language is often only
a sure proof of the scanty attainments of the complainant,
and gross mistakes are often made by the most experienced.
We once caught a sound like "Syria" as the name of a
country on the *other side* of a river.   It was *"Psidia,"*
and meant only the *" other side."*   A grave professor put
down in a scientific work "Kaia" as the native name of
a certain lizard.   Kaia simply means "I don't know!" the
answer which he received.   This name was also applied in
equal innocence to a range of mountains.   Every one can
recal mistakes, the remembrance of which, in after years,
brings a blush to his brow.   In general the opinion of an
intelligent missionary who has diligently studied the language
is superior to that of any traveller.   Quite as sensible if not
more pertinent answers will usually be given by Africans
to those who know their language, as are obtained from our
own uneducated poor; and could we but forget that a couple
of centuries back, the ancestors of common people in England—probably our own great-great-grandfathers—were as
unenlightened as the Africans are now, we might maunder
away about intellect, and fancy that the tacit inference
would be drawn that our own is Arch-Angelic.   The low
motives which often actuate the barbarians do, unfortunately, bear abundant crops of mean actions among servants
and even in higher ranks of more civilized people; but we
hope that these may decrease in the general improvement
of our race by the diffusion of true religion.

Dr. Kirk very properly divides the year into three seasons,
a cold, a hot, and a rainy season.   The cold period lasts
through May, June, and July; the hot prevails in August,

September, and October. The rains may be expected during the remaining months of the year.

The rainy season of Tette differs a little from that of some of the other intertropical regions; the quantity of rain-fall being considerably less. It begins in November and ends in April. During our first season in that place, only a little over nineteen inches of rain fell. In an average year, and when the crops are good, the fall amounts to about thirty-five inches. On many days it does not rain at all, and rarely is it wet all day; some days have merely a passing shower, preceded and followed by hot sunshine; occasionally an interval of a week, or even a fortnight, passes without a drop of rain, and then the crops suffer from the sun. These partial droughts happen in December and January. The heat appears to increase to a certain point in the different latitudes so as to necessitate a change, by some law similar to that which regulates the intense cold in other countries. After several days of progressive heat here, on the hottest of which the thermometer probably reaches 103° in the shade, a break occurs in the weather, and a thunderstorm cools the air for a time. At Kuruman, when the thermometer stood above 84°, rain might be expected; at Kolobeng, the point at which we looked for a storm was 96°. The Zambesi is in flood twice in the course of the year; the first flood, a partial one, attains its greatest height about the end of December or beginning of January; the second, and greatest, occurs after the river inundates the interior, in a manner similar to the overflow of the Nile, this rise not taking place at Tette until March. The Portuguese say that the greatest height which the March floods attain is thirty feet at Tette, and this happens only about every fourth year; their observations, however, have never been very accurate on anything but ivory, and they have in this case trusted to memory alone. The only fluviometer at Tette, or anywhere else on the river, was set up at our suggestion; and the first flood was at its greatest height of thirteen feet six inches on the 17th January, 1859, and then gradually fell a few feet, until succeeded by the greater flood of March. The river rises suddenly, the water is highly discoloured and impure, and there is a four-knot current in many places; but in a day or two after the first rush of waters is passed, the current becomes more equally spread over the whole bed of the river, and resumes its usual rate in the channel, although continuing in flood. The Zambesi water at other times is almost chemically pure, and the photographer would find that it is nearly as good as distilled water for the nitrate of silver bath.

A third visit to Kebrabasa was made for the purpose of ascertaining whether it might be navigable when the Zambesi was in flood, the chief point of interest being of course Morumbwa; it was found that the rapids observed in our first trip had disappeared, and that while they were smoothed over, in a few places the current had increased in strength. As the river fell rapidly while we were on the journey, the cataract of Morumbwa did not differ materially from what it was when discovered. Some fishermen assured us that it was not visible when the river was at its fullest, and that the current was then not very strong. On this occasion we travelled on the right bank, and found it, with the additional inconvenience of rain, as rough and fatiguing as the left had been. Our progress was impeded by the tall wet grass and dripping boughs, and consequent fever. During the earlier part of the journey we came upon a few deserted hamlets only; but at last in a pleasant valley we met some of the people of the country, who were miserably poor and hungry. The women were gathering wild fruits in the woods. A young man having consented for two yards of cotton cloth to show us a short path to the cataract led us up a steep hill to a village perched on the edge of one of its precipices; a thunderstorm coming on at the time, the headman invited us to take shelter in a hut until it had passed. Our guide having informed him of what he knew and conceived to be our object, was favoured in return with a long reply in well-sounding blank verse; at the end of every line the guide, who listened with deep attention, responded with a grunt, which soon became so ludicrous that our men burst into a loud laugh. Neither the poet nor the responsive guide took the slightest notice of their rudeness, but kept on as energetically as ever to the end. The speech, or more probably our bad manners, made some impression on our guide, for he declined, although offered double pay, to go any further.

We brought cotton-seed to Africa, in ignorance that the cotton already introduced was equal, if not superior, to the common American, and offered it to any of the Portuguese and natives who chose to cultivate it; but, though some tried this source of wealth, it was evident that their ideas could not soar beyond black ivory, as they call slaves, elephant's tusks, and a little gold-dust.

A great deal of fever comes in with March and April; in March, if considerable intervals take place between the rainy days, and in April always, for then large surfaces of mud and decaying vegetation are exposed to the hot sun. In general an attack does not continue long, but it pulls one down quickly; though when the fever is checked the strength is as quickly restored.　It had long been observed that those who were stationed for any length of time in one spot, and lived sedentary lives, suffered more from fever than others who moved about and had both mind and body occupied; but we could not all go in the small vessel when she made her trips, during which the change of place and scenery proved so conducive to health; and some of us were obliged to remain in charge of the expedition's property, making occasional branch trips to examine objects of interest in the vicinity.　Whatever may be the cause of the fever, we observed that all were often affected at the same time, as if from malaria.　This was particularly the case during a north wind: it was at first commonly believed that a daily dose of quinine would prevent the attack. For a number of months all our men, except two, took quinine regularly every morning.　The fever sometimes attacked the believers in quinine, while the unbelievers in its prophylactic powers escaped.　Whether we took it daily, or omitted it altogether for months, made no difference; the fever was impartial, and seized us on the days of quinine as regularly and as severely as when it remained undisturbed in the medicine chest, and we finally abandoned the use of it as a prophylactic altogether.　The best preventive against fever is plenty of interesting work to do, and abundance of wholesome food to eat.　To a man well housed and clothed, who enjoys these advantages, the fever at Tette will not prove a more formidable enemy than a common cold; but let one of these be wanting—let him be indolent, or guilty of excesses in eating or drinking, or have poor, scanty fare,—and the fever will probably become a more serious matter.　It is of a milder type at Tette than at Quillimane or on the low seacoast; and, as in this part of Africa one is as liable to fever, as to colds in England, it would be advisable for strangers always to hasten from the coast to the higher lands, in order that when the seizure does take place, it may be of the mildest type. This having been pointed out by Dr. Kirk, the Portuguese authorities afterwards took the hint, and sent the next detachment of soldiers at once up to Tette. It consisted of eighty men, and in spite of the irregularities committed, most of them being of the class termed "incorrigibles," in three years only ten died, and but five of fever. Although quinine was not found to be a preventive, except possibly in the way of acting as a tonic, and rendering the system more able to resist the influence of malaria, it was found invaluable in the cure of the complaint, as soon as pains in the back, sore bones, headache, yawning, quick and sometimes intermittent pulse, noticeable pulsations of the jugulars, with suffused eyes, hot skin, and foul tongue, began.*

Very curious are the effects of African fever on certain

---

* A remedy composed of from six to eight grains of resin of jalap, the same of rhubarb, and three each of calomel and quinine, made up into four pills, with tincture of cardamoms, usually relieved all the symptoms in five or six hours. Four pills are a full dose for a man—one will suffice for a woman. They received from our men the name of "rousers," from their efficacy in rousing up even those most prostrated. When their operation is delayed, a dessert-spoonful of Epsom salts should be given. Quinine after or during the operation of the pills, in large doses every two or three hours, until deafness or cinchonism ensued, completed the cure. The only cases in which we found ourselves completely helpless, were those in which obstinate vomiting ensued. We had received from Viscount Torrington a handsome supply of "Warburgh's fever drops," a medicine much esteemed in India; and in consideration of his lordship's kindness in furnishing the drug at a considerable expense, as well as from a desire to find out a remedy that might be relied on for this formidable disease, we gave it as fair a trial as was in our power. In the shivering stage it caused warmth, but did not cure. One old man seemed cured, but died a day or two afterwards. We regret that we cannot recommend it for Africa, though we know of its high repute in India.

minds. Cheerfulness vanishes, and the whole mental horizon is overcast with black clouds of gloom and sadness. The liveliest joke cannot provoke even the semblance of a smile. The countenance is grave, the eyes suffused, and the few utterances are made in the piping voice of a wailing infant. An irritable temper is often the first symptom of approaching fever. At such times a man feels very much like a fool, if he does not act like one. Nothing is right, nothing pleases the fever-stricken victim. He is peevish, prone to find fault and to contradict, and think himself insulted, and is exactly what an Irish naval surgeon before a court-martial defined a drunken man to be : "a man unfit for society." If a party were all soaked full of malaria at once, the life of the leader of the expedition would be made a burden to him. One might come with lengthened visage, and urge as a good reason for his despair, if further progress were attempted, that "he had broken the photograph of his wife ;" another, "that his proper position was unjustly withheld because special search was not directed towards 'the ten lost tribes.'" It is dangerous to rally such a one, for the irate companion may quote Scripture, and point to their habitat "beyond the rivers of Ethiopia." When a man begins to feel that everything is meant to his prejudice,— he either takes a dose of "rousers," or writes to the newspapers, according to the amount of sense with which nature has endowed him.

Finding that it was impossible to take our steamer of only ten-horse power through Kebrabasa, and convinced that, in order to force a passage when the river was in flood, much greater power was required, due information was forwarded to Her Majesty's Government, and application made for a more suitable vessel. Our attention was in the mean time turned to the exploration of the river Shire, a northern tributary of the Zambesi, which joins it about a hundred miles from the sea. We could learn nothing satisfactory from the Portuguese regarding this affluent; no one, they said, had ever been up it, nor could they tell whence it came. Years ago a Portuguese expedition is said, however, to have attempted the ascent, but to have abandoned it on account of the impenetrable duckweed (*Pistia stratiotes*). Many asserted, on the strength of this, that not even canoes could force their way through the masses of aquatic plants that covered its surface.   Others, however, hinted in a private way that it was not the duckweed which drove back the expedition, but the poisoned arrows by which the hostile natives repulsed the Portuguese with heavy loss. No one sent native traders up the Shire, nor had intercourse with the treacherous savages who lived on its banks. A merchant of Senna told us that he once fitted out a trading party which went a short distance up the river, but the men of it were robbed and barely escaped with their lives. " Our Government," said one Commandant, " has sent us orders to assist and protect you, but you go where we dare not follow, and how can we protect you?" We could not learn from any record that the Shire had ever been ascended by Europeans. As far, therefore, as we were concerned, the exploration was absolutely new.   All the Portuguese believed the Manganja to be brave but bloodthirsty savages; and on our return we found that soon after our departure a report was widely spread that our temerity had been followed by fatal results, Dr. Livingstone having been shot, and Dr. Kirk mortally wounded by poisoned arrows.

Our first trip to the Shire was in January, 1859. A considerable quantity of duckweed floated down the river for the first twenty-five miles, but not sufficient to interrupt navigation with canoes or with any other craft. Nearly the whole of this aquatic plant proceeds from a marsh on the west, and comes into the river a little beyond a lofty hill called Mount Morambala. Above that there is hardly any. As we approached the villages, the natives collected in large numbers, armed with bows and poisoned arrows; and some, dodging behind trees, were observed taking aim as if on the point of shooting. All the women had been sent out of the way, and the men were evidently prepared to resist aggression. At the village of a Chief named Tingane, at least five hundred natives collected and ordered us to stop. Dr. Livingstone went ashore; and on his explaining that we were English and had come neither to take slaves nor to fight, but only to open a path by which our countrymen might follow to purchase cotton, or whatever else they might have to sell, except slaves, Tingane became at once quite friendly. The presence of the steamer, which showed that they had an entirely new people to deal with, probably contributed to this result; for Tingane was notorious for being the barrier to all intercourse between the Portuguese black traders and the natives further inland; none were allowed to pass him either way. He was an elderly, well-made man, grey-headed, and over six feet high. Though somewhat excited by our presence, he readily complied with the request to call his people together, in order that all might know what our objects were.

In commencing intercourse with any people we almost always referred to the English detestation of slavery. Most of them already possess some information respecting the efforts made by the English at sea to suppress the slave-trade; and our work being to induce them to raise and sell cotton, instead of capturing and selling their fellow-men, our errand appears quite natural; and as they all have clear ideas of their own self-interest, and are keen traders, the reasonableness of the proposal is at once admitted; and as a belief in a Supreme Being, the Maker and Ruler of all things, and in the continued existence of departed spirits is universal, it becomes quite appropriate to explain that we possess a Book containing a Revelation of the will of Him, to whom in their natural state they recognise no relationship. The fact that His Son appeared among men, and left His words in His Book, always awakens attention; but the great difficulty is to make them feel that they have any relationship to Him, and that He feels any interest in them. The numbness of moral perception exhibited, is often discouraging; but the mode of communication, either by interpreters, or by the imperfect knowledge of the language, which not even missionaries of talent can overcome save by the labour of many years, may, in part, account for the phenomenon. However, the idea of the Father of all being displeased with His children, for selling or killing each other, at once gains their ready assent: it harmonizes so exactly with their own ideas of right and wrong. But, as in our own case at home, nothing less than the instruction and example of many years will secure their moral elevation.

The dialect spoken here closely resembles that used at Senna and Tette. We understood it at first only enough to know whether our interpreter was saying what we bade him, or was indulging in his own version. After stating pretty nearly what he was told, he had an inveterate tendency to wind up with " The Book says you are to grow cotton, and the English are to come and buy it," or with. some joke of his own, which might have been ludicrous, had it not been seriously distressing.

In the first ascent of the Shire our attention was chiefly directed to the river itself. The delight of threading out the meanderings of upwards of 200 miles of a hitherto unexplored river must be felt to be appreciated. All the lower part of the river was found to be at least two fathoms in depth. It became shallower higher up, where many departing and re-entering branches diminished the volume of water, but the absence of sandbanks made it easy of navigation. We had to exercise the greatest care lest anything we did should be misconstrued by the crowds who watched us. After having made, in a straight line, one hundred miles, although the windings of the river had fully doubled the distance, we found further progress with the steamer arrested, in 15° 55′ south, by magnificent cataracts, which we called "The Murchison," after one whose name has already a world-wide fame, and whose generous kindness we can never repay. The native name of that figured in the woodcut is Mamvira. It is that at which the progress of the steamer was first stopped. The angle of descent is much smaller than that of the five cataracts above it; indeed, so small as compared with them, that after they were discovered this was not included in the number.

A few days were spent here in the hope that there might be an opportunity of taking observations for longitude, but it rained most of the time, or the sky was overcast. It was deemed imprudent to risk a land journey whilst the natives were so very suspicious as to have a strong guard on the banks of the river night and day; the weather also was unfavourable. After sending presents and messages to two of the Chiefs, we returned to Tette. In going down stream our progress was rapid, as we were aided by the current. The hippopotami never made a mistake, but got out of our way. The crocodiles, not

MAMʼVERA CATARACT, THE FIRST OR LOWEST OF MURCHISON'S CATARACTS.

so wise, sometimes rushed with great velocity at us, thinking that we were some huge animal swimming. They kept about a foot from the surface, but made three well-defined ripples from the feet and body, which marked their rapid progress; raising the head out of the water when only a few yards from the expected feast, down they went to the bottom like a stone, without touching the boat.

In the middle of March of the same year (1859), we started again for a second trip on the Shire. The natives were now friendly, and readily sold us rice, fowls, and corn. We entered into amicable relations with the Chief, Chibisa, whose village was about ten miles below the cataract. He had sent two men on our first visit to invite us to drink beer; but the steamer was such a terrible apparition to them, that, after shouting the invitation, they jumped ashore, and left their canoe to drift down the stream. Chibisa was a remarkably shrewd man, the very image, save his dark hue, of one of our most celebrated London actors, and the most intelligent Chief, by far, in this quarter. A great deal of fighting had fallen to his lot, he said; but it was always others who began; he was invariably in the right, and they alone were to blame. He was moreover a firm believer in the divine right of kings. He was an ordinary man, he said, when his father died, and left him the chieftainship; but directly he succeeded to the high office, he was conscious of power passing into his head, and down his back; he felt it enter, and knew that he was a Chief, clothed with authority, and possessed of wisdom; and people then began to fear and reverence him. He mentioned this, as one would a fact of natural history, any doubt being quite out of the question. His people, too, believed in him, for they bathed in the river without the slightest fear of crocodiles, the Chief having placed a powerful medicine

there, which protected them from the bite of these terrible
reptiles.

Leaving the vessel opposite Chibisa's village, Drs. Livingstone and Kirk and a number of the Makololo started on foot
for Lake Shirwa. They travelled in a northerly direction
over a mountainous country. The people were far from
being well-disposed to them, and some of their guides tried
to mislead them, and could not be trusted. Masakasa, a Makololo headman, overheard some remarks, which satisfied him
that the guide was leading them into trouble. He was quiet
till they reached a lonely spot, when he came up to Doctor
Livingstone, and said, " That fellow is bad, he is taking us into
mischief; my spear is sharp, and there is no one here; shall I
cast him into the long grass?" Had the Doctor given the
slightest token of assent, or even kept silence, never more
would any one have been led by that guide, for in a twinkling he would have been where "the wicked cease from
troubling." It was afterwards found that in this case there
was no treachery at all; but a want of knowledge on their
part of the language, and of the country. They asked to be
led to "Nyanja Mukulu," or Great Lake, meaning, by this,
Lake Shirwa; and the guide took them round a terribly rough
piece of mountainous country, gradually edging away towards
a long marsh, which from the numbers of those animals we
had seen there we had called the Elephant Marsh, but which
was really the place known to him by the name "Nyanja
Mukulu," or Great Lake. Nyanja or Nyanza means, generally,
a marsh, lake, river, or even a mere rivulet.

The party pushed on at last without guides, or only
with crazy ones; for, oddly enough, they were often
under great obligations to the madmen of the different
villages: one of these honoured them, as they slept

in the open air, by dancing and singing at their feet the whole night. These poor fellows sympathized with the explorers, probably in the belief that they belonged to their own class; and, uninfluenced by the general opinion of their countrymen, they really pitied, and took kindly to the strangers, and often guided them faithfully from place to place, when no sane man could be hired for love or money.

The bearing of the Manganja at this time was very independent; a striking contrast to the cringing attitude they afterwards assumed, when the cruel scourge of slave-hunting passed over their country. Signals were given from the different villages by means of drums, and notes of defiance and intimidation were sounded in the travellers' ears by day; and occasionally they were kept awake the whole night, in expectation of an instant attack. Drs. Livingstone and Kirk were desirous that nothing should occur to make the natives regard them as enemies; Masakasa, on the other hand, was anxious to show what he could do in the way of fighting them.

The perseverance of the party was finally crowned with success; for on the 18th of April they discovered Lake Shirwa, a considerable body of bitter water, containing leeches, fish, crocodiles, and hippopotami. From having probably no outlet, the water is slightly brackish, and it appears to be deep, with islands like hills rising out of it. Their point of view was at the base of Mount Pirimiti or Mopeu-peu, on its S.S.W. side. Thence the prospect northwards ended in a sea horizon with two small islands in the distance—a larger one, resembling a hill-top and covered with trees, rose more in the foreground. Ranges of hills appeared on the east; and on the west stood Mount Chikala,

G

which seems to be connected with the great mountain-mass called Zomba.

The shore, near which they spent two nights, was covered with reeds and papyrus. Wishing to obtain the latitude by the natural horizon, they waded into the water some distance towards what was reported to be a sandbank, but were so assaulted by leeches, they were fain to retreat; and a woman told them that in enticing them into the water the men only wanted to kill them. The information gathered was that this lake was nothing in size compared to another in the north, from which it is separated by only a tongue of land. The northern end of Shirwa has not been seen, though it has been passed; the length of the lake may probably be 60 or 80 miles, and about 20 broad. The height above the sea is 1800 feet, and the taste of the water is like a weak solution of Epsom salts. The country around is very beautiful, and clothed with rich vegetation; and the waves, at the time they were there, breaking and foaming over a rock on the south-eastern side, added to the beauty of the picture. Exceedingly lofty mountains, perhaps 8000 feet above the sea-level, stand near the eastern shore. When their lofty steep-sided summits appear, some above, some below the clouds, the scene is grand. This range is called Milanje; on the west stands Mount Zomba, 7000 feet in height, and some twenty miles long.

Their object being rather to gain the confidence of the people by degrees, than to explore, they considered that they had advanced far enough into the country for one trip; and believing that they could secure their end by a repetition of their visit, as they had done on the Shire, they decided to return to the vessel at Dakanamoio island; but, instead of returning by the way they came, they passed down southwards close by Mount Chiradzuru, among the relatives of Chibisa, and thence by the pass Zedi, down to the Shire. And it was well that they got to the ship when they did; for our excellent Quartermaster, John Walker, who had been left in charge, had been very ill of fever all the time of their absence; while those who had been roughing it for twenty-two days on the hills, and sleeping every night, except one, in the open air, came back well and hearty. Rowe, his companion, who had charge of the medicine, had not given him any, because he did not know what his illness was. One can scarcely mistake the fever if he attends to the symptoms already enumerated, or remembers that almost every complaint in this country is a form of fever, or is modified by the malaria. Walker's being a very severe case, a large dose of calomel was at once administered. This sometimes relieves when other remedies fail, but the risk of salivation must be run. When 20 grains are taken, it may cause an abundant flow of bile, and a cure be the result. This is mentioned not as a course to be followed, except when other remedies fail, or when jaundice supervenes. We have seen a case of this kind cured by a large dose of calomel, when a blister put on the pit of the stomach, to allay vomiting, brought out serum as black as porter, as if the blood had been impregnated with bile. These hints are given, though we believe, as we have before stated, that no Mission or Expedition ought to enter the country, without a skilful surgeon as an essential part of its staff.

Quartermaster Walker soon recovered, though, from the long continuance of the fever, his system was very much more shaken than it would have been, had the medicine been administered at once. The Kroomen had, while we were away, cut a good supply of wood for steaming, and we soon proceeded down the river.

The steamer reached Tette on the 23rd of June, and, after undergoing repairs, proceeded to the Kongone to receive provisions from one of H.M. cruisers. We had been very abundantly supplied with first-rate stores, but were unfortunate enough to lose a considerable portion of them, and had now to bear the privation as best we could. On the way down, we purchased a few gigantic cabbages and pumpkins at a native village below Mazaro. Our dinners had usually consisted of but a single course; but we were surprised the next day by our black cook from Sierra Leone bearing in a second course. "What have you got there?" was asked in wonder. "A tart, sir." "A tart! of what is it made?" "Of cabbage, sir." As we had no sugar, and could not "make, believe," as in the days of boyhood, we did not enjoy the feast that Tom's genius had prepared. Her Majesty's brig "Persian," Lieutenant Saumarez commanding, called on her way to the Cape; and, though somewhat short of provisions herself, generously gave us all she could spare. We now parted with our Kroomen, as, from their inability to march, we could not use them in our land journeys. A crew was picked out from the Makololo, who, besides being good travellers, could cut wood, work the ship, and required only native food.

While at the Kongone it was found necessary to beach the steamer for repairs. She was built of a newly-invented sort of steel plates, only a sixteenth of an inch in thickness, patented, but unfortunately never tried before. To build an exploring ship of untried material was a mistake. Some chemical action on this preparation of steel caused a minute hole; from this point, branches like lichens, or the little ragged stars we sometimes see in thawing ice, radiated in all directions. Small holes went through wherever a bend occurred in these branches. The bottom very soon became like a sieve, completely full of minute holes, which leaked perpetually. The engineer stopped the larger ones, but the vessel was no sooner afloat, than new ones broke out. The first news of a morning was commonly the unpleasant announcement of another leak in the forward compartment, or in the middle, which was worse still.

Frequent showers fell on our way up the Zambesi, in the beginning of August. On the 8th we had upwards of three inches of rain, which large quantity, more than falls in any single rainy day during the season at Tette, we owed to being near the sea. Sometimes the cabin was nearly flooded; for, in addition to the leakage from below, rain poured through the roof, and an umbrella had to be used whenever we wished to write : the mode of coupling the compartments, too, was a new one, and the action of the hinder compartment on the middle one pumped up the water of the river, and sent it in streams over the floor and lockers, where lay the cushions which did double duty as chairs and beds. In trying to form an opinion of the climate, it must be recollected that much of the fever, from which we suffered, was caused by sleeping on these wet cushions. Many of the botanical specimens, laboriously collected and carefully prepared by Dr. Kirk, were destroyed, or double work imposed, by their accidentally falling into wet places in the cabin.

When lying off an island a few miles below Mazaro, the owner of it, Paul, a relative of the rebel Mariano, paid us a visit. He had just returned from Mosambique, having, to use the common phrase of the country, "arranged" with the authorities. He told us that Governor-General d'Almeida knew nothing of the Kongone, and thought, with others, that the Zambesi entered the sea at Quillimane. His Excellency had been making inquiries of him, respecting the correctness

of Dr. Livingstone's map in this particular.   This is mentioned because lately the Portuguese have seriously attempted
to show that the Kongone was previously well known to their
slavers.   Paul is of mixed breed, but seems to thrive, being
the only really fat man of the descendants of the Portuguese
in East Africa.   It is a pity that a certain class of diseases,
self-induced and inherited, have become so universal among
half-castes, that no conclusion can here be drawn as to their
permanence as a race.

CHAPTER IV.

Up the Shire again, August, 1859 — Mount Morambala — Hot fountain — Chase by a buffalo — Nyanja Pangono, or Little Lake — Nyanja Mukulu, or Great Lake — Ancient Portuguese geographical knowledge unavailable — Chikanda-kadzo — Accident from unsuitability of steamer — Hippopotamus traps — Mosquitoes — Elephants — View of the Shire marshes — Birds — Palm wine, or *Sura* — Salt-making — Brackish soil and superior cotton — Dakanamoio Island — A loving hornbill — Chibisa — Child sold into slavery.

ABOUT the middle of August, after cutting wood at Shamoara, we again steamed up the Shire, with the intention of becoming better acquainted with the people, and making another and longer journey on foot to the north of Lake Shirwa, in search of Lake Nyassa, of which we had already received some information, under the name Nyinyesi (the stars). The Shire is much narrower than the Zambesi, but deeper, and more easily navigated. It drains a low, and exceedingly fertile valley of from fifteen to twenty miles in breadth. Ranges of wooded hills bound this valley on both sides. For the first twenty miles the hills on the left bank are close to the river; then comes Morambala, whose name means "the lofty watch-tower," a detached mountain 500 yards from the river's brink, which rises, with steep sides on the west, to 4000 feet in height, and is about seven miles in length. It is wooded up to the very top, and very beautiful. The southern end, seen from a distance, has a fine gradual slope, and looks as if it might be of easy ascent; but the side which faces the Shire is steep and rocky, especially in the upper half.

A small village peeps out about halfway up the mountain; it has a pure and bracing atmosphere; and is perched above mosquito range. The people on the summit have a very different climate and vegetation, from those of the plains; but they have to spend a great portion of their existence amidst white fleecy clouds, which, in the rainy season, rest daily on the top of their favourite mountain. We were kindly treated by these mountaineers on our first ascent; before our second they were nearly all swept away by Mariano. Dr. Kirk found upwards of thirty species of ferns on this and other mountains, and even good-sized tree-ferns; though scarcely a single kind is to be met with on the plains. Lemon and orange trees grew wild, and pineapples had been planted by the people. Many large hornbills, hawks, monkeys, antelopes, and rhinoceroses found a home and food among the great trees round its base. A hot fountain boils up on the plain near the north end. It bubbles out of the earth, clear as crystal, at two points, or eyes, a few yards apart from each other, and sends off a fine flowing stream of hot water. The temperature was found to be 174° Fahr., and it boiled an egg in about the usual time. Our guide threw in a small branch to show us how speedily the Madse-awira (boiling water) could kill the leaves. Unlucky lizards and insects did not seem to understand the nature of a hot-spring, as many of their remains were lying at the bottom. A large beetle had alighted on the water, and been killed before it had time to fold its wings. An incrustation, smelling of sulphur, has been deposited by the water on the stones. About a hundred feet from the eye of the fountain the mud is as hot as can be borne by the body. In taking a bath there, it makes the skin perfectly clean, and none of the mud adheres: it is strange that the Portuguese do not resort to it for the numerous cutaneous diseases, with which they are so often afflicted.

A few clumps of the palm and acacia trees appear west of Morambala, on the rich plain forming the tongue of land between the rivers Shire and Zambesi. This is a good place for all sorts of game. The Zambesi canoe-men were afraid to sleep on it from the idea of lions being there; they preferred to pass the night on an island. Some black men, who accompanied us as volunteer workmen from Shupanga, called out one evening that a lion stood on the bank. It was very dark, and we could only see two sparkling lights, said to be the lion's eyes looking at us; for here, as elsewhere, they have a theory that the lion's eyes always flash fire at night. Not being fireflies—as they did not move when a shot was fired in their direction—they were probably glowworms.

Beyond Morambala the Shire comes winding through an extensive marsh. For many miles to the north a broad sea of fresh green grass extends, and is so level, that it might be used for taking the meridian altitude of the sun. Ten or fifteen miles north of Morambala, stands the dome-shaped mountain Makanga, or Chi-kanda; several others with granitic-looking peaks stretch away to the north, and form the eastern boundary of the valley; another range, but of metamorphic rocks, commencing opposite Senna, bounds the valley on the west. After steaming through a portion of this marsh, we came to a broad belt of palm, and other trees, crossing the fine plain on the right bank. Marks of large game were abundant. Elephants had been feeding on the palm nuts, which have a pleasant fruity taste, and are used as food by man. Two pythons were observed coiled together among the branches of a large tree, and were both

shot. The larger of the two, a female, was ten feet long. They
are harmless, and said to be good eating. The Makololo
having set fire to the grass where they were cutting wood, a
solitary buffalo rushed out of the conflagration, and made a
furious charge at an active young fellow named Mantlanyane.
Never did his fleet limbs serve him better than during the few
seconds of his fearful flight before the maddened animal.
When he reached the bank, and sprang into the river, the
infuriated beast was scarcely six feet behind him. Towards
evening, after the day's labour in wood-cutting was over,
some of the men went fishing. They followed the common African custom of agitating the water, by giving it
a few sharp strokes with the top of the fishing-rod, immediately after throwing in the line, to attract the attention
of the fish to the bait. Having caught nothing, the
reason assigned was the same as would have been given in
England under like circumstances, namely, that "the wind
made the fish cold, and they would not bite." Many gardens
of maize, pumpkins, and tobacco, fringed the marshy banks
as we went on. They belong to natives of the hills, who come
down in the dry season, and raise a crop on parts at other
times flooded. While the crops are growing, large quantities
of fish are caught, chiefly *Clarias capensis*, and *Mugil Africanus;* they are dried for sale or for future consumption.

As we ascended, we passed a deep stream about thirty yards
wide, flowing in from a body of open water several miles
broad. Numbers of men were busy at different parts of it,
filling their canoes with the lotus root, called *Nyika*, which,
when boiled or roasted, resembles our chestnuts, and is
extensively used in Africa as food. Out of this lagoon, and by
this stream, the chief part of the duckweed of the Shire flows.
The lagoon itself is called Nyanja ea Motope (Lake of Mud).

It is also named Nyanja Pangono (Little Lake), while the elephant marsh goes by the name of Nyanja Mukulu (Great Lake).   It is evident from the shore line still to be observed on the adjacent hills, that in ancient times these were really lakes, and the traditional names thus preserved are only another evidence of the general desiccation which Africa has undergone.   No one would believe that beyond these little and great Nyanjas Portuguese geographical knowledge never extended.   But the Viscount Sa da Bandeira, in an official letter to the Governor-General of Mosambique, in his patriotic anxiety to prove that we did not discover *Lake Nyassa*, actually quotes as the only information the ancient archives of Lisbon can disclose, that the people of Senna held commercial intercourse with the people on Morambala, and of course, as he avers, must have sailed into the little and great marshes or Nyanjas referred to above.   As if either of these were Lake Nyassa!   The Shire cataracts are quite ignored. The great Victoria Falls of Mosi-oa-tunya, we are aware, were quite unknown to the Portuguese; but, until we read his Excellency's quotations from hearsay reports of some ancient author, we believed that the five great Murchison Cataracts, which form a descent of 1200 feet, only a hundred and fifty miles from Senna, must have been known to the old Portuguese, and we still incline to the belief that they must have been explored; but, since the discovery was hidden from the rest of the world, it takes rank with the explorations of illiterate Africans.   It is a pity, but the fact is, that the good Viscount now feels the inconvenience which follows the short-sighted policy of his ancestors in geographical matters, as much as his descendants will feel and lament the present "dog in the manger" commercial policy of his contemporaries.   One of the Jesuits formerly made a business-like proposal to explore

Lake Maravi, but nowhere is it stated that it ever was carried
into effect. This, we regret to say, is all the information we
have been able to gain on this subject from the Portuguese.
If we had been able to discover more particulars of their explorations, we certainly are not conscious of a desire to dwarf
them.

Late in the afternoon of the first day's steaming,
after we left the wooding-place, we called at the village of Chikanda-Kadze, a female Chief, to purchase rice
for our men; but we were now in the blissful region where
time is absolutely of no account, and where men may sit
down and rest themselves when tired; so they requested
us to wait till next day, and they would then sell us some
food. As our forty black men, however, had nothing to cook
for supper, we were obliged to steam on to reach a village a
few miles above. When we meet those who care not whether
we purchase or let it alone, or who think men ought only to be
in a hurry when fleeing from an enemy, our ideas about time
being money, and the power of the purse, receive a shock.
The state of eager competition, which in England wears out
both mind and body, and makes life bitter, is here happily
unknown. The cultivated spots are mere dots compared to
the broad fields of rich soil, which is never either grazed or
tilled. Pity that the plenty in store for all, from our Father's
bountiful hands, is not enjoyed by more.

The wretched little steamer could not carry all the hands
we needed; so, to lighten her, we put some into the boats
and towed them astern. In the dark, one of the boats was
capsized; but all in it, except one poor fellow who could not
swim, were picked up. His loss threw a gloom over us all,
and added to the chagrin we often felt at having been so ill-
served in our sorry craft by one of our own countrymen. Few

would have acted thus towards us: we had received the assurance that the steamer would carry from ten to twelve tons, and about thirty-six men; but we found that this made her draw so much as to be near sinking, and we adopted the expedient mentioned, with the unfortunate result described.

Next day we arrived at the village of Mboma (16° 56′ 30″ S.), where the people raised large quantities of rice, and were eager traders; the rice was sold at wonderfully low rates, and we could not purchase a tithe of the food brought for sale.

African Fiddle of one String.

A native minstrel serenaded us in the evening, playing several quaint tunes on a species of one-stringed fiddle, accompanied by wild, but not unmusical songs. He told the Makololo that he intended to play all night to induce us to give him a present. The nights being cold, the thermometer falling to 47°, with occasional fogs, he was asked if he was not afraid of perishing from cold; but, with the genuine spirit of an Italian organ-grinder, he replied, "Oh, no; I shall spend the night with my white comrades in the big canoe; I have often heard of the white men, but have never seen them till now, and I must sing and play well to them." A small piece of cloth, however, bought him off, and he moved away in good humour. The water of the river was 70° at sunrise, which was 23° warmer than the air at the same time, and this caused fogs, which rose like steam off the river. When this is the case cold bathing in the mornings at this time of the year is improper, for, instead of a glow on coming out, one is apt to get a chill; the air being so much colder than the water.

A range of hills, commencing opposite Senna, comes to within two or three miles of Mboma village, and then runs in a north-westerly direction; the principal hill is named Malawe; a number of villages stand on its tree-covered sides, and coal is found cropping out in the rocks. The country improves as we ascend, the rich valley becoming less swampy, and adorned with a number of trees.

Both banks are dotted with hippopotamus traps, over every track which these animals have made in going up out of the water to graze. The hippopotamus feeds on grass alone, and, where there is any danger, only at night. Its enormous lips act like a mowing-machine, and form a path of shortcropped grass as it feeds. We never saw it eat aquatic plants or reeds. The tusks seem weapons of both offence and defence. The hippopotamus trap consists of a beam five or six feet long, armed with a spear-head or hard-wood spike, covered with poison, and suspended to a forked pole by a cord, which, coming down to the path, is held by a catch, to be set free when the beast treads on it. Being wary brutes, they are still very numerous. One got frightened by the ship, as she was steaming close to the bank. In its eager hurry to escape it rushed on shore, and ran directly under a trap, when down came the heavy beam on its back, driving the poisoned spear-head a foot deep into its flesh. In its agony it plunged back into the river, to die in a few hours, and afterwards furnished a feast for the natives. The poison on the spear-head does not affect the meat, except the part around the wound, and that is thrown away. In some places the descending beam is weighted with heavy stones, but here the hard heavy wood is sufficient.

View of Steamer, Traps, and dead Hippopotamus.

About dusk we were hailed from the bank by an authoritative voice. "Where are you going to ? Where are you going to ? What is all this journeying about ? " " You may sleep there, so do not trouble yourself," was the answer returned by the Makololo.

"She is leaking worse than ever forward, sir, and there is a foot of water in the hold," was our first salutation on the morning of the 20th. But we have become accustomed to these things now, and are not surprised to hear of a new " cataclysm " at any time. The cabin-floor is always wet, and one is obliged to mop up the water many times a day, giving some countenance to the native idea that Englishmen, live in or on the water, and have no houses but ships. The cabin is now a favourite breeding-place for mosquitoes, and we have to support both the ship-bred and shore-bred bloodsuckers, of which several species show us their irritating attentions. A large brown sort, called by the Portuguese *mansos* (tame), flies straight to its victim, and goes to work at once, as though it were an invited guest. Some of the small kinds carry uncommonly sharp lancets, and very potent poison. " What would these insects eat, if we did not pass this way?" becomes a natural question.

The juices of plants, and decaying vegetable matter in the mud, probably form the natural food of mosquitoes, and blood is not necessary for their existence. They appear so commonly at malarious spots, that their presence may be taken as a hint to man to be off to more healthy localities. None appear on the high lands. On the low lands they swarm in myriads. The females alone are furnished with the biting apparatus, and their number appears to be out of all proportion in excess of the males. At anchor, on a still evening, they were excessively annoying; and the sooner we took refuge under our mosquito curtains, the better. The miserable and sleepless night that only one mosquito inside the curtain can cause, is so well known, and has been so often described, that it is needless to describe it here. One soon learns, from experience, that to beat out the curtains thoroughly before entering them, so that not one of these pests can possibly be harboured within, is the only safeguard against such severe trials to one's tranquillity and temper.

A few miles above Mboma we came again to the village (16° 44' 30" S.), of the Chief, Tingane, the beat of whose war-drums can speedily muster some hundreds of armed men.

The bows and poisoned arrows here are of superior work-manship to those below.   Mariano's slave-hunting parties stood in great awe of these barbed arrows, and long kept aloof from Tingane's villages.   His people were friendly enough with us now, and covered the banks with a variety of articles for sale.   The majestic mountain, Pirone, to which we have given the name of Mount Clarendon, now looms in sight, and further to the N.W. the southern end of the grand Milanje range rises in the form of an un-finished sphinx, looking down on Lake Shirwa.   The Ruo (16° 31' 0" S.) is said to have its source in the Milanje mountains, and flows to the S.W., to join the Shire some distance above Tingane's.   A short way beyond the Ruo lies the elephant marsh, or Nyanja Mukulu, which is fre-quented by vast herds of these animals.   We believe that we counted eight hundred elephants in sight at once.   In the choice of such a stronghold, they have shown their usual sagacity, for no hunter can get near them through the swamps.   They now keep far from the steamer; but, when she first came up, we steamed into the midst of a herd, and some were shot from the ship's deck.   A single lesson was sufficient to teach them that the puffing monster was a thing to be avoided; and at the first glimpse they are now off two or three miles to the midst of the marsh, which is furrowed in every direction by wandering branches of the Shire.   A fine young elephant was here caught alive, as he was climbing up the bank to follow his retreating dam.   When laid hold of, he screamed with so much energy that, to escape a visit from the enraged mother, we steamed off, and dragged him through the water by the proboscis.   As the men were holding his trunk over the gunwale, Monga, a brave Makololo elephant-hunter, rushed aft, and drew his

H

knife across it in a sort of frenzy peculiar to the chase. The
wound was skilfully sewn up, and the young animal soon
became quite tame, but, unfortunately, the breathing prevented the cut from healing, and he died in a few days from
loss of blood. Had he lived, and had we been able to bring
him home, he would have been the first *African* elephant
ever seen in England. The African male elephant is from
ten, to a little over eleven feet in height, and differs from the
Asiatic species, more particularly in the convex shape of his
forehead, and the enormous size of his ears. In Asia many
of the males, and all the females, are without tusks, but in
Africa both sexes are provided with these weapons. The
enamel in the molar teeth is arranged differently in the two
species. By an admirable provision, new teeth constantly
come up at the part, where in man the wisdom teeth appear, and these push the others along, and out at the front
end of the jaws, thus keeping the molars sound by renewal,
till the animal attains a very great age. The tusks of
animals from dry rocky countries are very much more dense
and heavier than those from wet and marshy districts, but
the latter attain much the larger size.

The Shire marshes support prodigious numbers of many
kinds of water-fowl. An hour at the mast-head unfolds
novel views of life in an African marsh. Near the edge,
and on the branches of some favourite tree, rest scores
of plotuses and cormorants, which stretch their snake-like
necks, and in mute amazement turn one eye and then
another towards the approaching monster. By-and-bye the
timid ones begin to fly off, or take "headers" into the
stream; but a few of the bolder, or more composed, remain,
only taking the precaution to spread their wings ready for instant flight. The pretty ardetta (*Herodias bubulcus*), of a light

yellow colour when at rest, but seemingly of a pure white when flying, takes wing, and sweeps across the green grass in large numbers, often showing us where buffaloes and elephants are, by perching on their backs.   Flocks of ducks, of which the kind called "Soriri" (*Dendrocygna personata*) is most abundant, being night feeders meditate quietly by the small lagoons, until startled by the noise of the steam machinery.   Pelicans glide over the water, catching fish, while the Scopus (*Scopus umbretta*) and large herons peer intently into pools.   The large black and white spur-winged goose (a constant marauder of native gardens) springs up, and circles round to find out what the disturbance can be, and then settles down again with a splash.   Hundreds of Linongolos (*Anastomus lamelligerus*) rise on the wing from the clumps of reeds, or low trees (the *Eschinomena*, from which pith hats are made), on which they build in colonies, and are speedily high in mid-air.   Charming little red and yellow weavers (*Ploceidæ*) remind one of butterflies, as they fly in and out of the tall grass, or hang to the mouths of their pendent nests, chattering briskly to their mates within.   These weavers seem to have "cock nests," built with only a roof, and a perch beneath, with a doorway on each side.   The natives say they are made to protect the bird from the rain.   Though her husband is very attentive, we have seen the hen bird tearing her mate's nest to pieces, but why we cannot tell.   Kites and vultures are busy overhead, beating the ground for their repast of carrion; and the solemn-looking, stately-stepping Marabout, with a taste for dead fish, or men, stalks slowly along the almost stagnant channels.   Groups of men and boys are searching diligently in various places for lotus and other roots.   Some are standing in canoes, on the weed-covered ponds, spearing fish, while others are punting over the small intersecting streams, to examine their sunken fish-baskets.

Fish-basket.

Towards evening, hundreds of pretty little hawks (*Erythropus vespertinus*) are seen flying in a southerly direction, and feeding on dragon-flies and locusts. They come, apparently, from resting on the palm-trees during the heat of the day. Flocks of scissor-bills (*Rhyncops*) are then also on the wing, and in search of food, ploughing the water with their lower mandibles, which are nearly half an inch longer than the upper ones.

At the north-eastern end of the marsh, and about three miles from the river, commences a great forest of palm-trees (*Borassus Æthiopium*). It extends many miles, and at one point comes close to the river. The grey trunks and green tops of this immense mass of trees give a pleasing tone of colour to the view. The mountain-range, which rises close behind the palms, is generally of a cheerful green, and has many trees, with patches of a lighter tint among them, as if spots of land had once been cultivated. The sharp angular rocks and dells on its sides have the appearance of a huge crystal broken; and this is so often the case in Africa, that one can guess pretty nearly at sight, whether a range is of the old crystalline rocks or not. The Borassus, though not an oil-bearing palm, is a useful tree. The fibrous pulp, round the large nuts, is of a sweet fruity taste, and is eaten by men and elephants. The natives bury the nuts until the kernels begin to sprout; when dug up and broken, the inside resembles coarse potatoes, and is prized in times of scarcity as nutritious food. During several months of the year, palm-wine, or *sura*, is obtained in large quantities; when fresh, it is a pleasant drink, somewhat like champagne, and not at all intoxicating; though, after standing a few hours, it becomes highly so. Sticks, a foot long, are driven into notches in the hard outside of the tree,—the inside being soft or hollow,—to serve as a ladder; the top of the fruit-shoot is cut off, and the sap, pouring out at the fresh wound, is caught in an earthen pot, which is hung at the point. A thin slice is taken off the end, to open the pores, and make the juice flow every time the owner ascends to empty the pot. Temporary huts are erected in the forest, and men and boys remain by their respective trees day and night; the nuts, fish, and wine, being their sole food. The Portuguese use the palm-wine as yeast, and it makes bread so light, that it melts in the mouth like froth.

Beyond the marsh the country is higher, and has a much larger population. We passed a long line of temporary huts, on a plain on the right bank, with crowds of men and women hard at work making salt. They obtain it by mixing the earth, which is here highly saline, with water, in a pot with a small hole in it, and then evaporating the liquid, which runs through, in the sun. From the number of women we saw carrying it off in bags, we concluded that vast quantities must be made at these works. It is worth observing that on soils like this, containing salt, the cotton is of larger and finer staple than elsewhere. We saw large tracts of this rich brackish soil both in the Shire and Zambesi valleys, and hence, probably, sea-island cotton would do well; a single plant of it, reared by Major Sicard, flourished and produced the long staple and peculiar tinge of this celebrated variety, though planted only in the street at Tette; and there also a salt efflorescence appears, probably from decomposition of the rock, off which the people scrape it for use.

Above the palm-trees, a succession of rich low islands stud the river. Many of them are cultivated and grow maize at all times of the year, for we saw it in different stages of growth; some patches ripe, and others half-grown, or just sprouting out of the ground. The shores are adorned with rows of banana-trees, and the fruit is abundant and cheap. Many of the reedy banks are so intertwined with convolvulus, and other creepers, as to be absolutely impenetrable. They are beautiful to the eye, a smooth wall of living green rising out of the crystal water, and adorned with lovely flowers; but so dense, that, if capsized in the water, one could scarcely pass through to land.

The large village of the Chief, Mankokwe, occupies a site on the right bank; he owns a number of fertile islands, and is said to be the Rundo, or paramount Chief, of a large district. Being of an unhappy suspicious disposition, he would not see us; so we thought it best to move on, rather than spend time in seeking his favour.

On the 25th August we reached Dakanamoio Island, opposite the perpendicular bluff on which Chibisa's village stands; he had gone, with most of his people, to live near the Zambesi, but his headman was civil, and promised us guides and whatever else we needed. A few of the men were busy cleaning, sorting, spinning, and weaving cotton. This is a common sight in nearly every village, and each family appears to have its patch of cotton, as our own ancestors in Scotland had each his patch of flax. Near sunset an immense flock of the largest species of hornbill (*Buceros cristatus*) came here to roost on the great trees which skirt the edge of the cliff. They leave early in the morning, often before sunrise, for their feeding-places, coming and going in pairs. They are evidently of a loving disposition, and strongly attached to each other, the male always nestling close beside his mate. A fine male fell to the ground, from fear, at the report of Dr. Kirk's gun; it was caught and kept on board; the female did not go off in the mornings to feed with the others, but flew round the ship, anxiously trying, by her plaintive calls, to induce her beloved one to follow her: she came again in the evenings to repeat the invitations. The poor disconsolate captive soon refused to eat, and in five days died of grief, because he could not have her company. No internal injury could be detected after death.

Chibisa and his wife, with a natural show of parental feeling, had told the Doctor, on his previous visit, that a few years before some of Chisaka's men had kidnapped and sold their little daughter, and that she was now a slave to the padrè at Tette. On his return to Tette, the Doctor tried hard to ransom and restore the girl to her parents, and offered twice the value of a slave; the padrè seemed willing, but she could not be found. This padrè was better than the average men of the country; and, being always civil and obliging, would probably have restored her gratuitously, but she had been sold, it might be, to the distant tribe Bazizulu, or he could not tell where. Custom had rendered his feelings callous, and Chibisa had to be told that his child would never return. It is this callous state of mind which leads some of our own blood to quote Scripture in support of slavery. If we could afford to take a backward step in civilization, we might find men among ourselves who would in like manner prove Mormonism or any other enormity to be divine.

CHAPTER V.

WE left the ship, on the 28th of August, 1859, for the discovery of Lake Nyassa. Our party numbered forty-two in all
—four whites, thirty-six Makololo, and two guides. We did
not actually need so many, either for carriage or defence;
but took them because we believed that, human nature
being everywhere the same, blacks are as ready as whites
to take advantage of the weak, and are as civil and respectful
to the powerful. We armed our men with muskets, which
gave us influence, although it did not add much to our
strength, as most of the men had never drawn a trigger,
and in any conflict would in all probability have been more
dangerous to us than to the enemy.

Our path crossed the valley, in a north-easterly direction,
up the course of a beautiful flowing stream. Many of the
gardens had excellent cotton growing in them. An hour's
march brought us to the foot of the Manganja hills, up

which lay the toilsome road. The vegetation soon changed; as we rose, bamboos appeared, and new trees and plants were met with, which gave such incessant employment to Dr. Kirk, that he travelled the distance three times over. Remarkably fine trees, one of which has oil-yielding seeds, and belongs to the mahogany family, grow well in the hollows along the rivulet courses. The ascent became very fatiguing, and we were glad of a rest. Looking back from an elevation of a thousand feet, we beheld a lovely prospect. The eye takes in at a glance the valley beneath, and the many windings of its silver stream Makubula, or Kubvula, from the shady hill-side, where it emerges in foaming haste, to where it slowly glides into the tranquil Shire; then the Shire itself is seen for many a mile above and below Chibisa's, and the great level country beyond, with its numerous green woods; until the prospect, west and north-west, is bounded far away by masses of peaked and dome-shaped blue mountains, that fringe the highlands of the Maravi country.

After a weary march we halted at Makolongwe, the village of Chitimba. It stands in a woody hollow on the first of the three terraces of the Manganja hills, and, like all other Manganja villages, is surrounded by an impenetrable hedge of poisonous euphorbia. This tree casts a deep shade, which would render it difficult for bowmen to take aim at the villagers inside. The grass does not grow beneath it, and this may be the reason why it is so universally used, for when dry the grass would readily convey fire to the huts inside; moreover, the hedge acts as a fender to all flying sparks. As strangers are wont to do, we sat down under some fine trees near the entrance of the village. A couple of mats, made of split reeds, were spread for the

white men to sit on; and the headman brought a seguati,
or present, of a small goat and a basket of meal. The full
value in beads and cotton cloth was handed to him in return.
He measured the cloth, doubled it, and then measured that
again. The beads were scrutinized; he had never seen beads
of that colour before, and should like to consult with his
comrades before accepting them, and this, after repeated
examinations and much anxious talk, he concluded to do.
Meal and peas were then brought for sale. A fathom of
blue cotton-cloth, a full dress for man or woman, was produced. Our Makololo headman, Sininyane, thinking a part
of it was enough for the meal, was proceeding to tear it,
when Chitimba remarked that it was a pity to cut such
a nice dress for his wife, he would rather bring more
meal. " All right," said Sininyane; " but look, the cloth is
very wide, so see that the basket which carries the meal be
wide too, and add a cock to make the meal taste nicely." A
brisk trade sprang up at once, each being eager to obtain as
fine things as his neighbour,—and all were in good humour.
Women and girls began to pound and grind meal, and men
and boys chased the screaming fowls over the village, until
they ran them down. In a few hours the market was
completely glutted with every sort of native food; the prices,
however, rarely fell, as they could easily eat what was not
sold.

We slept under the trees, the air being pleasant, and
no mosquitoes on the hills. According to our usual plan of
marching, by early dawn our camp was in motion. After a
cup of coffee, and a bit of biscuit we were on the way.
The air was deliciously cool, and the path a little easier than
that of yesterday. We passed a number of villages, occupying very picturesque spots among the hills, and in a few

hours gained the upper terrace, 3000 feet above the level of the sea. The plateau lies west of the Milanje Mountains, and its north-eastern border slopes down to Lake Shirwa. We were all charmed with the splendid country, and looked with never-failing delight on its fertile plains, its numerous hills, and majestic mountains. In some of the passes we saw bramble-berries growing; and the many other flowers, though of great beauty, did not remind us of youth and of home like the ungainly thorny bramble-bushes. We were a week in crossing the highlands in a northerly direction; then we descended into the Upper Shire Valley, which is nearly 1200 feet above the level of the sea. This valley is wonderfully fertile, and supports a large population. After leaving the somewhat flat-topped southern portion, the most prominent mountain of the Zomba range is Njongone, which has a fine stream running past its northern base. We were detained at the end of the chain some days by one of our companions being laid up with fever. One night we were suddenly aroused by buffaloes rushing close by the sick-bed. We were encamped by a wood on the border of a marsh, but our patient soon recovered, notwithstanding the unfavourable situation, and the poor accommodation.

The Manganja country is delightfully well watered. The clear, cool, gushing streams are very numerous. Once we passed seven fine brooks and a spring in a single hour, and this, too, near the close of the dry season. Mount Zomba, which is twenty miles long, and from 7000 to 8000 feet high, has a beautiful stream flowing through a verdant valley on its summit, and running away down into Lake Shirwa. The highlands are well wooded, and many trees, admirable for their height and timber, grow on the various watercourses. "Is this country good for cattle?" we inquired

of a Makololo herdsman, whose occupation had given him skill
in pasturage. " Truly," he replied, " do you not see abundance
of those grasses which the cattle love, and get fat upon ?" Yet
the people have but few goats, and fewer sheep. With the
exception of an occasional leopard, there are no beasts of prey
to disturb domestic animals. Wool-sheep would, without
doubt, thrive on these highlands. The Manganja generally live
in villages, each of which has its own headman, and he may be
ruler over several adjacent villages. The people are regarded
as his children. All the petty chiefs of a particular portion
of country give a sort of allegiance to a paramount chief,
called the Rondo, or Rundo. They are bound to pay him
a small annual tribute, and one of the tusks of every elephant killed; and it is his duty in return to assist and
protect them when attacked by an enemy. Mankokwe is
the Rundo of the southern portion of the highlands; but
he is a besotted character, who never visits nor aids them
as his father did, and so the tribute is rarely paid. Still
all acknowledge him as their Rundo, and admit that it is
wrong in them not to pay the tribute, though wrong in him
not to help them when in trouble. Part of the Upper Shire
Valley has a lady paramount, named Nyango; and in her
dominions, women rank higher and receive more respectful
treatment than their sisters on the hills.

The hill Chief, Mongazi, called his wife to take charge of a
present we had given him. She dropped down on her knees,
clapping her hands in reverence, before and after receiving
our present from his lordly hands. It was painful to see the
abject manner, in which the women of the hill tribes knelt
beside the path as we passed; but a great difference took
place when we got into Nyango's country. The headman of
the first of her villages, though told that the people of three

successive villages had refused to admit us, said "that it made no difference, we might sleep in his." He then asked that his wife also might be allowed to come and look at the watch, compass, and other curiosities. She came with other women, and seemed to be a modest and intelligent person. Her husband always consulted her before concluding a bargain, and was evidently influenced by her opinion. The sites of the villages are selected with judgment and good taste, as a flowing stream is always near, and shady trees grow around. In many cases the trees have been planted by the headman himself. The Boalo, or spreading-place, is generally at one end of the village; it is an area of twenty or thirty yards made smooth and neat, near the favourite banyan and other trees, which throw a grateful shade over it. Here the men sit at various sorts of work during the day, and smoke tobacco and bang; and here, on the clear delicious moonlight nights, they sing, dance, and drink beer.

On entering a village, we proceeded, as all strangers do, at once to the Boalo: mats of split reeds or bamboo were usually spread for us to sit on. Our guides then told the men who might be there, who we were, whence we had come, whither we wanted to go, and what were our objects. This information was duly carried to the Chief, who, if a sensible man, came at once; but, if he happened to be timid and suspicious, waited until he had used divination, and his warriors had time to come in from outlying hamlets. When he makes his appearance, all the people begin to clap their hands in unison, and continue doing so till he sits down opposite to us. His counsellors take their places beside him. He makes a remark or two, and is then silent for a few seconds. Our guides then sit down in front of the chief and his counsellors, and both parties lean forward, looking earnestly at each other;

the Chief repeats a word such as "Ambuiatu" (our Father, or master)—or "moio" (life), and all clap their hands. Another word is followed by two claps, a third by still more clapping, when each touches the ground with both hands placed together. Then all rise, and lean forward with measured clap, and sit down again with clap, clap, clap, fainter, and still fainter till the last dies away, or is brought to an end by a smart loud clap from the Chief. They keep perfect time in this species of court etiquette. Our guides now tell the Chief, often in blank verse, all they have already told his people, with the addition perhaps of their own suspicions of the visitors. He asks some questions, and then converses with us through the guides. Direct communication, between the chief and the head of the stranger party is not customary. In approaching they often ask who is the spokesman, and the spokesman of the Chief addresses the person indicated exclusively. There is no lack of punctilious good manners. The accustomed presents are exchanged, with civil ceremoniousness; until our men, wearied and hungry, call out, "English do not buy slaves, they buy food," and then the people bring meal, maize, fowls, batatas, yams, beans, beer, for sale.

The Manganja are an industrious race; and in addition to working in iron, cotton, and basket-making, they cultivate the soil extensively. All the people of a village turn out to labour in the fields. It is no uncommon thing to see men, women, and children hard at work, with the baby lying close by beneath a shady bush. When a new piece of woodland is to be cleared, they proceed exactly as farmers do in America. The trees are cut down with their little axes of soft native iron; trunks and branches are piled up and burnt, and the ashes spread on the soil. The corn is planted among the standing stumps which are left to rot. If grass land

is to be brought under cultivation, as much tall grass as the
labourer can conveniently lay hold of is collected together
and tied into a knot. He then strikes his hoe round the tufts
to sever the roots, and leaving all standing, proceeds until the
whole ground assumes the appearance of a field covered
with little shocks of corn in harvest. A short time before
the rains begin, these grass shocks are collected in small
heaps, covered with earth, and burnt, the ashes and
burnt soil being used to fertilize the. ground. Large crops
of the mapira, or Egyptian dura (*Holcus sorghum*), are raised,
with millet, beans, and ground-nuts; also patches of
yams, rice, pumpkins, cucumbers, cassava, sweet potatoes,
tobacco, and hemp, or bang (*Cannabis sativa*). Maize is grown
all the year round. Cotton is cultivated at almost every village.
Three varieties of cotton have been found in the country,
namely, two foreign, and one native. The tonje manga, or
foreign cotton, the name showing that it has been introduced,
is of excellent quality, and considered at Manchester to be
nearly equal to the best New Orleans. It is perennial, but requires replanting once in three years. A considerable amount
of this variety is grown in the Upper and Lower Shire Valleys.
Every family of any importance owns a cotton patch which,
from the entire absence of weeds, seemed to be carefully
cultivated. Most were small, none seen on this journey
exceeding half an acre; but on the former trip some were
observed of more than twice that size.

The tonje cadja, or indigenous cotton, is of shorter staple,
and feels in the hand like wool. This kind has to be
planted every season, in the highlands; yet, because it
makes stronger cloth, many of the people prefer it to the
foreign cotton; the third variety is not found here. It was
remarked to a number of men near the Shire Lakelet, a

little further on towards Nyassa, "You should plant plenty of cotton, and probably the English will come and buy it." "Truly," replied a far-travelled Babisa trader to his fellows, "the country is full of cotton, and if these people come to buy they will enrich us." Our own observation on the cotton cultivated convinced us that this was no empty flourish, but a fact. Everywhere we met with it, and scarcely ever entered a village, without finding a number of men cleaning, spinning, and weaving. It is first carefully separated from the seed by the fingers, or by an iron roller, on a little block of wood, and rove out into long soft bands without twist. Then it receives its first twist on the spindle, and becomes

Native web, and Weaver smoking the huge tobacco-pipe of the country.

about the thickness of coarse candlewick; after being taken off and wound into a large ball, it is given the final hard twist, and spun into a firm cop on the spindle again: all the processes being painfully slow.

Iron ore is dug out of the hills, and its manufacture is the staple trade of the southern highlands.   Each village has its smelting-house, its charcoal-burners, and blacksmiths. They make good axes, spears, needles, arrow-heads, bracelets and anklets, which, considering the entire absence of machinery, are sold at surprisingly low rates ; a hoe over two pounds in weight is exchanged for calico of about the value of

Blacksmith's Forge and Bellows of Goatskin.

fourpence.   In villages near Lake Shirwa and elsewhere, the inhabitants enter pretty largely into the manufacture of crockery, or pottery, making by hand all sorts of cooking, water, and grain pots, which they ornament with plumbago found in the hills.   Some find employment in weaving neat baskets from split bamboos, and others collect the fibre of the buaze, which grows abundantly on the hills, and make it into fish-nets.   These they either use themselves, or exchange with the fishermen on the river or lakes for dried fish and salt.   A great deal of native trade is carried on between the villages, by means of barter in tobacco, salt, dried fish,

I

skins, and iron. Many of the men are intelligent-looking, with well-shaped heads, agreeable faces, and high foreheads. We soon learned to forget colour, and we frequently saw countenances resembling those of white people we had known in England, which brought back the looks of forgotten ones vividly before the mind. The men take a good deal of pride in the arrangement of their hair; the varieties of style are endless. One trains his long locks till they take the admired form of the buffalo's horns; others prefer to let their hair hang in a thick coil down their backs, like that animal's tail; while another wears it in twisted cords, which, stiffened by fillets of the inner bark of a tree wound spirally round each curl, radiate from the head in all directions. Some have it hanging all round the shoulders in large masses; others shave it off altogether. Many shave part of it into ornamental figures, in which the fancy of the barber crops out conspicuously. About as many dandies run to seed among the blacks, as among the whites. The Manganja adorn their bodies extravagantly, wearing rings on their fingers and thumbs, besides throatlets, bracelets, and anklets of brass, copper, or iron. But the most wonderful of ornaments, if such it may be called, is the pelele, or upper-lip ring of the women. The middle of the upper lip of the girls is pierced close to the septum of the nose, and a small pin inserted to prevent the puncture closing up. After it has healed, the pin is taken out and a larger one is pressed into its place, and so on successively for weeks, and months, and years. The process of increasing the size of the lip goes on till its capacity becomes so great that a ring of two inches diameter can be introduced with ease. All the highland women wear the pelele, and it is common on the Upper and Lower Shire. The poorer classes make them of hollow, or of solid bamboo, but the wealthier of ivory, or tin. The tin pelele is often made in the form of a small dish. The ivory one is not unlike a napkin-ring. No woman ever appears in public without

Pelele, or Lip-ring of Manganja Woman.

the pelele, except in times of mourning for the dead. It is frightfully ugly to see the upper lip projecting two inches beyond the tip of the nose. When an old wearer of a hollow bamboo ring smiles, by the action of the muscles of the cheeks, the ring and lip outside it, are dragged back and thrown above the eyebrows. The nose is seen through the middle of the ring, and the exposed teeth show how carefully they have been chipped to look like those of a cat or crocodile. The pelele of an old lady, Chikanda Kadze, a Chieftainess, about twenty miles north of Mo-

I 2

rambala, hung down below her chin, with, of course,
a piece of the upper lip around its border. The labial
letters cannot be properly pronounced, but the under
lip has to do its best for them, against the upper teeth
and gum. Tell them it makes them ugly; they had
better throw it away; they reply, "Kodi! Really! it
is the fashion." How this hideous fashion originated is an
enigma. Can thick lips ever have been thought beautiful,
and this mode of artificial enlargement resorted to in consequence? The constant twiddling of the pelele with the
tongue by the younger women suggested the irreverent
idea that it might have been invented to give safe employment to that little member. "Why do the women wear
these things?" we inquired of the old Chief, Chinsunse.
Evidently surprised at such a stupid question, he replied,
"For beauty, to be sure! Men have beards and whiskers;
women have none; and what kind of creature would a woman
be without whiskers, and without the pelele? She would
have a mouth like a man, and no beard; ha! ha! ha!"
Afterwards on the Rovuma, we found men wearing the
pelele, as well as women. An idea suggested itself on
seeing the effects of the slight but constant pressure exerted on the upper gum and front teeth, of which our
medical brethren will judge the value. In many cases the
upper front teeth, instead of the natural curve outwards,
which the row presents, had been pressed so as to appear as
if the line of alveoli in which they were planted had an
inward curve. As this was produced by the slight pressure
of the pelele backwards, persons with too prominent teeth
might by slight, but long-continued pressure, by some appliance only as elastic as the lip, have the upper gum and teeth
depressed, especially in youth, more easily than is usually

imagined.   The pressure should be applied to the upper gum more than to the teeth.

The Manganja are not a sober people : they brew large quantities of beer, and like it well.   Having no hops, or other means of checking fermentation, they are obliged to drink the whole brew in a few days, or it becomes unfit for use.   Great merry-makings take place on these occasions, and drinking, drumming, and dancing continue day and night, till the beer is gone.   In crossing the hills we sometimes found whole villages enjoying this kind of mirth.   The veteran traveller of the party remarked, that he had not seen so much drunkenness during all the sixteen years he had spent in Africa.   As we entered a village one afternoon, not a man was to be seen ; but some women were drinking beer under a tree.   In a few moments the native doctor, one of the innocents, "nobody's enemy but his own," staggered out of a hut, with his cupping-horn dangling from his neck, and began to scold us for a breach of etiquette.   "Is this the way to come into a man's village, without sending him word that you are coming ?" Our men soon pacified the fuddled but good-humoured medico, who, entering his beer-cellar, called on two of them to help him to carry out a huge pot of beer, which he generously presented to us.   While the "medical practitioner" was thus hospitably employed, the Chief awoke in a fright, and shouted to the women to run away, or they would all be killed.   The ladies laughed at the idea of their being able to run away, and remained beside the beer-pots.   We selected a spot for our camp, our men cooked the dinner as usual, and we were quietly eating it, when scores of armed men, streaming with perspiration, came pouring into the village.   They looked at us, then at each other, and turning to the Chief upbraided him for

so needlessly sending for them. "These people are peaceable; they do not hurt you; you are killed with beer:"
so saying, they returned to their homes.

We remarked the different varieties of intoxication
among these topers, the talkative, the boisterous, the
silly, the stupid, and the pugnacious: the last, when the
Chief, at the head of his men, placed himself in ·front,
crying—"I stop this path, you must go back." He sprang
aside, however, with more speed than dignity, when an
angry Makololo made a lunge at him with the but of his
musket.

Native beer has a pinkish colour, and the consistency
of gruel. The grain is made to vegetate, dried in the
sun, pounded into meal, and gently boiled. When only
a day or two old, the beer is sweet, with a slight degree
of acidity, which renders it a most grateful beverage in
a hot climate, or when fever begets a sore craving for
acid drinks. A single draught of it satisfies this craving
at once. Only by deep and long-continued potations can
intoxication be produced: the grain being in a minutely
divided state, it is a good way of consuming it, and the decoction is very nutritious. At Tette a measure of beer is exchanged
for an equal-sized pot full of grain. A present of this beer,
so refreshing to our dark comrades, was brought to us in
nearly every village. Beer-drinking does not appear to
produce any disease, or to shorten life, on the hills. Never
before did we see so many old grey-headed men and women;
leaning on their staves they came with the others to see the
white men. The aged Chief, Muata Manga, could hardly have
been less than ninety years of age; his venerable appearance
struck the Makololo. "He is an old man," said they, "a very old
man; his skin hangs in wrinkles, just like that on elephants'

hips." "Did you never," he was asked, "have a fit of travelling come over you ; a desire to see other lands and people ?" No, he had never felt that, and had never been far from home in his life. For long life they are not indebted to frequent ablutions. An old man told us that he remembered to have washed once in his life, but it was so long since that he had forgotten how it felt. "Why do you wash?" asked Chinsunse's women of the Makololo; "our men never do."

On the Upper Shire Valley, a man, after favouring us with some queer geographical remarks, followed us for several days. The Makololo became very much annoyed with him, for he proclaimed in every village we entered—"These people have wandered; they do not know where they are going." In vain did they scold and order him away. As soon as we started, he appeared again in the line of march, with his little bag over his shoulder, containing all his worldly gear, and as ready with his uncalled-for remarks as before. Every effort failed to drive him away, until at length the happy expedient was hit on, of threatening to take him down to the river and wash him; he at once made off, and we saw him no more. Much skin disease is seen among the Manganja. Many had ulcers on their limbs; indeed, an indolent almost incurable ulcer is the worst complaint we saw. Some men appeared as if they had blotches of whitewash all over them, and some were afflicted with the leprosy of the Cape. Many fowls even have their feet deformed by a peculiar thickening of the skin. We noticed also some men marked with smallpox, and asked the Chief, Mongazi, if he knew whether it had come to them from the coast, or from the interior. Being, as usual, amiably tipsy and anxious to pay us a compliment, he graciously replied he did not know, but thought it must have come to them from the English.

The superstitious ordeal, by drinking the poisonous muave, obtains credit here; and when a person is suspected of crime, this ordeal is resorted to. If the stomach rejects the poison, the accused is pronounced innocent; but if it is retained, guilt is believed to be demonstrated. Their faith is so firm in its discriminating power, that the supposed criminal offers of his own accord to drink it, and even Chiefs are not exempted. Chibisa, relying on its efficacy, drank it several times, in order to vindicate his character. When asserting that all his wars had been just, it was hinted that, as every Chief had the same tale of innocence to tell, we ought to suspend our judgment. "If you doubt my word," said he, "give me the muave to drink." A Chief at the foot of Mount Zomba successfully went through the ordeal the day before we reached his village; and his people manifested their joy at his deliverance by drinking beer, dancing, and drumming for two days and nights. It is possible that the native doctor, who mixes the ingredients of the poisoned bowl, may be able to save those whom he considers innocent; but it is difficult to get the natives to speak about the matter, and no one is willing to tell what the muave poison consists of. We have been shown trees said to be used, but had always reason to doubt the accuracy of our informants. We once found a tree in a village, with many pieces of the bark chipped off, closely allied to the Tangena or Tanghina, the ordeal poison tree of Madagascar; but we could not ascertain any particulars about it. Death is inflicted on those found guilty of witchcraft, by the muave.

The women wail for the dead two days. Seated on the ground they chant a few plaintive words, and end each verse with the prolonged sound of a—a, or o—o, or ea-ea-ea—a. Whatever beer is in the house of the deceased, is poured out on the ground with the meal, and all cooking and water pots are broken, as being of no further use. Both men and women wear signs of mourning for their dead relatives. These consist of narrow strips of the palm-leaf wound round the head, the arms, legs, neck, and breasts, and worn till they drop off from decay. They believe in the existence of a Supreme Being, called Mpambè, and also Morungo, and in a future state. "We live only a few days here," said old Chin-sunse, "but we live again after death : we do not know where, or in what condition, or with what companions, for the dead never return to tell us. Sometimes the dead do come back, and appear to us in dreams ; but they never speak nor tell us where they have gone, nor how they fare."

Our path followed the Shire above the Cataracts, which is now a broad deep river, with but little current. It expands in one place into a lakelet, called Pamalombe, full of fine fish, and ten or twelve miles long by five or six in breadth. Its banks are low, and a dense wall of papyrus encircles it. On its western shore rises a range of hills running north. On reaching the village of the Chief Muana-Moesi, and about a day's march distant from Nyassa, we were told that no lake had ever been heard of there; that the River Shire stretched on as we saw it now to a distance of "two months," and then came out from between perpendicular rocks, which towered almost to the skies. Our men looked blank at this piece of news, and said, "Let us go back to the ship, it is of no use trying to find the lake." "We shall go and see those wonderful rocks at any rate," said the Doctor. "And when you see them," replied Masakasa, "you will just want to see something else." "But there *is* a lake," rejoined Masakasa, "for all their denying it, for it is down in a book." Masakasa, having unbounded faith in whatever was in a book, went and scolded the natives for telling him an untruth. "There is a lake," said he, "for how could the white men know about it in a book if it did not exist?" They then admitted that there was a lake a few miles off. Subsequent inquiries make it probable that the story of the "perpendicular rocks" may have had reference to a fissure, known to both natives and Arabs, in the north-eastern portion of the lake. The walls rise so high that the path along the bottom is said to be underground. It is probably a crack similar to that which made the Victoria Falls, and formed the Shire Valley.

The Chief brought a small present of meal in the evening, and sat with us for a few minutes. On leaving us he said that he wished we might sleep well. Scarce had he gone, when a wild sad cry arose from the river, followed by the shrieking of women. A crocodile had carried off his principal wife, as she was bathing. The Makololo snatched up their arms, and rushed to the bank, but it was too late, she was gone. The wailing of the women continued all night, and next morning we met others coming to the village to join in the general mourning. Their grief was evidently heartfelt, as we saw the tears coursing down their cheeks. In reporting this misfortune to his neighbours, Muana-Moesi said "that white men came to his village; washed themselves at the place where his wife drew water and bathed; rubbed themselves with a white medicine (soap); and his wife, having gone to bathe afterwards, was taken by a crocodile; he did not know whether in consequence of the medicine used or not." This we could not find fault with. On our return we were viewed with awe, and all the men fled at our approach; the women remained; and this elicited the remark from our men, "The women have the advantage of men, in not needing to dread the spear." The practice of bathing, which our first contact with Chinsunse's people led us to believe was unknown to the natives, we afterwards found to be common in other parts of the Manganja country.

We discovered Lake Nyassa a little before noon of the 16th September, 1859. Its southern end is in 14° 25' S. Lat., and 35° 30' E. Long. At this point the valley is about twelve miles wide. There are hills on both sides of the lake, but the haze from burning grass prevented us at the time from seeing far. A long time after our return from Nyassa, we received a letter from Captain R. B. Oldfield, R.N., then Commanding H.M.S. Lyra, with the information that Dr. Roscher, an enterprising German who unfortunately lost his life in his zeal for exploration, had also reached the Lake, but on the 19th of November following our discovery; and on his arrival had been informed by the natives that a party of white men were at the southern extremity. On comparing dates (16th September and 19th November) we were about two months before Dr. Roscher. Information, to the same effect as Captain Oldfield's, was also published in the Cape Newspapers in a letter to Sir George Grey, the Governor, from Colonel Rigby, H.M. Consul and Political Resident at Zanzibar, who derived his information from the depositions of Dr. Roscher's servants, after they had reached the coast.

It is not known where Dr. Roscher first saw its waters; as the exact position of Nusseewa on the borders of the Lake, where he lived some time, is unknown. He was three days north-east of Nusseewa, and on the Arab road back to the usual crossing-place of the Rovuma, when he was murdered. The murderers were seized by one of the Chiefs, sent to Zanzibar, and executed. He is said to have kept his discoveries to

himself, with the intention of publishing in Europe the whole
at once, in a splendid book of travels. Hence we can only
conjecture that as he travelled on the Arab route from
Kilwa (Quiloa), he struck the lake at the Arab crossing-place
Ngombo, adjacent to Tsenga, or possibly opposite Kotakota
Bay.* The regular publication of our letters by the Royal
Geographical Society we felt to be an inestimable benefit.
It fixed the date of, and perpetuated every discovery.

The Chief of the village near the confluence of the Lake
and River Shire, an old man, called Mosauka, hearing that
we were sitting under a tree, came and kindly invited us to his
village. He took us to a magnificent banyan-tree, of which he
seemed proud. The roots had been trained down to the ground
into the form of a gigantic arm-chair, without the seat. Four
of us slept in the space betwixt its arms. Mosauka brought
us a present of a goat and basket of meal " to comfort our
hearts." He told us that a large slave-party, led by Arabs,
were encamped close by. They had been up to Cazembe's
country the past year, and were on their way back, with plenty
of slaves, ivory, and malachite. In a few minutes half a dozen
of the leaders came over to see us. They were armed with
long muskets, and, to our mind, were a villanous-looking lot.
They evidently thought the same of us, for they offered
several young children for sale, but, when told that we were
English, showed signs of fear, and decamped during the night.
On our return to the Kongone, we found that H.M.S. Lynx
had caught some of these very slaves in a dhow; for a woman
told us she first saw us at Mosauka's, and that the Arabs had
fled for fear of an *uncanny* sort of Basungu.

This is one of the great slave-paths from the interior, others cross the Shire a little below, and some on

---

* See Appendix.

the lake itself. We might have released these slaves, but did not know what to do with them afterwards. On meeting men, led in slave-sticks, the Doctor had to bear

"Goree," or Slave-stick.

the reproaches of the Makololo, who never slave, " Ay, you call us bad, but are we yellow-hearted, like these fellows— why won't you let us choke them?" To liberate and leave them, would have done but little good, as the people of the surrounding villages would soon have seized them, and have sold them again into slavery. The Manganja Chiefs sell their own people, for we met Ajawa and slave-dealers in several highland villages, who had certainly been encouraged to come among them for slaves. The Chiefs always seemed ashamed of the traffic, and tried to excuse themselves. " We do not sell many, and only those who have committed crimes." As a rule the regular trade is supplied by the low and criminal classes, and hence the ugliness of slaves. Others are probably sold besides criminals, as on the accusation of witchcraft. Friendless orphans also sometimes disappear suddenly, and no one inquires what has become of them. The temptation to sell their people is peculiarly great, as there is but little ivory on the hills, and often the Chief has nothing but human flesh, with which to buy foreign goods. The Ajawa offer cloth, brass rings, pottery, and sometimes handsome young women, and agree to take the trouble of carrying off by night all those whom the Chief may point out to them. They give four yards of cotton cloth for a man, three for a woman, and two for a boy or girl, to be taken to the Portuguese at Mosambique, Iboe, and Quillimane.

Another channel of supply, fed by victims from all classes, but chiefly from the common people, is frequently opened, when one portion of a tribe, urged on by the greed of gain, begins to steal and sell their fellow-clansmen. The evil does not stop here. A feud is the consequence. The weaker part of the tribe is driven away, and wandering about, becomes so thoroughly demoralized, as to live by marauding and selling their captives, and even each other, without compunction. This was precisely the state of the portion of the Ajawa we first fell in with.

The Manganja were more suspicious and less hospitable than the tribes on the Zambesi. They were slow to believe that our object in coming into their country was really what we professed it to be. They naturally judge us by the motives which govern themselves. A Chief in the Upper Shire Valley, whose scared looks led our men to christen him Kitlabolawa (I shall be killed), remarked that parties had come before, with as plausible a story as ours, and, after a few days, had jumped up and carried off a number of his people as slaves. We were not allowed to enter some of the villages in the valley, nor would the inhabitants even sell us food; Zimika's men, for instance, stood at the entrance of the euphorbia hedge, and declared we should not pass in. We sat down under a tree close by. A young fellow made an angry oration, dancing from side to side with his bow and poisoned arrows, and gesticulating fiercely in our faces. He was stopped in the middle of his harangue by an old man, who ordered him to sit down, and not talk to strangers in that way; he obeyed reluctantly, scowling defiance, and thrusting out his large lips very significantly. The women were observed leaving the village; and, suspecting that mischief might ensue, we proceeded on our journey, to the great disgust of our men. They were very angry with the natives for their want of hospitality to strangers, and with us, because we would not allow them to give "the things a thrashing." "This is what comes of going with white men," they growled out, "had we been with our own Chief, we should have eaten their goats to-night, and had some of themselves to carry the bundles for us to-morrow." On our return, by a path which left his village on our right, Zimika sent to apologise, saying that "he was ill, and in another village at the time; it was not by his orders that we were sent away; his men did not know that we were a party wishing the land to dwell in peace."

We were not able, when hastening back to the men left in the ship, to remain in the villages belonging to this Chief; but the people came after us with things for sale, and invited us to stop, and spend the night with them, urging, "Are we to have it said that white people passed through our country and we did not see them?" We rested by a rivulet to gratify these sight-seers. We appear to them to be red rather than white; and, though light colour is admired among themselves, our clothing renders us uncouth in aspect. Blue eyes appear savage, and a red beard hideous. From the numbers of aged persons we saw on the highlands, and the increase of mental and physical vigour we experienced on our ascent from the lowlands, we inferred that the climate was salubrious, and that our countrymen might there enjoy good health, and also be of signal benefit, by leading the multitude of industrious inhabitants to cultivate cotton, buaze, sugar, and other valuable produce, to exchange for goods of European manufacture;

at the same time teaching them, by precept and example, the great truths of our Holy Religion.

Our stay at the Lake was necessarily short. We had found that the best plan for allaying any suspicions, that might arise in the minds of a people accustomed only to slave-traders, was to pay a hasty visit, and then leave for a while, and allow the conviction to form among the people that, though our course of action was so different from that of others, we were not dangerous, but rather disposed to be friendly. We had also a party at the vessel, and any indiscretion on their part might have proved fatal to the character of the Expedition.

The trade of Cazembe and Katanga's country, and of other parts of the interior, crosses Nyassa and the Shire, on its way to the Arab port, Kilwa, and the Portuguese ports of Iboe and Mosambique. At present, slaves, ivory, malachite, and copper ornaments, are the only articles of commerce. According to information collected by Colonel Rigby at Zanzibar, and from other sources, nearly all the slaves shipped from the above-mentioned ports come from the Nyassa district. By means of a small steamer, purchasing the ivory of the Lake and River above the cataracts, which together have a shore-line of at least 600 miles, the slave-trade in this quarter would be rendered unprofitable,—for it is only by the ivory being carried by the slaves, that the latter do not eat up all the profits of a trip. An influence would be exerted over an enormous area of country, for the Mazitu about the north end of the Lake will not allow slave-traders to pass round that way through their country. They would be most efficient allies to the English, and might themselves be benefited by more intercourse. As things are now, the native traders in ivory and malachite have to submit to heavy exactions; and if we could give them the same prices which they at present get after carrying their merchandise 300 miles beyond this to the Coast, it might induce them to return without going further. It is only by cutting off the supplies in the interior, that we can crush the slave-trade on the Coast. The plan proposed would stop the slave-trade from the Zambesi on one side and Kilwa on the other; and would leave, beyond this tract, only the Portuguese port of Inhambane on the south, and a portion of the Sultan of Zanzibar's dominion on the north, for our cruisers to look after. The Lake people grow abundance of cotton for their own consumption, and can sell it for a penny a pound, or even less. Water-carriage exists by the Shire and Zambesi all the way to England, with the single exception of a portage of about thirty-five miles past the Murchison Cataracts, along which a road of less than forty miles could be made at a trifling expense; and it seems feasible that a legitimate and thriving trade might, in a short time, take the place of the present unlawful traffic.

Colonel Rigby, Captains Wilson, Oldfield, and Chapman, and all the most intelligent officers on the Coast, were unanimous in the belief, that one small vessel on the Lake would have decidedly more influence, and do more good in suppressing the slave-trade, than half a dozen men-of-war on the ocean. By judicious operations, therefore, on a small scale inland, little expense would be incurred, and the English slave-trade policy on the East would have the same fair chance of success, as on the West Coast.

CHAPTER VI.

AFTER a land-journey of forty days, we returned to the ship on the 6th of October, 1859, in a somewhat exhausted condition, arising more from a sort of poisoning, than from the usual fatigue of travel. We had taken a little mulligatawney paste, for making soup, in case of want of time to cook other food. Late one afternoon, at the end of an unusually long march, we reached Mikena, near the base of Mount Njongone to the north of Zomba, and the cook was directed to use a couple of spoonfuls of the paste; but, instead of doing so, he put in the whole potful. The soup tasted rather hot,

but we added boiled rice to it, and, being very hungry,
partook freely of it; and, in consequence of the overdose,
we were delayed several days in severe suffering, and some
of the party did not recover till after our return to the ship.
Our illness may partly have arisen from another cause. One
kind of cassava (*Jatropha maligna*) is known to be, in its raw
state, poisonous, but by boiling it carefully in two waters,
which must be thrown off, the poison is extracted and the
cassava rendered fit for food. The poisonous sort is easily
known by raising a bit of the bark of the root, and putting
the tongue to it. A bitter taste shows poison, but it is
probable that even the sweet kind contains an injurious
principle. The sap, which, like that of our potatoes, is
injurious as an article of food, is used in the "Pepper-pot"
of the West Indies, under the name of "Cassereep," as a
perfect preservative of meat. This juice put into an earthen
vessel with a little water and Chili pepper is said to keep meat,
that is immersed in it, good for a great length of time; even
for years. No iron or steel must touch the mixture, or it
will become sour. This "Pepper-pot," of which we first heard
from the late Archbishop Whately, is a most economical
meat-safe in a hot climate; any beef, mutton, pork, or fowl
that may be left at dinner, if put into the mixture and a
little fresh cassereep added, keeps perfectly, though otherwise
the heat of the climate or flies would spoil it. Our cook,
however, boiled the cassava root as he was in the habit of
cooking meat, namely, by filling the pot with it, and then
pouring in water, which he allowed to stand on the fire
until it had become absorbed and boiled away. This method
did not expel the poisonous properties of the root, or render
it wholesome; for, notwithstanding our systematic caution
in purchasing only the harmless sort, we suffered daily

from its effects, and it was only just before the end of our trip, that this pernicious mode of boiling it was dis-covered by us.

In ascending 3000 feet from the lowlands to the high-lands, or on reaching the low valley of the Shire from the higher grounds, the change of climate was very marked. The heat was oppressive below, the thermometer standing at from 84° to 103° in the shade; and our spirits were as dull and languid, as they had been exhilarated on the heights in a temperature cooler by some 20°. The water of the river was sometimes 84° or higher, whilst that we had been drinking in the hill streams was only 65°.

It was found necessary to send two of our number across from the Shire to Tette; and Dr. Kirk, with guides from Chibisa, and accompanied by Mr. Rae, the engineer, ac-complished the journey. We had found the country to the north and east so very well watered, that no difficulty was anticipated in this respect in a march of less than a hundred miles; but on this occasion our friends suffered severely. The little water to be had at this time of the year, by digging in the beds of dry watercourses, was so brackish as to increase thirst, some of the natives indeed were making salt from it; and when at long intervals a less brackish supply was found, it was nauseous and muddy from the frequent visits of large game. The tsetse abounded. The country was level, and large tracts of it covered with mopane forest, the leaves of which afford but scanty shade to the baked earth, so that scarcely any grass grows upon it. The sun was so hot, that the men frequently jumped from the path, in the vain hope of cooling, for a moment, their scorched feet under the almost shadeless bushes; and the native who carried the provision of salt pork got lost, and came into

Tette two days after the rest of the party, with nothing but the fibre of the meat left, the fat, melted by the blazing sun, having all run down his back. This path was soon made a highway for slaving parties by Captain Raposo, the Commandant. The journey nearly killed our two active young friends; and what the slaves must have since suffered on it, no one can conceive; but slaving probably can never be conducted without enormous suffering and loss of life.

A series of magnetical observations, for ascertaining the dip and declination of the needle, was made by Charles Livingstone at Dakanamoio Island, as others had been made before at Expedition Island and at Tette; after which the ship left for the Kongone. All our provisions had been expended, except tea and salt pork; but fowls, beans, and mapira meal could be purchased from the natives. This meal does not, however, agree with the European stomach; and wheaten flour, in some form or other, is indispensable to the white man's health in Africa. Our ingenious first or leading stoker, Rowe, prepared mapira meal in many ways; at first he simply baked it pure, then tried a little pork gravy with it; next he mixed bananas, and finally bananas and cloves; but in whatever form the frightful Shire biscuit was baked, the same inevitable result ensued, gnawing heartburn throughout the entire process of digestion. It would therefore be advisable for missionaries and traders to secure a constant supply of wheat; and that could as easily be done by them as by the Portuguese, if only the proper season were selected for sowing it. April and May, the beginning of the cold weather, are the months in which no rain need be expected to fall; and irrigation must be resorted to, as at the Cape, for which there are abundant facilities. If wheat is sown in the rainy season, the crop runs all to stalk. Men of energy would never be dependent on any other country for their food in this.

Mankokwe now sent a message to say that he wished us to stop at his village on our way down. He came on board on our arrival there with a handsome present, and said that his young people had dissuaded him from visiting us before; but now he was determined to see what every one else was seeing. A bald square-headed man, who had been his Prime Minister when we came up, was now out of office, and another old man, who had taken his place, accompanied the Chief. In passing the Elephant Marsh, we saw nine large herds of elephants; they sometimes formed a line two miles long. On the 26th of October a heavy thunderstorm came on, and some large hailstones fell, to the surprise of our Senna men, who had never seen heavy hail before, though it is not at all unusual for it to fall further inland. A shower fell at Kuruman which killed kids, fowls, and antelopes; another at Kolobeng was destructive to the glass of the mission-house windows.

On the 2nd of November we anchored off Shamoara, and sent the boat to Senna for biscuit and other provisions. Senhor Ferrão, with his wonted generosity, gave us a present of a bullock, which he sent to us in a canoe. Wishing to know if a second bullock would be acceptable to us, he consulted his Portuguese and English dictionary, and asked the sailor in charge if he would take *another;* but Jack, mistaking the Portuguese pronunciation of the letter *h,* replied, "Oh no, sir, thank you, I don't want an *otter* in the boat, they are such terrible biters!"

We had to ground the vessel on a shallow sandbank every night; she leaked so fast, that in deep water she would have sunk, and the pump had to be worked all day to keep her afloat.   Heavy rains fell daily, producing the usual injurious effects in the cabin; and unable to wait any longer for our associates, who had gone overland from the Shire to Tette, we ran down to the Kongone and beached her for repairs. Her Majesty's ship Lynx, Lieut. Berkeley commanding, called shortly afterwards with supplies; the bar, which had been perfectly smooth for some time before, became rather rough just before her arrival, so that it was two or three days before she could communicate with us.   Two of her boats tried to come in on the second day, and one of them, mistaking the passage, capsized in the heavy breakers abreast of the island.   Mr. Hunt, gunner, the officer in charge of the second boat, behaved nobly, and by his skilful and gallant conduct succeeded in rescuing every one of the first boat's crew.   Of course the things that they were bringing to us were lost, but we were thankful that all the men were saved. The loss of the mail-bags, containing Government despatches and our friends' letters for the past year, was felt severely, as we were on the point of starting on an expedition into the interior, which might require eight or nine months; and twenty months is a weary time to be without news of friends and family.   In the repairing of our crazy craft, we received kind and efficient aid from Lieutenant Berkeley, and we were enabled to leave for Tette on December 16th.

On our way up, we met the Governor of Quillimane coming down in a boat.   He said that he was ordered by the Lisbon Government to select, after personal investigation, the best port for ships to enter, and the best landing-place for goods.   We gave him directions how to find Kongone.   He added that he was confident that the Portuguese of his own district knew of a mouth from which they exported slaves, but they would not tell him where it was, and it was on this account he applied to us. His Excellency next morning unfortunately caught fever, and returned before he reached the river's mouth. A Portuguese naval officer was subsequently sent by his Government to examine the different entrances. He *looked* only, and then made a report, in which our published soundings were used without acknowledgment. His own countrymen smiled at the silly vanity exhibited by their Government in thus seeking information, and all the while pretending to antecedent knowledge. When opposite Expedition Island, the furnace bridge of our steamer broke down, as it had often done before. Luckily it occurred at a good place for game, so we got buffalo beef and venison whilst it was undergoing repair.

On the 31st December, 1859, we reached Shupanga, where we had to remain eight days, awaiting the arrival of cotton cloth from Quillimane. Grey calico or sheeting is the usual currency of Eastern Africa, and this supply was to serve as money during our expedition into the interior. The governor and his two handsome grown-up daughters were staying in the Shupanga-house. It is seldom that the Portuguese show any repugnance to being served by blacks, but he preferred to be waited on by his daughters, and they performed their duty with graceful ease. This was the more agreeable to us, inasmuch as one rarely meets the Portuguese ladies at table in this country. His Excellency, talking in no way confidentially, but quite openly,—indeed it is here the common mode of speaking of lamentable truths —said, that the Portuguese in this country were a miserable lot, quite debased by debauchery, and with no enterprise whatever. A few of the large slaveholders, had they any vigour left, might each send fifty or a hundred slaves to the Cape, Mauritius, and England, to learn sugar-making

and trades; after which they could manufacture their own
cloth from cotton grown on the spot; and make their own
sugar too, instead of importing it from abroad: he saw
no reason even why they should not ere long have a railroad
across the continent to Angola!

His Excellency's remarks exhibit a failing often noticed
among the Portuguese, and resembling that of certain of our
countrymen, who take a foolish pride in deriding everything
English. If we may judge by our own impressions, strangers
would either regret to hear a man, as we often have, winding up a tirade with the climax "I am horribly ashamed
that I was born a Portuguese;" or would despise him. His
observations also showed the magnificent ideas that are
entertained, to the entire neglect of plain matter-of-fact
business and industry. Indigo six feet high was growing
self-sown in abundance at our feet; superior cotton was
found about a mile off, which had propagated itself in
spite of being burned off annually for many years; and
sugar-cane is said to be easily cultivated on the greater
part of the Zambesi delta; but, instead of taking the
benefit, in a common-sense way, of these obvious advantages, our friends, while indulging in magnificent dreams of
a second East India Company, to be established by English
capitalists in Eastern Africa, were all the while diligently
exporting the labour to the Island of Bourbon. The pro-
gramme of this English Company, carefully drawn out by a
Minister of the Crown at Lisbon, provides with commend-
able stringency for the erection of schools and bridges, the
making of roads, and deepening of harbours, in this land
of "Prester John," all to be delivered back to the Portuguese at the lapse of twenty years!

His Excellency adverted to the notorious fact, that the

Home Government of Portugal had to uphold the Settlements in Eastern Africa at an annual loss of £5000, while little or no trade went thence to Lisbon, and no Portuguese ever made a fortune and retired to spend it at home. It is indeed matter of intense regret, that statesmen, known by the laws they have enacted to be enlightened men, should be the means of perpetuating so much misery in this slave-making country, by keeping out other nations, with a pretence to dominion where they have absolutely no power for good. Is it not paying too dearly for a mere swagger in Europe, to have to bear the odium of united Christendom, as the first to begin the modern ocean slave-trade, and the last to abandon it ?

A worn out slave-trader, sadly diseased, and nearly blind, used to relate to us in a frank and open manner the moving incidents of his past career. It was evident that he did not see slavery in the same light as we did. His countrymen all knew that the plea of humanity was the best for exciting his liberality, and he was certainly most generous and obliging to us. On expressing our surprise that so humane a man could have been guilty of so much cruelty, as the exportation of slaves entailed, he indignantly denied that he had ever torn slaves away from their homes. He had exported "*brutos do mato,*" beasts of the field, alone, that is, natives still wild, or lately caught in forays. This way of viewing the matter made him gravely tell us, that when his wife died, to dull the edge of his grief he made a foray amongst the tribes near the mouth of the Shire, and took many captives. He had commenced slave-trading at Angola and made several fortunes; but somehow managed to dissipate them all in riotous living in a short time at Rio de Janeiro,—"The money a man makes in the slave-trade,"

said he, " is all bad, and soon goes back to the devil." Some
twelve years since, he embarked with a lot of ivory from
Quillimane, and the vessel was seized as a slaver and carried
to the Cape. Other ships of his had been captured by our
cruisers, and he had nothing to say against that, it was all
right and fair, for they were actually employed in the slave-
trade. But it was wrong, he thought, for the English to take
this vessel, as she was then on a lawful voyage. The English
officers had thought so too, and wished to restore it to
him, and would have done so, for they were gentlemen, but
a rascally countryman of his own at the Cape opposed them,
and his vessel was condemned. Many years afterwards a
naval officer, who had been in the cruiser that took his ship,
accompanied us up the river, and, recognising our friend, at
once informed him that the British Government, having subsequently ascertained that the capture of his vessel was
illegal, had paid to the Portuguese Government the full value
of both ship and cargo.

Senhor Vianna, a settler, had just purchased a farm of
three miles square, one side of which was the battle-field of
Mazaro ; and for this he was to pay nine hundred dollars, or
£180, in three years. He also rented from the Government
forty miles of Mariano's estate, situated on the Shire and
Zambesi. Mr. Azevedo rented for many years eighty miles
of the land on the Eastern side of Mazaro. The rental of a
few hundred dollars is made up by the colonos or serfs paying
him who farms the land a bag or two of grain annually,
and performing certain services somewhat as was done in our
" cottar " system. The Landeens or Zulus on the opposite or
southern bank had come down for their tribute, but Vianna
sent a small present, and begged them not to press for it until
the Governor had gone. Meanwhile sending all his goods to

the opposite side, he shortly after left with the Governor, the
Zulus being unpaid. The chief object in paying the Zulu tax
is to obtain permission to cut the gigantic Gunda trees, some
twenty miles inland, for the construction of the large "*coches*"
or canoes that are used on the Zambesi. He had, by felling
the timber, secured canoes enough from the estate to last
ten years, and trusted that, long ere that time had expired,
his sort of moonlight flitting would be forgotten. He complained bitterly, notwithstanding, of the want of respect shown
by these natives to the Governor and himself.

Whilst we were at Shupanga, Paul Mariano was carried
past, on his way to Senna, a prisoner in a canoe. He had
been accused of murdering *a few poor black fellows*, one of
whom was a carpenter, belonging to the well-known Senhor
Azevedo. An officer and some soldiers made a descent on
Mariano by night, and took him prisoner. His sister came
to the Governor and asked him outright, before a number of
gentlemen, how much money he required to let her brother
go free. His Excellency, of course, was very much shocked
at her audacity, and indignantly reprimanded her ; but,
singularly enough, within a few days Paul made his escape,
and returned to his island, where he has ever since remained
undisturbed. Before we knew where he had gone, a gentleman, well acquainted with the ways of the country, was
asked whither he imagined Paul had fled. "Bah! (qual!)"
said he, "to his own house to be sure ;" and thither he had
gone.

We had now frequent rains, and the river rose considerably ;
our progress up the stream was distressingly slow, and it was
not until the 2nd of February, 1860, that we reached Tette.
Mr. Thornton returned on the same day from a geological tour,
by which some Portuguese expected that a fabulous silver-

mine would be rediscovered. The tradition in the country is, that the Jesuits formerly knew and worked a precious lode at Chicova. Mr. Thornton had gone beyond Zumbo, in company with a trader of colour; he soon after this left the Zambesi, and, joining the expedition of the Baron van der Decken, explored the snow mountain Kilimanjaro, north-west of Zanzibar. Mr. Thornton's companion, the trader, brought back much ivory, having found it both abundant and cheap. He was obliged, however, to pay heavy fines to the Banyai and other tribes, in the country which is coolly claimed in Europe as Portuguese. During this trip of six months 200 pieces of cotton cloth of sixteen yards each, besides beads and brass wire, were paid to the different Chiefs, for leave to pass through their country. In addition to these sufficiently weighty exactions, the natives of *this dominion* have got into the habit of imposing fines for alleged milandos, or crimes, which the trader's men may have unwittingly committed. The merchants, however, submit rather than run the risk of fighting. The ivory is cheap enough to admit of the payment. Each merchant of Tette is said to be obliged to pay for the maintenance of a certain number of the soldiers in the garrison; and he who had just returned from the interior had to support five, although no services were rendered to him. The usual way of bringing the ivory down is by canoes from Zumbo to Chicova; there the canoes are left and land carriage takes their place past Kebrabasa. This trader hired the Banyai to carry the ivory past the rapids. They agreed to do so for three yards of cloth each a trip, but threw down their loads on the path repeatedly, demanding more and more until they raised their claims to ten yards. "I could have fought and beaten them all with my own men," said the trader, "but on reaching Tette the Governor would have fined me for disturbing the peace of the country. The Banyai would have robbed those of my party behind, of the ivory, and all the redress to be obtained from our authorities would have been the mortification of knowing, that, on hearing my complaint they had sent up to the Banyai to purchase my ivory at a cheap rate for themselves."

The senior officer, since deceased, was Acting Commandant of the fort at Tette, and was a rare specimen of a Governor. Soon after he came into power he passed a sumptuary law defining the market prices of native produce. Owing to the desolating wars of former years, the cost of provisions was nearly three times as much as in bygone days; so his Excellency determined to reduce prices to their former standard, and proclaimed that in future twenty-four fowls instead of eight were to be sold for two yards of calico, and that the prices of sheep, goats, and oil should be reduced in like proportion. The first native who came to market refused to sell his fowls at Government prices, and was at once hauled up before the irate Commandant, and, for contumacy to this new re-enactment of old laws, condemned to be marched up and down the street all day, with his cackling merchandise hung round his neck, and then sent to prison to pass the night. Another poor fellow brought a pot of ground-nut-oil for sale, and was condemned to drink of it largely, for refusing to sell it at the legal rate. The only difficulty that this gentleman met with in carrying out his reforms arose from the natives declining to come with their produce until the laws were repealed.

As there is a pretty high tariff on all imported wines and spirits, Tette for a mere village must yield a respectably large revenue. The climate is usually blamed for everything; thus the merchants, being of a social turn, have night parties in each other's houses. During these meetings, the curious debilitating effects of the climate may be witnessed. In the course of an hour a number of the members become too feeble to sit in their chairs, and slip unconsciously under the table; while others, who have been standing up loudly singing or talking, fall into one another's arms, swearing eternal friendship, but gradually losing control both of tongue and limb. Slaves sit at the door, who, understanding these symptoms, enter and bear their weak and prostrate masters home. We should not hesitate to ascribe these symptoms to inebriety, if intoxication was not described here by the phrase "he speaks English," that is, "he's drunk;" so that any such charge would have the appearance of a *tu quoque*. The shocking prevalence of intemperance and other vices among the Portuguese at Tette made us wonder, not that they had fever, but that they were not all swept off together. Their habits would be fatal in any climate; the natives marvelled even more than we did; our Makololo, for instance, looked on aghast at these convivial parties, and Sininyane described one in a way that might have done the actors good. "A Portuguese stands up," said he, "and cries 'Viva!' that means, I am pleased; another says, 'Viva!' I am pleased too; and then they all shout out 'Viva!' We are all pleased together; they are so glad just to get a little beer." One night he saw three inebriated officers in the midst of their enjoyment, quarrelling about a false report; one jumped on his superior and tried to bite him; and, whilst these two were rolling on the floor, the third caught up a chair and therewith pounded them both. Sininyane, horrified at such conduct, exclaimed, "What kind of people can these whites be, who treat even their chiefs in this manner?"

The general monotony of existence at Tette is sometimes relieved by an occasional death or wedding. When the deceased is a person of consequence, the quantity of gunpowder his slaves are allowed to expend is enormous. The expense may, in proportion to their means, resemble that incurred by foolishly gaudy funerals in England. When at Tette, we always joined with sympathizing hearts in aiding, by our presence at the last rites, to soothe the sorrows of the surviving relatives. We are sure that they would have done the same to us, had we been the mourners. We never had to complain of want of hospitality. Indeed the great kindness shown by many, of whom we have often spoken, will never be effaced from our memory till our dying day. When we speak of their failings it is in sorrow, not in anger. Their trading in slaves is an enormous mistake. Their Government places them in a false position by cutting them off from the rest of the world; and of this they always speak with a bitterness which, were it heard, might alter the tone of the statesmen of Lisbon. But here there is no press, no booksellers' shops, and scarcely a schoolmaster. Had we been born in similar untoward circumstances—we tremble to think of it!

The weddings are celebrated with as much jollity as weddings are anywhere. We witnessed one in the house of our friend the Padre. It being the marriage of his god-daughter, he kindly invited us to be partakers in his joy; and we there became acquainted with old Donna Eugenia, who was a married wife and had children, when the slaves came from Cassange, before any of us were born. The whole merry-making was marked by good taste and propriety.

Another marriage brought out a feature in the Catholic church, akin, we believe, to a custom in Scotland, which commended itself to us as right. Our friend Captain Terrazão was

WEDDING PROCESSION AT SETTE.

BRIDE AND BRIDEGROOM CARRIED IN MACHILAS, OR HAMMOCKS, BY SLAVES. FRIENDS FOLLOWING. TRIUMPHAL ARCH AT FATHER-IN-LAW'S HOUSE.
SLAVES DISCHARGING MUSKETS, AS IS USUALLY DONE AT MARRIAGES AND FUNERALS.

about to be married to a young lady of no less illustrious
a name than Victoria Alexandrina, the daughter of one of the
richest merchants of Tette.   But her mother had been living
only in a state of concubinage ; and, to legitimatize the children, the marriage of the parents was first celebrated, and then
Terrazão received his bride, and another gentleman her sister
on the same day.   With our laws it seems to be a pity that
those who have the misfortune to be born out of wedlock
should be condemned, for no sin of their own, to bear the
stain through life.

In the wedding processions, the brides and bridegrooms are
carried in hammocks slung to poles, called machillas.   The
female slaves, dressed in all their finery, rejoice in the happiness of their masters and mistresses.   The males carry the
machillas, or show their gladness by discharging their
muskets.   The friends of the young couple form part of the
procession behind the machillas, dressed usually in black
dress-coats and tall chimney-pot hats, which to us outlandish
spectators look more hideous now than they ever did at
home.   The women, as seen in the woodcut, stand admiring
their neighbour's finery, balancing their water-pots gracefully on their heads; while all the invited guests proceed to wash down the dust, raised by the crowd, in copious
potations, followed by feasting, dancing, and joyous merry-
making.

About the only interesting object in the vicinity of Tette is
the coal a few miles to the north.   There, in the feeders of
the stream Revubue, it crops out in cliff sections.   The seams
are from four to seven feet in thickness; one measured was
found to be twenty-five feet thick.   That on the surface
contains much shale, but, a shaft having been run in horizontally for some twenty-five or thirty feet, the quality improved,

L

and it gave good steam. The imbedded roots of plants showed it to be of old formation. It lies under a coarse grey sandstone, which often has the ripple mark, and impressions of plants and silicified wood on its surface. Gold also is found in many of the streams on the south of Tette; but so long as slavery maintains its sway, the coal and gold will be kept unworked, and safe for future generations.

Learning that it would be difficult for our party to obtain food beyond Kebrabasa before the new crop came in, and knowing the difficulty of hunting for so many men in the wet season, we decided on deferring our departure for the interior until May, and in the mean time to run down once more to the Kongone, in the hopes of receiving letters and despatches from the man-of-war that was to call in March. We left Tette on the 10th, and at Senna heard that our lost mail had been picked up on the beach by natives, west of the Milambe; carried to Quillimane; sent thence to Senna; and, passing us somewhere on the river, on to Tette. At Shupanga the Governor informed us that it was a very large mail; no great comfort, seeing it was away up the river.

Mosquitoes were excessively troublesome at the harbour, and especially when a light breeze blew from the north over the mangroves. We lived for several weeks in small huts, built by our men. Those who did the hunting for the party always got wet, and were attacked by fever, but generally recovered in time to be out again before the meat was all consumed. No ship appearing, we started off on the 15th of March, and stopped to wood on the Luabo, near an encampment of hippopotamus hunters; our men heard again, through them, of the canoe path from this place to Quillimane, but they declined to point it out. The Governor of Quillimane had already complained that the Portuguese of his district

keep it secret for slaving purposes, and refused to show it, even
to him.   Masakasa felt confident that he could get it out of
these hunters by his diplomacy, and said that a soft tongue
would eat them up, whilst a hard one would drive them
off; but they all left during the night.   We subsequently
ascertained that the entrance to it is by a natural opening
called Kushishone, between two and three miles above the
Kongone canal, but on the opposite bank of the Zambesi.
It is however of no importance, as it is at times capable of
passing only small canoes.

The Portuguese Government in Lisbon have since striven
with amusing earnestness to prove that these parts were
long ago well known to them.   To the rest of the world
this is a matter of perfect indifference.   *We* had to discover,
or at least to rediscover, them for ourselves; and considering the perfect knowledge possessed by that ministry, it is
odd that none of their information accompanied the orders
to the officials in Africa.   The Governor of Quillimane had
orders to examine the Kongone, but frankly confessed he did
not know where that harbour lay.   Our friend Major Sicard,
after receiving the assurance from us that no Zulus could
cross the creeks around it, with sly foresight resolved to
gain possession of a large slice of the soil for himself, and
sent slaves to make a garden, and build him a house at
Kongone, which gives the harbour its value.   They executed their orders at a point some twenty miles off; not
knowing that we had taken the name from the side of the
natural canal between the Kongone branch and the Zambesi.   We could see plainly, that we and our Portuguese
friends had different ranges of vision.   We looked for the
large result of benefit to all, both white and black, by
establishing free commercial intercourse.   They could see

nothing beyond our inducing English merchants to establish a company, of which the Portuguese would, by fictitious claims, reap all the benefit. The short-sighted " dog in the manger" policy was so transparent that we always warned our commercial friends in England that, without free navigation of the Zambesi, it was in vain for them to run any risk. Nothing but slaving will on any account be tolerated. W. Sunley, Esq., of Johanna, on the recommendation of the late Admiral Wyvil, took a cargo of goods to the River Angonsh, or Angoxe, in order to begin a legal traffic with the natives. He succeeded as well as he expected. He was then inveigled on false pretences, by two Portuguese officials, to Mosambique; and, as soon as he came under the guns of the fort, he was declared a prisoner, and his cargo and ship confiscated, for " illegal traffic in Portuguese territory." Had he been a slaver, without doubt, a little head-money would have secured him lodging and a feast in the Governor-General's palace instead.

We found our friend Major Sicard at Mazaro with picks, shovels, hurdles, and slaves, having come to build a fort and custom-house at the Kongone. As we had no good reason to hide the harbour, but many for its being made known, we supplied him with a chart of the tortuous branches, which, running among the mangroves, perplex the search; and with such directions as would enable him to find his way down to the river. He had brought the relics of our fugitive mail, and it was a disappointment to find that all had been lost, with the exception of a bundle of old newspapers, two photographs, and three letters which had been written before we left England.

Sininyane had exchanged names with a Zulu at Shupanga, and on being called next morning made no answer; to a second and third summons he paid no attention; but at length one of his men replied, " He is not Sininyane now, he is Moshoshoma;" and to this name he answered promptly. The custom of exchanging names with men of other tribes, is not uncommon ; and the exchangers regard themselves as close comrades, owing special duties to each other ever after. Should one by chance visit his comrade's town, he expects to receive food, lodging, and other friendly offices from him. While Charles Livingstone was at Kebrabasa during the rainy season, a hungry, shivering native traveller was made a comrade for life, not by exchanging names, but by some food and a small piece of cloth.   Eighteen months after, while on our journey into the interior, a man came into our camp, bringing a liberal present of rice, meal, beer, and a fowl, and reminding us of what had been done for him (which Charles Livingstone had entirely forgotten), said that now seeing us travelling he " did not like us to sleep hungry or thirsty." Several of our men, like some people at home, dropped their own names and adopted those of the Chiefs ; others were a little in advance of those who take the surnames of higher people, for they took those of the mountains, or cataracts we had seen on our travels. We had a Chibisa, a Morambala, a Zomba, and a Kebrabasa, and they were called by these names even after they had returned to their own country.

We had been so much hindered and annoyed by the " Ma Robert," *alias* "Asthmatic," that the reader, though a tithe is not mentioned, may think we have said more than enough. The man, who had been the chief means of imposing this wretched craft on us, had passed away, and with him all bitterness from our hearts.   We felt it to be a sad pity, however, that any one, for unfair gain, should do deeds which cannot be spoken of after he is gone.   We had still our much-esteemed and noble-hearted friend, the late Admiral Washington, at home to see that we did not again suffer; but the prospect of effecting a grand work on Lake Nyassa, by means of a steamer, made to be unscrewed and carried past the cataracts, was so fair,—indeed it promised, if carried out, so entirely to change the wretched system, which has been the bane of the country for ages,—that to have the vessel properly constructed we sent Mr. Rae, the engineer, home to superintend its construction. He could be of no further use in the "Asthmatic," as she was utterly beyond cure. We sent also five boxes of specimens, carefully collected and prepared by Dr. Kirk; four of them, to our very great sorrow and loss, never arrived at the Gardens at Kew. We all accompanied our engineer on foot to a small stream that runs into the Kwakwa, or river of Quillimane, on his way to that port to embark for England.

The distance from Mazaro, on the Zambesi side, to the Kwakwa at Nterra, is about six miles, over a surprisingly rich dark soil. We passed the night in the long shed, erected at Nterra, on the banks of this river, for the use of travellers, who have often to wait several days for canoes; we tried to sleep, but the mosquitoes and rats were so troublesome as to render sleep impossible. The rats, or rather large mice, closely resembling *Mus pumilio* (Smith), of this region, are quite facetious, and, having a great deal of fun in them, often laugh heartily. Again and again they woke us up by scampering over our faces, and then bursting into a loud laugh of He! he! he! at having performed the feat. Their sense of the ludicrous appears to be exquisite; they screamed with laughter at the attempts, which disturbed and angry human nature made in the dark to bring their ill-timed merriment to a close. Unlike their

prudent European cousins, which are said to leave a sinking
ship, a party of these took up their quarters in our leaky
and sinking vessel. Quiet and invisible by day, they emerged
at night, and cut their funny pranks. No sooner were we all
asleep, than they made a sudden dash over the lockers and
across our faces for the cabin door, where all broke out into
a loud He! he! he! he! he! he! showing how keenly they
enjoyed the joke. They next went forward with as much
delight, and scampered over the men. Every night they went
fore and aft, rousing with impartial feet every sleeper, and
laughing to scorn the aimless blows, growls, and deadly rushes
of outraged humanity. We observed elsewhere, a species of
large mouse, nearly allied to *Euryotis unisulcatus* (F. Cuvier),
escaping up a rough and not very upright wall, with six young
ones firmly attached to the perineum. They were old enough
to be well covered with hair, and some were not detached by
a blow which disabled the dam. We could not decide whether
any involuntary muscles were brought into play, in helping
the young to adhere. Their weight seemed to require a sort
of cataleptic state of the muscles of the jaw, to enable them
to hold on.

Scorpions, centipedes, and poisonous spiders also, were not
unfrequently brought into the ship with the wood, and occasionally found their way into our beds; but, in every
instance, we were fortunate enough to discover and destroy
them, before they did any harm. Naval officers on this coast
report, that when scorpions and centipedes remain a few
weeks after being taken on board in a similar manner, their
poison loses nearly all its virulence, but this we did not verify.
Snakes sometimes came in with the wood, but oftener floated
down the river to us, climbing on board with ease by the
chain-cable, and some poisonous ones were caught in the

cabin. A green snake lived with us several weeks, con-
cealing himself behind the casing of the deckhouse in the
daytime. To be aroused in the dark by five feet of cold
green snake gliding over one's face, is rather unpleasant,
however rapid the movement may be. Myriads of two
varieties of cockroaches infested the vessel; they not only
ate round the roots of our nails, but even devoured and
defiled our food, flannels, and boots; vain were all our
efforts to extirpate these destructive pests; if you kill one,
say the sailors, a hundred come down to his funeral! In the
work of Commodore Owen it is stated that cockroaches,
pounded into a paste, form a powerful carminative; this has
not been confirmed, but when monkeys are fed on them they
are sure to become so lean as to suggest the idea, that for fat
people a course of cockroach might be as efficacious as a
course of Banting.

On coming to Senna, we found that the Zulus had arrived in
force for their annual tribute. These men are under good discipline, and never steal from the people. The tax is claimed on
the ground of conquest, the Zulus having formerly completely
overcome the Senna people, and chased them on to the islands
in the Zambesi. Fifty-four of the Portuguese were slain on
the occasion, and, notwithstanding the mud fort, the village
has never recovered its former power. Fever was now very
prevalent, and most of the Portuguese were down with it.
The village has a number of foul pools, filled with green, fetid
mud, in which horrid long-snouted greyhound-shaped pigs
wallow with delight. The greater part of the space enclosed
in the stockade, which is an oblong of say a thousand yards
by five hundred, is covered with tall indigo-plants, cassia,
and bushes, with mounds on which once stood churches and
monasteries. The air is not allowed free circulation, so it

is not to be wondered at that men suffer from fever. The feeding of the pigs is indescribably shocking; but they are a favourite food themselves, and the owners may be heard, both here and at Tette, recalling them from their wanderings, by pet names, as "João," "Manoel," "kudia! kudia! (to eat, to eat), Antonio!" We saw a curious variety, which had accidentally appeared among these otherwise uninteresting brutes. A litter was beautifully marked with yellowish brown and white stripes alternately, and the bands, about an inch broad, were disposed, not as in the zebra, but horizontally along the body. Stripes appear occasionally in mules and in horses, and are supposed to show a reversion to the original wild type, in the same way that highly-bred domestic pigeons sometimes manifest a tendency to revert to the plumage of the rock-pigeon, with its black bar across the tail. This striped variety may betoken relationship to the original wild pig, the young of which are distinctly banded, though the marks fade as the animal grows up.

For a good view of the adjacent scenery, the hill, Baramuana, behind the village, was ascended. A caution was given about the probability of an attack of fever from a plant that grows near the summit. Dr. Kirk discovered it to be the *Pœdevia fœtida*, which, when smelt, actually does give headache and fever. It has a nasty fetor, as its name indicates. This is one instance in which fever and a foul smell coincide. In a number of instances offensive effluvia and fever seem to have no connexion. Owing to the abundant rains, the crops in the Senna district were plentiful; this was fortunate, after the partial failure of the past two years. It was the 25th of April, 1860, before we reached Tette; here also the crops were luxuriant, and the people said that they had not had such abundance since 1856, the year when Dr. Livingstone came down the river. It is astonishing to any one who has seen the works for irrigation in other countries, as at the Cape and in Egypt, that no attempt has ever been made to lead out the water either of the Zambesi or any of its tributaries; no machinery has ever been used to raise it even from the stream, but droughts and starvation are endured, as if they were inevitable dispensations of Providence, incapable of being mitigated. Our friends at Tette, though heedless of the obvious advantages which other nations would eagerly seize, have beaten the entire world in one branch of industry. It is a sort of anomaly that the animal, most nearly allied to man in structure and function, should be the most alien to him in respect to labour, or trusty friendship; but here the genius of the monkey is turned to good account He is made to work in the chase of certain " wingless insects better known than respected." Having been invited to witness this branch of Tette industry, we can testify that the monkey took to it kindly, and it seemed profitable to both parties.

CHAPTER VII.

FEELING in honour bound to return with those who had been the faithful companions of Dr. Livingstone, in 1856, and to whose guardianship and services was due the accomplishment of a journey which all the Portuguese at Tette had previously pronounced impossible, the requisite steps were taken to convey them to their homes.

We laid the ship alongside of the island Kanyimbe, opposite Tette; and, before starting for the country of the Makololo, obtained a small plot of land, to form a garden for the two English sailors who were to remain in charge during our absence. We furnished them with a supply of seeds, and they set to work with such zeal, that they certainly merited success. Their first attempt at African horticulture met with failure from a most unexpected source; every seed was dug up and the inside of it eaten by mice. "Yes," said an old native, next morning, on seeing the husks, "that is what happens this month; for it is the mouse month, and the seed should have been sown last month, when I sowed mine." The sailors, however, sowed more next day; and, being determined to outwit the mice, they this time covered the beds over with grass. The onions, with other seeds of plants cultivated by the Portuguese, are usually planted in the beginning of April, in order to have the advantage of the cold season; the wheat a little later, for the same reason. If sown at the beginning of the rainy season in November, it runs, as before remarked, entirely to straw; but, as the rains are nearly over in May, advantage is taken of low-lying patches, which have been flooded by the river. A hole is made in the mud with a hoe, a few seeds dropped in, and the earth shoved back with the foot. If not favoured with certain misty showers, which, lower down the river, are simply fogs, water is borne from the river to the roots of the wheat in earthen pots; and, in about four months, the crop is ready for the sickle. The wheat of Tette is exported, as the best grown in the country; but a hollow spot at Maruru, close by Mazaro, yielded very good crops, though just at the level of the sea, as a few inches rise of tide shows.

A number of days were spent in busy preparation for our journey; the cloth, beads, and brass wire, for the trip, were sewn up in old canvass, and each package had the bearer's name printed on it. The Makololo, who had worked for the Expedition, were paid for their services, and every one who had come down with the Doctor from the interior received a present of cloth and ornaments, in order to protect them from the greater cold of their own country, and to show that they had not come in vain. Though called Makololo by courtesy, as they were proud of the name, Kanyata, the principal headman, was the only real Makololo of the party; and he, in virtue of his birth, had succeeded to the chief place on the death of Sekwebu. The others belonged to the conquered tribes of the Batoka, Bashubia, BaSelea, and Barotse. Some of these men had only added to their own vices those of the Tette slaves; others, by toiling during the first two years in navigating canoes, and hunting elephants, had often managed to save a little, to take back to their own country, but had to part with it all for food to support the rest in times of hunger, and, latterly, had fallen into the improvident habits of slaves, and spent their surplus earnings in beer and agua ardiente.

Everything being ready on the 15th of May, we started at 2 P.M. from the village where the Makololo had dwelt. A number of the men did not leave with the good-will which their talk for months before had led us to anticipate; but some proceeded upon being told that they were not compelled to go unless they liked, though others altogether declined moving. Many had taken up with slave-women, whom they assisted in hoeing, and in con-suming the produce of their gardens. Some fourteen children had been born to them; and in consequence of now having no Chief to order them, or to claim their services, they thought that they were about as well off as they had been in their own country. They knew and regretted that they could call neither wives nor children their own; the slave-owners claimed the whole; but their natural affections had been so enchained, that they clave to the domestic ties. By a law of Portugal the baptized children of slave women are all free; by the custom of the Zambesi that law is void. When it is re-ferred to, the officers laugh and say, "These Lisbon-born laws are very stringent, but somehow, possibly from the heat of the climate, here they lose all their force." Only one woman joined our party—the wife of a Batoka man: she had been given to him, in consideration of his skilful dancing, by the chief, Chisaka. A merchant sent three of his men along with us, with a present for Sekeletu, and Major Sicard also lent

us three more to assist us on our return, and two Portuguese
gentlemen kindly gave us the loan of a couple of donkeys.
We slept four miles above Tette, and hearing that the
Banyai, who levy heavy fines on the Portuguese traders, lived
chiefly on the right bank, we crossed over to the left, as we
could not fully trust our men. If the Banyai had come
in a threatening manner, our followers might perhaps, from
having homes behind them, have even put down their bundles
and run. Indeed two of them, at this point, made up their
minds to go no further, and turned back to Tette. Another,
Monga, a Batoka, was much perplexed, and could not make
out what course to pursue, as he had, three years previously,
wounded Kanyata, the headman, with a spear. This is a capital
offence among the Makololo, and he was afraid of being put
to death for it on his return. He tried, in vain, to console
himself with the facts that he had neither father, mother,
sisters, nor brothers, to mourn for him, and that he could die
but once. He was good, and would go up to the stars to Yesu,
and, therefore, did not care for death. In spite, however, of
these reflections, he was much cast down, until Kanyata assured
him that he would never mention his misdeed to the Chief;
indeed, he had never even mentioned it to the Doctor, which
he would assuredly have done, had it lain heavy on his heart.
We were right glad of Monga's company, for he was a merry
good-tempered fellow, and his lithe manly figure had always
been in the front in danger; and, from being left-handed,
had been easily recognised in the fight with elephants.

We commenced, for a certain number of days, with short
marches, walking gently until broken in to travel. This is of so
much importance that it occurs to us that more might be made
out of soldiers if the first few days' marches were easy, and
gradually increased in length and quickness. The nights were

cold, with heavy dews and occasional showers, and we had
several cases of fever. Some of the men deserted every night,
and we fully expected that all who had children would prefer
to return to Tette, for little ones are well known to prove the
strongest ties, even to slaves. It was useless informing them,
that if they wanted to return they had only to come and tell
us so; we should not be angry with them for preferring Tette
to their own country. Contact with slaves had destroyed their
sense of honour, they would not go in daylight, but decamped in the night, only in one instance, however, taking
our goods, though, in two more, they carried off their
comrades' property. By the time we had got well into the
Kebrabasa hills, thirty men, nearly a third of the party, had
turned back, and it became evident that, if many more left
us, Sekeletu's goods could not be carried up. At last, when
the refuse had fallen away, no more desertions took place.

Stopping one afternoon at a Kebrabasa village, a man,
who pretended to be able to change himself into a lion, came
to salute us. Smelling the gunpowder from a gun which
had been discharged, he went on one side to get out of
the wind of the piece, trembling in a most artistic manner,
but quite overacting his part. The Makololo explained to
us that he was a Pondoro, or a man who can change his
form at will, and added that he trembles when he smells
gunpowder. "Do you not see how he is trembling now?"
We told them to ask him to change himself at once into a
lion, and we would give him a cloth for the performance.
"Oh, no," replied they; "if we tell him so, he may change himself and come when we are asleep and kill us." Having similar
superstitions at home, they readily became as firm believers
in the Pondoro as the natives of the village. We were told
that he assumes the form of a lion and remains in the woods

for days, and is sometimes absent for a whole month. His considerate wife had built him a hut or den, in which she places food and beer for her transformed lord, whose metamorphosis does not impair his human appetite. No one ever enters this hut except the Pondoro and his wife, and no stranger is allowed even to rest his gun against the Baobab-tree beside it: the Mfumo, or petty Chief, of another small village wished to fine our men for placing their muskets against an old tumble-down hut, it being that of the Pondoro. At times the Pondoro employs his acquired powers in hunting for the benefit of the village; and, after an absence of a day or two, his wife smells the lion, takes a certain medicine, places it in the forest, and there quickly leaves it, lest the lion should kill even her. This medicine enables the Pondoro to change himself back into a man, return to the village, and say "Go and get the game that I have killed for you." Advantage is of course taken of what a lion has done, and they go and bring home the buffalo or antelope killed when he was a lion, or rather found when he was patiently pursuing his course of deception in the forest. We saw the Pondoro of another village dressed in a fantastic style, with numerous charms hung round him, and followed by a troop of boys who were honouring him with rounds of shrill cheering.

It is believed also that the souls of departed Chiefs enter into lions and render them sacred. On one occasion, when we had shot a buffalo in the path beyond the Kafue, a hungry lion, attracted probably by the smell of the meat, came close to our camp, and roused up all hands by his roaring. Tuba Mokoro, imbued with the popular belief that the beast was a Chief in disguise, scolded him roundly during his brief intervals of silence. "You a Chief, eh? You call your-

self a Chief, do you? What kind of Chief are you to come
sneaking about in the dark, trying to steal our buffalo
meat! Are you not ashamed of yourself? A pretty Chief
truly; you are like the scavenger beetle, and think of yourself only. You have not the heart of a Chief; why don't you
kill your own beef? You must have a stone in your chest,
and no heart at all, indeed!" Tuba Mokoro producing no
impression on the transformed Chief, one of the men, the most
sedate of the party, who seldom spoke, took up the matter,
and tried the lion in another strain. In his slow quiet way
he expostulated with him on the impropriety of such conduct
to strangers, who had never injured him. "We were travelling
peaceably through the country back to our own Chief. We
never killed people, nor stole anything. The buffalo meat
was ours, not his, and it did not become a great Chief like
him to be prowling round in the dark, trying, like a hyena,
to steal the meat of strangers. He might go and hunt for
himself, as there was plenty of game in the forest." The
Pondoro, being deaf to reason, and only roaring the louder, the
men became angry, and threatened to send a ball through him
if he did not go away. They snatched up their guns to shoot
him, but he prudently kept in the dark, outside of the lumi-
nous circle made by our camp fires, and there they did not
like to venture. A little strychnine was put into a piece of
meat, and thrown to him, when he soon departed, and we
heard no more of the majestic sneaker.

The Kebrabasa people were now plumper and in better
condition than on our former visits; the harvest had been
abundant; they had plenty to eat and drink, and they were
enjoying life as much as ever they could. At Defwe's
village, near where the ship lay on her first ascent, we found
two Mfumos or headmen, the son and son-in-law of the former

Chief. A sister's son has much more chance of succeeding to a chieftainship than the Chief's own offspring, it being unquestionable that the sister's child has the family blood. The men are all marked across the nose and up the middle of the forehead, with short horizontal bars or cicatrices; and a single brass earring of two or three inches diameter, like the ancient Egyptia is worn by the men. Some wear the hair long like the ancient Assyrians and Egyptians, and a few have eyes with the downward and inward slant of the Chinese.

After fording the rapid Luia, we left our former path on the banks of the Zambesi, and struck off in a N.W. direction behind one of the hill ranges, the eastern end of which is called Mongwa, the name of an acacia, having a peculiarly strong fetor, found on it. Our route wound up a valley along a small mountain-stream which was nearly dry, and then crossed the rocky spurs of some of the lofty hills. The country was all very dry at the time, and no water was found except in an occasional spring and a few wells dug in the beds of watercourses. The people were poor, and always anxious to convince travellers of the fact. The men, unlike those on the plains, spend a good deal of their time in hunting; this may be because they have but little ground on the hill-sides suitable for gardens, and but little certainty of reaping what may be sown in the valleys. No women came forward in the hamlet, east of Chiperiziwa, where we halted for the night. Two shots had been fired at guinea-fowl a little way off in the valley; the women fled into the woods, and the men came to know if war was meant, and a few of the old folks only returned after hearing that we were for peace. The headman, Kambira, apologized for not having a present ready, and afterwards brought us some meal, a roasted coney (*Hyrax capensis*) and a pot of beer; he wished to be thought poor. The beer had

come to him from a distance; he had none of his own. Like
the Manganja, these people salute by clapping their hands.
When a man comes to a place where others are seated, before
sitting down he claps his hands to each in succession, and they
do the same to him. If he has anything to tell, both speaker
and hearer clap their hands at the close of every paragraph,
and then again vigorously at the end of the speech. The
guide, whom the headman gave us, thus saluted each of his
comrades before he started off with us. There is so little
difference in the language, that all the tribes of this region
are virtually of one family.

We proceeded still in the same direction, and passed
only two small hamlets during the day. Except the noise
our men made on the march, everything was still around us:
few birds were seen. The appearance of a whydah-bird
showed that he had not yet parted with his fine long plumes.
We passed immense quantities of ebony and lignum-vitæ,
and the tree from whose smooth and bitter bark granaries
are made for corn. The country generally is clothed with a
forest of ordinary-sized trees. We slept in the little village
near Sindabwe, where our men contrived to purchase plenty
of beer, and were uncommonly boisterous all the evening.
We breakfasted next morning under green wild date-
palms, beside the fine flowery stream, which runs through
the charming valley of Zibah. We now had Mount Chiperiziwa between us, and part of the river near Morumbwa,
having in fact come north about in order to avoid the difficulties of our former path. The last of the deserters, a
reputed thief, took French leave of us here. He left the
bundle of cloth he was carrying in the path a hundred
yards in front of where we halted, but made off with the
musket and most of the brass rings and beads of his comrade

Shirimba, who had unsuspectingly intrusted them to his care.

Proceeding S.W. up this lovely valley, in about an hour's time we reached Sandia's village. The Chief was said to be absent hunting, and they did not know when he would return. This is such a common answer to the inquiry after a headman, that one is inclined to think, that it only means that they wish to know the stranger's object, before exposing their superior to danger. As some of our men were ill, a halt was made here. Sandia's people were very civil: a kinsman of his came to see us in the evening, bringing a large pot of beer: he did not like to see us eating with nothing to drink, so brought it as a present. When at a distance from those who are engaged in the slave-trade, there is much in the manners of the natives, and their ways of speaking, to remind us of the Patriarchs. The inhabitants of Zibah are Badéma, and a wealthier class than those we have recently passed, with more cloth, ornaments, food and luxuries. Fowls, eggs, sugar-canes, sweet-potatoes, ground-nuts, turmeric, tomatoes, chillies, rice, mapira (*holcus sorghum*), and maize, were offered for sale in large quantities. The mapira may be called the corn of the country. It is known as Kaffir and Guinea corn, in the south and west; as dura in Egypt, and badjery in India; the grain is round and white, or reddish-white, about the size of the hemp-seed given to canaries. Several hundred grains form a massive ear, on a stalk as thick as an ordinary walking-staff, and from eight to eighteen feet high. Tobacco, hemp, and cotton were also cultivated, as, indeed, they are by all the people in Kebrabasa. In nearly every village here, as in the Manganja hills, men are engaged in spinning and weaving cotton of excellent quality.

As we were unable to march next morning, six of our young

men, anxious to try their muskets, went off to hunt elephants. For several hours they saw nothing, and some of them, getting tired, proposed to go to a village and buy food. " No !" said Mantlanyane, " we came to hunt, so let us go on." In a short time they fell in with a herd of cow elephants and calves. As soon as the first cow caught sight of the hunters on the rocks above her, she, with true motherly instinct, placed her young one between her fore-legs for protection. The men were for scattering, and firing into the herd indiscriminately. " That won't do," cried Mantlanyane, " let us all fire at this one." The poor beast received a volley, and ran down into the plain, where another shot killed her; the young one escaped with the herd. The men were wild with excitement, and danced round the fallen queen of the forest, with loud shouts and exultant songs. They returned, bearing as trophies, the tail and part of the trunk, and marched into camp as erect as soldiers, and evidently feeling that their stature had increased considerably since the morning.

Sandia's wife was duly informed of their success, as here a law decrees that half the elephant belongs to the Chief on whose ground it has been killed. The Portuguese traders always submit to this tax, and, were it of native origin, it could hardly be considered unjust. A Chief must have some source of revenue ; and, as many Chiefs can raise none except from ivory or slaves, this tax is more free from objections than any other that a black Chancellor of the Exchequer could devise. It seems, however, to have originated with the Portuguese themselves, and then to have spread among the adjacent tribes. The Governors look sharply after any elephant that may be slain on the Crown lands, and demand one of the tusks from their vassals. We did not find the law in operation in any tribe beyond the range of Portuguese traders, or further than the sphere of travel of those Arabs who imitated Portuguese customs in trade. At the Kafue in 1855 the Chiefs bought the meat we killed, and demanded nothing as their due ; and so it was up the Shire during our visits. The slaves of the Portuguese, who are sent by their masters to shoot elephants, probably connive at the extension of this law, for they strive to get the good will of the Chiefs to whose country they come, by advising them to make a demand of half of each elephant killed, and for this advice they are well paid in beer. When we found that the Portuguese argued in favour of this law, we told the natives that they might exact tusks from *them,* but that the English, being different, preferred the pure native custom. It was this which made Sandia, as afterwards mentioned, hesitate ; but we did not care to insist on exemption in our favour, where the prevalence of the custom might have been held to justify the exaction.

Sandia's wife said that she had sent a messenger to her husband on the day of our arrival, and soon expected his return ; but that some of his people would go with our men in the morning, and receive what we chose to give. We accompanied our hunters across the hills to the elephant vale, north of Zibah. It was a beautiful valley covered with tall heavy-seeded grass, on which the elephants had been quietly feeding when attacked. We found the carcass undisturbed, an enormous mass of meat.

The cutting up of an elephant is quite a unique spectacle. The men stand round the animal in dead silence, while the chief of the travelling party declares that, according to ancient law, the head and right hind-leg belong to him who killed the beast, that is, to him who inflicted the first wound ; the left leg to him who delivered the second, or first touched the animal after it fell. The meat around the eye to the English, or chief of the travellers, and different parts to the headmen of the different fires, or groups, of which the camp is composed; not forgetting to enjoin the preservation of the fat and bowels for a second distribution.   This oration finished, the natives soon become excited, and scream wildly as they cut away at the carcass with a score of spears, whose long handles quiver in the air above their heads.   Their excitement becomes momentarily more and more intense, and reaches the culminating point when, as denoted by a roar of gas, the huge mass is laid fairly open.   Some jump inside, and roll about there in their eagerness to seize the precious fat, while others run off, screaming, with pieces of the bloody meat, throw it on the grass, and run back for more : all keep talking and shouting at the utmost pitch of their voices.   Sometimes two or three, regardless of all laws, seize the same piece of meat, and have a brief fight of words over it.   Occasionally an agonized yell bursts forth, and a native emerges out of the moving mass of dead elephant and wriggling humanity, with his hand badly cut by the spear of his excited friend and neighbour: this requires a rag and some soothing words to prevent bad blood. In an incredibly short time tons of meat are cut up, and placed in separate heaps around.

Sandia arrived soon after the beast was divided: he is an elderly man, and wears a wig made of ife fibre (*sanseviera*) dyed black, and of a fine glossy appearance.   This plant is allied to the aloes, and its thick fleshy leaves, in shape somewhat like our sedges, when bruised yield much fine strong fibre, which is made into ropes, nets, and wigs.   It takes dyes readily, and the fibre might form a good article of commerce.   Ife wigs, as we afterwards saw, are not uncommon in this country, though perhaps not so common as hair wigs at home. Sandia's mosamela, or small carved wooden pillow, exactly resembling the ancient Egyptian one, was hung from the back of his neck; this pillow and a sleeping mat are usually carried by natives when on hunting excursions. The Chief visited the different camp-fires of our men, and accepted presents of meat from them; but said that he should like to consume it with his elders, as he wished to consult them whether he ought to receive the half of the elephant from the Englishmen. His Cabinet, seeing no good reason for departing from the established custom, concluded that it was best to treat white tax-payers as on a perfect equality with black ones, and to accept the half which belonged to Sandia's Government. In the afternoon the Chief returned with his counsellors, accompanied by his wife and several other women, carrying five pots of beer: three, he explained, were a present to the white men, and the other two were intended for sale. The women have a remarkably erect gait, probably from having been accustomed from infancy to carry heavy water-pots on their heads. This brings all the muscles of the back into play, and might prove beneficial as a practice to those who are troubled with weakness of spine among ourselves. They use a piece of wood between the head and pot, perhaps for elegance.

We had the elephant's fore-foot cooked for ourselves, in native fashion. A large hole was dug in the ground, in which a fire was made; and, when the inside was thoroughly heated, the entire foot was placed in it, and covered over with the hot ashes and soil; another fire was made above the whole, and kept burning all night. We had the foot thus cooked for breakfast next morning, and found it delicious. It is a whitish mass, slightly gelatinous, and sweet, like marrow. A long march, to prevent biliousness, is a wise precaution after a meal of elephant's foot. Elephant's trunk and tongue

are also good, and, after long simmering, much resemble
the hump of a buffalo, and the tongue of an ox; but all the
other meat is tough, and, from its peculiar flavour, only to be
eaten by a hungry man. The quantities of meat our men
devour is quite astounding. They boil as much as their
pots will hold, and eat till it becomes physically impossible
for them to stow away any more. An uproarious dance
follows, accompanied with stentorian song; and as soon
as they have shaken their first course down, and washed off
the sweat and dust of the after performance, they go to work
to roast more: a short snatch of sleep succeeds, and they are
up and at it again; all night long it is boil and eat, roast and
devour, with a few brief interludes of sleep. Like other car-
nivora these men can endure hunger for a much longer period
than the mere porridge-eating tribes. Our men can cook meat
as well as any reasonable traveller could desire; and, boiled in
earthen pots, like Indian chatties, it tastes much better than
when cooked in iron ones.

Their porridge is a failure, at least for a Scotch digestion that has been impaired by fever. When on a journey,
unaccompanied by women, as soon as the water is hot,
they tumble in the meal by handfuls in rapid succession,
until it becomes too thick to stir about, when it is
whipped off the fire, and placed on the ground; an assistant then holds the pot, whilst the cook, grasping the stick
with both hands, exerts his utmost strength in giving it a
number of circular turns, to mix and prevent the solid mass
from being burnt by the heat. It is then served up to us,
the cook retaining the usual perquisite of as much as can be
induced to adhere to the stick, when he takes it from the pot.
By this process, the meal is merely moistened and warmed,
but not boiled; much of it being raw, it always causes

heartburn. This is the only mode that the natives have of cooking the mapira meal. They seldom, if ever, bake it into cakes, like oatmeal; for, though finely ground and beautifully white, it will not cohere readily. Maize meal is formed into dough more readily, but that too is inferior to wheaten flour, or even oatmeal, for baking. It was rather difficult to persuade the men to boil the porridge for us more patiently; and they became witty, and joked us for being like women, when the weakness of fever compelled us to pay some attention to the cooking, evidently thinking that it was beneath the dignity of white men to stoop to such matters. They look upon the meal and water porridge of the black tribes as the English used to do upon the French frogs, and call the eaters "mere water-porridge fellows," while the Makololo's meal and milk porridge takes the character of English roast-beef.

Sandia gave us two guides; and on the 4th of June we left the Elephant valley, taking a westerly course; and, after crossing a few ridges, entered the Chingerere or Paguruguru valley, through which, in the rainy season, runs the streamlet Pajodze. The mountains on our left, between us and the Zambesi, our guides told us have the same name as the valley, but that at the confluence of the Pajodze is called Morumbwa. We struck the river at less than half a mile to the north of the cataract Morumbwa. On climbing up the base of this mountain at Pajodze, we found that we were distant only the diameter of the mountain from the cataract. In measuring the cataract we formerly stood on its southern flank; now we were perched on its northern flank, and at once recognised the onion-shaped mountain, here called Zakavuma, whose smooth convex surface overlooks the broken water. Its bearing by compass was 180° from the spot to which we had climbed and 700 or 800 yards distant. We now, from this standing-point, therefore, completed our inspection of all Kebrabasa, and saw what, as a whole, was never before seen by Europeans so far as any records show.

The difference of level between Pajodze and Tette, as shown by the barometer, was about 160 feet; but it must be remembered that we had no simultaneous observations at the two stations. The somewhat conical shape of Zaka-vuma standing on the right, and the more castellated form of Morumbwa on the left, constitute the narrow gate-way in which the cataract exists. The talus of each portal, keeping close together northwards, makes a narrow, upright-sided trough from the cataract up to Pajodze. The deep green river winds in it among massive black angular rocks; above this, as far as Chicova, the Zambesi again has a flood bed and a deep waterworn groove, like that near the lower end of Kebrabasa, but the flood bed is only 200 or 300 yards broad, and the stream in this part of the groove is adorned in various places with the white foam of a number of small rapids. By the motion of pieces of wood in the water, and timed by a watch, the current was ascertained to be from 3·3 to 4·1 knots per hour in the more rapid places. We breakfasted a short dis-tance above Pajodze. At a comparatively smooth part of the Zambesi, called Movuzi, still further up, where traders sometimes cross from the southern to the northern bank, a Banyai headman came over with a dozen armed followers, and in an insolent way demanded payment for leave to pass on our way. This was not a friendly request for a present, so our men told him that it was not the custom of the English to pay fines for nothing; and, being unsuccessful, he went quietly back again. One

Chief of the Banyai on the opposite bank is called Zuda, which the Portuguese translate into Judas, on account of his grasping propensities. Talking of us to some of our party, he said, "These men passed me going down and gave me nothing; the English cloth is good; I am come to clothe myself with it now as they go up." His messenger came and sat down impudently in our midst before we rose from breakfast, and began an oration, not to us, but to his attendant. This talking at us roused the Makololo's ire, and they replied that "English cloth was good; and Englishmen paid for all they ate. They were now walking on God's earth in peace, doing no harm to the country or gardens, though English guns had six mouths, and English balls travelled far, and hit hard." However, by keeping on the left bank, we avoided collision with these troublesome and exacting Banyai.

The remainder of the Kebrabasa path, on to Chicova, was close to the compressed and rocky river. Ranges of lofty tree-covered mountains, with deep narrow valleys, in which are dry watercourses, or flowing rivulets, stretch from the north-west, and are prolonged on the opposite side of the river in a south-easterly direction. Looking back, the mountain scenery in Kebrabasa was magnificent; conspicuous from their form and steep sides, are the two gigantic portals of the cataract; the vast forests still wore their many brilliant autumnal-coloured tints of green, yellow, red, purple, and brown, thrown into relief by the grey bark of the trunks in the background. Among these variegated trees were some conspicuous for their new livery of fresh light-green leaves, as though the winter of others was their spring. The bright sunshine in these mountain forests, and the ever-changing forms of the cloud shadows, gliding over portions of the surface, added fresh charms to scenes already surpassingly beautiful.

From what we have seen of the Kebrabasa rocks and
rapids, it appears too evident that they must always form a
barrier to navigation at the ordinary low water of the river;
but the rise of the water in this gorge being as much as eighty
feet perpendicularly, it is probable that a steamer might be
taken up at high flood, when all the rapids are smoothed
over, to run on the upper Zambesi. The most formidable cataract in it, Morumbwa, has only about twenty feet of fall, in
a distance of thirty yards, and it must entirely disappear when
the water stands eighty feet higher. Those of the Makololo
who worked on board the ship were not sorry at the steamer
being left below, as they had become heartily tired of cutting
the wood that the insatiable furnace of the "Asthmatic" required. Mbia, who was a bit of a wag, laughingly exclaimed
in broken English, "Oh, Kebrabasa good, very good; no let
shippee up to Sekeletu, too muchee work, cuttee woodyee,
cuttee woodyee: Kebrabasa good." It is currently reported,
and commonly believed, that once upon a time a Portuguese
named José Pedra,—by the natives called Nyamatimbira,—
Chief, or capitão mor, of Zumbo, a man of large enterprise
and small humanity,—being anxious to ascertain if Kebrabasa
could be navigated, made two slaves fast to a canoe, and
launched it from Chicova into Kebrabasa, in order to see if
it would come out at the other end. As neither slaves nor
canoe ever appeared again, his Excellency concluded that
Kebrabasa was unnavigable. A trader had a large canoe
swept away by a sudden rise of the river, and it was found
without damage below; but the most satisfactory information was that of old Sandia, who asserted that in flood
all Kebrabasa became quite smooth, and he had often seen
it so.

CHAPTER VIII.

WE emerged from the thirty-five or forty miles of Kebrabasa hills into the Chicova plains on the 7th of June, 1860, having made short marches all the way. The cold nights caused some of our men to cough badly, and colds in this country almost invariably become fever. The Zambesi suddenly expands at Chicova, and assumes the size and appearance it has at Tette. Near this point we found a large seam of coal exposed in the left bank.

We met with native travellers occasionally. Those on a long journey carry with them a sleeping-mat and wooden pillow, cooking-pot and bag of meal, pipe and tobacco-pouch, a knife, bow, and arrows, and two small sticks, of from two to three feet in length, for making fire, when obliged to sleep away from human habitations. Dry wood is always abundant, and they get fire by the following method. A notch is cut in one of the sticks, which, with a close-grained outside, has a small core of pith, and this notched stick is laid horizontally on a knife-blade on the ground; the operator squatting, places his great toes on each end to keep all steady, and taking the other wand, which is of very hard wood cut to a blunt point, fits it into the notch at right angles; the upright wand is made to spin rapidly backwards and forwards between the palms of the hands, drill fashion, and at the same time is pressed downwards; the friction, in the course of a minute or so, ignites portions of the pith of the notched stick, which, rolling over like live charcoal on to the knife-blade, are lifted into a handful of fine dry grass, and carefully blown, by waving backwards and forwards in the air. It is hard work for the hands to procure fire by this process, as the vigorous drilling and downward pressure requisite soon blister soft palms.

Having now entered a country where lions were numerous, our men began to pay greater attention to the arrangements of the camp at night. As they are accustomed to do with their Chiefs, they place the white men in the centre; Kanyata, his men, and the two donkeys, camp on our right; Tuba Mokoro's party of Bashubia are in front, Masakasa, and Sininyane's body of Batoka, on the left, and in the rear six Tette men have their fires. In placing their fires they are careful to put them where the smoke will not blow in our faces. Soon after we halt, the spot for the English is selected, and all regulate their places accordingly, and deposit their burdens. The men take it by turns to cut some of the tall dry grass, and spread it for our beds on a spot, either naturally level, or smoothed by the hoe; some, appointed to carry our bedding, then bring our rugs and karosses, and place the three rugs in a row on the grass; Dr. Livingstone's being in the middle, Dr. Kirk's on the right, and Charles Livingstone's on the left. Our bags, rifles, and revolvers are carefully placed at our heads, and a fire made near our feet. We have no tent nor covering of any kind except the branches of the tree under which we

may happen to lie; and it is a pretty sight to look up and
see every branch, leaf, and twig of the tree stand out, reflected against the clear star-spangled and moonlit sky. The
stars of the first magnitude have names which convey the
same meaning over very wide tracts of country. Here when
Venus comes out in the evenings, she is called Ntanda, the
eldest or first-born, and Manjika, the first-born of morning, at other times: she has so much radiance when shining
alone, that she casts a shadow. Sirius is named Kuewa usiko,
"drawer of night," because supposed to draw the whole night
after it. The moon has no evil influence in this country, so
far as we know. We have lain and looked up at her, till sweet
sleep closed our eyes, unharmed. Four or five of our men
were affected with moon-blindness at Tette; though they
had not slept out of doors there, they became so blind
that their comrades had to guide their hands to the general
dish of food; the affection is unknown in their own
country. When our posterity shall have discovered what it
is which, distinct from foul smells, causes fever, and what,
apart from the moon, causes men to be moon-struck, they
will pity our dulness of perception.

The men cut a very small quantity of grass for themselves, and sleep in fumbas or sleeping-bags, which are
double mats of palm-leaf, six feet long by four wide, and
sewn together round three parts of the square, and left
open only on one side. They are used as a protection
from the cold, wet, and mosquitoes, and are entered as we
should get into our beds, were the blankets nailed to the
top, bottom, and one side of the bedstead. When they
are all inside their fumbas, nothing is seen but sacks lying
all about the different fires. At times two persons sleep
inside one, which is, indeed, close packing. Matonga, one of

the men, has volunteered to take the sole charge of our fire, and is to receive for his services the customary payment of the heads and necks of all the beasts we kill; and, except on the days when only guinea-fowl are shot, he thus gets abundance of food. He bears our fowl diet resignedly for a few days, and then, if no large game is killed, he comes and expostulates as seriously, as he did with the lion that envied us our buffalo meat, "Morena, my lord, a hungry man cannot fill his stomach with the head of a bird; he is killed with hunger for want of meat, and will soon, from sheer weakness, be unable to carry the wood for the fire ; he ought to have an entire bird to save him from dying of starvation." His request being reasonable, and guinea-fowl abundant, it is of course complied with. Guinea-fowl are conveniently numerous on the Zambesi during the dry season; they then collect in large flocks and come daily to the river to drink, and roost at night on the tall acacia-trees on its banks. We usually fall in with two or three flocks in the course of the day's march, and find that they are all fat, and in excellent condition. In a few spots, as at Shupanga, a second variety is found, which has a pretty black feathery crest, and is a much handsomer bird than the common one; the native name is *Khanga Tore,* and its spots are a fine light blue. Naturalists call it *Numida cristata.*

A dozen fires are nightly kindled in the camp; and these, being replenished from time to time by the men who are awakened by the cold, are kept burning until daylight. Abundance of dry hard wood is obtained with little trouble; and burns beautifully. After the great business of cooking and eating is over, all sit round the camp-fires, and engage in talking or singing. Every evening one of the Batoka plays his sansa, and continues at it until far into

N

the night; he accompanies it with an extempore song, in
which he rehearses their deeds ever since they left their own
country. At times animated political discussions spring up,
and the amount of eloquence expended on these occasions
is amazing. The whole camp is aroused, and the men shout
to one another from the different fires; whilst some, whose
tongues are never heard on any other subject, now burst
forth into impassioned speech. The misgovernment of Chiefs
furnishes an inexhaustible theme. " We could govern ourselves better," they cry, "so what is the use of Chiefs at all?
they do not work. The Chief is fat, and has plenty of wives;
whilst we, who do the hard work, have hunger, only one wife,
or more likely none; now this must be bad, unjust, and
wrong." All shout to this a loud "ēhē," equivalent to our
" hear, hear." Next the headman, Kanyata, and Tuba with
his loud voice, are heard taking up the subject on the loyal
side. " The Chief is the father of the people; can there be
people without a father, eh? God made the Chief. Who says
that the Chief is not wise? He is wise; but his children are
fools." Tuba goes on generally till he has silenced all opposition; and if his arguments are not always sound, his voice
is the loudest, and he is sure to have the last word.

As a specimen of our mode of marching, we rise about
five, or as soon as dawn appears, take a cup of tea and a
bit of biscuit; the servants fold up the blankets and stow
them away in the bags they carry; the others tie their
fumbas and cooking-pots to each end of their carrying-sticks,
which are borne on the shoulder; the cook secures the
dishes, and all are on the path by sunrise. If a convenient spot can be found we halt for breakfast about nine
A.M. To save time, this meal is generally cooked the night
before, and has only to be warmed. We continue the march

after breakfast, rest a little in the middle of the day, and break off early in the afternoon. We average from two to two-and-a-half miles an hour in a straight line, or, as the crow flies, and seldom have more than five or six hours a day of actual travel. This in a hot climate is as much as a man can accomplish without being oppressed; and we always tried to make our progress more a pleasure than a toil. To hurry over the ground, abuse, and look ferocious at one's native companions, merely for the foolish vanity of boasting how quickly a distance was accomplished, is a combination of silliness with absurdity quite odious; while kindly consideration for the feelings of even blacks, the pleasure of observing scenery and everything new as one moves on at an ordinary pace, and the participation in the most delicious rest with our fellows, render travelling delightful. Though not given to over haste, we were a little surprised to find that we could tire our men out; and even the headman, who carried but little more than we did, and never, as we often had to do, hunted in the afternoon, was no better than his comrades. Our experience tends to prove that the European constitution has a power of endurance, even in the tropics, greater than that of the hardiest of the meat-eating Africans.

After pitching our camp, one or two of us usually go off to hunt, more as a matter of necessity than of pleasure, for the men, as well as ourselves, must have meat. We prefer to take a man with us to carry home the game, or lead the others to where it lies; but as they frequently grumble and complain of being tired, we do not particularly object to going alone, except that it involves the extra labour of our making a second trip to show the men where the animal that has been shot is to be found. When it is a couple of miles off it is rather fatiguing to have to go twice; more especially on the days when it is solely to supply their wants that, instead of resting ourselves, we go at all.   Like those who perform benevolent deeds at home, the tired hunter, though trying hard to live in charity with all men, is strongly tempted to give it up by bringing only sufficient meat for the three whites and leaving the rest; thus sending the " idle ungrateful poor " supperless to bed.   And yet it is only by continuance in well-doing, even to the length of what the worldly-wise call weakness, that the conviction is produced anywhere, that our motives are high enough to secure sincere respect.

The Chicova plains are very fertile, have rich dark soil, and formerly supported a numerous population; but desolating wars and slaving had swept away most of the inhabitants.   In spite of a rank growth of weeds, cotton still remains in the deserted gardens of ruined villages.   A jungle of mimosa, ebony, and " wait-a-bit " thorn lies between the Chicova flats and the cultivated plain, on which stand the villages of the Chief, Chitora. He brought us a present of food and drink, because, as he, with the innate politeness of an African, said, he " did not wish us to sleep hungry : he had heard of the Doctor when he passed down, and had a great desire to see and converse with him ; but he was a child then, and could not speak in the presence of great men.   He was glad that he had seen the English now, and was sorry that his people were away, or he should have made them cook for us."   All his subsequent conduct showed him to be sincere.

Many of the African women are particular about the water they use for drinking and cooking, and prefer that which is filtered through sand.   To secure this, they scrape holes in the sandbanks beside the stream, and scoop up the water, which slowly filters through, rather than take it from the equally clear and limpid river. This practice is common in the Zambesi, the Rovuma, and Lake Nyassa; and some of the Portuguese at Tette have adopted the native custom, and send canoes to a low island in the middle of the river for water. Chitora's people also obtained their supply from shallow wells in the sandy bed of a small rivulet close to the village. The habit may have arisen from observing the unhealthiness of the main stream at certain seasons. During nearly nine months in the year, ordure is deposited around countless villages along the thousands of miles drained by the Zambesi. When the heavy rains come down, and sweep the vast fetid accumulation into the torrents, the water is polluted with filth; and, but for the precaution mentioned, the natives would prove themselves as little fastidious as those in London who drink the abomination poured into the Thames by Reading and Oxford. It is no wonder that sailors suffered so much from fever after drinking African river water, before the present admirable system of condensing it was adopted in our Navy.

There must be something in the appearance of white men, frightfully repulsive to the unsophisticated natives of Africa; for, on entering villages previously unvisited by Europeans, if we met a child coming quietly and unsuspectingly towards us, the moment he raised his eyes, and saw the men in " bags," he would take to his heels in an agony of terror, such as we might feel if we met a live Egyptian mummy at the door of the British Museum. Alarmed by the child's wild outcries, the mother rushes out of her hut, but darts back again at the first glimpse of the same fearful apparition. Dogs turn tail, and scour off in dismay; and hens, abandoning their chickens, fly screaming to the tops of the houses. The so lately peaceful village becomes a scene of confusion and hubbub,

until calmed by the laughing assurance of our men, that
white people do not eat black folks; a joke having often-
times greater influence in Africa than solemn assertions.
Some of our young swells, on entering an African village,
might experience a collapse of self-inflation, at the sight of
all the pretty girls fleeing from them, as from hideous
cannibals; or by witnessing, as we have done, the conversion
of themselves into public hobgoblins, the mammas holding
naughty children away from them, and saying "Be good, or
I shall call the white man to bite you."

The scent of man is excessively terrible to game of all
kinds, much more so, probably, than the sight of him. A
herd of antelopes, a hundred yards off, gazed at us as we
moved along the winding path, and timidly stood their ground
until half our line had passed, but darted off the instant they
"got the wind," or caught the flavour of those who had gone
by. The sport is all up with the hunter who gets to the
windward of the African beast, as it cannot stand even
the distant aroma of the human race, so much dreaded
by all wild animals. Is this the fear and the dread of man,
which the Almighty said to Noah was to be upon every
beast of the field? A lion may, while lying in wait for his
prey, leap on a human being as he would on any other animal,
save a rhinoceros or an elephant, that happened to pass; or a
lioness, when she has cubs, might attack a man, who, passing
"up the wind of her," had unconsciously, by his scent,
alarmed her for the safety of her whelps; or buffaloes, and
other animals, might rush at a line of travellers, in apprehension of being surrounded by them; but neither beast nor snake
will, as a general rule, turn on man except when wounded,
or by mistake. If gorillas, unwounded, advance to do battle
with him, and beat their breasts in defiance, they are an

exception to all wild beasts known to us. From the way an elephant runs at the first glance of man, it is inferred that this huge brute, though really king of beasts, would run even from a child.

Our two donkeys caused as much admiration as the three white men. Great was the astonishment when one of the donkeys began to bray. The timid jumped more than if a lion had roared beside them. All were startled, and stared in mute amazement at the harsh-voiced one, till the last broken note was uttered; then, on being assured that nothing in particular was meant, they looked at each other, and burst into a loud laugh at their common surprise. When one donkey stimulated the other to try his vocal powers, the interest felt by the startled visitors, must have equalled that of the Londoners, when they first crowded to see the famous hippopotamus.

CHAPTER IX.

Seams of coal under Tette grey sandstone — Use of coal unknown to the natives — Mbia kills a hippopotamus — Traps and pitfalls — Sagacity of elephants at pitfalls — White ants and their galleries — Black soldier-ants lord it over the white ants — Language of ants — Biting ants — Rogue monkey respected — Native salt-making — The Mountains — Chikwanitsela — Afflictions of beasts — The human buffalo — Mpende — Chilondo — Monaheng murdered — Animals which have not been hunted with fire-arms — Pangola — A rifle-loving Chief — Undi and fate of African empires — Are Africans industrious? — Arrive at Zumbo on the Loangwa on 26th June — Results of no government — Murder of Mpangue — Sequasha.

WE were now, when we crossed the boundary rivulet Nyama-tarara, out of Chicova and amongst sandstone rocks, similar to those which prevail between Lupata and Kebrabasa. In the latter gorge, as already mentioned, igneous and syenitic masses have been acted on by some great fiery convulsion of nature; the strata are thrown into a huddled heap of confusion. The coal has of course disappeared in Kebrabasa, but is found again in Chicova. Tette grey sandstone is common about Sinjére, and, wherever it is seen with fossil wood upon it, coal lies beneath; and here, as at Chicova, some seams crop out on the banks of the Zambesi. Looking southwards, the country is open plain and woodland, with detached hills and mountains in the distance; but the latter are too far off, the natives say, for them to know their names. The principal hills on our right, as we look up stream, are from six to twelve miles away, and occasionally they send down spurs to the river, with brooks flowing through their narrow valleys.

The banks of the Zambesi show two well-defined terraces; the first, or lowest, being usually narrow, and of great fertility, while the upper one is a dry grassy plain, a thorny jungle, or a mopane (*Bauhinia*) forest.   One of these plains, near the Kafue, is covered with the large stumps and trunks of a petrified forest.   We halted a couple of days by the fine stream Sinjére, which comes from the Chiroby-roby hills, about eight miles to the north.   Many lumps of coal, brought down by the rapid current, lie in its channel.   The natives never seem to have discovered that coal would burn, and, when informed of the fact, shook their heads, smiled incredulously, and said "*Kodi*" (really), evidently regarding it as a mere traveller's tale.   They were astounded to see it burning freely on our fire of wood.   They told us that plenty of it was seen among the hills; but, being long ago aware that we were now in an immense coalfield, we did not care to examine it further.   Coal had been discovered to the south of this in 1856, and several seams were examined on the stream Revubue, a few miles distant from Tette.   This was evidently an extension of the same field, but the mineral was more bituminous.   In an open fire it bubbled up, and gave out gas like good domestic coal.

A dyke of black basaltic rock, called Kakolole, crosses the river near the mouth of the Sinjére; but it has two open gateways in it of from sixty to eighty yards in breadth, and the channel is very deep.

On a shallow sandbank, under the dyke, lay a herd of hippopotami in fancied security.   The young ones were playing with each other like young puppies, climbing on the backs of their dams, trying to take hold of one another by the jaws, and tumbling over into the water.   Mbia, one of the Makololo, waded across to within a dozen yards of the drowsy beasts, and shot the father of the herd; who, being very fat, soon floated, and was secured at the village below. The headman of the village visited us while we were at breakfast. He wore a black ife wig and a printed shirt. After

Group of Hippopotami.

a short silence he said to Masakasa, "You are with the white people, so why do you not tell them to give me a cloth?" "We are strangers," answered Masakasa, "why do you not bring us some food?" He took the plain hint, and brought us two fowls, in order that we should not report that in passing him we got nothing to eat; and, as usual, we gave a cloth in return. In reference to the hippopotamus he would make no demand, but said he would take what we chose to give him. The men gorged themselves with meat for two days, and cut large quantities into long narrow strips, which they half-dried and half-roasted on wooden frames over the fire. Much game is taken in this neighbourhood in pitfalls.   Sharp-pointed stakes are set in the bottom, on which the game tumbles and gets impaled.   The natives are careful to warn strangers of these traps, and also of the poisoned beams suspended on the tall trees for the purpose of killing elephants and hippopotami.   It is not difficult to detect the pitfalls after one's attention has been called to them; but in places where they are careful to carry the earth off to a distance, and a person is not thinking of such things, a sudden descent of nine feet is an experience not easily forgotten by the traveller.   The sensations of one thus instantaneously swallowed up by the earth are peculiar. A momentary suspension of consciousness is followed by the rustling sound of a shower of sand and dry grass, and the half-bewildered thought of where he is, and how he came into darkness.   Reason awakes to assure him that he must have come down through that small opening of daylight overhead, and that he is now where a hippopotamus ought to have been.   The descent of a hippopotamus pitfall is easy, like that of Avernus, but to get out again into the upper air is a work of labour.   The sides are smooth and treacherous, and the cross reeds, which support the covering, break in the attempt to get out by clutching them.   A cry from the depths is unheard by those around, and it is only by repeated and most desperate efforts that the buried alive can regain the upper world.   At Tette we were told of a white hunter, of unusually small stature, who plumped into a pit while stalking a guinea-fowl on a tree.   It was the labour of an entire forenoon to get out; and he was congratulating himself on his escape, and brushing off the clay from his clothes, when down he went into a second pit, which happened, as is often the case, to be close beside the first, and it was evening before he could work himself out of *that*.

Elephants and buffaloes seldom return to the river by the same path on two successive nights, they become so apprehensive of danger from this human art.   An old elephant will walk in advance of the herd, and uncover the pits with his trunk, that the others may see the openings and tread on firm ground. Female elephants are generally the victims: more timid by nature than the males, and very motherly in their anxiety for their calves, they carry their trunks up, trying every breeze for fancied danger, which often in reality lies at their feet.   The tusker, fearing less, keeps his trunk down, and, warned in time by that exquisitely sensitive organ, takes heed to his ways.

Our camp on the Sinjére stood under a wide-spreading wild fig-tree. From the numbers of this family, of large size, dotted over the country, the fig or banyan species would seem to have been held sacred in Africa from the remotest times. The soil teemed with white ants, whose clay tunnels, formed

Tunnels of Ants.

to screen them from the eyes of birds, thread over the ground, up the trunks of trees and along the branches, from which the little architects clear away all rotten or dead wood. Very often the exact shape of branches is left in tunnels on the ground and not a bit of the wood inside. The first night we passed here these destructive insects ate through our grass-beds, and attacked our blankets, and certain large red-headed ones even bit our flesh.

On some days not a single white ant is to be seen abroad; and on others, and during certain hours, they appear out of doors in myriads, and work with extraordinary zeal and energy in carrying bits of dried grass down into their nests. During these busy reaping-fits, the lizards and birds have a good time of it, and enjoy a rich feast at the expense of thousands of hapless workmen; and, when they swarm, they are caught in countless numbers by the natives, and their roasted bodies are spoken of in an unctuous manner as resembling grains of soft rice fried in delicious fresh oil.

A strong marauding party of large black ants attacked a nest of white ones near the camp: as the contest took place beneath the surface, we could not see the order of the battle; but it soon became apparent that the blacks had gained the day, and sacked the white town, for they returned in triumph, bearing off the eggs, and choice bits of the bodies of the vanquished. A gift, analogous to that of language, has not been withheld from ants: if part of their building is destroyed, an official is seen coming out to examine the damage; and, after a careful survey of the ruins, he chirrups a few clear and distinct notes, and a crowd of workers begin at once to repair the breach. When the work is completed, another order is given, and the workmen retire, as will appear on removing the soft freshly-built portion. We tried to sleep one rainy night in a native hut, but could not because of attacks by the fighting battalions of a very small species of formica, not more than one-sixteenth of an inch in length. It soon became obvious that they were under regular discipline, and even attempting to carry out the skilful plans and stratagems of some eminent leader. Our hands and necks were the first objects of attack. Large bodies of these little pests were massed in silence round the point to be assaulted. We could hear the sharp shrill word of command two or three times repeated, though, until then, we had not believed in the vocal power of an ant; the instant after we felt the storming hosts range over head and neck, biting the tender skin, clinging with a death-grip to the hair, and parting with their jaws, rather than quit their hold. On our lying down again in the hope of their having been driven off, no sooner was the light out, and all still, than the manœuvre was repeated. Clear and audible orders were issued, and the assault renewed. It was as hard to sleep in that hut, as in the trenches before Sebastopol. The white ant, being a vegetable feeder, devours articles of vegetable origin only, and leather, which, by tanning, is imbued with a vegetable flavour. "A man may be rich to-day and poor to-morrow, from the ravages of white ants," said a Portuguese merchant. "If he gets sick, and unable to look after his goods, his slaves neglect them, and they are soon destroyed by these insects." The reddish ant, in the west called drivers, crossed our path daily, in solid columns an inch wide, and never did the pugnacity of either man or beast exceed theirs. It is a sufficient cause of war if you only approach them, even by accident. Some turn out of the ranks and stand with open mandibles, or, charging with extended jaws, bite with savage ferocity. When hunting, we lighted among them too often; while we were intent on the game, and without a thought of ants, they quietly covered us from head to foot, then all began to bite at the same instant; seizing a piece of the skin with their powerful pincers, they twisted themselves round with it, as if determined to tear it out. Their bites are so terribly sharp that the bravest must run, and then strip to pick off those that still cling with their hooked jaws, as with steel forceps. This kind abounds in damp places, and is usually met with on the banks of streams. We have not heard of their actually killing any animal except the Python, and that only when gorged and quite lethargic, but they soon clear away any dead animal matter; this appears to be their principal food, and their use in the economy of nature is clearly in the scavenger line.

We started from the Sinjére on the 12th of June, our men carrying with them bundles of hippopotamus meat for sale, and for future use. We rested for breakfast opposite the Kakolole dyke, which confines the channel, west of the Manyerére mountain. A rogue monkey, the largest by far that we ever saw, and very fat and tame, walked off leisurely from a garden as we approached. The monkey is a sacred animal in this region, and is never molested or killed, because the people believe devoutly that the souls of their ancestors now occupy these degraded forms, and anticipate that they themselves must, sooner or later, be transformed in like manner; a future as cheerless for the black, as the spirit-rapper's heaven is for the whites. The gardens are separated from each other by a single row of small stones, a few handfuls of grass, or a slight furrow made by the hoe. Some are enclosed by a reed fence of the flimsiest construction, yet sufficient to keep out the ever wary hippopotamus, who dreads a trap. His extreme caution is taken advantage of by the women, who hang, as a miniature trap-beam, a kigelia fruit with a bit of stick in the end. This protects the maize, of which he is excessively fond.

The women are accustomed to transact business for themselves. They accompany the men into camp, sell their own wares, and appear to be both fair traders, and modest sensible persons. Elsewhere they bring things for sale on their heads, and, kneeling at a respectful distance, wait till their husbands or fathers, who have gone forward, choose to return, and to take their goods, and barter for them. Perhaps in this particular, the women here occupy the golden mean between the Manganja hill-tribes and the Jaggas of the north, who live on the mountain summits near Kilimanjaro. It is said that at the latter place the women do all the trading, have regular markets, and will on no account allow a man to enter the market-place.

The quantity of hippopotamus meat eaten by our men made some of them ill, and our marches were necessarily short. After three hours' travel on the 13th, we spent the remainder of the day at the village of Chasiribera, on a rivulet flowing through a beautiful valley to the north, which is bounded by magnificent mountain-ranges. Pinkwe, or Mbingwe, otherwise Moeu, forms the south-eastern angle of the range. On the 16th June we were at the flourishing village of Senga, under the headman Manyame, which lies at the foot of the mount Motemwa. Nearly all the mountains in this country are covered with open forest and grass, in colour, according to the season, green or yellow. Many are between 2000 and 3000 feet high, with the sky line fringed with trees; the rocks show just suffi-

ciently for one to observe their stratification, or their granitic
form, and though not covered with dense masses of climbing
plants, like those in moister eastern climates, there is still
the idea conveyed that most of the steep sides are fertile,
and none give the impression of that barrenness which, in
northern mountains, suggests the idea, that the bones of
the world are sticking through its skin.

The villagers reported that we were on the footsteps of
a Portuguese half-caste, who, at Senga, lately tried to
purchase ivory, but, in consequence of his having murdered a Chief near Zumbo and twenty of his men, the
people declined to trade with him.   He threatened to
take the ivory by force, if they would not sell it; but that
same night the ivory and the women were spirited out of
the village, and only a large body of armed men remained.
The trader, fearing that he might come off second best if it
came to blows, immediately departed. Chikwanitsela, or Se-
kuanangila is the paramount Chief of some fifty miles of the
northern bank of the Zambesi in this locality.   He lives on
the opposite, or southern side, and there his territory is still
more extensive. We sent him a present from Senga, and were
informed by a messenger next morning that he had a cough
and could not come over to see us.   "And has his present a
cough too," remarked one of our party, "that it does not come
to us?   Is this the way your Chief treats strangers, receives
their present, and sends them no food in return?"   Our
men thought Chikwanitsela an uncommonly stingy fellow;
but, as it was possible that some of them might yet wish
to return this way, they did not like to scold him more
than this, which was sufficiently to the point.

Men and women were busily engaged in preparing the
ground for the November planting.   Large game was abun-

dant; herds of elephants and buffaloes came down to the river in the night, but were a long way off by daylight. They soon adopt this habit in places where they are hunted.

The plains we travel over are constantly varying in breadth, according as the furrowed and wooded hills approach or recede from the river. On the southern side we see the hill Bungwe, and the long, level, wooded ridge Nyangombe, the first of a series bending from the S. E. to the N.W. past the Zambesi. We shot an old pallah on the 16th, and found that the poor animal had been visited with more than the usual share of animal afflictions. He was stone-blind in both eyes, had several tumours, and a broken leg, which showed no symptoms of ever having begun to heal. Wild animals sometimes suffer a great deal from disease, and wearily drag on a miserable existence before relieved of it by some ravenous beast. Once we drove off a maneless lion and lioness from a dead buffalo, which had been in the last stage of a decline. They had watched him staggering to the river to quench his thirst, and sprang on him as he was crawling up the bank. One had caught him by the throat, and the other by his high projecting backbone, which was broken by the lion's powerful fangs. The struggle, if any, must have been short. They had only eaten the intestines when we frightened them off. It is curious that this is the part that wild animals always begin with, and that it is also the first choice of our men. Were it not a wise arrangement that only the strongest males should continue the breed, one could hardly help pitying the solitary buffalo expelled from the herd for some physical blemish, or on account of the weakness of approaching old age. Banished from the softening influences of female society, he naturally becomes morose and savage; the necessary watchfulness against enemies

is now never shared by others; disgusted, he passes into a state
of chronic war with all who enjoy life, and the sooner after his
expulsion that he fills the lion's or the wild-dog's maw, the
better for himself and for the peace of the country.   Though
we are not disposed to be didactic, the idea of a crusty old
bachelor or of a cantankerous husband will rise up in our
minds; to this human buffalo, at whose approach wife and
children, or poor relations, hold their breath with awe, we
cannot extend one grain of pity; because it is not infirmity
of temper this brute can plead, seeing that, when in the herd
with his equals, he is invariably polite, and only exercises his
tyranny when with those who cannot thrash him into decency.

We encamped on the 20th of June at a spot, where Dr.
Livingstone, on his journey from the West to the East Coast,
was formerly menaced by a Chief named Mpende.   No offence
had been committed against him, but he had firearms, and, with
the express object of showing his power, he threatened to attack
the strangers.   Mpende's counsellors having, however, found
out that Dr. Livingstone belonged to a tribe of whom they
had heard that "they loved the black man and did not make
slaves," his conduct at once changed from enmity to kindness,
and, as the place was one well selected for defence, it was perhaps quite as well for Mpende that he decided as he did.
Three of his counsellors now visited us, and we gave them
a handsome present for their Chief, who came himself next
morning and made us a present of a goat, a basket of boiled
maize, and another of vetches.   A few miles above this, the
headman, Chilondo of Nyamasusa, apologized for not formerly
lending us canoes.   "He was absent, and his children were to
blame for not telling him when the Doctor passed; he did not
refuse the canoes."   The sight of our men, now armed with
muskets, had a great effect.   Without any bullying, firearms

command respect, and lead men to be reasonable who might otherwise feel disposed to be troublesome. Nothing, however, our fracas with Mpende excepted, could be more peaceful than our passage through this tract of country in 1856. We then had nothing to excite the cupidity of the people, and the men maintained themselves, either by selling elephant's meat, or by exhibiting feats of foreign dancing. Most of the people were very generous and friendly; but the Banyai, nearer to Tette than this, stopped our march with a threatening war-dance. One of our party, terrified at this, ran away, as we thought, insane, and could not, after a painful search of three days, be found. The Banyai, evidently touched by our distress, allowed us to proceed. Through a man we left on an island a little below Mpende's, we subsequently learned that poor Monaheng had fled thither and had been murdered by the headman for no reason except that he was defenceless. This headman had since become odious to his countrymen, and had been put to death by them.

Our path leads frequently through vast expanses of apparently solitary scenery; a strange stillness pervades the air; no sound is heard from bird or beast or living thing; no village is near; the air is still, and earth and sky have sunk into a deep, sultry repose, and like a lonely ship on the desert sea is the long winding line of weary travellers on the hot, glaring plain. We discover that we are not alone in the wilderness; other living forms are round about us, with curious eyes on all our movements. As we enter a piece of wood-land, an unexpected herd of pallahs, or waterbucks, suddenly appears, standing as quiet and still, as if constituting a part of the landscape; or, we pass a clump of thick thorns, and see through the bushes the dim phantom-like forms of buffaloes, their heads lowered, gazing at us with fierce untameable eyes. Again a sharp turn brings us upon a native, who has seen us from afar, and comes with noiseless footsteps to get a nearer view.

On the 23rd of June we entered Pangola's principal village, which is upwards of a mile from the river. The ruins of a mud wall showed that a rude attempt had been made to imitate the Portuguese style of building. We established ourselves under a stately wild fig-tree, round whose trunk witchcraft medicine had been tied, to protect from thieves the honey of the wild bees, which had their hive in one of the limbs. This is a common device. The charm, or the medicine, is purchased of the dice doctors, and consists of a strip of palm-leaf smeared with something, and adorned with a few bits of grass, wood, or roots. It is tied round the tree, and is believed to have the power of inflicting disease and death on the thief who climbs over it. Superstition is thus not without its uses in certain states of society ; it prevents many crimes and misdemeanors, which would occur, but for the salutary fear that it produces.

Pangola arrived, tipsy and talkative.—" We are friends, we are great friends ; I have brought you a basket of green maize —here it is ! " We thanked him, and handed him two fathoms of cotton cloth, four times the market-value of his present. No, he would not take so small a present ; he wanted a double-barrelled rifle—one of Dixon's best. " We are friends, you know ; we are all friends together." But although we were willing to admit that, we could not give him our best rifle, so he went off in high dudgeon. Early next morning, as we were commencing Divine service, Pangola returned, sober. We explained to him that we wished to worship God, and invited him to remain ; he seemed frightened and retired : but after service he again importuned us for the rifle. It was of no use telling him that we had a long journey before us, and needed it to kill game for ourselves.—"He too must obtain meat for himself and people, for they sometimes suffered from hunger." He then got sulky, and his people refused to sell food except at extravagant prices. Knowing that we had nothing to eat, they felt sure of starving us into compliance. But two of our young men, having gone off at sunrise, shot a fine waterbuck, and down came the provision market to the lowest figure; they even became eager to sell, but our men were angry with them for trying compulsion, and would not buy. Black greed had outwitted itself, as happens often with white cupidity; and not only here did the traits of Africans remind us of Anglo-Saxons elsewhere: the notoriously ready world-wide disposition to take an unfair advantage of a man's necessities shows that the same mean motives are pretty widely diffused among all races. It may not be granted that the same blood flows in all veins, or that all have descended from the same stock; but the traveller has no doubt that, practically, the white rogue and black are men and brothers.

Pangola is the child or vassal of Mpende. Sandia and Mpende are the only independent chiefs from Kebrabasa to Zumbo, and belong to the tribe Manganja. The country north of the mountains here in sight from the Zambesi is called Senga, and its inhabitants Asenga, or Basenga, but all appear to be of the same family as the rest of the Manganja and Maravi. Formerly all the Manganja were united under the government of their great Chief, Undi, whose Empire extended from Lake Shirwa to the River Loangwa; but after Undi's death it fell to pieces, and a large portion of it on the Zambesi was absorbed by their powerful southern neighbours the Banyai. This has been the inevitable fate of every African Empire from time immemorial. A Chief of more than ordinary ability arises and, subduing all his less powerful neighbours, founds a kingdom, which he governs more or less wisely till he dies. His successor not having the talents of the conqueror cannot retain the dominion, and some of the abler under-chiefs set up for themselves, and, in a few years, the remembrance only of the Empire remains. This, which may be considered as the normal state of African society, gives rise to frequent and desolating wars, and the people long in vain for a power able to make all dwell in peace. In this light, a European colony would be considered by the natives as an inestimable boon to intertropical Africa. Thousands of industrious natives would gladly settle round it, and engage in that peaceful pursuit of agriculture and trade of which they are so fond, and, undistracted by wars or rumours of wars, might listen to the purifying and ennobling truths of the Gospel of Jesus Christ. The Manganja on the Zambesi, like their countrymen on the Shire, are fond of agriculture; and, in addition to the usual varieties of food, cultivate tobacco and cotton in quantities more than equal to their wants. To the question, " Would they work for Europeans?" an affirmative answer may be given, if the Europeans belong to the class which can pay a reasonable price for labour, and not to that of adventurers who want employment for themselves. All were particularly well clothed from Sandia's to Pangola's; and it was noticed that all the cloth was of native manufacture, the product of their own looms. In Senga a great deal of iron is obtained from the ore and manufactured very cleverly.

As is customary when a party of armed strangers visits the village, Pangola took the precaution of sleeping in one of the outlying hamlets. No one ever knows, or at any rate will tell, where the Chief sleeps. He came not next morn-

ing, so we went on our way; but in a few moments we saw
the rifle-loving Chief approaching with some armed men.
Before meeting us, he left the path and drew up his "following" under a tree, expecting us to halt, and give him a
chance of bothering us again; but, having already had
enough of that, we held right on: he seemed dumb-
foundered, and could hardly believe his own eyes. For a few
seconds he was speechless, but at last recovered so far as to
be able to say, "You are passing Pangola. Do not you see
Pangola?" Mbia was just going by at the time with the
donkey, and, proud of every opportunity of airing his small
stock of English, shouted in reply, "All right! then get
on." "Click, click, click." This fellow, Pangola, would
have annoyed and harassed a trader until his unreasonable demands were complied with.

On the 26th June we breakfasted at Zumbo, on the left bank
of the Loangwa, near the ruins of some ancient Portuguese
houses. The Loangwa was too deep to be forded, and there were
no canoes on our side. Seeing two small ones on the opposite
shore, near a few recently-erected huts of two half-castes from
Tette, we halted for the ferry-men to come over. From their
movements it was evident that they were in a state of
rollicking drunkenness. Having a waterproof cloak, which
could be inflated into a tiny boat, we sent Mantlanyane across
in it. Three half-intoxicated slaves then brought us the shaky
canoes, which we lashed together and manned with our own
canoe-men. Five men were all that we could carry over at
a time; and after four trips had been made the slaves
began to clamour for drink; not receiving any, as we had
none to give, they grew more insolent, and declared
that not another man should cross that day. Sininyane was
remonstrating with them, when a loaded musket was pre-

sented at him by one of the trio.   In an instant the gun was
out of the rascal's hands, a rattling shower of blows fell on
his back, and he took an involuntary header into the river. He
crawled up the bank a sad and sober man, and all three at once
tumbled from the height of saucy swagger to a low depth of
slavish abjectness. The musket was found to have an enormous
charge, and might have blown our man to pieces, but for the
promptitude with which his companions administered justice
in a lawless land. We were all ferried safely across by
8 o'clock in the evening.

In illustration of what takes place where no government, or law exists, the two half-castes, to whom these men
belonged, left Tette, with four hundred slaves, armed with
the old Sepoy Brown Bess, to hunt elephants and trade
in ivory. On our way up, we heard from natives of their
lawless deeds, and again, on our way down, from several,
who had been eyewitnesses of the principal crime, and all
reports substantially agreed. The story is a sad one. After
the traders reached Zumbo, one of them, called by the natives
Sequasha, entered into a plot with the disaffected headman,
Namakusuru, to kill his Chief, Mpangwe, in order that Namakusuru might seize upon the chieftainship; and for the murder
of Mpangwe, the trader agreed to receive ten large tusks of
ivory. Sequasha, with a picked party of armed slaves, went
to visit Mpangwe, who received him kindly, and treated him
with all the honour and hospitality usually shown to distinguished strangers, and the women busied themselves in cooking the best of their provisions for the repast to be set before
him. Of this, and also of the beer, the half-caste partook
heartily. Mpangwe was then asked by Sequasha to allow his
men to fire their guns in amusement. Innocent of any suspicion of treachery, and anxious to hear the report of firearms,

Mpangwe at once gave his consent; and the slaves rose and
poured a murderous volley into the merry group of unsuspect-
ing spectators, instantly killing the chief and twenty of his
people. The survivors fled in horror. The children and young
women were seized as slaves, and the village sacked. Sequasha
sent the message to Namakusuru: "I have killed the lion
that troubled you, come and let us talk over the matter." He
came, and brought the ivory; "No," said the half-caste,
"let us divide the land:" and he took the larger share for
himself, and compelled the would-be usurper to deliver up
his bracelets, in token of subjection on becoming the child
or vassal of Sequasha. These were sent in triumph to the
authorities at Tette. The Governor of Quillimane had told
us that he had received orders from Lisbon to take advantage
of our passing to re-establish Zumbo; and, accordingly, these
traders had built a small stockade on the rich plain of the
right bank of Loangwa, a mile above the site of the ancient
mission church of Zumbo, as part of the royal policy. The
bloodshed was quite unnecessary, because, the land at Zumbo
having of old been purchased, the natives would have always
of their own accord acknowledged the right thus acquired;
they pointed it out to Dr. Livingstone in 1856 that, though
they were cultivating it, it was not theirs, but white man's
land. Sequasha and his mate had left their ivory in charge of
some of their slaves, who, in the absence of their masters,
were now having a gay time of it, and getting drunk every
day with the produce of the sacked villages. The head slave
came and begged for the musket of the delinquent ferryman, which was returned. He thought his master did perfectly right to kill Mpangwe, when asked to do it for the fee
of ten tusks, and he even justified it thus: "If a man invites
you to eat, will you not partake?"

CHAPTER X.

WE remained a day by the ruins of Zumbo. The early traders, guided probably by Jesuit missionaries, must have been men of taste and sagacity. They selected for their village the most charmingly picturesque site in the country, and had reason to hope that it would soon be enriched by the lucrative trade of the rivers Zambesi and Loangwa pouring into it from north and west, and by the gold and ivory of the Manica country on the south. The Portuguese of the present day have certainly reason to be proud of the enterprise of their ancestors. If ever in the Elysian fields the conversation of these ancient and honourable men, who dared so much for Christianity, turns on their African descendants, it will be difficult for them to reciprocate the feeling. The chapel, near which lies a broken church bell, commands a glorious view of the two noble rivers,—the green fields—the undulating forest—the pleasant hills, and the magnificent mountains in the distance. It is an utter ruin now, and desolation broods around. The wild bird, disturbed by the unwonted sound

of approaching footsteps, rises with a harsh scream. Thorn-
bushes, marked with the ravages of white ants, rank grass
with prickly barbed seeds, and noxious weeds, overrun the
whole place. The foul hyena has defiled the sanctuary,
and the midnight-owl has perched on its crumbling walls, to
disgorge the undigested remnant of its prey. One can
scarcely look without feelings of sadness on the utter desolation of a place where men have met to worship the Supreme
Being, or have united in uttering the magnificent words,
"Thou art the King of glory, O Christ!" and remember, that
the natives of this part know nothing of His religion, not even
His name; a strange superstition makes them shun this
sacred place, as men do the pestilence, and they never come
near it. Apart from the ruins, there is nothing to remind one
that a Christian power ever had traders here; for the natives
of to-day are precisely what their fathers were, when the
Portuguese first rounded the Cape. Their language, unless
buried in the Vatican, is still unwritten. Not a single art,
save that of distilling spirits by means of a gun-barrel, has
ever been learnt from the strangers; and, if all the progeny
of the whites were at once to leave the country, their only
memorial would be the ruins of a few stone and mud-built
walls, and that blighting relic of the slave-trade, the belief
that man may sell his brother man; a belief which is not
of native origin, for it is not found except in the track of
the Portuguese.

Since the early Missionaries were not wanting in either
wisdom or enterprise, it would be intensely interesting to
know the exact cause of their failing to perpetuate their
Faith. Our observation of the operations of the systems,
whether of native or of European origin, which sanction
slavery, tends to prove that *they* only perpetuate barbarism.

Raids like that of Sequasha,—also of Simoens, who carried his
foray up the river as far as Kariba,—and many others, have
exactly the same effect as the normal native policy already
mentioned: one tract of country is devastated after another,
and the slave-hunter attains great wealth and influence.
Pereira, the founder of Zumbo, gloried in being called "the
Terror." If the scourge is not fleeced by some needy Governor,
his wealth is usually scattered to the winds by the children
of mixed breed who succeed him. Can it be that the Missionaries of old, like many good men formerly among ourselves,
tolerated this system of slave-making, which inevitably leads
to warfare, and thus failed to obtain influence over the
natives by not introducing another policy than that which
had prevailed for ages before they came?

We continued our journey on the 28th of June. Game
was extremely abundant, and there were many lions. Mbia
drove one off from his feast on a wild pig, and appropriated
what remained of the pork to his own use. Lions are
particularly fond of the flesh of wild pigs and zebras, and
contrive to kill a large number of these animals. In the
afternoon we arrived at the village of the female Chief,
Ma-mburuma, but she herself was now living on the opposite side of the river. Some of her people called, and said
she had been frightened by seeing her son and other
children killed by Sequasha, and had fled to the other bank;
but when her heart was healed, she would return and live
in her own village, and among her own people. She constantly inquired of the black traders, who came up the river,
if they had any news of the white man who passed with the
oxen. "He has gone down into the sea," was their reply,
"but we belong to the same people." "Oh, no; you need
not tell me that; he takes no slaves, but wishes peace: you

are not of his tribe." This anti-slavery character excites such universal attention, that any Missionary, who winked at the gigantic evils involved in the slave-trade, would certainly fail to produce any good impression on the native mind.

We left the river here, and proceeded up the valley which leads to the Mburuma or Mohango pass. The nights were cold, and on the 30th of June the thermometer was as low as 39° at sunrise. We passed through a village of twenty large huts, which Sequasha had attacked on his return from the murder of the Chief, Mpangwe. He caught the women and children for slaves, and carried off all the food, except a huge basket of bran, which the natives are wont to save against a time of famine. His slaves had broken all the water-pots and the millstones for grinding meal.

The buaze-trees and bamboos are now seen on the hills; but the jujube or zisyphus, which has evidently been introduced from India, extends no further up the river. We had been eating this fruit, which, having somewhat the taste of apples, the Portuguese call Maçãas, all the way from Tette; and here they were larger than usual, though immediately beyond they ceased to be found. No mango-tree either is to be met with beyond this point, because the Portuguese traders never established themselves anywhere beyond Zumbo. Tsetse flies are more numerous and troublesome than we have ever before found them. They accompany us on the march, often buzzing round our heads like a swarm of bees. They are very cunning, and when intending to bite, alight so gently that their presence is not perceived till they thrust in their lance-like proboscis. The bite is acute, but the pain is over in a moment; it is followed by a little of the disagreeable itching of the musquito's bite. This fly invariably kills all domestic animals except goats and donkeys; man and the wild animals escape. We ourselves were severely bitten on this pass, and so were our donkeys, but neither suffered from any after effects.

Water is scarce in the Mburuma pass, except during the rainy season. We however halted beside some fine springs in the bed of the now dry rivulet, Podebode, which is continued down to the end of the pass, and yields water at intervals in pools. Here we remained a couple of days in consequence of the severe illness of Dr. Kirk. He had several times been attacked by fever; and observed that when we were on the cool heights he was comfortable, but when we happened to descend from a high to a lower altitude, he felt chilly, though the temperature in the latter case was 25° higher than it was above; he had been trying different medicines of reputed efficacy with a view to ascertain whether other combinations might not be superior to the preparation we generally used ; in halting by this water, he suddenly became blind, and unable to stand from faintness. The men, with great alacrity, prepared a grassy bed, on which we laid our companion, with the sad forebodings which only those who have tended the sick in a wild country can realize. We feared that in experimenting he had overdrugged himself; but we gave him a dose of our fever pills ; on the third day he rode the one of the two donkeys that would allow itself to be mounted, and on the sixth he marched as well as any of us. This case is mentioned in order to illustrate what we have often observed, that moving the patient from place to place is most conducive to the cure; and the more pluck a man has—the less he gives in to the disease—the less likely he is to die.

Supplied with water by the pools in the Podebode, we again joined the Zambesi at the confluence of the rivulet. When passing through a dry district the native hunter knows where to expect water by the animals he sees. The presence of the gemsbuck, duïker or diver, springbucks, or elephants, is no proof that water is near; for these animals roam over vast tracts of country, and may be met scores of miles from it. Not so, however, the zebra, pallah, buffalo, and rhinoceros; their spoor gives assurance that water is not far off, as they never stray any distance from its neighbourhood. But when amidst the solemn stillness of the woods, the singing of joyous birds falls upon the ear, it is certain that water is close at hand. While waiting here, under a great tamarind-tree, we heard many new and pleasant songs from strange little birds, with the love-notes of pigeons, in the trees overhanging these living springs.

Our men in hunting came on an immense herd of buffaloes, quietly resting in the long dry grass, and began to blaze away furiously at the astonished animals. In the wild excitement of the hunt, which heretofore had been conducted with spears, some forgot to load with ball, and, firing away vigorously with powder only, wondered for the moment that the buffaloes did not fall. The slayer of the young elephant, having buried his four bullets in as many buffaloes, fired three charges of number 1 shot he had for killing guinea-fowl. The quaint remarks and merriment after these little adventures seemed to the listener like the pleasant prattle of children. Mbia and Mantlanyane, however, killed one buffalo each; both the beasts were in prime condition; the meat was like really excellent beef, with a smack of venison. A troop of hungry, howling hyenas also thought the savour tempting, as they hung round the camp at night, anxious to partake of the feast. They are, fortunately, arrant cowards, and never attack either men or beasts, except they can catch them asleep, sick, or at some other disadvantage. With a bright fire at our feet their presence excites no uneasiness. A piece of meat hung on a tree, high enough to make him jump to reach it, and a short spear, with its handle firmly planted in the ground beneath, are used as a device to induce the hyena to commit suicide by impalement.

The honey-guide is an extraordinary bird; how is it that every member of its family has learned that all men, white or black, are fond of honey? The instant the little fellow gets a glimpse of a man, he hastens to greet him with the hearty invitation to come, as Mbia translated it, to a bees' hive, and take some honey. He flies on in the proper direction, perches on a tree, and looks back to see if you are following; then on to another and another, until he guides you to the spot. If you do not accept his first invitation he follows you with pressing importunities, quite as anxious to lure the stranger to the bees' hive as other birds are to draw him away from their own nests. Except while on the march, our men were sure to accept the invitation, and manifested the same by a peculiar responsive whistle, meaning, as they said, "All right, go ahead; we are coming." The bird never deceived them, but always guided them to a hive of bees, though some had but little honey in store. Has this peculiar habit of the honey-guide its origin, as the attachment of dogs, in friendship for man, or in love for the sweet pickings of the plunder left on the ground? Self-interest aiding in preservation from danger seems to be the rule in most cases, as, for instance, in the bird that guards the buffalo and rhinoceros. The grass is often so tall and dense that one could go close up to these animals quite unperceived; but the guardian bird, sitting on the beast, sees the approach of danger, flaps its wings and screams, which causes its bulky charge to rush off from a

P

foe he has neither seen nor heard; for his reward the vigilant little watcher has the pick of the parasites of his fat friend. In other cases a chance of escape must be given even by the animal itself to its prey; as in the rattle-snake, which, when excited to strike, cannot avoid using his rattle, any more than the cat can resist curling its tail when excited in the chase of a mouse, or the cobra can refrain from inflating the loose skin of the neck and extending it laterally, before striking its poison fangs into its victim.   There were many snakes in parts of this pass; they basked in the warm sunshine, but rustled off through the leaves as we approached.   We observed one morning a small one of a deadly poisonous species, named Kakone, on a bush by the way-side, quietly resting in a horizontal position, digesting a lizard for breakfast. Though openly in view, its colours and curves so closely resembled a small branch that some failed to see it, even after being asked if they perceived anything on the bush. Here also one of our number had a glance at another species, rarely seen, and whose swift lightning-like motion has given rise to the native proverb, that when a man sees this snake he will forthwith become a rich man.

We slept near the ruined village of the murdered chief, Mpangwe, a lovely spot, with the Zambesi in front, and extensive gardens behind, backed by a semicircle of hills, receding up to lofty mountains. Our path kept these mountains on our right, and crossed several streamlets, which seemed to be perennial, and among others the Selole, which apparently flows past the prominent peak Chiarapela. These rivulets have often human dwellings on their banks; but the land can scarcely be said to be occupied. The number of all sorts of game increases wonderfully every day. As a specimen of what may be met with where there are no human habitations, and where no firearms have been introduced, we may mention what at times has actually been seen by us. On the morning of July 3rd a herd of elephants passed within fifty yards of our sleeping-place, going down to the river along the dry bed of a rivulet. Starting a few minutes before the main body, we come upon large flocks of guinea-fowl, shoot what may be wanted for dinner, or next morning's breakfast, and leave them in the path to be picked up by the cook and his mates behind. As we proceed, francolins of three varieties run across the path, and hundreds of turtle-doves rise, with great blatter of wing, and fly off to the trees. Guinea-fowls, francolins, turtle-doves, ducks, and geese are the game birds of this region. At sunrise a herd of pallahs, standing like a flock of sheep, allow the first man of our long Indian file to approach within about fifty yards; but having meat, we let them trot off leisurely and unmolested. Soon afterwards we come upon a herd of waterbucks, which here are very much darker in colour, and drier in flesh, than the same species near the sea. They look at us and we at them; and we pass on to see a herd of doe koodoos, with a magnificently horned buck or two, hurrying off to the dry hill-sides. We have ceased shooting antelopes, as our men have been so often gorged with meat that they have become fat and dainty. They say that they do not want more venison, it is so dry and tasteless, and ask why we do not give them shot to shoot the more savoury guinea-fowl.

About eight o'clock the tsetse commence to buzz about us, and bite our hands and necks sharply. Just as we are thinking of breakfast, we meet some buffaloes grazing by the path; but they make off in a heavy gallop at the sight of man. We fire, and the foremost, badly wounded, separates from the herd, and is seen to stop amongst the trees; but, as it is a matter of great danger to follow a wounded buffalo, we hold on our way. It is this losing of wounded animals which makes firearms so annihilating to these beasts of the field, and will in time sweep them all away. The small Enfield bullet is worse than the old round one for this. It often goes through an animal without killing him, and he afterwards perishes, when he is of no value to man. After breakfast we draw near a pond of water, a couple of elephants stand on its bank, and, at a respectful distance behind these monarchs of the wilderness, is seen a herd of zebras, and another of waterbucks. On getting our wind the royal beasts make off at once; but the zebras remain till the foremost man is within eighty yards of them, when old and young canter gracefully away. The zebra has a great deal of curiosity; and this is often fatal to him, for he has the habit of stopping to look at the hunter. In this particular he is the exact opposite of the diver antelope, which rushes off like the wind, and never for a moment stops to look behind, after having once seen or smelt danger. The finest zebra of the herd is sometimes shot, our men having taken a sudden fancy to the flesh, which all declare to be the "king of good meat." On the plains of short grass between us and the river many antelopes of different species are calmly grazing, or reposing. Wild pigs are common, and walk abroad during the day; but are so shy as seldom to allow a close approach. On taking alarm they erect their slender tails in the air, and trot off swiftly in a straight line, keeping their bodies as steady as a locomotive on a railroad. A mile beyond the pool three cow buffaloes with their calves come from the woods, and move out into the plain. A troop of

monkeys, on the edge of the forest, scamper back to its depths
on hearing the loud song of Singeleka, and old surly fellows,
catching sight of the human party, insult it with a loud and
angry bark. Early in the afternoon we may see buffaloes
again, or other animals. We camp on the dry higher
ground, after, as has happened, driving off a solitary
elephant. The nights are warmer now, and possess nearly
as much of interest and novelty as the days. A new world
awakes and comes forth, more numerous, if we may judge
by the noise it makes, than that which is abroad by sunlight. Lions and hyenas roar around us, and sometimes come
disagreeably near, though they have never ventured into our
midst. Strange birds sing their agreeable songs, while others
scream and call harshly as if in fear or anger. Marvellous
insect-sounds fall upon the ear; one, said by natives to
proceed from a large beetle, resembles a succession of
measured musical blows upon an anvil, while many others
are perfectly indescribable. A little lemur was once seen to
leap about from branch to branch with the agility of a frog;
it chirruped like a bird, and is not larger than a robin-
red-breast. Reptiles, though numerous, seldom troubled
us; only two men suffered from stings, and that very
slightly, during the entire journey, the one supposed
that he was bitten by a snake, and the other was stung by
a scorpion.

Grass-burning has begun, and is producing the blue hazy
atmosphere of the American Indian summer, which in
Western Africa is called the "smokes." Miles of fire burn
on the mountain-sides in the evenings, but go out during the
night. From their height they resemble a broad zigzag line
of fire in the heavens.

We slept on the night of the 6th July on the left bank of

the Chongwe, which comes through a gap in the hills on our right, and is twenty yards wide. A small tribe of the Bazizulu, from the south, under Dadanga, have recently settled here and built a village. Some of their houses are square, and they seem to be on friendly terms with the Bakoa, who own the country. They, like the other natives, cultivate cotton, but of a different species from any we have yet seen in Africa, the staple being very long, and the boll larger than what is usually met with; the seeds cohere as in the Pernambuco kind. They brought the seed with them from their own country, the distant mountains of which in the south, still inhabited by their fellow-countrymen, who possess much cattle and use shields, can be seen from this high ground. These people profess to be children of the great paramount Chief, Kwanyakarombe, who is said to be lord of all the Bazizulu. The name of this tribe is known to geographers, who derive their information from the Portuguese, as the *Morusurus*, and the hills mentioned above are said to have been the country of Changamira, the warrior-chief of history, whom no Portuguese ever dared to approach. The Bazizulu seem, by report, to be brave mountaineers; nearer the river, the Sidima inhabit the plains; just as on the north side, the Babimpe live on the heights, about two days off, and the Makoa on or near the river. The Chief of the Bazizulu we were now with was hospitable and friendly. A herd of buffaloes came trampling through the gardens and roused up our men; a feat that roaring lions seldom achieved.

Our course next day passed over the upper terrace and through a dense thorn jungle. Travelling is always difficult where there is no path, but it is even more perplexing where the forest is cut up by many game-tracks. Here we got separated from one another, and a rhinoceros with angry snort dashed at Dr. Livingstone as he stooped to pick up a specimen of the wild fruit morula; but she strangely stopped stock-still when less than her own length distant, and gave him time to escape; a branch pulled out his watch as he ran, and turning half round to grasp it, he got a distant glance of her and her calf still standing on the selfsame spot, as if arrested in the middle of her charge by an unseen hand. When about fifty yards off, thinking his companions close behind, he shouted "Look out there!" when off she rushed, snorting loudly, in another direction. The Doctor usually went unarmed before this, but never afterwards.

A peculiar yelping came from one part of the jungle, and Charles Livingstone found it to proceed from a troop of wild dogs wrangling over the remains of a buffalo which they had killed and nearly devoured. The wild dog (*Hyæna venatica*) has a large head, and jaws of great power; the ears are long, the colour black and yellow in patches, with a white tuft at the tip of the tail. They hunt their game in packs, and perseveringly follow the animal they first start till they bring him down. The Balala of the Kalahari desert are said to have formerly tamed them and to have employed them to hunt. An intelligent native at Kolobeng remembered when a boy to have seen a pack of the dogs returning from a hunt in charge of their masters, who drove them like a herd of goats, and for safety kept them in a pit. A fine eland was shot by Dr. Kirk this afternoon, the first we have killed. It was in first-rate condition, and remarkably fat; but the meat, though so tempting in appearance, severely deranged all who partook of it heartily, especially those who ate of the fat. Natives who live in game countries, and are acquainted with the different kinds of wild animals, have a prejudice against the fat of the eland, the pallah, the zebra, hippopotamus, and pig: they never reject it however, the climate making the desire for all animal food very strong; but they consider that it causes ulcers and leprosy, while the fat of sheep and of oxen never produces any bad effects, unless the animal is diseased.

We frequently meet families flitting from one place to another, marching, like ourselves, in single file. The father and husband at the head, carrying his bow and arrow, bag, hatchet, and spear, and little else; next his son or sons, armed also, but carrying loads; then follow wife and daughters, with bulky loads of household gear on their heads. They meet us without fear, or any of the cringing ways of slaves, so common down the river, where the institution has been established. When we kill any animal these travelling parties are made welcome to a good portion of meat. At the foot or on the branches of the great wild fig-tree, at the public meeting-place of every village, a collection of the magnificent horns of buffaloes and antelopes shows the proud trophies of the hunter's success in the chase. At these spots were some of the most splendid buffalo heads we have ever seen: the horns after making a complete circle had commenced a second turn. This would be a rich country for a horn fancier.

On the morning of the 9th, after passing four villages, we breakfasted at an old friend's, Tombanyama, who lives now on the mainland, having resigned the reedy island, where he was first seen, to the buffaloes, which used to take his crops and show fight to his men. He keeps a large flock of tame pigeons, and some fine fat capons, one of which he gave us, with a basket of meal. They have plenty of salt in this part of the country, obtaining it from the plains in the usual way.

The half-caste partner of Sequasha and a number of his men were staying near. The fellow was very much frightened when he saw us, and trembled so much when he spoke, that the Makololo and other natives noticed and remarked on it. His fears arose from a sense of guilt, as we said nothing to frighten him, and did not allude to the murder till a few minutes before starting; when it was remarked that Dr. Livingstone having been accredited to the murdered Chief, it would be his duty to report on it; and that not even the Portuguese Government would approve of the deed. He defended it by saying that they had put in the right man, the other was a usurper. He was evidently greatly relieved when we departed. In the afternoon we came to an outlying hamlet of Kambadzo, whose own village is on an island, Nyampungo or Nyangalule, at the confluence of the Kafue. The Chief was on a visit here, and they had been enjoying a regular jollification in honour of his Highness. There had been much mirth, music, drinking, and dancing. The men, and women too, had taken " a wee drap too much," but had not passed the complimentary stage. The wife of the headman, after looking at us a few moments, called out to the others, " Black traders have come before, calling themselves Bazungu, or white men, but now, for the first time, have we seen the real Bazungu." Kambadzo also soon appeared; he was sorry that we had not come before the beer was all done, but he was going back to see if it was all really and entirely finished, and not one little potful left somewhere.

This was, of course, mere characteristic politeness, as he was perfectly aware that every drop had been swallowed; so we proceeded on to the Kafue, or Kafuje, accompanied by the most intelligent of his headmen. A high ridge, just before we reached the confluence, commands a splendid view of the two great rivers and the rich country beyond. Behind, on the north and east, is the high mountain-range, along whose base we have been travelling; the whole range is covered with trees, which appear even on the prominent peaks, Chiarapela, Morindi, and Chiava; at this last the chain bends away to the N.W., and we could see the distant mountains where the Chief, Semalembue, gained all our hearts in 1856.

CHAPTER XI.

On the 9th July, we tried to send Semalembue a present, but the people here refused to incur the responsibility of carrying it. We, who have the art of writing, cannot realize the danger one incurs of being accused of purloining a portion of goods sent from one person to another, when the carrier cannot prove that he delivered all committed to his charge. Rumours of a foray having been made, either by Makololo or Batoka, as far as the fork of the Kafue, were received here by our men with great indignation, as it looked as if the marauders were shutting up the country, which they had been trying so much to open. Below the junction of the rivers, on a shallow sandbank, lay a large herd of hippopotami, their bodies out of the water, like masses of black rock. Kambadzo's island, called Nyangalule, a name which occurs again at the mouth of the Zambesi, has many choice Motsikiri (*Trachelia*) trees on it; and four very conspicuous stately palms growing out of a single stem. The

Kafue reminds us a little of the Shire, flowing between steep banks, with fertile land on both sides. It is a smaller river, and has less current. Here it seems to come from the west. The headman of the village, near which we encamped, brought a present of meal, fowls, and sweet potatoes. They have both the red and white varieties of this potato. We have, on several occasions during this journey, felt the want of vegetables, in a disagreeable craving which our diet of meat and native meal could not satisfy. It became worse and worse till we got a meal of potatoes, which allayed it at once. A great scarcity of vegetables prevails in these parts of Africa. The natives collect several kinds of wild plants in the woods, which they use no doubt for the purpose of driving off cravings similar to those we experienced.

Owing to the strength of the wind, and the cranky state of the canoes, it was late in the afternoon of the 11th before our party was ferried over the Kafue. After crossing, we were in the Bawe country. Fishhooks here, of native workmanship, were observed to have barbs like the European hooks : elsewhere the point of the hook is merely bent in towards the shank, to have the same effect in keeping on the fish as the barb. We slept near a village a short distance above the ford. The people here are of Batoka origin, the same as many of our men, and call themselves Batonga (independents) or Balengi, and their language only differs slightly from that of the Bakoa, who live between the two rivers Kafue and Loangwa. The paramount Chief of the district lives to the west of this place, and is called Nchomokela—an hereditary title : the family burying-place is on a small hill near this village. The women salute us by clapping their hands and lullilooing as we enter and leave a village, and the men, as they think, respectfully clap their hands on their hips. Immense crops of mapira (*holcus sorghum*) are raised; one species of it forms a natural bend on the seed-stalk, so that the massive ear hangs down. The grain was heaped up on wooden stages, and so was a variety of other products. The men are skilful hunters, and kill elephants and buffaloes with long heavy spears. We halted a few minutes on the morning of the 12th July, opposite the narrow island of Sikakoa, which has a village on its lower end. We were here told that Moselekatse's chief town is a month's distance from this place. They had heard, moreover, that the English had come to Moselekatse, and told him it was wrong to kill men; and he had replied that he was born to kill people, but would drop the habit; and, since the English came, he had sent out his men, not to kill as of yore, but to collect tribute of cloth and ivory. This report referred to the arrival of the Rev. R. Moffat, of Kuruman, who, we afterwards found, had established a Mission. The statement is interesting as showing, that, though imperfectly expressed, the purport of the Missionaries' teaching had travelled, in a short time, over 300 miles, and we know not how far the knowledge of the English operations on the Coast spread inland.

When abreast of the high wooded island Kalabi we came in contact with one of the game-laws of the country, which has come down from the most ancient times. An old buffalo crossed the path a few yards in front of us; our guide threw his small spear at its hip, and it was going off scarcely hurt, when three rifle balls knocked it over. "It is mine," said the guide. He had wounded it first, and the established native game-law is that the animal belongs to the man who first draws blood; the two legs on one side, by the same law, belonged to us for killing it. This beast was very old, blind of one eye, and scabby; the horns, mere stumps, not a foot long, must have atrophied, when by age he lost the strength distinctive of his sex; some eighteen or twenty inches of horn could not well be worn down by mere rubbing against the trees. We saw many buffaloes next day, standing quietly amidst a thick thorn-jungle, through which we were passing. They often stood until we were within fifty or a hundred yards of them.

We had always mountains before us in the distance, and sometimes passed through hills that come close to or intersect the river. This is the case with those called Moio. They are generally of igneous or metamorphic rocks, clayslate, or trap, with porcellanite and zeolite; the principal rock in the central part of the country, where no syenite or gneiss had been upheaved, seems to be a grey coarse sandstone, known to us by the name of Tette sandstone. Large masses of it still lie horizontally or only slightly inclined. When much disturbed, it has been tilted up by the eruption of igneous rocks, and near the point of contact it has either been hardened or melted, and the coal which elsewhere still lies under the undisturbed stratum, is crystallized or entirely burned. The igneous rocks often form dykes, as that called Nakabele, which stretches like a dam across the western entrance to the Kariba gorge. In the vicinity of the erupted rocks we usually meet soft calcareous tufa, as if, after the igneous action, many hot fountains flowing had deposited lime from their water.

Previous, however, to this period of eruption and upheaval, it is probable that the sandstone formed the bed of prodigious inland seas, along the low shores of which the plants of the coal flourished, succeeded, as the land was gradually elevated, by the trees we now find silicified on the surface;

these may perhaps have been submerged, as the land again sank under some igneous agency, and became subjected to the action of water, at a high temperature, holding silica in solution.   However that may have been, it is certain that a coalfield of unknown extent exists, for coal is found cropping out near to the lava or basalt, which is the principal rock of the Victoria Falls district, and, with the "faults" alluded to, it extends to the east of Tette.   Then, again, we saw it in the Rovuma, with the same characteristic of fossil-wood lying on the grey sandstone.   With abundance of fine iron-ore, the existence of this prodigious coalfield leads to the belief that an important future is in store for Africa.

On the 14th July we left the river at the mountain-range, which, lying north-east and south-west across the river, forms the Kariba gorge.   Near the upper end of the Kariba rapids, the stream Sanyati enters from the south, and is reported to have Moselekatse's principal cattle-posts at its sources; our route went round the north end of the mountains, and we encamped beside the village of the generous Chief, Moloi, who brought us three immense baskets of fine mapira meal, ten fowls, and two pots of beer.   On receiving a present in return, he rose, and, with a few dancing gestures, said or sang, "Motota, Motota, Motota," which our men translated into "thanks."   He had visited Moselekatse a few months before our arrival, and saw the English Missionaries, living in their wagons.   "They told Moselekatse," said he, "they were of his family, or friends, and would plough the land and live at their own expense;" and he had replied, "The land is before you, and I shall come and see you plough."   This again was substantially what took place, when Mr. Moffat introduced the Missionaries to his old friend, and shows still further that the notion of losing their country by admitting foreigners does not come as the first idea to the native mind. One might imagine that, as mechanical powers are unknown to the heathen, the almost magic operations of machinery, the discoveries of modern science and art, or the presence of the prodigious force which, for instance, is associated with the sight of a man-of-war, would have the effect which miracles once had of arresting the attention and inspiring awe. But, though we have heard the natives exclaim in admiration at the sight of even small illustrations of what science enables us to do—" Ye are gods, and not men "—the heart is unaffected. In attempting their moral elevation, it is always more conducive to the end desired, that the teacher should come unaccompanied by any power to cause either jealousy or fear. The heathen, who have not become aware of the greed and hate which too often characterize the advancing tide of emigration, listen with most attention to the message of Divine love when delivered by men who evidently possess the same human sympathies with themselves. A Chief is rather envied his good fortune in first securing foreigners in his town. Jealousy of strangers belongs more to the Arab than to the African character; and if the women are let alone by the traveller, no danger need be apprehended from any save the slave-trading tribes, and not often even from them.

We saw large flocks of the beautiful Numidian cranes: guinea-fowls were still numerous, but rather shyer, as the natives here shoot many with arrows, and kill them by skilfully throwing their clubs. The Mambo, the name here for Chief, of the island Mochue sent his brother and principal men after us to present a gift, and to " hear the words which were to cause the land to rest." We apologized for passing without calling, by stating that strangers could not know

who was who. He proposed sending a deputation with us
to Sekeletu, in order to renew the friendly intercourse of
former years, which of late had been broken by marauding
and war : but the Doctor said he did not know whether
Sekeletu was governing wisely, or whether he was hearkening
to the counsels of the old warriors, who wished him to follow
in the footsteps of his warlike father, Sebetuane. As we
were spending the evening opposite Mochue, some men came
with a marimba and accompaniments of buffalo-horns beaten
with sticks ; but our men, knowing that we soon tired of
their monotonous tunes and ungainly dancing, ordered them
away. On the islands and on the left bank of the Zambesi,
all the way from the river Kafue, there is a large population ; the right bank is equally fertile, but depopulated,
because Moselekatse does not allow any one to live there
who might raise an alarm when he sends out marauders
beyond. From Moloi's village onwards, the people, though
Batoka, are called Bawe and Ba Selea. Much salt is made
on the rivulet Losito, and sold in large quantities, and very
cheap.

We passed through a fertile country, covered with open
forest, accompanied by the friendly Bawe. They are very
hospitable ; many of them were named, among themselves,
"the Baenda pezi," or "Go-nakeds," their only clothing
being a coat of red ochre. Occasionally stopping at their
villages we were duly lullilooed, and regaled with sweet
new-made beer, which, being yet unfermented, was not intoxicating. It is in this state called Liting or Makonde.
Some of the men carry large shields of buffalo-hide, and
all are well supplied with heavy spears. The vicinity
of the villages is usually cleared and cultivated in large
patches ; but nowhere can the country be said to be stocked

Q

with people. At every village stands were erected, and piles
of the native corn, still unthrashed, placed upon them; some
had been beaten out, put into oblong parcels made of grass,
and stacked in wooden frames.

We crossed several rivulets in our course, as the Mandora,
the Lofia, the Manzaia (with brackish water), the Rimbe, the
Chibue, the Chezia, the Chilola (containing fragments of coal),
which did little more than mark our progress. The island and
rapid of Nakansalo, of which we had formerly heard, were of no
importance, the rapid being but half-a-mile long, and only on
one side of the island. The island Kaluzi marks one of the
numerous places where astronomical observations were made;
Mozia, a station where a volunteer poet left us; the island
Mochenya, and Mpande island, at the mouth of the Zungwe
rivulet, where we left the Zambesi.

When favoured with the hospitality and company of the
" Go-nakeds," we tried to discover if nudity were the badge
of a particular order among the Bawe, but they could only
refer to custom. Some among them had always liked it for
no reason in particular: shame seemed to lie dormant, and
the sense could not be aroused by our laughing and joking
them on their appearance. They evidently felt no less
decent than we did with our clothes on; but, whatever may
be said in favour of nude statues, it struck us that man, in
a state of nature, is a most ungainly animal. Could we see a
number of the degraded of our own lower classes in like
guise, it is probable, that, without the black colour which
acts somehow as a dress, they would look worse still.

In domestic contentions the Bawe are careful not to kill
each other; but, when one village goes to war with another,
they are not so particular. The victorious party are said to
quarter one of the bodies of the enemies they may have killed,

and to perform certain ceremonies over the fragments. The vanquished call upon their conquerors to give them a portion also; and, when this request is complied with, they too perform the same ceremonies, and lament over their dead comrade, after which the late combatants may visit each other in peace. Sometimes the head of the slain is taken and buried in an ant-hill, till all the flesh is gone; and the lower jaw is then worn as a trophy by the slayer; but this we never saw, and the fore-going information was obtained only through an interpreter.

We left the Zambesi at the mouth of the Zungwe or Mozama or Dela rivulet, up which we proceeded, first in a westerly and then in a north-westerly direction. The Zungwe at this time had no water in its sandy channel for the first eight or ten miles. Willows, however, grow on the banks, and water soon began to appear in the hollows; and a few miles further up it was a fine flowing stream deliciously cold. As in many other streams from Chicova to near Si-namane, shale and coal crop out in the bank; and here the large roots of stigmaria or its allied plants were found. We followed the course of the Zungwe to the foot of the Batoka highlands, up whose steep and rugged sides of red and white quartz we climbed till we attained an altitude of upwards of 3000 feet. Here, on the cool and bracing heights, the ex-hilaration of mind and body was delightful, as we looked back at the hollow beneath covered with a hot sultry glare, not un-pleasant now that we were in the mild radiance above. We had a noble view of the great valley in which the Zambesi flows. The cultivated portions are so small in comparison to the rest of the landscape that the valley appears nearly all forest, with a few grassy glades. We spent the night of the 28th July high above the level of the sea, by the rivulet Tyotyo, near Tabacheu or Chirebuechina, names both signifying white

mountain; in the morning hoar frost covered the ground, and
thin ice was on the pools. Skirting the southern flank of Tabacheu, we soon passed from the hills on to the portion of the
vast table-land called Mataba, and looking back saw all the
way across the Zambesi valley to the lofty ridge some thirty
miles off, which, coming from the Mashona, a country in the
S.E., runs to the N.W. to join the ridge at the angle of
which are the Victoria Falls, and then bends far to the
N.E. from the same point.   Only a few years since,
these extensive highlands were peopled by the Batoka; numerous herds of cattle furnished abundance of milk, and
the rich soil amply repaid the labour of the husbandman;
now large herds of buffaloes, zebras, and antelopes fatten
on the excellent pasture; and on that land, which formerly
supported multitudes, not a man is to be seen.   In
travelling from Monday morning till late on Saturday
afternoon, all the way from Tabacheu to Moachemba,
which is only twenty-one miles of latitude from the
Victoria Falls, and constantly passing the ruined sites
of utterly deserted Batoka villages, we did not fall in
with a single person.   The Batoka were driven out of
their noble country by the invasions of Moselekatse and
Sebetuane.   Several tribes of Bechuana and Basutu, fleeing from the Zulu or Matebele Chief, Moselekatse, reached
the Zambesi above the Falls.   Coming from a land without
rivers, none of them knew how to swim; and one tribe, called
the Bamangwato, wishing to cross the Zambesi, was ferried
over, men and women separately, to different islands, by one
of the Batoka Chiefs; the men were then left to starve and
the women appropriated by the ferryman and his people.
Sekomi, the present Chief of the Bamangwato, then an infant in his mother's arms, was enabled, through the kindness

of a private Batoka, to escape. This act seems to have made an indelible impression on Sekomi's heart, for, though otherwise callous, he still never fails to inquire after the welfare of his benefactor.

Sebetuane, with his wonted ability, outwitted the treacherous Batoka, by insisting in the politest manner on their Chief remaining at his own side until the people and cattle were all carried safe across; the Chief was then handsomely rewarded, both with cattle and brass rings off Sebetuane's own wives. No sooner were the Makololo, then called Basuto, safely over, than they were confronted by the whole Batoka nation; and to this day the Makololo point with pride to the spot on the Lekone, near to which they were encamped, where Sebetuane, with a mere handful of warriors in comparison to the vast horde that surrounded him, stood waiting the onslaught, the warriors in one small body, the women and children guarding the cattle behind them. The Batoka, of course, melted away before those, who had been made veterans by years of continual fighting, and Sebetuane always justified his subsequent conquests in that country by alleging that the Batoka had come out to fight with a man fleeing for his life, who had never done them any wrong. They seem never to have been a warlike race; passing through their country, we once observed a large stone cairn, and our guide favoured us with the following account of it:—"Once upon a time, our forefathers were going to fight another tribe, and here they halted and sat down. After a long consultation, they came to the unanimous conclusion, that instead of proceeding to fight and kill their neighbours, and perhaps be killed themselves, it would be more like men to raise this heap of stones, as their protest against the wrong the other tribe had done them, which, having accomplished, they returned quietly home." Such men of peace could not stand before the Makololo, nor, of course, the more warlike Matebele, who coming afterwards drove even their conquerors, the Makololo, out of the country. Sebetuane, however, profiting by the tactics which he had learned of the Batoka, inveigled a large body of this new enemy on to another island, and after due starvation there overcame the whole. A much greater army of "Moselekatse's own" followed with canoes, but were now baffled by Sebetuane's placing all his people and cattle on an island and so guarding it that none could approach. Dispirited, famished, borne down by fever, they returned to the Falls, and all, except five, were cut off.

But though the Batoka appear never to have had much inclination to fight with men, they are decidedly brave hunters of buffaloes and elephants. They go fearlessly close up to these formidable animals, and kill them with large spears. The Banyai, who have long bullied all Portuguese traders, were amazed at the daring and bravery of the Batoka in coming at once to close quarters with the elephant; and Chisaka, a Portuguese rebel, having formerly induced a body of this tribe to settle with him, ravaged all the Portuguese villas around Tette. They bear the name of Basimilongwe, and some of our men found relations among them. Sininyane and Matenga also, two of our party, were once inveigled into a Portuguese expedition against Mariano, by the assertion that the Doctor had arrived and had sent for them to come down to Senna. On finding that they were entrapped to fight, they left, after seeing an officer with a large number of Tette slaves killed.

The Batoka had attained somewhat civilized ideas, in planting and protecting various fruit and oil-seed yielding trees of the country. No other tribe either plants or abstains from cutting down fruit trees, but here we saw some which had been planted in regular rows, and the trunks of which were quite two feet in diameter. The grand old Mosibe, a tree yielding a bean with a thin red pellicle, said to be very fattening, had probably seen two hundred summers. Dr. Kirk found that the Mosibe is peculiar, in being allied to a species met with only in the West Indies. The Motsikiri, sometimes called Mafuta, yields a hard fat, and an oil which is exported from Inhambane. It is said that two ancient Batoka travellers went down as far as the Loangwa, and finding the Macāā tree (*jujube* or *zisyphus*) in fruit, carried the seed all the way back to the great Falls, in order to plant them. Two of these trees are still to be seen there, the only specimens of the kind in that region.

The Batoka had made a near approach to the custom of more refined nations and had permanent graveyards, either on the sides of hills, thus rendered sacred, or under large old shady trees; they reverence the tombs of their ancestors, and plant the largest elephants' tusks, as monuments at the head of the grave, or entirely enclose it with the choicest ivory. Some of the other tribes throw the dead body into the river to be devoured by crocodiles, or, sewing it up in a mat, place it on the branch of a Baobab, or cast it in some lonely gloomy spot, surrounded by dense tropical vegetation, where it affords a meal to the foul hyenas; but the Batoka reverently bury their dead, and regard the spot henceforth as sacred. The ordeal by the poison of the muave is resorted to by the Batoka, as well as by the other tribes; but a cock is often made to stand proxy for the supposed witch. Near the confluence of the Kafue the Mambo, or Chief, with some of his headmen, came to our sleeping-place with a present; their foreheads were smeared with white flour, and an

unusual seriousness marked their demeanour.   Shortly before
our arrival they had been accused of witchcraft; conscious of
innocence, they accepted the ordeal, and undertook to
drink the poisoned muave.   For this purpose they made
a journey to the sacred hill of Nchomokela, on which repose
the bodies of their ancestors; and, after a solemn appeal to
the unseen spirits to attest the innocence of their children,
they swallowed the muave, vomited, and were therefore declared not guilty.   It is evident that they believe that the
soul has a continued existence; and that the spirits of the departed know what those they have left behind them are doing,
and are pleased or not, according as their deeds are good or evil;
this belief is universal.   The owner of a large canoe refused to
sell it, because it belonged to the spirit of his father, who helped
him when he killed the hippopotamus.   Another, when the bargain for his canoe was nearly completed, seeing a large serpent
on a branch of the tree overhead, refused to complete the sale,
alleging that this was the spirit of his father come to protest
against it.

Some of the Batoka Chiefs must have been men of considerable enterprise; the land of one, in the western part of this
country, was protected by the Zambesi on the S., and on
the N. and E. lay an impassable reedy marsh, filled with
water all the year round, leaving only his western border
open to invasion: he conceived the idea of digging a broad
and deep canal nearly a mile in length, from the reedy
marsh to the Zambesi, and, having actually carried the scheme
into execution, he formed a large island, on which his cattle
grazed in safety, and his corn ripened from year to year
secure from all marauders.

Another Chief, who died a number of years ago, believed
that he had discovered a remedy for tsetse-bitten cattle; his

son Moyara showed us a plant, which was new to our botanist, and likewise told us how the medicine was prepared; the bark of the root, and, what might please our homœopathic friends, a dozen of the tsetse are dried, and ground together into a fine powder. This mixture is administered internally; and the cattle are fumigated by burning under them the rest of the plant collected. The treatment must be continued for weeks, whenever the symptoms of poison appear. This medicine, he frankly admitted, would not cure all the bitten cattle. " For," said he, " cattle, and men too, die in spite of medicine; but should a herd by accident stray into a tsetse district and be bitten, by this medicine of my father, Kampa-kampa, some of them could be saved, while, without it, all would inevitably die." He stipulated that we were not to show the medicine to other people, and if ever we needed it in this region we must employ him; but if we were far off we might make it ourselves; and when we saw it cure the cattle think of him, and send him a present.

Our men made it known everywhere that we wished the tribes to live in peace, and would use our influence to induce Sekeletu to prevent the Batoka of Moshobo-twane and the Makololo under-chiefs making forays into their country: they had already suffered severely, and their remonstrances with their countryman, Moshobotwane, evoked only the answer, " The Makololo have given me a spear; why should I not use it ?" He, indeed, it was, who, being remarkably swift of foot, first guided the Makololo in their conquest of the country. In the character of peace-makers, therefore, we experienced abundant hospitality; and, from the Kafue to the Falls, none of our party were allowed to suffer hunger. The natives sent to our sleeping-places generous presents of the finest white meal, and fat capons to give it a relish, great pots of beer to comfort our hearts, together with pumpkins, beans, and tobacco, so that we "should sleep neither hungry nor thirsty."

In travelling from the Kafue to the Zungwe we frequently passed several villages in the course of a day's march. In the evening came deputies from the villages, at which we could not stay to sleep, with liberal presents of food. It would have pained them to have allowed strangers to pass without partaking of their hospitality; repeatedly were we hailed from huts, and asked to wait a moment and drink a little of the beer, which was brought with alacrity. Our march resembled a triumphal procession. We entered and left every village amidst the cheers of its inhabitants; the men clapping their hands, and the women lullilooing, with the shrill call, "Let us sleep," or "Peace." Passing through a hamlet one day, our guide called to the people, "Why do you not clap your hands and salute when you see men who are wishing to bring peace to the land?" When we halted for the night it was no uncommon thing for the people to prepare our camp entirely of their own accord; some with hoes quickly smoothed the ground for our beds, others brought dried grass and spread it carefully over the spot; some with their small axes speedily made a bush fence to shield us from the wind; and if, as occasionally happened, the water was a little distance off, others hastened and brought it with firewood to cook our food with. They are an industrious people, and very fond of agriculture. For hours together we marched through unbroken fields of mapira, or native corn, of a great width; but one can give no idea of the extent of land under the hoe as compared with any European country. The extent of surface is so great that the largest fields under culture, when viewed on a wide landscape, dwindle to mere spots.

When taken in connexion with the wants of the people, the cultivation on the whole is most creditable to their industry.   They erect numerous granaries which give their villages the appearance of being large; and, when the water of the Zambesi has subsided, they place large quantities of grain, tied up in bundles of grass, and well plastered over with clay, on low sand islands for protection from the attacks of marauding mice and men.   Owing to the ravages of the weevil, the native corn can hardly be preserved until the following crop comes in.   However largely they may cultivate, and however abundant the harvest, it must all be consumed in a year.   This may account for their making so much of it into beer.   The beer these Batoka or Bawe brew is not the sour and intoxicating boala or pombe, found among some other tribes, but sweet, and highly nutritive, with only a slight degree of acidity, sufficient to render it a pleasant drink. The people were all plump, and in good condition; and we never saw a single case of intoxication among them, though all drank abundance of this liting, or sweet beer.   Both men and boys were eager to work for very small pay.   Our men could hire any number of them to carry their burdens for a few beads a day.   Our miserly and dirty ex-cook had an old pair of trousers that some one had given to him; after he had long worn them himself, with one of the sorely decayed legs he hired a man to carry his heavy load a whole day; a second man carried it the next day for the other leg, and what remained of the old garment, without the buttons, procured the labour of another man for the third day.

Men of remarkable ability have risen up among the Africans from time to time, as amongst other portions of the human family.   Some have attracted the attention, and excited the admiration of large districts by their wisdom.

Others, apparently by the powers of ventriloquism, or by peculiar dexterity in throwing the spear, or shooting with the bow, have been the wonder of their generation; but the total absence of literature leads to the loss of all former experience, and the wisdom of the wise has not been handed down. They have had their minstrels too, but mere tradition preserves not their effusions. One of these, and apparently a genuine poet, attached himself to our party for several days, and, whenever we halted, sang our praises to the villagers in smooth and harmonious numbers. It was a sort of blank verse, and each line consisted of five syllables. The song was short when it first began, but each day he picked up more information about us, and added to the poem until our praises became an ode of respectable length. When distance from home compelled his return, he expressed his regret at leaving us, and was, of course, paid for his useful and pleasant flatteries. Another, though a less gifted son of song, belonged to the Batoka of our own party. Every evening, while the others were cooking, talking, or sleeping, he rehearsed his songs, containing a history of everything he had seen in the land of the white men, and on the way back. In composing, extempore, any new piece, he was never at a loss; for if the right word did not come, he halted not, but eked out the measure with a peculiar musical sound meaning nothing at all. He accompanied his recitations on the *sansa*, an instrument figured in the woodcut (*c*), the nine iron keys of which are played with the thumbs, while the fingers pass behind to hold it. The hollow end and ornaments face the breast of the player. Persons of a musical turn, if too poor to buy a sansa, may be seen playing vigorously on an instrument made with a number of thick corn-stalks sewn together, as a sansa frame, and keys of split bamboo, which, though making but little sound, seems to soothe the player himself.   When the instrument is played with a calabash (*a*) as a sounding-board, it emits a greater volume of sound.   Pieces of shells and tin are added to make a jingling accompaniment, and the calabash (*b*) is also ornamented.

(*a*) Calabash sounding-board.   (*b*) Calabash ornamented with figures.   (*c*) Sansa.

In musing over the peculiar habit indicated in the name "Baenda pezi" (Go-nakeds), we conjectured that it might be an order similar to that of Freemasons, but no secret society can be found among the native Africans. A sort of brotherhood, called by the Portuguese "Empacasseiros," exists in Angola, but it only enjoins community of right to food in each other's hut; and the qualification for admission is ability to shoot the empacasso (buffalo or gnu).   This is very much the same thing as that which distinguishes the bands into which the young Makololo are formed on circumcision. They thence forward consider each other as in a state of perfect equality, and bound to keep up the discipline of their troop, and, in case of cowardice, to inflict punishment.   No

good, as far as we could learn, would result to any one in
this country from his knowledge of Freemasonry. A noble
specimen of the Baenda pezi order once visited us and gained
our esteem, though the full dress in which he stood consisted
only of a tobacco-pipe, with a stem two feet long wound
round with polished iron. He brought a liberal present.
"God made him naked," he said, "and he had therefore
never worn any sort of clothing." This gentleman's philosophy is very much like that of some dirty people we have
known, who justified their want of fastidiousness by saying,
"fingers were made before forks." Early next morning we
had another interview with our naked friend, accompanied
this time by his wife and daughter, bearing two large pots
of beer, with which he wished us to refresh ourselves before
starting. Both the women, as comely and modest-looking
as any we have seen in Africa, were well-clothed, and
adorned, as indeed all their women are. Some wear tin
ear-rings all round the ear, and as many as nine often in
each ear. The men rub their bodies with red ochre. Some
plait a fillet two inches wide, of the inner bark of trees, and
shave the hair off the lower part of the head, an inch above
the ears being bare; the hair, on the upper part, having
been well smeared with red ochre in oil, the fillet is bound
on to it, and gives the head the appearance of having on
a neat forage-cap. Some strings of coarse beads, and a
little polished iron-wire round the arms, the never-failing
pipe, and a small pair of iron tongs to lift the lighted coal,
constitute the entire clothing of the most dandified young
men of the Baenda pezi. All their other faculties seem
fairly developed; but, as neither ridicule nor joking could
awaken the sense of shame, it is probable that clothing
alone would arouse the dormant feeling. Girls of eight or

ten years, nearly naked, were clothed and taken into the
Mission-house at Kolobeng as nurses to the children. In
a fortnight after, they hastily covered their bosoms, even
if one only passed through the sitting-room in which they
slept. Among Zulus the smaller the covering, the more
intense the shame on accidental exposure.

Large quantities of tobacco are raised on the lower bank
of the Zambesi during the winter months, and the people are
perhaps the most inveterate smokers in the world. The pipe
is seldom out of their mouths, and they are as polite smokers
as any ever met with in a railway-carriage. When they
came with a present, although we were in their own country
they asked before lighting their pipes if we had any objection to their smoking beside us, which, of course, we never
had. They think that they have invented an improved
method of smoking; a description of it may interest those
who are fond of the weed at home. They take a whiff,
puff out the grosser smoke, then, by a sudden inhalation,
contrive to catch and swallow, as they say, the real essence,
the very spirit of the tobacco, which in the ordinary way is
entirely lost. The Batoka tobacco is famed in the country
for its strength, and it certainly is both very strong and
very cheap: a few strings of beads will purchase enough
to last any reasonable man for six months. It caused
headache in the only smoker of our party, from its strength,
but this quality makes the natives come great distances to
buy it.

The people above Kariba had never been visited before by
foreigners; the chief of Koba, on being asked if any tradition
existed of strangers having formerly come into the country,
replied, "Not at all; our fathers all died without telling us
that they had seen men like you. To-day I am exalted in

seeing what they never saw." Others, in reference to old men being in the habit of telling wonderful tales, said, "We are the true ancients; we have seen stranger things than any of our ancestors, in seeing you." The only tradition of foreigners coming into the country refers to the ascent of Simoens as far as the Sanyati, at the entrance to the Kariba gorge. According to the testimony of the people of the country and the statement of the companion of this robber to us, it was a regular plundering foray similar to that of Sequasha. Like the Boers and others we have known, this man, who is still alive at Tette, eager to make the most of his conquest, represented the people attacked to have been Matebele, and on being told that they were Bawe, a tribe of Batoka, he answered, "Well, we thought them to be Matebele (Landeens), because they were naked." After accumulating large quantities of ivory and many slaves, by the aid of his followers' firearms, which the people had never before encountered, Simoens lost all the booty and his life by a combination of the Chiefs under Chisaka, at the rivulet Zingesi, near to Mpende.

After we had passed up, however, a party of slaves, belonging to the two native Portuguese who assassinated the Chief, Mpangwe, and took possession of his lands at Zumbo, followed on our footsteps, and, representing themselves to be our "children," bought great quantities of ivory, from the Bawe, for a few coarse beads a tusk. They also purchased ten large new canoes to carry it, at the rate of six strings of red or white beads, or two fathoms of grey calico, for each canoe, and, at the same cheap rate, a number of good-looking girls.

We had long ere this become thoroughly convinced that the Government of Lisbon had been guilty, possibly unin-

tentionally, of double dealing. Public instructions, as already
stated, had been sent from Portugal to all the officials to
render us every assistance in their power, but these were
to be understood with considerable reservation. From what
we observed it was clear that, with the public orders to the
officials to aid us, private instructions had come to thwart
us. It is possible that these private instructions meant
only that we were to be watched; but where nearly every
one, from Governor to convict soldier, is an eager slave-
dealer, such orders could only mean, "keep a sharp look
out that your slave-trade follows as near their heels as
possible." We were now so fully convinced that, in opening the country through which no Portuguese durst previously pass, we were made the unwilling instruments of
extending the slave-trade, that, had we not been under obligations to return with the Makololo to their own country,
we should have left the Zambesi and gone to the Rovuma,
or to some other inlet to the interior. It was with bitter
sorrow that we saw the good we would have done turned to
evil.

We afterwards learned that no sooner was it proposed that
we should go to the Rovuma, than the Governor-General
d'Almeida hastened up to Zanzibar, and tried to induce the
Sultan to agree to that river being made the boundary between him and the Portuguese. This movement, the effect
of instructions drawn up after information had been obtained
from our letters being read at the meetings of the Geographical Society, London, was happily frustrated by Colonel
Rigby; and the Governor-General had to be content with
Cape Delgado as the extreme limit of Portuguese claims
northward.

On the Batoka highlands, the invigorating breezes disposed

us to listen with pleasure to the singing of birds. It might be owing to the greater cold, but the variety of notes in their warblings seemed greater than with African birds in general. A pretty little black bird, with white shoulders, probably a weaver, but not seen elsewhere, sat on the topmost twigs of the huge trees, pouring forth its melody as if glad, among the deserted villages, once more to see the face of man. It flew from tree to tree, and sang on the wing, though not soaring like the lark. It bears frost, and to the bird-fancier or Acclimatization Society might be an interesting addition to their birds of song. It is not the honey-guide alone that is attached to man. The whydah-bird and waterwagtail are held sacred by the natives of different parts, and consequently come without fear close to human kind. Were our small birds not so much persecuted by small boys, their attachment would be more apparent, even in England.

Seabenzo, the chief whom we found on the Tyotyo rivulet, had accompanied us some distance over the undulating highland plains; and as he and our own men needed meat, we killed an elephant. This, unless one really needs the meat, or is eager for the ivory, can scarcely be looked back to without regret. These noble beasts, capable of being so useful to man in the domestic state, are, we fear, destined, at no distant date, to disappear from the face of the earth. Yet, in the excitement, all this and more was at once forgotten, and we joined in the assault as eagerly as those who think only of the fat and savoury flesh.

The writings of Harris and Gordon Cumming contain such full and nauseating details of indiscriminate slaughter of the wild animals, that one wonders to see almost every African book since besmeared with feeble imitations of these great hunters' tales. Some tell of escapes from situations which, from our knowledge of the nature of the animals, it requires a painful stretch of charity to believe ever existed, even in dreams; and others of deeds which lead one to conclude that the proportion of "born butchers," in the population, is as great as of public-house keepers to the people in Glasgow.

The amount of ivory taken to the marts of the world shows that about 30,000 elephants are annually slain.*   It is highly

---

* After a lecture by Professor Owen, F.R.S., at the Society of Arts, London, 17th Dec., 1856, on the "Ivory and Teeth of Commerce," Mr. P. L. Simmonds gave some trade statistics from which it was calculated that upwards of 30,000 elephants annually perished. In one cargo of 1276 elephants' tusks, weighing in all 20,953 lbs., the average weight was 16½ lbs. In another cargo 556 elephants' tusks weighed 9698 lbs., giving an average of 17½ lbs. In the accompanying note with which Mr. Simmonds has kindly obliged us, the ivory mentioned refers only to our own trade; the exports from India and Siam to China, from Zanzibar, and the East Coast to India and the United States, and from the French African possessions to France, are not included. He takes the average weight at 30 lbs., and estimates the number killed annually at 30,000—as stated in the text. Elephants, as a rule, never shed their tusks. We have only met with pieces broken off when the animal was engaged in digging up the roots of trees;—so, practically, every tusk seen in the market belonged to an elephant now dead; and, considering the number of calves destroyed before the tusk becomes of any value to the trader, it is probable that 40,000

is about the actual number annually killed.

We have made no reference to what may be called monster tusks, of from 130 to 150 lbs.—some are spoken of as upwards of 200 lbs. In some parts, the average tusk may weigh 60 lbs.; but as a set-off to this in the calculation it must be remembered that one of the places not included, namely, Zanzibar, for many years received annually 20,000 tusks.

"Importation of IVORY *of all kinds* into the United Kingdom—elephants' tusks, walruses, and hippopotamus teeth :—

	Cwts.	£
1856	9,866	343,517
1857	9,890	421,318
1858	12,279	410,608
1859	10,821	336,147
1860	10,854	332,166
1861	11,163	297,491
1862	11,605	262,962
1863	9,290	256,059
	8/85,768	2,660,268
Average	10,721	332,533

" The import of hippopotamus teeth and walrus is scarcely more than 10 or 12 tons a year; therefore it is scarcely worth considering. The difficulty is what average weight to take the tusks at. 30 lbs. may be considered a fair probable, that as the great size of the ears exhibited on ancient Roman coins prove the animals in use by that nation to have been of the African, and not of the Asiatic species, they must have been tamed by the negroes in the interior of Africa. This is the more likely, inasmuch as there is no instance on record of ancient Europeans daring to tame this animal. Never, since the time of the Romans and Carthaginians, has the African elephant been tamed, though it was believed to be much more sagacious than the Asiatic species.

In this hunt a small herd of female elephants, with their young, were encountered near a belt of open forest near Motunta. Three rifle-balls, including a Jacob's shell, were lodged in the body of the nearest; a smaller one charged back, but stopped on seeing so many enemies, and went off with the others. The herd waited twice for the wounded one, which was not able to keep up, and only left her to her fate when self-preservation became the more imperious law. This made us imagine that she was perhaps the mother of the herd. She ran a mile and a half, and then stopped to lean against a tree. A few of our men approached, and fired a volley, she went on a few paces, shook her trunk, dropped gently on one knee, then on the other; slowly the two hindlegs bent, and she fell.* We read it now with a pang.

---

average. If African do not average much more than 20 or 25 lbs., while for Zanzibar and Mosambique the average would be 60 to 80 lbs., taking the average at 30 lbs. this would imply the annual slaughter of 20,000 elephants a year; and, taking the eastern and other markets, the number may be fairly estimated at 30,000 animals killed every year for the ivory."

* The elephant was an ordinary sized female, and her measurement may be of interest to some :—

	Ft.	in.
Height at withers	8	2¼
Circumference of forefoot ..	3	7
Length from tip of trunk to eye	6	10
From eye to eye	0	14½
Eye to meatus of ear	1	3½

A shout of exultation rose from the men, who rushed up, and danced round the fallen animal with wild shouts of triumph. When we came up, Tuba Mokoro approached the Doctor, whose Jacob's shell had inflicted a mortal wound behind the orifice of the ear, and, with great self-complacency, said, " You see it was speed that did it—my speed. I kept up while all the others lagged behind, though I fell and hurt my knee. You will give me a cloth, won't you ? "

The men, having had no meat for the last three or four days, thought that they could eat the elephant all themselves, and were not disposed to let Seabenzo and his people have any ; but, after gorging themselves all night, and grumbling at the English for possessing so little practical sense as to kill an elephant, and then not wait long enough to eat it up, they gave Seabenzo upwards of three-quarters of it, and we presented him with the tusks. The proboscis of the African elephant is so full at the insertion into the upper part of the face, that the animal appears to have a very convex forehead. The trunk when cut off close to the bone is so

	Ft.	in.
Eye to lower jaw ., ..	0	16¾
Eye to insertion of tail ..	9	10
From insertion to end of tail	3	4½
Semi-circumference at middle of chest	6	0
Semi-circumference of abdomen to middle of back ..	7	1½
From neck to forefoot ..	5	1
From abdomen to hindfoot	3	3½
From meatus of ear horizontally to external edge ..	2	9
Diagonal breadth of ear ..	4	3
Height from hindfoot ..	7	6

Measurement of full-grown fœtal elephant, having four placentæ with cotyledons, and near its full time :—

	Ft.	in.
Height at withers	2	6
Circumference of forefoot ..	1	1
Height at hindleg	2	5
From tip of trunk to tip of tail	6	0
From tip of trunk to eye ..	1	7½
From eye to the meatus of ear	0	7½
Horizontal diameter of ear from meatus	0	8
Diagonal breadth of ear ..	1	3½
Semi-circumference of chest	1	7
Semi-circumference of abdomen	1	8½
Length of cord	3	7

heavy, that our companions declared only two or three men in their tribe could lift one.

A herd of elephants makes sad havoc among the trees, which cover the highlands only in patches. They break off great branches as easily as we could snap the shoots of celery ; and they often break down good-sized trees in the mere wantonness of strength, without even tasting them.

During the time we remained at Motunta a splendid meteor was observed to lighten the whole heavens. The observer's back was turned to it, but on looking round the streak of light was seen to remain on its path some seconds. This streak is usually explained to be only the continuance of the impression made by the shining body on the retina. This cannot be, as in this case the meteor was not actually seen and yet the streak was clearly perceived. The rays of planets and stars also require another explanation than that usually given.

Fruit-trees and gigantic wild fig-trees, and circles of stones on which corn safes were placed, with worn grindstones, point out where the villages once stood. The only reason now assigned, for this fine country remaining desolate, is the fear of fresh visitations by the Matebele. The country now slopes gradually to the west into the Makololo Valley. Two days' march from the Batoka village nearest the highlands, we met with some hunters who were burning the dry grass, in order to attract the game by the fresh vegetation which speedily springs up afterwards. The grass, as already re-marked, is excellent for cattle. One species, with leaves having finely serrated edges, and of a reddish-brown colour, we noticed our men eating: it tastes exactly like liquorice-root, and is named kezu-kezu. The tsetse, known to the

Batoka by the name ndoka, does not exist here, though buffaloes and elephants abound.

A small trap in the path, baited with a mouse, to catch spotted cats (*F. Genetta*), is usually the first indication that we are drawing near to a village; but when we get within the sounds of pounding corn, cockcrowing, or the merry shouts of children at play, we know that the huts are but a few yards off, though the trees conceal them from view. We reached, on the 4th of August, Moa-chemba, the first of the Batoka villages which now owe allegiance to Sekeletu, and could see distinctly with the naked eye, in the great valley spread out before us, the columns of vapour rising from the Victoria Falls, though upwards of 20 miles distant. We were informed that, the rains having failed this year, the corn crops had been lost, and great scarcity and much hunger prevailed from Sesheke to Linyanti. Some of the reports which the men had heard from the Batoka of the hills concerning their families, were here confirmed. Takelang's wife had been killed by Mashotlane, the headman at the Falls, on a charge, as usual, of witchcraft. Inchikola's two wives, believing him to be dead, had married again; and Masakasa was intensely disgusted to hear that two years ago his friends, upon a report of his death, threw his shield over the Falls, slaughtered all his oxen, and held a species of wild Irish wake, in honour of his memory: he said he meant to disown them, and to say, when they come to salute him, "I am dead. I am not here. I belong to another world, and should stink if I came among you."

All the sad news we had previously heard, of the disastrous results which followed the attempt of a party of missionaries, under the Rev. H. Helmore, to plant the Gospel at Linyanti, were here fully confirmed. Several of the missionaries and their native attendants, from Kuruman, had succumbed to the fever, and the survivors had retired some weeks before our arrival. We remained the whole of the 7th beside the village of the old Batoka chief, Moshobotwane, the stoutest man we have seen in Africa. The cause of our delay here was a severe attack of fever in Charles Livingstone. He took a dose of our fever pills; was better on the 8th, and marched three hours; then on the 9th marched eight miles to the Great Falls, and spent the rest of the day in the fatiguing exercise of sight-seeing. We were in the very same valley as Linyanti, and this was the same fever which treated, or rather maltreated, with only a little Dover's powder, proved so fatal to poor Helmore; the symptoms, too, were identical with those afterwards described by non-medical persons, as those of poison.

We gave Moshobotwane a present, and a pretty plain exposition of what we thought of his bloody forays among his Batoka brethren. A scolding does most good to the recipient, when put alongside some obliging act. He certainly did not take it ill, as was evident from what he gave us in return; which consisted of a liberal supply of meal, milk, and an ox. He has a large herd of cattle, and a tract of fine pasture-land on the beautiful stream Lekone. A home-feeling comes over one, even in the interior of Africa, at seeing once more cattle grazing peacefully in the meadows. The tsetse inhabits the trees which bound the pasture-land on the west; so, should the herdsman forget his duty, the cattle straying might be entirely lost. The women of this village were more numerous than the men, the result of the chief's marauding. The Batoka wife of Sima came up from the Falls, to welcome her husband back, bringing a present of the best fruits of the country. Her husband was the only one of the party who had brought a wife from Tette, namely, the girl whom he obtained from Chisaka for his feats of dancing. According to our ideas, his first wife could hardly have been pleased at seeing the second and younger one ; but she took her away home with her, while the husband remained with us. In going down to the Fall village we met several of the real Makololo. They are lighter in colour than the other tribes, being of a rich warm brown ; and they speak in a slow deliberate manner, distinctly pronouncing every word. On reaching the village opposite Kalai, we had an interview with the Makololo headman, Mashotlane : he came to the shed in which we were seated, a little boy carrying his low three-legged stool before him : on this he sat down with becoming dignity, looked round him for a few seconds, then at us, and, saluting us with "Rumela" (good morning, or hail), he gave us some boiled hippopotamus meat, took a piece himself, and then handed the rest to his attendants, who soon ate it up. He defended his forays on the ground that, when he went to collect tribute, the Batoka attacked him, and killed some of his attendants. The excuses made for their little wars are often the very same as those made by Cæsar in his 'Commentaries.' Few admit, like old Moshobotwane, that they fought because they had the power, and a fair prospect of conquering. We found here Pitsane, who had accompanied the Doctor to St. Paul de Loanda. He had been sent by Sekeletu to purchase three horses from a trading party of Griquas from Kuruman, who charged nine large tusks apiece for very wretched animals.

In the evening, when all was still, one of our men, Takelang, fired his musket, and cried out, " I am weeping for my wife : my court is desolate : I have no home ;" and then uttered a loud wail of anguish.

CHAPTER XII.

WE proceeded next morning, 9th August, 1860, to see the
Victoria Falls.   Mosi-oa-tunya is the Makololo name, and
means smoke sounding; Seongo or Chongwe, meaning the
Rainbow, or the place of the Rainbow, was the more ancient
term they bore. We embarked in canoes, belonging to Tuba
Mokoro, "smasher of canoes," an ominous name; but he alone
it seems knew the medicine which insures one against ship-
wreck in the rapids above the Falls. For some miles the
river was smooth and tranquil, and we glided pleasantly
over water clear as crystal, and past lovely islands densely
covered with a tropical vegetation. Noticeable among the
many trees were the lofty Hyphæne and Borassus palms;
the graceful wild date-palm, with its fruit in golden clusters,
and the umbrageous mokononga, of cypress form, with its
dark-green leaves and scarlet fruit. Many flowers peeped
out near the water's edge, some entirely new to us, and
others, as the convolvulus, old acquaintances.

But our attention was quickly called from the charming
islands to the dangerous rapids, down which Tuba might
unintentionally shoot us. To confess the truth, the very
ugly aspect of these roaring rapids could scarcely fail to
cause some uneasiness in the minds of new-comers. It is

only when the river is very low, as it was now, that any one durst venture to the island to which we were bound. If one went during the period of flood, and fortunately hit the island, he would be obliged to remain there till the water subsided again, if he lived so long. Both hippopotami and elephants have been known to be swept over the Falls, and of course smashed to pulp.

Before entering the race of waters, we were requested not to speak, as our talking might diminish the virtue of the medicine; and no one with such boiling eddying rapids before his eyes, would think of disobeying the orders of a " canoe-smasher." It soon became evident that there was sound sense in this request of Tuba's, although the reason assigned was not unlike that of the canoe-man from Sesheke, who begged one of our party not to whistle, because whistling made the wind come. It was the duty of the man at the bow to look out ahead for the proper course, and when he saw a rock or snag, to call out to the steersman. Tuba doubtless thought that talking on board might divert the attention of his steersman, at a time when the neglect of an order, or a slight mistake, would be sure to spill us all into the chafing river. There were places where the utmost exertions of both men had to be put forth in order to force the canoe to the only safe part of the rapid, and to prevent it from sweeping down broadside on, where in a twinkling we should have found ourselves floundering among the plotuses and cormorants, which were engaged in diving for their breakfast of small fish. At times it seemed as if nothing could save us from dashing in our headlong race against the rocks which, now that the river was low, jutted out of the water; but, just at the very nick of time, Tuba passed the word to the steersman, and then with ready pole turned the canoe a little aside, and we glided swiftly past the threatened danger. Never was canoe more admirably managed: once only did the medicine seem to have lost something of its efficacy. We were driving swiftly down, a black rock, over which the white foam flew, lay directly in our path, the pole was planted against it as readily as ever, but it slipped, just as Tuba put forth his strength to turn the bow off. We struck hard, and were half-full of water in a moment; Tuba recovered himself as speedily, shoved off the bow, and shot the canoe into a still shallow place, to bale out the water. Here we were given to understand that it was not the medicine which was at fault; *that* had lost none of its virtue; the accident was owing entirely to Tuba having started without his breakfast. Need it be said we never let Tuba go without that meal again?

We landed at the head of Garden Island, which is situated near the middle of the river and on the lip of the Falls. On reaching that lip, and peering over the giddy height, the wondrous and unique character of the magnificent cascade at once burst upon us.

It is rather a hopeless task to endeavour to convey an idea of it in words, since, as was remarked on the spot, an accomplished painter, even by a number of views, could but impart a faint impression of the glorious scene. The probable mode of its formation may perhaps help to the conception of its peculiar shape. Niagara has been formed by a wearing back of the rock over which the river falls; and, during a long course of ages, it has gradually receded, and left a broad, deep, and pretty straight trough in front. It goes on wearing back daily, and may yet discharge the lakes from which its river—the St. Lawrence—flows. But the Victoria

Falls have been formed by a crack right across the river, in the hard, black, basaltic rock which there formed the bed of the Zambesi. The lips of the crack are still quite sharp, save about three feet of the edge over which the river rolls. The walls go sheer down from the lips without any projecting crag, or symptom of stratification or dislocation. When the mighty rift occurred, no change of level took place in the two parts of the bed of the river thus rent asunder, consequently, in coming down the river to Garden Island, the water suddenly disappears, and we see the opposite side of the cleft, with grass and trees growing where once the river ran, on the same level as that part of its bed on which we sail. The first crack is, in length, a few yards more than the breadth of the Zambesi, which by measurement we found to be a little over 1860 yards, but this number we resolved to retain as indicating the year in which the Fall was for the first time carefully examined. The main stream here runs nearly north and south, and the cleft across it is nearly east and west. The depth of the rift was measured by lowering a line, to the end of which a few bullets and a foot of white cotton cloth were tied. One of us lay with his head over a projecting crag, and watched the descending calico, till, after his companions had paid out 310 feet, the weight rested on a sloping projection, probably 50 feet from the water below, the actual bottom being still further down. The white cloth now appeared the size of a crown-piece. On measuring the width of this deep cleft by sextant, it was found at Garden Island, its narrowest part, to be eighty yards, and at its broadest somewhat more. Into this chasm, of twice the depth of Niagara-fall, the river, a full mile wide, rolls with a deafening roar; and this is Mosi-oa-tunya or the Victoria Falls.

Looking from Garden Island, down to the bottom of the abyss, nearly half a mile of water, which has fallen over that portion of the Falls to our right, or west of our point of view, is seen collected in a narrow channel twenty or thirty yards wide, and flowing at exactly right angles to its previous course, to our left; while the other half, or that which fell over the eastern portion of the Falls, is seen in the left of the narrow channel below, coming towards our right. Both waters unite midway, in a fearful boiling whirlpool, and find an outlet by a crack situated at right angles to the fissure of the Falls. This outlet is about 1170 yards from the western end of the chasm, and some 600 from its eastern end; the whirlpool is at its commencement. The Zambesi, now apparently not more than twenty or thirty yards wide, rushes and surges south, through the narrow escape-channel for 130 yards; then enters a second chasm somewhat deeper, and nearly parallel with the first. Abandoning the bottom of the eastern half of this second chasm to the growth of large trees, it turns sharply off to the west, and forms a promontory, with the escape-channel at its point, of 1170 yards long, and 416 yards broad at the base. After reaching this base, the river runs abruptly round the head of another promontory, and flows away to the east, in a third chasm; then glides round a third promontory, much narrower than the rest, and away back to the west, in a fourth chasm; and we could see in the distance that it appeared to round still another promontory, and bend once more in another chasm towards the east. In this gigantic, zigzag, yet narrow trough, the rocks are all so sharply cut and angular, that the idea at once arises that the hard basaltic trap must have been riven into its present shape by a force acting from beneath, and that this probably took place, when the ancient inland seas were let off by similar fissures nearer the ocean.

The land beyond, or on the south of the Falls, retains, as already remarked, the same level as before the rent was made. It is as if the trough below Niagara were bent right and left, several times before it reached the railway bridge. The land in the supposed bends being of the same height as that above the Fall, would give standing-places, or points of view, of the same nature as that from the railway-bridge, but the nearest would be only eighty yards, instead of two miles (the distance to the bridge) from the face of the cascade. The tops of the promontories are in general flat, smooth, and studded with trees. The first with its base on the east, is at one place so narrow, that it would be dangerous to walk to its extremity. On the second, however, we found a broad rhinoceros path and a hut; but, unless the builder were a hermit, with a pet rhinoceros, we cannot conceive what beast or man ever went there for. On reaching the apex of this second eastern promontory we saw the great river, of a deep sea-green colour, now sorely compressed, gliding away, at least 400 feet below us.*

Garden Island, when the river is low, commands the best view of the Great Fall chasm, as also of the promontory op-

---

* We have twice used the word "glide" in the above description, and wish to convey the idea that the river, although so torn, tossed, and buffeted in the Fall chasm, slips round the points of the promontories with a resistless flow, unbroken save by a peculiar churning, eddying motion; this gave us the impression that the cleft must be prodigiously deep to allow all the water poured into it to pass so untumultuously away; and it may here be remarked that in the frontispiece, a sketch of which was sent to Sir Roderick Murchison from the spot in 1860, the land forming the promontories is necessarily depressed to exhibit the Falls, though it is not so in nature. The foreground of this bird's-eye view has more vegetation than actually appears; far away from the influence of the vapour, the rocks are rather bare.

posite, with its grove of large evergreen trees, and brilliant rainbows of three-quarters of a circle, two, three, and sometimes even four in number, resting on the face of the vast perpendicular rock, down which tiny streams are always running to be swept again back by the upward rushing vapour. But as, at Niagara, one has to go over to the Canadian shore to see the chief wonder—the Great Horseshoe Fall—so here we have to cross over to Moselekatse's side to the promontory of evergreens, for the best view of the principal Falls of Mosi-oa-tunya. Beginning, therefore, at the base of this promontory, and facing the Cataract, at the west end of the chasm, there is, first, a fall of thirty-six yards in breadth, and of course, as they all are, upwards of 310 feet in depth. Then Boaruka, a small island, intervenes, and next comes a great fall, with a breadth of 573 yards; a projecting rock separates this from a second grand fall of 325 yards broad; in all, upwards of 900 yards of perennial Falls. Further east stands Garden Island; then, as the river was at its lowest, came a good deal of the bare rock of its bed, with a score of narrow falls, which, at the time of flood, constitute one enormous cascade of nearly another half-mile. Near the east end of the chasm are two larger falls, but they are nothing at low water compared to those between the islands.

The whole body of water rolls clear over, quite unbroken; but, after a descent of ten or more feet, the entire mass suddenly becomes like a huge sheet of driven snow. Pieces of water leap off it in the form of comets with tails streaming behind, till the whole snowy sheet becomes myriads of rushing, leaping, aqueous comets. This peculiarity was not observed by Charles Livingstone at Niagara, and here it happens, possibly from the dryness of the atmosphere, or whatever the cause may be which makes every drop of Zambesi water appear to possess a sort of individuality. It runs off the ends of the paddles, and glides in beads along the smooth surface, like drops of quicksilver on a table. Here we see them in a conglomeration, each with a train of pure white vapour, racing down till lost in clouds of spray. A stone dropped in became less and less to the eye, and at last disappeared in the dense mist below.

Charles Livingstone had seen Niagara, and gave Mosi-oa-tunya the palm, though now at the end of a drought, and the river at its very lowest. Many feel a disappointment on first seeing the great American Falls, but Mosi-oa-tunya is so strange, it must ever cause wonder. In the amount of water, Niagara probably excels, though not during the months when the Zambesi is in flood. The vast body of water, separating in the comet-like forms described, necessarily encloses in its descent a large volume of air, which, forced into the cleft, to an unknown depth, rebounds, and rushes up loaded with vapour to form the three or even six columns, as if of steam, visible at the Batoka village Moachemba, twenty-one miles distant. On attaining a height of 200, or at most 300 feet from the level of the river above the cascade, this vapour becomes condensed into a perpetual shower of fine rain. Much of the spray, rising to the west of Garden Island, falls on the grove of evergreen trees opposite; and from their leaves, heavy drops are for ever falling, to form sundry little rills, which, in running down the steep face of rock, are blown off and turned back, or licked off their perpendicular bed, up into the column from which they have just descended.

The morning sun gilds these columns of watery smoke

s

with all the glowing colours of double or treble rainbows.
The evening sun, from a hot yellow sky, imparts a sul-
phureous hue, and gives one the impression that the yawning gulf might resemble the mouth of the bottomless pit. No
bird sits and sings on the branches of the grove of perpetual
showers, or ever builds its nest there.   We saw hornbills,
and flocks of little black weavers flying across from the
mainland, to the islands, and from the islands to the points
of the promontories and back again, but they uniformly
shunned the region of perpetual rain, occupied by the
evergreen grove. The sunshine, elsewhere in this land so
overpowering, never penetrates the deep gloom of that shade.
In the presence of the strange Mosi-oa-tunya, we can sympathize with those who, when the world was young, peopled
earth, air, and river, with beings not of mortal form. Sacred
to what deity would be this awful chasm and that dark
grove, over which hovers an ever-abiding "pillar of cloud?"

The ancient Batoka Chieftains used Kazeruka, now Garden
Island, and Boaruka, the island further west, also on the lip
of the Falls, as sacred spots for worshipping the Deity.   It
is no wonder that under the cloudy columns, and near the
brilliant rainbows, with the ceaseless roar of the cataract, with
the perpetual flow, as if pouring forth from the hand of the
Almighty, their souls should be filled with reverential awe.
It inspired wonder in the native mind throughout the interior.
Among the first questions asked by Sebituane of Mr. Oswell
and Dr. Livingstone, in 1851, was, "Have you any smoke
soundings in your country," and "what causes the smoke to
rise for ever so high out of water?"   In that year its fame
was heard 200 miles off, and it was approached within two
days; but it was seen by no European till 1855, when Dr.
Livingstone visited it on his way to the East Coast.   Being

then accompanied as far as this Fall by Sekeletu and 200
followers, his stay was necessarily short; and the two days
there were employed in observations for fixing the geographical position of the place, and turning the showers,
that at times sweep from the columns of vapour across the
island, to account, in teaching the Makololo arboriculture,
and making that garden from which the natives named
the island; so that he did not visit the opposite sides of
the cleft, nor see the wonderful course of the river beyond the Falls.   The hippopotami had destroyed the trees
which were then planted; and, though a strong stockaded
hedge was made again, and living orange-trees, cashew-
nuts, and coffee seeds, put in afresh, we fear that the perseverance of the hippopotami will overcome the obstacle of
the hedge.*   It would require a resident missionary to rear
European fruit-trees.   The period, at which the peach and
apricot come into blossom, is about the end of the dry season, and artificial irrigation is necessary.   The Batoka, the
only arboriculturists in the country, rear native fruit-trees
alone—the mosibe, the motsikiri, the boma, and others.   When
a tribe takes an interest in trees, it becomes more attached to

---

* The Victoria Falls were visited
by Sir Richard Glyn, Bart., and his
brother when on a hunting excursion
in 1863.   They visited Garden Island, and found that our fears of the
depredations of the hippopotami had
been only too well founded.   The fruit
trees had been destroyed.   Sir Richard
kindly deepened the initials "D. L.,
1855," made on a tree on the island
when the discovery took place, and
the only case in which the letters had
been cut by Dr. Livingstone in the
country.   Traders and others also
have visited the country south of the
Falls, but we have not seen any new
ground described in that quarter, nor
does any one else seem to have gone
over to the eastern side, and again
seen the chasms there.   The river
Loñkwe or Quai, said to have canoes upon it, and to join the Zambesi
between Mosi-oa-tunya and Sinamane's, might be interesting to explorers; and Moselekatse, the paramount lord of the people there, is
known to be favourable to the English.

the spot on which they are planted, and they prove one of the civilizing influences.

Before leaving the most wonderful Falls in the world, one may be excused for referring to the fact that, though they had produced a decided impression on the native mind in the interior, no intelligence of their existence ever reached the Portuguese. About 1809 two black slaves, named Pedro Baptista and Andre José, were sent from Cassange, a village three hundred miles from the West Coast, through the country of Cazembe, to Tette, nearly an equal distance from the East Coast. A lady now living at Tette, Donna Eugenia, re-members distinctly these slaves—their woolly hair dressed in the Londa fashion—arriving and remaining at Tette, till letters came from the Governor-General of Mosambique, which they successfully carried back to Cassange. On this slender fibre hangs all the Portuguese pretension to having possessed a road across Africa. Their maps show the source of the Zambesi S.S.W. of Zumbo, about where the Falls were found; and on this very questionable authority an untravelled English map-maker, with most amusing as-surance, asserts that the river above the Falls runs under the Kalahari Desert and is lost.

Where one Englishman goes, others are sure to follow. Mr. Baldwin, a gentleman from Natal, succeeded in reaching the Falls guided by his pocket-compass alone. On meeting the second subject of Her Majesty, who had ever beheld the greatest of African wonders, we found him a sort of prisoner at large. He had called on Mashotlane to ferry him over to the north side of the river, and, when nearly over, he took a bath, by jumping in and swimming ashore. "If," said Mashotlane, "he had been devoured by one of the crocodiles which abound there, the English would have blamed us for

his death.   He nearly inflicted a great injury upon us, therefore, we said, he must pay a fine."   As Mr. Baldwin had
nothing with him wherewith to pay, they were taking care
of him till he should receive beads from his wagon two days
distant.

Mashotlane's education had been received in the camp of
Sebituane, where but little regard was paid to human life.
He was not yet in his prime, and his fine open countenance
presented to us no indication of the evil influences which
unhappily, from infancy, had been at work on his mind.
The native eye was more penetrating than ours; for the
expression of our men was, "He has drunk the blood of
men—you may see it in his eyes."   He made no further
difficulty about Mr. Baldwin; but, the week after we left, he
inflicted a severe wound on the head of one of his wives with
his rhinoceros-horn club.   She, being of a good family, left
him, and we subsequently met her and another of his wives
proceeding up the country.

The ground is strewn with agates for a number of miles
above the Falls; but the fires, which burn off the grass yearly,
have injured most of those on the surface.   Our men were
delighted to hear that they do as well as flints for muskets;
and this, with the new ideas of the value of gold (*dalama*) and
malachite, that they had acquired at Tette, made them conceive that we were not altogether silly in picking up and
looking at stones.

CHAPTER XIII.

Condition of fugitives and captives in native tribes — Servitude in the interior light as compared to slavery on the coast — Molele's village — Scarcity of food — Tianyane identical with Ourebi — The Poku — Dr. Livingstone consulted on the value of horses — Mparira, village of Mokompa — Stingless bee — Take canoe for Sesheke — Sekeletu's attempt at enforcing quarantine — The Chiefs' messengers — "The argument" for learning to read — "Free pratique" — Native instructions — The cattle-post school — Sesheke old and new town — Sekeletu — Nothing like beef — "Beef with and beef without" — Visitors — Sekeletu's leprosy and its attendant evils — Disease pronounced incurable by native doctors — Taken in hand by a doctress — Handed over to Drs. Livingstone and Kirk — Improvement of patient — Description of disease — Tea and preserved fruits from Benguela — No ivory, no slave-trade — Effect of Sekeletu's orders in closing slave-market — Fashion — Horse-dealing — Peculiar style of racing — "The household cavalry" — Produce of interior in grain — No vegetables — No fruit — Mr. Baldwin, and Mr. Helmore's party — Sad breaking up of the Mission — Fever, not poison, the cause of deaths.

MARCHING up the river, we crossed the Lekone at its confluence, about eight miles above the island Kalai, and went on to a village opposite the Island Chundu. Nambowe, the headman, is one of the Matebele or Zulus, who have had to flee from the anger of Moselekatse, to take refuge with the Makololo. During our interview, his six handsome wives came and sat behind him. He had only two children. The ladies were amused with our question whether they ever quarrelled, to which the monster answered, "Oh, yes, they are always quarrelling amongst themselves." Among the coast tribes a fugitive is almost always sold, but here a man retains the same rank he held in his own tribe. The children of captives even have the same privileges as the children of their captors. The Rev. T. M. Thomas, a missionary now living with Moselekatse, finds the same system prevailing among his Zulus or Matebele.   He says that, " the African slave, brought by a foray to the tribe, enjoys, from the beginning, the privileges and name of a child, and looks upon his master and mistress in every respect as his new parents.   He is not only nearly his master's equal, but he may, with impunity, leave his master and go wherever he likes within the boundary of the kingdom : although a bondman or servant, his position, especially in Moselekatse's country, does not convey the true idea of a state of slavery ; for, by care and diligence, he may soon become a master himself, and even more rich and powerful than he who led him captive."

The practice pursued by these people, on returning from a foray, of selling the captives to each other for corn or cattle, might lead one to imagine that slavery existed in all its intensity among the native Africans ; but Mr. Thomas, observing, as we have often done, the actual working of the system, says very truly, " Neither the punctuality, quickness, thoroughness, nor amount of exertion is required by the African as by the European master.   In Europe the difficulty is want of time ; in Africa, what is to be done with it." Apart from the shocking waste of life, which takes place in these and all slave forays, their slavery is not so repulsive as it always becomes in European hands.   It is perhaps a failing in a traveller to be affected with a species of homesickness, so that the mind always turns from the conditions and circumstances of the poor abroad to the state of the lonely in our native land ; but so it is.   When we see with how much ease the very lowest class here can subsist, we cannot help remembering, with sorrow, with what difficulty our own poor can manage to live—with what timid eagerness employment is sought—how hard the battle of life; while so much of this fair earth remains unoccupied, and not put to the benevolent purpose for which it was intended by its Maker.

We spent Sunday, the 12th, at the village of Molele, a tall old Batoka, who was proud of having formerly been a great favourite with Sebituane. In coming hither we passed through patches of forest abounding in all sorts of game. The elephants' tusks, placed over graves, are now allowed to decay, and the skulls, which the former Batoka stuck on poles to ornament their villages, not being renewed, now crumble into dust. Here the famine, of which we had heard, became apparent, Molele's people being employed in digging up the *tsitla* root out of the marshes, and cutting out the soft core of the young palm-trees, for food.

The village, situated on the side of a wooded ridge, commands an extensive view of a great expanse of meadow and marsh lying along the bank of the river. On these holmes herds of buffaloes and waterbucks daily graze in security, as they have in the reedy marshes a refuge into which they can run on the approach of danger. The pretty little tianyane or ourebi is abundant further on,* and herds

---

* From being entirely unknown in the Bechuana country south of this, it was thought to be a new antelope, and is so mentioned by Dr. Livingstone; but the description of the appearance, gait, alarm-call, and habits (given by another African traveller, Mr. W. F. Webb) of the ourebi, as found in Natal, leaves no doubt but that the two animals are identical. Having made this mistake himself, Dr. Livingstone is quite disposed to be lenient to others; but would respectfully suggest a doubt, whether it be advisable to multiply names when there is no more variation than a bend in the shape of the horns, or a slight difference in the colour of the hair. An eland for instance, described, from specimens shot on these very plains in 1853, as retaining in maturity the stripes which appear on the young of all elands in the Kalahari Desert, ten years later has been rediscovered as *djikijunka*, named from specimens seen in West Africa. This has been the case also with the nakong or nzoe, and the reason assigned in this case was its being "faintly spotted." A young

of blue weldebeests or brindled gnus (*Katoblepas Gorgon*) amused us by their fantastic capers. They present a much more ferocious aspect than the lion himself, but are quite timid. We never could by waving a red handkerchief, according to the prescription, induce them to venture near to us. It may therefore be, that the red colour excites their fury only when wounded or hotly pursued. Herds of lechee or lechwé now enliven the meadows; and they and their younger brother, the graceful poku, smaller, and of a rounder contour, race together towards the grassy fens. We ventured to call the poku after the late Major Vardon, a noble-hearted African traveller; but fully anticipate that some aspiring Nimrod will prefer that his own name should go down to posterity on the back of this buck.

Midway between Tabacheu and the Great Falls the streams begin to flow westward. On the other side they flow east. Large round masses of granite, somewhat like old castles, tower aloft about the Kalomo. The country is an elevated plateau, and our men knew and named the different plains as we passed them by.

On the 13th we met a party from Sekeletu, who was now at Sesheke. Our approach had been reported, and they had been sent to ask the Doctor what the price of a horse ought to be; and what he said, that they were to give and no more. In reply they were told that by their having given nine large tusks for one horse before the Doctor came, the Griquas would naturally imagine that the price was already settled. It was exceedingly amusing to witness the exact imitation they gave of the swagger of a certain white with whom they

---

waterbuck's head has also been brought from West Africa and figured as a new species; and the common bushbuck was called *A. Roualeyni*, though well known and described before any of us were born.

had been dealing, and who had, as they had perceived, evidently wished to assume an air of indifference. Holding up the head and scratching the beard it was hinted might indicate not indifference, but vermin. It is well that we do not always know what they say about us. The remarks are often not quite complimentary, and resemble closely what certain white travellers say about the blacks.

We made our camp in the afternoon abreast of the large island called Mparira, opposite the mouth of the Chobe. Francolins, quails, and guinea-fowls, as well as larger game, were abundant. The Makololo headman, Mokompa, brought us a liberal present; and, in the usual way, which is considered politeness, regretted he had no milk, as his cows were all dry. We got some honey here from the very small stingless bee, called, by the Batoka, moandi, and by others, the kokomatsane. This honey is slightly acid, and has an aromatic flavour. The bees are easily known from their habit of buzzing about the eyes, and tickling the skin by sucking it as common flies do. The hive has a tube of wax like a quill, for its entrance, and is usually in the hollows of trees.

Mokompa feared that the tribe was breaking up, and lamented the condition into which they had fallen in consequence of Sekeletu's leprosy; he did not know what was to become of them. He sent two canoes to take us up to Sesheke; his best canoe had taken ivory up to the Chief, to purchase goods of some native traders from Benguela. Above the Falls the paddlers always stand in the canoes, using long paddles, ten feet in length, and changing from side to side without losing the stroke.

Mochokotsa, a messenger from Sekeletu, met us on the 17th, with another request for the Doctor to take ivory and purchase a horse. He again declined to interfere. None were to come up to Sekeletu but the Doctor; and all the men who had had

smallpox at Tette, three years ago, were to go back to
Moshobotwane, and he would sprinkle medicine over them,
to drive away the infection, and prevent it spreading in
the tribe. Mochokotsa was told to say to Sekeletu that the
disease was known of old to white men, and we even knew
the medicine to prevent it; and, were there any danger now,
we should be the first to warn him of it. Why did not he go
himself to have Moshobotane sprinkle medicine to drive away
his leprosy. We were not afraid of his disease, nor of the
fever that had killed the teachers and many Makololo at
Linyanti. As this attempt at quarantine was evidently
the suggestion of native doctors to increase their own importance, we added that we had no food, and would hunt
next day for game, and the day after; and, should we be
still ordered purification by their medicine, we should then
return to our own country.

The message was not all of our dictation, our companions
interlarded it with their own indignant protests, and said some
strong things in the Tette dialect about these " doctor things"
keeping them back from seeing their father; when to their
surprise Mochokotsa told them he knew every word they
were saying, as he was of the tribe Bazizulu, and defied
them to deceive him by any dialect, either of the Mashona
on the east, or of the Mambari on the west. Mochokotsa
then repeated our message twice, to be sure that he had it
every word, and went back again. These Chiefs' messengers have most retentive memories; they carry messages of
considerable length great distances, and deliver them almost
word for word. Two or three usually go together, and when
on the way the message is rehearsed every night, in order
that the exact words may be kept to. One of the native
objections to learning to write is, that these men answer the
purpose of transmitting intelligence to a distance as well

as a letter would; and, if a person wishes to communicate
with any one in the town, the best way to do so is either to
go to or send for him. And as for corresponding with friends
very far off, that is all very well for white people, but the
blacks have no friends to whom to write. The only effective
argument for their learning to read is, that it is their duty
to know the revelation from their Father in Heaven, as it
stands in the Book.

Our messenger returned on the evening of the following
day with "You speak truly," says Sekeletu, "the disease is
old, come on at once, do not sleep in the path; for I am
greatly desirous (*tlologelecoe*) to see the Doctor."

After Mochokotsa left us, we met some of Mokompa's men
bringing back the ivory, as horses were preferred to the West-
Coast goods. They were the bearers of instructions to Mokompa, and as these instructions illustrate the government
of people who have learned scarcely anything from Europeans, they are inserted, though otherwise of no importance.
Mashotlane had not behaved so civilly to Mr. Baldwin, as
Sekeletu had ordered him to do to all Englishmen. He
had been very uncivil to the messengers sent by Moselekatse with letters from Mr. Moffat, treated them as spies,
and would not land to take the bag until they moved off.
On our speaking to him about this, he justified his conduct
on the plea that he was set at the Falls for the very purpose of watching these, their natural enemies; and how was
he to know that they had been sent by Mr. Moffat? Our
men thereupon reported at head-quarters that Mashotlane
had cursed the Doctor. The instructions to Mokompa,
from Sekeletu, were to "go and tell Mashotlane that he
had offended greatly. He had not cursed Monare (Dr.
Livingstone) but Sebituane, as Monare was now in the
place of Sebituane, and he reverenced him as he had done

his father. Any fine taken from Mr. Baldwin was to be
returned at once, as he was not a Boer but an Englishman.
Sekeletu was very angry, and Mokompa must not conceal the
message."

On finding afterwards that Mashotlane's conduct had been
most outrageous to the Batoka, Sekeletu sent for him to come
to Sesheke, in order that he might have him more under his
own eye; but Mashotlane, fearing that this meant the punishment of death, sent a polite answer, alleging that he was ill
and unable to travel. Sekeletu tried again to remove Mashotlane from the Falls, but without success. In theory the Chief
is absolute and quite despotic; in practice his authority is
limited, and he cannot, without occasionally putting refrac-
tory headmen to death, force his subordinates to do his will.

Except the small rapids by Mparira island, near the mouth
of the Chobe, the rest of the way to Sesheke by water, is
smooth. Herds of cattle of two or three varieties graze on
the islands in the river: the Batoka possessed a very small
breed of beautiful shape, and remarkably tame, and many
may still be seen; a larger kind, many of which have horns
pendent, and loose at the roots; and a still larger sort, with
horns of extraordinary dimensions, apparently a burden for
the beast to carry. This breed was found in abundance
at Lake Ngami. We stopped at noon at one of the
cattle posts of Mokompa, and had a refreshing drink of
milk. Men of his standing have usually several herds
placed at different spots, and the owner visits each in
turn, while his head-quarters are at his village. His son,
a boy of ten, had charge of the establishment during
his father's absence. According to Makololo ideas, the
cattle-post is the proper school in which sons should be
brought up. Here they receive the right sort of education—
the knowledge of pasture and how to manage cattle.

Strong easterly winds blow daily from noon till midnight, and continue till the October or November rains set in. Whirlwinds, raising huge pillars of smoke from burning grass and weeds, are common in the forenoon. We were nearly caught in an immense one. It crossed about twenty yards in front of us, the wind apparently rushing into it from all points of the compass. Whirling round and round in great eddies, it swept up hundreds of feet into the air a continuous dense dark cloud of the black pulverized soil, mixed with dried grass, off the plain. Herds of the new antelopes, lechwé, and poku, with the kokong, or gnus, and zebras stood gazing at us as we passed. The mirage lifted them at times halfway to the clouds, and twisted them and the clumps of palms into strange unearthly forms. The extensive and rich level plains by the banks, along the sides of which we paddled, would support a vast population, and might be easily irrigated from the Zambesi. If watered, they would yield crops all the year round, and never suffer loss by drought. The hippopotamus is killed here with long lance-like spears. We saw two men, in a light canoe, stealing noiselessly down on one of these animals thought to be asleep; but it was on the alert, and they had quickly to retreat. Comparatively few of these animals now remain between Sesheke and the Falls, and they are uncommonly wary, as it is certain death for one to be caught napping in the daytime.

On the 18th we entered Sesheke. The old town, now in ruins, stands on the left bank of the river. The people have built another on the same side, a quarter of a mile higher up, since their headman Moriantsiane was put to death for bewitching the Chief with leprosy. Sekeletu was on the right bank, near a number of temporary huts. A man hailed us from the Chief's quarters, and requested us to rest under the old Kotla, or public meeting-place tree. A young Makololo, with the large thighs which Zulus and most of this tribe have, crossed over to receive orders from the Chief, who had not shown himself to the people since he was affected with leprosy. On returning he ran for Mokele, the headman of the new town, who, after going over to Seke-letu, came back and conducted us to a small but good hut, and afterwards brought us a fine fat ox, as a present from the Chief. "This is a time of hunger," he said, "and we have no meat, but we expect some soon from the Barotse Valley." We were entirely out of food when we reached Sesheke. Never was better meat than that of the ox Seke-letu sent, and infinitely above the flesh of all kinds of game is classic beef! We have partaken of the flesh of all the eatable animals in Africa, except the crocodile, and often under circumstances when a keen appetite might be sup-posed to give a bias to the judgment in favour of the game; yet all that could be said of the best was, it is nearly as good as the flesh of oxen. Possibly some ani-mals, still untamed, might be found to turn to good account land covered with pasture such as heather or brackens, other-wise useless for cattle; but we say, Let the "Acclimatization Society" increase and multiply the number of beeves, and it will please the taste, and benefit humanity, more than it possibly could by the introduction of every wild animal from the elephant down to the crocodile. It must be confessed, however, that to the uninitiated it is rather awkward to sit down to a meal of nothing but beef, however excellent. On taking a mouthful, hands and eyes turn instinctively in search of something in the form of bread, potatoes, or vegetables to accompany it, and there is an unpleasant sensation of wanting what the Scotch know by the word 'kitchen' (οψον). We made the fat *kitchen* the lean. The Makololo usually devour all the fat first, that being considered the best, and afterwards eat the lean, and, last of all, the porridge or bread, if they have any. The people who, like them, live much on milk and meat, can bear fatigue and privation much better than those whose sustenance is chiefly grain and pulse. When the Makololo go on a foray, as they sometimes do, a month distant, many of the subject tribes who accompany them, being grain eaters, perish from sheer fatigue, while the beef eaters scorn the idea of even being tired.

A constant stream of visitors rolled in on us the day after our arrival. Several of them, who had suffered affliction during the Doctor's absence, seemed to be much affected on seeing him again. All were in low spirits. A severe drought had cut off the crops, and destroyed the pasture of Linyanti, and the people were scattered over the country in search of wild fruits, and the hospitality of those whose ground-nuts (*Arachis hypogœa*) had not failed. Sekeletu's leprosy brought troops of evils in its train. Believing himself bewitched, he had suspected a number of his chief men, and had put some, with their families, to death; others had fled to distant tribes, and were living in exile. The Chief had shut himself up, and allowed no one to come into his presence but his uncle Mamire. Ponwane, who had been as "head and eyes" to him, had just died; evidence, he thought, of the potent spells of those who hated all who loved the Chief. The country was suffering grievously, and Sebituane's grand empire was crumbling to pieces. A large body of young Barotse had revolted and fled to the north; killing a man by the way, in order to put a blood-feud between Masiko, the Chief to whom they were going, and Sekeletu. The Batoka under Sinamane, and Muemba, were independent, and Mashotlane at the Falls was setting Sekeletu's authority virtually at defiance. Sebituane's wise policy in treating the conquered tribes on equal terms with his own Makololo, as all children of the Chief, and equally eligible to the highest honours, had been abandoned by his son, who married none but Makololo women, and appointed to office none but Makololo men. He had become unpopular among the black tribes, conquered by the spear but more effectually won by the subsequent wise and just government of his father.

Strange rumours were afloat respecting the unseen Sekeletu; his fingers were said to have grown like eagle's claws, and his face so frightfully distorted that no one could recognise him. Some had begun to hint that he might not really be the son of the great Sebituane, the founder of the nation, strong in battle, and wise in the affairs of state. "In the days of the Great Lion" (Sebituane), said his only sister, Moriantsiane's widow, whose husband Sekeletu had killed, " we had Chiefs and little Chiefs and elders to carry on the government, and the great Chief, Sebituane, knew them all, and everything they did, and the whole country was wisely ruled; but now Sekeletu knows nothing of what his underlings do, and they care not for him, and the Makololo power is fast passing away."*

The native doctors had given the case of Sekeletu up.

---

* In 1865, four years after these forebodings were penned, we received intelligence that they had all come to pass. Sekeletu died in the beginning of 1864—a civil war broke out about the succession to the chieftainship ; a large body of those opposed to the late Chief's uncle, Impololo, being regent, departed with their cattle to Lake Ngami ; an insurrection by the black tribes followed; Impololo was slain, and the kingdom, of which, under an able sagacious mission, a vast deal might have been made, has suffered the usual fate of African conquests. That fate we deeply deplore ; for, whatever other faults the Makololo might justly be charged with, they did not belong to the class who buy and sell each other, and the tribes who have succeeded them do.

T

They could not cure him, and pronounced the disease incurable. An old doctress from the Manyeti tribe had come to see what she could do for him, and on her skill he now hung his last hopes. She allowed no one to see him, except his mother and uncle, making entire seclusion from society an essential condition of the much longed-for cure. He sent, notwithstanding, for the Doctor; and on the following day we all three were permitted to see him. He was sitting in a covered wagon, which was enclosed by a high wall of close-set reeds; his face was only slightly disfigured by the thickening of the skin in parts, where the leprosy had passed over it; and the only peculiarity about his hands was the extreme length of his finger-nails, which, however, was nothing very much out of the way, as all the Makololo gentlemen wear them uncommonly long. He has the quiet, unassuming manners of his father, Sebituane, speaks distinctly, in a low pleasant voice, and appears to be a sensible man, except perhaps on the subject of his having been bewitched; and in this, when alluded to, he exhibits as firm a belief as if it were his monomania. "Moriantsiane, my aunt's husband, tried the bewitching medicine first on his wife, and she is leprous, and so is her head-servant; then, seeing that it succeeded, he gave me a stronger dose in the cooked flesh of a goat, and I have had the disease ever since. They have lately killed Ponwane, and, as you see, are now killing me." Ponwane had died of fever a short time previously. Sekeletu asked us for medicine and medical attendance, but we did not like to take the case out of the hands of the female physician already employed, it being bad policy to appear to undervalue any of the profession; and she, being anxious to go on with her remedies, said "She had not given him up yet, but would try for another month; if he was not cured by that time, then she would hand him over to the white doctors." But we intended to leave the country before a month was up; so Mamire, with others, induced the old lady to suspend her treatment for a little. She remained, as the doctors stipulated, in the Chief's establishment, and on full pay.

Sekeletu was told plainly that the disease was unknown in our country, and was thought exceedingly obstinate of cure; that we did not believe in his being bewitched, and we were willing to do all we could to help him. This was a case for disinterested benevolence; no pay was expected, but considerable risk incurred; yet we could not decline it, as we had the trading in horses. Having, however, none of the medicines usually employed in skin-diseases with us, we tried the local application of lunar caustic, and hydriodate of potash internally; and with such gratifying results, that Mamire wished the patient to be smeared all over with a solution of lunar caustic, which he believed to be of the same nature as the blistering fluid formerly applied to his own knee by Mr. Oswell. *Its* power he considered irresistible, and he would fain have had anything like it tried on Sekeletu.

The disease begins with slight discoloration of the surface, and at first affects only the cuticle, the patches spreading in the manner, and with somewhat of the appearance, of lichens, as if it were a fungus; small vesicles rise at the outer edges of the patches, and a discharge from the vesicles forms scabs. The true skin next thickens and rises in nodules, on the forehead, nose, and ears; and, when the disease is far advanced, foul fissures appear on the toes and fingers; these eventually drop off, and sometimes the deformed patient recovers. The natives believe it to be hereditary, and non-contagious; but, while working with this case, something very like it was transplanted to the hands of Drs. Kirk and Livingstone, and was cured only by the liberal use of the caustic. The Chief's health and spirits became better, as the skin became thinner, and the deformity of face disappeared. The aged doctress, naturally wishing to obtain some credit for the improvement, began secretly to superadd her remedies, which consisted of scraping the diseased skin, and rubbing it with an astringent bark in powder. She desisted on receiving a hint from Mamire, that perhaps the medicine of the white doctors and the medicine of the black doctors might not work well together.

It was a time of great scarcity and hunger, but Sekeletu treated us hospitably, preparing tea for us at every visit we paid him. With the tea we had excellent American biscuit and preserved fruits, which had been brought to him all the way from Benguela. The fruits he most relished were those preserved in their own juices; plums, apples, pears, strawberries, and peaches, which we have seen only among Portuguese and Spaniards. It made us anxious to plant the fruit-tree seeds we had brought, and all were pleased with the idea of having these same fruits in their own country.

Mokele, the headman of Sesheke, and Sebituane's sister, Manchunyane, were ordered to provide us with food, as Sekeletu's wives, to whom this duty properly belonged, were at Linyanti. We found a black trader from the West Coast, and some Griqua traders from the South, both in search of ivory. Ivory is dear at Sesheke; but cheaper in the Batoka country, from Sinamane's to the Kafue, than anywhere else. The trader from Benguela took orders for goods for his next year's trip, and offered to bring tea, coffee, and sugar at cent. per cent. prices. As, in consequence of a hint formerly given, the Makololo had secured all the ivory in the Batoka country to the east, by purchasing it with hoes, the Benguela traders found it unprofitable to go thither for slaves. They assured us that without ivory the trade in slaves did not pay. In this way, and by the orders of Sekeletu, an extensive slave-mart was closed. These orders were never infringed except secretly. We discovered only two or three cases of their infraction.

Fashion is as despotic in Sesheke and Linyanti as in London and Paris. The ladies will not wear beads which are out of fashion, however pretty they may be. The Chief is a great horse-fancier, and has invested pretty largely in horse-flesh; but he has been very unlucky, nearly all his horses having died soon after being purchased. A party was sent last year to Benguela with ivory to purchase five horses, said to have been imported from Lisbon; all the animals died on the road, and the grieved drivers brought the five melancholy tails, and laid them before the Chief. " A native Portuguese at Bihé, one of the sleeping-stations, bewitched them; they saw him look at the horses and touch them, and were sure that he bewitched them then, for they died soon after!" The universal belief in witchcraft, of which we ourselves have but recently got rid, is a great barrier to the progress of civilization. Two horses left by the Doctor in 1853 had lived, in spite of hard usage and perpetual hunting; this was, in the native opinion, because he loved the Makololo; while others, from whom they purchased horses, hated them and bewitched their horses. The treatment the poor beasts received could scarcely fail to prove fatal. A jolly set of young men, the Chief's bodyguard, had a rare sort of horse-racing; one mounted with neither saddle, bit, nor bridle, and, spreading out both arms, dashed

off at full speed. When he tumbled off, to the great amusement of the by-standers, the servants caught the horse and
rode off anywhere, leaving the fallen rider to return, rubbing
his bruises. The poor horse was kept at this work till completely exhausted, each of the guards being anxious to show
that he could keep on longer than the others. This racing,
and want of corn and care, would soon knock up any steeds
they may obtain. The Doctor, when in Angola, happening
to ride the horse of a gentleman at Pungo Andongo, remarked to his companions, "This would do for Sekeletu."
A party had been sent over a thousand miles to purchase
it; but it was now so altered as not to be recognisable.
They had no grain at the time we were there, and but a
little poor dry grass.

The native produce cultivated in this, the centre of the
continent, consists of mapira, or mabele (*holcus sorghum*),
lobelebele or meshwera (*pennisetum*), millet, maize, ground-
nuts (*Arachis hypogæa*), underground beans (*voandzeia*),
cucumbers, melons, pumpkins, mchae, or sweet-reed (*holcus
saccharatum*), sweet potatoes, tobacco, cotton, and Indian
hemp or Bang (*Cannabis sativa*); but wheat, rice, and yams
they have never seen. Sugar-cane, bananas, and cassava
grow in the Barotse valley. They have no garden vegetables, nor any of the fruits found nearer the sea, such as
mangoes and oranges, which have been introduced into
Africa from other countries.

We had ascertained at the Falls the sad fate of the
Missionaries of the London Society. Our friend from Natal,
Mr. Baldwin, had found them at a well in the desert suffering
from hunger; they had no horses, without which game there
cannot easily be procured. They had failed to kill the
rhinoceroses which came to the water at night; Mr. Bald-

win kindly shot a couple of animals for them; but was apprehensive when he left them, that they would hardly live to see the Makololo country.   They did reach Linyanti, however, though in that exhausted state on which the fever of the country is sure to fasten.   The severe drought of that year had dried up the great marshes around the village, and rendered fever more than usually virulent.   Aware, from Dr. Livingstone's description, of the extreme unhealthiness of the place, Mr. Helmore, who seems soon to have gained the people's confidence, told the Chief that he could not remain in that locality, but wished to go on to a higher and more healthy part, north-east of the Falls.   Sekeletu said that he offered to take him to Sesheke to see if he liked that better than Linyanti.   "You will take me also," said Mr. Helmore, "to see Mosi-oa-tunya," the picture of which, in 'Missionary Travels,' was readily recognised; but, while they were getting ready for the journey, the wagon-drivers were seized with fever; Mrs. Helmore was the first white person who fell a victim to the fatal malady.   The devoted missionary then told the people that, although his wife had died, he did not mean to leave them, but would remain and do his duty.   Notwithstanding the hunger, toil, and exhaustion, consequent on the long journey through the desert, and this heavy affliction at Linyanti, the good man, already knowing the native language, at once commenced the work of preaching the Gospel.   We heard some young men at Sesheke sing the hymns he had taught them.   All liked and spoke kindly of him; and his death was generally regretted.   It is probable that he would soon have exerted a powerful and happy influence over the tribe; but in a month he was cut down by fever.   Our information was derived entirely from the natives of the different tribes, which now form the Makololo. They are generally truthful, unless they have some self-interest at stake; and they cannot be made to combine to propagate any downright falsehood. Taking their statements as probably true, the whole party consisted of twenty-two persons, of whom nine were Europeans, and thirteen people of colour; of these five Europeans and four natives perished by fever in less than three months. The missionary associate of Helmore was then left in a somewhat trying position. Four out of the nine Europeans had succumbed to the disease, and his own wife was lying ill, and soon to be the fifth victim. He had been but a short time in Africa, his knowledge of the native language was of course limited, his influence small, and he had no experience: accordingly he took the wise course of leaving the country; his wife died before he reached the healthy desert. The native servants from the south, who had never seen the fever in their own country, thought that the party had been poisoned by the Makololo; but, although they are heathens, and have little regard for human life, they are not quite so bad as that. The spear, and not poison, is their weapon. There is no occasion for suspecting other poison than malaria, that being more than enough. We have witnessed all the symptoms of this poison scores of times, and, from the survivors' description, believe the deaths to have been caused by severe African fever, and nothing else. We much regretted that, though we were on the same river lower down, we were not aware of their being at Linyanti till too late to render the medical aid they so much needed. It is undoubtedly advisable that every Mission should have a medical man as an essential part of its staff.

CHAPTER XIV.

SEKELETU was well pleased with the various articles we brought for him, and inquired, if a ship could not bring his sugar-mill and the other goods we had been obliged to leave behind at Tette. On hearing that there was a possibility of a powerful steamer ascending as far as Sinamane's, but never above the Grand Victoria Falls, he asked, with charming simplicity, if a cannon could not blow away the Falls, so as to allow the vessel to come up to Sesheke.

To save the tribe from breaking up, by the continual loss of real Makololo, it ought at once to remove to the healthy Batoka highlands, near the Kafue. Fully aware of this, Sekeletu remarked that all his people, save two, were convinced, that if they remained in the lowlands, a few years would suffice to cut off all the real Makololo; they came originally from the healthy South, near the confluence of the Likwa and Namagari, where fever is almost unknown, and its ravages had been as frightful among them here, as amongst Europeans on the Coast. Sebituane's sister described its first appearance among the tribe, after their settling in the Barotse Valley on the Zambesi. Many of them were seized with a shivering sickness, as if from excessive cold: they had never seen the like before. They made great fires, and laid the shivering wretches down before them; but, pile on wood as they might, they could not raise heat enough to drive the cold out of the bodies of the sufferers, and they shivered on till they died. But, though all preferred the highlands, they were afraid to go there, lest the Matebele should come and rob them of their much-loved cattle. Sebituane, with all his veterans, could not withstand that enemy; and how could they be resisted, now that most of the brave warriors were dead? The young men would break, and run away the moment they saw the terrible Matebele; being as much afraid of them, as the black conquered tribes are of the Makololo. "But if the Doctor and his wife," said the Chief and counsellors, "would come and live with us, we would remove to the highlands at once, as Moselekatse would not attack a place where the daughter of his friend, Moffat, was living."

The Makololo are by far the most intelligent and enterprising of the tribes we have met. None but brave and daring men remained long with Sebituane, his stern discipline soon eradicated cowardice from his army. Death was the inevitable doom of the coward. If the Chief saw a man running away from the fight, he rushed after him with amazing speed, and cut him down; or waited till he

returned to the town, and then summoned the deserter
into his presence. "You did not wish to die on the field,
you wished to die at home, did you? you shall have your
wish!" and he was instantly led off and executed. The
present race of young men are inferior in most respects to
their fathers. The old Makololo had many manly virtues;
they were truthful, and never stole, excepting in what they
considered the honourable way of lifting cattle in fair fight.
But this can hardly be said of their sons; who, having
been brought up among the subjected tribes, have acquired
some of the vices peculiar to a menial and degraded race. A
few of the old Makololo cautioned us not to leave any of
our property exposed, as the blacks were great thieves; and
some of our own men advised us to be on our guard, as the
Makololo also would steal. A very few trifling articles were
stolen by a young Makololo; and he, on being spoken to on
the subject, showed great ingenuity in excusing himself, by a
plausible and untruthful story. The Makololo of old were hard
workers, and did not consider labour as beneath them; but
their sons never work, regarding it as fit only for the
Mashona and Makalaka servants. Sebituane, seeing that
the rival tribes had the advantage over his, in knowing how
to manage canoes, had his warriors taught to navigate;
and his own son, with his companions, paddled the Chief's
canoe. All the dishes, baskets, stools, and canoes, are
made by the black tribes called Manyeti and Matlotlora.
The houses are built by the women and servants. The Makololo women are vastly superior to any we have yet seen.
They are of a light warm brown complexion, have pleasant
countenances, and are remarkably quick of apprehension.
They dress neatly, wearing a kilt and mantle, and have
many ornaments. Sebituane's sister, the head lady of

Sesheke, wore eighteen solid brass rings, as thick as one's finger, on each leg, and three of copper under each knee; nineteen brass rings on her left arm, and eight of brass and copper on her right, also a large ivory ring above each elbow. She had a pretty bead necklace, and a bead sash encircled her waist. The weight of the bright brass rings round her legs impeded her walking, and chafed her ankles; but, as it was the fashion, she did not mind the inconvenience, and guarded against the pain, by putting soft rag round the lower rings.

The practice of polygamy, though intended to increase, tends to diminish the tribe. The wealthy old men, who have plenty of cattle, marry all the pretty young girls. An ugly but rich old fellow, who was so blind that a servant had to lead him along the path, had two of the very handsomest young wives in the town; one of them, the daughter of Mokele, being at least half-a-century younger than himself, was asked, "Do you like him?" "No," she replied; "I hate him, he is so disagreeable." The young men of the tribe, who happen to have no cattle, must get on without a wife, or be content with one who has few personal attractions. This state of affairs probably leads to a good deal of immorality, and children are few. By pointed inquiries, and laying oneself out for that kind of knowledge, one might be able to say much more; but if one behaves as he must do among the civilized, and abstains from asking questions, no improper hints even will be given by any of the native women we have met.

Polygamy, the sign of low civilization, and the source of many evils, is common, and, oddly enough, approved of even by the women. On hearing that a man in England could marry but one wife, several ladies exclaimed that they would

not like to live in such a country : they could not imagine
how English ladies could relish our custom ; for, in their
way of thinking, every man of respectability should have a
number of wives, as a proof of his wealth. Similar ideas
prevail all down the Zambesi. No man is respected by his
neighbour who has not several wives. The reason for this is,
doubtless, because, having the produce of each wife's garden,
he is wealthy in proportion to their number.

Wives are not bought and sold among the Makololo,
though the marriage looks like a bargain. The husband,
in proportion to his wealth, hands over to the father-in-
law a certain number of cows, not as purchase-money for
the bride, but to purchase the right to retain in his own
family the children she may have ; otherwise the children
would belong to the family of the wife's father. A man may
have perfect control over his wife without this payment, but
not of the children ; for, as the parents make a sacrifice of a
portion of the family circle in parting with their daughter,
the husband must sacrifice some of his property, to heal, as
it were, that breach. It is not absolute separation, for, when
a wife dies, the husband gives an ox again, to cause entire
severance, or make her family " give her up." The Makololo ladies have soft, small, delicate hands and feet; their
foreheads are well shaped and of good size; the nose not
disagreeably flat, though the *alæ* are full; the mouth,
chin, teeth, eyes, and general form are beautiful, and, contrasted with the West-Coast negro, quite ladylike. Having
maidservants to wait on them and perform the principal
part of the household work, abundance of leisure time is
left them, and they are sometimes at a loss to know what to
do with it. Unlike their fairer and more fortunate sisters
in Europe, they have neither sewing nor other needle-

work, nor pianoforte practice, to occupy their fingers, nor reading to improve their minds; few have children to attend to, and time does hang rather heavily on their hands. The men wickedly aver that their two great amusements, or modes for killing time, are sipping beer, and secretly smoking bang, or Indian hemp, here known as matokwane. Although the men indulge pretty freely in smoking it, they do not like their wives to follow their example, and many of the " monsters" prohibit it. Nevertheless, some women do smoke it secretly, and the practice causes a disease known by a minute eruption on the skin, quite incurable unless the habit be abandoned. The Chief himself is a slave to this deleterious habit, and could hardly be induced to give it up, even during the short time he was under medical treatment. We had ample opportunities for observing the effects of this matokwane smoking on our men. It makes them feel very strong in body, but it produces exactly the opposite effect upon the mind. Two of our finest young men became inveterate smokers, and partially idiotic. The performances of a group of matokwane smokers are somewhat grotesque: they are provided with a calabash of pure water, a split bamboo, five feet long, and the great pipe, which has a large calabash or kudu's horn chamber to contain the water, through which the smoke is drawn, Narghillé fashion, on its way to the mouth. Each smoker takes a few whiffs, the last being an extra long one, and hands the pipe to his neighbour. He seems to swallow the fumes; for, striving against the convulsive action of the muscles of chest and throat, he takes a mouthful of water from the calabash, waits a few seconds, and then pours water and smoke from his mouth down the groove of the bamboo. The smoke causes violent coughing in all, and in some a species of frenzy,

which passes away in a rapid stream of unmeaning words, or
short sentences, as, " the green grass grows," " the fat cattle
thrive," " the fish swim." No one in the group pays the
slightest attention to the vehement eloquence, or the sage or
silly utterance of the oracle, who stops abruptly, and, the
instant common sense returns, looks rather foolish.

Our visit to Sesheke broke in upon the monotony of
their daily life, and we had crowds of visitors both men
and women; especially at meal-times, for then they had
the double attraction, of seeing white men eat, and of eating with them. The men made an odd use of the spoon
in supping porridge and milk, employing it to convey the
food to the palm of the left hand, which passed it on to
the mouth. We shocked the over-refined sensibilities of
the ladies, by eating butter on our bread. " Look at them,
look at them, they are actually eating *raw* butter, ugh !
how nasty !" or pitying us, a goodwife would say, " Hand
it here to be melted, and then you can dip your bread
into it decently." They were as much disgusted as we
should be by seeing an Esquimaux eating raw whale's blub-
ber. In their opinion butter is not fit to be eaten until it
is cooked or melted. The principal use they make of it is
to anoint the body, and it keeps the skin smooth and glossy.
Men and women begged hard for such things as they
fancied, and were not at all displeased when refused : they
probably thought there was no harm in asking; it did not
hurt us, and cost their glib tongues no effort. Mamire
asked for a black frock-coat, because he admired the colour !
When told he might have it for a nice new kaross of young
lechwés' skins, he smiled, and asked no more ; a joke usually
stopped the begging.

The Chief receives the hump and ribs of every ox slaught-

ered by his people, and tribute of corn, beer, honey, wild
fruits, hoes, paddles, and canoes, from the Barotse, Manyeti,
Matlotlora, and other subject tribes. The principal revenue,
however, is derived from ivory. All the ivory of the country,
in theory, belongs to the Chief, and the tusks of every
elephant killed are placed at his disposal. This game-law
at first sight seems more stringent than that of the Portuguese, and of the tribes adjacent to them, where only one tusk
belongs to Government, and the hunter retains the other.
But here the Chief is expected to be generous, and, as a
father among his children, to share the proceeds of the ivory
with his people. They say, " Children require the guidance
of their fathers, so as not to be cheated by foreigners." This
reconciles them to the law. The upper classes, too, receive
the lion's share of the profits from the elephant-hunt without
undergoing much of the toil and danger; and the subject
tribes get the flesh, which is all they ever had, and no one
appears to have any wish to change the established custom.
Our own men, however, had often discussed the rights of
labour during their travels; and, having always been paid by
us for their work, had acquired certain new ideas, which
rather jostled against this old law. They thought it unjust
to be compelled to give up both tusks to the Chief: bad as
the Portuguese were, they were not so oppressive as that;
they allowed the hunter one of the tusks; Sekeletu's law was
wrong; they wished he would repeal it. This usage doubtless
preserves the elephants, though that is not the object in view.
Pitsane shot a few on his return from Angola, and then gave
up hunting altogether.

Moselekatse, too, claims all the ivory in his country, and
allows no stranger even to hunt the elephant. A gentleman
from Natal, ignorant of this prohibition, went with the inten-

tion of shooting these animals, but was soon taken up and carried before the Chief. He was kept a prisoner at large for three months, and allowed to hunt the buffalo, giraffe, rhinoceros, and antelope as much as he pleased; but the moment he began to follow the tracks of the elephant, his attendants, or keepers, turned his horse's head in the opposite direction.

The Makololo man, Seroke, who had recently returned from Benguela, with the tails of the poor bewitched horses, called on us with some of his companions soon after our arrival. They had found out that all the Doctor had told them about the land being surrounded by the ocean was true. They had seen the sea, and the wonders of the sea-shore, and ships, just as the Book had said: travellers alone knew anything, while those who knew not the Book, and remained at home, were mere children in knowledge. The merchants of Benguela had treated them kindly; and, to encourage trade with the Makololo, had given to each one a liberal present of clothing. Before coming to visit us they put on all these new clothes, and were certainly better dressed than we were ourselves. They wore shirts, well washed and starched, coats, and trousers, white socks and patent-leather boots, a red Kilmarnock cowl on the head, and a brown wide-awake on the top of that. They had a long conversation with our men about the wonderful things they had seen, and all agreed that the Makololo who tarried at home were mere game, or beasts of the field. But their wealthier neighbours, referred to as *poloholo*, or game, were by no means disposed to admit that the travellers knew more than they did. "They had seen the sea, had they, and what is that? Nothing but water; they could see plenty of water at home,—ay, more than they wanted to see; and white people came to their towns: why then travel to the Coast, to look at them?"

Justice appears upon the whole to be pretty fairly admi-

U

nistered among the Makololo. A headman took some beads
and a blanket from one of his men who had been with us;
the matter was brought before the Chief, and he immediately
ordered the goods to be restored, and decreed, moreover, that
no headman should take the property of the men who had
returned. In theory, all the goods brought back belonged to
the Chief; the men laid them at his feet, and made a formal
offer of them all; he looked at the articles, and told the men
to keep them. This is almost invariably the case. Tuba
Mokoro, however, fearing lest Sekeletu might take a fancy
to some of his best goods, exhibited only a few of his old and
least valuable acquisitions. Masakasa had little to show; he
had committed some breach of native law in one of the
villages on the way, and paid a heavy fine rather than have
the matter brought to the Doctor's ears. Each carrier is
entitled to a portion of the goods in his bundle, though purchased by the Chief's ivory, and they never hesitate to claim
their rights; but no wages can be demanded from the Chief,
if he fails to respond to the first application.

Our men, accustomed to our ways, thought that the English system of paying a man for his labour was the only
correct one, and some even said it would be better to live
under a Government where life and labour were more secure
and valuable than here. While with us, they always conducted
themselves with propriety during Divine service, and not only
maintained decorum themselves, but insisted on other natives
who might be present doing the same. When Moshobotwane,
the Batoka chief, came on one occasion with a number of his
men, they listened in silence to the reading of the Bible in
the Makololo tongue; but, as soon as we all knelt down to
pray, they commenced a vigorous clapping of hands, their
mode of asking a favour. Our indignant Makololo soon
silenced their noisy accompaniment, and looked with great

contempt on this display of ignorance. Nearly all our men
had learned to repeat the Lord's Prayer and the Apostles'
Creed in their own language, and felt rather proud of being
able to do so; and when they reached home, they liked to
recite them to groups of admiring friends. Their ideas of
right and wrong differ in no respect from our own, except
in their professed inability to see how it can be improper
for a man to have more than one wife. A year or two ago
several of the wives of those who had been absent with us
petitioned the Chief for leave to marry again. They thought
that it was of no use waiting any longer, their husbands must
be dead; but Sekeletu refused permission; he himself had
bet a number of oxen that the Doctor would return with
their husbands, and he had promised the absent men that
their wives should be kept for them. The impatient spouses
had therefore to wait a little longer. Some of them, however, eloped with other men; the wife of Mantlanyane, for
instance, ran off and left his little boy amongst strangers.
Mantlanyane was very angry when he heard of it, not
that he cared much about her deserting him, for he had
two other wives at Tette, but he was indignant at her
abandoning his boy.

While we were at Sesheke, an ox was killed by a crocodile; a man found the carcass floating in the river, and appropriated the meat. When the owner heard of this, he
requested him to come before the Chief, as he meant to
complain of him; rather than go, the delinquent settled the
matter by giving one of his own oxen in lieu of the lost one.
A headman from near Linyanti came with a complaint that
all his people had run off, owing to the "hunger." Sekeletu
said, " You must not be left to grow lean alone, some of them
must come back to you." He had thus an order to compel
their return, if he chose to put it in force. Families fre-

quently leave their own headman and flee to another village, and sometimes a whole village decamps by night, leaving the headman by himself. Sekeletu rarely interfered with the liberty of the subject to choose his own headman, and, as it is often the fault of the latter which causes the people to depart, it is punishment enough for him to be left alone. Flagrant disobedience to the Chief's orders is punished with death. A Moshubia man was ordered to cut some reeds for Sekeletu: he went off, and hid himself for two days instead. For this he was doomed to die, and was carried in a canoe to the middle of the river, choked, and tossed into the stream. The spectators hooted the executioners, calling out to them that they too would soon be carried out and strangled. Occasionally when a man is sent to beat an offender, he tells him his object, returns, and assures the Chief he has nearly killed him. The transgressor then keeps for a while out of sight, and the matter is forgotten. The river here teems with monstrous crocodiles, and women are frequently, while drawing water, carried off by these reptiles.

We met a venerable warrior, sole survivor, probably, of the Mantatee host which threatened to invade the colony in 1824. He retained a vivid recollection of their encounter with the Griquas: "As we looked at the men and horses, puffs of smoke arose, and some of us dropped down dead!" "Never saw anything like it in my life, a man's brains lying in one place and his body in another!" They could not understand what was killing them; a ball struck a man's shield at an angle; knocked his arm out of joint at the shoulder; and leaving a mark, or burn as he said, on the shield, killed another man close by. We saw the man with his shoulder still dislocated. Sebetuane was present at the fight, and had an exalted opinion of the power of white people ever afterwards.

The ancient costume of the Makololo consisted of the skin of a lamb, kid, jackal, ocelot, or other small animal, worn round and below the loins: and in cold weather a kaross, or skin mantle, was thrown over the shoulders. The kaross is now laid aside, and the young men of fashion wear a monkey-jacket and a skin round the hips; but no trousers, waistcoat, or shirt. The river and lake tribes are in general very cleanly, bathing several times a day. The Makololo women use water rather sparingly, rubbing themselves with melted butter instead: this keeps off parasites, but gives their clothes a rancid odour. One stage of civilization often leads of necessity to another—the possession of clothes creates a demand for soap; give a man a needle, and he is soon back to you for thread.

This being a time of mourning, on account of the illness of the Chief, the men were negligent of their persons, they did not cut their hair, or have merry dances, or carry spear and shield when they walked abroad. The wife of Pitsane was busy making a large hut, while we were in the town: she informed us that the men left house-building entirely to the women and servants. A round tower of stakes and reeds, nine or ten feet high, is raised and plastered; a floor is next made of soft tufa, or ant-hill material and cowdung. This plaster prevents the poisonous insects, called tampans, whose bite causes fever in some, and painful sores in all, from harbouring in the cracks or soil. The roof, which is much larger in diameter than the tower, is made on the ground, and then, many persons assisting, lifted up and placed on the tower, and thatched. A plastered reed fence is next built up to meet the outer part of the roof, which still projects a little over this fence, and a space of three feet remains between it and the tower. We slept in this space, instead of in the tower, as the inner door of the hut we occupied was uncomfortably small, being only nineteen inches high, and twenty-two inches wide at the floor. A foot from the bottom it measured seventeen inches in breadth, and close to the top only twelve inches, so it was a difficult matter to get through it. The tower has no light or ventilation, except through this small door. The reason a lady assigned for having the doors so very small was to keep out the mice!

The children have merry times, especially in the cool of the evening. One of their games consists of a little girl being carried on the shoulders of two others. She sits with outstretched arms, as they walk about with her, and all the rest clap their hands, and stopping before each hut sing pretty airs, some beating time on their little kilts of cowskin, others making a curious humming sound between the songs. Excepting this and the skipping-rope, the play of the girls consists in imitation of the serious work of their mothers, building little huts, making small pots, and cooking, pounding corn in miniature mortars, or hoeing tiny gardens. The boys play with spears of reeds pointed with wood, and small shields, or bows and arrows; or amuse themselves in making little cattle-pens, or in moulding cattle in clay; they show great ingenuity in the imitation of various-shaped horns. Some too are said to use slings, but as soon as they can watch the goats, or calves, they are sent to the field. We saw many boys riding on the calves they had in charge, but this is an innovation since the arrival of the English with their horses. Tselane, one of the ladies, on observing Dr. Livingstone noting observations on the wet and dry bulb thermometers, thought that he too was engaged in play; for on receiving no reply to her question, which was rather difficult to answer, as the native tongue has no scientific terms, she said, with roguish glee, "Poor thing, playing like a little child!"

Like other Africans, the Makololo have great faith in the power of medicine; they believe that there is an especial medicine for every ill that flesh is heir to. Mamire is anxious to have children; he has six wives, and only one boy, and he begs earnestly for "child medicine." The mother of Sekeletu came from the Barotse Valley to see her son. Thinks she has lost flesh since Dr. Livingstone was here before, and asks for "the medicine of fatness." The Makololo consider plumpness an essential part of beauty in women, but the extreme stoutness, mentioned by Captain Speke, in the north, would be considered hideous here, for the men have been overheard speaking of a lady whom we call "inclined to *embonpoint*," as "fat unto ugliness."

Two packages from the Kuruman, containing letters and newspapers, reached Linyanti previous to our arrival, and Sekeletu, not knowing when we were coming, left them there; but now at once sent a messenger for them. This man returned on the seventh day, having travelled 240 geographical miles. One of the packages was too heavy for him, and he left it behind. As the Doctor wished to get some more medicine and papers out of the wagon left at Linyanti in 1853, he decided upon going thither himself. The Chief gave him his own horse, now about twelve years old, and some men. He found everything in his wagon as safe as when he left it seven years before. The headmen, Mosale and Pekonyane, received him cordially, and lamented that they had so little to offer him. Oh! had he only arrived the year previous, when there was abundance of milk and corn and beer.

Very early the next morning the old town-crier, Ma-Pulenyane, of his own accord made a public proclamation, which, in the perfect stillness of the town long before dawn was striking: "I have dreamed! I have dreamed! I have dreamed! Thou Mosale and thou Pekonyane, my lords, be not fainthearted, nor let your hearts be sore, but believe all the words of Monare (the Doctor) for his heart is white as milk towards the Makololo. I dreamed that he was coming, and that the tribe would live, if you prayed to God and gave heed to the word of Monare." Ma-Pulenyane showed Dr. Livingstone the burying-place where poor Helmore and seven others were laid, distinguishing those whom he had put to rest, and those for whom Mafale had performed that last office. Nothing whatever marked the spot, and with the native idea of *hiding* the dead, it was said, "it will soon be all overgrown with bushes, for no one will cultivate there." None but Ma-Pulenyane approached the place, the others stood at a respectful distance; they invariably avoid everything connected with death, and no such thing as taking portions of human bodies to make charms of, as is the custom further north, has ever been known among the Makololo.

When the wagon was left eight years before, several loose articles, as the medicine-chest, magic lantern, tools, and books, were given, by Sekeletu, into the charge of his wives. Everything was now found in safety. The wagon was in sufficiently good condition for the Doctor to sleep in, though the covering had partly rotted off, and when the Chief was absent at the Barotse, the white ants had destroyed one of the wheels. Sekeletu's wives, Seipone and Mantu, without being asked, cooked abundance of good beef, and baked a large supply of little cakes after the pattern which the Makololo, who went to Loanda, had brought back to them. With gentle reproaches for not bringing Ma-Robert, or Mrs. Livingstone, they repeated some of the prattle of her children in Sechuana, and said, "Are we never more to know anything of them but their names?" These little points are noticed with feelings of gratitude for abundant and unvarying kindness on numerous occasions during many years. But no man in his senses would suppose that the confidence which inspired these kind expressions would be imparted at sight to any novice. It ought never to be forgotten that influence among the heathen can be acquired only by a patient continuance in well-doing, and that good manners are as necessary among barbarians, as among the civilized.

Among the articles put into the hands of Sekeletu's wives for greater security were two manuscript volumes of notes, which, on starting in 1853 from the interior to the West Coast, Dr. Livingstone wished, in the event of his never returning from that hazardous journey, to be transmitted to his family. A letter was left with them, addressed to any English traveller or trader, and expressing a desire that the volumes might be handed to Mr. Moffat. One contained notes on the discovery of Lake Ngami, and on the Kalahari Desert; the other, notes on its natural history. The Makololo, who had guarded all the rest of the property most faithfully, declared that they had delivered the books to one of the only two traders who had visited them. When they were now told that the person in question denied their reception, Seipone, one of Sekeletu's wives, said, "He lies, I gave them to him myself." Conscience seems to have worked; for the trader, having gone to Moselekatse's country, one of the volumes was put into the mail-bag coming from the south, which came to hand with the lock taken off in quite a scientific manner.

Taking a supply of the medicine, which had been lying only a hundred yards from the spot where the Missionaries helplessly perished, the Doctor returned towards Sesheke. The journey took three days each way. The path leads through a district infested by tsetse; to preserve the horses from being bitten, this was passed through by night. The party slept at the different Makololo cattle-stations. At one a lion had been killed by a serpent. We have often heard of animals being so killed; but in a twenty-two years' residence in the country, Dr. Livingstone has only met with one case in which the bite was fatal to a human being. Ipecacuanha mixed with ammonia, and rubbed into the wound, is much esteemed in India. A key, pressed on the puncture for some time, extracts the poison; and when ipecacuanha is not at hand, a little powder ignited on the spot will do instead. Very large herds of kualatas were seen on the plains, and many black bucks, though their habitat is generally on the hills.*

Sekeletu's health improved greatly during our visit, the melancholy foreboding left his spirits, and he became cheerful, but resolutely refused to leave his den, and appear in public till he was perfectly cured, and had regained what he considered his good looks. He also feared lest some of those who had bewitched him originally might still be among the people, and neutralize our remedies.†

As we expected another steamer to be at Kongone in

---

* A female kualata (*Aigoceros equina*) shot here measured—

	ft.	in.
At withers	4	8
Entire length..	6	3
Length of horn	2	2
Half circumference at chest	2	8

These measurements may be interesting to those who try to acclimatize animals. The elands in England are small. One we measured in Africa in 1849 was six feet four inches at the withers, and it seemed an animal of only ordinary size. Its power of taking on fat, and the quantity of fluid found in its stomach in the driest season, are quite remarkable. It browses chiefly on the leaves of trees.

† It was with sorrow that we learned by a letter from Mr. Moffat, in 1864, that poor Sekeletu was dead. As will be mentioned further on, men were sent with us to bring up more medicine. They preferred to remain on the Shire, and, as they were free men, we could do no more than try and persuade them to hasten back to their chief with iodine and other remedies. They took the parcel, but there being only two real Makololo among them, these could neither return themselves alone nor force their attendants to leave a part of the country where they were independent, and could support themselves with ease. Sekeletu, however, lived long enough to receive and acknowledge goods to the value of 50*l.*, sent, in lieu of those which remained in Tette, by Robert Moffat, jun., since dead.

November, it was impossible for us to remain in Sesheke more than one month.   Before our departure, the Chief and his principal men expressed in a formal manner their great desire to have English people settled on the Batoka highlands.   At one time he proposed to go as far as Phori, in order to select a place of residence; but as he afterwards saw reasons for remaining where he was, till his cure was completed, he gave orders to those sent with us, in the event of our getting, on our return, past the rapids near Tette, not to bring us to Sesheke, but to send forward a messenger, and he with the whole tribe would come to us.   Dr. Kirk being of the same age, Sekeletu was particularly anxious that he should come and live with him.   He said he would cut off a section of the country for the special use of the English; and on being told that in all probability their descendants would cause disturbance in his country, he replied, "These would be only domestic feuds, and of no importance."   The great extent of uncultivated land on the cool and now unpeopled highlands, has but to be seen, to convince the spectator how much room there is, and to spare, for a vastly greater population than ever, in our day, can be congregated there.

The agricultural tribes are more peaceful than the pastoral. The Makololo are both pastoral and agricultural, and their love for lifting cattle often leads them to great distances. This marauding, if sanctioned by the Chief, is not considered dishonest or dishonourable, for they laugh if they are charged with cattle-*stealing*, and assert that they have *lifted* them only.   As in the tribes nearer the Coast slave-trading is the gigantic evil, which must be grappled with, if any good is to be done; so here it was necessary frequently, yet in a kindly way, to point out the evils of marauding.   A wagon with Mr. Helmore's name on it being in the Chief's possession, a doubt was expressed whether the person said to have given it had any power to dispose of the property of the orphan children; and Sekeletu was told that should Mr. Moffat, in answer to a letter, say that the doubt had weight, the wagon ought to be paid for in ivory: this the Chief readily agreed to; and had it been possible for one with the wisdom, experience, and conciliating manners of Mr. Moffat to have visited the Makololo, he would have found them easily influenced to fairness, and not at all the unreasonable savages they were represented to be. Unquestionably a great amount of goodness exists in the midst of all their evil; and we know of no more desirable field for an active and sensible missionary.

In trying to benefit them it was often pointed out that the necessary consequence of these lawless forays, such as that they had made the year before against a tribe of Damaras to the west, was to produce a lawless state at home. They did not relish the idea of the reflected action on themselves, nor did they like being plainly told that those who shed the blood of other tribes, and then returned to kill each other at home on charges of witchcraft, were the only real sorcerers; that murdering the children of the same Great Father, for the sake of cattle which did not belong to them, entailed guilt in His sight; that those who gave no peace to others could hope from the Supreme Ruler for none among themselves. It all seemed reasonable and true; they would not dispute it; " They needed the Book of God. But the hearts of black men are not the same as those of the whites. They had real sorcerers among them. If that was guilt which custom led them to do, it lay between the white man and Jesus, who had not given them the Book, nor favoured them as He had the whites." None ever attempted to justify the shedding of human blood; but some, in reference to cattle-lifting, said, " Why should these Makalaka—" a term of contempt for all the blacker tribes—"possess cattle if they cannot fight for

them?"   Ma-Sekeletu asserted that it was Moselekatse who
had made the Makololo covetous, or yellow-hearted, *pelutsetla*.
He had taken their cattle, and subsequent hunger had made
them greedy of the oxen of other tribes. She being the
chief's mother, we may imagine what his education on the
maternal side has been. They often try to make peace, notwithstanding, amongst themselves. Two men were wrangling
and cursing each other one day, when Moikele, a Makololo
man, rose, and, to prevent mischief, quietly took their spears
from the corner in which they stood, and sitting down beside
Dr. Livingstone remarked, "It is the nature of bulls to gore
each other." This is probably the idea that lies at the
bottom of Muscular Heathenism, if not of Muscular Christianity.

On the last occasion of our holding Divine service at
Sesheke, the men were invited to converse on the subject on
which they had been addressed. So many of them had died
since we were here before, that not much probability existed
of our all meeting again, and this had naturally led to the
subject of a future state. They replied that they did not
wish to offend the speaker, but they could not believe that
all the dead would rise again: "Can those who have been
killed in the field and devoured by the vultures; or those
who have been eaten by the hyenas or lions; or those who
have been tossed into the river, and eaten by more than
one crocodile,—can they all be raised again to life?" They
were told that men could take a leaden bullet, change it
into a salt (acetate of lead), which could be dissolved as
completely in water, as our bodies in the stomachs of animals, and then reconvert it into lead; or that the bullet
could be transformed into the red and white paint of our
wagons, and again be reconverted into the original lead;
and that if men exactly like themselves could do so much,

how much more could He do, who had made the eye to
see, and the ear to hear! We added, however, that we believed in a resurrection, not because we understood how it
would be brought about, but because our Heavenly Father
assured us of it in His Book. The reference to the truth of
the Book and its Author seems always to have more influence
on the native mind than the cleverness of the illustration.
The knowledge of the people is scanty, but their reasoning
is generally clear as far as their information goes.

CHAPTER XV.

WE left Sesheke on the 17th September, 1860, convoyed by
Pitsane and Leshore with their men. Pitsane was ordered
by Sekeletu to make a hedge round the garden at the Falls,
to protect the seeds we had brought; and also to collect some
of the tobacco tribute below the Falls. Leshore, besides
acting as a sort of guard of honour to us, was sent on a
diplomatic mission to Sinamane. No tribute was exacted
by Sekeletu from Sinamane; but, as he had sent in his
adhesion, he was expected to act as a guard in case of the
Matebele wishing to cross and attack the Makololo. As we
intended to purchase canoes of Sinamane in which to descend
the river, Leshore was to commend us to whatever help this
Batoka chief could render. It must be confessed that Leshore's men, who were all of the black subject tribes, really
needed to be viewed by us in the most charitable light;
for Leshore, on entering any village, called out to the inhabitants, " Look out for your property, and see that my
thieves don't steal it."

Two young Makololo with their Batoka servants accompanied us to see if Kebrabasa could be surmounted, and
to bring a supply of medicine for Sekeletu's leprosy; and

half a dozen able canoe-men, under Mobita, who had previously gone with Dr. Livingstone to Loanda, were sent to
help us in our river navigation.   Some men on foot drove
six oxen which Sekeletu had given us as provisions for the
journey.   It was, as before remarked, a time of scarcity ;
and, considering the dearth of food, our treatment had been
liberal.

By day the canoe-men are accustomed to keep close under
the river's bank from fear of the hippopotami; by night,
however, they keep in the middle of the stream, as then
those animals are usually close to the bank on their way to
their grazing-grounds.   Our progress was considerably impeded by the high winds, which at this season of the year
begin about eight in the morning, and blow strongly up
the river all day.   The canoes were poor leaky affairs, and
so low in parts of the gunwale, that the paddlers were afraid
to follow the channel when it crossed the river, lest the
waves might swamp us.   A rough sea is dreaded by all
these inland canoe-men ; but, though timid, they are by
no means unskilful at their work.   The ocean rather astonished them afterwards ; and also the admirable way that
the Nyassa men managed their canoes on a rough lake, and
even amongst the breakers, where no small boat could possibly live.

On the night of the 17th we slept on the left bank of the
Majeele, after having had all the men ferried across.   An ox
was slaughtered, and not an ounce of it was left next morning.
Our two young Makololo companions, Moloka and Ramaku-
kane, having never travelled before, naturally clung to some
of the luxuries they had been accustomed to at home.
When they lay down to sleep, their servants were called to
spread their blankets over their august persons, not forgetting
their feet.   This seems to be the duty of the Makololo wife

to her husband, and strangers sometimes receive the honour. One of our party, having wandered, slept at the village of Nambowe. When he laid down, to his surprise two of Nambowe's wives came at once, and carefully and kindly spread his kaross over him.

A beautiful silvery fish with reddish fins, called Ngwesi, is very abundant in the river; large ones weigh fifteen or twenty pounds each. Its teeth are exposed, and so arranged that, when they meet, the edges cut a hook like nippers. The Ngwesi seems to be a very ravenous fish. It often gulps down the Konokono, a fish armed with serrated bones more than an inch in length in the pectoral and dorsal fins, which, fitting into a notch at the roots, can be put by the fish on full cock or straight out,—they cannot be folded down, without its will, and even break in resisting. The name "Konokono," elbow-elbow, is given it from a resemblance its extended fins are supposed to bear to a man's elbows stuck out from his body. It often performs the little trick of cocking its fins in the stomach of the Ngwesi, and, the elbows piercing its enemy's sides, he is frequently found floating dead. The fin bones seem to have an acrid secretion on them, for the wound they make is excessively painful. The Konokono barks distinctly when landed with the hook. Our canoe-men invariably picked up every dead fish they saw on the surface of the water, however far gone. An unfragrant odour was no objection; the fish was boiled and eaten, and the water drunk as soup. It is a curious fact that many of the Africans keep fish as we do woodcocks, until they are extremely offensive, before they consider them fit to eat. Our paddlers informed us on our way down that iguanas lay their eggs in July and August, and crocodiles in September. The eggs remain a month or two under the sand where they are laid, and the young come out when the rains have

x

fairly commenced. The canoe-men were quite positive that crocodiles frequently stun men by striking them with their tails, and then squat on them till they are drowned. We once caught a young crocodile, which certainly did use its tail to inflict sharp blows, and led us to conclude that the native opinion is correct. They believed also that, if a person shuts the beast's eyes, it lets go its hold. Crocodiles have been known to unite and kill a large one of their own species and eat it.* Some fishermen throw the bones of the fish into the river, but in most of the fishing villages there are heaps of them in various places. The villagers can walk over them without getting them into their feet; but the Makololo, from having softer soles, are unable to do so. The explanation offered was, that the fishermen have a medicine against fish-bones, but that they will not reveal it to the Makololo.

We spent a night on Mparira island, which is four miles long and about one mile broad. Mokompa, the headman, was away hunting elephants. His wife sent for him on our arrival, and he returned next morning before we left. Taking advantage of the long-continued drought, he had set fire to the reeds between the Chobe and Zambesi, in such a manner as to drive the game out at one corner, where his men laid in wait with their spears. He had killed five elephants and three buffaloes, wounding several others which escaped.

On our land party coming up, we were told that the oxen were bitten by the tsetse: they could see a great difference

---

* A greater variety of fishes are on the same authority found above than below the Falls. Of those above they name: — Mpofu—Mŏ—Nijnje—Ngwesi—Moshona—Nembwe—Seéo Lobotu—Lobangwa—Motome—Nembele—Litore—Leshuala or Ndombe — Linyonga — Mpala — Joruugo — Likeya—Moshiba—Bundo—Seto—Minga—Lisinje.

In addition to these, say twenty fishes, they mention Mumbo, called also by the Bashubia Mohumbwe, which seems to be a kind of saw-fish, and Likala, or ñala, the Lepidosiren in the Barotse Valley.

in their looks. One was already eaten, and they now wished to
slaughter another. A third fell into a buffalo-pit next day,
so our stock was soon reduced. A man, who accompanied
us to the Falls, was a great admirer of the ladies. Every
pretty girl he saw filled his heart with rapture. " Oh, what
a beauty! never saw her like before; I wonder if she is
married?" and earnestly and lovingly did he gaze after the
charming one till she had passed out of sight. He had four
wives at home, and hoped to have a number more before
long, but he had only one child; this Mormonism does not
seem to satisfy; it leads to a state of mind which, if not
disease, is truly contemptible. The Batoka Chief, Moshobotwane, again treated us with his usual hospitality, giving us
an ox, some meal, and milk. We took another view of the
grand Mosi-oa-tunya, and planted a quantity of seeds in the
garden on the island; but, as no one will renew the hedge,
the hippopotami will, doubtless, soon destroy what we planted.
Mashotlane assisted us. So much power was allowed to this
under-chief, that he appeared as if he had cast off the
authority of Sekeletu altogether. He did not show much
courtesy to his messengers; instead of giving them food, as
is customary, he took the meat out of a pot in their presence,
and handed it to his own followers. This may have been
because Sekeletu's men bore an order to him to remove to
Linyanti. He had not only insulted Baldwin, but had also
driven away the Griqua traders; but this may all end in
nothing. Some of the natives here, and at Sesheke, know
a few of the low tricks of more civilized traders. A pot
of milk was brought to us one evening, which was more
indebted to the Zambesi than to any cow. Baskets of fine-
looking white meal, elsewhere, had occasionally the lower half
filled with bran. Eggs are always a perilous investment.
The native idea of a good egg differs as widely from our own

as is possible on such a trifling subject. An egg is eaten here
with apparent relish, though an embryo chick be inside.

We left Mosi-oa-tunya on the 27th, and slept close to the
village of Bakwini. It is built on a ridge of loose red soil,
which produces great crops of mapira and ground-nuts; many
magnificent mosibe-trees stand near the village. Machimisi,
the headman of the village, possesses a herd of cattle and a
large heart; he kept us company for a couple of days to guide
us on our way.

We had heard a good deal of a stronghold some miles
below the Falls, called Kalunda. Our return path was
much nearer the Zambesi than that of our ascent,—in fact,
as near as the rough country would allow,—but we left it
twice before we reached Sinamane's, in order to see Kalunda
and a Fall called Moōmba, or Moamba. The Makololo had
once dispossessed the Batoka of Kalunda, but we could not
see the fissure, or whatever it is, that rendered it a place
of security, as it was on the southern bank. The crack of the
Great Falls was here continued: the rocks are the same as
further up, but perhaps less weather-worn—and now partially
stratified in great thick masses. The country through which
we were travelling was covered with a cindery-looking
volcanic tufa, and might be called "Katakaumena."

The description we received of the Moamba Falls seemed
to promise something grand. They were said to send up
"smoke" in the wet season, like Mosi-oa-tunya; but when
we looked down into the cleft, in which the dark-green
narrow river still rolls, we saw, about 800 or 1000 feet
below us, what, after Mosi-oa-tunya, seemed two insignificant cataracts. It was evident, that Pitsane, observing our
delight at the Victoria Falls, wished to increase our pleasure
by a second wonder. One Mosi-oa-tunya, however, is quite
enough for a continent.

The natives of Africa have an amiable desire to please, and often tell what they imagine will be gratifying, rather than the uninteresting naked truth.   Let a native from the interior be questioned by a thirsty geographer, whether the mountains round his youthful home are high; from a dim recollection of something of the sort, combined with a desire to please, the answer will be in the affirmative.   And so it will be if the subject of inquiry be gold or unicorns, or men with tails.   English sportsmen, though first-rate shots at home, are notorious for the number of their misses on first trying to shoot in Africa.   Everything is on such a large scale, and there is such a glare of bright sunlight, that some time is required to enable them to judge of distances.   "Is it wounded?" inquired a gentleman, of his dark attendant, after firing at an antelope, "Yes! the ball went right into his heart."   These mortal wounds never proving fatal, he asked a friend, who understood the language, to explain to the man, that he preferred the truth in every case.   "He is my father," replied the native, "and I thought he would be displeased if I told him that he never hits at all."   But great as this failing is among the free, it is much more annoying among the slaves.   One can scarcely induce a slave to translate anything truly: he is so intent on thinking of what will please.   By far the greatest wonder of Captain Speke and Grant's journey was, that they accomplished it with slaves.

We had now an opportunity of seeing more of the Batoka, than we had on the highland route to our north.   They did not wait till the evening before offering food to the strangers.   The aged wife of the headman of a hamlet, where we rested at midday, at once kindled a fire, and put on the cooking-pot to make porridge.   Both men and women are to be distinguished by greater roundness of feature than the other

natives, and the custom of knocking out the upper front
teeth gives at once a distinctive character to the face.   Their
colour attests the greater altitude of the country in which
many of them formerly lived.   Some, however, are as dark
as the Bashubia and Barotse of the great valley to their west,
in which stands Sesheke, formerly the capital of the Balui, or
Bashubia.

The assertion may seem strange, yet it is none the less
true, that in all the tribes we have visited we never saw a
really black person.   Different shades of brown prevail, and
often with a bright bronze tint, which no painter, except Mr.
Angus, seems able to catch.   Those who inhabit elevated,
dry situations, and who are not obliged to work much in
the sun, are frequently of a light warm brown, "dark but
comely."   Darkness of colour is probably partly caused by
the sun, and partly by something in the climate or soil which
we do not yet know.   We see something of the same sort
in trout and other fish which take their colour from the
ponds or streams in which they live.   The members of our
party were much less embrowned by free exposure to the sun
for years than Dr. Livingstone and his family were by passing
once from Kuruman to Cape Town, a journey which occupied
only a couple of months.

What the peculiarity of climate is, which favours the
deposition of colouring matter in the skin and hair, is yet
unknown; but, in some cases observed, colour was not a
matter of race, for, after long residence in a hot country, a
wound or boil heals much darker than the rest of the body.
The hair of the Africans, microscopists inform us, is not really
wool, but a growth of identically the same nature as our own,
only with a greater amount of the pigment deposited.   It is
not at all unusual to meet Europeans with hair darker than
the African; and with Africans, whose hair has a distinct

reddish tinge, and who have the same nervo-sanguineous temperament as the Xanthous varieties of other races.

But few good-looking women appear in the first Batoka villages; because the Makololo marry all the pretty girls. In one village we saw on a pole the head of a crocodile. It had entered by night the enclosure constructed to protect the women when drawing water, and caught one of them: the men rushed to the rescue, killed the monster, and stuck his head on a pole, as they were wont to do the heads of human criminals and of strangers.

A strong clannish feeling exists among the Batoka, as among all the other tribes. In travelling, those belonging to one tribe always keep by themselves, and help one another. The Batoka, like the Bushmen, excel in following the track of a wounded animal; it is part of their education. They are also good climbers, from being accustomed to collect wild fruits.

We passed over a rugged country, with many hills and perennial streams, of which the Sindi was the finest for irrigation. On returning from Moamba to the Sindi we found our luggage had gone on, and, as the chronometer was with it, we had to follow it up on Sunday; we all felt sorely the want of the Sabbath through the following week. Apart from any Divine command, a periodical day of repose is absolutely necessary for the human frame.

We encamped on the Kalomo, on the 1st of October, and found the weather very much warmer than when we crossed this stream in August. At 3 p.m., the thermometer, four feet from the ground, was 101° in the shade; the wet bulb only 61°: a difference of 40°. Yet, notwithstanding this extreme dryness of the atmosphere, without a drop of rain having fallen for months, and scarcely any dew, many of the shrubs and trees were putting forth fresh leaves of various hues, while others made a profuse display of lovely blossoms.

Near the sites of ruined Batoka villages are always seen the Mochenje Milo, Boma, Mosibe, Motsintsela, and several other kinds of native fruits; Dr. Kirk found the Mamosho-mosho, and Milo to be Cinchonaceous trees. The Mosibe he considered identical with *capaifera hymenœfolia* of Cuba, a tree of which but little is yet known. As this tree is absent from the eastern and western slopes of the continent of Africa, and not met with on the East Coast, our finding it in this remote part, with other trees showing a relationship to India, is very interesting, as indicating that much is unknown in the migrations of plants. The Boma is a Vitex nearly allied to a Madagascar tree. It yields a very valuable oil-nut, and grows abundantly at Lake Nyassa, as well as in these quarters. The Mamosho-mosho is the best fruit in the country, but we, being glad of any fruit, are unable to say whether Europeans in general would esteem it as highly as the natives do. The edible part of uncultivated fruits is usually very small. One of our men speared a conger eel, four feet seven inches in length, and ten-and-a-half inches round the neck; it is here called Mokonga.

Two old and very savage buffaloes were shot for our companions on the 3rd October. Our Volunteers may feel an interest in knowing that balls sometimes have but little effect: one buffalo fell, on receiving a Jacob's shell; it was hit again twice, and lost a large amount of blood; and yet it sprang up, and charged a native, who, by great agility, had just time to climb a tree, before the maddened beast struck it, battering-ram fashion, hard enough almost to have split both head and tree. It paused a few seconds—drew back several paces—glared up at the man—and then dashed at the tree again and again, as if determined to shake him out of it. It took two more Jacob's shells, and five other large solid rifle-balls to finish the beast at last. These old surly buffaloes had been wandering about in a sort of miserable fellowship; their skins were diseased and scabby, as if leprous, and their horns atrophied or worn down to stumps—the first was killed outright, by one Jacob's shell, the second died hard. There is so much difference in the tenacity of life in wounded animals of the same species, that the inquiry is suggested where the seat of life can be? We have seen a buffalo live long enough, after a large bullet had passed right through the heart, to allow firm adherent clots to be formed in the two holes.

One day's journey above Sinamane's, a mass of mountain called Gorongue, or Golongwe, is said to cross the river, and the rent through which the river passes is, by native report, quite fearful to behold. The country round it is so rocky, that our companions dreaded the fatigue and were not much to blame, if, as is probably the case, the way be worse than that over which we travelled. As we trudged along over the black slag-like rocks, the almost leafless trees affording no shade, the heat was quite as great as Europeans could bear. It was 102° in the shade, and a thermometer placed under the tongue or armpit showed that our blood was 99·5°, or 1·5° hotter than that of the natives, which stood at 98°. Our shoes, however, enable us to pass over the hot burning soil better than they can. Many of those who wear sandals have corns on the sides of the feet, and on the heels, where the straps pass. We have seen instances, too, where neither sandals nor shoes were worn, of corns on the soles of the feet. It is, moreover, not at all uncommon to see toes cocked up, as if pressed out of their proper places; at home, we should have unhesitatingly ascribed this to the vicious fashions perversely followed by our shoemakers.

The Longkwe, or, as the Makololo call it, the river of Quai, or tobacco, comes in from the country of Moselekatse, or from the south-east, and joins the Zambesi above Golongwe. This fact may corroborate what is said by Mr. Thomas, that all the rivers rising on the one side of Moselekatse's country run easterly, and into the Shashe, to join the Limpopo, while all the others run westerly, and then northerly, to the Zambesi. Golongwe was probably the dam which, before the rent was made, converted the whole Linyanti Valley into a lake; but we could not, on the path we came, observe any difference of level by the barometer. From the Falls to Sinamane's the country sloped, and was all lower than Sesheke; still a considerable difference of level must have taken place since the deep undisturbed mass of soft tufa was deposited on the great flats of Sesheke and Linyanti. The courses of the rivers in the country of Moselekatse, and on the Batoka highlands, west of the Kalomo, show that, in reference to the countries east of it, the great Makololo Valley is still a hollow.

On the 5th, after crossing some hills, we rested at the

Bellows and other Tools.

village of Simariango. The bellows of the blacksmith here

were somewhat different from the common goatskin bags, and more like those seen in Madagascar. They consisted of two wooden vessels, like a lady's bandbox of small dimensions, the upper ends of which were covered with leather, and looked something like the heads of drums, except that the leather bagged in the centre. They were fitted with long nozzles, through which the air was driven by working the loose covering of the tops up and down by means of a small piece of wood attached to their centres. The blacksmith said that tin was obtained from a people in the north, called Marendi, and that he had made it into bracelets; we had never heard before of tin being found in the country.

Our course then lay down the bed of a rivulet, called Mapatizia, in which there was much calc spar, with calcareous schist, and then the Tette grey sandstone, which usually overlies coal. On the 6th we arrived at the islet Chilombe, belonging to Sinamane, where the Zambesi runs broad and smooth again, and were well received by Sinamane himself. Never was Sunday more welcome to the weary than this, the last we were to spend with our convoy.

Sinamane is an active-looking man of a light complexion, and is the ablest and most energetic of the Batoka chiefs we have met. He was independent until lately, when he sent in his adhesion to Linyanti; and, as all that Sekeletu asks of him is not to furnish the Matebele with canoes when they wish to cross the Zambesi to attack the Makololo, he will probably continue loyal. Leshore's mission, as we have said, was to ratify this vassal-ship, to request Sinamane to furnish us with what canoes he could, and to assure him that Moshobotwane had not received, and never would receive, authority from Sekeletu to go on forays among his countrymen. This message was communicated also to the offending Batoka at the Falls, with whom it would have a good effect. We now saw many good-looking young men and women. The dresses of the ladies are identical with those of Nubian women in Upper Egypt. To a belt on the waist a great number of strings are attached to hang all round the person. These fringes are about six or eight inches long. The matrons wear in addition a skin cut like the tails of the coatee formerly worn by our dragoons. The younger girls wear the waist-belt exhibited in the woodcut, ornamented with shells, and

Waist-belt.

have the fringes only in front. Marauding parties of Batoka, calling themselves Makololo, have for some time had a wholesome dread of Sinamane's "long spears." Before going to Tette our Batoka friend, Masakasa, was one of a party that came to steal some of the young women; but Sinamane, to their utter astonishment, attacked them so furiously that the survivors barely escaped with their lives. Masakasa had to flee so fast that he threw away his shield, his spear, and his clothes, and returned home a wiser and a sadder man.

CHAPTER XVI.

Sinamane — Canoe navigation — Moemba — Water-drawing stockades — Generosity of the Batoka — Purchase of a canoe — Ant-lions — Herd of Hippopotami — Cataract doctor of Kariba — Albinos, human and hippopotamic —
Meet Sequasha, not quite so black as painted — Native mode of salutation
— Karivua — Gallant conduct of the Makololo — Breakfast interrupted by
Mambo Kazai — Dinner spoilt by pretended aid — Banyai — Rapids of Kebrabasa — Dr. Kirk in danger — Sad loss of MSS., &c. — Death of one of
our donkeys — Amiable squeamishness of Makololo — Dinner à la Panzo —
Reach Tette 23rd Nov. — " Jacks of all trades " — Imposition practised on
the King of Portugal's Colonial scheme.

SINAMANE'S people cultivate large quantities of tobacco,
which they manufacture into balls for the Makololo market.
Twenty balls, weighing about three-quarters of a pound each,
are sold for a hoe. The tobacco is planted on low moist
spots on the banks of the Zambesi; and was in flower at
the time we were there, in October. Sinamane's people appear to have abundance of food, and are all in good condition. He could sell us only two of his canoes; but lent us
three more to carry us as far as Moemba's, where he thought
others might be purchased. They were manned by his own
canoe-men, who were to bring them back. The river is
about 250 yards wide, and flows serenely between high
banks towards the North - East. Below Sinamane's the
banks are often worn down fifty feet, and composed of
shingle and gravel of igneous rocks, sometimes set in a
ferruginous matrix. The bottom is all gravel and shingle,
how formed we cannot imagine, unless in pot-holes in the
deep fissure above. The bottom above the Falls, save a
few rocks close by them, is generally sandy or of soft tufa.
Every damp spot is covered with maize, pumpkins, water-

melons, tobacco, and hemp. There is a pretty numerous Batoka population on both sides of the river. As we sailed slowly down, the people saluted us from the banks, by clapping their hands. A headman even hailed us, and brought a generous present of corn and pumpkins.

Moemba owns a rich island, called Mosanga, a mile in length, on which his village stands. He has the reputation of being a brave warrior, and is certainly a great talker; but he gave us strangers something better than a stream of words. We received a handsome present of corn, and the fattest goat we had ever seen; it resembled mutton. His people were as liberal as their Chief. They brought two large baskets of corn, and a lot of tobacco, as a sort of general contribution to the travellers. One of Sinamane's canoe-men, after trying to get his pay, deserted here, and went back before the stipulated time, with the story, that the Englishmen had stolen the canoes. Shortly after sunrise next morning, Sinamane came into the village with fifty of his "long spears," evidently determined to retake his property by force; he saw at a glance that his man had deceived him. Moemba rallied him for coming on a wildgoose chase. "Here are your canoes left with me, your men have all been paid, and the Englishmen are now asking me to sell my canoes." Sinamane said little to us; only observing that he had been deceived by his follower. A single remark of his Chief's caused the foolish fellow to leave suddenly, evidently much frightened and crestfallen. Sinamane had been very kind to us, and, as he was looking on when we gave our present to Moemba, we made him also an additional offering of some beads, and parted good friends. Moemba, having heard that we had called the people of Sinamane together to tell them about our Saviour's mission to man, and to pray with them, associated the idea of Sunday with the meeting, and, before anything of the sort was proposed, came and asked that he and his people might be "sundayed" as well as his neighbours; and be given a little seed wheat, and fruit-tree seeds; with which request of course we very willingly complied. The idea of praying direct to the Supreme Being, though not quite new to all, seems to strike their minds so forcibly that it will not be forgotten. Sinamane said that he prayed to God, Morungo, and made drink-offerings to him. Though he had heard of us, he had never seen white men before.

When bargaining with Moemba for canoes, we were gratified to observe, that he wished to deal fairly and honourably with us. "Our price was large; but he had only two spare canoes. One was good,—he would sell that; the other he would not sell us, because it had a bad trick of capsizing, and spilling whatever was inside it into the river; he would lend us his own two large ones, until we could buy others below." The best canoes are made from a large species of thorny acacia. These trees were now in seed; and some of the natives boiled the pods in water, and mixed the decoction with their beer, to increase its intoxicating qualities. In times of great hunger the beans too are eaten, though very astringent.

We touched at Makonde's village to buy a canoe. They were having a gay time, singing, dancing, and drinking their beer extra strong. A large potful was at once brought to us. The Chief spoke but little; his orator did the talking and trading for him, and seemed anxious to show him how cleverly he could do both. Many tiny stockades stand on the edge of the river; they are built there to protect the women from the crocodiles, while filling their waterpots. This is in advance of the Portuguese; for, although many women are annually carried off by crocodiles at Senna and

Tette, so little are the lives of these poor drawers of water valued by the masters, that they never think of erecting even a simple fence for their protection. Dr. Livingstone tried to induce the padre of Senna to move in this matter, offering to give twenty dollars himself, if a collection should be made after mass; but the padre merely smiled, shrugged his shoulders, and did nothing.

Beautiful crowned cranes, named from their note '*ma-wang*,' were seen daily, and were beginning to pair. Large flocks of spur-winged geese, or machikwe, were common. This goose is said to lay her eggs in March. We saw also pairs of Egyptian geese, as well as a few of the knob-nosed, or, as they are called in India, combed geese. When the Egyptian geese, as at the present time, have young, the goslings keep so steadily in the wake of their mother, that they look as if they were a part of her tail; and both parents, when on land, simulate lameness quite as well as our plovers, to draw off pursuers. The ostrich also adopts the lapwing fashion, but no quadrupeds do: they show fight to defend their young instead. In some places the steep banks were dotted with the holes which lead into the nests of bee-eaters. These birds came out in hundreds as we passed. When the red-breasted species settle on the trees, they give them the appearance of being covered with red foliage.

Our land party came up to us on the evening of the 11th, a number of men kindly carrying their bundles for them. They had received valuable presents of food on the way. One had been given a goat, another fowls and maize. They began to believe that these Batoka "have hearts," though at first, as those who inflict an injury usually are, they were suspicious, and blamed them for hating the Makololo and killing every one they met. Marauding parties of Makololo and subject Batoka had formerly made swoops on these very villages. A few mornings since, Moloka appeared in great grief and fear: his servant Ranyeu had disappeared the day before, and he was sure that the Batoka had caught and killed him. A few minutes after, this Ranyeu arrived, with two men who had found him wandering after sunset, had given him supper and lodging, and, carrying his load for him, had brought him on to us.

On the morning of the 12th October we passed through a wild, hilly country, with fine wooded scenery on both sides, but thinly inhabited. The largest trees were usually thorny acacias, of great size and beautiful forms. As we sailed by several villages without touching, the people became alarmed, and ran along the banks, spears in hand. We employed one to go forward and tell Mpande of our coming. This allayed their fears, and we went ashore, and took breakfast near the large island with two villages on it, opposite the mouth of the Zungwe, where we had left the Zambesi on our way up. Mpande was sorry that he had no canoes of his own to sell, but he would lend us two. He gave us cooked pumpkins and a water-melon. His servant had lateral curvature of the spine. We have often seen cases of humpback, but this was the only case of this kind of curvature we had met with. Mpande accompanied us himself in his own vessel, till we had an opportunity of purchasing a fine large canoe elsewhere. We paid what was considered a large price for it: twelve strings of blue cut glass neck-beads, an equal number of large blue ones of the size of marbles, and two yards of grey calico. Had the beads been coarser, they would have been more valued, because such were in fashion. Before concluding the bargain the owner said "his bowels yearned for his canoe, and we must give a little more to stop their yearning." This was irresistible. The trading party of Sequasha, which we now met, had purchased ten large

Y

new canoes for six strings of cheap coarse white beads each, or their equivalent, four yards of calico, and had bought for the merest trifle ivory enough to load them all. They were driving a trade in slaves also, which was something new in this part of Africa, and likely soon to change the character of the inhabitants. These men had been living in clover, and were uncommonly fat and plump. When sent to trade, slaves wisely never stint themselves of beer or anything else, which their master's goods can buy.

The insects called ant-lions (*Myrmecoleo*), were very numerous in sandy places under shady trees, even where but few ants were to be seen. These patient creatures lie in ambush, and have a great deal of extra labour at this season of the year. The high winds fill up their pitfalls with drifting sand, and no sooner have they carefully shovelled it all out, than it is again blown in, thus keeping them constantly at work till the wind goes down.

The temperature of the Zambesi had increased 10° since August, being now 80°. The air was as high as 96° after sunset; and, the vicinity of the water being the coolest part, we usually made our beds close by the river's brink, though there in danger of crocodiles. Africa differs from India in the air always becoming cool and refreshing long before the sun returns, and there can be no doubt that we can in this country bear exposure to the sun, which would be fatal in India. It is probably owing to the greater dryness of the African atmosphere that sunstroke is so rarely met with. In twenty-two years Dr. Livingstone never met or heard of a single case, though the protective head-dresses of India are rarely seen.

When the water is nearly at its lowest, we occasionally meet with small rapids which are probably not in existence during the rest of the year. Having slept opposite the rivulet

Bume, which comes from the south, we passed the island of
Nakansalo, and went down the rapids of the same name on
the 17th, and came on the morning of the 19th to the more
serious ones of Nakabele, at the entrance to Kariba. The
Makololo guided the canoes admirably through the opening in the dyke. When we entered the gorge we came on
upwards of thirty hippopotami: a bank near the entrance
stretches two-thirds across the narrowed river, and in the
still place behind it they were swimming about. Several
were in the channel, and our canoe-men were afraid to
venture down among them, because, as they affirm, there is
commonly an illnatured one in a herd, which takes a malig-
nant pleasure in upsetting canoes. Two or three boys on
the rocks opposite amused themselves by throwing stones
at the frightened animals, and hit several on the head. It
would have been no difficult matter to have shot the whole
herd. We fired a few shots to drive them off; the balls
often glance off the skull, and no more harm is done than
when a schoolboy gets a bloody nose; we killed one, which
floated away down the rapid current, followed by a number
of men on the bank. A native called to us from the left
bank, and said that a man on his side knew how to pray
to the Kariba gods, and advised us to hire him to pray for
our safety, while we were going down the rapids, or we should
certainly all be drowned. No one ever risked his life in
Kariba without first paying the river-doctor, or priest, for his
prayers. Our men asked if there was a cataract in front,
but he declined giving any information; they were not on
his side of the river; if they would come over, then he might
be able to tell them. We crossed, but he went off to the
village. We then landed and walked over the hills to have a
look at Kariba before trusting our canoes in it. The current
was strong, and there was broken water in some places, but

the channel was nearly straight, and had no cataract, so we determined to risk it. Our men visited the village while we were gone, and were treated to beer and tobacco. The priest who knows how to pray to the god that rules the rapids followed us with several of his friends, and they were rather surprised to see us pass down in safety, without the aid of his intercession. The natives who followed the dead hippopotamus caught it a couple of miles below, and, having made it fast to a rock, were sitting waiting for us on the bank beside the dead animal. As there was a considerable current there, and the rocky banks were unfit for our beds, we took the hippopotamus in tow, telling the villagers to follow, and we would give them most of the meat. The crocodiles tugged so hard at the carcass, that we were soon obliged to cast it adrift, to float down in the current, to avoid upsetting the canoe. We had to go on so far before finding a suitable spot to spend the night in, that the natives concluded we did not intend to share the meat with them, and returned to the village. We slept two nights at the place were the hippopotamus was cut up.* The crocodiles had a busy time of it in the dark, tearing away at what was left in the river, and thrashing the water furiously with their powerful tails. The hills on both sides of Kariba are much like those of Kebrabasa, the strata tilted and twisted in every direction, with no level ground.

Although the hills confine the Zambesi within a narrow channel for a number of miles, there are no rapids beyond those near the entrance. The river is smooth and apparently very deep. Only one single human being was seen in the gorge, the country being too rough for culture. Some rocks

---

* The animal was a female, and fat; it was 10 ft. in length and 4 ft. 1 in. in height. A young bull obtained higher up was 4 ft. 3 in. at withers; 9 ft. 7 in. from snout to insertion of tail.

in the water, near the outlet of Kariba, at a distance look
like a fort; and such large masses dislocated, bent, and even
twisted to a remarkable degree, at once attest some tremendous upheaving and convulsive action of nature, which
probably caused Kebrabasa, Kariba, and the Victoria Falls
to assume their present forms; it took place after the formation of the coal, that mineral having then been tilted up.
We have probably nothing equal to it in the present quiet
operations of nature.

On emerging we pitched our camp by a small stream,
the Pendele, a few miles below the gorge. The Palabi
mountain stands on the western side of the lower end of
the Kariba strait; the range to which it belongs crosses the
river, and runs to the south-east.   Chikumbula, a hospitable
old headman, under Nchomokela, the paramount Chief of a
large district, whom we did not see, brought us next morning a great basket of meal, and four fowls, with some beer,
and a cake of salt, " to make it taste good."   Chikumbula
said that the elephants plagued them, by eating up the
cotton-plants; but his people seem to be well off.

A few days before we came, they caught three buffaloes in
pitfalls in one night, and, unable to eat them all, left one
to rot.   During the night the wind changed and blew from
the dead buffalo to our sleeping-place; and a hungry lion,
not at all dainty in his food, stirred up the putrid mass, and
growled and gloated over his feast, to the disturbance of our
slumbers.   Game of all kinds is in most extraordinary abundance, especially from this point to below the Kafue, and so
it is on Moselekatse's side, where there are no inhabitants.
The drought drives all the game to the river to drink.
An hour's walk on the right bank, morning or evening, reveals
a country swarming with wild animals : vast herds of pallahs,
many waterbucks, koodoos, buffaloes, wild pigs, elands, zebras,

and monkeys appear ; francolins, guinea-fowls, and myriads
of turtledoves attract the eye in the covers, with the fresh
spoor of elephants and rhinoceroses, which had been at the
river during the night. Every few miles we came upon a
school of hippopotami, asleep on some shallow sandbank ;
their bodies, nearly all out of the water, appeared like
masses of black rock in the river. When these animals
are hunted much, they become proportionably wary, but
here no hunter ever troubles them, and they repose in
security, always however taking the precaution of sleeping
just above the deep channel, into which they can plunge
when alarmed. When a shot is fired into a sleeping herd,
all start up on their feet, and stare with peculiar stolid looks
of hippopotamic surprise, and wait for another shot before
dashing into deep water. A few miles below Chikumbula's
we saw a white hippopotamus in a herd. Our men had never
seen one like it before. It was of a pinkish white, exactly
like the colour of the Albino. It seemed to be the father of
a number of others, for there were many marked with large
light patches. The so-called *white* elephant, is just such a
pinkish Albino as this hippopotamus. A few miles above
Kariba, we observed that, in two small hamlets, many of the
inhabitants had a similar affection of the skin. The same
influence appeared to have affected man and beast. A dark
coloured hippopotamus stood alone, as if expelled from
the herd, and bit the water, shaking his head from side to
side in a most frantic manner. This biting the water with
his huge jaws is the hippopotamus' way of " slamming
the door." When the female has twins, she is said to kill
one of them.

We touched at the beautiful tree-covered island of Kalabi,
opposite where Tuba-mokoro lectured the lion in our way up.
The ancestors of the people who now inhabit this island pos-

sessed cattle. The tsetse has taken possession of the country since "the beeves were lifted." No one knows where these insects breed; at a certain season all disappear, and as suddenly come back, no one knows whence. The natives are such close observers of nature, that their ignorance in this case surprised us. A solitary hippopotamus had selected the little bay in which we landed, and where the women drew water, for his dwelling-place. Pretty little lizards, with light blue and red tails, run among the rocks, catching flies and other insects. These harmless—though to new-comers repulsive—creatures sometimes perform good service to man, by eating great numbers of the destructive white ants.

At noon on the 24th October, we found Sequasha in a village below the Kafue, with the main body of his people. He said that 210 elephants had been killed during his trip; many of his men being excellent hunters. The numbers of animals we saw renders this possible. He reported that, after reaching the Kafue, he went northwards into the country of the Zulus, whose ancestors formerly migrated from the south and set up a sort of Republican form of government. Sequasha is the greatest Portuguese traveller we ever became acquainted with, and he boasts that he is able to speak a dozen different dialects; yet, unfortunately, he can give but a very meagre account of the countries and people he has seen, and his statements are not very much to be relied on. But considering the influences among which he has been reared, and the want of the means of education at Tette, it is a wonder that he possesses the good traits that he sometimes exhibits. Among his wares were several cheap American clocks; a useless investment rather, for a part of Africa where no one cares for the artificial measurement of time. These clocks got him into trouble among the Banyai: he set them all agoing in the presence of a Chief, who became frightened at the strange sounds they made, and looked upon them as so many witchcraft agencies at work to bring all manner of evils upon himself and his people. Sequasha, it was decided, had been guilty of a milando or crime, and he had to pay a heavy fine of cloth and beads for his exhibition. He alluded to our having heard that he had killed Mpangwe, and he denied having actually done so; but in his absence his name had got mixed up in the affair, in consequence of his slaves, while drinking beer one night with Namakusuru, the man who succeeded Mpangwe, saying that they would kill the Chief for him. His partner had not thought of this when we saw him on the way up, for he tried to excuse the murder, by saying that now they had put the right man into the Chieftainship.

From Tombanyama's onwards the Zambesi is full of islands, and many buffaloes had been attracted by the fresh young grass and reeds. One was shot on the forenoon of the 27th. Distant thunder was heard during the night, and, as usually happens in this state of the atmosphere, the meat spoiled so rapidly, that it was not fit to eat next morning. Hunger in this case, and with no choice but want, made a bitter thing sweet. The same rapid decomposition is also produced if meat is hung on a papaw-tree for four or five hours; an hour or two, however, makes it tender only.

Three of Ma-mburuma's men brought us a present of meal and fowls, as we rested on the 28th on an island near Podebode. Their mode of salutation, intended to show good manners and respectful etiquette, was to clap the thigh with one hand while approaching with the present in the other; and, on sitting down before us, to clap the hands together, then to continue clapping on the thigh when they handed the present to our men, and with both hands when they received one in return, and also on their departure. This ceremonious procedure is gone through with grave composure, and mothers may be observed enjoining on their children the proper clapping of the hands, as good manners are taught among ourselves.

After three hours' sail, on the morning of the 29th, the river was narrowed again by the mountains of Mburuma, called Karivua, into one channel, and another rapid dimly appeared. It was formed by two currents guided by rocks to the centre. In going down it, the men sent by Sekeletu behaved very nobly. The canoes entered without previous survey, and the huge jobbling waves of mid-current began at once to fill them. With great presence of mind, and without a moment's hesitation, two men lightened each by jumping overboard; they then ordered a Batoka man to do the same, as "the white men must be saved." "I cannot swim," said the Batoka. "Jump out, then, and hold on to the canoe;" which he instantly did. Swimming alongside, they guided the swamping canoes down the swift current to the foot of the rapid, and then ran them ashore to bale them out. A boat could have passed down safely, but our canoes were not a foot above the water at the gunwales.

Thanks to the bravery of these poor fellows, nothing was lost, although everything was well soaked. This rapid is nearly opposite the west end of the Mburuma mountains or Karivua. Another soon begins below it. They are said to be all smoothed over when the river rises. The canoes had to be unloaded at this the worst rapid, and the goods carried about a hundred yards. By taking the time in which a piece of stick floated past 100 feet, we found the current to be running six knots, by far the greatest velocity noted in the river. As the men were bringing the last canoe down close to the shore, the stern swung round into the current, and all except one man let go, rather than be dragged off. He

clung to the bow, and was swept out into the middle of the
stream. Having held on when he ought to have let go, he
next put his life in jeopardy by letting go when he ought to
have held on ; and was in a few seconds swallowed up by a
fearful whirlpool. His comrades launched out a canoe below,
and caught him as he rose the third time to the surface, and
saved him, though much exhausted and very cold.

The scenery of this pass reminded us of Kebrabasa, although
it is much inferior. A band of the same black shining glaze
runs along the rocks about two feet from the water's edge.
There was not a blade of grass on some of the hills, it being
the end of the usual dry season succeeding a previous severe
drought; yet the hill-sides were dotted over with beautiful
green trees. A few antelopes were seen on the rugged slopes,
where some people too appeared lying down, taking a cup of
beer. The Karivua narrows are about thirty miles in length.
They end at the mountain Roganora. Two rocks, twelve or
fifteen feet above the water at the time we were there, may
in flood be covered and dangerous. Our chief danger was the
wind, a very slight ripple being sufficient to swamp canoes.

We arrived at Zumbo, at the mouth of the Loangwa,
on the 1st of November. The water being scarcely up to
the knee, our land party waded this river with ease. A
buffalo was shot on an island opposite Pangola's, the ball
lodging in the spleen. It was found to have been wounded
in the same organ previously, for an iron bullet was imbedded in it, and the wound entirely healed. A great deal
of the plant *Pistia stratiotes* was seen floating in the
river. Many people inhabit the right bank about this
part, yet the game is very abundant.

As we were taking our breakfast on the morning of the
2nd, the Mambo Kazai, of whom we knew nothing, and
his men came with their muskets and large powder-horns

to levy a fine, and obtain payment for the wood we used
in cooking. But on our replying to his demand that we were
English, "Oh! are you?" he said; "I thought you were
Bazungu (Portuguese). They are the people I take pay-
ments from:" and he apologized for his mistake. Bazungu,
or Azungu, is a term applied to all foreigners of a light colour,
and to Arabs; even to trading slaves if clothed; it probably
means foreigners or visitors,—from *zunga*, to visit or wander,—
and the Portuguese were the only foreigners these men had
ever seen. As we had no desire to pass for people of that
nation—quite the contrary—we usually made a broad line
of demarcation by saying that we were English, and the
English neither bought, sold, nor held black people as slaves,
but wished to put a stop to the slave-trade altogether.

We called upon our friend, Mpende, in passing. He provided a hut for us, with new mats spread on the floor.
Having told him that we were hurrying on because the rains
were near; "Are they near?" eagerly inquired an old
counsellor, "and are we to have plenty of rain this year?"
We could only say that it was about the usual time for the
rains to commence; and that there were the usual indications
in great abundance of clouds floating westwards, but that we
knew nothing more than they did themselves. Some people
occasionally take advantage of the supposed credulity of the
natives to gain temporary applause; but Africans are usually
shrewd enough to detect some discrepancy, and no one is
duped but the traveller himself. Mpende had been blamed
for driving the clouds away during the past drought, and had
to pay a heavy fine to the Pondoro, as an atonement for his
offence. It blew a gale on the night of the 4th, after which
the wind suddenly chopped round, and blew down the river,
and we had thunder, lightning, and rain. The temperature
of both air and water was lowered next morning, the river

having fallen 7°, or to 78°. There were thunderstorms all around us during the day, and the Zambesi rose several inches, and became highly discoloured.

The hippopotami are more wary here than higher up, as the natives hunt them with guns. Having shot one on a shallow sandbank, our men undertook to bring it over to the left bank, in order to cut it up with greater ease. It was a fine fat one, and all rejoiced in the hope of eating the fat for butter, with our hard dry cakes of native meal. Our cook was sent over to cut a choice piece for dinner, but returned with the astonishing intelligence that the carcass was gone. They had been hoodwinked, and were very much ashamed of themselves. A number of Banyai came to assist in rolling it ashore, and asserted that it was all shallow water. They rolled it over and over towards the land, and, finding the rope we had made fast to it, as they said, an encumbrance, it was unloosed. All were shouting and talking as loud as they could bawl, when suddenly our expected feast plumped into a deep hole, as the Banyai intended it should do. When sinking, all the Makololo jumped in after it. One caught franticly at the tail; another grasped a foot, a third seized the hip; "but, by Sebituane! it would go down, in spite of all that we could do." Instead of a fat hippopotamus, we had only a lean fowl for dinner, and were glad enough to get even that. The hippopotamus, however, floated during the night, and was found about a mile below. The Banyai then assembled on the bank, and disputed our right to the beast: "It might have been shot by somebody else." Our men took a little of it and then left it, rather than come into collision with them.

A fine waterbuck was shot in the Kakolole narrows, at Mount Manyerere; it dropped beside the creek where it was feeding; an enormous crocodile, that had been watching it at the moment, seized and dragged it into the water, which was not very deep. The mortally-wounded animal made a desperate plunge, and, hauling the crocodile several yards, tore itself out of the hideous jaws. To escape the hunter, the waterbuck jumped into the river, and was swimming across, when another crocodile gave chase, but a ball soon sent it to the bottom. The waterbuck swam a little longer, the fine head dropped, the body turned over, and one of the canoes dragged it ashore. Below Kakolole, and still at the base of Manyerere mountain, several coal-seams, not noticed on our ascent, were now seen to crop out on the right bank of the Zambesi.

Chitora, of Chicova, treated us with his former hospitality. Our men were all much pleased with his kindness, and certainly did not look upon it as a proof of weakness. They meant to return his friendliness when they came this way on a marauding expedition to eat the sheep of the Banyai, for insulting them in the affair of the hippopotamus; they would then send word to Chitora not to run away for they, being his friends, would do such a good-hearted man no harm.

In our voyage down we had gleaned the following information respecting the river itself. From the point where we embarked at Sinamane's to Kansalo, the river is more navigable than between Tette and Senna, though much of it is only from 250 to 300 yards broad, or like the Thames at London-bridge. It is deep, and flows gently. A little below Kansalo, at Kariba, a basaltic dyke, called Nakabele, with a wide opening in it, dangerous only for canoes, stretches like an artificial dam across the stream. The deep and narrow river then flows on for several miles through a range of lofty mountains. Still further down, and from the Kafue eastward, it is at least half a mile wide; the current is gentle, and there are many sandy islands. Then there is the rapid at Karivua, mentioned above, about 100 yards in length, with a current of

nearly six knots an hour; this is the most rapid part of the
Zambesi, except in actual cataracts. In the space below
Zumbo, and on to Chicova, the river is again broad and of easy
navigation. Chicova, of which geographers have spoken sometimes as a kingdom, and sometimes as a cataract, is a district
having a fertile plain on the south bank, and both sides of
the river were formerly well cultivated; but now it has no
population.

We entered Kebrabasa rapids, at the east end of Chicova,
in the canoes, and went down a number of miles, until the
river narrowed into a groove of fifty or sixty yards wide, of
which we have already spoken in describing the flood-bed and
channel of low water. The navigation then became difficult
and dangerous. A fifteen feet fall of the water in our absence
had developed many cataracts. Two of our canoes passed safely
down a narrow channel, which, bifurcating, had an ugly whirlpool at the rocky partition between the two branches, the deep
hole in the whirls at times opening and then shutting. The
Doctor's canoe came next, and seemed to be drifting broadside
into the open vortex, in spite of the utmost exertions of the
paddlers. The rest were expecting to have to pull to the
rescue; the men saying, "Look where these people are going!—
look, look!"—when a loud crash burst on our ears. Dr. Kirk's
canoe was dashed on a projection of the perpendicular rocks,
by a sudden and mysterious boiling up of the river, which
occurs at irregular intervals. Dr. Kirk was seen resisting the
sucking-down action of the water, which must have been
fifteen fathoms deep, and raising himself by his arms on to
the ledge, while his steersman, holding on to the same rocks,
saved the canoe; but nearly all its contents were swept away
down the stream. Dr. Livingstone's canoe meanwhile, which
had distracted the men's attention, was saved by the cavity in
the whirlpool filling up as the frightful eddy was reached. A

few of the things in Dr. Kirk's canoe were left; but all that
was valuable, including a chronometer, a barometer, and, to
our great sorrow, his notes of the journey and botanical
drawings of the fruit-trees of the interior, perished.

We now left the river, and proceeded on foot, sorry that
we had not done so the day before. The men were
thoroughly frightened, they had never seen such perilous
navigation. They would carry all the loads, rather than
risk Kebrabasa any longer; but the fatigue of a day's march
over the hot rocks and burning sand changed their tune
before night; and then they regretted having left the canoes;
they thought they should have dragged them past the
dangerous places, and then launched them again. One of
the two donkeys died from exhaustion near the Luia.
Though the men eat zebras and quaggas, blood relations
of the donkey, they were shocked at the idea of eating the
ass; "it would be like eating man himself, because the donkey
lives with man, and is his bosom companion." We met two
large trading parties of Tette slaves on their way to Zumbo,
leading, to be sold for ivory, a number of Manganja women,
with ropes round their necks, and all made fast to one long
rope.

Panzo, the headman of the village east of Kebrabasa,
received us with great kindness. After the usual salutation
he went up the hill, and, in a loud voice, called across the
valley to the women of several hamlets to cook supper for
us. About eight in the evening he returned, followed by a
procession of women, bringing the food. There were eight
dishes of nsima, or porridge, six of different sorts of very
good wild vegetables, with dishes of beans and fowls; all
deliciously well cooked, and scrupulously clean. The wooden
dishes were nearly as white as the meal itself: food also was
brought for our men. Ripe mangoes, which usually indicate

the vicinity of the Portuguese, were found on the 21st
November; and we reached Tette early on the 23rd, having
been absent a little over six months.

The two English sailors, left in charge of the steamer, were
well, had behaved well, and had enjoyed excellent health all
the time we were away. Their farm had been a failure. We
left a few sheep, to be slaughtered when they wished for fresh
meat, and two dozen fowls. Purchasing more, they soon had
doubled the number of the latter, and anticipated a good supply
of eggs; but they also bought two monkeys, and *they* ate all
the eggs. A hippopotamus came up one night, and laid waste
their vegetable garden; the sheep broke into their cotton
patch, when it was in flower, and ate it all, except the stems;
then the crocodiles carried off the sheep, and the natives stole
the fowls. Nor were they more successful as gunsmiths: a
Portuguese trader, having an exalted opinion of the ingenuity
of English sailors, showed them a double-barreled rifle, and
inquired if they could put on the *browning*, which had
rusted off. "I think I knows how," said one, whose
father was a blacksmith, "it's very easy; you have only to
put the barrels in the fire." A great fire of wood was made
on shore, and the unlucky barrels put over it, to secure the
handsome rifle colour. To Jack's utter amazement the
barrels came asunder. To get out of the scrape, his companion and he stuck the pieces together with resin, and sent
it to the owner, with the message, "It was all they could do
for it, and they would not charge him anything for the job!"
They had also invented an original mode of settling a
bargain; having ascertained the market price of provisions,
they paid that, but no more. If the traders refused to
leave the ship till the price was increased, a chameleon, of
which the natives have a mortal dread, was brought out
of the cabin; and the moment the natives saw the creature,

they at once sprang overboard. The chameleon settled every dispute in a twinkling.

But besides their goodhumoured intercourse, they showed humanity worthy of English sailors. A terrible scream roused them up one night, and they pushed off in a boat to the rescue. A crocodile had caught a woman, and was dragging her across a shallow sandbank. Just as they came up to her, she gave a fearful shriek : the horrid reptile had snapped off her leg at the knee. They took her on board, bandaged the limb as well as they could, and, not thinking of any better way of showing their sympathy, gave her a glass of rum, and carried her to a hut in the village. Next morning they found the bandages torn off, and the unfortunate creature left to die. "I believe," remarked Rowe, one of the sailors, " her master was angry with us for saving her life, seeing as how she had lost her leg."

Having heard a great deal about a military and agricultural colony, which was sent out by the late King of Portugal, Don Pedro V., well known as a true-hearted man, we felt much interest in an experiment begun under his enlightened auspices. Immediately after our arrival at Tette, we called upon the new Governor. His Excellency coolly said that the king had been grossly deceived by those appointed to select the men. He smiled at his Government sending out military convicts as colonists; and said, "These men are not fitted to do anything in the country ; they know how to keep their arms clean, and nothing else. Of what possible use was it to send agricultural implements for men like these ? The Government is deceived respecting Africa."

CHAPTER XVII.

THE Zambesi being unusually low, we remained at Tette till it rose a little, and then left on the 3rd December for the Kongone. It was hard work to keep the vessel afloat; indeed we never expected her to remain above water. New leaks broke out every day; the engine-pump gave way; the bridge broke down; three compartments filled at night; except the cabin and front compartment all was flooded; and in a few days we were assured by Rowe that "she can't be worse than she is, sir." He and Hutchins had spent much of their time, while we were away, in patching her bottom, puddling it with clay, and shoring it, and it was chiefly to please them that we again attempted to make use of her. We had long been fully convinced that the steel plates were thoroughly unsuitable. On the morning of the 21st the uncomfortable "Asthmatic" grounded on a sandbank and filled. She could neither be emptied nor got off. The river rose during the night, and all that was visible of the worn-out craft next day was about six feet of her two masts. Most of the property we had on board was saved; and we spent the Christmas of 1860 encamped on the island of Chimba. Canoes were sent for from Senna; and we reached it on the 27th, to be again hospitably entertained by our friend, Senhor Ferrão.

A large party of slaves, belonging to the Commandant, after having been away the greater part of a year, had just returned from a trading expedition to Moselekatse's country. They had taken in-land a thousand muskets and a large quantity of gunpowder; these being, they said, the only articles Moselekatse cares to purchase. They started on their journey back, with ivory, ostrich feathers, a thousand sheep and goats, and thirty head of fine cattle. Moselekatse sent, in addition, as a token that the traders and he had parted good friends, a splendid white bull to the Commandant. The ostrich feathers had been packed in reeds, a fire broke out in the camp one night, and most of them were burned. On their way the cattle had to pass through a tsetse country, and they all died from the effects of the bite. The white bull perished within two days of Senna; six hundred of the sheep and goats had been eaten, either because they became lame, or because the drivers were hungry. The Commandant having an attack of fever was unable to calculate his losses, but intended to imprison the slaves who, as usual, thought more of their own comfort than of their master's gain. Slave labour is certainly very dear; for an Englishman with two wagons and ten people could have made a more profitable trip to Moselekatse's— from the much greater distances of Natal or the Cape—than was made by these hundreds of slaves.

When we met Sequasha, he confessed to having already amassed 800 arrobas or 25,600 lbs. of ivory, the most of it purchased for a mere trifle. His comrade had about half that amount, or 12,800 lbs. When Sequasha returned to Tette, in the following year, he was cast into prison in the Fort. He had brought down several tons of ivory, and was soon a free man again. The ostensible reason for his imprisonment was the disorders he had been guilty of in the interior; but this was only like the customary manipulation by which, in pisciculture, the salmon is made to yield her spawn, before she

z 2

swims off a free light fish again. We do not envy the position of the colonist in these Portuguese convict settlements. But we do regret that our own countrymen of the Cape are prevented, by an unwise policy, from carrying their freedom and love of fair play into the country which is, so far as discovery goes, by right their own. And we may be permitted to record our heartfelt sorrow, that Robert Moffat, the son of the celebrated Missionary, was so soon cut off in the midst of his days, and at the commencement of his noble endeavours to carry lawful commerce into all the interior.

It may be interesting to our Cape friends to know that, notwithstanding their occasionally laudable growling about the fickleness of Kaffir labourers, such labourers are much better than slaves. The coal here, as we have mentioned, lies quite exposed in cliff sections, in the sides of streams, which could easily be made available for carriage by lighters. A small vessel, exactly like the Ma-Robert, was sent out by Don Pedro V. for the navigation of the Zambesi; and orders were forwarded to Tette to have a supply of coal ready for her from the seam at which we had supplied our vessel. This order was carried out by slaves; and from information supplied to us by the officer who superintended this easy mining operation, we found that the mineral cost 1*l.* per ton, or at least twice as much as it does by free labour at the pit's mouth in England. Indeed, it would have been more expensive, if taken to the river's mouth, than coal brought by sea round the Cape to India. The facts mentioned showed that the chief expense incurred was in the food required by the slaves. The wages allowed in the calculation to the masters were very small. Coal from the mines at Tette, according to the present system of labour, could not be delivered at Kongone much under 10*l.* per ton. The contrast is more striking if we remember the great depth at which the coal

in England is obtained.   We saw the vessel referred to above,
lying in Mosambique harbour in 1864; it had not been used
for the purpose it was sent out for, though it had been nearly
three years there.   What a howl would have rung through
the Cape Colony, if our Governor there had kept a vessel,
sent from Europe for the development of the colonial trade,
for his Excellency's own amusement!

We reached the Kongone on the 4th of January, 1861.   A
flagstaff and a Custom-house had been erected during our
absence; a hut, also, for a black lance-corporal and three
privates.   By the kind permission of the lance-corporal, who
came to see us as soon as he had got into his trousers and
shirt, we took up our quarters in the Custom-house, which,
like the other buildings, is a small square floorless hut of
mangrove stakes overlaid with reeds.   The soldiers complained of hunger, they had nothing to eat but a little mapira,
and were making palm wine to deaden their cravings.   While
waiting for a ship, we had leisure to read the newspapers and
periodicals we found in the mail which was waiting our
arrival at Tette.   Several were a year and a half old.

Our provisions began to run short; and towards the end
of the month there was nothing left but a little bad biscuit
and a few ounces of sugar.   Coffee and tea were expended,
but scarcely missed, as our sailors discovered a pretty good
substitute in roasted mapira.   Fresh meat was obtained in
abundance from our antelope preserves on the large island
made by a creek between the Kongone and East Luabo.

Large herds of waterbuck (*Aigocerus ellipsiprymnus*) feed
there on the grassy plains; when they desire fresh pasture
they wait on the bank till the tide is low, and then swim the
creeks, half a mile or more, with the greatest ease.   These
animals are difficult to kill, and seem at times to have as
many lives as a cat.   A shot in the neck is generally fatal,

but they have frequently gone off, as if unhurt, with two or three Enfield bullets in the lungs or other parts of the body. The lungs seemed to have numerous fibrous septa running into their substance, so as to form a congeries of small lobes, one of which might be wounded without much injury to the others; but while trying to find in this an explanation of the fact that a wound in the lungs of waterbucks did not kill, we never had the means and time for careful dissection. A fine male ran full speed upwards of two hundred yards with part of the heart blown out by a Jacob's shell. It was hoped that Jacob's shells would put animals out of pain at once; but from exploding on a bone near the skin, or even on the skin, they were found not to answer our expectations. The Enfield ball, too, though propelled with prodigious velocity, is much too small to prove speedily fatal; the large two-ounce round bullet is the best of all, if it is well driven home. Near the sea the meat of the waterbuck is always juicy and well-flavoured, reminding one of beef; but in the interior the flesh of the same kind of antelope is so dry and tough, that at last even our black men, though far from being fastidious, refused to eat it; and we gave up shooting antelopes there altogether. It is said to be a well-attested fact that the flesh of the sheep of the island of Halki is highly esteemed, and has a delicious flavour, in consequence, it is believed, of the animals drinking salt-water only. The vegetation here has usually a quantity of fine salt in efflorescence on it, and much of the water is brackish. The excellence of the flesh may in this case also, perhaps, be attributed to the salt. It was only after partaking of it in the interior, that we understood why Captain Harris had so low an opinion of it.

The reedbuck (*Redunca eleotragus*) commonly lies close in the long grass during the extreme heat of the day, and waits till the hunter is near, before bounding off and uttering its whistle of alarm. A better acquaintance with the habits of animals might aid in their division into groups, as they appear in nature, on the hills, plains, and marshes. The koodoo, pallah, blackbuck or kualata, klipspringer or kololo, are generally seen on the hills, and, when pursued, flee to them for safety. The gemsbuck or kukama, kama, tsessebe, gnu, eland, puti or diver, steinbuck, giraffe, nuni or blesbuck, springbuck or tsepe, and ourebi, are always on the plains; while the waterbuck, reed-buck, lechwe, poku, nakong, and bushbuck inhabit swampy places, and flee to waters or swamps for protection.

In the mornings and evenings the pretty-spotted bushbuck (*Tragelaphus sylvatica*) ventures, though only a short distance, out of the mangroves, to feed. When startled, its call of danger is a loud bark, the imitation of which is its name among most of the native tribes—"mpabala," "mpsware." The waterbuck keeps the open plains, and seldom lies down during the day. On clear windy days all the game are extremely wild and wary, and can only be stalked with the greatest difficulty; while in still, sultry weather, they may be approached with ease.

A few leopards (*Felis leopardus*), called "tigre" by the Portuguese, and troops of a green monkey called "pusi," find food and shelter among the mangroves. The hunting leopard, (*Felis jubata*) with small round black spots, we never saw.

In this focus of decaying vegetation, nothing is so much to be dreaded as inactivity. We had, therefore, to find what exercise and amusement we could, when hunting was not required, in peering about in the fetid swamps; to have gone mooning about, in listless idleness, would have ensured fever in its worst form, and probably with fatal results.

A curious little blenny-fish swarms in the numerous creeks which intersect the mangrove topes. When alarmed, it hurries across the surface of the water in a series of leaps. It may be considered amphibious, as it lives as much out of the water as in it, and its most busy time is during low water. Then it appears on the sand or mud, near the little pools left by the retiring tide; it raises itself on its pectoral fins into something of a standing attitude, and with its large projecting eyes keeps a sharp look-out for the light-coloured fly, on which it feeds. Should the fly alight at too great a distance for even a second leap, the blenny moves slowly towards it like a cat to its prey, or like a jumping spider; and, as soon as it gets within two or three inches of the insect, by a sudden spring contrives to pop its underset mouth directly over the unlucky victim. He is, moreover, a pugnacious little fellow; and rather prolonged fights may be observed between him and his brethren. One, in fleeing from an apparent danger, jumped into a pool a foot square, which the other evidently regarded as his by right of prior discovery; in a twinkling the owner, with eyes flashing fury and with dorsal fin bristling up in rage, dashed at the intruding foe. The fight waxed furious, no tempest in a teapot ever equalled the storm of that miniature sea. The warriors were now in the water, and anon out of it, for the battle raged on sea and shore. They struck hard, they bit each other; until, becoming exhausted, they seized each other by the jaws like two bull-dogs, then paused for breath, and at it again as fiercely as before, until the combat ended by the precipitate retreat of the invader.

The muddy ground under the mangrove-trees is covered with soldier-crabs, which quickly slink into their holes on any symptom of danger. When the ebbing tide retires, myriads of minute crabs emerge from their undergound quarters, and begin to work like so many busy bees. Soon many miles of the smooth sand become rough with the results of their labour. They are toiling for their daily bread: a round bit of moist sand appears at the little labourer's mouth, and is quickly brushed off by one of the claws; a second bit follows the first; and another, and still another come as fast as they can be laid aside. As these pellets accumulate, the crab moves sideways, and the work continues. The first impression one receives is, that the little creature has swallowed a great deal of sand, and is getting rid of it as speedily as possible: a habit he indulges in of darting into his hole at intervals, as if for fresh supplies, tends to strengthen this idea; but the size of the heaps formed in a few seconds shows that this cannot be the case, and leads to the impression that, although not readily seen, at the distance at which he chooses to keep the observer, yet that possibly he raises the sand to his mouth, where whatever animalcule it may contain is sifted out of it, and the remainder rejected in the manner described. At times the larger species of crabs perform a sort of concert; and from each subterranean abode strange sounds arise, as if, in imitation of the songsters of the groves, for very joy they sang! The wart-hogs (*Phacochœrus Africanus*), seem to be rather partial to these large, sound-producing crabs; they dig them out of the muddy swamps during the night, and devour them. Shoals of small fish abound in the shallows between the Kongone and the land, Nyangalule, and this is the favourite fishing-station of a large flock of pelicans, during the months they remain on the coast. These birds destroy an immense number of fish; they breed in April on the low island off Kongone, and also on that off East Luabo. The eggs, of which we got a good supply, are so fishy in taste, that anchovy sauce is necessary to render them palatable. At Luabo Island, the turtles come at stated times to lay their eggs, which have a tough membrane instead of a shell, and are pleasant in flavour.

The mangrove itself is worth examining; and Dr. Kirk found it, and trees and plants brought from a distance and stranded on these shores, an interesting and instructive study. One species of mangrove stands, at ebb tide, on its fantastic roots, raised high above the ground, while, at flood tide, the trunk seems as if planted on the surface of the water. Another has flat, broad, tortuous roots, placed on edge in the mud, so as to give it, even on that soft substance, a firm foundation to stand upon. The seeds of one species are formed somewhat like arrow-heads, and, in falling, are by their own weight shot into the soft ground, and self-planted. Another fruit nearly as large as a child's head, of no use, as far as we can guess, to man or beast, splits into pieces when it drops. The wood, however, makes excellent fuel, and possesses the valuable quality of burning freely in the furnace, even when green. It also makes capital rafters, which, from their straightness and length, are much esteemed by the Portuguese.

We found some natives pounding the woody stems of a poisonous climbing-plant (*Dirca palustris*) called Busungu, or poison, which grows abundantly in the swamps. When a good quantity was bruised, it was tied up in bundles. The stream above and below was obstructed with bushes, and with a sort of rinsing motion the poison was diffused through the water. Many fish were soon affected, swam in shore, and died, others were only stupified. The plant has pink, pea-shaped blossoms, and smooth, pointed, glossy leaves, and the brown bark is covered with minute white points. The knowledge of it might prove of use to a shipwrecked party by enabling them to catch the fish.

The poison is said to be deleterious to man if the water is drunk; but not when the fish is cooked. The Busungu is repulsive to some insects, and is smeared round the shoots of the palm-trees to prevent the ants from getting into the palm wine while it is dropping from the tops of the palm-trees into the little pots suspended to collect it.

We were in the habit of walking from our beds into the salt water at sunrise, for a bath, till a large crocodile appeared at the bathing place, and from that time forth, we took our dip in the sea, away from the harbour, about midday. This is said to be unwholesome, but we did not find it so. It is certainly better not to bathe in the mornings, when the air is colder than the water—for then, on returning to the cooler air, one is apt to get a chill and fever. In the mouth of the river, many saw-fish are found. Rowe saw one while bathing—caught it by the tail, and shoved it, "snout on," ashore. The saw is from a foot to eighteen inches long. We never heard of any one being wounded by this fish; nor, though it goes hundreds of miles up the river in fresh water, could we learn that it was eaten by the people. The hippopotami delighted to spend the day among the breakers, and seemed to enjoy the fun as much as we did.

Severe gales occurred during our stay on the Coast, and many small sea-birds (*Prion Banksii*, Smith) perished : the beach was strewn with their dead bodies, and some were found hundreds of yards inland ; many were so emaciated as to dry up without putrefying. We were plagued with myriads of mosquitoes, and had some touches of fever; the men we brought from malarious regions of the interior suffered almost as much from it here, as we did ourselves. This gives strength to the idea that the civilized withstand the evil influences of strange climates better than the uncivilized. When negroes return to their own country from healthy lands, they suffer as severely as foreigners ever do.

CHAPTER XVIII.

On the 31st January, 1861, our new ship, "The Pioneer,"
arrived from England, and anchored outside the bar; but the
weather was stormy, and she did not venture in till the 4th
of February.

Two of H.M. cruisers came at the same time, bringing
Bishop Mackenzie, and the Oxford and Cambridge Mission to
the tribes of the Shire and Lake Nyassa. The Mission consisted of six Englishmen, and five coloured men from the Cape.
It was a puzzle to know what to do with so many men. The
estimable Bishop, anxious to commence his work without delay,
wished the Pioneer to carry the Mission up the Shire, as
far as Chibisa's, and there leave them. But there were
grave objections to this. The Pioneer was under orders to
explore the Rovuma, as the Portuguese Government had refused to open the Zambesi to the ships of other nations, and
their officials were very effectually pursuing a system, which,
by abstracting the labour, was rendering the country of no
value either to foreigners or to themselves. She was already
two months behind her time, and the rainy season was half over.
Then, if the party were taken to Chibisa's, the Mission would be

left without a medical attendant, in an unhealthy region, at the beginning of the most sickly season of the year, and without means of reaching the healthy highlands, or of returning to the sea. We dreaded that in the absence of medical aid, and all knowledge of the treatment of fever, there might be a repetition of the sorrowful fate which befell the similar non-medical Mission at Linyanti. It was well that we objected so strongly, for we afterwards found that the Bishop had purchased our fever pills at the Cape, which must have been made of *dirt* instead of drugs. The Bishop at last consented to proceed in the Lyra man-of-war to Johanna, and there leave the members of the Mission with H.M.'s Consul, Mr. Sunley, while he himself should accompany us up the Rovuma, in order to ascertain whether the country round its head-waters, which were reported to flow out of Nyassa, was a suitable place for a settlement.

On the 25th of February the Pioneer anchored in the mouth of the Rovuma, which, unlike most African rivers, has a magnificent bay and no bar. We wooded, and then waited for the Bishop till the 9th of March, when he came in the Lyra. On the 11th we proceeded up the river, and saw that it had fallen four or five feet during our detention. The scenery on the lower part of the Rovuma is superior to that on the Zambesi, for we can see the highlands from the sea. Eight miles from the mouth the mangroves are left behind, and a beautiful range of well-wooded hills on each bank begins. On these ridges the tree resembling African blackwood, of finer grain than ebony, grows abundantly, and attains a large size. Few people were seen, and those were of Arab breed, and did not appear to be very well off. The current of the Rovuma was now as strong as that of the Zambesi, but the volume of water is very much less. Several of the crossings had barely water enough for our ship, drawing five feet, to pass. When we were thirty miles up the river, the water fell suddenly seven inches in twenty-four hours. As the March flood is the last of the season, and it appeared to be expended, it was thought prudent to avoid the chance of a year's detention, by getting the ship back to the sea without delay. Had the Expedition been alone, we would have pushed up in boats, or afoot, and done what we could towards the exploration of the river and upper end of the lake; but, though the Mission was a private one, and entirely distinct from our own, a public one, the objects of both being similar, we felt anxious to aid our countrymen in their noble enterprise; and, rather than follow our own inclination, decided to return to the Shire, see the Mission party settled safely, and afterwards explore Lake Nyassa and the Rovuma, from the Lake downwards. Fever broke out on board the Pioneer, at the mouth of the Rovuma, as we thought from our having anchored close to a creek coming out of the mangroves; and it remained in her until we completely isolated the engine-room from the rest of the ship. The coal-dust rotting sent out strong effluvia, and kept up the disease for more than a twelvemonth.

Soon after we started, the fever put the Pioneer almost entirely into the hands of the original Zambesi Expedition, and not long afterwards the leader had to navigate the ocean as well as the river. The habit of finding the geographical positions on land renders it an easy task to steer a steamer with only three or four sails at sea; where, if one does not run ashore, no one follows to find out an error and where a current affords a ready excuse for every blunder.

Touching at Mohilla, one of the Comoro Islands, on our return, we found a mixed race of Arabs, Africans, and their conquerors, the natives of Madagascar. Being Mahometans, they have mosques and schools, in which we were pleased to see girls as well as boys taught to read the Koran. The teacher said he was paid by the job, and received ten dollars for teaching each child to read. The clever ones learn in six months; but the dull ones take a couple of years. We next went over to Johanna for our friends; and, after a sojourn of a few days at the beautiful Comoro islands, we sailed for the Kongone mouth of the Zambesi with Bishop Mackenzie and his party. We reached the coast in seven days, and passed up the Zambesi to the Shire.

The Pioneer, constructed under the skilful supervision of Admiral Sir Baldwin Walker and the late Admiral Washington, warm-hearted and highly esteemed friends of the Expedition, was a very superior vessel, and well suited for our work in every respect, except in her draught of water. Five feet were found to be too much for the navigation of the upper part of the Shire. Designed to draw three feet only, the weight necessary to impart extra strength, and fit her for the ocean, brought her down two feet more, and caused us a great deal of hard and vexatious work, in laying out anchors, and toiling at the capstan to get her off sandbanks.   We should not have minded this much, but for the heavy loss of time which might have been more profitably, and infinitely more pleasantly, spent in intercourse with the people, exploring new regions, and otherwise carrying out the objects of the Expedition.   Once we were a fortnight on a bank of soft yielding sand, having only two or three inches less water than the ship drew ; this delay was occasioned by the anchors coming home, and the current swinging the ship broadside on the bank, which, immediately on our touching, always formed behind us.   We did not like to leave the ship short of Chibisa's, lest the crew should suffer from the malaria of the lowland around; and it would have been difficult to have got the Mission goods carried up.   We were daily visited by crowds of natives, who brought us abundance of provisions far beyond our ability to consume. In hauling the Pioneer over the shallow places, the Bishop, with Horace Waller and Mr. Scudamore, were ever ready and anxious to lend a hand, and worked as hard as any on board. Had our fine little ship drawn but three feet, she could have run up and down the river at any time of the year, with the greatest ease, but, as it was, having once passed up over a few shallow banks, it was impossible to take her down again until the river rose in December. She could go up over a bank, but not come down over it, as a heap of sand always formed instantly astern, while the current washed it away from under her bows.

From the period of our second entrance among the tribes on the Shire, Charles Livingstone had very zealously turned his energies to inducing the people to cultivate cotton for exportation. The Ma-Robert was so leaky that nothing more could be done, while we had her, than purchase small quantities of cleaned cotton and yarn of native manufacture, to be submitted to our friends at Manchester, and to inculcate the probability of our countrymen coming to buy as much as could be raised. Much of what we bought in this way was inevitably spoiled by the wet state of the vessel; but the specimens sent home were pronounced to be "the very kind of cotton most needed in Lancashire," and the yarn, or rather rove, which we bought at about a penny per pound, excited the admiration of practical manufacturers there.

Now that we had more accommodation, Charles Livingstone pursued the same system of attempting to turn the industrial energies of the natives to good account, and with very gratifying success. Cotton was bought, and cleaned with cotton-gins, and, though we were restricted by the great draught of the Pioneer to an area of less than seven miles, in three months he had collected 300 lbs. of clean cotton-wool, at less than a penny per pound.   No great amount, certainly, when compared with the thousands of bales which come from other countries; but still sufficient to prove that cotton of superior quality can be raised by native labour alone; and but for the slave-trade, which soon afterwards swept all these people away, it is highly probable, that in a few years, the free-labour could have been turned to account in the markets of the world.

It was never intended that a Government Expedition should become a mere cotton collecting or mercantile specu-lation.   We ascertained that the part of Africa in which we laboured was pre-eminently suited for the better varie-ties of the cotton-plant; that two species of excellent cotton had already been introduced, and so widely distributed by the natives themselves, as to render new seed unnecessary, and the indigenous kind quite an exception in the country. The climate and soil were found to be so well adapted for raising this product, that no danger need ever be appre-hended of the crops being cut off by frosts; and, from all we could learn, free-labour was as available here as it is in any other country in the world.   But a mighty want was felt in the entire absence of those blessings which England has unquestionably conferred on the West Coast.   There were none of those Christian natives that can be numbered by thousands at Sierra-Leone and elsewhere, who, whatever defects they may have, do possess the qualification of being trustworthy trade-agents among their countrymen.   Having carefully examined and compared both Coasts, and making allowance for the fact that perhaps a majority of those on whom English benevolence has been expended have been the lowest of the low—liberated African slaves,—and likewise giving all due weight to the assertions of the traders who have used strong language to express their injured feelings

2 A

in being prevented from using the people as brutes, we must say that the conduct of England on the West Coast of late years deserves the world's admiration. Her generosity will appear grand in the eyes of posterity. Here, on the East Coast, we have the contrast. No trustworthy agents can be employed; no education has been imparted; and not even slave agents can be sent to a distance except on the promise of plunder and rapine. In the Mission we had now with us, we trusted that we saw the dawn of a better system for both Portuguese and natives, than that which has been the bane of all progress for ages past.

The Expedition, in spite of several adverse circumstances, was up to this point eminently successful in its objects. As will be afterwards seen, we had opened a cotton-field, which, taking in the Shire and Lake Nyassa, was 400 miles in length. We had gained the confidence of the people wherever we had gone; and, supposing the Mission of the Universities to be only moderately successful, as all we had previously known of the desire of the natives to trade had been amply confirmed, a perfectly new era had commenced in a region much larger than the cotton-fields of the Southern States of America.

We had, however, as will afterwards be seen, arrived at the turning-point of our prosperous career, and soon came into contact with the Portuguese slave-trade; and let any one reflect on the injury that any country sustains, even by laws which only hamper trade and free commercial intercourse, and he may judge how utterly destructive to all prosperity that system must be, which not only fosters internecine wars, but renders the pursuit of agriculture perilous in times of peace.

On at last reaching Chibisa's, we heard that there was war in the Manganja country, and the slave-trade was going on briskly. A deputation from a Chief near Mount Zomba had just passed on its way to Chibisa, who was in a distant village, to implore him to come himself, or send medicine, to drive off the Waiao, Waiau, or Ajawa, whose marauding parties were desolating the land. A large gang of recently enslaved Manganja crossed the river, on their way to Tette, a few days before we got the ship up. Chibisa's deputy was civil, and readily gave us permission to hire as many men to carry the Bishop's goods up to the hills as were willing to go. With a sufficient number, therefore, we started for the highlands on the 15th of July, to show the Bishop the country, which, from its altitude and coolness, was most suitable for a station. Our first day's march was a long and fatiguing one. The few hamlets we passed were poor, and had no food for our men, and we were obliged to go on till 4 P.M., when we entered the small village of Chipindu. The inhabitants complained of hunger, and said they had no food to sell, and no hut for us to sleep in ; but, if we would only go on a little further, we should come to a village where they had plenty to eat ; but we had travelled far enough, and determined to remain where we were. Before sunset as much food was brought as we cared to purchase, and, as it threatened to rain, huts were provided for the whole party.

Next forenoon we halted at the village of our old friend Mbame, to obtain new carriers, because Chibisa's men, never before having been hired, and not having yet learned to trust us, did not choose to go further. After resting a little, Mbame told us that a slave party on its way to Tette would presently pass through his village. " Shall we interfere ?" we inquired of each other. We remembered that all our valuable private baggage was in Tette, which, if we freed the slaves, might, together with some Government property, be destroyed in retaliation ; but this system of slave-hunters dogging us

2 A 2

where previously they durst not venture, and, on pretence of being " our children," setting one tribe against another, to furnish themselves with slaves, would so inevitably thwart all the efforts, for which we had the sanction of the Portuguese Government, that we resolved to run all risks, and put a stop, if possible, to the slave-trade, which had now followed on the footsteps of our discoveries. A few minutes after Mbame had spoken to us, the slave party, a long line of manacled men, women, and children, came wending their way round the hill and into the valley, on the side of which the village stood. The black drivers, armed with muskets, and bedecked with various articles of finery, marched jauntily in the front, middle, and rear of the line; some of them blowing exultant notes out of long tin horns. They seemed to feel that they were doing a very noble thing, and might proudly march with an air of triumph. But the instant the fellows caught a glimpse of the Eng- lish, they darted off like mad into the forest; so fast, indeed, that we caught but a glimpse of their red caps and the soles of their feet. The chief of the party alone remained; and he, from being in front, had his hand tightly grasped by a Makololo! He proved to be a well-known slave of the late Commandant at Tette, and for some time our own attendant while there. On asking him how he obtained these captives, he replied, he had bought them; but on our inquiring of the people themselves all, save four, said they had been captured in war. While this inquiry was going on, he bolted too. The captives knelt down, and, in their way of expressing thanks, clapped their hands with great energy. They were thus left entirely on our hands, and knives were soon busy at work cutting the women and children loose. It was more difficult to cut the men adrift, as each had his neck in the fork of a stout stick, six or seven feet long, and

GANG OF CAPTIVES MET AT MBAME'S ON THEIR WAY TO TETTE.

kept in by an iron rod which was riveted at both ends across
the throat. With a saw, luckily in the Bishop's baggage,
one by one the men were sawn out into freedom. The
women, on being told to take the meal they were carrying
and cook breakfast for themselves and the children, seemed
to consider the news too good to be true; but after a little
coaxing went at it with alacrity, and made a capital fire
by which to boil their pots with the slave sticks and bonds,
their old acquaintances through many a sad night and
weary day. Many were mere children about five years of age
and under. One little boy, with the simplicity of childhood,
said to our men, " The others tied and starved us, you cut
the ropes and tell us to eat; what sort of people are you?—
Where did you come from?" Two of the women had been
shot the day before for attempting to untie the thongs.
This, the rest were told, was to prevent them from attempting
to escape. One woman had her infant's brains knocked out,
because she could not carry her load and it. And a man
was despatched with an axe, because he had broken down
with fatigue. Self-interest would have set a watch over the
whole rather than commit murder; but in this traffic we
invariably find self-interest overcome by contempt of human
life and by bloodthirstiness.

The Bishop was not present at this scene, having gone to
bathe in a little stream below the village; but on his return he
warmly approved of what had been done; he at first had doubts,
but now felt that, had he been present, he would have joined
us in the good work. Logic is out of place when the question
with a true-hearted man is, whether his brother-man is to be
saved or not. Eighty-four, chiefly women and children, were
liberated; and on being told that they were now free, and
might go where they pleased, or remain with us, they all chose
to stay; and the Bishop wisely attached them to his Mission,

to be educated as members of a Christian family. In this way a great difficulty in the commencement of a Mission was overcome. Years are usually required before confidence is so far instilled into the natives' mind as to induce them, young or old, to submit to the guidance of strangers professing to be actuated by motives the reverse of worldly wisdom, and inculcating customs strange and unknown to them and their fathers.

We proceeded next morning to Soche's with our liberated party, the men cheerfully carrying the Bishop's goods. As we had begun, it was of no use to do things by halves, so eight others were freed in a hamlet on our path; but a party of traders, with nearly a hundred slaves, fled from Soche's on hearing of our proceedings. Dr. Kirk and four Makololo followed them with great energy, but they made clear off to Tette. Six more captives were liberated at Mongazi's, and two slave-traders detained for the night, to prevent them from carrying information to a large party still in front. Of their own accord they volunteered the information that the Governor's servants had charge of the next party; but we did not choose to be led by them, though they offered to guide us to his Excellency's own agents. Two of the Bishop's black men from the Cape, having once been slaves, were now zealous emancipators, and volunteered to guard the prisoners during the night. So anxious were our heroes to keep them safe, that instead of relieving each other, by keeping watch and watch, both kept watch together, till towards four o'clock in the morning, when sleep stole gently over them both; and the wakeful prisoners, seizing the opportunity, escaped: one of the guards, perceiving the loss, rushed out of the hut, shouting, "They are gone, the prisoners are off, and they have taken my rifle with them, and the women too! Fire! everybody fire!" The rifle and the women, however, were all safe enough, the slave-traders being only too glad to escape alone. Fifty more slaves were freed next day in another village; and, the whole party being stark-naked, cloth enough was left to clothe them, better probably than they had ever been clothed before. The head of this gang, whom we knew as the agent of one of the principal merchants of Tette, said that they had the licence of the Governor for all they did. This we were fully aware of without his stating it. It is quite impossible for any enterprise to be undertaken there without the Governor's knowledge and connivance.

The portion of the highlands which the Bishop wished to look at before deciding on a settlement, belonged to Chiwawa or Chibaba, the most manly and generous Manganja Chief we had met with on our previous journey. On reaching Nsambo's, near Mount Chiradzuru, we heard that Chibaba was dead, and that Chigunda was Chief instead. Chigunda, apparently of his own accord, though possibly he may have learnt that the Bishop intended to settle somewhere in the country, asked him to come and live with him at Magomero, adding that there was room enough for both. This hearty and spontaneous invitation had considerable influence on the Bishop's mind, and seemed to decide the question. A place nearer the Shire would have been chosen, had he expected his supplies to come up that river; but the Portuguese, claiming the river Shire, though never occupying even its mouth, had closed it, as well as the Zambesi.

Our hopes were turned to the Rovuma, as a free highway into Lake Nyassa and the vast interior. A steamer was already ordered for the Lake, and the Bishop, seeing the advantageous nature of the highlands which stretch an immense way to the north, was more anxious to be near the Lake and the Rovuma, than the Shire. When he decided to settle at Magomero, it was thought desirable, to prevent the country from being depopulated, to visit the Ajawa Chief, and to try and persuade him to give up his slaving and kidnapping courses, and turn the energies of his people to peaceful pursuits.

On the morning of the 22nd we were informed that the Ajawa were near, and were burning a village a few miles off. Leaving the rescued slaves, we moved off to seek an interview with these scourges of the country. On our way we met crowds of Manganja fleeing from the war in front. These poor fugitives from the slave hunt had, as usual, to leave all the food they possessed, except the little they could carry on their heads. We passed field after field of Indian corn or beans, standing ripe for harvesting, but the owners were away. The villages were all deserted: one where we breakfasted two years before, and saw a number of men peacefully weaving cloth, and, among ourselves, called it the "Paisley of the hills," was burnt; the stores of corn were poured out in cartloads, and scattered all over the plain, and all along the paths, neither conquerors nor conquered having been able to convey it away. About two o'clock we saw the smoke of burning villages, and heard triumphant shouts, mingled with the wail of the Manganja women, lamenting over their slain. The Bishop then engaged us in fervent prayer; and, on rising from our knees, we saw a long line of Ajawa warriors, with their captives, coming round the hill-side. The first of the returning conquerors were entering their own village below, and we heard women welcoming them back with "lilliloo-ings." The Ajawa headman left the path on seeing us, and stood on an anthill to obtain a complete view of our party. We called out that we had come to have an interview with them, but some of the Manganja who followed us shouted "Our Chibisa is come:" Chibisa being well known as a great conjurer and general. The Ajawa ran off yelling and scream-

ing, "Nkondo! Nkondo!" (War! War!) We heard the words
of the Manganja, but they did not strike us at the moment
as neutralizing all our assertions of peace. The captives
threw down their loads on the path, and fled to the hills: and
a large body of armed men came running up from the village,
and in a few seconds they were all around us, though mostly
concealed by the projecting rocks and long grass. In vain
we protested that we had not come to fight, but to talk with
them. They would not listen, having, as we remembered
afterwards, good reason, in the cry of "Our Chibisa."
Flushed with recent victory over three villages, and confident
of an easy triumph over a mere handful of men, they began
to shoot their poisoned arrows, sending them with great
force upwards of a hundred yards, and wounding one of our
followers through the arm. Our retiring slowly up the
ascent from the village only made them more eager to
prevent our escape ; and, in the belief that this retreat was
evidence of fear, they closed upon us in bloodthirsty fury.
Some came within fifty yards, dancing hideously; others
having quite surrounded us, and availing themselves of the
rocks and long grass hard by, were intent on cutting us off,
while others made off with their women and a large body of
slaves. Four were armed with muskets, and we were obliged
in self-defence to return their fire and drive them off. When
they saw the range of the rifles, they very soon desisted, and
ran away; but some shouted to us from the hills the con-
soling intimation, that they would follow, and kill us where
we slept. Only two of the captives escaped to us, but
probably most of those made prisoners that day fled elsewhere in the confusion. We returned to the village which
we had left in the morning, after a hungry, fatiguing, and
most unpleasant day.

Though we could not blame ourselves for the course we had

followed, we felt sorry for what had happened. It was the first time we had ever been attacked by the natives or come into collision with them; though we had always taken it for granted that we might be called upon to act in self-defence, we were on this occasion less prepared than usual, no game having been expected here. The men had only a single round of cartridge each; their leader had no revolver, and the rifle he usually fired with was left at the ship to save it from the damp of the season. Had we known better the effect of slavery and murder, on the temper of these blood-thirsty marauders, we should have tried messages and presents before going near them.

The old chief, Chinsunse, came on a visit to us next day, and pressed the Bishop to come and live with him. " Chigunda," he said, " is but a child, and the Bishop ought to live with the father rather than with the child." But the old man's object was so evidently to have the Mission as a shield against the Ajawa, that his invitation was declined. While begging us to drive away the marauders, that he might live in peace, he adopted the stratagem of causing a number of his men to rush into the village, in breathless haste, with the news that the Ajawa were close upon us. And having been reminded that we never fought, unless attacked, as we were the day before, and that we had come among them for the purpose of promoting peace, and of teaching them to worship the Supreme, to give up selling His children, and to cultivate other objects for barter than each other, he replied, in a huff, " Then I am dead already."

The Bishop, feeling, as most Englishmen would, at the prospect of the people now in his charge being swept off into slavery by hordes of men-stealers, proposed to go at once to the rescue of the captive Manganja, and drive the marauding Ajawa out of the country. All were warmly in favour of this, save Dr. Livingstone, who opposed it on the ground that it would be better for the Bishop to wait, and see the effect of the check the slave-hunters had just experienced. The Ajawa were evidently goaded on by Portuguese agents from Tette, and there was no bond of union among the Manganja on which to work. It was possible that the Ajawa might be persuaded to something better, though, from having long been in the habit of slaving for the Quillimane market, it was not very probable. But the Manganja could easily be overcome piecemeal by any enemy; old feuds made them glad to see calamities befall their next neighbours. We counselled them to unite against the common enemies of their country, and added distinctly that we English would on no account enter into their quarrels. On the Bishop inquiring whether, in the event of the Manganja again asking aid against the Ajawa, it would be his duty to accede to their request,—"No," replied Dr. Livingstone, " you will be oppressed by their importunities, but do not interfere in native quarrels." This advice the good man honourably mentions in his journal. We have been rather minute in relating what occurred during the few days of our connexion with the Mission of the English Universities, on the hills, because, the recorded advice having been discarded, blame was thrown on Dr. Livingstone's shoulders, as if the Missionaries had no individual responsibility for their subsequent conduct. This, unquestionably, good Bishop Mackenzie had too much manliness to have allowed. The connexion of the members of the Zambesi Expedition, with the acts of the Bishop's Mission, now ceased, for we returned to the ship and prepared for our journey to Lake Nyassa. We cheerfully, if necessary, will bear all responsibility up to this point; and if the Bishop afterwards made mistakes in certain collisions with the slavers, he had the votes of all his party with him, and those who best knew the peculiar circumstances, and the loving disposition of this good-hearted man, will blame him least. In this position, and in these circumstances, we left our friends at the Mission Station.

As a temporary measure the Bishop decided to place his Mission Station on a small promontory formed by the windings of the little, clear stream of Magomero, which was so cold that the limbs were quite benumbed by washing in it in the July mornings. The site chosen was a pleasant spot to the eye, and completely surrounded by stately, shady trees. It was expected to serve for a residence, till the Bishop had acquired an accurate knowledge of the adjacent country, and of the political relations of the people, and could select a healthy and commanding situation, as a permanent centre of Christian civilization. Everything promised fairly. The weather was delightful, resembling the pleasantest part of an English summer; provisions poured in very cheap and in great abundance. The Bishop, with characteristic ardour, commenced learning the language, Mr. Waller began building, and Mr. Scudamore improvised a sort of infant school for the children, than which there is no better means for acquiring an unwritten tongue.

CHAPTER XIX.

ON the 6th of August, 1861, a few days after returning from Magomero, Drs. Livingstone and Kirk, and Charles Livingstone started for Nyassa with a light four-oared gig, a white sailor, and a score of attendants. We hired people along the path to carry the boat past the forty miles of the Murchison Cataracts for a cubit of cotton cloth a day. This being deemed great wages, more than twice the men required eagerly offered their services. The chief difficulty was in limiting their numbers. Crowds followed us; and, had we not taken down in the morning the names of the porters engaged, in the evening claims would have been made by those who only helped during the last ten minutes of the journey. The men of one village carried the boat to the next, and all we had to do was to tell the headman that we wanted fresh men in the morning. He saw us pay the first party, and had his men ready at the time appointed, so there was no delay in waiting for carriers. They often make a loud noise when carrying heavy loads, but talking

and bawling does not put them out of breath. The country
was rough and with little soil on it, but covered with grass
and open forest. A few small trees were cut down to clear
a path for our shouting assistants, who were good enough
to consider the boat as a certificate of peaceful intentions
at least to them. Several small streams were passed, the
largest of which were the Mukuru-Madse and Lesungwe.
The inhabitants on both banks were now civil and obliging. Our possession of a boat, and consequent power of
crossing independently of the canoes, helped to develop
their good manners, which were not apparent on our previous visit.

There is often a surprising contrast between neighbouring villages. One is well off and thriving, having good huts,
plenty of food, and native cloth; and its people are frank,
trusty, generous, and eager to sell provisions; while in the
next the inhabitants may be ill-housed, disobliging, suspicious, ill fed, and scantily clad, and with nothing for sale,
though the land around is as fertile as that of their wealthier
neighbours. We followed the river for the most part to
avail ourselves of the still reaches for sailing; but a comparatively smooth country lies further inland, over which a
good road could be made. Some of the five main cataracts
are very grand, the river falling 1200 feet in the 40 miles.
After passing the last of the cataracts, we launched our boat
for good on the broad and deep waters of the Upper Shire,
and were virtually on the lake, for the gentle current shows
but little difference of level. The bed is broad and deep,
but the course is rather tortuous at first, and makes a long
bend to the east till it comes within five or six miles of
the base of Mount Zomba. The natives regarded the Upper
Shire as a prolongation of Lake Nyassa; for where what we
called the river approaches Lake Shirwa, a little north of

the mountains, they said that the hippopotami, "which are great night travellers," pass from *one lake into the other.* There the land is flat, and only a short land journey would be necessary. Seldom does the current here exceed a knot an hour, while that of the Lower Shire is from two to two-and-a-half knots. Our land party of Makololo accompanied us along the right bank, and passed thousands of Manganja fugitives living in temporary huts on that side, who had recently been driven from their villages on the opposite hills by the Ajawa.

The soil was dry and hard, and covered with mopane-trees; but some of the Manganja were busy hoeing the ground and planting the little corn they had brought with them. The effects of hunger were already visible on those whose food had been seized or burned by the Ajawa and Portuguese slave-traders. The spokesman or prime minister of one of the Chiefs, named Kaloñjeré, was a humpbacked dwarf, a fluent speaker, who tried hard to make us go over and drive off the Ajawa; but he could not deny that by selling people Kaloñjeré had invited these slave-hunters to the country. This is the second humpbacked dwarf we have found occupying the like important post, the other was the prime minister of a Batonga Chief on the Zambesi.

As we sailed along, we disturbed many white-breasted cormorants; we had seen the same species fishing between the cataracts. Here, with many other wild-fowl, they find subsistence on the smooth water by night, and sit sleepily on trees and in the reeds by day. Many hippopotami were seen in the river, and one of them stretched its wide jaws, as if to swallow the whole stern of the boat, close to Dr. Kirk's back; the animal was so near, that in opening its mouth it lashed a quantity of water on to the stern-sheets, but did no damage. To avoid large marauding parties of

Ajawa, on the left bank of the Shire, we continued on the right, or western side, with our land party, along the shore of the small lake Pamalombe. This lakelet is ten or twelve miles in length, and five or six broad. It is nearly surrounded by a broad belt of papyrus, so dense that we could scarcely find an opening to the shore. The plants, ten or twelve feet high, grew so closely together that air was excluded, and so much sulphuretted hydrogen gas evolved that by one night's exposure the bottom of the boat was blackened. Myriads of mosquitoes showed, as probably they always do, the presence of malaria.

We hastened from this sickly spot, trying to take the attentions of the mosquitoes as hints to seek more pleasant quarters on the healthy shores of Lake Nyassa; and when we sailed into it, on the 2nd September, we felt refreshed by the greater coolness of the air off this large body of water. The depth was the first point of interest. This is indicated by the colour of the water, which, on a belt along the shore, varying from a quarter to half a mile in breadth, is light green, and this is met by the deep blue or indigo tint of the Indian Ocean, which is the colour of the great body of Nyassa. We found the Upper Shire from nine to fifteen feet in depth; but skirting the western side of the lake about a mile from the shore the water deepened from nine to fifteen fathoms; then, as we rounded the grand mountainous promontory, which we named Cape Maclear, after our excellent friend the Astronomer Royal at the Cape of Good Hope, we could get no bottom with our lead-line of thirty-five fathoms. We pulled along the western shore, which was a succession of bays, and found that where the bottom was sandy near the beach, and to a mile out, the depth varied from six to fourteen fathoms. In a rocky bay about latitude 11° 40' we had soundings at

100 fathoms, though outside the same bay we found none with a fishing-line of 116 fathoms; but this cast was unsatisfactory, as the line broke in coming up. According to our present knowledge, a ship could anchor only near the shore.

Looking back to the southern end of Lake Nyassa, the arm from which the Shire flows was found to be about thirty miles long and from ten to twelve broad. Rounding Cape Maclear, and looking to the south-west, we have another arm, which stretches some eighteen miles southward, and is from six to twelve miles in breadth. These arms give the southern end a forked appearance, and with the help of a little imagination it may be likened to the "boot-shape" of Italy. The narrowest part is about the ankle, eighteen or twenty miles. From this it widens to the north, and in the upper third or fourth it is fifty or sixty miles broad. The length is over 200 miles. The direction in which it lies is as near as possible due north and south. Nothing of the great bend to the west, shown in all the previous maps, could be detected by either compass or chronometer, and the watch we used was an excellent one. The season of the year was very unfavourable. The "smokes" filled the air with an impenetrable haze, and the equinoctial gales made it impossible for us to cross to the eastern side. When we caught a glimpse of the sun rising from behind the mountains to the east, we made sketches and bearings of them at different latitudes, which enabled us to secure approximate measurements of the width. These agreed with the times taken by the natives at the different crossing-places—as Tsenga, and Molamba. About the beginning of the upper third the lake is crossed by taking advantage of the island Chizumara, which name in the native tongue means the "ending;" further north they go round the end instead, though that takes several days.

2 B

The lake appeared to be surrounded by mountains, but it was afterwards found that these beautiful tree-covered heights were, on the west, only the edges of high table-lands. Like all narrow seas encircled by highlands, it is visited by sudden and tremendous storms. We were on it in September and October, perhaps the stormiest season of the year, and were repeatedly detained by gales. At times, while sailing pleasantly over the blue water with a gentle breeze, suddenly and without any warning was heard the sound of a coming storm, roaring on with crowds of angry waves in its wake. We were caught one morning with the sea breaking all around us, and, unable either to advance or recede, anchored a mile from shore, in seven fathoms. The furious surf on the beach would have shivered our slender boat to atoms, had we tried to land. The waves most dreaded came rolling on in threes, with their crests, driven into spray, streaming behind them. A short lull followed each triple charge. Had one of these white-maned seas struck our frail bark, nothing could have saved us; for they came on with resistless force; seaward, in shore, and on either side of us, they broke in foam, but we escaped. For six weary hours we faced those terrible trios, any one of which might have been carrying the end of our Expedition in its hoary head. A low, dark, detached, oddly-shaped cloud came slowly from the mountains, and hung for hours directly over our heads. A flock of night-jars (*Cometornis vexillarius*), which on no other occasion come out by day, soared above us in the gale, like birds of evil omen. Our black crew became sea-sick and unable to sit up or keep the boat's head to the sea. The natives and our land party stood on the high cliffs looking at us and exclaiming, as the waves seemed to swallow up the boat, "They are lost! they are all dead!" When at last the gale moderated and we got safely ashore, they saluted us warmly, as after a long absence. From this time we trusted implicitly to the opinions of our seaman, John Neil, who, having been a fisherman on the coast of Ireland, understood boating on a stormy coast, and by his advice we often sat cowering on the land for days together waiting for the surf to go down. He had never seen such waves before. We had to beach the boat every night to save her from being swamped at anchor; and, did we not believe the gales to be peculiar to one season of the year, would call Nyassa, the "Lake of Storms."

Lake Nyassa receives no great affluents from the west. The five rivers we observed in passing did not at this time appear to bring in as much water as the Shire was carrying out. They were from fifteen to thirty yards wide, and some too deep to ford; but the evaporation must be very considerable. These streams, with others of about the same size from the mountains on the east and north, when swollen by the rains may be sufficient to account for the rise in the lake without any large river. The natives nearest the northern end denied the existence of a large river there, though at one time it seemed necessary to account for the Shire's perennial flow. Distinct white marks on the rocks showed that, for some time during the rainy season, the water of the lake is three feet above the point to which it falls towards the close of the dry period of the year. The rains begin here in November, and the permanent rise of the Shire does not take place till January. The western side of Lake Nyassa, with the exception of the great harbour to the west of Cape Maclear, is, as has been said before, a succession of small bays of nearly similar form, each having an open sandy beach and pebbly shore, and being separated from its neighbour by a rocky headland, with detached rocks extending some distance out to sea. The great south-western bay referred

to would form a magnificent harbour, the only really good one
we saw to the west.

The land immediately adjacent to the lake is low and
fertile, though in some places marshy and tenanted by large
flocks of ducks, geese, herons, crowned cranes, and other birds.
In the southern part we have sometimes ten or a dozen miles
of rich plains, bordered by what seem high ranges of well-
wooded hills, running nearly parallel with the lake. Northwards the mountains become loftier and present some magnificent views, range towering beyond range, until the dim,
lofty outlines projected against the sky bound the prospect.
Still further north the plain becomes more narrow,
until, near where we turned, it disappears altogether, and
the mountains rise abruptly out of the lake, forming the
north-east boundary of what was described to us as an extensive table-land, well suited for pasturage and agriculture, and
now only partially occupied by a tribe of Zulus, who came
from the south some years ago. These people own large
herds of cattle, and are constantly increasing in numbers by
annexing other tribes.

Never before in Africa have we seen anything like the dense
population on the shores of Lake Nyassa. In the southern
part, there was an almost unbroken chain of villages. On
the beach of wellnigh every little sandy bay, dark crowds
were standing, gazing at the novel sight of a boat under sail;
and wherever we landed we were surrounded in a few seconds
by hundreds of men, women, and children, who hastened to
have a stare at the "chirombo" (wild animals). To see the
animals feed was the greatest attraction; never did the Zoo-
logical Society's lions or monkeys draw more sightseers,
than we did. Indeed, we equalled the hippopotamus on his first
arrival among the civilized on the banks of the Thames. The
wondering multitude crowded round us at meal-times and

formed a thicket of dark bodies, all looking on, apparently, with the deepest interest; but they goodnaturedly kept each other to a line we made on the sand, and left us room to dine. They were civil upon the whole. Twice they went the length of lifting up the edge of our sail, which we used as a tent, as boys do the curtains of travelling menageries at home. They named us indeed "chirombo," which means only the wild beasts that may be eaten, but they had no idea that we understood their meaning. No fines were levied on us, nor dues demanded. At one village only were they impudent, but they were "elevated" by beer. They cultivate the soil pretty extensively, and grow large quantities of rice and sweet potatoes, as well as maize, mapira, and millet. In the north, however, cassava is the staple product, which, with fish kept till the flavour is high, constitutes the main support of the inhabitants. During a portion of the year, the northern dwellers on the lake have a harvest which furnishes a singular sort of food. As we approached our limit in that direction, clouds, as of smoke rising from miles of burning grass, were observed bending in a south-easterly direction, and we thought that the unseen land on the opposite side was closing in, and that we were near the end of the lake. But next morning we sailed through one of the clouds on our own side, and discovered that it was neither smoke nor haze, but countless millions of minute midges called "kungo" (a cloud or fog). They filled the air to an immense height, and swarmed upon the water, too light to sink in it. Eyes and mouth had to be kept closed while passing through this living cloud: they struck upon the face like fine drifting snow. Thousands lay in the boat when she emerged from the cloud of midges. The people gather these minute insects by night, and boil them into thick cakes, to be used as a relish—millions of midges in a cake. A kungo cake, an inch thick and as large as the blue bonnet of a Scotch ploughman, was offered to us; it was very dark in colour, and tasted not unlike caviare, or salted locusts.

Abundance of excellent fish are found in the lake, and nearly all were new to us. The mpasa or sanjika, found by Dr. Kirk to be a kind of carp, was running up the rivers to spawn, like our salmon at home: the largest we saw was over two feet in length; it is a splendid fish, and the best we have ever eaten in Africa. They were ascending the rivers in August and September, and furnished active and profitable employment to many fishermen, who did not mind their being out of season. Weirs were constructed full of sluices, in each of which was set a large basket-trap, through whose single tortuous opening the fish once in has but small chance of escape. A short distance below the weir, nets are stretched across from bank to bank, so that it seemed a marvel how the most sagacious sanjika could get up at all without being taken. Possibly a passage up the river is found at night; but this is not the country of Sundays or " close times " for either men, or fish. The lake fish are caught chiefly in nets, although men, and even women with babies on their backs, are occasionally seen fishing from the rocks with hooks.

A net with small meshes is used for catching the young fry of a silvery kind like pickerel, when they are about two inches long; thousands are often taken in a single haul. We had a present of a large bucketful one day for dinner: they tasted as if they had been cooked with a little quinine, probably from their gall-bladders being left in. In deep water, some sorts are taken by lowering fish-baskets attached by a long cord to a float, around which is often tied a mass of grass or weeds, as an alluring shade for the deep-sea fish. Fleets of fine canoes are engaged in the fisheries. The men have long paddles, and stand erect while using them. They sometimes venture out when a considerable sea is running. Our Makololo acknowledged that, in handling canoes, the Lake men beat them; they were unwilling to cross the Zambesi even, when the wind blew fresh. The first impression one receives of the Lake Nyassa men is, that they are far from being industrious—or, to be more explicit, are troubled with downright laziness. Groups may be seen during the day lying fast asleep under the shady trees along the shore, and apparently taking life very easily: but, on a little better acquaintance, this first impression is modified, and it is found that these forenoon sleepers have been hard at work the greater part of the night. In the afternoon they begin to bestir themselves; examining and mending their nets, carrying them to the canoes, and coiling in their lines. In the evening they paddle off to the best fishing station, and throughout most of the night the poor fellows are toiling in the water, dragging their nets. They too suffer from fever. We saw the herpetic eruptions round their mouths which often mark its cure, and found that the chills act on them, though their skin is much more torpid in function than ours. Hence that conformity to the customs of the natives, which some people enjoin, would require modification for our highly excitable skins. Our beards grow as much in a week as theirs do in a month.

Though there are many crocodiles in the lake, and some of an extraordinary size, the fishermen say that it is a rare thing for any one to be carried off by these reptiles. When crocodiles can easily obtain abundance of fish — their natural food—they seldom attack men; but when unable to see to catch their prey, from the muddiness of the water in floods, they are very dangerous.

Many men and boys are employed in gathering the buaze, in preparing the fibre, and in making it into long nets. The knot of the net is different from ours, for they invariably use what sailors call the reef knot, but they net with a needle like that we use. From the amount of native cotton cloth worn in many of the southern villages, it is evident that a goodly number of busy hands, and patient heads, must be employed in the cultivation of cotton and in the various slow processes through which it has to pass, before the web is finished in the native loom. In addition to this branch of industry, an extensive manufacture of cloth, from the inner bark of an undescribed tree, of the botanical group, *Cæsalpineæ,* is ever going on, from one end of the lake to the other; and both toil and time are required to procure the bark, and to prepare it by pounding and steeping it to render it soft and pliable. The prodigious amount of the bark clothing worn indicates the destruction of an immense number of trees every year; yet the adjacent heights seem still well covered with timber.

The Lake people are by no means handsome: the women— to use our mildest term to the fair sex—are *very* plain; and really make themselves hideous by the means they adopt to render their persons beautiful and attractive. The *pelele,* or ornament for the upper lip, is universally worn by the ladies; the most valuable is of pure tin, hammered into the shape of a small dish; some are made of white quartz, and give the wearer the appearance of having an inch or more of one of Price's patent candles thrust through the lip, and projecting beyond the tip of the nose. Some ladies, not content with the upper pelele, go to extremes, as ladies will, and insert another in the under lip through a hole almost opposite the lower gums. A few peleles are made of a blood-red kind of pipeclay, much in fashion,—"sweet things" in the way of lip-rings; but so hideous to behold, that no time nor usage could make our eyes rest upon them without aversion.

All the natives are tattooed from head to foot, the figures

being characteristic of the tribes, and varying with them. The Matumboka, or Atimboka, raise up little knobs on the skin of their faces, after a fashion that makes them look as if covered all over with warts or pimples. The young girls are good-looking before this ugly adornment hardens the features, and gives them the appearance of age. Their gowns are indescribable, owing to the extreme scantiness of the material from which they are cut, and their beautiful teeth are notched or clipped to points like those of cats.

In character, the Lake tribes are very much like other people; there are decent men among them, while a good many are no better than they should be. They are open-handed enough: if one of us, as was often the case, went to see a net drawn, a fish was always offered. Sailing one day past a number of men, who had just dragged their nets ashore, at one of the fine fisheries at Pamalombe, we were hailed and asked to stop, and received a liberal donation of beautiful fish. Arriving late one afternoon at a small village on the lake, a number of the inhabitants manned two canoes, took out their seine, dragged it, and made us a present of the entire haul. The northern Chief, Marenga, a tall handsome man, with a fine aquiline nose, whom we found living in his stockade in a forest about twenty miles north of the mountain Kowirwe, behaved like a gentleman to us. His land extended from Dambo to the north of Makuza hill. He was specially generous, and gave us bountiful presents of food and beer. " Do they wear such things in your country ? " he asked, pointing to his iron bracelet, which was studded with copper, and highly prized. The Doctor said he had never seen such in his country, whereupon Marenga instantly took it off, and presented it to him, and his wife also did the same with hers. On our return south from the mountains near the north end of the Lake, we reached

Marenga's on the 7th October. When he could not prevail upon us to forego the advantage of a fair wind for his invitation to "spend the whole day drinking his beer, which was," he said "quite ready," he loaded us with provisions, all of which he sent for before we gave him any present. In allusion to the boat's sail, his people said that they had no Bazimo, or none worth having, seeing they had never invented the like for them. The Chief, Mankambira, likewise treated us with kindness; but wherever the slave-trade is carried on, the people are dishonest and uncivil; that invariably leaves a blight and a curse in its path. The first question put to us at the lake crossing-places, was, "Have you come to buy slaves?" On hearing that we were English, and never purchased slaves, the questioners put on a supercilious air, and sometimes refused to sell us food. This want of respect to us may have been owing to the impressions conveyed to them by the Arabs, whose dhows have sometimes been taken by English cruisers when engaged in lawful trade. Much foreign cloth, beads, and brass-wire, were worn by these ferrymen—and some had muskets.

By Chitanda, near one of the slave crossing-places, we were robbed for the first time in Africa, and learned by experience that these people, like more civilized nations, have expert thieves among them. It might be only a coincidence; but we never suffered from impudence, loss of property, or were endangered, unless among people familiar with slaving. We had such a general sense of security, that never, save when we suspected treachery, did we set a watch at night. Our native companions had, on this occasion, been carousing on beer, and had removed to a distance of some thirty yards, that we might not overhear their free and easy after-dinner remarks, and two of us had a slight touch of fever; between three and four o'clock in the morning some light-fingered gentry came, while we slept ingloriously—rifles and revolvers all ready,—and relieved us of most of our goods. The boat's sail, under which we slept, was open all around, so the feat was easy. One of us felt his pillow moving, but in the delicious dreamy state in which he lay, thought it was one of the attendants adjusting his covering, and so, as he fancied, let well alone.

Awaking as honest men do, at the usual hour, the loss of one was announced by "My bag is gone—with all my clothes; and my boots too!" "And mine!" responded a second. "And mine also!" chimed in the third, "with the bag of beads, and the rice!" "Is the cloth taken?" was the eager inquiry, as that would have been equivalent to all our money. It had been used for a pillow that night, and thus saved. The rogues left on the beach, close to our beds, the Aneroid Barometer and a pair of boots, thinking, possibly, that they might be of use to us, or, at least, that they could be of none to them. They shoved back some dried plants and fishes into one bag, but carried off many other specimens we had collected; some of our notes also, and nearly all our clothing; one of our party, indeed, rose with nothing belonging to him but what he happened to have on at the time; another was indebted to female curiosity for the safety of his best suit; for, having on the day previous, Sunday, retired from the crowd to have a bath and change among the reeds, he looked about before being quite undressed, and found a crowd of ladies peering at the apparition. He retired without either bath or change of apparel. One feels ashamed of the white skin; it seems unnatural, like blanched celery—or white mice. On returning to the camp, which was surrounded with perpetual clatter and crowds of visitors all day, he changed his clothing after dark, putting on and sleeping in his best, as it

was too late to change it again, so the worst only was
stolen.

We could not suspect the people of the village near which
we lay. We had probably been followed for days by the
thieves watching for an opportunity. And our suspicions
fell on some persons who had come from the East Coast; but
having no evidence, and expecting to hear if our goods were
exposed for sale in the vicinity, we made no fuss about it,
and began to make new clothing. That our rifles and revolvers
were left untouched was greatly to our advantage: yet we
felt it was most humiliating for armed men to have been so
thoroughly fleeced by a few black rascals.

Some of the best fisheries appear to be private property.
We found shelter from a storm one morning in a spacious
lagoon, which communicated with the lake by a narrow
passage. Across this strait stakes were driven in, leaving
only spaces for the basket fish-traps. A score of men were
busily engaged in taking out the fish. We tried to purchase
some, but they refused to sell. The fish did not belong to
them, they would send for the proprietor of the place. The
proprietor arrived in a short time, and readily sold what we
wanted.

Some of the burying-grounds are very well arranged, and
well cared for ; this was noticed at Chitanda, and more particularly at a village on the southern shore of the fine harbour
at Cape Maclear. Wide and neat paths were made in the bury-
ing-ground on its eastern and southern sides. A grand old fig-
tree stood at the north-east corner, and its wide-spreading
branches threw their kindly shade over the last resting-place
of the dead. Several other magnificent trees grew around
the hallowed spot. Mounds were raised as they are at
home, but all lay north and south, the neads apparently
north. The graves of the sexes were distinguished by

the various implements which the buried dead had used
in their different employments during life; but they were
all broken as if to be employed no more. A piece of
fishing-net and a broken paddle told that a fisherman
slept beneath that sod. The graves of the women had the
wooden mortar, and the heavy pestle used in pounding
the corn, and the basket in which the meal is sifted, while
all had numerous broken calabashes and pots arranged
around them. The idea that the future life is like the present does not appear to prevail; yet a banana-tree had been
carefully planted at the head of several of the graves, and,
if not merely for ornament, the fruit might be considered an
offering to those who still possess human tastes. The people
of the neighbouring villages were friendly and obliging, and
willingly brought us food for sale.

Pursuing our exploration, we found that the northern
part of the lake was the abode of lawlessness and bloodshed. The Mazite or Mazitu live on the highlands, and
make sudden swoops on the villages of the plains. They
are Zulus who came originally from the south, inland of
Sofalla and Inhambane; and are of the same family as those
who levy annual tribute from the Portuguese on the Zambesi.
All the villages north of Mankambira's (lat. 11° 44′ south)
had been recently destroyed by these terrible marauders,
but they were foiled in their attacks upon that Chief and
Marenga. The thickets and stockades round their villages
enabled the bowmen to pick off the Mazitu in security,
while they were afraid to venture near any place where
they could not use their shields. Beyond Mankambira's we
saw burned villages, and the putrid bodies of many who had
fallen by Mazitu spears only a few days before. Our land
party were afraid to go further, and dreaded meeting the
inflicters of the terrible vengeance, of which they saw

the evidence at every turning, without a European in
their company. This reluctance on the part of the native
land party to proceed without the presence of a white man
was very natural, because bands of the enemy who had
ravaged the country were supposed to be still roaming
about; and, if these marauders saw none but men of their
own colour, our party might forthwith be attacked. Compliance with their request led to an event which might have
been attended by very serious consequences. Dr. Livingstone got separated from the party in the boat for four
days. Having taken the first morning's journey along with
them, and directing the boat to call for him in a bay in
sight, both parties proceeded north. In an hour Dr. Livingstone and his party struck inland, on approaching the foot of
the mountains which rise abruptly from the lake. Supposing
that they had heard of a path behind the high range
which there forms the shore, those in the boat held on
their course; but it soon began to blow so fresh that they
had to run ashore for safety. While delayed a couple of
hours, two men were sent up the hills to look for the land
party, but they could see nothing of them, and the boat
party sailed as soon as it was safe to put to sea, with the
conviction that the missing ones would regain the lake in
front.

In a short time a small island or mass of rocks was passed,
on which were a number of armed Mazitu with some young
women apparently their wives. The headman said that he
had been wounded in the foot by Mankambira, and that
they were staying there till he could walk to his Chief, who
lived over the hills. They had several large canoes, and it
was evident that this was a nest of lake pirates, who sallied
out by night to kill and plunder. They reported a path behind the hills, and, the crew being reassured, the boat sailed on.

A few miles further, another and still larger band of pirates were fallen in with, and hundreds of crows and kites hovered over and round the rocks on which they lived. Dr. Kirk and Charles Livingstone, though ordered in a voice of authority to come ashore, kept on their course. A number of canoes then shot out from the rocks and chased them. One with nine strong paddlers persevered for some time after all the others gave up the chase. A good breeze, however, enabled the gig to get away from them with ease. After sailing twelve or fifteen miles, north of the point where Dr. Livingstone had left them, it was decided that he must be behind; but no sooner had the boat's head been turned south, than another gale compelled her to seek shelter in a bay. Here a number of wretched fugitives from the slave-trade on the opposite shore of the lake were found; the original inhabitants of the place had all been swept off the year before by the Mazitu. In the deserted gardens beautiful cotton was seen growing, much of it had the staple an inch and a half long, and of very fine quality. Some of the plants were uncommonly large, deserving to be ranked with trees.

On their trying to purchase food, the natives had nothing to sell except a little dried cassava-root, and a few fish: and they demanded two yards of calico for the head only of a large fish. When the gale admitted of their return, their former pursuers tried to draw them ashore by asserting that they had quantities of ivory for sale. Owing to a succession of gales, it was the fourth day from parting that the boat was found by Dr. Livingstone, who was coming on in search of it with only two of his companions.

After proceeding a short distance up the path in which they had been lost sight of, they learned that it would take several days to go round the mountains, and rejoin the lake; and they therefore turned down to the bay, expecting to find

the boat, but only saw it disappearing away to the north.
They pushed on as briskly as possible after it, but the
mountain flank which forms the coast proved excessively
tedious and fatiguing; travelling all day, the distance
made, in a straight line, was under five miles. As soon as
day dawned, the march was resumed; and, after hearing at
the first inhabited rock that their companions had passed it
the day before, a goat was slaughtered out of the four which
they had with them, when suddenly, to the evident con-
sternation of the men, seven Mazitu appeared armed with
spears and shields, with their heads dressed fantastically
with feathers.   To hold a parley, Dr. Livingstone and
Moloka, a Makololo man who spoke Zulu, went unarmed
to meet them.   On Dr. Livingstone approaching them,
they ordered him to stop, and sit down in the sun,
while they sat in the shade.   "No, no!" was the reply,
"if you sit in the shade, so will we." They then
rattled their shields with their clubs, a proceeding which
usually inspires terror; but Moloka remarked, "It is not the
first time we have heard shields rattled."   And all sat down
together.   They asked for a present, to show their Chief
that they had actually met strangers—something as evidence
of having seen men who were not Arabs.   And they were
requested in turn to take these strangers to the boat or to their
Chief. All the goods were in the boat, and to show that no present
sent such as they wanted was in his pockets, Dr. Livingstone
emptied them, turning out, among other things, a note-book:
thinking it was a pistol they started up, and said, "Put
that in again." The younger men then became boisterous, and
demanded a goat.   That could not be spared, as they were the
sole provisions.   When they insisted, they were asked how
many of the party they had killed, that they thus began to
divide the spoil; this evidently made them ashamed.   The

elders were more reasonable; they dreaded treachery, and were as much afraid of Dr. Livingstone and his party as his men were of them; for on leaving they sped away up the hills like frightened deer. One of them, and probably the leader, was married, as seen by portions of his hair sewn into a ring; all were observed by their teeth to be people of the country, who had been incorporated into the Zulu tribe.

The way still led over a succession of steep ridges with ravines of from 500 to 1000 feet in depth; some of the sides had to be scaled on hands and knees, and no sooner was the top reached than the descent began again. Each ravine had a running stream; and the whole country, though so very rugged, had all been cultivated, and densely peopled. Many banana-trees, uncared for patches of corn, and Congo-bean bushes attested former cultivation. The population had all been swept away; ruined villages, broken utensils, and human skeletons, met with at every turn, told a sad tale of "man's inhumanity to man." So numerous were the slain, that it was thought the inhabitants had been slaughtered in consequence of having made raids on the Zulus for cattle.

We conjectured this to be the cause of the wholesale butchery, because Zulus do not usually destroy any save the old, and able-bodied men. The object of their raids in general is that the captured women and children may be embodied into the tribe, and become Zulus. The masters of the captives are kind to them, and the children are put on the same level as those of any ordinary man. In their usual plan, we seem to have the condition so bepraised by some advocates for slavery. The members of small dis-united communities are taken under a powerful government —obtain kind masters, whom they are allowed to exchange for any one else within the tribe, and their children become freemen. It is, as our eyes and nostrils often found by the

2 c

putrid bodies of the slain, a sad system nevertheless—yet
by no means so bad as that which, causing a still greater
waste of human life, consigns the surviving victims to perpetual slavery.   The Zulus are said never to sell their
captives.

Several Senna men were of the land party; one of these,
a dice diviner, being mortally afraid of the Mazitu bolted the
moment he saw our visitors.   Before again starting, his comrades shouted for him, and called him by firing their muskets
for a long time; but he could not be induced to come out
from his hiding-place.

Continuing the journey that night as long as light served,
they slept unconsciously on the edge of a deep precipice, without fire lest the Mazitu should see it.   Next morning most
of the men were tired out, the dread of the apparition of the
day before tending probably to increase the lameness of
which they complained.   When told, however, that all might
return to Mankambira's save two, Moloka and Charlie, they
would not, till assured that the act would not be considered
one of cowardice.   Giving them one of the goats as provision,
another was slaughtered for the remainder of the party who,
having found on the rocks a canoe which had belonged to one
of the deserted villages, determined to put to sea again; but
the craft was very small, and the remaining goat, spite of
many a threat of having its throat cut, jumped and rolled
about so, as nearly to capsize it; so Dr. Livingstone took to
the shore again, and after another night spent without fire,
except just for cooking, was delighted to see the boat coming
back.

We pulled that day to Mankambira's, a distance that on
shore, with the most heartbreaking toil, had taken three days
to travel.   This was the last latitude taken, 11° 44' S.   The
boat had gone about 24' further to the north, the land party

probably half that distance, but fever prevented the instruments being used. Dr. Kirk and Charles Livingstone were therefore furthest up the lake, and they saw about 20' beyond their turning-point, say into the tenth degree of south latitude. From the heights of at least a thousand feet, over which the land party toiled, the dark mountain masses on both sides of the lake were seen closing in. At this elevation the view extended at least as far as that from the boats, and it is believed the end of the lake lies on the southern borders of 10°, or the northern limits of 11°, south latitude.

Mankambira thought that our diviner would die of starvation in the mountains; but he promised that, if he survived and came to him, he would give him food, and send him after us. A week afterwards the poor fellow overtook us, to the great delight of his comrades, who ran back to meet and salute him; they danced and shouted with joy, and fired off their muskets. He had heard, from his place of concealment his comrades calling for him and firing, but did not answer, because he thought that they were fighting with the Mazitu. Hunger at length drove him from the mountains. Mankambira treated him kindly, gave him food, and sent him on, as he had promised; but a set of lawless fellows between Mankambira's and Marenga's seized and robbed him, and put a slave-stick on his neck, intending to sell him as a slave, when some of the older men said that the English would come back and avenge the deed if they stole him. He was then let go, and Marenga also gave him food, and a piece of bark cloth as a covering.

Elephants are numerous on the borders of the lake, and surprisingly tame, being often found close to the villages. Hippopotami swarm very much at their ease in the creeks and lagoons, and herds are sometimes seen in the lake itself.

Their tameness arises from the fact that poisoned arrows have no effect on either elephant or hippopotamus. Five of each were shot for food during our journey. Two of the elephants were females, and had only a single tusk apiece, and were each killed by the first shot. It is always a case of famine or satiety, when depending on the rifle for food—a glut of meat or none at all. Most frequently it is scanty fare, except when game is abundant, as it is far up the Zambesi. We had one morning two hippopotami and an elephant, perhaps in all some eight tons of meat, and two days after the last of a few sardines only for dinner.

One morning when sailing past a pretty-thickly inhabited part, we were surprised at seeing nine large bull-elephants standing near the beach quietly flapping their gigantic ears. Glad of an opportunity of getting some fresh meat, we landed and fired into one. They all retreated into a marshy piece of ground between two villages. Our men gave chase, and fired into the herd. Standing on a sand hummock, we could see the bleeding animals throwing showers of water with their trunks over their backs. The herd was soon driven back upon us, and a wounded one turned to bay. Yet neither this one, nor any of the others, ever attempted to charge. Having broken his legs with a rifle-ball, we fired into him at forty yards as rapidly as we could load and discharge the rifles. He simply shook his head at each shot, and received at least sixty Enfield balls before he fell. Our excellent sailor from the north of Ireland happened to fire the last, and, as soon as he saw the animal fall, he turned with an air of triumph to the Doctor and exclaimed, "It was *my* shot that done it, sir!"

In a few minutes, upwards of a thousand natives were round the prostrate king of beasts; and, after our men had taken all they wanted, an invitation was given to the villagers to take

the remainder.   They rushed at it like hungry hyenas, and
in an incredibly short time every inch of it was carried off.
It was only by knowing that the meat would all be used, that
we felt justified.in the slaughter of this noble creature.   The
tusks weighed 62 lbs. each.   A large amount of ivory might
be obtained from the people of Nyassa, and we were frequently
told of their having it in their huts.

While detained by a storm on the 17th October at the
mouth of the Kaombe, we were visited by several men belonging to an Arab who had been for fourteen years in the interior
at Katanga's, south of Cazembe's.   They had just brought
down ivory, malachite, copper rings, and slaves to exchange
for cloth at the lake.   The malachite was said to be dug out
of a large vein on the side of a hill near Katanga's.   They
knew Lake Tanganyika well, but had not heard of the Zambesi.
They spoke quite positively, saying that the water of Lake
Tanganyika flowed out by the opposite end to that of Nyassa.
As they had seen neither of the overflows, we took it simply as
a piece of Arab geography.   We passed their establishment
of long sheds next day, and were satisfied that the Arabs must
be driving a good trade.   It is difficult to get at facts, or
draw out of the natives any reliable information respecting
the country in front.   Some are so suspicious of strangers that
they show extreme caution in their answers, and are unwilling
to commit themselves by any statement; while others draw
largely upon their imagination, and tell marvels equal to the
most romancing tales of ancient travellers, or say just what
they think will please one.

" How far is it to the end of the lake ? " we inquired of an
intelligent-looking native at the south part.   " The other end
of the lake ! " he exclaimed, in real or well-feigned astonishment, " who ever heard of such a thing ?   Why, if one started
when a mere boy to walk to the other end of the lake, he

would be an old grey-headed man before he got there. I never heard of such a thing being attempted." We were told on the Rovuma that that river flowed out of Nyassa; and on the lower half of the lake every one assured us that a canoe could sail out of Nyassa into the Rovuma; but above that, their testimony differed, some saying that it ran near the lake but not out of it, and others were equally positive that it was several days' journey from Lake Nyassa. Mankambira had never heard of any large river in the north, and even denied its existence altogether; giving us at the same time the names of the different halting-places round the head of the lake, and the number of days required to reach the coast opposite his village; which corresponded, as nearly as we could judge, with the distance at which we have placed its end.

The Lake slave-trade was going on at a terrible rate. Two enterprising Arabs had built a dhow, and were running her, crowded with slaves, regularly across the Lake. We were told she sailed the day before we reached their head-quarters. This establishment is in the latitude of the Portuguese slave-exporting town of Iboe, and partly supplies that vile market; but the greater number of the slaves go to Kilwa.* We did not see much evidence of a wish to

---

* On one occasion one of our cruisers, the Wasp, when calling at Iboe, was taken for a large slaver just then expected. The slaves in the vicinity were all hurried into the town, and, when Captain J. C. Stirling landed, it was full of them. Our friend Major Sicard was at the time Acting-Governor of Iboe, though very much against his own wishes. It had become public that the late Governor had left, in certain boxes, vast sums of money accumulated by slave-trading, and the Governor-General was said to be very much shocked that his confidential subordinate should have behaved so shamefully. Major Sicard had just received the thanks of our Government for his most disinterested kindness to the Expedition (and now that he has gone, as we trust, to a better world, we would say never were public thanks accompanied by more fervent private gratitude), and he was selected by the Governor-General to fill the vacant post of Governor at Iboe, until the then recent scandal had passed away

barter.   Some ivory was offered for sale; but the chief
traffic was in human chattels.   Would that we could give a
comprehensive account of the horrors of the slave-trade,
with an approximation to the number of lives it yearly
destroys! for we feel sure that were even half the truth told
and recognised, the feelings of men would be so thoroughly
roused, that this devilish traffic in human flesh would be put
down at all risks; but neither we, nor any one else, have the
statistics necessary for a work of this kind.   Let us state
what we do know of one portion of Africa, and then every
reader who believes our tale, can apply the ratio of the
known misery to find out the unknown.   We were informed
by Colonel Rigby, late H.M. Political Agent, and Consul at
Zanzibar, that 19,000 slaves from this Nyassa country alone
pass annually through the Custom-house of that island.   This
is exclusive of course of those sent to Portuguese slave-ports.
Let it not be supposed for an instant that this number,
19,000, represents all the victims.   Those taken out of the
country are but a very small section of the sufferers.   We
never realized the atrocious nature of the traffic, until we
saw it at the fountain-head.   There truly "Satan has his
seat."   Besides those actually captured, thousands are killed

---

and been forgotten.   Major Sicard
protested against being thus placed
over a nest of slave-dealers, from
which it is scarcely possible for any
Portuguese to escape with untarnished
honour; and naturally feared that the
position he had acquired by receiving
the thanks of the English Government
would be seriously affected by such
questionable promotion.   His remonstrances were all in vain, for the
Governor-General insisted, and as a soldier our friend had nothing left but to
obey.   When Captain Stirling landed,

Major Sicard was so much taken
aback by his own false position and
the crowd of slaves ready for exportation, that he could scarcely articulate,
and, forgetting his usual prompt politeness, did not even ask his visitor to
sit down.   It is scarcely possible to
conceive the force of temptation which
must assail officers in a place like
Iboe, which exists only by its extensive trade in slaves, and where any
man who might feel squeamish as to
the profits would be universally esteemed a fool.

and die of their wounds and famine, driven from their villages by the slave raid proper. Thousands perish in internecine war waged for slaves with their own clansmen and neighbours, slain by the lust of gain, which is stimulated, be it remembered always, by the slave purchasers of Cuba and elsewhere. The many skeletons we have seen, amongst rocks and woods, by the little pools, and along the paths of the wilderness, attest the awful sacrifice of human life, which must be attributed, directly or indirectly, to this trade of hell. We would ask our countrymen to believe us when we say, as we conscientiously can, that it is our deliberate opinion from what we know and have seen, that not one-fifth of the victims of the slave-trade ever become slaves. Taking the Shire Valley as an average, we should say not even one-tenth arrive at their destination. As the system, therefore, involves such an awful waste of human life,—or shall we say of human labour?—and moreover tends directly to perpetuate the barbarism of those who remain in the country, the argument for the continuance of this wasteful course because, forsooth, a fraction of the enslaved may find good masters, seems of no great value. This reasoning, if not the result of ignorance, may be of maudlin philanthropy. A small armed steamer on Lake Nyassa could easily, by exercising a control, and furnishing goods in exchange for ivory and other products, break the neck of this infamous traffic in that quarter; for nearly all must cross the Lake or the Upper Shire.

Our exploration of the Lake extended from the 2nd September to the 27th October, 1861; and, having expended or lost most of the goods we had brought, it was necessary to go back to the ship. When near the southern end, on our return, we were told that a very large slave-party had just crossed to the eastern side. We heard the fire of three guns in the evening, and judged by the report that they must be at least six-pounders.   They were said to belong to an Ajawa Chief named Mukata.

In descending the Shire, we found concealed in the broad belt of papyrus round the lakelet Pamalombe, into which the river expands, a number of Manganja families who had been driven from their homes by the Ajawa raids.   So thickly did the papyrus grow, that when beat down it supported their small temporary huts, though when they walked from one hut to another, it heaved and bent beneath their feet as thin ice does at home.

A dense and impenetrable forest of the papyrus was left standing between them and the land, and no one passing by on the same side would ever have suspected that human beings lived there.   They came to this spot from the south by means of their canoes, which enabled them to obtain a living from the fine fish which abound in the lakelet.   They had a large quantity of excellent salt sewed up in bark, some of which we bought, our own having run out.   We anchored for the night off their floating camp, and were visited by myriads of mosquitoes.   Some of the natives show a love of country quite surprising.   We saw fugitives on the mountains, in the north of the lake, who were persisting in clinging to the haunts of their boyhood and youth, in spite of starvation and the continual danger of being put to death by the Mazitu.

A few miles below the lakelet is the last of the great slave-crossings.   Since the Ajawa invasion the villages on the left bank had been abandoned, and the people, as we saw in our ascent, were living on the right or western bank.

As we were resting for a few minutes opposite the valuable fishery at Movunguti, a young effeminate-looking man from some sea-coast tribe came in great state to have a look at us. He walked under a large umbrella, and was followed by five

handsome damsels gaily dressed and adorned with a view to
attract purchasers. One was carrying his pipe for smoking
bang, here called "chamba;" another his bow and arrows;
a third his battle-axe; a fourth one of his robes; while the
last was ready to take his umbrella when he felt tired. This
show of his merchandise was to excite the cupidity of any
Chief who had ivory, and may be called the lawful way of
carrying on the slave-trade. What proportion it bears to the
other ways in which we have seen this traffic pursued, we
never found means of forming a judgment. He sat and looked
at us for a few minutes, the young ladies kneeling behind
him; and, having satisfied himself that we were not likely to
be customers, he departed.

On our first trip we met, at the landing opposite this place,
a middle-aged woman of considerable intelligence, and possessing more knowledge of the country than any of the

An old Manganja Woman, showing the pelele or lip-ring and the tattooing in intersecting
lines on face, arms, and body.

men. Our first definite information about Lake Nyassa was obtained from her. Seeing us taking notes, she remarked that she had been to the sea, and had there seen white men writing. She had seen camels also, probably among the Arabs. She was the only Manganja woman we ever met, who was ashamed of wearing the "pelele," or lip-ring. She retired to her hut, took it out, and kept her hand before her mouth to hide the hideous hole in the lip while conversing with us. All the villagers respected her, and even the headmen took a secondary place in her presence. On inquiring for her now, we found that she was dead. We never obtained sufficient materials to estimate the relative mortality of the highlands and lowlands; but, from many very old white-headed blacks having been seen on the highlands, we think it probable that even native races are longer lived the higher their dwelling-places are.

We landed below at Mikena's and took observations for longitude, to verify those taken two years before. The village was deserted, Mikena and his people having fled to the other side of the river. A few had come across this morning to work in their old gardens. After completing the observations we had breakfast; and, as the last of the things were being carried into the boat, a Manganja man came running down to his canoe, crying out, "The Ajawa have just killed my comrade!" We shoved off, and in two minutes the advanced guard of a large marauding party were standing with their muskets on the spot where we had taken breakfast. They were evidently surprised at seeing us there, and halted; as did also the main body of perhaps a thousand men. "Kill them," cried the Manganja; "they are going up to the hills to kill the English," meaning the Missionaries we had left at Magomero. But having no prospect of friendly communication with them, nor confidence in Manganja's testimony, we proceeded down the river; leaving the Ajawa sitting under a large baobab, and the Manganja cursing them most energetically across the river.

On our way up, we had seen that the people of Zimika had taken refuge on a long island in the Shire, where they had placed stores of grain to prevent it falling into the hands of the Ajawa; supposing afterwards that the invasion and war were past, they had removed back again to the mainland on the east, and were living in fancied security. On approaching the Chief's village, which was built in the midst of a beautiful grove of lofty wild-fig and palm trees, sounds of revelry fell upon our ears. The people were having a merry time —drumming, dancing, and drinking beer—while a powerful enemy was close at hand, bringing death or slavery to every one in the village. One of our men called out to several who came to the bank to look at us, that the Ajawa were coming and were even now at Mikena's village; but they were dazed with drinking, and took no notice of the warning.

In passing a temporary village of Manganja fugitives, we saw a poor fellow with his neck in a slave-stick, and landed a few hundred feet below; but when we walked up to the spot at which he had been, he had vanished, and every one denied having seen such a person there. Though suffering so terribly from the slave-trade themselves, these Manganja still patronized it. A man, near whose temporary hut we slept among a crowd of fugitives, started even before sunrise, to sell a boy to some black Portuguese who were purchasing slaves in a neighbouring village. The fortune of war had brought this poor boy into the fellow's power, and the heartlessness of the ruffian, who had himself suffered the loss of everything by the slave-hunters, made us look upon him and his race as without natural affection. Selling each other, when on the point of perishing by

starvation, not for grain, but cloth, of which there was no
great lack, was so very unnatural, that at first we felt as if no
mortal men, except blacks, could be guilty of such cruelty;
and began to speculate how the idea of property in human kind
could ever enter into beings possessing reasonable minds like
our own.   We remembered, however, having seen a man who
was reputed humane, and in whose veins no *black* blood flowed,
parting for the sum of twenty dollars, or about 4*l.*, with a
good-looking girl, who stood in a closer relationship to him,
than this boy did to the man who excited our ire; and, she
being the nurse of his son besides, both son and nurse made
such a pitiable wail for an entire day, that even the half-
caste who had bought her relented, and offered to return her
to the white man, but in vain.   Community in suffering
does not always beget sympathy, though we naturally
expect it should.   This was proved in the case of the wreck
of the French transport ship Medusa, on the West Coast,
and may not be peculiar to black men.

The Tette slavers subsequently brought over corn (mapira)
and therewith bought many slaves.   This might be considered in one sense humane, as it actually kept many
poor creatures from death by starvation; but, as in the
case of the "removal to kind masters" scheme, the saviours
of lives are actually the destroyers of all the lives that are
lost.

A number of elephants were standing near the spot where
we left the boat, and one of the herd was engaged in the
elephantine amusement of breaking down trees; he did not
eat any part of them, but simply rejoicing in his strength
was knocking them over for the mere fun of the thing.
Three Enfield and other rifle balls in the head sent him
rushing through the thick bush with apparently as much ease,
as if it were only grass: an immense number of trees are

destroyed by these huge beasts.   They frequently chew the
branches for the bark and the sap alone.

Crowds of carriers offered their services after we left the
river.   Several sets of them placed so much confidence in
us, as to decline receiving payment at the end of the first
day; they wished to work another day, and so receive both
days' wages in one piece.   The young headman of a new
village himself came on with his men.   The march was a
pretty long one, and one of the men proposed to lay the
burdens down beside a hut a mile or more from the next
village.   The headman scolded the fellow for his meanness
in wishing to get rid of our goods where we could not
procure carriers, and made him carry them on.   The village,
at the foot of the cataracts, had increased very much
in size and wealth since we passed it on our way up.   A
number of large new huts had been built; and the people
had a good stock of cloth and beads.   We could not
account for this sudden prosperity, until we saw some fine
large canoes, instead of the two old, leaky things which lay
there before.   This had become a crossing-place for the slaves
that the Portuguese agents were carrying to Tette, because
they were afraid to take them across nearer to where the ship
lay, about seven miles off.   Nothing was more disheartening
than this conduct of the Manganja, in profiting by the entire
breaking up of their nation.   It was nearly as bad as the
behaviour of our own countrymen, who bought up muskets
and sent them out to the Chinese engaged in war with our
own soldiers; or of those who, at the Cape, supplied ammunition to the Kaffirs, under similar circumstances, and coolly
fathered the traffic on the Missionaries.

Extract of Despatch from Lieut.-Col. C. P. RIGBY, H. M. Consul and British Agent, Zanzibar, to H. L. ANDERSON, Esq., Secretary to Government, Bombay.

" BRITISH CONSULATE, ZANZIBAR,
" SIR, "15th July, 1860.

"I have the honour to report, for the information of the Right Hon. the Governor in Council, that Dr. Albrect Roscher, a gentleman who was sent by His Majesty the King of Bavaria on a scientific mission to E. Africa, was murdered on the 19th of March last, at the village of Kisoongoonee, three days' journey to the north-east of Lake Nyassa."

*   *   *   *   *   *

After some information bearing on Dr. Roscher's other movements, the despatch proceeds :—

" 4. He again left Zanzibar in June, 1859, to explore the great lake of Nyassa, and, having joined a caravan at Keelwa, started from that part on the 24th of August last, and reached the Lake on the 19th of November, being the first white man who has ever reached its shores."

[The reason of Col. Rigby's mistake was, that sufficient time had not elapsed for the news of our discovery of Nyassa to reach him at Zanzibar; nor was it then known that the Lake Dr. Roscher and we had both visited was one and the same. It does not in the least detract from the honour due to Dr. Roscher for reaching the Lake by a path totally distinct from ours, that others had preceded him in the discovery; but, for the sake of accuracy, it is necessary to produce the grounds on which the precedence in the exploration is claimed by the English.]

" He was in very bad health when he left Zanzibar, and became so weak on the journey, that he was carried in a cot all the latter part of it.

" He remained at *Nussewa*, on the borders of the Lake, nearly four months. On the 16th of March last he left *Nussewa* to go to the River Rovuma, which is crossed about twelve' days' journey from Lake Nyassa on the road to *Keelwa*. He evidently intended to return to the Lake from the *Rovuma*, as he left nearly all his baggage in charge of the Sultan of *Nussewa*, and was only accompanied by two negro-servants and two porters for his luggage, viz., one man and one woman."

The despatch is long and full of details and depositions. Dr. Roscher's friend Kingomanga, the Sultan of Nussewa, lives three days from the Lake, and probably opposite *Kotakota* Bay, or even further south, and is of the Waiao tribe.

The depositions of the natives are very interesting, as they show conclusively that Roscher heard of us. Colonel Rigby thinks that Dr. Roscher had been told of the trip we had made to Shirwa, or as he writes it Kirwa, "where," he remarks, "the natives of Nussewa go for salt." But it is more likely that he heard of our arrival at the southern end of Nyassa where the Shire flows from it, where there are immense salt washings, and where we came in contact with a party of coast Arabs who fled by night, and would take the road through the Ajawa country in which Roscher arrived two months later.

CHAPTER XX.

Encouraging prospects — Bishop Mackenzie — Our progress down river arrested — River flooded in January, 1862 — Mariano resumes his career of slave-hunting — The Governor plays at hide and seek with him — Captain Alvez — Reach the Zambesi — A slave-owner's ideas of his slaves — Wisdom and humanity of Napoleon III. — At Luabo — Arrival of H.M.S. Gorgon — The Pioneer out of repair — Captain Wilson proceeds up the Shire — Continuation of story of the Bishop's Mission — He descends the Shire in a small canoe — Loses clothing, medicine, &c. — Fever — Death and burial — His character — Kindness of Makololo — Death of Mr. Burrup — Captain Wilson returns to Shupanga — The Rev. James Stewart examines the country previous to attempting a Mission by the Free Church of Scotland — Portuguese policy and slave-trading are the chief obstacles to any Mission — Personal responsibility ignored and blame put on others — Mrs. Livingstone's illness, and death 27th April, 1862.

WE reached the ship on the 8th of November, 1861, in a very weak condition, having suffered more from hunger than on any previous trip. Heavy rains commenced on the 9th, and continued several days; the river rose rapidly, and became highly discoloured. Bishop Mackenzie came down to the ship on the 14th, with some of the Pioneer's men, who had been at Magomero for the benefit of their health, and also for the purpose of assisting the Mission. The Bishop appeared to be in excellent spirits, and thought that the future promised fair for peace and usefulness. The Ajawa having been defeated and driven off while we were on the Lake, had sent word that they desired to live at peace with the English. Many of the Manganja had settled round Magomero, in order to be under the protection of the Bishop; and it was hoped that the slave-trade would soon cease in the highlands, and the people be left in the secure enjoyment of their industry. The Mission, it was also anticipated, might soon become, to a considerable degree, self-supporting, and raise certain kinds of food, like the Portuguese of Senna and Quillimane.   Mr. Burrup, an energetic young man, had arrived at Chibisa's the day before the Bishop, having come up the Shire in a canoe.   A surgeon and a lay brother followed behind in another canoe.   The Pioneer's draught being too much for the upper part of the Shire, it was not deemed advisable to bring her up, on the next trip, further than the Ruo; the Bishop, therefore, resolved to explore the country from Magomero to the mouth of that river, and to meet the ship with his sisters and Mrs. Burrup, in January. This was arranged before parting, and then the good Bishop and Burrup, whom we were never to meet again, left us; they gave and received three hearty English cheers as they went to the shore, and we steamed off.

The rains ceased on the 14th, and the waters of the Shire fell, even more rapidly than they had risen.   A shoal, twenty miles below Chibisa's, checked our further progress, and we lay there five weary weeks, till the permanent rise of the river took place.   During this detention, with a large marsh on each side, the first death occurred in the Expedition which had now been three-and-a-half years in the country.   The carpenter's mate, a fine, healthy young man, was seized with fever.   The usual remedies had no effect; he died suddenly while we were at evening prayers, and was buried on shore. He came out in the Pioneer, and, with the exception of a slight touch of fever at the mouth of the Rovuma, had enjoyed perfect health all the time he had been with us. The Portuguese are of opinion that the European who has immunity from this disease for any length of time after he enters the country is more likely to be cut off by it when it does come, than the man who has it frequently at first.

The rains became pretty general towards the close of December, and the Shire was in flood in the beginning of January, 1862. At our wooding-place, a mile above the Ruo, the water was three feet higher than it was when we were here in June; and on the night of the 6th it rose eighteen inches more, and swept down an immense amount of brushwood and logs which swarmed with beetles, and the two kinds of shells which are common all over the African continent. Natives in canoes were busy spearing fish in the meadows and creeks, and appeared to be taking them in great numbers. Spur-winged geese, and others of the knob-nosed species, took advantage of the low gardens being flooded, and came to pilfer the beans. As we passed the Ruo, on the 7th, and saw nothing of the Bishop, we concluded that he had heard from his surgeon of our detention, and had deferred his journey. He arrived there five days after, on the 12th.

We heard at Mboma's village, that the notorious rebel-robber and murderer, Mariano, had been allowed to return from Mosambique, and was at his old trade again, of kidnapping the Manganja, and selling them to the people of Quillimane as slaves. He had already desolated a large portion of the right bank, and the people of this village were living in constant dread of a visit from his armed marauders. On coming to the Zambesi, we found that the Portuguese had lately made a station on an island opposite the mouth of the Shire. Captain Alvez,—Mozinga, or Big Gun, as the natives called him,—was the officer in command, and came on board after we dropped anchor. The Governor had desired him to assure us that the occupation of the island was only temporary, and solely in consequence of Mariano's escape and rebellion.

It appears that this half-caste rebel, notwithstanding all his notorious robberies and murders, and his actual rebellion and war, had been tried at Mosambique, and had been let off with the mild sentence of imprisonment for three years, and a fine. Not having money enough with him to pay the fine, the Mosambique authorities considerately allowed him to go back to Quillimane, to collect some debts which he asserted were due to him; but, when he got there, it was found that his debts were due somewhere up the country. His Quilli- mane creditors, however, most feelingly petitioned the Govern- ment to allow Mariano to go thither, in order to obtain ivory to pay both debts and fine. Permission was graciously given, and he was also allowed to take several hundreds of muskets and much ammunition; but, instead of collecting ivory, he returned to his own people up the Shire, and betook himself at once to his former course of robbery, murder, and kidnap- ping, and set the Portuguese authority at defiance. The Governor of Quillimane then declared war against his old enemy, and with all his available soldiers and slaves in a fleet of boats and canoes, sailed up the Shire to capture the rebel, but could not find him—so sailed down again. The whole thing had the appearance—to the uncharitable, who knew that nothing could be done in a district, without the knowledge of the Governor—of Mariano's having been allowed to run away with a large assortment of arms and ammunition, out of a small hamlet, where every one, by means of his slaves, knows the affairs of every one else. It is true the Governor ran after him, but at the pace one does after a child in play—and, of course, could not catch him. A captain was afterwards sent across the country with a force, and was more fortunate than the Governor, for he reached Mariano. Unluckily, however, instead of capturing the rebel, the rebel captured him, in a night attack it was said, with all his ammunition and a number of his men. The captain, according to the account of his brother officers, was allowed to depart, after receiving a present of ivory. To us, this was

2 D 2

incredible, but it is mentioned, to show the way that these men, who have been convicts, speak of each other.

Captain Alvez was suffering from fever, and had been, ever since he came to this low marshy place. The island would be under water, he said, if the river rose two feet higher, which it was extremely likely to do. The lonely life of a solitary officer, living with a number of debased black soldiers, on such a spot as this, is something frightful to think of. It is next door to imprisonment, if not to solitary confinement; and this was the lot of a brave artillery officer, who was sent here for some political offence, and who had done all the hard fighting with the rebels for a number of years back. While he, who crushed out the rebellion, was living thus, Mariano, the rebel, was reported for the last three years, to have been living sumptuously in the capital of the province; and even dining at the tables of the highest in the land. Seeing that this sentence of imprisonment at Mosambique was carried out so mildly as not to amount to confinement at all, it is not to be wondered at that men's tongues should speak hard things against the Governor-General, and that, though, of course, it cannot be actually known, bribery should be openly declared to have taken place. We know nothing more than the probability and general report, which may be false. We never met Mozinga again; he succumbed in a few months to fever.

After paying our Senna men, as they wished to go home, we landed them here. All were keen traders, and had invested largely in native iron-hoes, axes, and ornaments. Many of the hoes and spears had been taken from the slaving parties whose captives we liberated; for on these occasions our Senna friends were always uncommonly zealous and active. The remainder had been purchased with the old clothes we had given them, and their store of hippopotamus meat: they had no fears of losing them, or of being punished for aiding us. The system, in which they had been trained, had eradicated the idea of personal responsibility from their minds. The Portuguese slaveholders would blame the English alone, they said; they were our servants at the time. No white man on board could purchase so cheaply as these men could. Many a time had their eloquence persuaded a native trader to sell for a bit of dirty worn cloth things for which he had, but a little before, refused twice the amount of clean new calico. "Scissors" being troubled with a cough at night, received a present of a quilted coverlet, which had seen a good deal of service. A few days afterwards, a good chance of investing in hoes offering itself, he ripped off both sides, tore them into a dozen pieces, and purchased about a dozen hoes with them.

We entered the Zambesi on the 11th of January, and steamed down towards the coast, taking the side on which we had come up; but the channel had changed to the other side during the summer, as it sometimes does, and we soon grounded. A Portuguese gentleman, formerly a lieutenant in the army, and now living on Sangwisa, one of the islands of the Zambesi, came over with his slaves, to aid us in getting the ship off. He said frankly, that his people were all great thieves, and we must be on our guard not to leave anything about. He next made a short speech to his men, told them he knew what thieves they were, but implored them not to steal from us, as we would give them a present of cloth when the work was done. "The natives of this country," he remarked to us, "think only of three things, what they shall eat and drink, how many wives they can have, and what they may steal from their master, if not how they may murder him." He always slept with a loaded musket by his side. This opinion may apply to slaves, but

decidedly does not in our experience apply to freemen. We
paid his men for helping us, and believe that even they,
being paid, stole nothing from us. Our friend farms pretty
extensively the large island called Sangwisa,—lent him for
nothing by Senhor Ferrão,—and raises large quantities of
mapira and beans, and also beautiful white rice, grown
from seed brought a few years ago from South Carolina.
He furnished us with some, which was very acceptable; for,
though not in absolute want, we were living on beans, salt
pork, and fowls, all the biscuit and flour on board having
been expended.

We fully expected that the owners of the captives we had
liberated would show their displeasure, at least by their
tongues; but they seemed ashamed; only one ventured a
remark, and he, in the course of common conversation, said,
with a smile, " You took the Governor's slaves, didn't you?"
" Yes, we did free several gangs that we met in the Manganja
country." The Portuguese of Tette, from the Governor downwards, were extensively engaged in slaving. The trade is
partly internal and partly external: they send some of the
captives, and those bought, into the interior, up the Zambesi;
some of these we actually met on their way up the river.
The young women were sold there for ivory: an ordinary-
looking one brought two arrobas, sixty-four pounds weight,
and an extra beauty brought twice that amount. The men
and boys were kept as carriers, to take the ivory down from
the interior to Tette, or were retained on farms on the
Zambesi, ready for export if a slaver should call: of this
last mode of slaving we were witnesses also. The slaves
were sent down the river chained, and in large canoes.
This went on openly at Tette, and more especially so while
the French "Free Emigration" system was in full operation.
This double mode of disposing of the captives pays better

than the single system of sending them down to the Coast for exportation.   One merchant at Tette, with whom we were well acquainted, sent into the interior three hundred Manganja women to be sold for ivory, and another sent a hundred and fifty.   The process by which the Island of Bourbon was supplied with slaves was carried on with even greater effrontery than the Manganja raids.   The Commandant at Tette, having found that a cargo of slaves had been taken down the river by a woman of bad character, for form's sake sent an officer after her.   He followed, overtook her, but returned without her.   When spoken to on the subject, the Commandant said, with an air of triumph, " The English cannot now interfere, while we have the French flag to protect us."   And this flag did protect slaving till May, 1864. Of all the benefits which the reign of Napoleon III. has conferred on his kind, none does more credit to his wisdom and humanity than his having stopped this wretched system. As much was done as lay in his power, in the way of regulating the system of abstraction of labour from Africa, by the appointment of officers to prevent abuses in its working; but, in spite of every precaution, the "engagee system" became neither more nor less than the abominable slave-trade in all its horrors, not so much by French agency, as by that of Portuguese and half-castes.   Until the people are enlightened, every attempt of the kind must always promote the slave-trade and nothing else.

We anchored on the Great Luabo mouth of the Zambesi, because wood was much more easily obtained there than at the Kongone.   On the 30th, H. M. S. Gorgon arrived, towing the brig which brought Mrs. Livingstone, some ladies about to join their relatives in the Universities' Mission, and the twenty-four sections of a new iron steamer intended for the navigation of Lake Nyassa.   The Pioneer steamed out,

and towed the brig into the Kongone harbour. The new
steamer was called the Lady of the Lake, or the Lady
Nyassa, and as much as could be carried of her in one
trip was placed, by the help of the officers and men of the
Gorgon, on board the Pioneer, and the two large paddle-box
boats of H.M.'s ship. We steamed off for the Ruo on the
10th of February, having on board Captain Wilson, with a
number of his officers and men to help us to discharge the
cargo. Our progress up was distressingly slow. The river was
in flood, and we had a three-knot current against us in many
places. The engines of the Pioneer were of the best quality,
but had been entirely neglected by the engineer—the packing not having been renewed during twenty months. These
causes delayed us six months in the delta, instead of, as we
anticipated, only six days; for, finding it impossible to carry
the sections up to the Ruo without great loss of time, it was
thought best to land them at Shupanga, and, putting the
hull of the Lady Nyassa together there, to tow her up to the
foot of the Murchison Cataracts.

A few days before the Pioneer reached Shupanga, Captain
Wilson, seeing the hopeless state of our engines, generously
resolved to hasten with the Mission ladies up to those who,
we thought, were anxiously awaiting their arrival, and therefore started in his gig for the Ruo, taking Miss Mackenzie,
Mrs. Burrup, and his surgeon, Dr. Ramsay. They were
accompanied by Dr. Kirk and Mr. Sewell, paymaster of the
Gorgon, in the whale-boat of the Lady Nyassa. As our slow-
paced-launch, Ma-Robert, had formerly gone up to the foot of
the cataracts in nine days steaming, it was supposed that the
boats might easily reach the expected meeting-place at the
Ruo in a week; but the Shire was now in flood, and in its
most rapid state; and they were longer in getting up about
half the distance, than it was hoped they would be in the

whole navigable part of the river. They could hear nothing of the Bishop from the Chief of the island, Malo, at the mouth of the Ruo. "No white man had ever come to his village," he said. They proceeded on to Chibisa's, suffering terribly from mosquitoes at night. Their toil in stemming the rapid current made them estimate the distance, by the windings, as nearer 300 than 200 miles. The Makololo who had remained at Chibisa's told them the sad news of the death of the good Bishop and of Mr. Burrup. Other information received there awakened fresh anxiety on behalf of the survivors; so, leaving the ladies with Dr. Ramsay and the Makololo, Captain Wilson and Dr. Kirk went up the hills, in hopes of being able to render assistance, and on the way they met some of the Mission party at Soche's. The excessive fatigue that our friends had undergone in the voyage up to Chibisa's in no wise deterred them from this further attempt for the benefit of their countrymen, but the fresh labour, with diminished rations, was too much for their strength. They were reduced to a diet of native beans and an occasional fowl. Both became very ill of fever, Captain Wilson so dangerously that his fellow-sufferer lost all hopes of his recovery. His strong able-bodied cockswain did good service in cheerfully carrying his much-loved Commander, and they managed to return to the boat, and brought the two bereaved and sorrow-stricken ladies back to the Pioneer.

We learnt that the Bishop, wishing to find a shorter route down to the Shire, had sent two men to explore the country between Magomero and the junction of the Ruo; and in December Messrs. Proctor and Scudamore, with a number of Manganja carriers, left Magomero for the same purpose. They were to go close to Mount Choro, and then skirt the Elephant Marsh, with Mount Clarendon on their left. Their guides seem to have led them away to the east, instead of south;

to the upper waters of the Ruo in the Shirwa valley, instead of to its mouth. Entering an Anguro slave-trading village, they soon began to suspect that the people meant mischief, and just before sunset a woman told some of their men that if they slept there they would all be killed. On their preparing to leave, the Anguro followed them and shot their arrows at the retreating party. Two of the carriers were captured, and all the goods were taken by these robbers. An arrow-head struck deep into the stock of Proctor's gun; and the two Missionaries, barely escaping with their lives, swam a deep river at night, and returned to Magomero famished and exhausted.

The wives of the captive carriers came to the Bishop day after day weeping and imploring him to rescue their husbands from slavery. The men had been caught while in his service, no one else could be entreated; there was no public law nor any power superior to his own, to which an appeal could be made; for in him Church and State were, in the disorganized state of the country, virtually united. It seemed to him to be clearly his duty to try and rescue these kidnapped members of the Mission family. He accordingly invited the veteran Makololo to go with him on this somewhat hazardous errand. Nothing could have been proposed to them which they would have liked better, and they went with alacrity to eat the sheep of the Anguro, only regretting that the enemy did not keep cattle as well. Had the matter been left entirely in their hands, they would have made a clean sweep of that part of the country; but the Bishop restrained them, and went in an open manner, thus commending the measure to all the natives, as one of justice. This deliberation, however, gave the delinquents a chance of escape.*

---

* On the way the Bishop is said to have had an opportunity of correcting a slight geographical mistake made by Dr. Livingstone when Lake Shirwa

The Missionaries were successful; the offending village was burned, and a few sheep and goats were secured, which could not be considered other than a very mild punishment for the offence committed; the headman, Muana-somba, afraid to retain the prisoners any longer, forthwith liberated them, and they returned to their homes. This incident took place at the time we were at the Ruo and during the rains, and proved very trying to the health of the Missionaries; they were frequently wetted, and had hardly any food but roasted maize. Mr. Scudamore was never well afterwards. Directly on their return to Magomero, the Bishop and Mr. Burrup, both suffering from diarrhœa in consequence of wet, hunger, and exposure, started for Chibisa's to go down to the Ruo by the Shire. So fully did the Bishop expect a renewal of the soaking wet from which he had just returned, that on leaving Magomero he walked through the stream. The rivulets were so swollen that it took five days to do a journey that would otherwise have occupied only two days and a half.

None of the Manganja being willing to take them down the river during the flood, three Makololo canoe-men agreed to go with them. After paddling till near sunset, they decided to stop and sleep on shore; but the mosquitoes were so numerous that they insisted on going on again; the Bishop, being a week behind the time he had engaged to be at the Ruo, reluctantly consented, and in the darkness the canoe was upset in one of the strong eddies or whirl-pools, which suddenly boil up in flood time near the out-going branches of the river; clothing, medicines, tea, coffee, and sugar were all lost. Wet and weary, and tormented by

---

was discovered. A white vapour, at that time resting on the rich valley at the southern end of the lake, had led to the inference that the lake stretched a little further south than it actually does.

mosquitoes, they lay in the canoe till morning dawned, and
then proceeded to Malo, an island at the mouth of the Ruo,
where the Bishop was at once seized with fever.

Had they been in their usual health, they would doubtless have pushed on to Shupanga, or to the ship; but fever
rapidly prostrates the energies, and induces a drowsy stupor,
from which, if not roused by medicine, the patient gradually
sinks into the sleep of death. Still mindful, however, of
his office, the Bishop consoled himself by thinking, that he
might gain the friendship of the Chief, which would be of
essential service to him in his future labours. That heartless
man, however, probably suspicious of all foreigners from the
knowledge he had acquired of white slave-traders, wanted to
turn the dying Bishop out of the hut, as he required it for
his corn, but yielded to the expostulations of the Makololo.
Day after day for three weeks did these faithful fellows
remain beside his mat on the floor; till, without medicine
or even proper food, he died. They dug his grave on the
edge of the deep dark forest where the natives buried their
dead. Mr. Burrup, himself far gone with dysentery, staggered
from the hut, and, as in the dusk of evening they committed
the Bishop's body to the grave, repeated from memory portions of our beautiful service for the Burial of the Dead—
"earth to earth, ashes to ashes, dust to dust; in sure and
certain hope of the resurrection of the dead through our
Lord Jesus Christ." And in this sad way ended the earthly
career of one, of whom it can safely be said that for un-
selfish goodness of heart, and earnest devotion to the noble
work he had undertaken, none of the commendations of his
friends can exceed the reality. The grave in which his body
rests is about a hundred yards from the confluence of the Ruo,
on the left bank of the Shire, and opposite the island of Malo.
The Makololo then took Mr. Burrup up in the canoe as far

as they could, and, making a litter of branches, carried him themselves, or got others to carry him, all the way back to his countrymen at Magomero. They hurried him on lest he should die in their hands, and blame be attached to them. Soon after his return he expired, from the disease which was on him when he started to meet his wife.

Captain Wilson arrived at Shupanga on the 11th of March, having been three weeks on the Shire. On the 15th the Pioneer steamed down to the Kongone. The Gorgon had been driven out to sea in a gale, and had gone to Johanna for provisions, and it was the 2nd of April before she returned. It was fortunate for us that she had obtained a supply, as our provisions were exhausted, and we had to buy some from the master of the brig. The Gorgon left for the Cape on the 4th, taking all, except one, of the Mission party who had come in January. We take this opportunity of expressing our heartfelt gratitude to the gallant Captain Wilson and his officers for innumerable acts of kindness and hearty co-operation. Our warmest thanks are also due to Captain R. B. Oldfield and the other officers from the Admiral downwards, and we beg to assure them that nothing could be more encouraging to us in our difficulties and trials, than the knowledge that we possessed their friendship and sympathy in our labours.

The Rev. James Stewart, of the Free Church of Scotland, arrived in the Gorgon. He had wisely come out to inspect the country, before deciding on the formation of a Mission in the interior. To this object he devoted many months of earnest labour. This Mission was intended to embrace both the industrial and the religious element; and, as the route by the Zambesi and Shire forms the only one at present known, with but a couple of days' land journey to the highlands, which stretch to an unknown distance into the continent, and as no jealousy was likely to be excited in the mind of a man of Bishop Mackenzie's enlarged views—there being moreover room for hundreds of Missions—we gladly extended the little aid in our power to an envoy from the energetic and most respectable body above mentioned, but recommended him to examine the field with his own eyes.

During our subsequent detention at Shupanga, he proceeded as far up the Shire as the Upper Cataracts, and saw the mere remnants of that dense population, which we at first had found living in peace and plenty, but which was now scattered and destroyed by famine and slave-hunting. The land, which both before and after we found so fair and fruitful, was burned up by a severe drought; in fact, it was at its very worst. With most praiseworthy energy, and in spite of occasional attacks of fever, he then ascended the Zambesi as far as Kebrabasa; and, what may be of interest to some, compared it, in parts, to the Danube. His estimate of the highlands would naturally be lower than ours. The main drawbacks in his opinion, however, were the slave-trade, and the power allowed the effete Portuguese of shutting up the country from all except a few convicts of their own nation. The time of his coming was inopportune; the disasters, which from inexperience had befallen the Mission of the Universities, had a depressing effect on the minds of many at home, and rendered a new attempt unadvisable; though, had the Scotch perseverance and energy been introduced, it is highly probable that they would have reacted, most beneficially, on the zeal of our English brethren, and desertion would never have been heard of. After examining the country, Mr. Stewart descended the Zambesi in the beginning of the following year, and proceeded homewards with his report, by Mosambique and the Cape.

On the 7th of April we had only one man fit for duty; all the rest were down with fever, or with the vile spirit secretly sold to them by the Portuguese officer of customs, in spite of our earnest request to him to refrain from the pernicious traffic.

We started on the 11th for Shupanga with another load of the Lady Nyassa. As we steamed up the Delta, we observed many of the natives wearing strips of palm-leaf, the signs of sickness and mourning; for they too suffer from fever. This is the unhealthy season; the rains are over, and the hot sun draws up malaria from the decayed vegetation; disease seemed peculiarly severe this year. On our way up we met Mr. Waller, who had come from Magomero for provisions; the missionaries were suffering severely from want of food; the liberated people were starving, and dying of diarrhœa, and loathsome sores. The Ajawa, stimulated in their slave raids by supplies of ammunition and cloth from the Portuguese, had destroyed the large crops of the past year; a drought had followed, and little or no food could be bought. With his usual energy, Mr. Waller hired canoes, loaded them with stores, and took them up the long weary way to Chibisa's. Before he arrived he was informed that the Mission of the Universities, now deprived of its brave leader, had fled from the highlands down to the Low Shire Valley. This appeared to us, who knew the danger of leading a sedentary life, the greatest mistake they could have made, and was the result of no other counsel or responsibility than their own. Waller would have reascended at once to the higher altitude, but various objections stood in the way. The loss of poor Scudamore and Dickinson, in this low-lying situation, but added to the regret that the highlands had not received a fair trial.

When the news of the Bishop's unfortunate collisions with the natives, and of his untimely end, reached England, much blame was imputed to him. The policy, which with the formal sanction of all his companions he had adopted,

being directly contrary to the advice which Dr. Livingstone
tendered, and to the assurances of the peaceable nature of
the Mission which the Doctor had given to the natives,
a friendly disapproval of a bishop's engaging in war was
ventured on, when we met him at Chibisa's in November.
But when we found his conduct regarded with so much
bitterness in England, whether from a disposition to "stand
by the down man," or from having an intimate knowledge
of the peculiar circumstances of the country in which he
was placed, or from the thorough confidence which intimacy
caused us to repose in his genuine piety, and devout service
of God, we came to think much more leniently of his proceedings, than his assailants did. He never seemed to doubt
but that he had done his duty; and throughout he had
always been supported by his associates. One of them
subsequently, and in a weak moment, ignoring personal
responsibility, rested all the blame on Dr. Livingstone; and
the gentleman who was designated as the Bishop's successor,
declared in public meetings at Cambridge and elsewhere, in
spite of the proof to the contrary in Bishop Mackenzie's own
journal, "that the warlike measures of the Mission were the
consequences of following Dr. Livingstone's advice." The
question whether a Bishop, in the event of his flock being
torn from his bosom, may make war to rescue them, requires
serious consideration. It seems to narrow itself into whether
a Christian man may lawfully use the civil power or the
sword at all in defensive war, as police, or otherwise. We
would do almost anything to avoid a collision with degraded
natives; but in case of an invasion—our blood boils at the
very thought of our wives, daughters, or sisters being touched
—we, as men with human feelings, would unhesitatingly
fight to the death, with all the fury in our power.

The good Bishop was as intensely averse to using arms,

before he met the slave-hunters, as any man in England. In the course he pursued he may have made a mistake, but it is a mistake which very few Englishmen on meeting bands of helpless captives, or members of his family in bonds, would have failed to commit likewise.

During unhealthy April, the fever was more severe in Shupanga and Mazaro than usual. We had several cases on board—they were quickly cured, but, from our being in the Delta, as quickly returned. About the middle of the month Mrs. Livingstone was prostrated by this disease; and it was accompanied by obstinate vomiting. Nothing is yet known that can allay this distressing symptom, which of course renders medicine of no avail, as it is instantly rejected. She received whatever medical aid could be rendered from Dr. Kirk, but became unconscious, and her eyes were closed in the sleep of death as the sun set on the evening of the Christian Sabbath, the 27th April, 1862. A coffin was made during the night, a grave was dug next day under the branches of the great Baobab-tree, and with sym- pathizing hearts the little band of his countrymen assisted the bereaved husband in burying his dead. At his request, the Rev. James Stewart read the burial-service; and the seamen kindly volunteered to mount guard for some nights at the spot where her body rests in hope. Those who are not aware how this brave, good, English wife made a delightful home at Kolobeng, a thousand miles inland from the Cape, and as the daughter of Moffat and a Christian lady exercised most beneficial influence over the rude tribes of the interior, may wonder that she should have braved the dangers and toils of this down-trodden land. She knew them all, and, in the disinterested and dutiful attempt to renew her labours, was called to her rest instead. "*Fiat, Domine, voluntas tua!*"

CHAPTER XXI.

On the 5th of May Dr. Kirk and Charles Livingstone started in the boat for Tette, in order to see the property of the Expedition brought down in canoes. They took four Mazaro canoe-men to manage the boat, and a white sailor to cook for them; but, unfortunately, he caught fever the very day after leaving the ship, and was ill most of the trip; so they had to cook for themselves, and to take care of him besides. The natives behaved remarkably well, and were very cleanly in their habits, bathing every day after sunset, although the weather was rather chilly. If a little food was given to one, according almost to universal custom he shared it with the others, although often there was not more than a mouthful for each. They preferred punting to paddling, and chose, in going up the river, the parts that had from two to four feet of water, instead of the deep channel where the current is strong. They kept admirable time with their poles, raising them, bringing them down, pushing, and giving the final

shove all at the same instant. The helm had hardly to
be touched at all, so well did they keep the boat on her
course. Many of their canoe songs are very fine; some are
peculiarly plaintive, like the one which appears to be a
lament over a dying Chief. There being but little wind
during the first day, the sail could not be used; but towards
sunset a pleasant breeze sprang up and sail was set.
The canoe-men were of course much pleased to see the boat
moving on without their exertions. The Makololo of our first
party always maintained that a sailing-boat was the perfection
of navigation—it was vastly superior to a steamer, because no
wood had to be cut—and you had merely to sit still, and let
the wind drive you along. After dark the wind increased,
the boat swept swiftly through the water; the men, who
are of an excitable temperament, felt the influence, and
began an extemporary and very energetic song. As the
breeze freshened, the boat dashed through the waves;
then, wild with excitement the men sprang to their feet, and
sang still louder, gesticulating with might and main. Suddenly the career of song ceased—the singers were sprawling
on their backs—the boat was on a sandbank.

On an island opposite Shiramba the party found a large
number of fugitive Manganja, who had fled from the war on
the mainland. A man banished from Portugal, called Belchior, who had married a sister of the half-caste Chief below
Tette, and had settled near Lupata, was encamped on an
island in Shigogo. They were challenged as they sailed past
it after dark. The fife and drums called to arms. "The
English! the English!" our men answered, and no molesta-
tion ensued. Chibisa, he told them, had sent an insulting
message to him, so he attacked him, and, with seventy men
armed with muskets, drove him from his principal village
near the Zambesi, and burned it. Even private persons

imitate military manners, and make what they call war and peace, as if no other authority existed. At a subsequent period this adventurer forced Chibisa to flee to the new Mission-station opposite Dakanamoio island, and threatened to follow him thither. To prevent this Dr. Livingstone applied to the Governor of Tette, Antonio Tavares d'Almeida, and we have much pleasure in stating that his Excellency had already laid an injunction on Belchior, not to proceed with his intended foray. This very creditable order had preceded the application.

Dr. Kirk and Charles Livingstone arrived at Tette on the 17th, and found its wonted dull monotony agreeably broken by the marriage of the Governor's daughter to one of the officers. The slaves were celebrating the joyful event in the usual way, by drinking, drumming, dancing, singing, and firing off muskets. Our companions were hospitably received by the Governor, which was more than they had reason to expect, after having so recently freed his slave-gangs in the Manganja country. His Excellency alluded to the subject one evening, remarking to Dr. Kirk that he had received from his brother, the Governor-General, a despatch, saying that as the slave-trade was legal under Portuguese law, if any slave-party, out of the Portuguese territory, was attacked, they were to resist force by force; in plain words, they were to fight the next time we attempted to rescue the kidnapped Manganja. This is mentioned not that it is in any way remarkable for a representative of the Portuguese Crown to connive at slaving, but because the Governor-General Almeida, by speaking English and professing to have an intense desire to suppress the slave-trade, gained a character for uprightness among the officers of H.M. cruisers, which none of his countrymen would for a moment endorse. On finding afterwards that his less powerful brother at Tette had unwittingly revealed to us the real sentiments of the big brother at Mosambique, his Excellency could not conceal a little, perhaps excusable, chagrin, though he must have known, that, living behind the scenes, we had never been misled by his English palavers, and that we should have rejoiced, had it been possible to have held him in higher esteem. Some of the slaves, captured by his brother's agents, are sent inland for ivory, and others kept on farms, whence he and every one else know they will be shipped by means of large canoes whenever an opportunity occurs. This inland slave-trade feeds the foreign one ; and, if Portuguese legislation has any meaning, the whole thing is forbidden. If, as the laws profess, they wish to get rid of slavery, no more slaves can be made, unless the laws be only enacted to please the English, and gratify the self-esteem of the legislators.

The Portuguese Government is really famous for passing good laws in Lisbon, and no less for allowing those respecting slavery to remain a dead letter. It has been decreed that slavery is to be abolished in this province in 1878, and the Government slaves to be free in the year 1864.   An officer told us that they were working the Government slaves tremendously, making streets and tiles, in order to get all the work they could out of them before they were set free.

Tette is very much improved since the present Governor came into office.   Two good roads or streets have been made, which is something new for this country.   The Governor himself is nearly walked off his feet looking after them.   There are some hundreds of black soldiers in the town, who are very much better clothed, than a tithe of the number used to be in former years.   We were told, on what seemed good authority, that Tette now costs the Home Government 3000l. a year, and yields an annual revenue of 300l.   The ivory-trade has declined very materially, from the elephants being nearly all killed, or driven off from the part of the country formerly hunted.

The canoes hired at Mazaro for the return voyage were at Tette when we arrived. They had brought up stores for the Portuguese Government, and had been accompanied by an officer who had a number of the men flogged, though they were freemen, because he said they were lazy, and lost time in coming up. The backs of the poor fellows were badly cut. Public law exists in theory; in practice punishment is often inflicted at the caprice of individuals. On one occasion we sent a couple of the Shupanga thieves, caught with the booty on them, to the nearest official; we received a note next day asking what punishment was to be inflicted; we preferred letting the criminals go free to giving a sentence. Between men of equal standing, a threat is often made of using the musket, by the name of the "minister of justice." The canoe-men receive their pay and food for the trip before starting. When the canoes are heavily laden, and the water low, they often eat up all their food before they reach Tette, and have none left for the return passage, unless they purchase more with their wages. This was the case with our men. Food was cheap, and, wishing to make them strong for their work, we gave them considerably more than they were accustomed to receive, with a pig and a goat besides, and they worked remarkably well. Starting, of their own accord, at the first dawn of day, and keeping on till dusk, they resolutely kept up with the boat, and reached Shupanga in four days and three-quarters. The merchants complain much of the dishonesty of the canoe-men, and sometimes they actually do make off with a whole cargo of cloth, and no punishment can reach them. One thing is certain, there is no love lost between these parties.

We now proceeded with preparations for the launch of the Lady Nyassa. Ground was levelled on the bank at Shupanga, for the purpose of arranging the compartments in order : she was placed on palm-trees which were brought from a place lower down the river for ways, and the engineer and his assistants were soon busily engaged; about a fortnight after they were all brought from Kongone, the sections were screwed together. The blacks are more addicted to stealing where slavery exists than elsewhere. We were annoyed by thieves who carried off the iron screw-bolts, but were gratified to find that strychnine saved us from the man-thief as well as the hyena-thief. A hyena was killed by it, and after the natives saw the dead animal and knew how we had destroyed it, they concluded that it was not safe to steal from men who possessed a medicine so powerful. The half-caste, who kept Shupanga-house, said he wished to have some to give to the Zulus, of whom he was mortally afraid, and to whom he had to pay an unwilling tribute.

The Pioneer made several trips to the Kongone, and returned with the last load on the 12th of June. On the 23rd the Lady Nyassa was safely launched, the work of putting her together having been interrupted by fever and dysentery, and many other causes which it would only weary the reader to narrate in detail. Natives from all parts of the country came to see the launch, most of them quite certain that, being made of iron she must go to the bottom as soon as she entered the water. Earnest discussions had taken place among them with regard to the propriety of using iron for ship-building. The majority affirmed that it would never answer. They said, " If we put a hoe into the water, or the smallest bit of iron, it sinks immediately. How then can such a mass of iron float? it must go to the bottom." The minority answered that this might be true with them, but white men had medicine for everything. "They could even make a woman, all except the speaking; look at that one on the figure-head of the vessel." The unbelievers were astonished, and could hardly believe their eyes, when they saw the ship float lightly and gracefully on the river, instead of going to the bottom, as they so confidently predicted. "Truly," they said, "these men have powerful medicine."

Our distinguished countryman, Professor Owen, recommended our attention to be directed to the genesis of the tsetse, in order to discover a means for the extirpation of this pest. We frequently inquired of the different tribes if they could help us in our inquiries; and one of the Makololo remembered that this very question was once under public discussion at Linyanti, and as usual a bet was laid that no one could tell. After a number of days had elapsed, an old man claimed the prize, asserting that the tsetse laid its eggs, which were of a red colour, on the leaves of the mopane-tree. These were probably only the eggs of an insect described in the 'Missionary Travels' as depositing over its eggs a sweet gum, which is collected and eaten. Some denied that he had seen them; others affirmed that the red eggs were laid on the twigs of trees, and not on the leaves; and others insisted that the eggs were placed in the droppings of buffaloes, and these last were probably in the right. The destruction of all game by the advance of civilization is the only chance of getting rid of the tsetse.

We remember to have heard a furious discussion among the natives on the question whether the two toes of the ostrich represent the thumb and forefinger in man, or the little and ring fingers. On these occasions it is amusing to observe the freedom and earnestness with which men of the lowest grade assault the opinions of their betters. It is not often that they can bring themselves into importance, and they make the most of an opportunity. "We are little infants; we are still clinging to the bosoms of our mothers; we cannot walk alone; we know nothing at all; but on this little subject we know that the elder gentlemen talk like all those who speak about that of which they know nothing. We never heard such nonsense," and so forth; or two men of the same age may be the disputants. He who is most glib of tongue covers his opponent with confusion; that, however, does not end the argument. Why should it? The sensation of choking in his throat, the pressure of blood on his heart, make the vanquished, when unable to argue still, gasp out "Can you outrun me then?" and off they start, run a mile, bring a branch of a tree at the end of the usual race-course, and, the mental and bodily excitement by this means equalized, they settle down in peace. If our editors, after allowing the paper war to rage till both the "esteemed correspondents" are ready to go into fits from the blood being lashed into fury round the heart and brain, instead of the usual atrocious way' (!) of proposing the next letters to be paid for as advertisements, would only advise that they should "run a race," far fewer cases of heart disease and apoplexy would be traceable to the "sanctum" door.

Birds are numerous on the Shupanga estate. Some kinds remain all the year round, while many others are there only for a few months. Flocks of green pigeons come in April to feed on the young fruit of the wild fig-trees, which is also eaten by a large species of bat in the evenings. The pretty little black weaver, with yellow shoulders, appears to enjoy life intensely after assuming his wooing dress. A hearty breakfast is eaten in the morning, and then come the hours for making merry. A select party of three or four perch on the bushes which skirt a small grassy plain, and cheer themselves with the music of their own quiet

and self-complacent song.   A playful performançe on the
wing succeeds.   Expanding his soft velvet-like plumage,
one glides with quivering pinions to the centre of the open
space, singing as he flies, then turns with a rapid whirring sound
from his wings—somewhat like a child's rattle—and returns
to his place again.   One by one the others perform the same
feat, and continue the sport for hours, striving which can
produce the loudest brattle while turning.   These games are
only played during the season of courting and of the gay
feathers, the merriment seems never to be thought of while
the bird wears his winter suit of sober brown.

We received two mules from the Cape to aid us in transporting the pieces of the Lady Nyassa past the cataracts
and landed them at Shupanga, but they soon perished.   A
Portuguese gentleman kindly informed us, *after* both the
mules were dead, that he knew they would die; for the land
there had been often tried, and nothing would live on it—
not even a pig.   He said he had not told us so before,
because he did not like to appear officious!

We obtained from the Gorgon an assistant in the shape of
an old quartermaster; an excellent sailor, and exceedingly
useful man when sober, but uncommonly apt to get drunk,
when he had the chance.   He would have done well, had
we been able, as we intended, to proceed up the river
at once; for then he must soon have been a total abstainer;
but so long as we were near the Portuguese he was
useless, and the power which impelled him must have
been terribly strong.   He knew not a word of the language,
and the natives were equally ignorant of English; yet
he succeeded in getting a native to go seven miles for some
gin, and smuggle it, mixed with native beer, into the ship.
When sober he was quiet, respectful, obliging, quick to see what
should be done, constantly at work, and taking particularly

good care of everything. We felt sorry for the poor fellow, but, as we could not get up the river, we had to put him on board the first man-of-war we were able. Those who have never acquired the intense craving for stimulants that these men feel, can scarcely realize the force of the temptation they have to resist. In the words of the Scotch toper—" We know about the drinking, but nothing of the drouth."

By the time everything had been placed on board the Lady Nyassa, the waters of the Zambesi and the Shire had fallen so low that it was useless to attempt taking her up to the cataracts before the rains in December. Draught oxen and provisions also were required, and could not be obtained nearer than the Island of Johanna. The Portuguese, without refusing positively to let trade enter the Zambesi, threw impediments in the way; they only wanted a small duty! They were about to establish a river police, and re-arrange the Crown lands, which have long since become Zulu lands; meanwhile they were making the Zambesi, by slaving, of no value to any one.

The Rovuma, which was reported to come from Lake Nyassa, being out of their claims and a free river, we determined to explore it in our boats immediately on our return from Johanna, for which place after some delay at the Kongone, in repairing engines, paddle-wheel, and rudder, we sailed on the 6th of August. A store of naval provisions had been formed on a hulk in Pomone Bay of that island for the supply of the cruisers, and was in charge of Mr. Sunley, the Consul, from whom we always received the kindest attentions and assistance. He now obliged us by parting with six oxen, trained for his own use in sugar-making. Though sadly hampered in his undertaking by being obliged to employ slave labour, he has by indomitable energy overcome obstacles under which most persons would have sunk. He has done all that

under the circumstances could be done to infuse a desire
for freedom, by paying regular wages; and has established
a large factory, and brought 300 acres of rich soil under
cultivation with sugar-cane. We trust he will realize the
fortune, which he so well deserves to earn. Had Mr.
Sunley performed the same experiment on the mainland,
where people would have flocked to him for the wages he
now gives, he would certainly have inaugurated a new era
on the East Coast of Africa. On a small island where the
slaveholders have complete power over the slaves, and
where there is no free soil such as is everywhere met with
in Africa, the experiment ought not to be repeated. Were
Mr. Sunley commencing again, it should neither be in Zanzibar nor Johanna, but on African soil, where, if even a slave
is ill-treated, he can easily by flight become free. On an
island under native rule a joint manufacture by Arabs and
Englishmen might only mean that the latter were to escape
the odium of flogging the slaves.

On leaving Johanna and our oxen for a time, H.M.S.
Orestes towed us thence to the mouth of the Rovuma at the
beginning of September. Captain Gardner her commander,
and several of his officers, accompanied us up the river
for two days in the gig and cutter. The water was unusually
low, and it was rather dull work for a few hours in the
morning; but the scene became livelier and more animated
when the breeze began to blow. Our four boats then swept
on under full sail, the men on the look-out in the gig and
cutter calling, " Port, sir!" " Starboard, sir!" " As you go,
sir!" while the black men in the bows of the others shouted
the practical equivalents, " Pagombe! Pagombe!" " Enda
quete!" " Berane! Berane!" Presently the leading-boat
touches on a sandbank; down comes the fluttering sail;
the men jump out to shove her off, and the other boats,

shunning the obstruction, shoot on ahead to be brought up each in its turn by mistaking a sandbank for the channel, which had often but a very little depth of water.

A drowsy herd of hippopotami were suddenly startled by a score of rifle-shots, and stared in amazement at the strange objects which had invaded their peaceful domains, until a few more bullets compelled them to seek refuge at the bottom of the deep pool, near which they had been quietly reposing. On our return, one of the herd retaliated. He followed the boat, came up under it, and twice tried to tear the bottom out of it; but fortunately it was too flat for his jaws to get a good gripe, so he merely damaged one of the planks with his tusks, though he lifted the boat right up, with ten men and a ton of ebony in it.

We slept, one of the two nights Captain Gardner was with us, opposite the lakelet Chidia, which is connected with the river in flood time, and is nearly surrounded by hills some 500 or 600 feet high, dotted over with trees. A few small groups of huts stood on the hill-sides, with gardens off which the usual native produce had been reaped. The people did not seem much alarmed by the presence of the large party which had drawn up on the sandbanks below their dwellings. There is abundance of large ebony in the neighbourhood. The pretty little antelope (*Cephalophus cœruleus*), about the size of a hare, seemed to abound, as many of their skins were offered for sale. Neat figured date-leaf mats of various colours are woven here, the different dyes being obtained from the barks of trees. Cattle could not live on the banks of the Rovuma on account of the tsetse, which are found from near the mouth, up as far as we could take the boats. The navigation did not improve as we ascended; snags, brought down by the floods, were common, and left in the channel on the sudden subsidence of the water. In many

places, where the river divided into two or three channels,
there was not water enough in any of them for a boat drawing three feet, so we had to drag ours over the shoals; but
we saw the river at its very lowest, and it may be years
before it is so dried up again.

The valley of the Rovuma, bounded on each side by a
range of highlands, is from two to four miles in width, and
comes in a pretty straight course from the W.S.W.; but
the channel of the river is winding, and now at its lowest
zigzagged so perversely, that frequently the boats had to pass
over three miles to make one in a straight line. With a
full stream it must of course be much easier work. Few
natives were seen during the first week. Their villages are
concealed in the thick jungle on the hill-sides, for protection
from marauding slave-parties. Not much of interest was observed on this part of the silent and shallow river. Though
feeling convinced that it was unfit for navigation, except for
eight months of the year, we pushed on, resolved to see if,
further inland, the accounts we had received from different
naval officers of its great capabilities would prove correct;
or if, by communication with Lake Nyassa, even the upper
part could be turned to account. Our exploration showed us,
that the greatest precaution is required in those who visit
new countries.

The reports we received from gentlemen, who had entered
the river and were well qualified to judge, were that the
Rovuma was infinitely superior to the Zambesi, in the absence of any bar at its mouth, in its greater volume of
water, and in the beauty of the adjacent lands. We probably came at a different season from that in which they
visited it, and our account ought to be taken with theirs to
arrive at the truth. It might be available as a highway
for commerce during three quarters of each year; but casual

visitors, like ourselves and others, are ill able to decide.   The
absence of bird or animal life was remarkable.   Occasionally
we saw pairs of the stately jabirus, or adjutant-looking mara-
bouts, wading among the shoals, and spurwinged geese, and
other water-fowl, but there was scarcely a crocodile or a
hippopotamus to be seen.

At the end of the first week, an old man called at our
camp, and said he would send a present from his village,
which was up among the hills.   He appeared next morning
with a number of his people, bringing meal, cassava-root,
and yams.   The language differs considerably from that on
the Zambesi, but it is of the same family.   The people are
Makonde, and are on friendly terms with the Mabiha, and
the Makoa, who live south of the Rovuma.   When taking
a walk up the slopes of the north bank, we found a great
variety of trees we had seen nowhere else.   Those usually
met with far inland seem here to approach the coast.
African ebony, generally named *mpingu*, is abundant within
eight miles of the sea; it attains a larger size, and has
more of the interior black wood than usual.   A good timber
tree called *mosoko* is also found; and we saw half-caste Arabs
near the coast cutting up a large log of it into planks.   Before reaching the top of the rise we were in a forest of
bamboos.   On the plateau above, large patches were cleared
and cultivated.   A man invited us to take a cup of beer; on
our complying with his request, the fear previously shown by
the bystanders vanished.   Our Mazaro men could hardly
understand what they said.   Some of them waded in the
river and caught a curious fish in holes in the claybank.
Its ventral fin is peculiar, being unusually large, and of a
circular shape, like boys' playthings called "suckers."   We
were told that this fish is found also in the Zambesi, and is
called Chirire.   Though all its fins are large, it is asserted

that it rarely ventures out into the stream, but remains near its hole, where it is readily caught by the hand.

The Zambesi men thoroughly understood the characteristic marks of deep or shallow water, and showed great skill in finding out the proper channel. The Molimo is the steersman at the helm, the Mokadamo is the head canoe-man, and he stands erect on the bows with a long pole in his hands, and directs the steersman where to go, aiding the rudder, if necessary, with his pole. The others preferred to stand and punt our boat, rather than row with our long oars, being able to shove her ahead faster than they could pull her. They are accustomed to short paddles. Our Mokadamo was affected with moon-blindness, and could not see at all at night. His comrades then led him about, and handed him his food. They thought that it was only because his eyes rested all night, that he could see the channel so well by day. At difficult places the Mokadamo sometimes, however, made mistakes, and ran us aground; and the others, evidently imbued with the spirit of resistance to constituted authority, and led by João an aspirant for the office, jeered him for his stupidity. "Was he asleep? Why did he allow the boat to come there? Could he not see the channel was somewhere else?" At last the Mokadamo threw down the pole in disgust, and told João he might be a Mokadamo himself. The office was accepted with alacrity; but in a few minutes he too ran us into a worse difficulty than his predecessor ever did, and was at once disrated amidst the derision of his comrades.

In travelling it is best to enjoy the little simple incidents of this kind, which, at most, exemplify the tendencies woven into the being of the whole human family. It is a pity to hear that some of our countrymen rudely interfere in what really does no harm. Blows even have been inflicted under the silly assumption that the negro is this, that, and the other thing, and not, like other men, a curious mixture of good and evil, wisdom and folly, cleverness and stupidity. An Englishman possessed of a gun, which had the ugly trick of going off of itself, came up the Zambesi in a canoe manned by natives. He scarcely knew another word of the language than the verb "*to kill*." The gun, as was its wont, accidentally went off close to the head of one of the party, who, before going to sleep, expressed his fears to his comrades that this unlucky gun might "*kill*" some of them. Our hero caught the word, and spent the whole night revolver in hand, ready to punish the treachery which existed only in his own excited brain. This adventure he afterwards published in a newspaper as a terrible situation, a hairbreadth escape from bloodthirsty savages. Another British Lion, having to travel some two hundred miles in a canoe, and being unable to speak a word of the language, thought it clever to fire off all the barrels of his revolver every time his canoe-men proposed to land during the live-long day. The torrid sun right overhead was at its hottest. The poor fellows made signs they wished to purchase some beer. Off went the revolver, " No, no, no, paddle you must." This madness, as described to us by himself, was evidently thought clever. Another, whose estimate of himself and that formed of him by a tribe he visited did not at all coincide, after complaining at a public meeting of the un-truthfulness of a previous traveller to whom that same tribe had shown distinguished kindness and respect, stated, as we learn on the authority of a clergyman who was present, that he had tied up one of his people before reaching the tribe referred to, "and given him a sound thrashing." Let us fancy the effect on an English village if a black man came to it, and a white servant complained that he had been maltreated by him on the way. We have felt heartily ashamed sometimes on discovering how causelessly we have been angry. No doubt the natives are at times as perversely stupid as servants at home can be when they like; but our conduct must often appear to the native mind as a mixture of silliness and insanity.

On the 16th September, we arrived at the inhabited island of Kichokomane. The usual way of approaching an unknown people is to call out in a cheerful tone "Malonda!" Things for sale, or do you want to sell anything? If we can obtain a man from the last village, he is employed, though only useful in explaining to the next that we come in a friendly way. The people here were shy of us at first, and could not be induced to sell any food; until a woman, more adventurous than the rest, sold us a fowl. This opened the market, and crowds came with fowls and meal, far beyond our wants. The women are as ugly as those on Lake Nyassa, for who can be handsome wearing the pelele or upper-lip ring of large dimensions? We were once surprised to see young men wearing the pelele, and were told that in the tribe of the Mabiha, on the south bank, men as well as women wore them.

Along the left bank, above Kichokomane, is an exceedingly fertile plain, nearly two miles broad, and studded with a number of deserted villages. The inhabitants were living in temporary huts on low naked sandbanks; and we found this to be the case as far as we went. They leave most of their property and food behind, because they are not afraid of these being stolen, but only fear being stolen themselves. The great slave-route from Nyassa to Kilwa passes to N. E. from S.W., just beyond them; and it is dangerous to remain in their villages at this time of year, when the kidnappers are abroad. In one of the tempo-

rary villages, we saw, in passing, two human heads lying
on the ground. We slept a couple of miles above this
village.

Before sunrise next morning, a large party armed with
bows and arrows and muskets came to the camp, two or
three of them having a fowl each, which we refused to purchase, having bought enough the day before. They followed
us all the morning, and after breakfast those on the left
bank swam across and joined the main party on the other
side. It was evidently their intention to attack us at a
chosen spot, where we had to pass close to a high bank,
but their plan was frustrated by a stiff breeze sweeping
the boats past, before the majority could get to the place.
They disappeared then, but came out again ahead of us, on a
high wooded bank, walking rapidly to the bend, near which
we were obliged to sail. An arrow was shot at the foremost
boat; and seeing the force at the bend, we pushed out from
the side, as far as the shoal water would permit, and tried
to bring them to a parley, by declaring, that we had not come
to fight, but to see the river. "Why did you fire a gun, a
little while ago?" they asked. "We shot a large puff-adder,
to prevent it from killing men; you may see it lying dead on
the beach." With great courage, our Mokadamo waded to
within thirty yards of the bank, and spoke with much
earnestness, assuring them that we were a peaceable party,
and had not come for war, but to see the river. We were
friends, and our countrymen bought cotton and ivory, and
wished to come and trade with them. All we wanted was to
go up quietly to look at the river, and then return to the sea
again. While he was talking with those on the shore, the
old rogue, who appeared to be the ringleader, stole up the
bank, and with a dozen others, waded across to the island, near
which the boats lay, and came down behind us. Wild with

2 F 2

excitement, they rushed into the water, and danced in our rear, with drawn bows, taking aim, and making various savage gesticulations. Their leader urged them to get behind some snags, and then shoot at us. The party on the bank in front had many muskets—and those of them, who had bows, held them with arrows ready set in the bowstrings. They had a mass of thick bush and trees behind them, into which they could in a moment dart, after discharging their muskets and arrows, and be completely hidden from our sight; a circumstance that always gives people who use bows and arrows the greatest confidence. Notwithstanding these demonstrations, we were exceedingly loath to come to blows. We spent a full half-hour exposed at any moment to be struck by a bullet or poisoned arrow. We explained that we were better armed than they were, and had plenty of ammunition, the suspected want of which often inspires them with courage, but that we did not wish to shed the blood of the children of the same Great Father with ourselves; that if we must fight, the guilt would be all theirs.

This being a common mode of expostulation among themselves, we so far succeeded, that with great persuasion the leader and others laid down their arms, and waded over from the bank to the boats to talk the matter over. "This was their river; they did not allow white men to use it. We must pay toll for leave to pass." It was somewhat humiliating to do so, but it was pay or fight; and, rather than fight, we submitted to the humiliation of paying for their friendship, and gave them thirty yards of cloth. They pledged themselves to be our friends ever afterwards, and said they would have food cooked for us on our return. We then hoisted sail, and proceeded, glad that the affair had been amicably settled. Those on shore walked up to

the bend above to look at the boat, as we supposed;
but, the moment she was abreast of them, they gave us
a volley of musket-balls and poisoned arrows, without a
word of warning. Fortunately we were so near, that all
the arrows passed clear over us, but four musket-balls went
through the sail just above our heads. All our assailants
bolted into the bushes and long grass, the instant after
firing, save two, one of whom was about to discharge a
musket and the other an arrow, when arrested by the
fire of the second boat. Not one of them showed their
faces again, till we were a thousand yards away. A
few shots were then fired over their heads, to give them
an idea of the range of our rifles, and they all fled into
the woods. Those on the sandbank rushed off too,
with the utmost speed; but, as they had not shot at us,
we did not molest them, and they went off safely with
their cloth. They probably expected to kill one of our
number, and in the confusion rob the boats. It is only
where the people are slavers, that the natives of this part
of Africa are bloodthirsty.

These people have a bad name in the country in front,
even among their own tribe. A slave-trading Arab we met
above, thinking we were then on our way down the river,
advised us not to land at the villages, but to stay in the
boats, as the inhabitants were treacherous, and attacked
at once, without any warning or provocation. Our experience of their conduct fully confirmed the truth of what
he said. There was no trade on the river where they
lived, but beyond that part there was a brisk canoe-
trade in rice and salt; those further in the interior cultivating rice, and sending it down the river to be exchanged
for salt, which is extracted from the earth in certain places
on the banks. Our assailants hardly anticipated resist-

ance, and told a neighbouring Chief, that if they had known who we were, they would not have attacked English, who can "bite hard." They offered no molestations on our way down, though we were an hour in passing their village. Our canoe-men plucked up courage on finding that we had come off unhurt. One of them named Chiku, acknowledging that he had been terribly frightened, said "His fear was not the kind which makes a man jump overboard and run away; but that which brings the heart up to the mouth, and renders the man powerless, and no more able to fight than a woman."

In the country of Chonga Michi, about 80 or 90 miles up the river, we found decent people, though of the same tribe, who treated strangers with civility. A body of Makoa had come from their own country in the south, and settled here. The Makoa are known by a cicatrice in the forehead shaped like the new moon with the horns turned downwards. The tribe possesses all the country west of Mosambique; and they will not allow any of the Portuguese to pass into their country more than two hours' distance from the fort. A hill some ten or twelve miles distant, called Pau, has been visited during the present generation only by one Portuguese and one English officer, and this visit was accomplished only by the influence of the private friendship of a Chief for this Portuguese gentleman. Our allies have occupied the Fort of Mosambique for three hundred years, but in this, as in all other cases, have no power further than they can see from a gun-carriage.

The Makoa chief, Matingula, was hospitable and communicative, telling us all he knew of the river and country beyond. He had been once to Iboe and once at Mosambique with slaves. Our men understood his language easily. A useless musket he had bought at one of the above places was

BEEHIVE.

NEAR THE CATARACTS OF THE ROVUMA.

BASKET EMPLOYED BY WOMEN TO CATCH FISH.

offered us for a little cloth. Having received a present of food from him, a railway rug was handed to him: he looked at it —had never seen cloth like that before—did not approve of it, and would rather have cotton cloth. " But this will keep you warm at night."—" Oh I do not wish to be kept warm at night."—We gave him a bit of cotton cloth, not one-third the value of the rug, but it was more highly prized. His people refused to sell their fowls for ou splendid prints and drab cloths. They had probably been taken in with gaudy-patterned sham prints before. They preferred a very cheap, plain, blue stuff of which they had experience. A great quantity of excellent honey is collected all along the river, by bark hives being placed for the bees on the high trees on both banks. Large pots of it, very good and clear, were offered in exchange for a very little cloth. No wax was brought for sale; there being no market for this commodity it is probably thrown away as useless.

At Michi we lose the table-land which, up to this point, bounds the view on both sides of the river, as it were, with ranges of flat-topped hills, 600 or 800 feet high; and to this plateau a level fertile plain succeeds, on which stand detached granite hills. That portion of the table-land on the right bank seems to bend away to the south, still preserving the appearance of a hill range. The height opposite extends a few miles further west, and then branches off in a northerly direction. A few small pieces of coal were picked up on the sandbanks, showing that this useful mineral exists on the Rovuma, or on some of its tributaries: the natives know that it will burn. At the lakelet Chidia, we noticed the same sandstone rock, with fossil wood on it, which we have on the Zambesi, and knew to be a sure evidence of coal beneath. We mentioned this at the time to Captain

Gardner, and our finding coal now seemed a verification
of what we then said; the coalfield probably extends from
the Zambesi to the Rovuma, if not beyond it. Some of the
rocks lower down have the permanent water-line three feet
above the present height of the water.

A few miles west of the Makoa of Matingula, we came
again among the Makonde, but now of good repute. War
and slavery have driven them to seek refuge on the sandbanks. A venerable-looking old man hailed us as we
passed, and asked us if we were going by without speaking.
We landed, and he laid down his gun and came to us; he
was accompanied by his brother, who shook hands with every
one in the boat, as he had seen people do at Kilwa. "Then
you have seen white men before?" we said. "Yes," replied
the polite African, "but never people of your quality." These
men were very black, and wore but little clothing. A young
woman, dressed in the highest style of Makonde fashion,
punting as dexterously as a man could, brought a canoe full
of girls to see us. She wore an ornamental head-dress of red
beads tied to her hair on one side of her head, a necklace of
fine beads of various colours, two bright figured brass bracelets on her left arm, and scarcely a farthing's worth of cloth,
though it was at its cheapest.

As we pushed on westwards, we found that the river makes
a little southing, and some reaches were deeper than any
near the sea; but when we had ascended about 140 miles by
the river's course from the sea, soft tufa rocks began to
appear; ten miles beyond, the river became more narrow
and rocky, and when, according to our measurement, we had
ascended 156 miles, our further progress was arrested. We
were rather less than two degrees in a straight line from
the Coast. The incidents worth noticing were but few:
seven canoes with loads of salt and rice kept company with

us for some days, and the further we went inland, the more civil the people became.

When we came to a stand, just below the island of Nyamatolo, Long. 38° 36′ E., and Lat. 11° 53′, the river was narrow, and full of rocks. Near the island there is a rocky rapid with narrow passages fit only for native canoes; the fall is small, and the banks quite low; but these rocks were an effectual barrier to all further progress in boats. Previous reports represented the navigable part of this river as extending to the distance of a month's sail from its mouth; we found that, at the ordinary heights of the water, a boat might reach the obstructions which seem peculiar to all African rivers in six or eight days. The Rovuma is remarkable for the high lands that flank it for some eighty miles from the ocean. The cataracts of other rivers occur in mountains, those of the Rovuma are found in a level part, with hills only in the distance. Far away in the west and north we could see high blue heights, probably of igneous origin from their forms, rising out of a plain.

The distance from Ngomano, a spot thirty miles further up, to the Arab crossing-places of Lake Nyassa Tsenga or Kotakota was said to be twelve days. The way we had discovered to Lake Nyassa by Murchison's Cataracts had so much less land carriage, that we considered it best to take our steamer thither, by the route in which we were well known, instead of working where we were strangers; and accordingly we made up our minds to return.

The natives reported a worse place above our turning-point —the passage being still narrower than this. An Arab, they said, once built a boat above the rapids, and sent it down full of slaves; but it was broken to pieces in these upper narrows. Many still maintained that the Rovuma came from Nyassa, and that it is very narrow as it issues out of the lake. One man declared that he had seen it with his own eyes as it left the lake, and seemed displeased at being cross-questioned, as if we doubted his veracity.

More satisfactory information, as it appeared to us, was obtained from others. Two days, or thirty miles, beyond where we turned back, the Rovuma is joined by the Liende, which, coming from the south-west, rises in the mountains on the east side of Nyassa. The great slave route to Kilwa runs up the banks of this river, which is only ankle-deep at the dry season of the year. The Rovuma itself comes from the W.N.W., and after the traveller passes the confluence of the Liende at Ngomano or "meeting-place," the Chief of which part is named Ndonde, he finds the river narrow, and the people Ajawa.

The Nyamatolo people have a great abundance of food, and they cultivate the land extensively. The island is simply their summer residence; their permanent villages being in the woods. While hunting, we entered some of these villages, and saw that large quantities of grain were left in them, and in some parts of the forest away from the villages we found many pots of oil-yielding seeds (sesamum), besides grain. The sesamum was offered to us both for sale and as a present, under the name *mafuta*, or fat; and small quantities of gum copal were also brought to us, which led us to think that these articles may have been collected by the Arabs. Tobacco, formed into lumps, was abundant and cheap. Cotton-bushes were seen, but no one was observed spinning or weaving cotton for anything but fishing-nets. The article of most value was a climbing dye-wood, which attains the thickness of a man's leg, and which Dr. Kirk has found experimentally to be of considerable value as a fast yellow colour. Baobab-trees on the Rovuma, though not nearly so gigantic in size as those on the Zambesi, bear fruit more than twice as large.   The great white blossoms were just out, and much of last year's fruit was still hanging on the branches.

Crocodiles in the Rovuma have a sorry time of it. Never before were reptiles so persecuted and snubbed. They are hunted with spears, and spring traps are set for them. If one of them enters an inviting pool after fish, he soon finds a fence thrown round it, and a spring trap set in the only path out of the enclosure. Their flesh is eaten, and relished. The banks, on which the female lays her eggs by night, are carefully searched by day, and all the eggs dug out and devoured. The fish-hawk makes havoc among the few young ones that escape their other enemies. Our men were constantly on the look-out for crocodiles' nests. One was found containing thirty-five newly-laid eggs, and they declared that the crocodile would lay as many more the second night in another place. The eggs were a foot deep in the sand on the top of a bank ten feet high. The animal digs a hole with its foot, covers the eggs, and leaves them till the river rises over the nest in about three months afterwards, when she comes back, and assists the young ones out.   We once saw opposite Tette young crocodiles in December, swimming beside an island in company with an old one.   The yolk of the egg is nearly as white as the real white.   In taste they resemble hen's eggs with perhaps a smack of custard, and would be as highly relished by whites as by blacks, were it not for their unsavoury origin in men-eaters.

Hunting the Senze (*Aulacodus Swindernianus*), an animal the size of a large cat, but in shape more like a pig, was the chief business of men and boys as we passed the reedy banks and low islands.   They set fire to a mass of reeds, and, armed with sticks, spears, bows and arrows, stand in groups guarding the outlets through which the scared Senze may run from

the approaching flames.   Dark dense volumes of impenetrable smoke now roll over on the lee side of the islet, and
shroud the hunters.   At times vast sheets of lurid flames
bursting forth, roaring, crackling and exploding, leap wildly
far above the tall reeds.   Out rush the terrified animals, and
amid the smoke are seen the excited hunters dancing about
with frantic gesticulations, and hurling stick, spear, and
arrow at their burned out victims.   Kites hover over the
smoke, ready to pounce on the mantis and locusts as they
spring from the fire.   Small crows and hundreds of swallows
are on eager wing, darting into the smoke and out again,
seizing fugitive flies.   Scores of insects, in their haste to
escape from the fire, jump into the river, and the active fish
enjoy a rare feast.

We returned to the Pioneer on the 9th of October, having
been away one month.   The ship's company had used distilled
water, a condenser having been sent out from England; and
there had not been a single case of sickness on board since
we left, though there were so many cases of fever the few
days she lay in the same spot last year.   Our boat party
drank the water of the river, and the three white sailors, who
had never been in an African river before, had some slight
attacks of fever.

CHAPTER XXII.

WE put to sea on the 18th of October, and, again touching at Johanna, obtained a crew of Johanna men and some oxen, and sailed for the Zambesi; but our fuel failing before we reached it, and the wind being contrary, we ran into Quillimane for wood.

Quillimane must have been built solely for the sake of carrying on the slave-trade, for no man in his senses would ever have dreamed of placing a village on such a low, muddy, fever-haunted, and mosquito-swarming site, had it not been for the facilities it afforded for slaving. The bar may at springs and floods be easily crossed by sailing-vessels, but, being far from the land, it is always dangerous for boats Slaves, under the name of "free emigrants," have gone by thousands from Quillimane, during the last six years, to the ports a little to the south, particularly to Massangano. Some excellent brick-houses still stand in the place, and the owners

View of Quillimane and of the Pioneer.

are generous and hospitable: among them our good friend, Colonel Nuñez. His disinterested kindness to us and to all our countrymen can never be forgotten. He is a noble example of what energy and uprightness may accomplish even here. He came out as a cabin-boy, and, without a single friend to help him, he has persevered in an honourable course until he is the richest man on the East Coast. When Dr. Livingstone came down the Zambesi in 1856, Colonel Nuñez was the chief of the only four honourable, trustworthy men in the country. But while he has risen, a whole herd has sunk, making loud lamentations, through puffs of cigar-smoke, over negro laziness; they might add, their own.

All agricultural enterprise is virtually discouraged by the Quillimane Government. A man must purchase a permit from the Governor, when he wishes to visit his country farm; and this tax, in a country where labour is unpopular, causes the farms to be almost entirely left in the hands of a head slave, who makes returns to his master as interest or honesty prompts him. A passport must also be bought whenever a man wishes to go up the river to Mazaro, Senna, or Tette, or even to reside for a month at Quillimane. With a soil and a climate well suited for the growth of the cane, abundance of slave labour, and water communication to any market in the world, they have never made their own sugar. All they use is imported from Bombay. "The people of Quillimane have no enterprise," said a young European Portuguese, "they do nothing, and are always wasting their time in suffering, or in recovering from fever."

We entered the Zambesi about the end of November and found it unusually low, so we did not get up to Shupanga till the 19th of December. The friends of our Mazaro men, who had now become good sailors and very attentive servants, turned out and gave them a hearty welcome back from the perils of the sea: they had begun to fear that they would never return. We hired them at a sixteen-yard piece of cloth a month—about ten shillings' worth, the Portuguese market-price of the cloth being then sevenpence halfpenny a yard,—and paid them five pieces each, for four-and-a-half months' work. A merchant at the same time paid other Mazaro men three pieces for seven months, and they were with him in the interior. If the merchants do not prosper, it is not because labour is dear, but because it is scarce, and because they are so eager on every occasion to sell the workmen out of the country. Our men had also received quantities of good clothes from the sailors

of the Pioneer and of the Orestes, and were now regarded by their neighbours and by themselves as men
of importance. Never before had they possessed so much
wealth : they believed that they might settle in life,
being now of sufficient standing to warrant their entering
the married state; and a wife and a hut were among
their first investments. Sixteen yards were paid to the
wife's parents, and a hut cost four yards. We should have
liked to have kept them in the ship, for they were well-
behaved and had learned a great deal of the work required.
Though they would not themselves go again, they engaged
others for us; and brought twice as many as we could take, of
their brothers and cousins, who were eager to join the ship
and go with us up the Shire, or anywhere else. They all
agreed to take half-pay until they too had learned to work;
and we found no scarcity of labour, though all that could be
exported is now out of the country.

There had been a drought of unusual severity during the
past season in the country between Lupata and Kebrabasa,
and it had extended north-east to the Manganja highlands.
All the Tette slaves, except a very few household ones,
had been driven away by hunger, and were now far off
in the woods, and wherever wild fruit, or the prospect of
obtaining anything whatever to keep the breath of life in
them, was to be found. Their masters were said never to
expect to see them again. There have been two years of
great hunger at Tette since we have been in the country,
and a famine like the present prevailed in 1854, when
thousands died of starvation. If men like the Cape farmers
owned this country, their energy and enterprise would soon
render the crops independent of rain. There being plenty of
slope or fall, the land could be easily irrigated from the
Zambesi and its tributary streams. A Portuguese colony can

never prosper : it is used as a penal settlement, and everything must be done military fashion. " What do I care for this country ? " said the most enterprising of the Tette merchants, " all I want is to make money as soon as possible, and then go to Bombay and enjoy it." All business at Tette was now suspended. Carriers could not be found to take the goods into the interior, and the merchants could barely obtain food for their own families. At Mazaro more rain had fallen, and a tolerable crop followed. The people of Shupanga were collecting and drying different wild fruits, nearly all of which are far from palatable to a European taste. The root of a small creeper called " bisé " is dug up and eaten. In appearance it is not unlike the small white sweet potato, and has a little of the flavour of our potato. It would be very good, if it were only a little larger. From another tuber, called " ulanga," very good starch can be made. A few miles from Shupanga there is an abundance of large game, but the people here, though fond enough of meat, are not a hunting race, and seldom kill any.

The Shire having risen, we steamed off on the 10th of January, 1863, with the Lady Nyassa in tow. It was not long before we came upon the ravages of the notorious Mariano. The survivors of a small hamlet, at the foot of Morambala, were in a state of starvation, having lost their food by one of his marauding parties. The women were in the fields collecting insects, roots, wild fruits, and whatever could be eaten, in order to drag on their lives, if possible, till the next crop should be ripe. Two canoes passed us, that had been robbed by Mariano's band of everything they had in them ; the owners were gathering palm-nuts for their subsistence. They wore palm-leaf aprons, as the robbers had stripped them of their clothing and ornaments. Dead bodies floated past us daily, and in the mornings the paddles had to

2 G

be cleared of corpses, caught by the floats during the night. For scores of miles the entire population of the valley was swept away by this scourge Mariano, who is again, as he was before, the great Portuguese slave-agent. It made the heart ache to see the wide-spread desolation; the river-banks, once so populous, all silent; the villages burned down, and an oppressive stillness reigning where formerly crowds of eager sellers appeared with the various products of their industry. Here and there might be seen on the bank a small dreary deserted shed, where had sat, day after day, a starving fisherman, until the rising waters drove the fish from their wonted haunts, and left him to die. Tingane had been defeated; his people had been killed, kidnapped, and forced to flee from their villages. There were a few wretched survivors in a village above the Ruo; but the majority of the population was dead. The sight and smell of dead bodies was everywhere. Many skeletons lay beside the path, where in their weakness they had fallen and expired. Ghastly living forms of boys and girls, with dull dead eyes, were crouching beside some of the huts. A few more miserable days of their terrible hunger, and they would be with the dead.

Oppressed with the shocking scenes around, we visited the Bishop's grave; and though it matters little where a good Christian's ashes rest, yet it was with sadness that we thought over the hopes which had clustered around him, as he left the classic grounds of Cambridge, all now buried in this wild place. How it would have torn his kindly heart to witness the sights we now were forced to see!

In giving vent to the natural feelings of regret, that a man so eminently endowed and learned, as was Bishop Mackenzie, should have been so soon cut off, some have expressed an opinion that it was wrong to use an instrument so

valuable *merely* to convert the heathen. If the attempt is
to be made at all, it is "penny wise and pound foolish" to
employ any but the very best men, and those who are
specially educated for the work. An ordinary clergyman,
however well suited for a parish, will not, without special
training, make a Missionary; and as to their comparative
usefulness, it is like that of the man who builds an hospital, as
compared with that of the surgeon who in after years only
administers for a time the remedies which the founder had
provided in perpetuity. Had the Bishop succeeded in introducing Christianity, his converts might have been few, but
they would have formed a continuous roll for all time to come.

The Shire fell two feet, before we reached the shallow
crossing where we had formerly such difficulty, and we had
now two ships to take up. A hippopotamus was shot two
miles above a bank on which the ship lay a fortnight: it
floated in three hours. As the boat was towing it down, the
crocodiles were attracted by the dead beast, and several shots
had to be fired to keep them off. The bullet had not entered
the brain of the animal, but driven a splinter of bone into it.
A little moisture with some gas issued from the wound, and
this was all that could tell the crocodiles down the stream
of a dead hippopotamus; and yet they came up from miles
below. Their sense of smell must be as acute as their
hearing; both are quite extraordinary. Dozens fed on the
meat we left. Our Krooman, Jumbo, used to assert, that
the crocodile never eats fresh meat, but always keeps it till
it is high and tender—and the stronger it smells, the better
he likes it. There seems to be some truth in this. They
can swallow but small pieces at a time, and find it difficult
to tear fresh meat. In the act of swallowing, which is like
that of a dog, the head is raised out of the water. We
tried to catch some, and one was soon hooked; it required half-

a-dozen hands to haul him up the river, and the shark-hook straightened, and he got away. A large iron hook was next made, but, as the creatures could not swallow it, their jaws soon pressed it straight — and our crocodile-fishing was a failure. As one might expect,—from ·the power even of a salmon—the tug of a crocodile was terribly strong.

The corpse of a boy floated past the ship; a monstrous crocodile rushed at it with the speed of a greyhound, caught it and shook it, as a terrier dog does a rat. Others dashed at the prey, each with his powerful tail causing the water to churn and froth, as he furiously tore off a piece. In a few seconds it was all gone. The sight was frightful to behold. The Shire swarmed with crocodiles; we counted sixty-seven of these repulsive reptiles on a single bank, but they are not as fierce as they are in some rivers. "Crocodiles" says Captain Tuckey, "are so plentiful in the Congo, near the rapids, and so frequently carry off the women, who at daylight go down to the river for water, that, while they are filling their calabashes, one of the party is usually employed in throwing large stones into the water outside." Here, either a calabash on a long pole is used in drawing water, or a fence is planted. The natives eat the crocodile, but to us the idea of tasting the musky-scented, fishy-looking flesh carried the idea of cannibalism. Humboldt remarks, that in South America the alligators of some rivers are more dangerous than in others. Alligators differ from crocodiles in the fourth or canine tooth going into a hole or socket in the upper jaw, while, in the crocodile it fits into a notch. The forefoot of the crocodile has five toes not webbed, the hindfoot has four toes which are webbed; in the alligator the web is altogether wanting. They are so much alike that they would no doubt breed together.

One of the crocodiles which was shot had a piece snapped off the end of his tail, another had lost a forefoot in fighting; we saw actual leeches between the teeth, such as are mentioned by Herodotus, but we never witnessed the plover picking them out. Their greater fierceness in one part of the country than another is doubtless owing to a scarcity of fish; in fact, Captain Tuckey says, of that part of the Congo, mentioned above, "There are no fish here but catfish," and we found, that the lake crocodiles, living in clear water, and with plenty of fish, scarcely ever attacked man. The Shire teems with fish of many different kinds. The only time, as already remarked, when its crocodiles are particularly to be dreaded, is when the river is in flood. Then the fish are driven from their usual haunts, and no game comes down to the river to drink, water being abundant in pools inland. Hunger now impels the crocodile to lie in wait for the women who come to draw water, and on the Zambesi numbers are carried off every year. The danger is not so great at other seasons; though it is never safe to bathe, or to stoop to drink, where one cannot see the bottom, especially in the evening. One of the Makololo ran down in the dusk to the river; and, as he was busy tossing the water to his mouth with his hand, in the manner peculiar to the natives, a crocodile rose suddenly from the bottom, and caught him by the hand. The limb of a tree was fortunately within reach, and he had presence of mind to lay hold of it. Both tugged and pulled; the crocodile for his dinner, and the man for dear life. For a time, it appeared doubtful whether a dinner or a life was to be sacrificed; but the man held on, and the monster let the hand go, leaving the deep marks of his ugly teeth in it.

During our detention, in expectation of the permanent rise of the river in March, Dr. Kirk and Mr. C. Livingstone collected numbers of the wading-birds of the marshes—and made pleasant additions to our salted provisions, in geese, ducks, and hippopotamus flesh. One of the comb or knob-nosed geese, on being strangled in order to have its skin preserved without injury, continued to breathe audibly by the broken humerus, or wing-bone, and other means had to be adopted to put it out of pain. This was as if a man on the gallows were to continue to breathe by a broken arm-bone, and afforded us an illustration of the fact, that in birds, the vital air penetrates every part of the interior of their bodies. The breath passes through and round about the lungs—bathes the surfaces of the viscera, and enters the cavities of the bones; it even penetrates into some spaces between the muscles of the neck—and thus not only is the most perfect oxygenation of the blood secured, but, the temperature of the blood being very high, the air in every part is rarefied, and the great lightness and vigour provided for, that the habits of birds require. Several birds were found by Dr. Kirk, to have marrow in the tibiæ, though these bones are generally described as hollow.

During the period of our detention on the shallow part of the river in March, Mr. Thornton came up to us from Shu-panga: he had, as before narrated, left the expedition in 1859, and joined Baron van der Decken, in the journey to Kilimanjaro, when, by an ascent of the mountain to the height of 8000 feet, it was first proved to be covered with perpetual snow, and the previous information respecting it, given by the Church of England Missionaries, Krapf and Rebman, con-firmed. It is now well known that the Baron subsequently ascended the Kilimanjaro to 14,000 feet, and ascertained its highest peak to be at least 20,000 feet above the sea. Mr. Thornton made the map of the first journey, at Shu-panga, from materials collected when with the Baron; and when that work was accomplished, followed us. He was then directed to examine geologically, the Cataract district, but not to expose himself to contact with the Ajawa until the feelings of that tribe should be ascertained.

The members of Bishop Mackenzie's party had, on the loss of their head, fled from Magomero on the highlands, down to Chibisa's, in the low-lying Shire Valley; and Thornton, finding them suffering from want of animal food, kindly volunteered to go across thence to Tette, and bring a supply of goats and sheep. We were not aware of this step, to which the generosity of his nature prompted him, till two days after he had started. In addition to securing supplies for the Universities' Mission, he brought some for the Expedition, and took bearings, by which he hoped to connect his former work at Tette with the mountains in the Shire district. The toil of this journey was too much for his strength, as with the addition of great scarcity of water, it had been for that of Dr. Kirk and Rae, and he returned in a sadly haggard and exhausted condition; diarrhœa supervened, and that ended in dysentery and fever, which terminated fatally on the 21st of April, 1863. He received the un-remitting attentions of Dr. Kirk, and Dr. Meller, surgeon of the Pioneer, during the fortnight of his illness; and as he had suffered very little from fever, or any other disease, in Africa, we had entertained strong hopes that his youth and unimpaired constitution would have carried him through. During the night of the 20th, his mind wandered so much, that we could not ascertain his last wishes; and on the morn-ing of the 21st, to our great sorrow, he died. He was buried on the 22nd, near a large tree on the right bank of the Shire, about five hundred yards from the lowest of the Murchison Cataracts—and close to a rivulet, at which the Lady Nyassa and Pioneer lay.

No words can convey an adequate idea of the scene of wide-spread desolation, which the once pleasant Shire Valley now presented. Instead of smiling villages and crowds of people coming with things for sale, scarcely a soul was to be seen; and, when by chance one lighted on a native, his frame bore the impress of hunger, and his countenance, the look of a cringing broken-spiritedness. A drought had visited the land after the slave-hunting panic swept over it. Had it been possible to conceive the thorough depopulation which had ensued, we should have avoided coming up the river. Large masses of the people had fled down to the Shire, only anxious to get the river between them and their enemies. Most of the food had been left behind; and famine and starvation had cut off so many, that the remainder were too few to bury the dead. The corpses we saw floating down the river were only a remnant of those that had perished, whom their friends, from weakness, could not bury, nor over-gorged crocodiles devour. It is true that famine caused a great portion of this waste of human life: but the slave-trade must be deemed the chief agent in the ruin, because, as we were informed, in former droughts all the people flocked from the hills down to the marshes, which are capable of yielding crops of maize in less than three months, at any time of the year, and now they were afraid to do so. A few, encouraged by the Mission in the attempt to cultivate, had their little patches robbed as successive swarms of fugitives came from the hills. Who can blame these outcasts from house and home for stealing to save their wretched lives, or wonder that the owners protected the little all, on which their own lives depended, with club and spear? We were informed by Mr. Waller of the dreadful blight which had befallen the once smiling Shire Valley. His words, though strong, failed to impress us with the reality. In fact, they were received, as some may accept our own, as tinged with exaggeration; but when our eyes beheld the last mere driblets of this cup of woe, we for the first time felt that the enormous wrongs inflicted on our fellow-men by slaving are beyond exaggeration.

The plan adopted by these Manganja highlanders to raise crops on the soft black mud of the marshes might not occur to agriculturists of other coumtries. Coarse river-sand is put down on the rich dark ooze in spadefuls, at about two feet from each other, and the maize planted therein. In vegetating, the roots are free to take what they require from the too fat soil beneath, and also atmospheric constituents through the sand. Nearly the same thing is done when the soil is more solid, but too damp. A hole is dug about a foot in depth, the seed is thrown in and covered with a spadeful of sand, and the result is a flourishing crop; where, without the sand, the rich but too wet loam would yield nothing. In this way, the people saved their lives in former droughts, but now the slave-hunting panic seemed to have destroyed all presence of mind. The few wretched survivors, even after our arrival, were overpowered by an apathetic lethargy. They attempted scarcely any cultivation, which, for people so given to agriculture as they are, was very remarkable; they were seen daily devouring the corn-stalks which had sprung up in the old plantations, and which would, if let alone, have yielded corn in a month. They could not be aroused from their lethargy. Famine benumbs all the faculties. We tried to induce some to exert themselves to procure food—but failed. They had lost all their former spirit, and with lacklustre eyes, scarcely meeting ours, and in whining tones, replied to every proposition for their benefit—" No, no!" (Ai! ai!)

Wherever we took a walk, human skeletons were

seen in every direction, and it was painfully interesting to observe the different postures in which the poor
wretches had breathed their last. A whole heap had been
thrown down a slope behind a village, where the fugitives
often crossed the river from the east; and in one hut
of the same village no fewer than twenty drums had been
collected, probably the ferryman's fees. Many had ended
their misery under shady trees—others under projecting
crags in the hills — while others lay in their huts, with
closed doors, which when opened disclosed the mouldering
corpse with the poor rags round the loins — the skull
fallen off the pillow—the little skeleton of the child, that
had perished first, rolled up in a mat between two large
skeletons. The sight of this desert, but eighteen months
ago a well peopled valley, now literally strewn with human
bones, forced the conviction upon us, that the destruction
of human life in the middle passage, however great, constitutes but a small portion of the waste, and made us feel
that unless the slave-trade—that monster iniquity, which
has so long brooded over Africa—is put down, lawful commerce cannot be established.

We believed that, if it were possible to get a steamer upon
the Lake, we could by her means put a check on the slavers
from the East Coast; and aid more effectually still in the
suppression of the slave-trade, by introducing, by way of the
Róvuma, a lawful traffic in ivory. We therefore unscrewed
the Lady Nyassa at a rivulet about five hundred yards
below the first cataract, and began to make a road over the
thirty-five or forty miles of land portage, by which to carry
her up piecemeal. After mature consideration, we could not
imagine a more noble work of benevolence, than thus to
introduce light and liberty into a quarter of this fair earth,
which human lust has converted into the nearest possible

resemblance of what we conceive the infernal regions to be—and we sacrificed much of our private resources as an offering for the promotion of so good a cause.

The chief part of the labour of road-making consisted in cutting down trees and removing stones. The country being covered with open forest, a small tree had to be cut about every fifty or sixty yards. The land near the river was so very much intersected by ravines, that search had to be made, a mile from its banks, for more level ground. Experienced Hottentot drivers would have taken Cape wagons without any other trouble than that of occasionally cutting down a tree. No tsetse infested this district and the cattle brought from Johanna flourished on the abundant pasture. The first half-mile of road led up, by a gradual slope, to an altitude of two hundred feet above the ship, and a sensible difference of climate was felt even there. For the remainder of the distance the height increased,—till, at the uppermost Cataract, we were more than 1200 feet above the sea. The country here, having recovered from the effects of the drought, was bright with young green woodland, and mountains of the same refreshing hue. But the absence of the crowds, which had attended us as we carried up the boat, when the women followed us for miles with fine meal, vegetables, and fat fowls for sale, and the boys were ever ready for a little job — and the oppressive stillness bore heavily on our spirits. The Portuguese of Tette had very effectually removed our labourers. Not an ounce of fresh provisions could be obtained, except what could be shot, and even the food for our native crew had to be brought one hundred and fifty miles from the Zambesi.

The diet of salt provisions and preserved meats without vegetables, with the depression of spirits caused by seeing how effectually a few wretched convicts, aided by the connivance of officials, of whom better might have been hoped, could counteract our best efforts, and turn intended good to certain evil, brought on attacks of dysentery, which went the round of the Expedition—and, Dr. Kirk and Charles Livingstone having suffered most severely, it was deemed advisable that they should go home. This measure was necessary, though much to the regret of all—for having done so much, they were naturally anxious to be present, when, by the establishing ourselves on the Lake, all our efforts should be crowned with success. After it had been decided that these two officers, and all the whites who could be spared, should be sent down to the sea for a passage to England, Dr. Livingstone was seized in May with a severe attack of dysentery, which continued for a month, and reduced him to a shadow. Dr. Kirk kindly remained in attendance till the worst was passed. The parting took place on the 19th of May.

We had still the hope, that by means of a strong remonstrance sent to Lisbon, against the Portuguese officials in Tette engaging in the slave-hunting forays, some means would be resorted to for preventing slavers for the future following on our footsteps and neutralizing our efforts. The appeal, however, we subsequently ascertained, produced only a shoal of promises from the Portuguese Ministry. New orders were to be sent out to the officials, to render us every assistance, and a request was made for information respecting Dr. Livingstone's geographical discoveries, for the especial use of the Minister of Marine and the Colonies: though it was notorious that his Excellency had made use of our previous information in constructing a map, in which by changing the spelling he had attempted to prove that Dr. Livingstone had made no discoveries at all. Truly our object was not so much discovery, as a desire to lead the nation, which his Excellency's countrymen had so enslaved and degraded, to a state of freedom and civilization. We regret to have to make this statement—but it was a monstrous mistake to believe in the honour of the Government of Portugal, or in their having a vestige of desire to promote the amelioration of Africa. One ought to hope the best of every one, giving, if possible, credit for good intentions; but, though deeply sensible of obligations to individuals of the nation, and anxious to renew the expressions of respect formerly used, we must declare the conduct of Portuguese statesmen to Africa to be simply infamous.

After a few miles of road were completed, and the oxen broken in, we resolved to try and render ourselves independent of the South for fresh provisions, by going in a boat up the Shire, above the Cataracts, to the tribes at the foot of Lake Nyassa, who were still untouched by the Ajawa invasion. In furtherance of this plan Dr. Livingstone and Mr. Rae determined to walk up to examine, and, if need be, mend the boat which had been left two seasons previously hung up to the limb of a large shady tree, before attempting to carry another past the Cataracts. The Pioneer, which was to be left in charge of our active and most trustworthy gunner, Mr. Edward Young, R.N., was thoroughly roofed over with euphorbia branches and grass, so as completely to protect her decks from the sun: she also received daily a due amount of man-of-war scrubbing and washing; and, besides having everything put in shipshape fashion, was every evening swung out into the middle of the river, for the sake of the greater amount of air which circulated there. In addition to their daily routine work of the ship, the three stokers, one sailor, and one carpenter—now our complement—were encouraged to hunt for guinea-fowl, which in June, when the water inland is dried up, come in large

flocks to the river's banks, and roost on the trees at night.
Everything that can be done to keep mind and body employed, tends to prevent fever.

During the period of convalescence, repairs were carried
on on the Pioneer's engines. Trees were sawn into planks
for paddle-floats, by two carpenters from Senna—and a
garden made for vegetables, to be irrigated by a pump from
the stream : our plot of ground was manured—a new style
of agriculture to the people of this country,—the wheat was
sown in May, when the weather was cold and damp, and it
grew beautifully ; this was interesting, as showing how easily
a Mission might be supplied with corn, by leading out one
of the numerous springs which run among the hills. Good
Bishop Mackenzie was fully aware of this, but unfortunately
sowed his crop at the wrong time of the year. Had we
been able to continue to attend to ours, we should have
had a crop in about four months' time ; but duty soon called
us elsewhere.

While we were employed in these operations, some of the
poor starved people about had been in the habit of crossing the river, and reaping the self-sown mapira, in the old
gardens of their countrymen. In the afternoon of the 9th,
a canoe came floating down empty, and shortly after a
woman was seen swimming near the other side, which was
about two hundred yards distant from us. Our native crew
manned the boat, and rescued her ; when brought on board,
she was found to have an arrow-head, eight or ten inches
long in her back, below the ribs, and slanting up through
the diaphragm and left lung, towards the heart — she had
been shot from behind when stooping. Air was coming out
of the wound, and, there being but an inch of the barbed
arrow-head visible, it was thought better not to run the risk
of her dying under the operation necessary for its removal ;

so we carried her up to her own hut. One of her relatives was less scrupulous, for he cut out the arrow and part of the lung. Mr. Young sent her occasionally portions of native corn, and strange to say found that she not only became well, but stout. The constitution of these people seems to have a wonderful power of self-repair—and it could be no slight privation which had cut off the many thousands that we saw dead around us.

We regretted that, in consequence of Dr. Meller having now sole medical charge, we could not have his company in our projected trip; but he found employment in botany and natural history, after the annual sickly season of March, April, and May was over; and his constant presence was not so much required at the ship. Later in the year, when he could be well spared, he went down the river to take up an appointment he had been offered in Madagascar; but unfortunately was so severely tried by illness while detained at the coast, that for nearly two years, he was not able to turn his abilities as a naturalist to account by proceeding to that island. We have no doubt but he will yet distinguish himself in that untrodden field.

CHAPTER XXIII.

June 16th, 1863, start for Upper Cataracts — Cultivation — Cotton — Huts, empty, or tenanted by skeletons — Buffalo-birds and dread of the poisoned arrow — *Kombi*, a species of strophanthus, the poison employed — The 'Nga poison — Its effects — Instinct in man — Mukuru-Madse — *Sanu*, or prickly-seeded grass — Its use — Native paths — Guinea-fowls — Cotton patches — Expedition recalled — No other course open to us, labour being all swept away by Portuguese slave-trading — Mr. Waller witnesses a small part of the trade — Friendliness of Ajawa and Makololo to English — Try to take another boat past the Cataracts — Loss of the boat — Penitence of the losers — The Cataracts — Geology.

On the 16th of June, we started for the Upper Cataracts, with a mule-cart, our road lying a distance of a mile west from the river. We saw many of the deserted dwellings of the people who formerly came to us; and were very much struck by the extent of land under cultivation, though that, compared with the whole country, is very small. Large patches of mapira continued to grow,—as it is said it does from the roots for three years. The mapira was mixed with tall bushes of the Congo-bean, castor-oil plants, and cotton. The largest patch of this kind we paced, and found it to be six hundred and thirty paces on one side—the rest were from one acre to three, and many not more than one-third of an acre. The cotton—of very superior quality—was now dropping off the bushes, to be left to rot—there was no one to gather what would have been of so much value in Lancashire. The huts, in the different villages we entered, were standing quite perfect. The mortars for pounding corn—the stones for grinding it—the water and beer pots—the empty corn-safes and kitchen utensils, were all untouched; and most of the doors were shut, as if the starving owners had gone out to wander in search of roots or fruits in the forest, and had never returned.   When opened, several huts revealed a ghastly sight of human skeletons.   Some were seen in such unnatural positions, as to give the idea that they had expired in a faint, when trying to reach something to allay the gnawings of hunger.

We took several of the men as far as the Mukuru-Madse for the sake of the change of air and for occupation, and also to secure for the ships a supply of buffalo meat—as those animals were reported to be in abundance on that stream.   But though it was evident from the tracks that the report was true, it was impossible to get a glimpse of them.   The grass being taller than we were, and pretty thickly planted, they always knew of our approach before we saw them.   And the first intimation we had of their being near was the sound they made in rushing over the stones, breaking the branches, and knocking their horns against each other.   Once, when seeking a ford for the cart, at sunrise, we saw a herd slowly wending up the hill-side from the water.   Sending for a rifle, and stalking with intense eagerness for a fat beefsteak, instead of our usual fare of salted provisions, we got so near that we could hear the bulls uttering their hoarse deep low, but could see nothing except the mass of yellow grass in front; suddenly the buffalo-birds sounded their alarm-whistle, and away dashed the troop, and we got sight of neither birds nor beasts.   This would be no country for a sportsman except when the grass is short.   The animals are wary, from the dread they have of the poisoned arrows.   Those of the natives who do hunt are deeply imbued with the hunting spirit, and follow the game with a stealthy perseverance and cunning, quite extraordinary.   The arrow, making no noise, the herd is followed up until the poison takes effect, and the wounded animal falls out.   It is then patiently watched till it drops—

a portion of meat round the wound is cut away, and all the rest eaten.

Poisoned arrows are made in two pieces. An iron barb is firmly fastened to one end of a small wand of wood, ten inches or a foot long, the other end of which, fined down to a long point, is nicely fitted, though not otherwise secured, in

A. Common form of Ajawa arrow iron head, with barbs.
B. 　　　„　　　„　　 Manganja, poisoned at head and barbs, and neck.
C. Manner of inserting arrow-head into the shaft.
D. Entire arrow nearly four feet long, and feathered.

the hollow of the reed, which forms the arrow shaft. The wood immediately below the iron head is smeared with the poison. When the arrow is shot into an animal, the reed either falls to the ground at once, or is very soon brushed off by the bushes; but the iron barb and poisoned upper part of the wood remain in the wound. If made in one piece, the arrow would often be torn out, head and all, by the long shaft catching in the underwood, or striking against trees. The poison used here, and called *kombi*, is obtained from a species of *strophanthus*, and is very virulent. Dr. Kirk found by an accidental experiment on himself that it acts by lowering the pulse. In using his tooth-brush, which had been in a pocket containing a little of the poison, he noticed a bitter taste, but attributed it to his having sometimes used the handle in taking quinine. Though the quantity was small, it immediately showed its power by lowering his pulse which at the time had been raised by a cold, and next day he was perfectly restored. Not much can be inferred from a single case of this kind, but it is possible that the kombi may turn out a valuable remedy; and, as Professor Sharpey has conducted a series of experiments with this substance, we look with interest for the results. An alkaloid has been obtained from it similar to strychnine. There is no doubt that all kinds of wild animals die from the effects of poisoned arrows, except the elephant and hippopotamus. The amount of poison that this little weapon can convey into their systems being too small to kill those huge beasts, the hunters resort to the beam trap instead.

Another kind of poison was met with on Lake Nyassa, which was said to be used exclusively for killing men. It was put on small wooden arrow-heads, and carefully protected by a piece of maize-leaf tied round it. It caused numbness of the tongue when the smallest particle was tasted. The Bushmen of the northern part of the Kalahari were seen applying the entrails of a small caterpillar which they termed 'Ngā to their arrows. This venom was declared to be so powerful in producing delirium, that a man in dying returned in imagination to a state of infancy, and would call for his mother's breast. Lions when shot with it are said to perish in agonies. The poisonous ingredient in this case may be derived from the plant on which the caterpillar feeds. It is difficult to conceive by what sort of experiments the properties of these poisons, known for generations, were proved. Probably the animal instincts, which have become so obtuse by civilization, that children in England eat the berries of the deadly nightshade (*Atropa belladonna*) without suspicion, were in the early uncivilized state much more keen. In some points instinct is still retained among savages. It is related that in the celebrated voyage of the French navigator, Bougainville, a young lady, who had assumed the male attire, performed all the hard duties incident to the calling of a common sailor; and, even as servant to the geologist, carried a bag of stones and specimens over hills and dales without a complaint, and without having her sex suspected by her associates; but on landing among the savages of one of the South Sea Islands, she was instantly recognised as a female. They began to show their impressions in a way that compelled her to confess her sex, and throw herself on the protection of the commander, which of course was granted. In like manner, the earlier portions of the human family may have had their instincts as to plants, more highly developed than any of their descendants—if indeed much more knowledge than we usually suppose be not the effect of direct revelation from above.

The Mukuru-Madse has a deep rocky bed. The water is generally about four feet deep, and fifteen or twenty yards broad. Before reaching it, we passed five or six gullies; but beyond it the country, for two or three miles from the river, was comparatively smooth. The long grass was overrunning all the native paths, and one species (*sanu*), which has a sharp barbed seed a quarter of an inch in length, enters every pore of woollen clothing, and highly irritates the skin. From its hard, sharp point a series of minute barbs are laid back, and give the seed a hold wherever it enters: the slightest touch gives it an entering motion, and the little hooks prevent its working out. These seeds are so abundant in some spots, that the inside of the stocking becomes worse than the roughest hair shirt. It is, however, an excellent self-sower, and fine fodder; it rises to the height of common meadow-grass in England, and would be a capital plant for spreading over a new country not so abundantly supplied with grasses as this is.

We have sometimes noticed two or three leaves together pierced through by these seeds, and thus made, as it were, into wings to carry them to any soil suited to their growth.

We always follow the native paths, though they are generally not more than fifteen inches broad, and so often have deep little holes in them, made for the purpose of setting traps for small animals, and are so much obscured by the long grass, that one has to keep one's eyes on the ground more than is pleasant. In spite, however, of all drawbacks, it is vastly more easy to travel on these tracks, than to go straight over uncultivated ground, or virgin forest. A path usually leads to some village, though sometimes it turns out to be a mere game track leading nowhere.

In going north, we came into a part called Mpemba where Chibisa was owned as chief, but the people did not know that he had been assassinated by the Portuguese Terera. A great deal of grain was lying round the hut, where we spent the night. Very large numbers of turtledoves feasted undisturbed on the tall stalked mapira ears, and we easily secured plenty of fine fat guinea-fowls—now allowed to feed leisurely in the deserted gardens. The reason assigned for all this listless improvidence was "There are no women to grind the corn—all are dead."

The cotton patches in all cases seemed to have been so well cared for, and kept so free of weeds formerly, that, though now untended, but few weeds had sprung up ; and the bushes were thus preserved in the annual grass burnings. Many baobab-trees grow in different spots, and the few people seen were using the white pulp found between the seeds to make a pleasant subacid drink.

On passing Malango, near the uppermost Cataract, not
a soul was to be seen; but, as we rested opposite a beautiful
tree-covered island, the merry voices of children at play
fell on our ears—the parents had fled thither for protection from the slave-hunting Ajawa, still urged on by
the occasional visits of the Portuguese agents from Tette.
The Ajawa, instead of passing below the Cataracts, now avoided
us, and crossed over to the east side near to the tree on which
we had hung the boat.   Those of the Manganja, to whom we
could make ourselves known, readily came to us; but the
majority had lost all confidence in themselves, in each
other, and in every one else.   The boat had been burned
about three months previously, and the Manganja were
very anxious that we should believe that this had been
the act of the Ajawa; but on scanning the spot we saw
that it was more likely to have caught fire in the grass-
burning of the country.   Had we intended to be so long in
returning to it, we should have hoisted it bottom upwards;
for, as it was, it is probable that a quantity of dried leaves
lay inside, and a spark ignited the whole.   All the trees
within fifty yards were scorched and killed, and the nails,
iron, and copper sheathing, all lay undisturbed beneath.
Had the Ajawa done the deed, they would have taken
away the copper and iron.

Our hopes of rendering ourselves independent of the south
for provisions, by means of this boat, being thus disappointed,
we turned back with the intention of carrying another up to
the same spot; and, in order to find level ground for this,
we passed across from the Shire at Malango to the upper part
of the stream Lesungwe.   A fine, active, intelligent fellow,
called Pekila, guided us, and was remarkable as almost the
only one of the population left with any spirit in him.   The
depressing effect which the slave-hunting scourge has upon

the native mind, though little to be wondered at, is sad, very sad to witness. Musical instruments, mats, pillows, mortars for pounding meal, were lying about unused, and becoming the prey of the white ants. With all their little comforts destroyed, the survivors were thrown still further back into barbarism.

It is of little importance perhaps to any but travellers, to notice that in occupying one night a well-built hut, which had been shut up for some time, the air inside at once gave us a chill, and an attack of fever ; both of which vanished when the place was well-ventilated by means of a fire. We have frequently observed that lighting a fire early in the mornings, even in the hottest time of the year, gives fresh-ness to the whole house, and removes that feeling of closeness and languor, which a hot climate induces.

On the night of the 1st July, 1863, several loud peals of thunder awoke us; the moon was shining brightly, and not a cloud to be seen. All the natives remarked on the clear-ness of the sky at the time, and next morning said, " We thought it was God ".(Morungo).

On arriving at the ship on the 2nd July, we found a despatch from Earl Russell, containing instructions for the withdrawal of the Expedition. The devastation caused by slave-hunting and famine lay all around. The labour had been as completely swept away from the Great Shire Valley, as it had been from the Zambesi, wherever Portuguese in-trigue or power extended. The continual forays of Mariano had spread ruin and desolation on our south-east as far as Mount Clarendon.

While this was going on in our rear, the Tette slave-hunters from the West had stimulated the Ajawa to sweep all the Manganja off the hills on our East; and slaving parties for this purpose were still passing the Shire above the Cataracts. In addition to the confession of the Governor of Tette, of an intention to go on with this slaving in accordance with the counsel of his elder brother at Mosambique, we had reason to believe that slavery went on under the eye of his Excellency, the Governor-General himself; and this was subsequently corroborated by our recognising two women at Mosambique who had lived within a hundred yards of the Mission-station at Magomero. They were well known to our attendants, and had formed a part of a gang of several hundreds taken to Mosambique by the Ajawa at the very time when his Excellency was entertaining English officers with anti-slavery palavers. To any one who understands how minute the information is, which Portuguese governors possess by means of their own slaves, and through gossiping traders who seek to curry their favour, it is idle to assert that all this slaving goes on without their approval and connivance.

If more had been wanted to prove the hopelessness of producing any change in the system which has prevailed ever since our allies, the Portuguese, entered the country, we had it in the impunity with which the freebooter, Terera, who had murdered Chibisa, was allowed to carry on his forays. Belchior, another marauder, had been checked, but was still allowed to make war, as they term slave-hunting.

Mr. Horace Waller was living for some five months on Mount Morambala, a position from which the whole process of the slave-trade, and depopulation of the country around could be well noted. The mountain overlooks the Shire, the beautiful meanderings of which are distinctly seen, on clear days, for thirty miles. This river was for some time supposed to be closed against Mariano, who, as a mere matter of form, was declared a rebel against the Portuguese flag. When, however, it became no longer possible to keep up the sham, the river was thrown open to him; and Mr. Waller has seen in a single day from fifteen to twenty canoes of different sizes going down, laden with slaves, to the Portuguese settlements from the so-called rebel camp. These cargoes were composed entirely of women and children. For three months this traffic was incessant, and at last, so completely was the mask thrown off, that one of the officials came to pay a visit to Bishop Tozer on another part of the same mountain, and, combining business with pleasure, collected payment for some canoe work done for the Missionary party, and with this purchased slaves from the rebels, who had only to be hailed from the bank of the river. When he had concluded the bargain he trotted the slaves out for inspection in Mr. Waller's presence. This official, Senhor Mesquita, was the only officer who could be forced to live at the Kongone. From certain circumstances in his life, he had fallen under the power of the local Government; all the other Custom-house officers refused to go to Kongone, so here poor Mesquita must live on a miserable pittance—must live, and perhaps slave, sorely against his will. His name is not brought forward with a view of throwing any odium on his character. The disinterested kindness which he showed to Dr. Meller, and others, forbids that he should be mentioned by us with anything like unkindness.

Other parties were out to the south-east of Senna, slaving for exportation from Inhambane. While we were at Shupanga, an embassy was sent to us with an offer of ivory, and all the land not occupied by the Zulus, if we would only send a few people to expel the Senna slave-hunters from the neighbourhood. Here, as with what are called the emigrant Boers of the interior of the Cape, the secret of power is, the possession of gunpowder; bowmen cannot stand the attack of muskets, and whoever possesses access to a seaport has the power of carrying on slaving to any extent; for on the East Coast there is no restriction in the introduction of arms and ammunition. The *laws* are quite as stringent against these articles as at the Cape; but, like the laws for the abolition of slavery, no one obeys them—they are only for quotation and self-glorification in Europe.

Under all these considerations, with the fact that we had not found the Rovuma so favourable for navigation at the time of our visit as we expected, it was impossible not to coincide in the wisdom of our withdrawal; but we deeply regretted that we had ever given credit to the Portuguese Government for any desire to ameliorate the condition of the African race; for, with half the labour and expense anywhere else, we should have made an indelible mark of improvement on a section of the Continent. Viewing Portuguese statesmen in the light of the laws they have passed for the suppression of slavery and the slave-trade, and by the standard of the high character of our own public men, it cannot be considered weakness to have believed in the sincerity of the anxiety to aid our enterprise, professed by the Lisbon Ministry. We hoped to benefit both Portuguese and Africans by introducing free-trade and Christianity. Our allies, unfortunately, cannot see the slightest benefit in any measure, that does not imply raising themselves up by thrusting others down. The official* paper

---

* The Portuguese Government lately employed a gentleman named Lacerda to write a series of papers in their official journal, the 'Diario de Lisboa,' to prove that Dr. Livingstone made a great mistake in ascribing any merit to Speke and Grant's discovery of what appears to be the main source of the Nile. The ancient Portuguese missionaries, Jeronymo Lobo and João dos Santos, and others, it seems, preceded our countrymen. In fact, this clever writer proves to his own satisfaction that the English have discovered next to nothing in Africa. As no one out of Portugal requires a refutation of these loose statements, we turn to a question of more import-

of the Lisbon Government has since let us know " that their policy was directed to frustrating the grasping designs of the British Government to the dominion of Eastern Africa." We, who were on the spot, and behind the scenes, knew that feelings of private benevolence had the chief share in the operations undertaken for introducing the reign of peace and good will on the Lakes and central regions, which for ages

---

ance. Do the Portuguese Ministry, by employing the writer of these papers, mean to endorse the deeds of their officials in Africa? We have believed them to be incapable of so doing; but they quoted with so much eagerness a private note from the Rev. Henry Rowley, which he never intended for publication, that we give our friend's opinion as to the chief cause of the disasters which befell the Mission of which he was a member. In the intercourse between the Mission and Expedition not a single break occurred in our friendly intercourse and good will.

" BATH, *February* 22, 1865.

" DEAR DR. LIVINGSTONE,

"Waller has written to me on the subject of my letter to Mr. Glover, and he tells me that a certain Portuguese publication, professedly quoting from that letter, says in substance—

"'The Rev. Mr. Rowley states that the attack by Dr. Livingstone on the Ajawa was the cause of the final non-success of the Mission.'

"I never said that; nor have I at any time said anything from which such a statement could be justly inferred.

"The misfortunes of the Mission were owing to loss of stores, the famine, and, *above all*, to the evil prac-

tices of the Portuguese, who kindled and kept up wars between the tribes, in order that they might purchase the prisoners for slaves.

"The Portuguese were in our hour of need of great service to us in supplying us with food. Personally, we missionaries had much to thank them for; but their conduct towards the natives is past description bad; and I am entirely one with you in your denouncement of such conduct.

"I have always said and thought you did well in releasing the slaves, and in going against the Ajawa under the idea that they were a mere slaving horde. My letter to Mr. Glover was not written to blame you for what you had done, nor to throw the responsibility of our acts upon you, but to make known to our friends at the Cape that you had done what we had done, and that you were the first to do it.

"Had you at that time been in the same mind about our attack upon the Ajawa as you were when you wrote to Sir Culling Eardley, my letter would never have been written; and seeing the ill effect it appears to have produced, I am very sorry it was ever written.

"I hope what I have said will meet your wishes.

" Very truly yours,
        " HENRY ROWLEY,"

have been the abodes of violence and bloodshed. But that
great change was not to be accomplished. The narrow-minded
would ascribe all that was attempted to the grasping pro-
pensity of the English. But the motives that actuate many
in England, both in public and private life, are much more
noble than the world gives them credit for.

Seeing, then, that we were not yet arrived at "the good
time coming," and that it was quite impossible to take the
Pioneer down to the sea till the floods of December, we
made arrangements to screw the Lady Nyassa together;
and, in order to improve the time intervening, we resolved
to carry a boat past the Cataracts a second time, sail along
the eastern shore of the Lake, and round the northern end,
and also collect data by which to verify the information
collected by Colonel Rigby, that the 19,000 slaves, who go
through the Custom-house of Zanzibar annually, are chiefly
drawn from Lake Nyassa and the Valley of the Shire.

The people attached to the Mission by Bishop Mackenzie
now formed a little free community near Chibisa's, supporting
themselves by cultivating the soil. They imitated in this
respect the Makololo, who had formed very extensive
gardens, and were now able to sell grain and vegetables
to the Expedition. The friendly feelings of both these
people towards the English were unmistakeable. An
instance in proof of this may be cited. The Makololo
village was about a quarter of a mile distant from the
Mission-huts, one of which was accidentally set on fire by
the owner; some loaded guns inside went off as the fire
reached the powder, and the Makololo, hearing the unwonted
sounds of guns in the evening, seized their arms and
rushed to the rescue of the English, supposing that they
were attacked by an enemy with firearms.

Notwithstanding their refusal to return with medicine for

their Chief, and in spite of several accusations made against
them by the black men from the Cape, which, after a good
deal of careful inquiry, could not be proved ; we remembered their noble conduct in saving our lives in the river
at Karivua, and, with this fresh proof of their willingness
to risk their lives for our countrymen, we selected five of
the best rowers among them, in the belief that these
five were worth fifty of any other tribe for the navigation
of the Lake, or for any difficulty which might occur in
the course of our journey northwards.   Our party consisted
of twenty natives, some of whom were Johanna men, and
were supposed to be capable of managing the six oxen which
drew the small wagon with a boat on it.   A team of twelve
Cape oxen, with a Hottentot driver and leader, would
have taken the wagon over the country we had to pass
through with the greatest ease ; but no sooner did we get
beyond the part of the road already made, than our drivers
encountered obstructions in the way of trees and gullies,
which it would have been a waste of time to have overcome by felling timber and hauling out the wagon by
block and tackle purchases.   The Ajawa and Manganja
settled at Chibisa's were therefore sent for, and they took
the boat on their shoulders and carried it briskly, in a
few days, past all the Cataracts except one ; then coming to
a comparatively still reach of the river, they took advantage
of it to haul her up a couple of miles.   The Makololo had
her then entirely in charge ; for, being accustomed to rapids
in their own country, no better boatmen could be desired.
The river here is very narrow, and even in what are called
still places, the current is very strong, and often obliged
them to haul the boat along by the reeds on the banks, or to
hand a tow-rope ashore.   The reeds are full of cowitch
(*Dolichos pruriens*), the pods of which are covered with

what looks a fine velvety down, but is in reality a multitude of fine prickles, which go in by the million, and caused an itching and stinging in the naked bodies of those who were pulling the tow-rope, that made them wriggle as if stung by a whole bed of nettles. Those on board required to be men of ready resource with oars and punting-poles, and such they were. But, nevertheless, they found after attempting to pass by a rock, round which the water rushed in whirls, that the wiser plan would be to take the boat ashore, and carry her past the last Cataract. When this was reported, the carriers were called from the various shady trees under which they had taken refuge from the sun. This was midwinter, but the sun is always hot by day here, though the nights are cold. Five Zambesi men, who had been all their lives accustomed to great heavy canoes,—the chief recommendation of which is said to be, that they can be run against a rock with the full force of the current without injury—were very desirous to show how much better they could manage our boat than the Makololo; three jumped into her when our backs were turned, and two hauled her up a little way; the tide caught her bow, we heard a shout of distress, the rope was out of their hands in a moment, and there she was, bottom upwards; a turn or two in an eddy, and away she went, like an arrow, down the Cataracts. One of the men in swimming ashore saved a rifle. The whole party ran with all their might along the bank, but never more did we see our boat.

The five performers in this catastrophe approached with penitential looks. They had nothing to say, nor had we. They bent down slowly, and touched our feet with both hands. "Ku kuata moendo"—"to catch the foot"—is their way of asking forgiveness. It was so like what we have seen a little child do—try to bring a dish unbidden

to its papa, and letting it fall, burst into a cry of distress—
that they were only sentenced to go back to the ship,
get provisions, and, in the ensuing journey on foot, carry
as much as they could, and thus make up for the loss of
the boat.

It was excessively annoying to lose all this property,
and be deprived of the means of doing the work proposed,
on the east and north of the Lake; but it would have
been like crying over spilt milk, to do otherwise now than
make the best use we could of our legs. The men were
sent back to the ship for provisions, cloth, and beads;
and while they are gone, we may say a little of the Cataracts
which proved so fatal to our boating plan.

They begin in 15° 20' S., and end in lat. 15° 55' S., the
difference of latitude is therefore 35'. The river runs
in this space nearly north and south, till we pass Malango;
so the entire distance is under 40 miles. The principal
Cataracts are five in number, and are called Pamofunda
or Pamozima, Morewa, Panoreba or Tedzane, Pampatamanga,
and Papekira. Besides these, three or four smaller ones
might be mentioned; as, for instance, Mamvira, where in our
ascent we first met the broken water, and heard that gushing sound, which, from the interminable windings of some
200 miles of river below, we had come to believe the tranquil
Shire could never make. While these lesser cataracts descend at an angle of scarcely 20°, the greater fall 100 feet
in 100 yards, at an angle of about 45°, and one at an angle
of 70°. One part of Pamozima is perpendicular, and, when
the river is in flood, causes a cloud of vapour to ascend,
which, in our journey to Lake Shirwa, we saw at a distance
of at least eight miles. The entire descent from the Upper
to the Lower Shire is 1200 feet. Only on one spot in all that
distance is the current moderate—namely, above Tedzane.

The rest is all rapid, and much of it being only fifty or eighty yards wide, and rushing like a mill-race, it gives the impression of water-power, sufficient to drive all the mills in Manchester, running to waste. Pamofunda, or Pamozima, has a deep shady grove on its right bank. When we were walking alone through its dark shade, we were startled by a shocking smell like that of a dissecting-room; and on looking up saw dead bodies in mats suspended from the branches of the trees, a mode of burial somewhat similar to that which we subsequently saw practised by the Parsees in their "towers of silence" at Poonah near Bombay. The name Pamozima means, "the departed spirits or gods"— a fit name for a place over which, according to the popular belief, the disembodied souls continually hover.

The rock lowest down in the series is dark reddish-grey syenite. This seems to have been an upheaving agent, for the mica schists above it are much disturbed. Dark trappean rocks full of hornblende have in many places burst through these schists, and appear in nodules on the surface. The highest rock seen is a fine sandstone of closer grain than that at Tette, and quite metamorphosed where it comes into contact with the igneous rocks below it. It sometimes gives place to quartz and reddish clay schists, much baked by heat. This is the usual geological condition on the right bank of the Cataracts. On the other side we pass over masses of porphyritic trap, in contact with the same mica schists, and these probably give to the soil the great fertility we observed. The great body of the mountains is syenite. So much mica is washed into the river, that on looking attentively on the stream one sees myriads of particles floating and glancing in the sun; and this, too, even at low water.

CHAPTER XXIV.

Travelling beverage — Good behaviour of the English sailors — Motola island — Starvation fare of natives — New course of march — The Rivi-rivi — A country after the scourge of war has passed over it — Lose our way — Hospitality of the people — Kirk's Range — Valley of Gōa or Gova — Disintegration of rocks in a hot climate — Our party viewed as slave-traders — Matunda — Reach the heel of Lake Nyassa — Kotosa's village — Ajawa migrations — Native agriculture — Bishop Mackenzie's idea of cotton — Chinsamba — The Assyrian countenance, the true negro type — The Babisa — Laugh of native women — Cry of children — Course N.E. to the shores of Lake Molamba — The Chia fish-net — Hoes — Savages could not have continued to live, had they been entirely uninstructed — They needed a superhuman instructor.

It was the 15th of August before the men returned from the ship, accompanied by Mr. Rae and the steward of the Pioneer. They brought two oxen, one of which was instantly slaughtered to put courage into all hearts, and some bottles of wine, a present from Waller and Alington. We never carried wine before, but this was precious as an expression of kindheartedness on the part of the donors. If one attempted to carry either wine or spirits, as a beverage, he would require a whole troop of followers for nothing else. Our greatest luxury in travelling was tea or coffee. We never once carried sugar enough to last a journey, but coffee is always good, while the sugarless tea is only bearable, because of the unbearable gnawing feeling of want and sinking which ensues if we begin to travel in the mornings without something warm in the stomach. Our drink generally was water, and if cool, nothing can equal it in a hot climate. We usually carried a bottle of brandy rolled up in our blankets, but that was used only as a medicine; a spoonful in hot water before going to bed, to fend off a chill and fever.

Spirits always do harm, if the fever has fairly begun; and it is probable that brandy-and-water has to answer for a good many of the deaths in Africa.

Mr. Rae had made gratifying progress in screwing together the Lady Nyassa. He had the zealous co-operation of three as fine steady workmen as ever handled tools; and, as they were noble specimens of English sailors, we would fain mention the names of men who are an honour to the British navy—John Reid, John Pennell, and Richard Wilson. The reader will excuse our doing so, but we desire to record how much they were esteemed, and how thankful we felt for their good behaviour. The weather was delightfully cool; and, with full confidence in those left behind, it was with light hearts we turned our faces north. Mr. Rae accompanied us a day in front; and, as all our party had earnestly advised that at least two Europeans should be associated together on the journey, the steward was at the last moment taken. Mr. Rae returned to get the Lady Nyassa ready for sea; and, as she drew less water than the Pioneer, take her down to the ocean in October. One reason for taking the steward is worth recording. Both he and a man named King,* who, though only a leading stoker in the Navy, had been a promising student in the University of Aberdeen, had got into that weak bloodless-looking state which residence in the lowlands without much to do or think about often induces. The best thing for this is change and an active life. A couple of days' march only as far as the Mukuru-Madse, infused so much vigour into King that he was able to walk briskly back. Consideration for the steward's health led to his being selected for this northern journey, and the measure was so com-

---

* A brother, we believe, of one who | famous but unfortunate Australian
accompanied Burke and Willis in the | Expedition.

pletely successful that it was often, in the hard march, a subject of regret, that King had not been taken too. A removal of only a hundred yards is sometimes so beneficial that it ought in severe cases never to be omitted.

We were fairly on the march on the 19th August. The island Motola, at which the boat had been hung, was soon reached. Two men, who had taken refuge on the island, were walking along one of the paths which wound among the trees and bushes. The noise of the Cataract, on the other side of their island home, prevented them from hearing the sound of our footsteps till we were within a yard of them. A start—and the bundles of roots they were carrying fell to the ground, and they made off as if to jump into the river; but we stopped beside the roots, and called them to come back and take their food. They thought that we were Ajawa, but a glance assured them to the contrary, and we were gratified to see, in their look of confidence when told who we were, the wide-spread influence of the English name. The roots were about the size of common turnips, and called Malapa. The natives said that a person who did not know how to cook them would kill himself by using them as food. This is probable; for it is necessary to boil them in a strong ley of woodashes, pour that away, and boil them in the same kind of mixture a second and third time before they are eatable. The tamarinds of this country were now ripe, and the people were collecting them and neutralizing their excessive acidity by boiling the pods with the ashes of the lignum-vitæ tree, which are beautifully white, and sometimes cake as if they contained a large amount of alkali; the same ashes are used too as a whitewash. When we came upon men like these poor fugitives, they were employed to carry our luggage, and were paid for their labour. This seemed to inspire more confidence than giving a present would have done.

Our object now was to get away to the N.N.W.,
proceed parallel with Lake Nyassa, but at a considerable
distance west of it, and thus pass by the Mazitu or Zulus
near its northern end without contact—ascertain whether any
large river flowed into the Lake from the west—visit Lake
Moelo, if time permitted, and collect information about the
trade on the great slave route, which crosses the Lake at
its southern end, and at Tsenga and Kota-kota.   The
Makololo were eager to travel fast, because they wanted
to be back in time to hoe their fields before the rains,
and also because their wives needed looking after.   Indeed
Masiko had already been obliged to go back and settle
some difference, of which a report was brought by other
wives who followed their husbands about twenty miles
with goodly supplies of beer and meal.   Masiko went off
in a fury; nothing less than burning the offenders' houses
would satisfy him; but a joke about the inevitable fate of
polygamists, and our inability to manage more than one
wife, and sometimes not even her, with a walk of a good
many miles in the hot sun, mollified him so much, that a
week afterwards he followed and caught us up without having
used any weapon more dangerous than his tongue.

In going in the first instance N.E. from the uppermost
Cataract, we followed in a measure the great bend of the river
towards the foot of Mount Zomba.   Here we had a view of
its most imposing side, the west, with the plateau some 3000
feet high, stretching away to its south, and Mounts Chiradzuru and Mochiru towering aloft to the sky.   From that
goodly highland station, it was once hoped by the noble
Mackenzie, who, for largeness of heart and loving disposition,
really deserved to be called the "Bishop of Central Africa,"
that light and liberty would spread to all the interior.
We still think it may be a centre for civilizing influences;

for any one descending from these cool heights, and stepping into a boat on the Upper Shire, can sail three hundred miles without a check into the heart of Africa.

We passed through a tract of country covered with mopane trees, where the hard baked soil refused to let the usual thick crops of grass grow; and here we came upon very many tracks of buffaloes, elephants, antelopes, and the spoor of one lion.   An ox we drove along with us, as provision for the way, was sorely bitten by the tsetse. The effect of the bite was, as usual, quite apparent two days afterwards, in the general flaccidity of the muscles, the drooping ears, and looks of illness.   It always excited our wonder that we, who were frequently much bitten too by the same insects, felt no harm from their attacks.   Man shares the immunity of the wild animals.

Though this was the dry, or rather hot season, many flowers were in blossom along our path.   The euphorbia, baobab, and caparidaceous trees were in full bloom.   A number of large hornbills attracted our attention, and Masiko, approaching the root of a tree in order to take sure aim at the birds, did not observe that within a few yards of the same tree two elephants stood in the cool shade fanning themselves with their huge ears.   Dr. Livingstone fired a ball into the ear of one of the animals at thirty yards distance, but he only went off shaking his head, and Masiko for the first time perceived his danger as the beast began to tear away through the bush.   Many Manganja skeletons were passed on entering a grove of lofty trees, under whose deep shade stood the ruins of a large village.   Wild animals had now taken possession of what had lately been the abodes of men living in peace and plenty.

Finding a few people on the evening of the 20th of August, who were supporting a wretched existence on tamarinds and mice, we ascertained that there was no hope of our being able to buy food anywhere nearer than the Lakelet Pamalombe, where the Ajawa Chief, Kainka, was now living; but that plenty could be found with the Maravi female Chief, Nyango. We turned away north-westwards, and struck the stream Ribve-ribve, or Rivi-rivi, which rises in the Maravi range, and flows into the Shire. Here, except below its sandy bed, the channel was without any water, but higher up it has pools at intervals with dry spaces between, and still further west it becomes a fast-flowing stream, forty feet wide, and one or two feet deep. Its name implies that it has Cataracts in it, and the sanjika ascends it to spawn; but the evaporation is so great in the hot season, that before it reaches the Shire it is quite dry.

The country here has been divided into districts, that on the south of the Rivi-rivi is called Nkwesi, and that on the north, Banda; and these extend along the boundary stream from its source to its confluence. This is interesting, as indicating an appreciation of the value of land. In many parts the idea has not taken root, and any one may make a garden wherever he pleases. The garden becomes property, the uncultivated land no one claims. The villages, of the number of which we never previously had the smallest idea, from our route having been along the river, seem always to have been selected with a view to shade—they were now all deserted. The lofty sterculias, with trunks of fifty feet without a branch, of a yellowish-green, stand around, and many of the huts have been overshadowed by wide-spreading wild fig-trees, on which the elephants now feed undisturbed. The ground was strewn with branches which they had broken off. One species of sterculia has roundish pods the size of one's fist, with seeds covered with canary-coloured pulp which yields abundance of fine oil. The motsikiri-trees have also been preserved for the sake of the fat and oil which may be obtained from their seeds.

As the Rivi-rivi came from the N.W. we continued to travel along its banks, until we came to people who had successfully defended themselves against the hordes of the Ajawa.   By employing the men of one village to go forward and explain who we were to the next, we managed to prevent the frightened inhabitants from considering us a fresh party of Ajawa, or of Portuguese slaving agents. Here they had cultivated maize, and were willing to sell, but no persuasion could induce them to give us guides to the Chieftainess, Nyango.   They evidently felt that we were not to be trusted; though, as we had to certify to our own character, our companions did not fail "to blow our own trumpet," with blasts in which modesty was quite out of the question.   To allay suspicion we had at last to refrain from mentioning the lady's name.

It would be wearisome to repeat the names of the villages we passed on our way to the north-west.   One was the largest we ever saw in Africa, and quite deserted, with the usual sad sight of many skeletons lying about.   Another was called Tette.   We know three places of this name, which fact shows it to be a native word; it seems to mean a place where the water rushes over rocks.   A third village was called Chipanga (a great work), a name identical with the Shupanga of the Portuguese.   This repetition of names may indicate that the same people first took these epithets in their traditional passage from north to south.   The country generally was covered with open forest of moderate growth, and very large trees fringed the watercourses.   One, a fig-tree with a peculiar leaf, had been struck by lightning.   On the lines which the electric fluid had made in streaming down its trunk, masses of new growth were shooting out to repair the damage, and a great deal of gum, of a kind never observed before by us on any tree, had exuded. Beyond the village of Tette, the scourge of slave war had not passed westward; and now, when we came to human dwellings, the people welcomed us in words, the full meaning of which we, whose happy country has never suffered from an invasion, can scarcely realize, "We are glad that it is not war you bring, but peace."

At this season of the year the nights are still cold, and the people having no crops to occupy their attention do not stir out till long after the sun is up. At other times they are off to their fields before the day dawns, and the first sound one hears is the loud talking of men and women, in which they usually indulge in the dark to scare off beasts by the sound of the human voice. When no work is to be done, the first warning of approaching day is the hemp-smoker's loud ringing cough.

Having been delayed one morning by some negotiation about guides, who were used chiefly to introduce us to other villages, we two whites walked a little way ahead, taking the direction of the stream. The men having been always able to find out our route by the prints of our shoes, we went on for a number of miles. This time, however, they lost our track and failed to follow us. The path was well marked by elephants, hyenas, pallahs, and zebras, but for many a day no human foot had trod it. When the sun went down a deserted hamlet was reached, where we made comfortable beds for ourselves of grass. Firing muskets to attract the attention of those who have strayed is the usual resource in these cases. On this occasion the sound of firearms tended to mislead us; for, hearing shots next morning, a long weary march led us only to some native hunters, who had been shooting buffaloes. Returning to a small village we met with some people who remembered our passing up to the Lake in the boat; they were as kind as they could be.   The only food they possessed was tamarinds, prepared with ashes, and a little cowitch meal.   The cowitch, as mentioned before, has a velvety brown covering of minute prickles, which, if touched, enter the pores of the skin and cause a painful tingling.   The women in times of scarcity collect the pods, kindle a fire of grass over them to destroy the prickles, then steep the beans till they begin to sprout, wash them in pure water, and either boil them or pound them into meal, which resembles our bean-meal.   This plant climbs up the long grass, and abounds in all reedy parts, and, though a plague to the traveller who touches its pods, it performs good service in times of famine by saving many a life from starvation.   Its name here is Kitedzi.

Having travelled at least twenty miles in search of our party that day, our rest on a mat in the best hut of the village was very sweet.   We had dined the evening before on a pigeon each, and had eaten only a handful of kitedzi porridge this afternoon.   The good wife of the village took a little corn which she had kept for seed, ground it after dark, and made it into porridge, this, and a cup of wild vegetables of a sweetish taste for a relish, a little boy brought in and put down, with several vigorous claps of his hands, in the manner which is esteemed polite, and which is strictly enjoined on all children.   The repast was so scanty that even the smaller of the two starvelings, who was awake, thought that it was all for him, and set to work at once, while his fellow-sufferer, overcome with sleep, had just commenced a pleasant dream of being at a grand feast.   Awaking just in time to save a mere fragment of the tiny meal, he was amused to hear the excuses offered by the ruthless devourer, which, from feeling the same cravings of appetite, his companion perfectly understood.

On the third day of separation, Akosanjere, the headman of this village, conducted us forward to our party who had gone on to Nseze, a district to the westward. This incident is mentioned, not for any interest it possesses, apart from the idea of the people it conveys. We were completely separated from our men for nearly three days, and had nothing wherewith to purchase food. The people were sorely pressed by famine and war, and their hospitality, poor as it was, did them great credit, and was most grateful to us. Our own men had become confused and wandered, but had done their utmost to find us; on our rejoining them, the ox was slain, and all, having been on short commons, rejoiced in this " day of slaughter." Akosanjere was, of course, rewarded to his heart's content.

On the 26th August we left the village of Chasundu, where the party had reunited, and crossed several running streams of fine cold water. We had now attained a considerable altitude, as was evident from the change in the vegetation;— the masuko-tree, with its large hard leaves, never met with in the lowlands, was here covered with unripe fruit,—fine rhododendrons,—the trees (*Cæsalpineæ*), with pinnated leaves, from which bark cloth is made,—the molompi (*Pterocarpus*), which, when wounded, exudes large quantities of a red juice so astringent that it might answer the purposes of kino, and furnishes a wood, as elastic and light as ash, from which the native paddles are made. These trees, with everlasting flowers shaped like daisies, and ferns, betokened an elevated habitat, and the boiling-point of water showed that our altitude was 2500 feet above the sea.

As we pursued our way, we came close up to a range of mountains, the most prominent peak of which is called Mvai.

This is a great, bare, rounded block of granite shooting up from the rest of the chain. It and several other masses of rock are of a light grey colour, with white patches, as if of lichens; the sides and summits are generally thinly covered with rather scraggy trees. There are several other prominent peaks—one, for instance, still further north, called Chirobve. Each has a name, but we could never ascertain that there was an appellation which applied to the whole. This fact, and our wish to commemorate the name of Dr. Kirk, induced us afterwards, when we could not discover a particular peak mentioned to us formerly as Molomo-ao-koku, or Cock's-bill, to call the whole chain from the west of the Cataracts up to the north end of the Lake, " Kirk's Range." The part we slept at opposite Mvai was named Paudio, and was evidently a continuation of the district of one of our stations on the Shire, at which observations for latitude were formerly taken.

Leaving Paudio, we had Kirk's Range close on our left and at least 3000 feet above us, and probably not less than 5000 feet above the sea. Far to our right extended a long green wooded country rising gradually up to a ridge, ornamented with several detached mountains, which bounded the Shire Valley. In front, northwards, lay a valley as rich and lovely as we ever saw anywhere, terminating at the mountains, which, stretched away some thirty miles beyond our range of vision and ended at Cape Maclear. The groups of trees had never been subjected to the landscape gardener's art; but had been cut down mercilessly, just as suited the convenience of the cultivator; yet the various combinations of open forest, sloping woodland, grassy lawns, and massive clumps of dark green foliage along the running streams, formed as beautiful a landscape as could be seen on the Thames. This valley is named Gõa or Gova, and as

we moved through it we found that what was smooth to the
eye was very much furrowed by running streams winding
round innumerable knolls. These little brooklets came
down from the range on our left, and the water was deliciously cool.

Gova had been invaded by the Ajawa under Kaiñka, now
living at the lakelet Pamalombe, and a party of Babisa,
both eager slave-traders. The consequence of this visitation was, that, in the spots where women had ventured back
to their former gardens, our appearance was the signal for
instant flight. A very large portion of the land had once
been under cultivation, but it was now abandoned to buffaloes
and elephants. The deep dark euphorbia hedges stood
round the hamlets, and shady trees cast a grateful coolness
over the smooth Boalo, where basket-making, spinning, and
weaving, or dancing, drinking, and gossip formerly went on.
Everything was beautiful to the eye; but no people could
be seen—except here and there a few dejected-looking
men. No food could be bought, and but a miserably small
present of wild fruits was brought as the accustomed offering
to strangers. We, therefore, tried to induce some of the
villagers we fell in with to take us over the range on our
left; but, though we knew that the Maravi lived on its
western side, they stoutly maintained that there were none
within two days of it. Several of the mountain-sides in
this country are remarkably steep, and the loose blocks
on them sharp and angular, without a trace of weathering.
For a time we considered the angularity of the loose fragments as evidence that the continent was of comparatively
recent formation, but we afterwards heard the operation actually going on, by which the boulders are split into these
sharp fragments. The rocks are heated by the torrid sun
during the day to such an extent that one is sometimes

startled on sitting down on them after dusk to find them quite too hot for the flesh, protected by only thin trousers, to bear. The thermometer placed on them rises to 137° in the sun. These heated surfaces, cooling from without by the evening air, contract more externally than within, and the unyielding interior forces off the outer parts, to a distance of one or two feet. Let any one in a rocky place observe the fragments that have been thus shot off, and he will find in the vicinity pieces from a few ounces to one or two hundred pounds in weight, which exactly fit the new surface of the original block; and he may hear in the evenings among the hills, where sound travels readily, the ringing echo of the report, which the natives ascribe to Mchesi or evil spirits, and the more enlightened to these natural causes.

It would have been no great feat to have scaled these mountains without any path to guide us; but we could not afford to waste the time necessary for a prolonged ascent. Our provisions were nearly expended, so we pushed onward to the north, in hopes of finding what we needed there.

We afterwards discovered that the poor people had good reason for not leading strangers, of whom they knew nothing, to the stores of corn which, after the invasion, they had been fain to hide amongst the crags of the hills.

When we came abreast of the peak Chirobve, the people would no longer give us guides. They were afraid of their enemies, whose dwellings we now had on our east; and, proceeding without any one to lead us, or to introduce us to the inhabitants, we were perplexed by all the paths running zigzag across instead of along the valley. They had been made by the villagers going from the hamlets on the slopes to their gardens in the meadows below. To add to our difficulties, the rivulets and mountain-torrents had worn gullies some thirty or forty feet deep, with steep sides that could not be climbed except at certain points. The remaining inhabitants on the flank of the range when they saw strangers winding from side to side, and often attempting to cross these torrent beds at impossible places, screamed out their shrill war-alarm, and made the valley ring with their wild outcries. It was war, and war alone, and we were too deep down in the valley to make our voices heard in explanation. Fortunately, they had burned off the long grass to a great extent. It only here and there hid them from us. Selecting an open spot, we spent a night regarded by all around us as slave-hunters, but were undisturbed, though the usual way of treating an enemy in this part of the country is by night attack.

The nights at the altitude of the valley were cool, the lowest temperature shown being 37°; at 9 A.M. and 9 P.M. it was 58°, about the average temperature of the day; at midday 82°, and sunset 70°. Our march was very much hindered by the imperfectly burned corn and grass stalks having fallen across the paths. To a reader in England this will seem a very small obstacle. But he must fancy the grass stems as thick as his little finger, and the cornstalks like so many walkingsticks lying in one direction, and so supporting each other that one has to lift his feet up as when wading through deep high heather. The stems of grass showed the causes of certain explosions as loud as pistols, which are heard when the annual fires come roaring over the land. The heated air inside expanding bursts the stalk with a loud report, and strews the fragments on the ground.

A very great deal of native corn had been cultivated here, and we saw buffaloes feeding in the deserted gardens, and some women, who ran away very much faster than the beasts did.

On the 29th, seeing some people standing under a tree by a village, we sat down, and sent Masego, one of our party, to communicate. The headman, Matunda, came back with him, bearing a calabash with water for us. He said that all the people had fled from the Ajawa, who had only just desisted from their career of pillage on being paid five persons as a fine for some offence for which they had commenced the invasion. Matunda had plenty of grain to sell, and all the women were soon at work grinding it into meal. We secured an abundant supply, and four milk goats. The Manganja goat is of a very superior breed to the general African animal, being short in the legs and having a finely-shaped broad body. By promising the Makololo that, when we no longer needed the milk, they should have the goats to improve the breed of their own at home, they were induced to take the greatest possible care of both goats and kids in driving and pasturing.

After leaving Matunda, we came to the end of the highland valley; and, before descending a steep declivity of a thousand feet towards the part which may be called the heel of the Lake, we had the bold mountains of Cape Maclear on our right, with the blue water at their base, the hills of Tsenga in the distance in front, and Kirk's Range on our left, stretching away northwards, and apparently becoming lower. As we came down into a fine rich undulating valley, many perennial streams running to the east from the hills on our left were crossed, while all those behind us on the higher ground seemed to unite in one named Leküe, which flowed into the Lake.

After a long day's march in the valley of the Lake, where the temperature was very much higher than in that we had just left, we entered the village of Katosa, which is situated on the bank of a stream among gigantic timber trees, and found there a large party of Ajawa—Waiau, they called themselves—all armed with muskets. We sat down among them, and were soon called to the Chief's court, and presented with an ample mess of porridge, buffalo meat, and beer. Katosa was more frank than any Manganja Chief we had met, and complimented us by saying that "we must be his ' Bazimo ' (good spirits of his ancestors); for when he lived at Pamalombe, we lighted upon him from above— men the like of whom he had never seen before, and coming he knew not whence." He gave us one of his own large and clean huts to sleep in; and we may take this opportunity of saying that the impression we received, from our first journey on the hills among the villages of Chisunsé, of the excessive dirtiness of the Manganja was erroneous. This trait was con- fined to the cool highlands. Here crowds of men and women were observed to perform their ablutions daily in the stream that ran past their villages; and this we have observed elsewhere to be a common custom with both Manganja and Ajawa.

Before we started on the morning of the 1st September, Katosa sent an enormous calabash of beer, containing at least three gallons, and then came and wished us to "stop a day and eat with him." On explaining to him the reasons for our haste, he said that he was in the way by which travellers usually passed, he never stopped them in their journeys, but would like to look at us for a day. On our promising to rest a little with him on our return, he gave us about two pecks of rice, and three guides to conduct us to a subordinate female Chief, Nkwinda, living on the borders of the Lake in front.

The Ajawa, from having taken slaves down to Quillimane

and Mosambique, knew more of us than Katosa did.   Their muskets were carefully polished, and never out of these slavers' hands for a moment, though in the Chief's presence. We naturally felt apprehensive that we should never see Katosa again.   A migratory afflatus seems to have come over the Ajawa tribes.   Wars among themselves, for the supply of the Coast slave-trade, are said to have first set them in motion.   The usual way in which they have advanced among the Manganja has been by slave-trading in a friendly way.   Then, professing to wish to live as subjects, they have been welcomed as guests, and the Manganja, being great agriculturists, have been able to support considerable bodies of these visitors for a time.   When the provisions became scarce, the guests began to steal from the fields; quarrels arose in consequence, and, the Ajawa having firearms, their hosts got the worst of it, and were expelled from village after village, and out of their own country. The Manganja were quite as bad in regard to slave-trading as the Ajawa, but had less enterprise, and were much more fond of the home pursuits of spinning, weaving, smelting iron, and cultivating the soil, than of foreign travel.   The Ajawa had little of a mechanical turn, and not much love for agriculture, but were very keen traders and travellers. This party seemed to us to be in the first or friendly stage of intercourse with Katosa; and, as we afterwards found, he was fully alive to the danger.

Our course was shaped towards the N.W., and we traversed a large fertile tract of rich soil extensively cultivated, but dotted with many gigantic thorny acacias which had proved too large for the little axes of the cultivators.   After leaving Nkwinda, the first village we spent a night at in the district Ngabi was that of Chembi, and it had a stockade around it.   The Azitu or Mazitu were said to be ravaging

2 K

the country to the west of us, and no one was safe except in a stockade. We have so often, in travelling, heard of war in front, that we paid little attention to the assertion of Chembi, that the whole country to the N.W. was in flight before these Mazitu, under a Chief with the rather formidable name of Mowhiriwhiri; we therefore resolved to go on to Chinsamba's, still further in the same direction, and hear what he said about it.

In marching across the same kind of fertile plains, there was little to interest the mind. The air was very sultry, for this is the " hot season " of the year. A thick haze restricted our view on all sides to a few miles. The blazing glare of the torrid sun on this haze gives to one, accustomed to mists elsewhere, the impression of being enveloped in a hot fog. The cultivation was very extensive and naturally drew our thoughts to the agriculture of the Africans. On one part of this plain the people had fields of maize, the plants of which towered far over our heads. A succession of holes three feet deep and four wide had been made in a sandy dell, through which flowed a perennial stream. The maize sown in the bottom of these holes had the benefit of the moisture, which percolated from the stream through the sand; and the result was a flourishing crop at a time of year when all the rest of the country was parched and dusty. On our counting the grains in one large cob or ear of maize, it was found to contain 360, and as one stalk has at times two or three cobs, it may be said to yield three or four hundred-fold.

While advantage is taken of the moist stratum in these holes during the dry season, grain, beans, and pumpkins, which are cultivated only in the rainy time of the year, are planted on ridges a foot high, allowing the superabundant moisture to run off. Another way in which the natives

show their skill in agriculture is by collecting all the weeds
and grass into heaps, covering them with soil and then setting fire to them.   They burn slowly, and all the ashes and
much of the smoke is retained in the overlying soil.   The
mounds thus formed, when sown upon, yield abundantly.   The
only instrument of husbandry here is the short-handled hoe ;
and about Tette the labour of tilling the soil, as represented
in the woodcut, is performed entirely by female slaves.   On

Females Hoeing.

the West Coast a double-handled hoe is employed.   Here
the small hoe is seen in the hands of both men and women.
In other parts of Africa a hoe with a handle four feet long is
used, but the plough is quite unknown.

In illustration of the manner in which the native knowledge of agriculture strikes an honest intelligent observer, it
may be mentioned that the first time good Bishop Mackenzie
beheld how well the fields of the Manganja were cultivated

on the hills, he remarked to Dr. Livingstone, then his fellow-traveller—"When telling the people in England what were my objects in going out to Africa, I stated that, among other things, I meant to teach these people agriculture; but I now see that they know far more about it than I do." This, we take it, was an honest straightforward testimony, and we believe that every unprejudiced witness, who has an opportunity of forming an opinion of Africans who have never been debased by slavery, will rank them very much higher in the scale of intelligence, industry, and manhood, than others who know them only in a state of degradation.

In two days' march we counted twenty-four cotton patches, each at least one-fourth of an acre in extent. One was 240 paces broad. All, as before observed, had been kept so clear of weeds, that the fires passed by the cotton bushes in the regular grass-burnings without touching them.

Men and women were seen carrying their grain from villages towards the stockades; much corn strewed along the path evinced the haste with which it had been borne to the places of safety. Some were cutting down the large old euphorbia-trees and an umbelliferous tree, which surrounded the villages, in order that a clear view of the approach of the enemy might be obtained. Then one dead body lay in our path with a wound in the back; then another, and another, lying in the postures assumed in mortal agony, which no painter can reproduce. On coming near Chinsamba's two stockades, on the banks of the Lintipe, we were told that the Mazitu had been repulsed there the day before, and we had evidence of the truth of the report of the attack in the sad sight of the bodies of the slain. The Zulus had taken off large numbers of women laden with corn; and, when driven back, had cut off the ears of a male prisoner, as a sort of credential that he had been with the Mazitu, and with grim

humour sent him to tell Chinsamba "to take good care
of the corn in the stockades, for they meant to return for
it in a month or two."

Chinsamba's people were drumming with might and main
on our arrival, to express their joy at their deliverance from
the Mazitu. The drum is the chief instrument of music
among the Manganja, and with it they express both their
joy and grief. They excel in beating time. Chinsamba
called us into a very large hut, and presented us with a
huge basket of beer. The glare of sunlight from which we
had come enabled him, in diplomatic fashion, to have a
good view of us before our eyes became enough accustomed
to the dark inside to see him. He has a Jewish cast of
countenance, or rather the ancient Assyrian face, as seen
in the monuments brought to the British Museum by Mr.
Layard. This form of face is very common in this country,
and leads to the belief that the true type of the negro is
not that met on the West Coast, from which most people
have derived their ideas of the African. The majority of
heads here are as well shaped as those depicted in the ancient Assyrian and Egyptian monuments. The lips are more
like those of Europeans than of the West Coast negroes.
They may be described as full, but not unpleasantly so;
and more heads may be observed prolonged a little backwards and upwards like that of Julius Cæsar, than among
ourselves. A large ring in one ear reminds one of the
Egyptian monuments, and so do some of the fashions of
dressing the hair. The legs do not, as a rule, present the
high calves, which are supposed to distinguish the African
race; nor do we meet what is termed the lark-heel any
oftener here than among the civilized races of Europe. We
have noticed a peculiar length of thigh-bone in several
instances, but have not had an opportunity of ascertaining

whether it is as common as the long arms, which formerly gave so much advantage in the use of the broadsword among ourselves.

Chinsamba had many Abisa or Babisa in his stockade, and it was chiefly by the help of their muskets that he had repulsed the Mazitu. These Babisa are great travellers and traders, and, in fact, occupy somewhat the same position in this country, as the Greeks do in the Levant. About the first words they addressed to us were—"I have seen the sea; I have been to Iboe, Mosambique, Quillimane; I know ships, steamers, Englishmen; I am a great trader." On this knowledge a claim was founded for familiarity, such as probably is permitted by half-caste traders on the coast. While the Manganja viewed us with awe, as totally unlike any people they had ever seen before, the Babisa entered our hut, and sat down with the air of men accustomed to good society. Wishing to be civil to the intruders, we complimented them on their extensive travels, and trading, and expressed the hope that, as they had learned so much, and become so rich, they would be more than usually generous towards the weary, hungry, and thirsty strangers; but this had no effect. We never here or elsewhere received the smallest present from the Babisa. The Makololo usually put the matter pretty forcibly by telling intrusive visitors of this tribe, " that from presuming to sit near to Englishmen, it was plain that they had never seen one before— that their travels were lies from end to end—that they never could have met the real English of the sea, but only mongrel things with hair like this" (pointing to their own heads). Without being rude, we usually obtained only just as much of their company as we required, and found that they had more knowledge of the interior than of the seaboard.

We liked Chinsamba very well, and found that he was decidedly opposed to our risking our lives by going further to the N.W. The Mazitu were believed to occupy all the hills in that direction, so we spent the 4th September with him. His district, called Mosapo, is undulating, with some conical hills, but the haze only permitted us to see short distances. The grass was now all yellow, and some black patches showed where it had been burned off. The tall trees were bare except on the banks of the Lintipe which runs here in a deep rocky channel. Where we formerly crossed it, at the Lake, it was still and deep, and a hippopotamus played in one of its reaches. A thick grove stood at the stockade in which we lived, and our men shot many guinea-fowls in it. The women and children were seen constantly bathing in the stream, and the men did not approach, until they had asked leave to pass. We have frequently observed that the Manganja women are very particular in avoiding any spot where men are supposed to be washing, and it is only the chance of a first sight of the white skin that makes them at times forget their good manners. The laugh of the women is brimful of mirth. It is no simpering smile, nor senseless loud guffaw; but a merry ringing laugh, the sound of which does one's heart good. One begins with Hă, Héé, then comes the chorus in which all join, Hăééé! and they end by slapping their hands together, giving the spectator the idea of great heartiness. When first introduced to a Chief, if we have observed a joyous twinkle of the eye accompanying his laugh, we have always set him down as a good fellow, and we have never been disappointed in him afterwards.

It is rather a minute thing to mention, and it will only be understood by those who have children of their own, but the cries of the little ones, in their infant sorrows, are the same

in tone, at different ages, here as all over the world. We
have been perpetually reminded of home and family by the
wailings which were once familiar to parental ears and heart,
and felt thankful that to the sorrows of childhood our children
would never have superadded the heartrending woes of the
slave-trade.

Taking Chinsamba's advice to avoid the Mazitu in their
marauding, we started on the 5th September away to the
N.E., and passed mile after mile of native cornfields, with
an occasional cotton-patch. Many of the thick corn-stalks
had been broken in the haste of the reapers, and lay across
the paths much to our inconvenience in walking. Men
and women were eagerly reaping the remaining ears, and
in haste conveying them to the stockades which were
crammed with corn, and contained each three or four thousand souls; some took us for Mazitu, and fled in dismay;
but returned when assured by our guides that we were the
English, who had sailed up the Lake. So much corn had
been scattered along the paths by the Mazitu and the fugitives in their haste, that some women were collecting and
winnowing it from the sand. Three dead bodies, and several burned villages, showed that we were close upon the
heels of the invaders, and that the system of securing "kind
masters" in the Zulu's hands is a sad system enough. All
that can be alleged in its favour is, that it entails much less
loss of life than that which secures "kind masters" across
the ocean for far fewer survivors.

After a long march through cornfields, we passed over
a waterless plain about N.N.W. of the hills of Tsenga to
a village on the Lake, and thence up its shores to Chitanda.
The banks of the Lake were now crowded with fugitives, who
had collected there for the poor protection which the reeds
afforded. For miles along the water's edge was one con-

tinuous village of temporary huts. The people had brought
a little corn with them; but they said, " What shall we eat
when that is done? When we plant corn, the wild beasts
(Zinyama, as they call the Mazitu) come and take it. When
we plant cassava, they do the same. How are we to live?"
A poor blind woman, thinking we were Mazitu, rushed off in
front of us with outspread arms, lifting the feet high, in the
manner peculiar to those who have lost their sight, and
jumped into the reeds of a stream for safety.

In our way along the shores we crossed several running
rivulets of clear cold water, which, from having reeds at their
confluences, had not been noticed in our previous exploration
in the boat. One of these was called Mokola, and another
had a strong odour of sulphuretted hydrogen. We reached
Molamba on the 8th September, and found our old acquaintance, Nkomo, there still. One of the advantages of travelling along the shores of the Lake was, that we could bathe
anywhere in its clear fresh water. To us, who had been
obliged so often to restrain our inclination in the Zambesi and
Shire for fear of crocodiles, this was pleasant beyond measure. The water now was of the same temperature as it was
on our former visit, or 72° Fahr. The immense depth of
the Lake prevents the rays of the sun from raising the temperature as high as that of the Shire and Zambesi; and
the crocodiles, having always clear water in the Lake,
and abundance of fish, rarely attack man; many of these
reptiles could be seen basking on the rocks.

A day's march beyond Molamba brought us to the lakelet
Chia, which lies parallel with the Lake. It is three or four
miles long, by from one to one and a half broad, and communicates with the Lake by an arm of good depth, but·with
some rocks in it. As we passed up between the Lake and
the eastern shore of this lakelet, we did not see any

streams flowing into it. It is quite remarkable for the abundance of fish; and we saw upwards of fifty large canoes engaged in the fishery, which is carried on by means of hand-nets with side-frame poles about seven feet long. These nets are nearly identical with those now in use in

Chia Hand Net.

Normandy — the difference being that the African net has a piece of stick lashed across the handle-ends of the side poles to keep them steady, which is a great improvement. The fish must be very abundant to be scooped out of the water in such quantities as we saw, and by so many canoes. There is quite a trade here in dried fish.

The country around is elevated, undulating, and very extensively planted with cassava. The hoe in use has a handle of four feet in length, and the iron part is exactly of the same form as that in the country of the Bechuanas. The baskets here, which are so closely woven together as to hold beer, are the same with those employed to hold milk in Kaffirland—a thousand miles distant.

Marching on foot is peculiarly conducive to meditation— one is glad of any subject to occupy the mind, and relieve the monotony of the weary treadmill-like trudge-trudging. This Chia net brought to our mind that the smith's bellows made here of a goatskin bag, with sticks along the open ends, are the same as those in use in the Bechuana country far to the south-west. These, with the long-handled hoe, may only show that each successive horde from north to south took inventions with it from the same original source. Where that source may have been is probably indicated by another pair of bellows, which we observed below the Victoria Falls, being found in Central India and among the Gipsies of Europe.

Men in remote times may have had more highly-developed instincts, which enabled them to avoid or use poisons; but the late Archbishop Whately has proved, that wholly untaught savages never could invent anything, or even subsist' at all. Abundant corroboration of his arguments is met with in this country, where the natives require but little in the way of clothing, and have remarkably hardy stomachs. Although possessing a knowledge of all the edible roots and fruits in the country, having hoes to dig with, and spears, bows, and arrows to kill the game,—we have seen that, notwithstanding all these appliances and means to boot, they have perished of absolute starvation.

Manganja Spears with iron paddles or dibbles in the ends of the handles and weighted with iron rings.

Three kinds of wild grasses are met with, the seeds of which may be used as food—one of them, called *Noanje*, has been cultivated, and when the grain is separated from the husks, and cooked, it yields a tolerable meal; but without the art of pounding these grains, and separating the husks, the stomachs of the lowest savages could not endure the sharp scales which form at least a half of the grain. The same form of pestle and mortar for clearing grain is met with from Egypt to the southern extremity of the continent; the existence of this seems to show that the same want has been felt and provided for from the period of the earliest migrations of the Africans.

Since we find that men, who already possess a knowledge of the arts needed by even the lowest savages, are swept off the earth when reduced to a dependence on wild roots and fruits alone, it is nearly certain that if they ever had been in what is called a state of nature, from being so much less fitted for supporting and taking care of themselves than the brutes, they could not have lived long enough to have attained even to the ordinary state of savages. They could not have survived for a sufficient period to invent any-thing, such as we who are not savages, and know how to make the egg stand on its end, think that *we* easily could have invented. The existence, therefore, of the various instruments in use among the Africans, and other partially civilized people, indicates the communication of instruction at some period from some Being superior to man himself.

The art of making fire is the same in India as in Africa. The smelting furnaces, for reducing iron and copper from the ores, are also similar. Yellow hæmatite, which bears not the smallest resemblance either in colour or weight to the metal, is employed near Kolobeng for the production of iron. Mala-chite, the precious green stone used in civilized life for vases, would never be suspected by the uninstructed to be a rich ore of copper, and yet it is extensively smelted for rings and other ornaments in the heart of Africa. A copper bar of native manufacture four feet long was offered to us for sale at Chinsamba's. These arts are monuments attesting the fact, that some instruction from above must at some time or other have been supplied to mankind; and, as Archbishop Whately says, "the most probable conclusion is, that man when first created, or very shortly afterwards, was ad-vanced, by the Creator himself, to a state above that of a mere savage."

The argument for an original revelation to man, though quite independent of the Bible history, tends to confirm that history. It is of the same nature with this, that man could not have *made* himself, and therefore must have had a Divine *Creator*. Mankind could not, in the first instance, have *civilized* themselves, and therefore must have had a superhuman *Instructor*.

In connexion with this subject, it is remarkable that throughout successive generations no change has taken place in the form of the various inventions. Hammers, tongs, hoes, axes, adzes, handles to them; needles, bows and arrows, with the mode of feathering the latter; spears, for killing game, with spear-heads having what is termed "dish" on both sides to give them, when thrown, the rotatory motion of rifle-balls; the arts of spinning and weaving, with that of pounding and steeping the inner bark of a tree till it serves as clothing; millstones for grinding corn into meal; the manufacture of the same kind of pots or *chatties* as in India; the art of cooking, of brewing beer and straining it as was done in ancient Egypt; fish-hooks, fishing and hunting nets, fish-baskets, and weirs, the same as in the Highlands of Scotland; traps for catching animals, &c. &c.,—have all been so very permanent from age to age, and some of them of identical patterns are so widely spread over the globe, as to render it probable that they were all, at least in some degree, derived from one Source. The African traditions, which seem possessed of the same unchangeability as the arts to which they relate, like those of all other nations refer their origin to a superior Being. And it is much more reasonable to receive the hints given in Genesis, concerning direct instruction from God to our first parents or their children in religious or moral duty, and probably in the knowledge of the arts of life,* than to give credence to the theory that untaught savage man subsisted in a state which would prove fatal to all his descendants, and that in such helpless state he made many inventions which most of his progeny retained, but never improved upon during some thirty centuries.

We crossed in canoes the arm of the Lake, which joins Chia to Nyassa, and spent the night on its northern bank. The whole country adjacent to the Lake, from this point up to Kota-kota Bay, is densely peopled by thousands who have fled from the forays of the Mazitu in hopes of protection from the Arabs who live there. In three running rivulets we saw the *Shuare* palm, and an oil palm which is much inferior to that on the West Coast. Though somewhat similar in appearance, the fruit is not much larger than hazel-nuts, and the people do not use them, on account of the small quantity of oil which they afford.

The idea of using oil for light never seems to have entered the African mind. Here a bundle of split and dried bamboo, tied together with creeping plants, as thick as a man's body, and about twenty feet in length, is employed in the canoes as a torch to attract the fish at night. It would be considered a piece of the most wasteful extravagance to burn the oil they obtain from the castor-oil bean and other seeds, and also from certain fish, or in fact to do anything with it but anoint their heads and bodies.

---

* Genesis, chap. iii., verses 21 and 23, " make coats of skins, and clothed them "—" sent him forth from the garden of Eden to till the ground " imply teaching. Vide Archbishop Whately's 'History of Religious Worship.' John W. Parker, West Strand, London, 1849.

CHAPTER XXV.

WE arrived at Kota-kota Bay in the afternoon of the 10th September, 1863; and sat down under a magnificent wild fig-tree with leaves ten inches long, by five broad, about a quarter of a mile from the village of Juma ben Saidi, and Yakobe ben Arame, whom we had met on the River Kaombe, a little north of this, in our first exploration of the Lake. We had rested but a short time when Juma, who is evidently the chief person here, followed by about fifty people, came to salute us and to invite us to take up our quarters in his village. The hut which, by mistake, was offered, was so small and dirty that we preferred sleeping in an open space a few hundred yards off.

Juma afterwards apologized for the mistake, and presented us with rice, meal, sugar-cane, and a piece of malachite. We returned his visit on the following day, and found him engaged in building a dhow or Arab vessel, to replace one which he said had been wrecked. This new one was fifty

feet long, twelve feet broad, and five feet deep. The planks
were of a wood like teak, here called *Timbati*, and the
timbers of a closer grained wood called *Msoro*. The sight
of this dhow gave us a hint which, had we previously received it, would have prevented our attempting to carry a
vessel of iron past the Cataracts. The trees around Katosa's
village were *Timbati*, and they would have yielded planks
fifty feet long and thirty inches broad. With a few native
carpenters a good vessel could be built on the Lake nearly
as quickly as one could be carried past the Cataracts, and at
a vastly less cost. Juma said that no money would induce
him to part with this dhow. He was very busy in transporting
slaves across the Lake by means of two boats, which we saw
returning from a trip in the afternoon. As he did not know
of our intention to visit him, we came upon several gangs of
stout young men slaves, each secured by the neck to one
common chain, waiting for exportation, and several more
in slave-sticks. These were all civilly removed before our
interview was over, because Juma knew that we did not
relish the sight.

When we met the same Arabs in 1861, they had but
few attendants: according to their own account they had now,
in the village and adjacent country, 1500 souls. It is certain
that tens of thousands had flocked to them for protection,
and all their power and influence must be attributed to
the possession of guns and gunpowder. This crowding of
refugees to any point where there is a hope for security
for life and property is very common in this region, and
the knowledge of it made our hopes beat high for the success
of a peaceful Mission on the shores of the Lake. The rate,
however, in which the people here will perish by the next
famine, or be exported by Juma and others, will, we fear,
depopulate those parts which we have just described as

crowded with people. Hunger will ere long compel them to sell each other. An intelligent man complained to us of the Arabs often seizing slaves, to whom they took a fancy, without the formality of purchase ; but the price is so low— from two to four yards of calico—that one can scarcely think this seizure and exportation without payment worth their while. The boats were in constant employment, and, curiously enough, Ben Habib, whom we met at Linyanti in 1855, had been taken across the Lake, the day before our arrival at this Bay, on his way from Sesheke to Kilwa, and we became acquainted with a native servant of the Arabs, called Selele Saidallah, who could speak the Makololo language pretty fairly from having once spent some months in the Barotse Valley.

From boyhood upwards we have been accustomed, from time to time, to read in books of travels about the great advances annually made by Mohammedanism in Africa. The rate at which this religion spreads was said to be so rapid, that in after days, in our own pretty extensive travels, we have constantly been on the look out for the advancing wave from North to South, which, it was prophesied, would soon reduce the entire continent to the faith of the false prophet. The only foundation that we can discover for the assertions referred to, and for others of more recent date, is the fact that in a remote corner of North-Western Africa the Fulahs, and Mandingoes, and some others in Northern Africa, as mentioned by Dr. Barth, have made conquests of territory ; but even they care so very little for the extension of their faith, that after conquest no pains whatever are taken to indoctrinate the adults of the tribe. This is in exact accordance with the impression we have received from our intercourse with Mohammedans and Christians. The followers of Christ alone are anxious to propagate their faith. A

2 L

quasi philanthropist would certainly never need to recommend the followers of Islam, whom we have met, to restrain
their benevolence by preaching that " Charity should begin at
home."

Though Selele and his companions were bound to their
masters by domestic ties, the only new idea they had imbibed
from Mohammedanism was, that it would be wrong to eat meat
killed by other people. They thought it would be " unlucky." Just as the inhabitants of Kolobeng, before being
taught the requirements of Christianity, refrained from
hoeing their gardens on Sundays, lest they should reap an
unlucky crop. So far as we could learn, no efforts had been
made to convert the natives, though these two Arabs, and
about a dozen half-castes, had been in the country for
many years; and judging from our experience with a dozen
Mohammedans in our employ at high wages for sixteen months,
the Africans would be the better men in proportion as they
retained their native faith. This may appear only a harsh
judgment from a mind imbued with Christian prejudices;
but without any pretension to that impartiality, which leaves
it doubtful to which side the affections lean, the truth may
be fairly stated by one who viewed all Mohammedans and
Africans with the sincerest good will.

Our twelve Mohammedans from Johanna were the least
open of any of our party to impression from kindness. A
marked difference in general conduct was apparent. The
Makololo, and other natives of the country, whom we had
with us, invariably shared with each other the food they had
cooked, but the Johanna men partook of their meals at a
distance. This, at first, we attributed to their Moslem prejudices; but when they saw the cooking process of the others
nearly complete, they came, sat beside them, and ate the
portion offered without ever remembering to return the

compliment when their own turn came to be generous. The Makololo and the others grumbled at their greediness, yet always followed the common custom of Africans of sharing their food with all who sit around them. What vexed us most in the Johanna men was their indifference to the welfare of each other. Once, when they were all coming to the ship after sleeping ashore, one of them walked into the water with the intention of swimming off to the boat, and while yet hardly up to his knees was seized by a horrid crocodile and dragged under; the poor fellow gave a shriek, and held up his hand for aid, but none of his countrymen stirred to his assistance, and he was never seen again. On asking his brother-in-law why he did not help him, he replied, "Well, no one told him to go into the water. It was his own fault that he was killed." The Makololo on the other hand rescued a woman at Senna by entering the water, and taking her out of the crocodile's mouth.

It is not assumed that their religion had much to do in the matter. Many Mohammedans might contrast favourably with indifferent Christians; but, so far as our experience in East Africa goes, the moral tone of the follower of Mahomed is pitched at a lower key than that of the untutored African. The ancient zeal for propagating the tenets of the Koran has evaporated, and been replaced by the most intense selfishness and grossest sensuality. The only known efforts made by Mohammedans, namely, those in the North-West and North of the continent, are so linked with the acquisition of power and plunder, as not to deserve the name of religious propagandism; and the only religion that now makes proselytes is that of Jesus Christ. To those who are capable of taking a comprehensive view of this subject, nothing can be adduced of more telling significance than the well-attested fact, that while the Mohammedans, Fulahs, and others towards Central Africa, make a few proselytes by a process which gratifies their own covetousness, three small sections of the Christian converts, the Africans in the South, in the West Indies, and on the West Coast of Africa actually contribute for the support and spread of their religion upwards of 15,000*l.* annually.* That religion which so far overcomes the selfishness of the human heart must be Divine.

Leaving Kota-kota Bay, we turned away due West on the great slave-route to Katanga's and Cazembe's country in Londa. Juma lent us his servant, Selele, to lead us the first day's march. He said that the traders from Kilwa and Iboe cross the Lake either at this bay, or at Tsenga, or at the southern end of the Lake; and that wherever they may cross they all go by this path to the interior. They have slaves with them to carry their goods, and when they reach a spot where they can easily buy others, they settle down and begin the traffic, and at once cultivate grain. So much of the land lies waste, that no objection is ever made to any one taking possession of as much as he needs; they can purchase a field of cassava for their present wants for very little, and they continue trading in the country for two or three years, and giving what weight their muskets possess to the Chief who is most liberal to them.

The first day's march led us over a rich, well-cultivated plain. This was succeeded by highlands, undulating, stony, and covered with scraggy trees. Many banks of well rounded shingle appear. The disintegration of the rocks, now going on, does not round off the angles; they are split up by the

---

* "In 1854 the native church at Sierra-Leone undertook to pay for their primary schools, and thereby effected a saving to the Church Missionary Society of 80*l.* per annum. In 1861 the contributions of this one section of native Christians had amounted to upwards of 10,000*l.*"—'Manual of Church Missionary Society's African Missions.'

heat and cold into angular fragments. On these high downs we crossed the River Kaombe. Beyond it we came among the upland vegetation—rhododendrons, proteas, the masuko, and molompi. At the foot of the hill, Kasuko-suko, we found the River Bua running north to join the Kaombe. We had to go a mile out of our way for a ford; the stream is deep enough at parts for hippopotami. The various streams not previously noticed, crossed in this journey, had before this led us to the conclusion, independently of the testimony of the natives, that no large river ran into the north end of the Lake. No such affluent was needed to account for the Shire's perennial flow.

In looking forward we seemed to be ascending the long slope of a range of mountains; but the nearer view consisted of a succession of beautiful tree-covered rounded hills; the narrow footpaths were perpetually leading up steep inclines and down descents to running rills, whose sides were fringed with fine, large evergreen trees; the deciduous trees having parted with their leaves, were now enjoying the rest of winter, though only twelve degrees from the Equator. The people in the villages into which we entered were generally employed in making very neat fish and other baskets of split bamboos, or in beating the bark of trees into cloth. The bark cloth, made to the north of this district, is from a species of fig-tree. The cassava is the chief food cultivated on the heights; the castor-oil plant is extensively grown also, and oil is extracted from the seeds for the purpose of lubricating the body and more especially the hair, which is worn very long. From the careful way in which many train out their hair into different-shaped masses, it has less of wavy curl than the wool of a long-fleeced sheep—the oil seems to keep it straight.

In one village we found all the women engaged in celebrating, with dancing and singing, a ceremony for two girls of twelve or fourteen, analogous to the *boguera* which among the Bechuana and Makololo forms the young men into bands or regiments for life. The Bechuana call it *boyale* when the novices are girls, and here the ceremony is named *moari*, evidently a cognate word. These girls were dressed with a profusion of beads, and painted over the head and face with pipeclay, which gave them the appearance of wearing an ancient helmet with chin-straps. The women were so eager in the dance and in teaching their young protegées to perform their part in it properly, that they paid no attention to the entreaties of the men to go and grind meal, and clothe themselves with the cloth the strangers had brought. Whence these customs, and from whom a number of laws which are recognised for thousands of miles, have been derived, no one can divine. They seem to have made an indelible impression on the native mind, and abide in it unchanged, from age to age. The *boguera* has something of the Jewish ceremony of initiation, but it is a political, not a religious institution. It cannot be traced to Arab origin, and is spoken of, by those who have undergone it, under the breath, and with a circumlocution which shows that they regard it in a very serious light.

On September 15th we reached the top of the ascent which, from its many ups and downs, had often made us puff and blow as if broken-winded. The water of the streams we crossed was deliciously cold, and now that we had gained the summit at Ndonda, where the boiling-point of water showed an altitude of 3440 feet above the sea, the air was delightful. Looking back we had a magnificent view of the Lake, but the haze prevented our seeing beyond the sea horizon. The scene was beautiful, but it was impossible to dissociate the lovely landscape whose hills and dales had so sorely tried our legs and lungs, from the sad fact that this was part of the great slave-route now actually in use. By this road many "Ten thousands" have here seen "the Sea," "the Sea," but with sinking hearts; for the universal idea among the captive gangs is, that they are going to be fattened and eaten by the whites. They cannot of course be so much shocked as we should be—their sensibilities are far from fine, their feelings are more obtuse than ours—in fact, "the live eels are used to being skinned," perhaps they rather like it. We who are not philosophic, blessed the Providence which at Thermopylæ in ancient days rolled back the tide of Eastern conquest from the West, and so guided the course of events that light and liberty and Gospel truth spread to our distant isle, and emancipating our race freed them from the fear of ever again having to climb fatiguing heights and descend wearisome hollows in a slave-gang, as we suppose they did when the fair English youths were exposed for sale at Rome.

Looking westwards we perceived that, what from below had the appearance of mountains, was only the edge of a table-land which, though at first undulating, soon became smooth, and sloped towards the centre of the country. To the south a prominent mountain called Chipata, and to the south-west another named Ngalla, by which the Bua is said to rise, gave character to the landscape. In the north, masses of hills prevented our seeing more than eight or ten miles.

The air which was so exhilarating to Europeans had an opposite effect on five men who had been born and reared in the malaria of the Delta of the Zambesi. No sooner did they reach the edge of the plateau at Ndonda, than they lay down prostrate, and complained of pains all over them. The temperature was not much lower than that on the shores of the Lake below, 76° being the mean temperature of the day, 52° the lowest, and 82° the highest during the twenty-four hours;

at the Lake it was about 10° higher. Of the symptoms they complained of—pains everywhere—nothing could be made. And yet it was evident that they had good reason for saying that they were ill. They scarified almost every part of their bodies as a remedial measure; medicines, administered on the supposition that their malady was the effect of a sudden chill, had no effect, and in two days one of them actually died in consequence of, as far as we could judge, a change from a malarious to a purer and more rarefied atmosphere.

As we were on the slave route, we found the people more churlish than usual. On being expostulated with about it, they replied, " We have been made wary by those who come to buy slaves." The calamity of death having befallen our party, seemed, however, to awaken their sympathies. They pointed out their usual burying-place, lent us hoes, and helped to make the grave. When we offered to pay all expenses, they showed that they had not done these friendly offices without fully appreciating their value; for they enumerated the use of the hut, the mat on which the deceased had lain, the hoes, the labour, and the medicine which they had scattered over the place to make him rest in peace.

The power ascribed to certain medicines, made from plants known only to the initiated, is the most prominent feature in the religion of the Africans. According to their belief there is not only a specific for every ill that flesh is heir to, but for every woe of the wounded spirit. The good spirits of the departed, Azimo or Bazimo, may be propitiated by medicines, or honoured by offerings of beer or meal, or anything they loved while in the body; and the bad spirits, " *Mchesi*," of whom we have heard only at Tette, and therefore cannot be certain that they belong to the pure native faith, may be prevented by medicine from making raids and mischief in the gardens. A man with headache

was heard to say, " My departed father is now scolding me;
I feel his power in my head ; " and then was observed to remove from the company, make an offering of a little food on
a leaf and pray, looking upwards to where he supposed his
father's spirit to be.   They are not, like Mohammedans,
ostentatious in their prayers.   They speak of the spirit world
with reverence, and court the shade and silence for their acts
of worship.   The Mohammedan is right in making the great·
show he does, bowing down to the earth before all, and using
the repetitions which belong to his creed, because his religion
enjoins great show of piety, and fosters the idea of proud
superiority in the self-complacent Pharisee over the whole
human family; while the African retires from view, somewhat
like the Christian, who enters into his closet, and, when he
has shut the door, prays to his Father who sees in secret.

The primitive African faith seems to be that there is one
Almighty Maker of heaven and earth ; that he has given
the various plants of earth to man to be employed as mediators
between him and the spirit world, where all who have ever
been born and died continue to live ; that sin consists in
offences against their fellow-men, either here or among the
departed, and that death is often a punishment of guilt,
such as witchcraft.   Their idea of moral evil differs in no
respect from ours, but they consider themselves amenable
only to inferior beings, not to the Supreme.   Evil speaking—
lying—hatred—disobedience to parents—neglect of them—
are said by the intelligent to have been all known to be sin, as
well as theft, murder, or adultery, before they knew aught
of Europeans or their teaching.   The only new addition to
their moral code is, that it is wrong to have more wives
than one.   This, until the arrival of Europeans, never entered
into their minds even as a doubt.

Everything not to be accounted for by common causes,

whether of good or evil, is ascribed to the Deity. Men are inseparably connected with the spirits of the departed, and when one dies he is believed to have joined the hosts of his ancestors. All the Africans we have met with are as firmly persuaded of their future existence as of their present life. And we have found none in whom the belief in the Supreme Being was not rooted. He is so invariably referred to as the Author of everything supernatural, that, unless one is ignorant of their language, he cannot fail to notice this prominent feature of their faith. When they pass into the unseen world, they do not seem to be possessed with the fear of punishment. The utensils placed upon the grave are all broken as if to indicate that they will never be used by the departed again. The body is put into the grave in a sitting posture, and the hands are folded in front. In some parts of the country there are tales which we could translate into faint glimmerings of a resurrection; but whether these fables, handed down from age to age, convey that meaning to the natives themselves we cannot tell. The true tradition of faith is asserted to be "though a man die he will live again;" the false, that when he dies he is dead for ever.

Though cheerless enough to a Christian, the African's religion is mild in its character. In one very remote and small corner of the country, called Dahomey, it has degenerated into a bloody superstition. Human blood there takes the place of the propitiatory plants which are used over ninetenths of the continent. The reckless disregard of human life mentioned by Speke and Grant is quite exceptional. We have heard from natives that a former possessor of Matiamvo's Chieftainship was subject to fits of a similar bloodthirstiness, but he was clearly insane; and the great reverence for royalty, with which the Africans are imbued, alone saved him, and probably Speke's Chief, Mtesi, also, from decapitation. In two or three other places, parts of the human body are also employed to mediate between man and the spirit world; but a cruel character can no more be ascribed to the African religion, as a whole, on such grounds as these, than cannibalism can be imputed to the whole African family, because human flesh is eaten in one or two places in Africa.

The idea of witchcraft flows naturally from their religious belief. The evil-disposed may, by a knowledge of the bark' and roots of plants, inflict disaster. A horn, or rude image, is sometimes made use of as a means of preserving the medicines of defence, and is worn as an amulet. These images, horns, or other articles, called greegrees, or jeujeus, are not held sacred for a moment after the medicine is found to have lost its power; and mere idol-worship, which they seem to indicate, is as much ignored among the natives, as the worship of pictures and images is asserted to be in the churches of the more enlightened. A greegree, or fetish, is thrown away as useless as soon as the consecrating nostrum is discovered to be inoperative for the purpose for which it was procured. On this subject Mr. Wilson, whom we have quoted before, gives much information, which, from observation elsewhere, we have found to be the fruit of accurate personal investigation.

In our course westwards, we at first passed over a gently undulating country, with a reddish clayey soil, which, from the heavy crops, appeared to be very fertile. Many rivulets were crossed, some running southwards into the Bua, and others northwards into the Loangwa, a river which we formerly saw flowing into the Lake. Further on, the water was chiefly found in pools and wells. Then still further, in the same direction, some watercourses were said to flow into that same " Loangwa of the Lake," and others into the Loangwa, which flows to the south-west, and enters the Zambesi at Zumbo, and is here called the "Loangwa of the Maravi." The trees were in general scraggy, and covered, exactly as they are in the damp climate of the Coast, with lichens, resembling orchilla-weed. The maize, which loves rather a damp soil, had been planted on ridges to allow the superfluous moisture to run off. Everything indicated a very humid climate, and the people warned us that, as the rains were near, we were likely to be prevented from returning by the country becoming flooded and impassable.

Villages, as usual encircled by euphorbia hedges, were numerous, and a great deal of grain had been cultivated around them. Domestic fowls, in plenty, and pigeons with dovecots like those in Egypt were seen. The people call themselves Matumboka, but the only difference between them and the rest of the Manganja is in the mode of tattooing the face. Their language is the same. Their distinctive mark consists of four tattooed lines diverging from the point between the eyebrows, which, in frowning, the muscles form into a furrow. The other lines of tattooing, as in all Manganja, run in long seams, which crossing each other at certain angles form a great number of triangular spaces on the breast, back, arms, and thighs. The cuticle is divided by a knife, and the edges of the incision are drawn apart till the true skin appears. By a repetition of this process, lines of raised cicatrices are formed, which are thought to give beauty, no matter how much pain the fashion gives.

The teeth here, as also among the Babisa, are filed to points; other Manganja notch each of the upper fore-teeth by means of small quartz stones: the notch in some is angular, in others round; this latter style gives the edges of the upper front teeth a semilunar shape; other tribes make an opening of a triangular shape between the central front teeth. It is surprising that the filing and chipping which the teeth undergo, that the possessor may be in the fashion, do not produce toothache, as is the case with us when a piece is chipped off by accident. But teeth here are more solid, and often wear down to the gums in old persons without decay, like those found in Egyptian mummies. A phrase used to express a very aged person is, " that he lived so long that his gums and teeth were worn quite smooth together." Cases of toothache are not at all uncommon nevertheless, though probably not so usually met with as among ourselves. This abuse of the fine teeth, which they possess by nature, is common among both sexes. They delight also in wearing the hair so as to give the head the appearance of being prolonged backwards and upwards. The Babisa are partial to making their locks into the form of a dragoon's helmet.

It would not be worth while to advert for a moment to the routine of travelling, or the little difficulties that beset every one who attempts to penetrate into a new country, were it not to show the great source of the power here possessed by slave-traders. We needed help in carrying our goods, while our men were ill, though still able to march. When we had settled with others for hire, we were often told, that the dealers in men had taken possession of some, and had taken them away altogether. Other things led us to believe that the slave-traders carry matters with a high hand; and no wonder, for the possession of gunpowder gives them almost absolute power. The mode by which tribes armed with bows and arrows carry on warfare, or defend themselves, is by ambuscade. They never come out in open fight, but wait for the enemy ensconced behind trees, or in the long grass of the country, and shoot at him unawares. Consequently, if men come against them with firearms, when, as is usually the case, the long grass is all burned off, the tribe attacked are as helpless, as a wooden ship, possessing only signal guns, would be before an iron-clad steamer. The time of year selected for this kind of warfare is nearly always that in which the grass is actually burnt off, or is so dry as readily to take fire. The dry grass in Africa looks more like ripe English wheat late in the autumn, than anything else we can compare it to. Let us imagine an English village standing in a field of this sort, bounded only by the horizon, and enemies setting fire to a line of a mile or two, by running along with bunches of burning straw in their hands, touching here and there the inflammable material,—the wind blowing towards the doomed village—the inhabitants with only one or two old muskets, but ten to one no powder,—the long line of flames, leaping thirty feet into the air with dense masses of black smoke— and pieces of charred grass falling down in showers. Would not the stoutest English villager, armed only with the bow and arrow against the enemy's musket, quail at the idea of breaking through that wall of fire? When at a distance, we once saw a scene like this, and had the charred grass, literally as thick as flakes of black snow, falling around us, there was no difficulty in understanding the secret of the slave-trader's power.

On the 21st of September, we arrived at the village of the Chief Muasi, or Muazi; it is surrounded by a stockade, and embowered in very tall euphorbia-trees; their height, thirty or forty feet, shows that it has been inhabited for at least one generation. A visitation of disease or death causes the headmen to change the site of their villages, and plant new hedges; but, though Muazi has suffered from the attacks of the Mazitu, he has evidently clung to his birthplace. The village is situated about two miles south-west of a high hill called Kasungu, which gives the name to a district extending to the Loangwa of the Maravi. Several other detached granite hills have been shot up on the plain, and many stockaded villages, all owing allegiance to Muazi, are scattered over it.

On our arrival, the Chief was sitting in the smooth shady place, called Boalo, where all public business is transacted, with about two hundred men and boys around him. We paid our guides with due ostentation. Masiko, the tallest of our party, measured off the fathom of cloth agreed upon, and made it appear as long as possible, by facing round to the crowd, and cutting a few inches beyond what his outstretched arms could reach, to show that there was no deception. This was by way of advertisement. The people are mightily gratified at having a tall fellow to measure the cloth for them. It pleases them even better than cutting it by a tape-line— though very few men of six feet high can measure off their own length with their outstretched arms. Here, where Arab traders have been, the cubit called *mokono*, or elbow, begins to take the place of the fathom in use further south. The measure is taken from the point of the bent elbow to the end of the middle finger.

We found, on visiting Muazi on the following day, that he was as frank and straightforward as could reasonably be expected. He did not wish us to go to the N.N.W., because he carries on a considerable trade in ivory there. We were anxious to get off the slave route, to people not visited before by traders; but Muazi naturally feared, that if we went to what is said to be a well-watered country, abounding in elephants, we might relieve him of the ivory which he now obtains at a cheap rate, and sells to the slave-traders as they pass Kasungu to the east; but at last he consented, warning us that "great difficulty would be experienced in obtaining food—a district had been depopulated by slave wars—and a night or two must be spent in it; but he would give us good guides, who would go three days with us, before turning, and then further progress must depend on ourselves." Some of our men having been ill ever since we mounted this highland plain, we remained two days with Muazi.

A herd of fine cattle showed that no tsetse existed in the district. They had the Indian hump, and were very fat, and very tame. The boys rode on both cows and bulls without fear, and the animals were so fat and lazy, that the old ones only made a feeble attempt to kick their young tormentors. Muazi never milks the cows; he complained that, but for the Mazitu having formerly captured some, he should now have had very many. They wander over the country at large, and certainly thrive.

Cotton-bushes are rarely seen along the slave route; this is not from soil or climate being unsuitable for them, for we passed some specimens which had grown well, and yielded cotton of superior quality, but from the fact that the people can supply their wants by exchanging grain for foreign calico, as the slave-traders pass. Many of these highlanders wear goatskins. Though they have plenty of food, they are not eager sellers. They are accustomed to eager purchasers at a very high rate.

After leaving Muazi's, we passed over a flat country sparsely covered with the scraggy upland trees, but brightened with many fine flowers. The grass was short, reaching no higher than the knee, and growing in tufts with bare spaces between, though the trees were draped with many various lichens, and showed a moist climate. A high and very sharp wind blew over the flats; its piercing keenness was not caused by low temperature, for the thermometer stood at 80°.

We now began to notice a very curious circumstance. Wherever a Manganja village was placed, a Babisa one was sure to appear in the vicinity. The former are the owners of the soil, but the latter did not seem to be considered intruders. Indeed, the uncultivated tracts are so large, that

it would scarcely occur to a people, who have few or no cattle
or goats, to quarrel about land which they cannot use themselves. The shallow valleys, along the sides of which the
villages were dotted, have, at certain times of the year, rivers
running through them, which at this time formed only a
succession of pools, with boggy and sedgy spaces between.
When the sun is vertical over any part in the tropics on
his way south, the first rains begin to fall, and the effect of
these, though copious, is usually only to fill the bogs and
pools. When, on his way north, he again comes over the
same part, we have the great rains of the year, and the pools
and bogs, being already filled, overflow, and produce the great
floods which mark the Zambesi, and probably in the same
manner cause the inundations of the Nile. The luxuriant
vegetation which the partial desiccation of many of these
rivers annually allows to grow, protects their bottoms and
banks from abrasion, and hence the comparative clearness
of their water in the greater floods. We were now on the
sources of the Loangwa of the Maravi, which enters the
Zambesi at Zumbo, and were struck by the great resemblance which the boggy and sedgy streams here presented
to the sources of the Leeba, an affluent of the Zambesi
formerly observed in Londa, and of the Kasai, which some
believe to be the principal branch of the Congo or Zaire.

The first or lesser rains take place in this region in
November, when the sun is vertical, going south. The greater
rains fall in January, February, and March, when he is on his
way back to the Equator. Supposing our observation of the
cause of inundating floods in south intertropical Africa to
be applicable to the north intertropical district, the pools,
bogs, and rivers there might be expected to fill, when the
sun became vertical, on his way south, and overflow on his
return. But this must be decided on the spot. We know from

the observations made for a number of years at Loanda, by the late Edmund Gabriel, that the same rule as to rainfall, which we have noticed from 12° to 20° south, applies in the eighth degree from the Equator.

The great source of the supply of moisture for South Africa is undoubtedly the Indian Ocean. The prevailing winds are from the east or south-east. Laden with moisture from this great reservoir, the air sweeps up the coast-ranges, and cooling in its passage over, deposits the chief portion of its aqueous vapour on the heights. Passing westwards, it is now the dry air that floats, during most of the year, as an east, or east-south-east wind, over the Kalahari Desert, and other arid plains. That this view is correct appears evident from the facts, that where no coast-range, or only a low one, exists the central region is not so devoid of moisture, as it is where, as in the case of the Drakensberg, the air must rise upwards of a mile in perpendicular height, before it can reach the plains beyond; and that wherever hills in the interior rise higher than those near the coast, their tops are covered with vegetation different from that on the plains below them, and requiring a more abundant supply of moisture. This is seen even on the hills close to the Kalahari Desert; and on other mountain-tops many species of ferns and some peppers flourish, which are never met with at lower altitudes.

As we approach nearer the Equator, the south-west winds from the Atlantic, robbed of their moisture by the western slopes, prevail for a certain distance into the continent, and probably meet the south-easterly breezes from the Indian Ocean. Whether this meeting produces a greater amount of rainfall on the Line than elsewhere, as has been asserted, appears to require confirmation. Theoretically, the confluence of dry winds under the Equator, would be followed by an upward and overlapping motion of the currents to the

north or south. But a hot, dry north wind is quite exceptional on the Kalahari Desert, and lasts usually but three
days at a time. The chief supply for the South African
rainfall comes from the Indian Ocean to the south-east, in
the same way that at a later period of the year the south-
west monsoon takes refreshing rains from the same great
reservoir to the plains of India.

We had taken pains to ascertain from the travelled Babisa
and Arabs as much as possible about the country in front,
which, from the lessening time we had at our disposal, we
feared we could scarcely reach, and had heard a good deal
of a small lake called Bemba. As we proceeded west, we
passed over the sources not only of the Loangwa, but of
another stream, called Moitawa or Moitala, which was represented to be the main feeder of Lake Bemba. This would be
of little importance, but for the fact that the considerable river
Luapula, or Loapula, is said to flow out of Bemba to the westward, and then to spread out into another and much larger
lake, named Moero, or Moelo. Flowing still further in the
same direction, the Loapula forms Lake Mofue, or Mofu, and
after this it is said to pass the town of Cazembe, bend to
the north, and enter Lake Tanganyika. Whither the water
went after it entered the last lake, no one would venture an assertion. But that the course indicated is the
true watershed of that part of the country, we believe from
the unvarying opinion of native travellers. There could be
no doubt that our informants had been in the country beyond
Cazembe's, for they knew and described Chiefs whom we afterwards met about thirty-five or forty miles west of his town.
The Lualaba is said to flow into the Loapula—and when, for
the sake of testing the accuracy of the travelled, it was asserted
that all the water of the region round the town of Cazembe
flowed into the Luambadzi, or Luambezi (Zambesi), they

remarked with a smile, " He says, that the Loapula flows
into the Zambesi—did you ever hear such nonsense ?" or words
to that effect. We were forced to admit, that according to
native accounts, our previous impression of the Zambesi's
draining the country about Cazembe's had been a mistake.
Their geographical opinions are now only stated, without any
further comment than that the itinerary given by the Arabs
and others shows that the Loapula is twice crossed on the
way to Cazembe's; and we may add that we have never
found any difficulty from the alleged incapacity of the negro
to tell which way a river flows.

The boiling-point of water showed a descent, from the edge
of the plateau to our furthest point west, of 170 feet; but
this can only be considered as an approximation, and no de-
pendance could have been placed on it, had we not had the
courses of the streams to confirm this rather rough mode of
ascertaining altitudes. The slope, as shown by the watershed,
was to the "Loangwa of the Maravi," and towards the Moitala,
or south-west, west, and north-west. After we leave the feeders
of Lake Nyassa, the water drains towards the centre of the
continent. The course of the Kasai, a river seen during Dr.
Livingstone's journey to the West Coast, and its feeders
was to the north-east, or somewhat in the same direction.
Whether the water thus drained off finds its way out by the
Congo, or by the Nile, has not yet been ascertained. Some
parts of the continent have been said to resemble an inverted
dinner-plate. This portion seems more of the shape, if shape
it has, of a wide-awake hat, with the crown a little depressed.
The altitude of the brim in some parts is considerable ; in
others, as at Tette and the bottom of Murchison's Cataracts,
it is so small that it could be ascertained only by elimina-
ting the daily variations of the barometer, by simultaneous
observations on the Coast, and at points some two or three

hundred miles inland. So long as African rivers remain in what we may call the brim, they present no obstructions; but no sooner do they emerge from the higher lands than their utility is impaired by cataracts. The low lying belt is very irregular. At times sloping up in the manner of the rim of an inverted dinner-plate—while in other cases, a high ridge rises near the sea, to be succeeded by a lower district inland before we reach the central plateau. The breadth of the low lands is sometimes as much as three hundred miles, and that breadth determines the limits of navigation from the seaward.

The ascent to the Maravi country, and all along from the west shore of the lake for at least three hundred miles on the same meridian of longitude, is, as we subsequently found, simply what Indians call a ghaut, like that on the way from Bombay to Poonah. The African ghaut from the west coast of the lake, which is 1300 feet above the sea, rises as high above our point of starting here, as the Indian one does from the level of the sea at Bombay. The African Deccan is a little higher and cooler than the Indian one is at Poonah. The African huts resemble the native Indian ones near Dapoore, but are much better built; in the possession of the plough, the Indians have the advantage over the Africans, though both cultivate very nearly the same grain. The soil and general appearance of the country, trees, nullahs, rivers, and undulating plains, are remarkably alike in both the African and Indian Deccan. But, in Africa, we see patches of fine long-stapled cotton, nearly equal to the Egyptian, instead of the miserable stuff grown in India. The contrast between the two countries, however, is very striking. In India, the evidences of human labour are everywhere apparent in roads, bridges, stone walls, ruins of temples, and palaces.

In Africa, the whole country looks, for all that man has done,
just as it did when it came from the hands of its Maker.
The only roads are footpaths worn by the feet of the natives
into hollows a few inches deep, and about fifteen or eighteen
inches wide, winding from village to village, as if made by
believers in the curved line being that of beauty, or by
people who had already attained that state of competence
to which we all aspire, when we may toddle round our
own little wavy walks without hurry.   The huts built
here have no ruins, except when they are burned, and
then a thin layer of the red clay, with which they were
plastered, and the impressions of the reeds which formed
the walls, remain with the colour and consistence of soft
bricks.   But these soon moulder away; the only durable
monuments to be met with, are mill-stones, worn in the
middle a couple of inches or more in depth; and cairns
in the passes of the mountains, of which tradition has no
record, but the salutation addressed to them —" Hail! O
Chief—let it be well with us in the country to which we
are going !"—may mean, that they are supposed to be the
resting-places of departed Chiefs.

It is a very remarkable fact, that while in many parts of
the world the stone, bronze, and iron instruments of men who
have passed away have been found, no flint arrow-heads,
spears, axes, or other implements of this kind, as far as we
can ascertain, have ever been discovered in Africa.   Dr. Kirk,
while botanizing in the Delta of the Zambesi, came upon a bed
of gravel, in which the fossil bones of nearly all the animals
now living in the country, as hippopotami, wild hogs, buffaloes,
antelopes, turtles, crocodiles, and hyenas, were associated with
pottery of the same nature and ornamental designs, as that
now in common use by the inhabitants.   Similar animal
remains were observed in a bed of gravel in the Zambesi in

1856, and now, in 1863, in the sand on the shores of Lake
Nyassa, pottery was found, with buffalo and other large
bones; but in no case have we found a specimen of the
weapons with which these animals may have been killed for
human food.

In attempting to decipher the testimony of the rocks
in the Lake and other regions of southern Africa, it had
always been a sore puzzle, that few or none of the regular
geological series, as described in books, could be made
out. The absence of marine limestone, and the evidences of
the oscillations of land and sea, which are so common in
other countries, baffled our unaided inquiries.   No chalk nor
flints were ever met with.   The nearest resemblance to the
cretaceous strata, were immense flat masses of calcareous
tufa, and this, from the impressions of reeds and leaves of the
same kind as those now growing in the vicinity, was evidently
a deposit from land springs, which formerly flowed much more
copiously than at the present day.   In association with these
tufaceous deposits, ferruginous masses, with gravel imbedded,
were observed, having all the appearance of the same origin
as the tufa.   Coal was discovered in sandstone, and that had
been disturbed only by the undulations of local igneous
irruptions.   It was only when our far-seeing and sagacious
countryman, Sir Roderick I. Murchison, collected all the
rays of light on the subject, from various sources, into the
focus of his mind, that what we had before but dimly guessed,
at length became apparent.   Those great submarine depres-
sions and elevations which have so largely affected Europe,
Asia, and America, during the secondary, tertiary, and quasi-
modern periods, have not affected Africa.   In fact, Africa is
the oldest continent in the world.   " It is unquestionably a
grand type of a region which has preserved its ancient ter-
restrial conditions during a very long period, unaffected by

any changes except those which are dependent on atmospheric and meteoric influences." *

According to the present state of our knowledge, the Africans never had a stone period. The proof of this is merely negative, but of the same nature as the evidence, that while the stone period lasted, no bronze implements were in use. And it does seem a difficulty worth remarking, that while it is assumed that, in ancient times, stone for lengthened periods alone was in use; we have the evidence of the late Admiral Fitzroy (whose recent death—the result of over fatigue in the pursuit of his valuable researches—all so greatly lament), that the present time is the stone period in Tierra del Fuego and some countries whose inhabitants resemble our remote ancestors—and in other parts it is the age of iron.

It is possibly only a display of ignorance, but we trust it will not be imagined to be a proof of conceit, when some of the ideas, which beguiled our weary marches, are put forth as materials for thought in younger minds. Here at every third or fourth village, we see a kiln-looking structure, about six feet high, by two-and-a-half or three feet in diameter. It is a clay, fire-hardened furnace, for smelting iron. No flux is used, whether the specular iron, the yellow hæmatite, or magnetic iron ore is fused, and yet capital metal is produced. Native manufactured iron is so good, that the natives declare English iron to be "rotten" in comparison, and specimens of African hoes were pronounced at Birmingham to be nearly equal to the best Swedish iron. As we passed along, men sometimes ran from the fields they were working in, and offered for sale new hoes, axes, and spears of their own workmanship. It is certainly the iron age here; copper, according to the ideas of the natives who smelt it from malachite, is much more

---

* Address to the Royal Geographical Society of London, at the anniversary meeting, 23rd May, 1864.

intractable than the metal from ironstone, which needs no
flux ; and as yet, so far as we can learn, neither tin nor zinc
has ever been used to form an amalgam with copper in this
country, so that we may expect the bronze age to come in
an inverted order.   Of the flint age as applied to Africa, we
are compelled to doubt, because no flints, with the exception
of a few small agates, are to be found in the southern parts
of the continent we have examined.   A stone period might
have its course without flints, as other rocks might have
been used, but the evidence must all be underground.

We made three long marches beyond Muazi's in a north-
westerly direction ; the people were civil enough, but refused to
sell us any food.   We were travelling too fast, they said ; in fact,
they were startled, and before they recovered their surprise, we
were obliged to depart.   We suspected that Muazi had sent them
orders to refuse us food, that we might thus be prevented from
going into the depopulated district ; but this may have been
mere suspicion, the result of our own uncharitable feelings.

We spent one night at Machambwe's village, and another
at Chimbuzi's.   It is seldom that we can find the headman on
first entering a village.   He gets out of the way till he has
heard all about the strangers, or he is actually out in the
fields looking after his farms.   We once thought that when
the headman came in from a visit of inspection, with his spear,
bow and arrows, they had been all taken up for the occasion,
and that he had all the while been hidden in some hut slily
watching till he heard that the strangers might be trusted ;
but on listening to the details given by these men of the appearances of the crops at different parts, and the astonishing
minuteness of the speakers' topography, we were persuaded
that in some cases we were wrong, and felt rather humiliated.
Every knoll, hill, mountain, and every peak on a range has a
name ; and so has every watercourse, dell, and plain.   In fact,

every feature and portion of the country is so minutely distinguished by appropriate names, that it would take a lifetime to
decipher their meaning.   It is not the want, but the super-
abundance of names that misleads travellers, and the terms
used are so multifarious that good scholars will at times scarcely
know more than the subject of conversation.   Though it is a
little apart from the topic of the attention which the headmen
pay to agriculture, yet it may be here mentioned, while speaking of the fulness of the language, that we have heard about
a score of words to indicate different varieties of gait—one
walks leaning forward, or backward, swaying from side to
side, loungingly, or smartly, swaggeringly, swinging the arms,
or only one arm, head down or up, or otherwise; each of
these modes of walking was expressed by a particular verb;
and more words were used to designate the different varieties
of fools than we ever tried to count.

Mr. Moffat has translated the whole Bible into the language
of the Bechuana, and has diligently studied this tongue for
the last forty-four years; and, though knowing far more of the
language than any of the natives who have been reared on
the Mission-station of Kuruman, he does not pretend to have
mastered it fully even yet.   However copious it may be in terms
of which we do not feel the necessity, it is poor in others, as in
abstract terms, and words used to describe mental operations.

Our third day's march ended in the afternoon of the
27th September, 1863, at the village of Chinanga on
the banks of a branch of the Loangwa.   A large, rounded
mass of granite, a thousand feet high, called $\tilde{N}ombe$ $rume$,
stands on the plain a few miles off.   It is quite remarkable,
because it has so little vegetation on it.   Several other granitic
hills stand near it, ornamented with trees, like most heights
of this country, and a heap of blue mountains appears away
in the north.

CHAPTER XXVI.

Reasons for returning — Despatch from H. M.'s Government — A thief —
   African women rarely address strangers — Employments of women — Grinding corn — Brewing beer — Drinking-bouts.

The effect of the piercing winds upon the men had never
been got rid of. Several had been unable to carry a load
ever since we ascended to the highlands; we had lost one,
and another poor lad was so ill as to cause us great anxiety.
By waiting in this village, which was so old that it was full
of vermin, all became worse. Our European food was entirely
expended, and native meal, though finely ground, has so
many sharp angular particles in it, that it brought back
dysentery, from which we had suffered so much in May. We
could scarcely obtain food for the men. The headman of
this village of Chinanga was off in a foray against some
people further north to supply slaves to the traders expected
along the slave route we had just left; and was said, after
having expelled the inhabitants, to be living in their
stockade, and devouring their corn. The conquered tribe
had purchased what was called a peace by presenting the
conqueror with three women.

This state of matters afforded us but a poor prospect of
finding more provisions in that direction than we could
with great difficulty and at enormous prices obtain here.
But neither want of food, dysentery, nor slave wars would
have prevented our working our way round the Lake in some
other direction, had we had time; but we had received orders
from the Foreign Office to take the Pioneer down to the sea
in the previous April. The salaries of all the men in her

were positively " in any case to cease by the 31st of December." The despatch from the Foreign Office having been
sent open to the Governor of the Cape, it seems to have been
forwarded in the same free and easy way to its destination;
for the new Bishop's chaplain had commented freely before
a number of Portuguese, Dr. Kirk, and Mr. Charles Livingstone, at Quillimane, on its different paragraphs, and more
especially on the omission of all notice of the Lady Nyassa.
When his servant brought it up to the Pioneer, he hailed
the crew in strong Surrey dialect with, " I say, no more pay
for you chaps after December. I brings the letter as says it."
Though we never for a single moment entertained the idea
that this grossly disrespectful way of treating a despatch
from H. M. Principal Secretary of State for Foreign Affairs
was anything more than the result of want of knowledge of
the world on the part of those who had probably never in
their lives seen a Government despatch before, yet the conviction that all the Pioneer's men knew that their wages
might not be forthcoming, if we were in the river after
December, had some influence on a mind borne down by
that most depressing of diseases, dysentery. We were said
to be only ten days' distant from Lake Bemba. We might
speculate on a late rise of the river. A month or six weeks
would secure a geographical feat, but the rains were near.
We had been warned by different people that the rains were
close at hand, and that we should then be bogged and unable
to travel. The flood in the river might be an early one, or
so small in volume as to give but one chance of the Pioneer
descending to the ocean. The Makololo too were becoming
dispirited by sickness and want of food, and were naturally
anxious to be back to their fields in time for sowing.
But in addition to all this and more, it was felt that it would
not be dealing honestly with the Government, were we, for

the sake of a little éclat, to risk the detention of the
Pioneer up the river during another year; so we decided
to return; and though we had afterwards the mortification to
find that we were detained two full months at the ship waiting for the flood which we expected immediately after our
arrival there, the chagrin was lessened by a consciousness of
having acted in a fair, honest, above-board manner throughout.

On the night of the 29th of September a thief came to the
sleeping-place of our men and stole a leg of a goat. On
complaining to the deputy headman, he said that the thief
had fled, but would be caught. He suggested a fine, and
offered a fowl and her eggs; but wishing that the thief
alone should be punished, it was advised that *he* should be
found and fined. The Makololo thought it best to take the
fowl as a means of making the punishment certain. After
settling this matter on the last day of September, we commenced our return journey. We had just the same time to go
back to the ship, that we had spent in coming to this point,
and there is not much to interest one in marching over the
same ground a second time.

While on our journey north-west, a cheery old woman, who
had once been beautiful, but whose white hair now contrasted
strongly with her dark complexion, was working briskly in her
garden as we passed. She seemed to enjoy a hale, hearty old
age. She saluted us with what elsewhere would be called a
good address; and, evidently conscious that she deserved the
epithet, " dark but comely," answered each of us with a
frank " Yes, my child." Another motherly-looking woman,
sitting by a well, began the conversation by " You are
going to visit Muazi, and you have come from afar, have you
not ? " But in general women never speak to strangers
unless spoken to, so anything said by them attracts attention. Muazi once presented us with a basket of corn. On

hinting that we had no wife to grind our corn, his buxom
spouse struck in with roguish glee, and said, "I will grind
it for you; and leave Muazi, to accompany and cook for
you in the land of the setting sun." As a rule the women
are modest and retiring in their demeanour, and, without
being oppressed with toil, show a great deal of industry.
The crops need about eight months' attention. Then when
the harvest is home, much labour is required to convert it
into food as porridge, or beer. The corn is pounded in a
large wooden mortar, like the ancient Egyptian one, with
a pestle six feet long and about four inches thick. The
pounding is performed by two or even three women at one
mortar. Each, before delivering a blow with her pestle, gives
an upward jerk of the body, so as to put strength into the
stroke, and they keep exact time, so that two pestles are
never in the mortar at the same moment. The measured
thud, thud, thud, and the women standing at their vigorous
work, are associations inseparable from a prosperous African
village. By the operation of pounding, with the aid of a
little water, the hard outside scale or husk of the grain is
removed, and the corn is made fit for the millstone. The
meal irritates the stomach unless cleared from the husk; without considerable energy in the operator, the husk sticks fast
to the corn. Solomon thought that still more vigour than is
required to separate the hard husk or bran from wheat would
fail to separate "a fool from his folly." "Though thou
shouldst bray a fool in a mortar among wheat with a pestle,
yet will not his foolishness depart from him." The rainbow,
in some parts, is called the "pestle of the Barimo," or gods.
Boys and girls, by constant practice with the pestle, are able
to plant stakes in the ground by a somewhat similar action,
in erecting a hut, so deftly that they never miss the first hole
made.

Let any one try by repeatedly jobbing a pole with all his force to make a deep hole in the ground, and he will understand how difficult it is always to strike it into the same spot.

As we were sleeping one night outside a hut, but near enough to hear what was going on within, an anxious mother began to grind her corn about 2 o'clock in the morning. "Ma," inquired a little girl, "why grind in the dark?" Mamma advised sleep, and administered material for a sweet dream to her darling, by saying, "I grind meal to buy a cloth from the strangers, which will make you look a little lady." An observer of these primitive races is struck continually with such little trivial touches of genuine human nature.

The mill consists of a block of granite, syenite, or even mica schist, fifteen or eighteen inches square and five or six thick, with a piece of quartz or other hard rock about the size of a half brick, one side of which has a convex surface, and fits into a concave hollow in the larger and stationary stone. The

Woman grinding.

workwoman kneeling, grasps this upper millstone with both hands, and works it backwards and forwards in the hollow of the lower millstone, in the same way that a baker works his dough, when pressing it and pushing from him. The weight of the person is brought to bear on the moveable stone, and while it is pressed and pushed forwards and backwards, one

Native Mill foɩ grinding Corn.

hand supplies every now and then a little grain to be thus at first bruised and then ground on the lower stone, which is placed on the slope, so that the meal, when ground, falls on to a skin or mat spread for the purpose. This is perhaps the most primitive form of mill, and anterior to that in oriental countries, where two women grind at one mill, and may have been that used by Sarah of old when she entertained the Angels.

Another part of the work of women is in the preparation of beer. The malted grain is sun-dried and pounded into meal, then cooked or brewed. A merrymaking often implies that all who come to make merry shall bring their hoes and let off the excitement of the liquor by a substantial day's hoeing. At other times, a couple shut themselves up in their huts, on pretence of sickness, and drink the whole brewing themselves. But a more common mode is to invite all the friends and relatives of the woman whose beer is to be drunk, and they rejoice in the entertainment, and praise the goodwife's ale, as so good that the "taste reaches right to the back of the neck," or in proper native gourmand's phrase declare the feast to be so *recherché* that every step they take homewards will cause their stomachs to say "tobu, tobu, tobu." None but a churl would grudge them this, the enjoyment, though a poor one, of their lives. Bless their hearts, let them rejoice in the fruits of their labour! We confess, however, that we have never witnessed the plenty which their land yields, without turning in imagination to the streets and lanes of our cities, and lamenting that the squalid offspring of poverty and sin has not more pleasant lines in this world, where there is so much and to spare.

CHAPTER XXVII.

Clearings in forests — Resemblance of hunters to ancient Egyptian figures — Muazi — Difficulty about guides — Babisa undertake to lead us to Chinsamba s — Babisa and Manganja heads — Different characteristics — Dialects different though akin — Nkoma — The Bua — We are taken for Mazitu, and treated accordingly — Intractable headman — Well-broken-in husband — Oppressive stillness of the deserted country — Bangwé — Meet the Mazitu — Show a bold front with success — Zachariah mends his pace — We are taken for a war party — Oct. 8th, we reach Molamba on Lake Nyassa — The unpaid guide and his doings — Polygamy — Loapula and Tanganyika — Babisa's knowledge of interior tested — False alarm of Mazitu — Prevailing direction of wind easterly — Shores of the Lake — Fugitives and their distress — Tobacco-traders attacked by Mazitu — Guns *versus* bows — Mosapo — Chinsamba's — Minute information of Chief — Africans not so degraded as described — Presents — Guides — Brisk slave-trading — Sad thoughts — 15th Oct., Katosa's — His description of the conduct of the Ajawa — Their admiration of red hair — Sugar-cane probably indigenous — Bamboos — Katosa is invested in an officer's coat and epaulets — His present village and his former one — 20th Oct , we arrive at Motunda's — Hidden stores of provisions — Kabambe and Nyango — The Gōa or Gova valley — The Lesungwe — Kindness of native women — 31st Oct., we reach the Mukuru-Madse — Thunder and rain — Wet clothes and fever.

WE passed several clearings, each a mile or more square, in which all the trees had been cut down, and the stumps left only two or three feet high. The felled wood was gathered into heaps, about fifty yards long, by thirty broad, and when dry was burned. The ashes were spread on these cleared spots, and a species of millet called *Maere* was raised, of which the natives seemed very fond, though to our stomachs the meal was as indigestible as so much coarse sand. On one side of these cleared spaces the hunters set large strong nets made of baobab bark, into which they drive the game. We saw about a dozen hartebeests which were small in size, and a few zebras on these uplands. We were struck with the resemblance the men carrying their hunting-nets bore to figures in ancient Egyptian tombs, but the proportion of these hunters to the population was very small.   The Africans here, as a rule, are of the agricultural class, and, when they have a prospect of reaping their grain in peace, must enjoy a pretty comfortable life.

On 2nd October we applied to Muazi for guides to take us straight down to Chinsamba's at Mosapo, and thus cut off an angle, which we should otherwise make, by going back to Kota-kota Bay.   He replied that his people knew the short way to Chinsamba's that we desired to go, but that they all were afraid to venture there, on account of the Zulus, or Mazitu.   We therefore started back on our old route, and, after three hours' march, found some Babisa in a village, who promised to lead us to Chinsamba.

We meet with these keen traders everywhere.   They are easily known by a line of horizontal cicatrices, each half an inch long, down the middle of the forehead and chin.   They often wear the hair collected in a mass on the upper and back part of the head, while it is all shaven off the forehead and temples.   The Babisa and Waiau or Ajawa heads have more of the round bullet-shape than those of the Manganja, indicating a marked difference in character; the former people being great traders and travellers, the latter being attached to home and agriculture.   The Manganja usually intrust their ivory to the Babisa to be sold at the Coast, and complain that the returns made never come up to the high prices which they hear so much about before it is sent. In fact, by the time the Babisa return, the expenses of the journey, in which they often spend a month or two at a place where food abounds, usually eat up all the profits.

The Babisa have a different dialect from the Manganja, but all readily converse together.   In passing among the different tribes, it is only necessary to know one dialect well, and then interpreters are easily found.   Masiko, one of the

2 N 2

Makololo, had already acquired a fair knowledge of the
Manganja dialect, and proved a good medium of communication. To our ears the tongue of the Matumboka seemed
more fully developed than that of the same tribe, Manganja
or Wanyassa, further south. The verb, for instance, shows
the passive and past tenses here, while, among tribes in contact with foreigners on the Zambesi, these distinctions are
seldom noticed. Our new companions were trading in tobacco, and had collected quantities of the round balls, about
the size of nine-pounder shot, into which it is formed. One
of them owned a woman, whose child had been sold that
morning for tobacco. The mother followed him, weeping
silently, for hours along the way we went; she seemed to be
well known, for, at several hamlets, the women spoke to
her with evident sympathy; we could do nothing to alleviate
her sorrow—the child would be kept until some slave-trader
passed, and then sold for calico. The different cases of slave-
trading observed by us are mentioned, in order to give a
fair idea of its details.

We spent the first night, after leaving the slave route,
at the village of Nkoma, among a section of Manganja,
called Machewa, or Macheba, whose district extends to the
Bua. Nkoma might be called an agricultural smith, for he
had a smelting furnace, and abundance of grain and goats,
with which he showed much more generosity than we had
met with on the slave route. On the 5th October, we came
to the Bua, which has here quite as rocky a bed as where we
crossed it lower down. Mount Ngalla was on our right, and
several hills on our left; the country generally is undulating
and covered with scraggy trees, many of which seemed pol-
larded, from having been cut down to make clearings for
hunting. Everywhere we came upon people in their gardens,
busily preparing for the approaching rains. The men were

up the trees, lopping off the branches, to prevent the shade injuring the crops below, or were clearing away the shoots from stumps formerly cut. Sometimes a woman is seen hoeing alone, or she has a couple of boys collecting the weeds and grass into bundles to be burned. At other times the whole family is working briskly, or all the neighbours are collected to give a day's hoeing for a quantity of beer. Our guides always asked these gatherings "if all the beer were drunk." Some of the women were watering their patches of maize and pumpkins from the running streams with calabashes and pots. About the end of the hot dry season, they make holes about the gardens, and sow maize in them, and water it till the rains begin. This plan gives the maize and pumpkins a start in the race towards harvest. The consequence is, that the owner has fresh green maize to eat some six weeks after the commencement of the regular showers.

The next village at which we slept was also that of a Manganja smith. It was a beautiful spot, shaded with tall euphorbia-trees. The people at first fled, but after a short time returned, and ordered us off to a stockade of Babisa, about a mile distant. We preferred to remain in the smooth shady spot outside the hamlet, to being pent up in a treeless stockade. Twenty or thirty men came dropping in, all fully armed with bows and arrows, some of them were at least six feet four in height, yet these giants were not ashamed to say, "We thought that you were Mazitu, and, being afraid, ran away." Their orders to us were evidently inspired by terror, and so must the refusal of the headman to receive a cloth, or lend us a hut have been; but as we never had the opportunity of realizing what feelings a successful invasion would produce, we did not know whether to blame them or not. The headman, a tall old smith, with an enormous, well-made knife of his own workmanship, came quietly round, and, inspecting the shelter, which, from there being abundance of long grass and bushes near, our men put up for us in half an hour, gradually changed his tactics, and, in the evening, presented us with a huge pot of porridge and a deliciously well-cooked fowl, and made an apology for having been so rude to strangers, and a lamentation that he had been so foolish as to refuse the fine cloth we had offered. Another cloth was of course presented, and we had the pleasure of parting good friends next day.

We were not always so fortunate. Once, after a long weary march, we were seeking a convenient spot to spend the night in: the path led through a village, but the headman tried to prevent our entering it. Without paying any attention to his vociferations, we went on and had reached the other side of his hamlet, intending to sleep elsewhere, when something he said induced us to turn back and sit down in the open space in the centre of his castles. He ran off, and, though we spent two nights there, we laboured in vain to bring him to terms. During the first night he tried to steal a blanket off one of the sleepers, and threw a horn among us containing witchcraft medicine : the next night he hurled a more potent missile into our midst in the shape of a big stone. His neighbours, to whom we spoke about his conduct, seemed to think little of it; " It was like the man, and it was no matter."

Our guide, who belonged to the stockade near to which we had slept, declined to risk himself further than his home. While waiting to hire another, Masiko attempted to purchase a goat, and had nearly concluded the bargain, when the wife of the would-be seller came forward, and said to her husband, " You appear as if you were unmarried; selling a goat without consulting your wife; what an insult to a woman! What sort of man are you ?" Masiko urged the man, saying,

" Let us conclude the bargain, and never mind her;" but he being better instructed, replied, "No, I have raised a host against myself already," and refused. If this was a fair specimen of domestic life, the women here have the same influence that they have in Londa, further west, and in many parts north of the Zambesi ; where we have known a wife order a husband not to sell a fowl, merely, as we supposed, to show us strangers that she had the upper hand. We conjectured that deference was commonly shown to women here, because, as in the west, the exclamation most commonly used was, "O my mother!" We heard it frequently some thirty miles east of this, when the inhabitants took us for the Mazitu. South of the Zambesi the exclamation oftenest heard is, "My father."

We now pushed on to the east, so as to get down to the shores of the Lake, and into the parts where we were known. The country was beautiful, well wooded, and undulating, but the villages were all deserted ; and the flight of the people seemed to have been quite recent, for the grain was standing in the corn-safes untouched. The tobacco, though ripe, remained uncut in the gardens, and the whole country was painfully quiet : the oppressive stillness quite unbroken by the singing of birds, or the shrill calls of women watching their corn.

On passing a beautiful village, called Bangwé, surrounded by shady trees, and placed in a valley among mountains, we were admiring the beauty of the situation, when some of the much dreaded Mazitu, with their shields, ran out of the hamlet, from which we were a mile distant. They began to scream to their companions to give us chase. Without quickening our pace we walked on, and soon were in a wood, through which the footpath we were· following led. The first intimation we had of the approaching Mazitu was given by the

Johanna man, Zachariah, who always lagged behind, running up, screaming as if for his life. The bundles were all put in one place to be defended; and Masiko and Dr. Livingstone walked a few paces back to meet the coming foe. Masiko knelt down anxious to fire, but was ordered not to do so. For a second or two dusky forms appeared among the trees, and the Mazitu were asked, in their own tongue, "What do you want?" Masiko adding, "What do you say?" No answer was given, but the dark shade in the forest vanished. They had evidently taken us for natives, and the sight of a white man was sufficient to put them to flight. Had we been nearer the Coast, where the people are accustomed to the slave-trade, we should have found this affair a more difficult one to deal with; but, as a rule, the people of the interior are much more mild in character than those on the confines of civilization.

The above very small adventure was all the danger we were aware of in this journey; but a report was spread from the Portuguese villages on the Zambesi, similar to several rumours that had been raised before, that Dr. Livingstone had been murdered by the Makololo; and very unfortunately the report reached England before it could be contradicted.

One benefit arose from the Mazitu adventure. Zachariah, and others who had too often to be reproved for lagging behind, now took their places in the front rank; and we had no difficulty in making very long marches for several days, for all believed that the Mazitu would follow our footsteps, and attack us while we slept.

Before commencing the actual descent to the valley of the lake, we passed through a very hilly district, cut up with many gullies, and covered with trees. Several times, as we entered a deep valley, or climbed a steep hill, our ears were saluted by the cry of "Nkondo! Nkondo!" (War! War!)

and with the shrill wail of the women, "O Mae!" (O mother!) The inhabitants answered our inquiries about the paths from the heights, but none came near us. The path we descended by at last was very cleverly chosen, it ran along the spurs rising from different points of the side of the great valley, and was comparatively level for thirty miles. The distance from the top of the plateau to the valley below was about fifty miles; and when we met people coming from the plains to collect wild fruit in the forests, they took it as great news that we had actually seen live Mazitu. The district into which we descended was still called Bango, and a fine stream, named Furisa, flowed through it into the Lake. Here the people had large fields of maize in ear, which had been raised in holes in the dry season by the aid of the water, that percolates from the Furisa through the sand.

On the 8th October we arrived at Molamba, on the banks of the Lake, and had a delicious bath. We were desirous of seeing Nkomo, the headman, again, because a guide whom he had given us had not been paid. Occasionally we have been ill served, and sometimes deserted by the men we have employed. Indeed, if one were inclined to make a wail about the miseries of travelling, an important item would be the difficulties about guides; they don't much relish the task of serving vagrants; nor should we. In this case, however, we had been the delinquents. The man, after going fifteen miles, suddenly stopped on the march, and said that he was going to leave us. He was told to come on to the next village, and that we should rest there and pay him his wages. We never saw him again. On telling this to Nkomo, we ascertained that in taking this particular guide we had been unconsciously aiding an elopement of two of the headman's wives. While marching along with us, the guide had been telegraphing to the ladies behind, and appeared to have received the signal to strike off to the west of our course when he proposed to leave us. From the numerous instances of the polygamist's sorrows which we have observed, we should suppose that he can have but few joys; but still there is something to be said, we dare say, on both sides. Polygamy is certainly a cause of misery to the children; who become partakers of all the petty jealousies, hate, and quarrels of the different mothers.

A party of Babisa tobacco-traders came from the N.W. to Molamba, while we were there; and one of them asserted several times that the Loapula, after emerging from Moelo, received the Lulua, and then flowed into Lake Mofu, and thence into Tanganyika; and from the last-named Lake into the sea. This is the native idea of the geography of the interior; and, to test the general knowledge of our informant, we asked him about our acquaintances in Londa; as Moene, Katema, Shinde or Shinte, who live south-west of the rivers mentioned, and found that our friends there were perfectly well-known to him and to others of these travelled natives. In the evening two of the Babisa came in, and reported that the Mazitu had followed us to the village called Chigaragara, at which we slept at the bottom of the descent. The whole party of traders set off at once, though the sun had set. We ourselves had given rise to the report, for the women of Chigaragara, supposing us in the distance to be Mazitu, fled, with all their household utensils on their heads, and had no opportunity afterwards of finding out their mistake. We spent the night where we were, and next morning, declining Nkomo's entreaty to go and kill elephants, took our course along the shores of the Lake southwards.

We have only been at the Lake at one season of the year: then the wind blows strongly from the east, and indeed this is its prevailing direction hence to the Orange River; a north or a south wind is rare, and seldom lasts more than three days. As the breeze now blew over a large body of water, towards us, it was delightful; but when facing it on the table-land it was so strong as materially to impede our progress, and added considerably to the labour of travelling. Here it brought large quantities of the plant (*Vallisneriæ*), from which the natives extract salt by burning, and which, if chewed, at once shows its saline ~~rerties~~ by the taste. Clouds of the kungo, or edible mʲ ~~the Lake,~~ and many rested on the bushes on/

The reeds along the shores of the Lake ~~..~~ with fugitives, and a great loss of life must since have taken place; for, after the corn they had brought with them was expended, famine would ensue. Even now we passed many women and children digging up the roots, about the size of peas, of an aromatic grass; and their wasted forms showed that this poor hard fare was to allay, if possible, the pangs of hunger. The babies at the breast crowed to us as we passed, their mothers kneeling and grubbing for the roots; the poor little things still drawing nourishment from the natural fountain were unconscious of that sinking of heart which their parents must have felt in knowing that the supply for the little ones must soon fail. No one would sell a bit of food to us: fishermen, even, would not part with the produce of their nets, except in exchange for some other kind of food. Numbers of newly-made graves showed that many had already perished, and hundreds were so emaciated that they had the appearance of human skeletons swathed in brown and wrinkled leather. In passing mile after mile, marked with these sad proofs that "man's inhumanity to man makes countless thousands mourn," one experiences an overpowering sense of helplessness to alleviate human woe, and breathes a silent prayer to the Almighty to hasten the good time coming when "man and man the world o'er, shall brothers be for all that." One small redeeming consideration in all this misery could not but be felt; these ills were inflicted by heathen Mazitu, and not by, or for, those who say to Him who is higher than the highest, "We believe that thou shalt come to be our Judge."

We crossed the Mokole, rested at Chitanda, and then left the Lake, and struck away N.W. to Chinsamba's. Our companions, who were so much oppressed by the rarefied air of the plateau, still showed signs of exhaustion, though now only 1300 feet above the sea, and did not recover flesh and spirits till we again entered the Lower Shire Valley, which is of so small an altitude, that, without simultaneous observations with the barometer there and on the sea-coast, the difference would not be appreciable.

On a large plain on which we spent one night, we had the company of eighty tobacco traders on their way from Kasungu to Chinsamba's. The Mazitu had attacked and killed two of them, near the spot where the Zulus fled from us without answering our questions. The traders were now so frightened that, instead of making a straight course with us, they set off by night to follow the shores of the Lake to Tsenga, and then turn west. It is the sight of shields, or guns that inspires terror. The bowmen feel perfectly helpless when the enemy comes with even the small protection the skin shield affords, or attacks them in the open field with guns. They may shoot a few arrows, but they are such poor shots that ten to one if they hit. The only thing that makes the arrow formidable is the poison; for if the poisoned barb goes in nothing can save the wounded. A bow is in use in the lower end of Lake Nyassa, but is more common in the Maravi country, from six to eight inches broad, which is intended to be used as a shield as well as a bow; but we never saw one with the mark on it of an enemy's arrow. It certainly is no match for the Zulu shield, which is between four and five feet long, of an oval shape, and about two feet broad. So great is the terror this shield inspires that we

Maravi Bow.

sometimes doubted whether the Mazitu here were Zulus at all, and suspected that the people of the country took advantage of that fear, and, assuming shields, pretended to belong to that nation.

On the 11th October we arrived at the stockade of Chinsamba in Mosapo, and had reason to be very well satisfied with his kindness. A paraffin candle was in his eyes the height of luxury, and the ability to make a light instantaneously by a lucifer match, a marvel that struck him with wonder. He brought all his relatives in different groups to see the strange sights,—instantaneous fire-making, and a light, without the annoyance of having fire and smoke in the middle of the floor. When they wish to look for anything in the dark, a wisp of dried grass is lighted. Our books, too, were objects of admiration. The idea that enters their minds is that books are our instruments of divination. Theirs are bits of wood, horn, and knuckle-bones of different animals, or the scales of the Manis, which, according to the way they alight when thrown on the ground, indicate which way the diviner is to answer the inquiries which have been put to him. The sextant and artificial horizon—the weight of the mercury—called by our men "foreign water," were all pondered over with the same kind of interest that we should take for the first time in any new and wonderful thing. In

many hundreds of instances in which we have sat with a
lantern star-gazing, we never once, as far as we know, excited
the suspicion of being engaged in the practice of witchcraft.
Being fully aware of the general belief in wizards and
witches, it has often been a matter of surprise to us that no
accusation ever reached our ears that this "foreign water"
must be used for something else than measuring distances,
and to help in writing down the paths of the new country.
The only reason we can conceive for our immunity is the
fact that we have invariably tried to give a truthful explanation of what we were doing. In the case of Sequasha,
mentioned in an earlier portion of this work, we suspect that
he told the people that the clocks for which he was fined
were his fetishes or charms.

Chinsamba gave us a great deal of his company during
our visits. As we have often remarked in other cases, a
Chief has a great deal to attend to in guiding the affairs of
his people. He is consulted on all occasions, and gives his
advice in a stream of words, which show a very intimate
acquaintance with the topography of his district; he knows
every rood cultivated, every weir put in the river, every
hunting-net, loom, gorge, and every child of his tribe. Any
addition made to the number of these latter is notified to
him; and he sends thanks and compliments to the parents.

After a great deal of intercourse with different rulers, we
have been unable to discover the grounds on which "sensation
writers" have managed to envelop African Chiefs with an
air of ridicule. As the headmen and people, too, are found
to deteriorate as we approach the borders of civilization, it
is probable that the stupid bestiality, described by the writers
referred to, on the West Coast, may be a reflection from the
low trading characters with whom many of the Chieftains
there have had their only intercourse. When a Chief has

made any inquiries from us, we have found that we gave most satisfaction in our answers when we tried to fancy ourselves in the position of the interrogator, and him in that of a poor uneducated fellow-countryman in England. The polite, respectful way of speaking and behaviour of what we call a " thorough gentleman," almost always secure the friendship and goodwill of the Africans.

The presents which, following the custom of the country, we gave to every headman, where we either spent a night or a longer period, varied from four to eight yards of calico. We had some Manchester cloths made in imitation of the native manufactured robes of the West Coast, each worth five or six shillings. To the more important of the Chiefs, for calico we substituted one of these strong gaudy dresses, iron spoons, a knife, needles, a tin dish, or pannikin, and found these presents to be valued more than three times their value in cloth would have been. Eight or ten shillings' worth gave abundant satisfaction to the greediest; but this is to be understood as the prime cost of the articles, and a trader would sometimes have estimated similar generosity as equal to from 30l. to 50l. In some cases the presents we gave exceeded the value of what was received in return; in others the excess of generosity was on the native side.

We never asked for leave to pass through the country; we simply told where we were going, and asked for guides; if they were refused, or if they demanded payment beforehand, we requested to be put into the beginning of the path, and said that we were sorry we could not agree about the guides, and usually they and we started together. Greater care would be required on entering the Mazitu or Zulu country, for there the government extends over very large districts, while among the Manganja each little district is independent of every other. The people here have not adopted the exacting system of the Banyai, or of the people whose country was traversed by Speke and Grant.

In our way back from Chinsamba's to Chembi's, and from his village to Nkwinda's, and thence to Katosa's, we only saw the people working in their gardens, near to the stockades. These strongholds were strengthened with branches of acacias, covered with strong hooked thorns; and were all crowded with people. The air was now clearer than when we went north, and we could see the hills of Kirk's Range five or six miles to the west of our path. The sun struck very hot, and the men felt it most in their feet. Every one who could get a bit of goatskin made it into a pair of sandals.

While sitting at Nkwinda's, a man behind the court hedge-wall said, with great apparent glee, that an Arab slaving party on the other side of the confluence of the Shire and Lake were "giving readily two fathoms of calico for a boy, and two and a half for a girl; never saw trade so brisk, no haggling at all." This party was purchasing for the supply of the ocean slave-trade. One of the evils of this traffic is that it profits by every calamity that happens in a country. The slave-trader naturally reaps advantage from every disorder, and though in the present case some lives may have been saved that otherwise would have perished, as a rule he intensifies hatreds, and aggravates wars between the tribes, because the more they fight and vanquish each other the richer his harvest becomes. Where slaving and cattle are unknown the people live in peace. As we sat leaning against that hedge, and listened to the harangue of the slave-trader's agent, it glanced across our mind that this was a terrible world; the best in it unable, from conscious imperfections, to say to the worst "Stand by! for I am holier than thou." The slave-trader, imbued no doubt with certain kindly feelings, yet pursuing a calling which makes him a fair specimen

of a human fiend, stands grouped, with those by whom the
slave-traders are employed, and with all the workers of sin
and misery in more highly-favoured lands, an awful picture
to the All-seeing Eye.

We arrived at Katosa's village on the 15th October, and
found about thirty young men and boys in slave-sticks.
They had been bought by other agents of the Arab slavers,
still on the east side of the Shire. They were resting in the
village, and their owners soon removed them. The weight of
the goree seemed very annoying when they tried to sleep.
This taming instrument is kept on, until the party has crossed
several rivers and all hope of escape has vanished from the
captive's mind.

On explaining to Katosa the injury he was doing in selling
his people as slaves, he assured us that those whom we had
seen belonged to the Arabs, and added that he had far too
few people already. He said he had been living in peace
at the lakelet Pamalombe ; that the Ajawa, or Machinga,
under Kaiñka and Karamba, and a body of Babisa, under
Maonga, had induced him to ferry them over the Shire ; that
they had lived for a considerable time at his expense, and at
last stole his sheep, which induced him to make his escape to
the place where he now dwelt, and in this flight he had lost
many of his people. His account of the usual conduct of the
Ajawa quite agrees with what these people have narrated
themselves, and gives but a low idea of their moral tone.
They have repeatedly broken all the laws of hospitality by
living for months on the bounty of the Manganja, and then,
by a sudden uprising, overcoming their hosts, and killing or
chasing them out of their inheritances. The secret of their
success is the possession of firearms. There were several of
these Ajawa here again, and on our arrival they proposed to
Katosa that they should leave ; but he replied that they

need not be afraid of us. They had red beads strung so thickly on their hair that at a little distance they appeared to have on red caps. It is curious that the taste for red hair should be so general among the Africans here and further north; in the south black mica, called *Sebilo*, and even soot are used to deepen the colour of the hair; here many smear the head with red-ochre, others plait the inner bark of a tree stained red into it; and a red powder called *Mukuru* is employed, which some say is obtained from the ground, and others from the roots of a tree.

It having been doubted whether sugar-cane is indigenous to this country or not, we employed Katosa to procure the two varieties commonly cultivated, with the intention of conveying them to Johanna. One is yellow, and the other, like what we observed in the Barotse Valley, is variegated with dark red and yellow patches, or all red. We have seen it "arrow" or blossom. Bamboos also run to seed, and the people are said to use the seed as food. The sugar-cane has native names, which would lead us to believe it to be indigenous. Here it is called *Zimbi*, further south *Mesari*, and in the centre of the country *Meshuati*. Anything introduced in recent times, as maize, superior cotton, or cassava, has a name implying its foreign origin.

As Katosa was very bountiful, and seemed, from calling Dr. Livingstone his good spirit, to have given us his confidence, a present was made him of a marine officer's coat and epaulets, which was sent by the officers of H.M.S. Lyra, under Captain Oldfield, to the Chief who had seized and delivered up to justice the murderers of the late Dr. Roscher. We carried it up the Rovuma, intending to present it, should we be fortunate enough to meet that Chief; but, at the point where we were obliged to turn back, we could hear nothing about him. Dr. Roscher, having gone with an Arab party, was not recognised among the people as a European, and we found it rather an awkward thing to inquire about one who had been murdered. Those who knew anything about the matter were naturally suspicious that our inquiries implied blood-relationship, and its attendant blood-feud ; so, after unavailing search, we brought the present here, and, it being unlikely that we should soon go to the east side of the Lake, after a full explanation of the reasons why we were carrying this present, we gave it to Katosa, and believe that, if any future traveller should require his aid, he would cheerfully render it to the utmost of his ability.

Katosa's village was embowered among gigantic trees of fine timber : several caffiaceous bushes, with berries closely resembling those of the common coffee, grew near, but no use had ever been made of them.   There are several cinchonaceous trees also in the country ; and some of the wild fruits are so good as to cause a feeling of regret that they have not been improved by cultivation, or whatever else brought ours to their present perfection.   Katosa lamented that this locality was so inferior to his former place at Pamalombe ; there he had maize at the different stages of growth throughout the year.   To us, however, he seemed, by digging holes, and taking advantage of the moisture beneath, to have succeeded pretty well in raising crops at this the driest time.   The Makololo remarked that "here the maize had no season,"— meaning that the whole year was proper for its growth and ripening.   By irrigation a succession of crops of grain might be raised anywhere within the south intertropical region of Africa.

When we were with Motunda, on the 20th October, he told us frankly that all the native provisions were hidden in Kirk's range, and his village being the last place where a supply of grain could be purchased before we reached the ship, we waited till he had sent to his hidden stores. The upland country, beyond the mountains now on our right, is called Deza, and is inhabited by Maravi, who are only another tribe of Manganja. The paramount Chief is called Kabambe, and he, having never been visited by war, lives in peace and plenty. Goats and sheep thrive; and Nyango, the Chieftainess further to the south, has herds of horned cattle. The country being elevated is said to be cold, and there are large grassy plains on it which are destitute of trees. The Maravi are reported to be brave, and good marksmen with the bow; but, throughout all the country we have traversed, guns are enabling the trading tribes to overcome the agricultural and manufacturing classes.

In marching up the Gõa or Gova Valley the haze had gone, and the mountains were all quite clear. In the lines of dark-green massive trees along the watercourses, sang swarms of cicadæ, with a stridulous chorus, which at spots resembled the noise of fifty fryingpans in active operation. A heavy shower of rain, which had fallen some time before, had cleared the atmosphere and called forth insect life.

On the ascent at the end of the valley just opposite Mount Mvai, we looked back for a moment to impress the beauties of the grand vale on our memory. The heat of the sun was now excessive, and Masiko, thinking that it was overpowering, proposed to send forward to the ship and get a hammock, in which to carry any one who might knock up. He was truly kind and considerate. Dr. Livingstone having fallen asleep after a fatiguing march, a hole in the roof of the hut he was in allowed the sun to beat on his head, and caused a splitting headache and deafness: while he was nearly insensible, he felt Masiko repeatedly lift him back to the bed off which he had rolled, and cover him up.

On the 24th we were again in Banda, at the village of Chasundu, and could now see clearly the hot valley in which the Shire flows, and the mountains of the Manganja beyond to our south-east. Instead of following the road by which we had come, we resolved to go south along the Lesungwe, which rises at Zunje, a peak on the same ridge as Mvai, and a part of Kirk's range, which bounds the country of the Maravi on our west. This is about the limit of the beat of the Portuguese native traders, and it is but recently that, following our footsteps, they have come so far. It is not likely that their enterprise will lead them further north, for Chasundu informed us that the Babisa under-sell the agents from Tette. He had tried to deal with the latter when they first came; but they offered only ten fathoms of calico for a tusk, for which the Babisa gave him twenty fathoms and a little powder. Ivory was brought to us for sale again and again, and, as far as we could judge, the price expected would be about one yard of calico per pound, or possibly more, for there is no scale of prices known. The rule seems to be that buyer and seller shall spend a good deal of time in trying to cheat each other before coming to any conclusion over a bargain.

We found the Lesungwe a fine stream near its source, and about forty feet wide and knee-deep, when joined by the Lekudzi, which comes down from the Maravi country. The banks and slopes down to the stream are dry and hard. The soil is largely mixed with disintegrated gneiss and mica schist, and is not so fertile as is common in this country. The gneiss and mica schist have been given their present dip away from the chain, or eastwards, by the granitic masses which form Kirk's range. The people had been subjected to the slave-trading scourge of the Ajawa and Tette dealers. Indeed, a party of the latter was actually on the Lesungwe at this very time, headed by a white Portuguese—probably one of the convict soldiers of the Governor.

Guinea-fowl abounded, but no grain could be purchased, for the people had cultivated only the holmes along the banks with maize and pumpkins. Time enough had not elapsed since the slave-trader's invasion, and destruction of their stores, for them to raise crops of grain on the adjacent lands. To deal with them for a few heads of maize was the hungry bargaining with the famished, so we hastened on southwards as fast as the excessive heat would allow us. It was impossible to march in the middle of the day, the heat was so intolerable; and we could not go on at night, because, if we had chanced to meet any of the inhabitants, we should have been taken for marauders. In making a detour one day in search of buffaloes or guinea-fowls, in company with Masego, we came upon some women working in their maize-gardens. They drew water for us, and spoke to us cheerily as we sat under a tree. One of their husbands soon came running up in alarm, and made a great demonstration of fighting. It was amusing to notice the effect of Masego's quiet chaff on our pugnacious visitor, who took up a defensible position on a slope some fifty yards off while we rested in the shade. "The women," said Masego, "had understood our civil petition for water perfectly; they showed no fear of peaceable men; we asked water from them because we had no vessel to draw with and they had; but if he insisted on fighting, he had better call all his friends and come on; it was daylight, and all would see who was the coward, and who was not." The arrow was first taken from the bow-string and put alongside the bow, then it was placed in the quiver, and, though he continued talking and justifying his alarm, he listened, sat down, followed us at a distance, and, uninvited,

eventually proved himself very useful as a guide.   He afterwards explained that he had been smoking hemp, and had
been excited to this mad sort of conduct.

We had now thunder every afternoon; but while occasional
showers seemed to fall at different parts, none fell on us.   The
air was deliciously clear, and revealed all the landscape covered everywhere with forest, and bounded by beautiful mountains.   On the 31st October we reached the Mukuru-Madse,
after having travelled 660 geographical miles, or 760 English
miles in a straight line.   This was accomplished in fifty-five
travelling days, twelve miles per diem on an average.   If the
numerous bendings and windings, and ups and downs of the
paths could have been measured too, the distance would have
been found at least fifteen miles a day.   A pedometer
showed more, but in coming back from one short trip we
found that the instrument varied so much that we did not
use it again.   A very good chronometer was employed to
measure the differences of longitude.   It was carried in a box
of clothing, on the head of a man of steady gait.   In order
to secure a chronometer being of any use, no dependence
ought to be placed on its rate, when stationary.   Its travelling
rate must be ascertained by taking a series of altitudes of
the sun or stars at certain spots in the outward journey;
and a second series of observations must be made at the same
stations in the return journey.   By this means the exact
travelling rate can be found.   The same plan should be
followed in a boat; for, if this or some similar precaution be
not taken, a chronometer when carried is of little value in
measuring distances.   This will be evident when it is mentioned that the chronometer we used, when at the ship,
had the rate -11^s; in travelling $+1^s$ daily, which would
amount to a daily error of three miles.

The night we slept at the Mukuru-Madse, it thundered

heavily, but, as this had been the case every afternoon, and no rain had followed, we erected no shelter, but during this night a pouring rain came on. When very tired a man feels determined to sleep in spite of everything, and the sound of dropping water is said to be conducive to slumber, but that does not refer to an African storm. If, when half asleep in spite of a heavy shower on the back of the head, he unconsciously turns on his side, the drops from the branches make such capital shots into his ear, that the brain rings again.

We were off next morning, the 1st of November, as soon as the day dawned. In walking about seven miles to the ship, our clothes were thoroughly dried by the hot sun, and an attack of fever followed. We relate this little incident to point out the almost certain consequence of getting wet in this climate, and allowing the clothes to dry on the person. Even if we walk in the mornings when the dew is on the grass, and only get our feet and legs wet, a very uneasy feeling and partial fever with pains in the limbs ensue, and continue till the march onwards bathes them in perspiration. Had Bishop Mackenzie been aware of this, which, before experience alone had taught us, entailed many a severe lesson, we know no earthly reason why his valuable life might not have been spared. The difference between getting the clothes soaked in England and in Africa is this: in the cold climate the patient is compelled, or, at any rate, warned, by discomfort to resort at once to a change of raiment; while in Africa it is cooling and rather pleasant to allow the clothes to dry on the person. A Missionary in proportion as he possesses an athletic frame, hardened by manly exercises, in addition to his other qualifications, will excel him who is not favoured with such bodily endowments; but in a hot climate efficiency mainly depends on husbanding the resources. He must never forget that, in the tropics, he is an exotic plant.

CHAPTER XXVIII.

Gratifying confidence of Ajawa — Annual rest of tropical trees — Rise in the Shire insufficient — Bishop Mackenzie's successor — Unfulfilled hopes — What a Missionary ought to be — Abandonment of Mission unnecessary — Success of West Coast Missions — Jan. 19th, the Shire in flood — Leave Chibisa's — Delayed — Reach Morambala 2nd Feb. — Effluvium from the water — Its effects — Take on board orphans and widows — Zambesi in flood — Islands in Zambesi — Formation of delta — Death of Mariano — Very moderate exports—Taken in tow—Heavy gale — Behaviour of the "Lady of the Lake" — Promptitude and skill of Capt. Chapman, of H.M.S. Ariel — Close packing of live cargoes perhaps necessary — The Pioneer takes rescued orphans and widows with Mr. Waller to Cape — Caboceira — M. Soares — New Governor of Mosambique — New species of Pedalia — 16th April we reach Zanzibar — Hospitality of foreigners, and of our own countrymen — 30th April we leave Zanzibar on board the Lady Nyassa for Bombay — African sailors — Arrival at Bombay.

WE were delighted and thankful to find all those left at the ship in good health, and that from the employments in which they had been occupied they had suffered less from fever than usual during our absence. The steward, after having performed his part in the march right bravely, rejoined his comrades stronger than he had ever been before.

An Ajawa Chief, named Kapeni, had so much confidence in the English name that he, with most of his people, visited the ship; and asserted that nothing would give his countrymen greater pleasure than to receive the associates of Bishop Mackenzie as their teachers. This declaration, coupled with the subsequent conduct of the Ajawa, was very gratifying, inasmuch as it was clear that no umbrage had been taken at the check which the Bishop had given to their slaving; their consciences had told them that the course he had pursued was right.

When we returned, the contrast between the vegetation

about Muazi's and that near the ship was very striking. We had come so quickly down, that while on the plateau, in latitude 12° S., the young leaves had in many cases passed from the pink or other colour they have on first coming out to the light fresh green which succeeds it, here, on the borders of 16° S., or from 150 to 180 miles distant, the trees were still bare, the grey colour of the bark pre-dominating over every other hue. The trees in the tropics here have a very well-marked annual rest. On the Rovuma even, which is only about ten degrees from the equator, in September the slopes up from the river some sixty miles inland were of a light ashy-grey colour; and on ascending them, we found that the majority of the trees were without leaves; those of the bamboo even lay crisp and crumpled on the ground. As the sun is usually hot by day, even in the winter, this withering process may be owing to the cool nights; Africa differing so much from Central India in the fact that, in Africa, however hot the day may be, the air generally cools down sufficiently by the early morning watches to render a covering or even a blanket agreeable.

The first fortnight after our return to the ship was employed in the delightful process of resting, to appreciate which a man must have gone through great exertions. In our case the muscles of the limbs were as hard as boards, and not an ounce of fat existed on any part of the body. We now had frequent showers; but, these being only the earlier rains, the result on the rise of the river was but a few inches. The effect of these rains on the surrounding scenery was beautiful in the extreme. All trace of the dry season was soon obliterated, and hills and mountains from base to summit were covered with a mantle of living green. The sun passed us on his way south without causing a flood, so all our hopes of a release were centred on his

return towards the Equator, when, as a rule, the waters
of inundation are made to flow. Up to this time the rains
descended simply to water the earth, fill the pools, and make
ready for the grand overflow for which we had still to wait
six weeks. It is of no use to conceal that we waited with
much chagrin; for had we not been forced to return from
the highlands west of Nyassa we might have visited Lake
Bemba; but unavailing regrets are poor employment for the
mind; so we banished them to the best of our power.

About the middle of December, 1863, we were informed
that Bishop Mackenzie's successor, after spending a few
months on the top of a mountain about as high as Ben Nevis
in Scotland, at the mouth of the Shire, where there were
few or no people to be taught, had determined to leave
the country. This unfortunate decision was communicated
to us at the same time that six of the boys reared by
Bishop Mackenzie were sent back into heathenism. The
boys were taken to a place about seven miles from the ship,
but immediately found their way up to us, lamenting that
they had no longer that Bishop who had a heart, and who was
more than a father to them. We told them that if they wished
to remain in the country they had better so arrange at once,
for we were soon to leave. The sequel will show their choice.

As soon as the death of Bishop Mackenzie was known at
the Cape, Dr. Gray, the excellent Bishop there, proceeded at
once to England, with a view of securing an early appointment of another head to the Mission, which in its origin owed
so much to his zeal for the spread of the Gospel among the
heathen, and whose interests he had continually at heart.
About the middle of 1862 we heard that Dr. Gray's efforts
had been successful, and that another clergyman would
soon take the place of our departed friend. This pleasing intelligence was exceedingly cheering to the Mis-

sionaries, and gratifying also to the members of the
Expedition.   About the beginning of 1863 the new Bishop
arrived at the mouth of the river in a man-of-war, and after
some delay proceeded inland.   The Bishop of the Cape had
taken a voyage home at considerable inconvenience to himself,
for the sole object of promoting this Mission to the heathen;
and it was somehow expected that the man he would secure
would be an image of himself; and we must say, that whatever others, from the representations that have gone abroad,
may think of his character, we invariably found Dr. Gray
to be a true, warmhearted promoter of the welfare of his
fellow-men; a man whose courage and zeal have provoked
very many to good works.

It was hoped that the presence of a new head to the Mission would infuse new energy and life into the small band of
Missionaries, whose ranks had been thinned by death; and
who, though discouraged by the disasters which the slave war
and famine had induced, and also dispirited by the depressing
influences of a low and unhealthy position in the swampy
Shire Valley, were yet bravely holding out till the much-
needed moral and material aid should arrive.

These expectations, we regret to say, were not fulfilled.   We
would here be understood as expressing only a general opinion.
The qualities required in a Missionary leader are not of the
common kind.   He ought to have physical and moral courage
of the highest order, and a considerable amount of cultivation
and energy, balanced by patient determination; and above
all these are necessary a calm Christian zeal and anxiety for
the main spiritual results of the work.   We repeat, that we
are expressing no opinion about the qualification of any
individual; but we assert that not every one has this rare
combination of power; and that a man who may be quite
in his natural sphere in a quiet round of common duties as

the minister of a town, or rural parish in England, may be very much out of it as a Missionary in Central Africa.

We believe that we are uttering the sentiments of many devout members of different sections of Christians, when we say, it was a pity that the Mission of the Universities was abandoned. The ground had been consecrated in the truest sense by the lives of those brave men who first occupied it. In bare justice to Bishop Mackenzie, who was the first to fall, it must be said, that the repudiation of all he had done, and the sudden abandonment of all that had cost so much life and money to secure, was a serious line of conduct for one so unversed in Missionary operations as his successor, to inaugurate. It would have been no more than fair that Bishop Tozer, before winding up the affairs of the Mission, should actually have examined the highlands of the Upper Shire; he would thus have gratified the associates of his predecessor, who believed that the highlands had never had a fair trial, and he would have gained from personal observation a more accurate knowledge of the country and the people than he could possibly have become possessed of by information gathered chiefly on the coast. With this examination, rather than with a stay of a few months on the humid, dripping top of misty Morambala, we should have felt much more satisfied.

To those who have not paid much attention to the labours of different bodies of Christians it may be mentioned, that, before success appeared at the Mission-stations on the West Coast, upwards of forty Missionaries had succumbed to the climate. Let it be said, if you will, that the Societies and the men were alike unwise to sacrifice so much valuable life. These may be proofs of folly to some, but to others they are telling evidence that our religion has lost none of its pristine power. Nothing in our opinion is wanting to complete the title of many of these men to take rank with the Saints and Martyrs of primitive times. More experience of the climate has since greatly diminished the mortality, and in 1861 there were, on the West Coast, one hundred and ten principal Mission-stations, thirteen thousand scholars in the schools, and nineteen thousand members in the churches.

Bishop Mackenzie had in a short time gained the first step, he had secured the confidence of the people. This step it often takes several years to attain; and we cannot but regret that subsequently the Mission of the Universities, when contrasted with others, should appear to so much disadvantage. In fact, though representing all that is brave and good and manly, in the chief seats of English learning, the Mission, in fleeing from Morambala to an island in the Indian Ocean, acted as St. Augustine would have done, had he located himself on one of the Channel Islands, when sent to christianize the natives of Central England. This is, we believe, the first case of a Protestant Mission having been abandoned without being driven away.

In January, 1864, the natives all confidently asserted that at next full moon the river would have its great and permanent flood. It had several times risen as much as a foot, but fell again as suddenly. It was curious that their observation coincided exactly with ours, that the flood of inundation happens when the sun comes overhead on his way back to the Equator. We mention this more minutely because, from the observation of several years, we believe that in this way the inundation of the Nile is to be explained. On the 19th the Shire suddenly rose several feet, and we started at once; and stopping only for a short time at Chibisa's to bid adieu to the Ajawa and Makololo, who had been extremely useful to us of late in supplying maize and fresh provisions, we hastened on

our way to the ocean. In order to keep steerage way on
the Pioneer, we had to go quicker than the stream, and
unfortunately carried away her rudder in passing suddenly
round a bank. The delay required for the repairs prevented
our reaching Morambala till the 2nd of February.

The flood-water ran into a marsh some miles above the
mountain, and became as black as ink; and when it returned
again to the river emitted so strong an effluvium of sulphuretted hydrogen, that one could not forget for an instant that
the air was most offensive. The natives said this stench
did not produce disease. We spent one night in it, and
suffered no ill effects, though we fully expected an attack of
fever. Next morning every particle of white paint on both
ships was so deeply blackened, that it could not be cleaned by
scrubbing with soap and water. The brass was all turned
to a bronze colour, and even the iron and ropes had taken a
new tint. This is an additional proof that malaria and offensive
effluvia are not always companions. We did not suffer more
from fever in the mangrove swamps, where we inhaled so
much of the heavy mousey smell that it was distinguishable
in the odour of our shirts and flannels, than we did elsewhere.

We tarried in the foul and blackening emanations from
the marsh because we had agreed to receive on board
about thirty poor orphan boys and girls, and a few helpless widows whom Bishop Mackenzie had attached to his
Mission. All who were able to support themselves had
been encouraged by the Missionaries to do so by cultivating
the ground, and they now formed a little free community.
But the boys and girls who were only from seven to twelve
years of age, and orphans without any one to help them,
could not be abandoned without bringing odium on the
English name. The effect of an outcry by some persons
in England, who knew nothing of the circumstances in which

Bishop Mackenzie was placed, and who certainly had not given up their own right of appeal to the sword of the magistrate, was, that the new head of the Mission had gone to extremes in the opposite direction from his predecessor; not even protesting against the one monstrous evil of the country, the slave-trade. The most heartless axiom that ever issued from a Missionary's mouth, "one black face is as good as another to me," was never uttered by Mackenzie; nor did it find a chord of sympathy in true English hearts. We believed that we ought to leave the English name in the same good repute among the natives that we had found it; and in removing the poor creatures, who had lived with Mackenzie as children with a father, to a land where the education he began would be completed, we had the aid and sympathy of the best of the Portuguese, and of the whole native population. The difference between shipping slaves and receiving these free orphans struck us as they came on board. As soon as permission to embark was given, the rush into the boat nearly swamped her—their eagerness to be safe on the Pioneer's deck had to be repressed.

Bishop Tozer had already left for Quillimane when we took these people and the last of the Universities' Missionaries on board and proceeded to the Zambesi. It was in high flood. We have always spoken of this river as if at its lowest, for fear lest we should convey an exaggerated impression of its capabilities for navigation. Instead of from five to fifteen feet, it was now from fifteen to thirty feet, or more, deep. All the sandbanks and many of the islands had disappeared, and before us rolled a river capable, as one of our naval friends thought, of carrying a gunboat. Some of the sandy islands are annually swept away, and the quantities of sand carried down are prodigious.

The process by which a delta, extending eighty or one hundred miles from the sea, has been formed may be seen

going on at the present day—the coarser particles of sand are
driven out into the ocean, just in the same way as we see they
are over banks in the beds of torrents. The finer portions are
caught by the returning tide, and, accumulating by successive
ebbs and flows, become, with the decaying vegetation, arrested
by the mangrove roots. The influence of the tide in bringing
back the finer particles gives the sea near the mouth of the
Zambesi a clean and sandy bottom. This process has been
going on for ages, and, as the delta has enlarged eastwards, the
river has always kept a channel for itself behind. Wherever
we see an island all sand, or with only one layer of mud in it,
we know it is one of recent formation, and that it may be swept
away at any time by a flood ; while those islands which are
all of mud are the more ancient, having in fact existed ever since
the time when the ebbing and flowing tides originally formed
them as parts of the delta. This mud resists the action of
the river wonderfully. It is a kind of clay on which the
eroding power of water has little effect. Were maps made,
showing which banks and which islands are liable to erosion,
it would go far to settle where the annual change of the
channel would take place ; and, were a few stakes driven
in year by year to guide the water in its course, the river
might be made of considerable commercial value in the
hands of any energetic European nation. No canal or
railway would ever be thought of for this part of Africa.
A few improvements would make the Zambesi a ready means
of transit for all the trade that, with a population thinned by
Portuguese slaving, will ever be developed in our day. Here
there is no instance on record of the natives flocking in
thousands to the colony, as they did at Natal, and even to the
Arabs on Lake Nyassa. This keeping aloof renders it unlikely that in Portuguese hands the Zambesi will ever be
of any more value to the world than it has been.

Mariano died, from the effects of debauchery, while we were coming down the Shire. His sad career affords another illustration of that system which, whether in African or half European hands, obstructs the prosperity of this country. We must say that, notwithstanding all the mismanagement and injustice with which the French and English stand chargeable in their treatment of barbarians, the commercial results of their enterprises are usually appreciable; while the total exports from the port of Quillimane, which is the trade outlet of the Zambesi, yield an annual revenue of about half the amount of the Governor's salary!

After a hurried visit to Senna, in order to settle with Major Sicard and Senhor Ferrão for supplies we had drawn thence after the depopulation of the Shire, we proceeded down to the Zambesi's mouth, and were fortunate in meeting, on the 13th February, with H.M.S. Orestes. She was joined next day by H.M.S. Ariel. The Orestes took the Pioneer, and the Ariel the Lady Nyassa in tow, for Mosambique. On the 16th a circular storm proved the sea-going qualities of the "Lady of the Lake;" for on this day a hurricane struck the Ariel, and drove her nearly backwards at a rate of six knots. The towing hawser wound round her screw and stopped her engines. No sooner had she recovered from this shock than she was again taken aback on the other tack, and driven stem on towards the Lady Nyassa's broadside. We who were on board the little vessel saw no chance of escape unless the crew of the Ariel should think of heaving ropes when the big ship went over us; but she glided past our bow, and we breathed freely again. We had now an opportunity of witnessing man-of-war-seamanship. Captain Chapman, though his engines were disabled, did not think of abandoning us in the heavy gale, but crossed the bows of the Lady Nyassa again and again, dropping a cask with a line by which to give us another hawser. We might never have picked it up, had not a Krooman jumped overboard and fastened a second line to the cask; and then we drew the hawser on board, and were again in tow. During the whole time of the hurricane the little vessel behaved admirably, and never shipped a single green sea. When the Ariel pitched forwards we could see a large part of her bottom, and when her stern went down we could see all her deck. A boat, hung at her stern davits, was stove in by the waves. The officers on board the Ariel thought that it was all over with us: we imagined that they were suffering more than we were. Nautical men may suppose that this was a serious storm only to landsmen; but the Orestes, which was once in sight, and at another time forty miles off during the same gale, split eighteen sails; and the Pioneer had to be lightened of parts of a sugar-mill she was carrying; her round-house was washed away, and the cabin was frequently knee-deep in water. When the Orestes came into Mosambique harbour nine days after our arrival there, our vessel, not being anchored close to the Ariel, for we had run in under the lee of the fort, led to the surmise on board the Orestes that we had gone to the bottom. Captain Chapman and his officers pronounced the Lady Nyassa to be the finest little sea-boat they had ever seen. She certainly was a contrast to the Ma-Robert, and did great credit to her builders, Tod and Macgregor of Glasgow. We can but regret that she was not employed on the Lake after which she was named, and for which she was intended and was so well adapted.

What struck us most, during the trip from the Zambesi to Mosambique, was the admirable way in which Captain Chapman handled the Ariel in the heavy sea of the hurricane; the promptitude and skill with which, when we had broken three hawsers, others were passed to us by the rapid evolutions of a big ship round a little one; and the ready appliance

2 P 2

of uncommon shewn in cutting the hawser off the screw nine feet under water with long chisels made for the occasion; a task which it took three days to accomplish. Captain Chapman very kindly invited us on board the Ariel, and we accepted his hospitality after the weather had moderated.

The little vessel was hauled through and against the huge seas with such force that two hawsers measuring eleven inches each in circumference parted. Many of the blows we received from the billows made every plate quiver from stem to stern, and the motion was so quick that we had to hold on continually to avoid being tossed from one side to the other or into the sea. Ten of the late Bishop's flock whom we had on board became so sick and helpless that do what we could to aid them they were so very much in the way that the idea broke in upon us, that the close packing resorted to by slavers is one of the necessities of the traffic. If this is so, it would account for the fact that even when the trade was legal the same injurious custom was common, if not universal. If, instead of ten such passengers, we had been carrying two hundred, with the wind driving the rain and spray, as by night it did, nearly as hard as hail against our faces, and nothing whatever to be seen to windward but the occasional gleam of the crest of a wave, and no sound heard save the whistling of the storm through the rigging, it would have been absolutely necessary for the working of the ship and safety of the whole that the live cargo should all have been stowed down below, whatever might have been the consequences.

Having delivered the Pioneer over to the Navy, she was towed down to the Cape by Captain Forsyth of the Valorous, and after examination it was declared that with repairs to the amount of 300l. she would be as serviceable as ever. Those of the Bishop's flock whom we had on board were kindly allowed a passage to the Cape. The boys went in the Orestes,

and we are glad of the opportunity to record our heartfelt
thanks to Captains Forsyth, Gardner, and Chapman for
rendering us, at various times, every aid in their power.
Mr. Waller went in the Pioneer, and continued his generous
services to all connected with the Mission, whether white or
black, till they were no longer needed; and we must say that
his conduct to them throughout was truly noble, and worthy
of the highest praise.

After beaching the Lady Nyassa at Caboçeira, opposite the
house of a Portuguese gentleman well known to all Englishmen, João da Costa Soares, we put in brine cocks, and
cleaned and painted her bottom.   Mr. Soares appeared to us
to have been very much vilified in a publication in England
a few years ago; our experience proved him to be extremely
kind and obliging.   All the members of the Expedition who
passed Mosambique were unanimous in extolling his generosity, and, from the general testimony of English visitors in
his favour, we very much regret that his character was so
grievously misrepresented.   To the authorities at Mosambique
our thanks are also due for obliging accommodation; and
though we differ entirely from the Portuguese officials as to the
light in which we regard the slave-trade, we trust our exposure
of the system, in which unfortunately they are engaged, will
not be understood as indicating any want of kindly feeling
and good will to them personally.   Senhor Canto e
Castro, who arrived at Mosambique two days after our
departure to take the office of Governor-General, was well
known to us in Angola.   We lived two months in his house
when he was Commandant of Golungo Alto; and, knowing
him thoroughly, believe that no better man could have been
selected for the office.   We trust that his good principles may
enable him to withstand the temptations of his position; but
we should be sorry to have ours tried in a den of slave-

traders with the miserable pittance he receives for his support.

While at Mosambique, a species of Pedalia called by Mr. Soares *Dadeleira*, and by the natives—from its resemblance to *Gerzilin*, or sesamum—"wild sesamum," was shown to us, and is said to be well known among native nurses as a very gentle and tasteless aperient for children. A few leaves of it are stirred in a cup of cold water for eight or nine seconds, and a couple of teaspoonfuls of the liquid given as a dose. The leaves form a sort of mucilage in the water by longer stirring, which is said to have diuretic properties besides.

On the 16th April we steamed out from Mosambique; and, the currents being in our favour, in a week reached Zanzibar. Here we experienced much hospitality from our countrymen, and especially from Dr. Seward, then acting consul and political agent for Colonel Playfair. A peculiarity in all our countrymen whom we have met abroad is the attention they pay to the comfort of the stranger. We cannot complain of a want of hospitality in other nations, but we have to wait till the time of the usual meal comes round; and, in the interval, our Dutch and other friends used to put a string of questions: "Where do you come from? Where are you bound for? What do you mean to do? Are you married? If not, why not?" and many more of the same kind; but, so far as our experience goes, the Englishman's first inquiries were, "Have you breakfasted? What will you take? Have some cold meat?" All were kind; but, from being English ourselves, we preferred our own countrymen's way of showing hospitality.

Dr. Seward was very doubtful if we could reach Bombay before what is called the break of the monsoon took place. This break occurs usually between the end of May and the 12th of June. The wind still blows from Africa to India, but with so much violence, and with such a murky atmosphere that few or no observations for position can be taken. We were, however, at the time very anxious to dispose of the Lady Nyassa, and, the only market we could reach being Bombay, we resolved to run the risk of getting there before the stormy period commenced ; and, after taking fourteen tons of coal on board, we started on the 30th April from Zanzibar.

Our complement consisted of seven native Zambesians, two boys, and four Europeans; namely, one stoker, one sailor, one carpenter, whose names have been already mentioned, and Dr. Livingstone, as navigator. The Lady Nyassa had shown herself to be a good sea-boat. The natives had proved themselves capital sailors, though before volunteering not one of them had ever seen the sea. They were not picked men, but, on paying a dozen whom we had in our employment for fifteen months, they were taken at random from several hundreds who offered to accompany us. Their wages were ten shillings per mensem, and it was curious to observe, that so eager were they to do their duty that only one of them lay down from sea-sickness during the whole voyage. They took in and set sail very cleverly in a short time, and would climb out along a boom, reeve a rope through the block, and come back with the rope in their teeth, though at each lurch the performer was dipped in the sea. The sailor and carpenter, though anxious to do their utmost, had a week's severe illness each, and were unfit for duty.

It is pleasant enough to take the wheel for an hour or two, or even for a watch, but when it comes to be for every alternate four hours, it is utterly wearisome. We set our black men to steer, showing them which arm of the compass needle was to be kept towards the vessel's head, and soon three of them could manage very well, and they only needed watching. In going up the East Coast to take advantage of the current of one hundred miles a day, we would fain have gone into the Juba or Webbe River, the mouth of which is only 15' south of the line, but we were too shorthanded. We passed up to about ten degrees north of the Equator, and then steamed out from the coast. Here Maury's wind chart showed that the calm-belt had long been passed, but we were in it still; and, instead of a current carrying us north, we had a contrary current which bore us every day four miles to the south. We steamed as long as we dared, knowing as we did that we must use the engines on the coast of India.

After losing many days tossing on the silent sea, with innumerable dolphins, flying-fish, and sharks around us, we had six days of strong breezes, then calms again tried our patience; and the near approach of that period, " the break of the Monsoon," in which it was believed no boat could live, made us sometimes think our epitaph would be "Left Zanzibar on 30th April 1864, and never more heard of." At last, in the beginning of June the chronometers showed that we were near the Indian coast. The black men believed it was true because we told them it was so, but only began to dance with joy when they saw sea-weed and serpents floating past. These serpents are peculiar to these parts, and are mentioned as poisonous in the sailing directions. We ventured to predict that we should see land next morning, and at midday the high coast hove in sight, wonderfully like Africa before the rains begin. Then a haze covered all the land, and a heavy swell beat towards it. A rock was seen, and a latitude showed it to be the Choule rock. Making that a fresh starting-point, we soon found the light-ship, and then the forest of masts loomed through the haze in Bombay harbour. We had sailed over 2500 miles. The vessel was so small, that no one noticed our arrival.

CHAPTER XXIX.

Conclusion.

Recapitulation of the results of the Expedition — Discovery of a port, and a
means of transit to healthy highlands — Fertility of soil — Indigo — Cotton
— Climate and soil admirably suited for its cultivation — Large cotton-bushes
of interior — Tobacco and castor-oil plants, and sugar-cane — Grasses — Continuous crops — Fat cattle — Droughts — Hard woods common — Timber
scarce — Sarsaparilla — Calumba-root — Fibrous and oil-yielding plants and
trees — Want of heart to describe discoveries in Africa — Gloom of the slave-
trade — Different ways in which it is carried on — Direct European agency
in the traffic — Napoleon III. — "Engagé system" — Slave-trade a barrier
to all progress — Its effects on slave-owners' country — Cause of the war in
America — Similar effect of centuries of barbarism on African and other
nations — The African physically, his lightheartedness — Fitness for servitude
not attributable to climate — Form of Government Patriarchal — African
stagnation from same cause as that of other nations — Man an unconscious
co-operator — Guided by wisdom not his own — Is the greatest power
derivable from science reserved for Christians? — The African's capability
for Christianity — Kindness the best road to the heart — Sierra Leone Missions — Sunday at Sierra Leone — Statement of Capt. Burton — Statistics
of Sierra Leone — Continuance of Lord Palmerston's policy needed — Trade
returns — Colonel Ord's report — Influences of Settlements — Mortality on
board the West Coast Squadron — Treatment of fever — Missionary Societies
on West Coast — Our American Missionary brethren — Suggestions for a
solution of our Convict Question — Colonel Ord on Settlements.

It may be useful to recount the more important results
enumerated in the foregoing pages. Among the first the
discovery of a port which could easily be made available
for commercial purposes, and of the exact value of the
Zambesi as a speedy means of transit to that interior of highlands, which in all probability will yet become the sphere of
European enterprise. The condition in which the river will be
found at its lowest has been carefully ascertained, and stated
in the same way as the depth of harbours usually is, namely,
at low water. However much higher the waters of the Zam-

besi and Shire may be found during several months of the year, they will never be found lower than what we have mentioned.

The fertility of the soil has been amply proved by its productions. Indigo, for instance, has been found growing wild over large tracts of country, and often attains the height of a man. It has probably been introduced from India, but a species was found at Lake Nyassa equally tall, though it differs from that on the Zambesi in having straight instead of curved pods. In order to remove all doubt as to the value of the latter sort, Dr. Kirk extracted some of the colouring matter from the indigo growing wild at Shupanga, and it exhibited the peculiar coppery streak when a scratch was made on it, which is characteristic of the best article of commerce.

The cotton collected from a great many districts of the country was found to be of very superior quality. Large spaces are so much impregnated with salt that an efflorescence of it appears all over the surface. In these spaces superior cotton flourishes with very little care. We saw some men who had been employed to take canoes down to the coast, sitting on the bank, on soil like this, cleaning and spinning their cotton. When we returned twelve months afterwards, the seeds thrown away had germinated, flourished, and yielded cotton wool, which, when sent to Manchester, was pronounced to be twopence per pound better in quality than common New Orleans; and not only is the cotton produced of good quality, but it is persistent in the soil to an extent quite unknown in America. We have observed cotton-bushes yielding vigorously in parts where they had not only to struggle for existence against grass towering over their heads, but had for at least ten years to bear up against the fires which annually burnt down them and the grass together.

During Dr. Livingstone's journey from Loanda on the West Coast to Quillimane on the East Coast, no particular attention was paid to the plant, because the question of cotton supply was then but little mooted. The statements made subsequently in England embodied only the results of casual observation, but they led to an official inquiry by the Portuguese Government, and Dr. Welweitch, a botanist well qualified from his general attainments and long residence in Angola, conducted the investigation. Dr. Livingstone's impressions as to the fitness of Angola for the growth of cotton were abundantly borne out by this gentleman's report.

Our late investigations prove that the former statements as to the suitability of the climate and soil north of the 15° or 16° of south latitude were very much within the truth. In fact, the region indicated is preeminently a cotton-field; crops never running any danger of being cut off by frost. The natives have paid a good deal of attention to the cultivation of the plant, and find that the best requires renewal only once in three years.

No cotton-plants were observed in the middle of the country during Dr. Livingstone's journey across Africa, but our attention had since been so carefully directed to the subject that a single cotton-bush never escaped observation. We found that not only was the plant well known to the people of the interior, but that a variety not met with on either Coast was under cultivation inland. Thus, for instance, the Bazizulu living near the Kafue had a variety yielding cotton of very fine quality and long staple, which can only be described as of the Pernambuco kind; and at Sesheke the stem of a tree of this species had attained a diameter of eight inches, and was so tall that Dr. Kirk had to climb up it for specimens as one would up an apple-tree.

Two other varieties were found cultivated over large tracts

of country. The indigenous kind had nearly been super-
seded by a very superior sort called "foreign cotton." This
had been introduced by the natives themselves; and the district included in the Shire Valley and shores adjacent to
Lake Nyassa, in which it abounds, is about 400 miles in
length, and may confidently be stated as one of the finest
cotton-fields in the world. Cotton already cultivated there
is superior to common American, and nearly equal to Egyptian. The favourable soil and climate render it probable that
with skill in cultivation this country might be made to excel
many others.

In further illustration of the fertility of the soil, we found
that those plants which require much care in the cultivation
in other countries grow wild here as well as cotton. Tobacco,
though a delicate plant, was frequently found growing self-
sown. The *Ricinus communis*, or castor-oil plant, was met
with everywhere under similar circumstances. In some
parts indigo is known by the name of "occupier of deserted
gardens," from its habit of springing up wherever it has a
chance. Sugar-cane is not a self-planter, but it blossoms,
and when cultivated in rich loam grows, without manure, as
large as that which can only be reared by the help of guano
in the Mauritius and Bourbon; and, from crystals at once
appearing on the cut surfaces, seems to contain much sugar.

In addition to these evidences of the richness of the soil,
we have the face of the country in the lowlands covered with
gigantic grasses; they tower over men's heads, and render
hunting quite impossible. The inhabitants of Natal and of
the Cape colony will understand us perfectly, when we say
that the low belt adjacent to the East Coast, from one to
three hundred miles broad, is "*zour velt*," and well suited for
cattle. In fact, the only fault that can be found with the
soil is its over luxuriance; and though Speke and Grant mention a very fertile zone near the Equator, we cannot conceive
that it exhibits greater fecundity than the districts between

10° and 15° South, otherwise it would be perfectly impassable. On the islands in the Shire crops are raised continuously, without any regard to the season, and, by irrigation, wheat during the four colder months.   Europeans can always secure one crop of European corn and two or three of maize annually.

On the highlands the natural grasses are less luxuriant, but the average crop is as heavy as could be obtained from rich meadow-land in England.   This self-sown pasturage, which extends over hundreds of miles of grassy valley and open woodland, is the best in Africa.   This was shown by the cattle, which were left almost in a wild state, becoming so fat and lazy that bulls allowed the boys to play with them, and to jump on their backs.   We have seen cows feeding on grass alone become as heavy as prize beasts.

In general no tsetse is found on the highlands to injure cattle, nor mosquitoes to annoy man.

It would not be fair, while giving the results of our inquiries, to keep out of view one serious drawback, which we believe is characteristic of every part of Central Africa.   Periodical droughts must be expected.   If a rainy zone exists under the Equator, that is the only exception known.   These droughts are always partial, but may prevail over areas of from one to three hundred miles in extent.   Our inquiries led us to believe that from 10° to 15° South they may be looked for once in every ten or fifteen years, and from 15° to 20° South once in every five years.   What the cause of them may be, we cannot tell; but lack of vegetation cannot be assigned as any reason either for their occurrence, or greater frequency now than at any former period.   The hills are covered with trees and grass to their summits.   The valleys are often encumbered with profuse and rank vegetation—but suddenly, and without any warning, the years of plenty are succeeded by one in which there is neither earing nor harvest.   A shower has fallen on one spot a mile square; there the grass has sprung up, but has died off again.   The rest of the country

is parched and brown, the grass of the preceding year, which
may have escaped the annual fires, is discoloured and crumbles
into powder in the hand; and the leaves of the trees, though
alive, look withered.   One who had seen the landscape in
all its glorious freshness and verdure after rains, could
scarcely believe that the brown and dusty world before him
was ever green.

Though the country is well supplied with trees, really
large timber is to be obtained only in limited districts.   The
Gunda is valuable for its durability and size, and is hollowed
out into canoes capable of carrying two or three tons each.
The Mosokoso and Mukundu-kundu also are good timber trees.
The Lignum-vitæ attains a larger size here than anywhere
else.   We have measured specimens four feet in diameter;
but though the wood is in appearance exactly like the lignum-
vitæ of other countries it is said to be inferior in toughness.
Africa is more remarkable for the abundance of its hard
woods than for its timber.   African ebony, or black wood,
though not the same botanically as the ebony of commerce,
attains a large size and is of a deeper black.   It abounds on
the Rovuma, within eight miles of the sea, and so do other
valuable woods, as for instance, the Fustic, which yields a
permanent yellow dye.   The Molompi is widely distributed,
and seems to be identical with the *Pterocarpus erinaceus*,
which produces the African kino on the West Coast; for when
wounded it exudes large quantities of gum resembling this
drug.   The wood is excellent for paddles and oars, from its
toughness and lightness.   In addition to these we have the
Mopane, or iron-wood, and the Mangroves, which are much
esteemed for rafters.

A species of sarsaparilla, probably *Smilax Krausiana*, is
abundant on the highlands; Calumba-root on the plains;
the Buaze, with a fibre stronger and finer than flax, and the
fibrous Sansiviera, or ife, are both common.   The Buaze, the
Motsikiri, the Boma,—one of the Sterculias, and a species of

mahogany—all yield oil, or a kind of oleaginous matter; the oil of the Buaze has fine drying properties.

In addition to these wild products we have the Sesamum widely and extensively cultivated; from its seeds, which are now an article of export, and ground-nuts, most of the salad oil used in England is expressed. A large species of cucumber called Makaka is much cultivated by the natives, both as an article of food and for the sake of its fine oil.

We confess that we do not attempt to describe the productions of the country with that fulness they deserve, nor with that hopeful heartiness we once felt. Nor do we cite the discoveries of Lakes Shirwa and Nyassa, or the patient examination of the Zambesi to a point beyond the Victoria Falls, or other important geographical feats, with any degree of pride. These were all incidental to our main design. What we have seen of the slave-trade has thrown a gloom over all. Our notes tell of a country entirely different from most preconceived notions of Africa; and though in the cozy room, which by grace we occupy in Newstead Abbey, the eye now falls on the lawn all covered with snow, it is no difficult task to recall the bright warm glow reflected from East African ghauts. We can easily fancy the slopes furrowed by valleys lined with trees, with here and there a rocky bluff jutting out. Or we can bring back to our memory the rich upland plateaux like open prairies covered with grass, or dotted over with clumps of foliage, and watered by numerous streams, all bathed in a flood of sunlight; but that sad slave-trade hangs like a pall over the whole. The picturesque undulations, the deep gorges and ravines leading down from the edges of the table-lands to lower levels where the Shire meanders in green meadows like a silver thread, or the broad lake, backed with its mountain masses, can all be pictured to the mind's eye; but their natural beauties are now inseparably associated with human sorrow and woe.

We have been careful to mention in the text the different ways in which the slave-trade is carried on, because we believe that, though this odious traffic baffled many of our efforts to ameliorate the condition of the natives, our Expedition is the first that ever saw slavery at its fountain-head, and in all its phases. The assertion has been risked, because no one was in a condition to deny it, that the slave-trade was like any other branch of commerce, subject to the law of supply and demand, and that therefore it ought to be free. From what we have seen, it involves so much of murder in it, as an essential element, that it can scarcely be allowed to remain in the catalogue of commerce, any more than garotting, thuggee, or piracy.

We have the system nearest to that of justice, indeed the only one that approaches it, when the criminal is sold for his crimes. Then, on the plea of witchcraft, the child taken from the poorer classes of parents as a fine, or to pay a debt, and sold to a travelling native slave-trader. Then children kidnapped by a single robber, or by a gang going from their own village to neighbouring hamlets, to steal the children who are out drawing water or gathering wood. We have seen places where every house was a stockade, and yet the people were not safe. Next comes the system of retaliation of one hamlet against another to make reprisals, and the same thing on a larger scale between tribes; the portion of the tribe which flees becomes vagrant, and eventually armed with muskets, the produce of previous slaving, attacks peaceful tribes, and depopulates the country for the supply of the ocean slave-trade. Again, we have the slave-traders from the Coast, who may be either Arabs or half-caste Portuguese. For them slaves are collected, by the natives who possess most of a commercial turn, along the most frequented routes. In this branch the Ajawa and Babisa are conspicuous. The lowering effects of this trade in man are quite apparent even in the natives. The Ajawa and Babisa, though

superior in intellect to many others, are so thoroughly degraded morally, that they have been known to sell, for a
tusk that took their fancy, their own daughters or newly-
married wives.   The members of the same tribes who are
settled, and have never engaged in slaving, would be shocked
at the bare mention of such enormities.

And lastly, we have still another and more ample source of
supply for the ocean slave-trade, and we regret to say the
means for its success are drawn directly from Europeans.
Trading parties are sent out from Portuguese and Arab coast
towns with large quantities of muskets, ammunition, cloth,
and beads.   The two last articles are used for paying their
way during the earlier part of the journey from the Coast,
and for the purchase of ivory.   From a great number of cases
we have examined, these slaving-parties seem to preserve the
mercantile character for a large portion of the trip.   They
usually settle down with some Chieftain and cultivate the
soil ; but we know of no instance in which they have not, at
one part of their journey, joined one tribe in attacking another
for the sake of the captives they could take.   This is so frequent an occurrence, that the system causes a frightful loss of
life.   The bow cannot stand for a moment against the musket.
Flight, starvation, and death ensue ; and we must again record
our conviction that the mortality after these slave wars, in
addition to the losses on the journey to the Coast and during
the middle passage, makes it certain that not more than one
in five ever reach the " kind masters " in Cuba and elsewhere,
whom, according to slave-owners' interpretation of Scripture,
Providence intended for them.

The Portuguese at Tette followed the last of these systems.
The waste of life we witnessed is beyond description.   As
members of the medical profession our eyes were familiar
with scenes truly sad enough, but this misery by the slave-
trade fairly outstrips all we ever saw.   Part of the captives
realized were sent up the Zambesi above Tette to be sold for

ferry—a woman fetched two arrobas, or sixty pounds weight.
A large portion of the males were sent to Bourbon. We
were witnesses of both these modes of disposing of the captives, as well as of the results following their capture. We
again allude to this nauseating subject, because it is of importance to observe that all this waste of life happened under
the direction of an enlightened and far-reaching intelligence.
His Majesty, Napoleon III., meant to supply the lack of labour
in Bourbon by engaging free emigrants from Africa. A Government Officer was appointed over every vessel, and he was to
see that the engagements with the natives were just and fair;
that no overcrowding took place, and that proper food was
supplied in sufficient quantity. With all the Emperor's care,
his policy actually produced the effects which we witnessed.
It became the accursed slave-trade in an aggravated form,
and with a powerful, energetic Government to back it. All
honour to the Emperor for freeing his people from the calamity
of being engaged in slaving; and to our Government for
patiently pointing out the evils of which he was unconsciously
guilty, and, at considerable sacrifice, enabling a supply of
labour to be exported from India. That there may be no
mistake in supposing that we have been misled in ascribing
the sad effects we have faintly described to the enlightened
and careful "French engagé system," we will mention one of
the proofs. When we were at Johanna, a "free emigrant,"
who had been bought at Kilwa for twenty-two dollars, swam
on board the Pioneer from a vessel long known at the Cape
as the Mazurka, but then belonging to a French owner, and
under the supervision of the French Government Officer.
This emigrant had slipped overboard from the Mazurka at
early dawn, when she was getting under way; and we found
that he was a Manganja, and had actually come from Banda.
We saw also the Manganja "free emigrants" going down in
canoe-loads *chained*. The Commandant of Tette remarked,
with a grin, "You can't interfere with us now that we have

the French flag to support us." We thought that there were thousands in France who would have kicked him for his compliment to the tricolor.

The result of our observation of the actual working of the slave-trade at its source is, that it must prove an insurmountable barrier to all moral and commercial progress. The different English statesmen, who have laboured for its suppression, have shown profound wisdom and great political foresight. Instead of viewing our leading politicians as eager only for place and power, the efforts of Liberals and Conservatives in this one direction would tend to prove them, in the widest sense, promoters of peace and good-will among men. The truth of this will become more evident, if we reflect on the ultimate effects of the traffic. It perpetuates barbarism in the country from which the slaves are drawn, and it has a most injurious influence on the land to which they are taken. The introduction of African labourers to compete with Europeans renders labour unpopular among the latter, and throws an obstacle in the way of the progress of society; because nothing tends more to elevate a people than that the best minds should be bent to, and delight in, labour dignified by being undertaken for the general improvement.

We would speak tenderly of the terrible revolution now going on in America, which is so destructive to life and property; for we deeply deplore the sufferings of our brethren—the sad effects of slavery. The war is entirely due to the presence in one section of that great country of a slave population, whose number does not form more than one-sixth part of the entire American community. The introduction of an inferior race from a barbarous country was a great mistake. To degrade and deny that race the rights of manhood, a still greater blunder; for the debasement was sure to react on the master and on his children. In fact, the degradation of the slave must not only demoralize the master, but probably the master is the

2 Q 2

greater loser of the two. Then the presence of millions of a degraded race makes amalgamation or transportation impossible; there they must remain; if they cannot be elevated, they must prove a down-drag, a moral millstone on the neck, an evil beyond remedy; a severe retribution on the descendants of those who were goaded on by our own forefathers in the slave-trade. But we do not believe in any incapacity of the African in either mind or heart; and our American brethren deserve our warmest sympathy in the gigantic task before them. From the evils connected with the slave-trade our statesmen have nobly striven to rescue and defend us; and no reasonable expense, that preserves us from contamination, should be esteemed a sacrifice: if we escape, it is not because, as a nation, we are innocent.

In reference to the status of the Africans among the nations of the earth, we have seen nothing to justify the notion that they are of a different " breed " or " species " from the most civilized. The African is a man with every attribute of human kind. Centuries of barbarism have had the same deteriorating effects on Africans, as Pritchard describes them to have had on certain of the Irish who were driven, some generations back, to the hills in Ulster and Connaught. And these depressing influences have had such moral and physical effects on some tribes, that ages probably will be required to undo what ages have done. This degradation, however, would hardly be given as a reason for holding any race in bondage, unless the advocate had sunk morally to the same low state. Apart from the frightful loss of life in the process by which, it is pretended, the negroes are better provided for than in a state of liberty in their own country, it is this very system that perpetuates, if not causes, the unhappy condition with which the comparative comfort of some of them in slavery is contrasted.

Ethnologists reckon the African as by no means the lowest of the human family. He is nearly as strong physically as the European, and, as a race, is wonderfully persistent among the nations of the earth.   Neither the diseases nor the ardent spirits which proved so fatal to North American Indians, South Sea Islanders, and Australians, seem capable of annihilating the negroes.   Even when subjected to that system so destructive to human life, by which they are torn from their native soil, they spring up irrepressibly and darken half the new continent.   They are gifted by nature with physical strength capable of withstanding the sorest privations, and a lightheartedness which, as a sort of compensation, enables them to make the best of the worst situations.   It is like that power which the human frame possesses of withstanding heat, and to an extent which we should never have known, had not an adventurous surgeon gone into an oven and burnt his fingers with his own watch.   The Africans have wonderfully borne up under unnatural conditions, that would have proved fatal to most races.

It is remarkable that the power of resistance under calamity, or, as some would say, adaptation for a life of servitude, is peculiar only to certain tribes on the Continent of Africa.   Climate cannot be made to account for the fact that many would pine in a state of slavery, or voluntarily perish.   No Krooman can be converted into a slave, and yet he is an inhabitant of the low, unhealthy West Coast.   Nor can any of the Zulu or Kaffir tribes be reduced to bondage, though all these live on comparatively elevated regions.   We have heard it stated by men familiar with some of the Kaffirs, that a blow, given even in play by a European, must be returned.   A love of liberty is observable in all who have the Zulu blood, as the Makololo, the Watuta, and probably the Masai.   But blood does not explain the fact.   A beautiful Barotse woman at Naliele, on refusing to marry a man whom she did not like, was in a pet given by the headman to some Mambari slave-traders from Benguela.   Seeing her fate, she seized one of their spears, and, stabbing herself, fell down dead.

The African form of government is patriarchal, and, according to the temperament of the Chief, despotic, or guided
by the counsel of the elders of the tribe.   Reverence for
royalty sometimes leads the mass of the people to submit to
great cruelty, and even murder, at the hands of a despot or
madman; but on the whole the rule is mild, and the same
remark applies in a degree to their religion.   The races
of this Continent seem to have advanced to a certain point
and no further; their progress in the arts of working iron and
copper, in pottery, basket-making, spinning, weaving, making
nets, fish-hooks, spears, axes, knives, needles, and other
things, whether originally invented by this people or communicated by another instructor, appears to have remained
in the same rude state for a great number of centuries.   This
apparent stagnation of mind in certain nations we cannot
understand; but, since we have in the later ages of the world
made what we consider great progress in the arts, we have
unconsciously got into the way of speaking of some other
races in much the same tone as that used by the Celestials in
the Flowery Land.   These same Chinese anticipated us in
several most important discoveries by as many centuries as we
may have preceded others.   In the knowledge of the properties of the magnet, the composition of gunpowder, the
invention of printing, the manufacture of porcelain, of silk,
and in the progress of literature, they were before us.   But
then the power of making further discoveries was arrested,
and a stagnation of the intellect prevented their advancing
in the path of improvement or invention.

To the Asiatics we owe cotton, sugar, clepsydras, and sun-
dials.   From the East we have derived algebra, the game of
chess, coffee, tea, alcohol, and steel.   The servile imitation,
which took the place of mental activity and invention, seems
to have fallen on Chinese, Japanese, Asiatics, Arabians, and
Africans alike.   Does this paralysis of the inventive faculties
indicate that each race is destined to perform its own part in

the one vast plan of creative Providence, of which our finite
minds can take in only so minute a portion that we shall never
comprehend it as a whole till the end of all things? In our
smaller sphere we can see many instances of unconscious co-
operation. Archbishop Whately points out the example of the
city of London, "a province covered with houses," supplied
with food with a certainty, completeness, and regularity to
which probably the most diligent benevolence, under the
guidance of the greatest human wisdom, could never have
attained. All the agency in this case is made up of men who
each thinks of nothing beyond his own immediate interest, and
yet they all unconsciously co-operate in carrying on a system,
which no human wisdom could have conducted so well. If
perfect adaptation of means to ends indicates wisdom and
design, we have in this instance both in full play; for each
man, acting by motives addressed to his own free will, advances
as regularly and passively to an object, which the co-operators
as a whole never contemplated, as if he were one of the
wheels of a machine. The proofs of man in society being
guided by wisdom not his own, and to beneficial results he
never intended, are abundant wherever the human race is so
far advanced as to live under a form of government however
rude; and indicate a plan of Providence which will at last be
clear to all, as one of consummate wisdom.

The stagnation of mind in certain nations which have
preceded us in the line of discovery may also have been
intended, in order that the greatest power derivable from
science and art might be associated with the religion which
proclaims peace and good will to man. Had the power
given by inventions to the nations of Christendom been
awarded in the natural course of things to the men who were
first in the race, we see no earthly reason why the Buddhists
and Mohammedans should not now have lorded it over us
poor islanders with steamers, and all the improvements in
artillery, or that the Lancashire witches and Edinburgh

"bonny lasses" should not now have been exported regularly to the harems of the East.*

We have been so often asked whether the Africans were capable of embracing the Christian religion, that we venture to make the following observations, although our doing so may appear to be a work of supererogation to all who have witnessed the effects already produced in West and South Africa by teaching supplied entirely by private benevolence, or who have watched the Missionary movements of various Christian Churches during the last quarter of a century. The question seems to imply a belief on the part of those who put it, that the reception of the Gospel involves a high development and exercise of the reasoning powers. Some men, indeed, are constitutionally prone to reason out every subject as far as their intellects can lead them; but those who are led through life by pure reason constitute a very small minority of any race. To quote from one of Sir James Stephen's excellent Historical Essays :—"The Apostles assume in all men the existence of a *spiritual discernment,* enabling the mind, when unclouded by

---

* The peculiar convexity of face, and enormous size of ears, which mark the African species of elephant, are so clearly defined in an Egyptian sarcophagus in the British Museum, of the 26th Dynasty, some 500 years before our era, as to render it probable that the sculptor saw the animal alive ; and it is more likely that it was a tame one than that the sculptor was a traveller, or that a wild elephant was driven down to Egypt. The elephants used by the Romans and Carthaginians were certainly African ; and in a treaty, pointed out by Mr. R. S. Poole, the Romans bound down the Carthaginians *not to tame any more elephants.* "Perfugas, fugitivosque, et captivos omnes redderent Romanis, et naves rostratas, præter decem triremes, traderent : elephantasque, quos haberent domitos, neque domarent alios."—Livy xxx. 37. This indicates the close of one branch of African industry. The Egyptian monuments show that other wild animals also were tamed; but the stagnation of intellect common to the later Egyptians and other tribes on that and the Indian Continent, seems to have taken place at very remote periods. In speaking of the African race, the reader will observe that we do not, as those do who know little of the great interior, take the negro inhabiting the minute fringe by the low West Coast as typical of the whole family.

appetite or passion, to recognise and distinguish the Divine voice, whether uttered from within by the intimations of conscience, or speaking from without in the language of the inspired oracles; they presuppose that vigour of reason may consist with feebleness of understanding; and that the power of discriminating between religious truth and error does not chiefly depend on the culture or on the exercise of the merely argumentative faculty.   The Gospel, the especial patrimony of the poor and the illiterate, has been the stay of millions who never framed a syllogism.   Of the great multitudes who, before and since the birth of Grotius, have lived in the peace and died in the consolations of our faith, how incomparably few are they whose convictions have been derived from argumentative works like his!"

We prefer to use the words of this able writer rather than our own, to express the belief that our divine religion suits the lowest as well as the highest of our race.   But in dealing with the different classes of the human family the teaching must be adapted to the individual circumstances. The stately ceremonial, the ritual observances, the sedative sermon, and the austere look of those who think it right to indulge in a little spiritual pride, may suit some minds; but the degraded of our race in every land must be treated in somewhat the same manner as is adopted in dealing with the outcasts of London.   Whether we approach the downtrodden victims of the slave-trade in sultry Africa, or our poor brethren in the streets, who have neither warmth, shelter, nor home, we must employ the same agency to secure their confidence,—the magic power of kindness—a charm which may be said to be one of the discoveries of modern days.   This charm may not act at once, nor may its effects always be permanent; the first feeling of the wretched, of whatever colour, may be that of distrust; or a suspicion that kindness is a proof of weakness; but the feelings which the severity of their lot has withered will in time spring up like the tender grass after rain. It was the fruit of Bishop Mackenzie's grappling in the true missionary spirit with the gigantic evil of the country, and affording a home and shelter to the oppressed, that gave him so soon the confidence of the people. In every case the means of amelioration must be adapted to the special circumstances of the people. Charity must adopt every effort that charity can devise to rouse the slothful, civilize the brutal, instruct the ignorant, and preach the Gospel of love and mercy to all.

With respect to the results already obtained by the labours of Missionaries, we have been led to the discovery of some very curious and unexpected facts. Having visited Sierra Leone and some other parts of the West Coast, as well as a great part of South Africa, we were very much gratified by the evidences of success which came under our own personal observation. The crowds of well-dressed, devout, and intelligent-looking worshippers, in both the West and South, formed a wonderful contrast to the same people still in their heathen state. At Sierra Leone, Kuruman, and other places, the Sunday, for instance, seemed as well observed as it is anywhere in Scotland. The sight produced an indelible impression on the mind, that England had done an amount of good by her philanthropy that will be recognised and appreciated by posterity. Had we not previously been intimately acquainted by long personal intercourse with the people at Kuruman, who have enjoyed nearly half a century of Mr. Moffat's missionary labours, and had we not known the state of mind of the stock from which all his converts had been drawn, we might have been misled, and have given a lower value to the appearances presented than they deserved. But we have had ample opportunities of forming an estimate of the amount of real Christianity among professing converts; and we are satisfied from observation and inquiry that the assertion of Captain Burton that Mohammedans alone make proselytes in Africa is not correct; and we believe that in making it he rather intended to shock the prejudices of those whom he thought weak-minded than to state a fact. The quotation of this statement in an English periodical led us to make a few inquiries, the results of which we give with satisfaction, because wherever Christianity spreads it makes men better.

By the Government census of 1861 the population of Sierra Leone was 41,000 souls. Of the entire population 27,000 were Christians. The Mohammedans numbered altogether 1734 souls, which does not seem a very large proportion for the sect which "alone makes proselytes." In 1854 the 12,000 Christians in the Colony belonging to the Church of England took the entire cost of the schools, £800 per annum, upon themselves. We are not aware at what stage of the growth of the native churches on the West Coast the wish to support and spread the religion they had received became apparent; but in 1861 the contributions to the Church Missionary Society for this purpose among these African Christians had amounted to £10,000. These facts show pretty conclusively that they have an earnest desire to communicate the blessings they have received to their children and to others.

No attempt has been made to collect information from all the African Missions, but from the replies of unimpeachable witnesses it appears that the contributions from negroes in the West Indies, and in West and South Africa, for the support and spread of the Christian Faith, amount to upwards of £15,000 annually. We therefore repeat, that while in exceptional cases Mohammedans have propagated their religion, and at the same time gratified their lust of plunder or selfishness, the rule is, that native Christians make sacrifices of their property to spread Christianity, though always instructed that they never thereby purchase their own salvation.

Having failed to find the grounds on which the spread of Mohammedanism is asserted as a fact, we cannot help associat-

ing the assertion with others made against the English anti
slave-trade policy, which, on examination on the spot, we
found to be groundless. These latter seem to have emanated
from traders on the Coast, who in their cups would have no objection to see the slave-trade revived. With all due deference
to our countrymen abroad, and in spite of the conviction that
they have a higher sense of justice than the members of some
other nations, we must confess that the low English trader is
so much of a bully, that he needs looking after; and, putting
out of the question the national duty of the strong to protect
the weak, we think that the amount of trade* already developed

---

* The Annual Trade Returns presented to Parliament show that the
declared value of British and Irish
produce and manufactures exported
to the West Coast of Africa, arranged
in periods of five years each, has been
as follows:—

EXPORTS FROM GREAT BRITAIN.

		£				£
1846–50	.. .. ..	2,773,408,	or a yearly average of			554,681
1851–55	.. .. ..	4,314,752,	„	„	•	862,950
1856–60	.. .. ..	5,582,941,	„	„		1,116,588
1861–63	.. .. ..	4,216,045,	„	„		1,405,348

IMPORTS.

The same Trade Returns show that
the imports of African produce from
the West Coast into Great Britain have
been as follows. The "official value"
is given before 1856, after that date
the "computed real value" is given:—

		£		£
Official value	1851–55	4,154,725;	average	830,945
Computed real value { 1856–60		9,376,251;	„	1,875,250
1861–63		5,284,611;	„	1,761,537

The value of African produce has
decreased during the last three years
in consequence of the discovery of the
petroleum or rock-oil in America. In
1864 between 4000 and 5000 bales of
cotton were shipped to England.

It is to be borne in mind that under
the system which existed when Sierra
Leone, the Gambia, and Gold Coast
settlements were maintained for the
promotion of the slave-trade, the lawful
commerce was only 20,000l. annually;
and that now the amount of tonnage
employed in carrying legal merchandise is greater than was ever engaged
in carrying slaves.

by Lord Palmerston's policy on the West Coast demands the continuance of that policy in unabated strictness.

The Report of Colonel Ord,—the Commissioner appointed to inquire into the condition of the British Settlements on the West Coast of Africa,—which was ordered to be printed by the House of Commons, 29th March, 1865, says: "As regards the slave-trade, it is a well established fact that it has disappeared from the neighbourhood of every spot on the West Coast which has been made a British settlement; the distance to which it has been removed depending in a great measure on the extent to which the authorities of the Settlement have been able to make their influence felt. Nor need this statement be limited to British territory, the Dutch and Danish possessions on the Gold Coast, and the Republic of Liberia, having been equally the means of banishing the traffic from their vicinity" (p. 28).

Although it is a little apart from the point to which our observations tend, and we would not willingly be thought indifferent to the loss of even a single human life, it is desirable that it should be more widely known than it is, that the employment of our squadron does not now involve the mortality that it once did. The men are not so much employed in the rivers as formerly; condensed water has been brought into common use, and the treatment of fever is better understood. In our own experience, instead of bleeding, as was the practice, we found an aperient combined with quinine so efficacious, that an attack of fever was generally not much worse than a common cold, and no strength was lost by the patient. Somewhat similar treatment has reduced the rate of mortality in H. M. Ships on the Coast of Africa lower than on the West Indies and North American Station.*

---

* The following table shows the ratio per 1000 of mean force, at the different Stations, of men daily sick from all diseases and injuries, of invalidings, and of deaths :—

STATIONS.

We certainly never met with any benevolent person who lavished all his charity abroad, and refused to extend a kind and helping hand to the children of sin and sorrow at home. Indeed we consider his existence to be a mere figment in the brain of croakers, whose own benevolence shines nowhere. So we anticipate no objection from those who are most alive to the pressing wants of the home population to our quoting with pride the Missionary Societies which are at work on the West Coast of Africa. The societies are sixteen in number. Of these six are British, seven American, two German, and one West Indian. These societies maintain 104 European or American Missionaries, have 110 stations, 13,000 scholars in 236 schools, and 19,000 registered communicants, a number which probably represents a Christian population of 60,000.

It is particularly pleasing to see the zeal of our American brethren; they show the natural influences and effects of our Holy Religion. With the genuine and true-hearted it is never a question of distance, but of need. The Americans

STATIONS.	Ratio per 1000 of men sick daily.	Ratio per 1000 of invalidings.	Ratio per 1000 of deaths.
Home	48·1	31·2	9·6
Mediterranean	61·8	45·4	10·4
North America and West Indies	60·4	36·2	42·1
Brazils	43·4	27·7	16·1
Pacific	58·9	36·2	7·9
West Coast of Africa	62·0	38·0	34·1
Cape of Good Hope	76·7	31·3	18·1
East Indies and China	86·7	61·6	26·1
Australia	40·0	28·4	13·7
Irregular Force	77·4	26·5	10 4

"No detailed information has been obtained respecting the loss by death of the civil servants of the Government on the West Coast; but it may be stated that the loss of life from climate amongst this class is by no means large. The facility with which officers of all the Services who suffer to any dangerous extent from disease are permitted to return home on sick leave, must operate to diminish considerably the number of fatal cases." — *Report of Colonel Ord,* p. 30.

make capital Missionaries; and it is only a bare act of justice
to say that their labours and success on the West Coast are
above all praise.   And not on that shore alone does their
benevolence shine.   In India, China, South Seas, Syria,
South Africa, and their own far West, they have proved
themselves worthy children of the old country—the asylum
for the oppressed of every nation—the source of light for all
lands.

Now that we have given but a faint outline of what has
been done on the West Coast, we ask with what face can the
Portuguese shut some 900 miles of the East Coast from these
civilizing and humanizing influences.   Looking at the lawful
trade which has been developed in one section of Africa, is
it to be endured by the rest of the world that most of a
continent so rich and fertile should be doomed to worse than
sterility till the Spaniards and Portuguese learn to abandon
their murderous traffic in man?   When these effete nations
speak of their famous ancestors they tacitly admit that the
same sort of mental stagnation has fallen on themselves as
on the Africans and others; the United States would confer
a blessing on Spain and tear away much of the veil that
blinds her, by annexing Cuba; and England would perform
a noble service to Portugal by ignoring those pretences to
dominion on the East Coast, by which, for the sake of mere
swagger in Europe, she secures for herself the worst name in
Christendom.   As we have mentioned, the more enlightened
Lisbon statesmen would fain effect by an English mercantile
company what has been accomplished elsewhere by English
philanthropy, protected by English cruisers.   Here, on the
East Coast, not a single native has been taught to read, not
one branch of trade has been developed, and wherever Portuguese power, or rather intrigue, extends, we have that traffic
in full force which may be said to reverse every law of Christ,
and to defy the vengeance of Heaven.

All the efforts of England for its permanent suppression

used only for convicts, why should not the English send theirs thither too? It does not belong to the Portuguese any more than China belongs to them because they possess Macao. Bad as our convicts are, they would be an improvement on those already sent. Neither officers nor men would deal in slaves. The climate certainly mollifies and subdues the passions. This we observed at Loando, where every night the whole of the arms of the city are in the hands of men who have once been convicts. The subject deserves consideration, in the present difficulty of disposing of our convict population.

In the able Report of Colonel Ord it is stated, that while the presence of the squadron has had some share in suppressing the slave-trade, the result is mainly due to the existence of the Settlements. This is supported by the fact that, even in those least visited by men-of-war, it has been as effectually suppressed as in those which have been their most constant resort. We have continually had the conviction in our minds that an expedition or settlement inland would produce greater results than men-of-war on the ocean, and be upheld with half the expense of one of Her Majesty's cruisers.

THE END.

ALBEMARLE STREET, LONDON,
January, 1865.

MR. MURRAY'S

GENERAL LIST OF WORKS.

ALBERT (PRINCE). THE SPEECHES AND ADDRESSES
on Public Occasions of H.R.H. THE PRINCE CONSORT; with an
Introduction giving some Outlines of his Character. Portrait. 8vo.
10s. 6d.; or Popular Edition, fcap. 8vo, 1s.

ABBOTT'S (REV. J.) Philip Musgrave; or, Memoirs of a Church of
England Missionary in the North American Colonies. Post 8vo. 2s.

ABERCROMBIE'S (JOHN) Enquiries concerning the Intellectual
Powers and the Investigation of Truth. 16th Edition. Fcap. 8vo. 6s. 6d.

———————————— Philosophy of the Moral Feelings. 12th Edition.
Fcap. 8vo. 4s.

ACLAND'S (REV. CHARLES) Popular Account of the Manners and
Customs of India. Post 8vo. 2s.

ÆSOP'S FABLES. A New Translation. With Historical
Preface. By Rev. THOMAS JAMES. With 100 Woodcuts, by TENNIEL
and WOLF. 50th Thousand. Post 8vo. 2s. 6d.

AGRICULTURAL (THE) JOURNAL. Of the Royal Agricultural
Society of England. 8vo. Published half-yearly.

AIDS TO FAITH: a Series of Essays. By various Writers. Edited
by WILLIAM THOMSON, D.D., Lord Archbishop of York. 8vo. 9s.

CONTENTS.

Rev. H. L. MANSEL—Miracles.
BISHOP OF KILLALOE—Christian Evi-
dences.
Rev. DR. MCCAUL—Prophecy and the
Mosaic Record of Creation.
Rev. CANON COOK — Ideology and
Subscription.

Rev. GEORGE RAWLINSON—The Pen-
tateuch.
ARCHBISHOP OF YORK—Doctrine of
the Atonement.
BISHOP OF ELY.—Inspiration.
BISHOP OF GLOUCESTER AND BRIS-
TOL.—Scripture and its Interpre-
tation.

AMBER-WITCH (THE). The most interesting Trial for Witchcraft ever known. Translated from the German by LADY DUFF
GORDON. Post 8vo. 2s.

ARMY LIST (THE). Published Monthly by Authority. 18mo. 1s. 6d.

ARTHUR'S (LITTLE) History of England. By LADY CALLCOTT.
130th Thousand. Woodcuts. Fcap. 8vo. 2s. 6d.

ATKINSON'S (MRS.) Recollections of Tartar Steppes and their
Inhabitants. Illustrations. Post 8vo. 12s.

AUNT IDA'S Walks and Talks; a Story Book for Children. By
a LADY. Woodcuts. 16mo. 5s.

AUSTIN'S (JOHN) LECTURES ON JURISPRUDENCE; or, the Philosophy
of Positive Law. 3 Vols. 8vo. 39s.

———————— (SARAH) Fragments from German Prose Writers.
With Biographical Notes. Post 8vo. 10s.

B

ADMIRALTY PUBLICATIONS; Issued by direction of the Lords
    Commissioners of the Admiralty:—

A MANUAL OF SCIENTIFIC ENQUIRY, for the Use of Travellers.
    Edited by Sir JOHN F. HERSCHEL, and Rev. ROBERT MAIN. *Third
    Edition.* Woodcuts. Post 8vo. 9s.

AIRY'S ASTRONOMICAL OBSERVATIONS MADE AT GREENWICH.
    836 to 1847. Royal 4to. 50s. each.

————— ASTRONOMICAL RESULTS. 1848 to 1858. 4to. 8s. each.

————— APPENDICES TO THE ASTRONOMICAL OBSERVA-
    TIONS.

> 1836.—I. Bessel's Refraction Tables.
>   II. Tables for converting Errors of R.A. and N.P.D. }8s.
>   into Errors of Longitude and Ecliptic P.D.
> 1837.—I. Logarithms of Sines and Cosines to every Ten }
>   Seconds of Time.   }8s.
>   II. Table for converting Sidereal into Mean Solar Time. }
> 1842.—Catalogue of 1439 Stars. 8s.
> 1845.—Longitude of Valentia. 8s.
> 1847.—Twelve Years' Catalogue of Stars. 14s.
> 1851.—Maskelyne's Ledger of Stars. 6s.
> 1852.—I. Description of the Transit Circle. 5s.
>   II. Regulations of the Royal Observatory. 2s.
> 1853.—Bessel's Refraction Tables. 3s.
> 1854.—I. Description of the Zenith Tube. 3s.
>   II. Six Years' Catalogue of Stars. 10s.
> 1856.—Description of the Galvanic Apparatus at Greenwich Ob-
>   servatory. 8s.

————— MAGNETICAL AND METEOROLOGICAL OBSERVA-
    TIONS. 1840 to 1847. Royal 4to. 50s. each.

————— ASTRONOMICAL, MAGNETICAL, AND METEOROLO-
    GICAL OBSERVATIONS, 1848 to 1862. Royal 4to. 50s. each.

————— ASTRONOMICAL RESULTS. 1848 to 1862. 4to.

————— MAGNETICAL AND METEOROLOGICAL RESULTS.
    1848 to 1862. 4to. 8s. each.

————— REDUCTION OF THE OBSERVATIONS OF PLANETS.
    1750 to 1830. Royal 4to. 50s.

——————————————————— LUNAR OBSERVATIONS. 1750
    to 1830. 2 Vols. Royal 4to. 50s. each.

———————————— 1831 to 1851. 4to. 20s.

BERNOULLI'S SEXCENTENARY TABLE. *London,* 1779. 4to.

BESSEL'S AUXILIARY TABLES FOR HIS METHOD OF CLEAR-
    ING LUNAR DISTANCES. 8vo.

————— FUNDAMENTA ASTRONOMIÆ: *Regiomontii,* 1818. Folio. 60s.

BIRD'S METHOD OF CONSTRUCTING MURAL QUADRANTS.
    London, 1768. 4to. 2s. 6d.

————— METHOD OF DIVIDING ASTRONOMICAL INSTRU-
    MENTS. *London,* 1767. 4to. 2s. 6d.

COOK, KING, AND BAYLY'S ASTRONOMICAL OBSERVATIONS.
    London, 1782. 4to. 21s.

ENCKE'S BERLINER JAHRBUCH, for 1830. *Berlin,* 1828. 8vo. 9s.

GROOMBRIDGE'S CATALOGUE OF CIRCUMPOLAR STARS.
    4to. 10s.

HANSEN'S TABLES DE LA LUNE. 4to. 20s.

HARRISON'S PRINCIPLES OF HIS TIME-KEEPER. PLATES
    1797. 4to. 5s.

ADMIRALTY PUBLICATIONS—*continued.*

HUTTON'S TABLES OF THE PRODUCTS AND POWERS OF NUMBERS. 1781. Folio. 7s. 6d.

LAX'S TABLES FOR FINDING THE LATITUDE AND LONGI-TUDE. 1821. 8vo. 10s.

LUNAR OBSERVATIONS at GREENWICH. 1783 to 1819. Compared with the Tables, 1821. 4to. 7s. 6d.

MASKELYNE'S ACCOUNT OF THE GOING OF HARRISON'S WATCH. 1767. 4to. 2s. 6d.

MAYER'S DISTANCES of the MOON'S CENTRE from the PLANETS. 1822, 3s.; 1823, 4s. 6d. 1824 to 1835, 8vo. 4s. each.

———— THEORIA LUNÆ JUXTA SYSTEMA NEWTONIANUM. 4to. 2s. 6d.

———— TABULÆ MOTUUM SOLIS ET LUNÆ. 1770. 4to. 5s.

———— ASTRONOMICAL OBSERVATIONS MADE AT GOT-TINGEN, from 1756 to 1761. 1826. Folio. 7s. 6d.

NAUTICAL ALMANACS, from 1767 to 1868. 8vo. 2s. 6d. each.

———— SELECTIONS FROM THE ADDITIONS up to 1812. 8vo. 5s. 1834-54. 8vo. 5s.

———— SUPPLEMENTS, 1828 to 1833, 1837 and 1838. 8vo. 2s. each.

———— TABLE requisite to be used with the N.A. 1781. 8vo. 5s.

POND'S ASTRONOMICAL OBSERVATIONS. 1811 to 1835. 4to. 21s. each.

RAMSDEN'S ENGINE for DIVIDING MATHEMATICAL INSTRUMENTS. 4to. 5s.

———— ENGINE for DIVIDING STRAIGHT LINES. 4to. 5s.

SABINE'S PENDULUM EXPERIMENTS to DETERMINE THE FIGURE OF THE EARTH. 1825. 4to. 40s.

SHEPHERD'S TABLES for CORRECTING LUNAR DISTANCES. 1772. Royal 4to. 21s.

———— TABLES, GENERAL, of the MOON'S DISTANCE from the SUN, and 10 STARS. 1787. Folio. 5s. 6d.

TAYLOR'S SEXAGESIMAL TABLE. 1780. 4to. 15s.

———— TABLES OF LOGARITHMS. 4to. 3l.

TIARK'S ASTRONOMICAL OBSERVATIONS for the LONGITUDE of MADEIRA. 1822. 4to. 5s.

———— CHRONOMETRICAL OBSERVATIONS for DIFFERENCES of LONGITUDE between DOVER, PORTSMOUTH, and FALMOUTH. 1823. 4to. 5s.

VENUS and JUPITER: OBSERVATIONS of, compared with the TABLES. *London*, 1822. 4to. 2s.

WALES' AND BAYLY'S ASTRONOMICAL OBSERVATIONS. 1777. 4to. 21s.

WALES' REDUCTION OF ASTRONOMICAL OBSERVATIONS MADE IN THE SOUTHERN HEMISPHERE. 1764—1771. 1788. 4to. 10s. 6d.

BABBAGE'S (CHARLES) Economy of Machinery and Manufactures. *Fourth Edition.* Fcap. 8vo. 6s.

———— Reflections on the Decline of Science in England, and on some of its Causes. 4to. 7s. 6d.

B 2

BAIKIE'S (W. B.) Narrative of an Exploring Voyage up the Rivers Quorra and Tshadda in 1854. Map. 8vo. 16s.

BANKES' (GEORGE) STORY OF CORFE CASTLE, with documents relating to the Time of the Civil Wars, &c. Woodcuts. Post 8vo. 10s. 6d.

BARBAULD'S (MRS.) Hymns in Prose for Children. With 112 Original Designs. Small 4to. 5s.

BARROW'S (SIR JOHN) Autobiographical Memoir, including Reflections, Observations, and Reminiscences at Home and Abroad. From Early Life to Advanced Age. Portrait. 8vo. 16s.

———— Voyages of Discovery and Research within the Arctic Regions, from 1818 to the present time. 8vo. 15s.

———— Life and Voyages of Sir Francis Drake. With numerous Original Letters. Post 8vo. 2s.

BATES' (H. W.) Records of a Naturalist on the River Amazons during eleven years of Adventure and Travel. *Second Edition.* Illustrations. Post 8vo. 12s.

BEES AND FLOWERS. Two Essays. By Rev. Thomas James. Reprinted from the "Quarterly Review." Fcap. 8vo. 1s. each.

BELL'S (SIR CHARLES) Mechanism and Vital Endowments of the Hand as evincing Design. *Sixth Edition.* Woodcuts. Post 8vo. 6s.

BERTHA'S Journal during a Visit to her Uncle in England. Containing a Variety of Interesting and Instructive Information. *Seventh Edition.* Woodcuts. 12mo.

BIRCH'S (SAMUEL) History of Ancient Pottery and Porcelain : Egyptian, Assyrian, Greek, Roman, and Etruscan. With 200 Illustrations. 2 Vols. Medium 8vo. 42s.

BLUNT'S (REV. J. J.) Undesigned Coincidences in the Writings of the Old and New Testament, an Argument of their Veracity : containing the Books of Moses. Historical and Prophetical Scriptures, and the Gospels and Acts. *8th Edition.* Post 8vo. 6s.

———— History of the Church in the First Three Centuries. *Third Edition.* Post 8vo. 7s. 6d.

———— Parish Priest; His Duties, Acquirements and Obligations. *Fourth Edition.* Post 8vo. 7s. 6d.

———— Lectures on the Right Use of the Early Fathers. *Second Edition.* 8vo. 15s.

———— Plain Sermons Preached to a Country Congregation. *Second Edition.* 3 Vols. Post 8vo. 7s. 6d. each.

———— Essays on various subjects. 8vo. 12s.

BISSET'S (ANDREW) History of England during the Interregnum, from the Death of Charles I. to the Battle of Dunbar, 1648—50. Chiefly from the MSS. in the State Paper Office. 8vo. 15s.

BLAKISTON'S (CAPT.) Narrative of the Expedition sent to explore the Upper Waters of the Yang-Tsze. Illustrations. 8vo. 18s.

BLOMFIELD'S (BISHOP) Memoir, with Selections from his Correspondence. By his Son. 2nd Edition. Portrait, post 8vo. 12s.

BOOK OF COMMON PRAYER. Illustrated with Coloured Borders, Initial Letters, and Woodcuts. A new edition. 8vo. 18s. cloth; 31s. 6d. calf; 36s. morocco.

BORROW'S (GEORGE) Bible in Spain; or the Journeys, Adventures, and Imprisonments of an Englishman in an Attempt to circulate the Scriptures in the Peninsula. 3 Vols. Post 8vo. 27s.; or Popular Edition, 16mo, 3s. 6d.

———————— Zincali, or the Gipsies of Spain; their Manners, Customs, Religion, and Language. 2 Vols. Post 8vo. 18s.; or Popular Edition, 16mo, 3s. 6d.

———————— Lavengro; The Scholar—The Gipsy—and the Priest. Portrait. 3 Vols. Post 8vo. 30s.

———————— Romany Rye; a Sequel to Lavengro. Second Edition. 2 Vols. Post 8vo. 21s.

BOSWELL'S (JAMES) Life of Samuel Johnson, LL.D. Including the Tour to the Hebrides. Edited by Mr. CROKER. Portraits. Royal 8vo. 10s.

BRACE'S (C. L.) History of the Races of the Old World. Designed as a Manual of Ethnology. Post 8vo. 9s.

BRAY'S (MRS.) Life of Thomas Stothard, R.A. With Personal Reminiscences. Illustrated with Portrait and 60 Woodcuts of his chief works. 4to.

BREWSTER'S (SIR DAVID) Martyrs of Science, or the Lives of Galileo, Tycho Brahe, and Kepler. Fourth Edition. Fcap. 8vo. 4s. 6d.

———————— More Worlds than One. The Creed of the Philosopher and the Hope of the Christian. Eighth Edition. Post 8vo. 6s.

———————— Stereoscope: its History, Theory, Construction, and Application to the Arts and to Education. Woodcuts. 12mo. 5s. 6d.

———————— Kaleidoscope: its History, Theory, and Construction, with its application to the Fine and Useful Arts. Second Edition. Woodcuts. Post 8vo. 5s. 6d.

BRINE'S (Capt.) Narrative of the Rise and Progress of the Taeping Rebellion in China. Plans. Post 8vo. 10s. 6d.

BRITISH ASSOCIATION REPORTS. 8vo. York and Oxford, 1831-32, 13s. 6d. Cambridge, 1833, 12s. Edinburgh, 1834, 15s. Dublin, 1835, 13s. 6d. Bristol, 1836, 12s. Liverpool, 1837, 16s. 6d. Newcastle, 1838, 15s. Birmingham, 1839, 13s. 6d. Glasgow, 1840, 15s. Plymouth, 1841, 13s. 6d. Manchester, 1842, 10s. 6d. Cork, 1843, 12s. York, 1844, 20s. Cambridge, 1845, 12s. Southampton, 1846, 15s. Oxford, 1847, 18s. Swansea, 1848, 9s. Birmingham, 1849, 10s. Edinburgh, 1850, 15s. Ipswich, 1851. 16s. Belfast, 1852, 15s. Hull, 1853, 10s. 6d. Liverpool, 1854, 18s. Glasgow, 1855, 15s.; Cheltenham, 1856, 18s.; Dublin, 1857, 15s.; Leeds, 1858, 20s. Aberdeen, 1859, 15s. Oxford, 1860, 25s. Manchester, 1861, 15s. Cambridge, 1862, 20s. Newcastle, 1863.

BRITISH CLASSICS. A New Series of Standard English Authors, printed from the most correct text, and edited with notes. 8vo.

Already Published.

I. GOLDSMITH'S WORKS. Edited by PETER CUNNINGHAM, F.S.A. Vignettes. 4 Vols. 30s.

II. GIBBON'S DECLINE AND FALL OF THE ROMAN EMPIRE. Edited by WILLIAM SMITH, LL.D Portrait and Maps. 8 Vols. 60s.

III. JOHNSON'S LIVES OF THE ENGLISH POETS. Edited by PETER CUNNINGHAM, F.S.A. 3 Vols. 22s. 6d.

IV. BYRON'S POETICAL WORKS. Edited, with Notes. 6 vols. 45s.

In Preparation.

WORKS OF POPE. With Life, Introductions, and Notes, by REV. WHITWELL ELWIN. Portrait.

HUME'S HISTORY OF ENGLAND. Edited, with Notes.

LIFE AND WORKS OF SWIFT. Edited by JOHN FORSTER.

BROUGHTON'S (LORD) Journey through Albania and other Provinces of Turkey in Europe and Asia, to Constantinople, 1809—10. *Third Edition.* Illustrations. 2 Vols. 8vo. 30s.

———————— Visits to Italy. *3rd Edition.* 2 vols. Post 8vo. 18s.

BUBBLES FROM THE BRUNNEN OF NASSAU. By an Old MAN. *Sixth Edition.* 16mo. 5s.

BUNYAN (JOHN) and Oliver Cromwell. Select Biographies. By ROBERT SOUTHEY. Post 8vo. 2s.

BUONAPARTE'S (NAPOLEON) Confidential Correspondence with his Brother Joseph, sometime King of Spain. *Second Edition.* 2 vols. 8vo. 26s.

BURGON'S (Rev. J. W.) Memoir of Patrick Fraser Tytler. *Second Edition.* Post 8vo. 9s.

———————— Letters from Rome, written to Friends at Home. Illustrations. Post 8vo. 12s.

BURN'S (LIEUT.-COL.) French and English Dictionary of Naval and Military Technical Terms. *Fourth Edition.* Crown 8vo. 15s.

BURNS' (ROBERT) Life. By JOHN GIBSON LOCKHART. Fifth *Edition.* Fcap. 8vo. 3s.

BURR'S (G. D.) Instructions in Practical Surveying, Topographical Plan Drawing, and on sketching ground without Instruments. *Fourth Edition.* Woodcuts. Post 8vo. 6s.

BUTTMAN'S LEXILOGUS; a Critical Examination of the Meaning of numerous Greek Words, chiefly in Homer and Hesiod. Translated by Rev. J. R. FISHLAKE. *Fifth Edition.* 8vo. 12s.

BUXTON'S (SIR FOWELL) Memoirs. With Selections from his Correspondence. By his Son. Portrait. *Fifth Edition.* 8vo. 16s. *Abridged Edition,* Portrait. Fcap. 8vo. 2s. 6d.

BYRON'S (LORD) Life, Letters, and Journals. By THOMAS MOORE.
Plates. 6 Vols. Fcap. 8vo. 18s.

————— Life, Letters, and Journals. By THOMAS MOORE.
Portraits. Royal 8vo. 9s.

————— Poetical Works. Portrait. 6 Vols. 8vo. 45s.

————— Poetical Works. Plates. 10 Vols. Fcap. 8vo. 30s.

————— Poetical Works. 8 Vols. 24mo. 20s.

————— Poetical Works. Plates. Royal 8vo. 9s.

————— Poetical Works. Portrait. Crown 8vo. 6s.

————— Childe Harold. With 80 Engravings. Small 4to. 21s.

————— Childe Harold. With 30 Vignettes. 12mo. 6s.

————— Childe Harold. 16mo. 2s. 6d.

————— Childe Harold. Vignettes. 16mo. 1s.

————— Childe Harold. Portrait. 16mo. 6d.

————— Tales and Poems. 24mo. 2s. 6d.

————— Miscellaneous. 2 Vols. 24mo. 5s.

————— Dramas and Plays. 2 Vols. 24mo. 5s.

————— Don Juan and Beppo. 2 Vols. 24mo. 5s.

————— Beauties. Selected from his Poetry and Prose. Portrait.
Fcap. 8vo. 3s. 6d.

CARNARVON'S (LORD) Portugal, Gallicia, and the Basque
Provinces. From Notes made during a Journey to those Countries.
Third Edition. Post 8vo. 3s. 6d.

————— Recollections of the Druses of Lebanon. With
Notes on their Religion. *Third Edition.* Post 8vo. 5s. 6d.

CAMPBELL'S (LORD) Lives of the Lord Chancellors and Keepers
of the Great Seal of England. From the Earliest Times to the Death of
Lord Eldon in 1838. *Fourth Edition.* 10 Vols. Crown 8vo. 6s. each.

————— Lives of the Chief Justices of England. From the
Norman Conquest to the Death of Lord Tenterden. *Second Edition.*
3 Vols. 8vo. 42s.

————— Shakspeare's Legal Acquirements Considered.
8vo. 5s. 6d.

————— Life of Lord Chancellor Bacon. Fcap. 8vo. 2s. 6d.

————— (GEORGE) Modern India. A Sketch of the System
of Civil Government. With some Account of the Natives and Native
Institutions. *Second Edition.* 8vo. 16s.

————— India as it may be. An Outline of a proposed
Government and Policy. 8vo. 12s.

————— (THOS.) Short Lives of the British Poets. With an
Essay on English Poetry. Post 8vo. 3s. 6d.

CALLCOTT'S (LADY) Little Arthur's History of England.
130th *Thousand.* With 20 Woodcuts. Fcap. 8vo. 2s. 6d.

CASTLEREAGH (The) DESPATCHES, from the commencement of the official career of the late Viscount Castlereagh to the close of his life. Edited by the Marquis of Londonderry. 12 Vols. 8vo. 14s. each.

CATHCART'S (Sir George) Commentaries on the War in Russia and Germany, 1812-13. Plans. 8vo. 14s.

CAVALCASELLE and CROWE'S New History of Painting in Italy, from the Second to the Sixteenth Century, from recent researches in the Archives, as well as from personal inspection of the Works of Art in that Country. With 70 Illustrations. Vols. I. and II. 8vo. 42s.

———————————— Notices of the Lives and Works of the Early Flemish Painters. Woodcuts. Post 8vo. 12s.

CHAMBERS' (G. F.) Handbook of Descriptive and Practical Astronomy. Illustrations. Post 8vo. 12s.

CHARMED ROE (The); or, The Story of the Little Brother and Sister. By Otto Speckter. Plates. 16mo. 5s.

CHURTON'S (Archdeacon) Gongora. An Historical Essay on the Age of Philip III. and IV. of Spain. With Translations. Portrait. 2 Vols. Small 8vo. 15s.

CLAUSEWITZ'S (Carl Von) Campaign of 1812, in Russia. Translated from the German by Lord Ellesmere. Map. 8vo. 10s. 6d.

CLIVE'S (Lord) Life. By Rev. G. R. Gleig, M.A. Post 8vo. 3s. 6d.

COLCHESTER (The) PAPERS. The Diary and Correspondence of Charles Abbott, Lord Colchester, Speaker of the House of Commons, 1802–1817. Edited by His Son. Portrait. 3 Vols. 8vo. 42s.

COLERIDGE'S (Samuel Taylor) Table-Talk. *Fourth Edition.* Portrait. Fcap. 8vo. 6s.

COLONIAL LIBRARY. [See Home and Colonial Library.]

COOK'S (Rev. Canon) Sermons Preached at Lincoln's Inn Chapel, and on Special Occasions. 8vo. 9s.

COOKERY (Modern Domestic). Founded on Principles of Economy and Practical Knowledge, and adapted for Private Families. By a Lady. *New Edition.* Woodcuts. Fcap. 8vo. 5s.

CORNWALLIS (The) Papers and Correspondence during the American War,—Administrations in India,—Union with Ireland, and Peace of Amiens. Edited by Charles Ross. *Second Edition.* 3 Vols. 8vo. 63s.

COWPER'S (Mary Countess) Diary while Lady of the Bedchamber to Caroline Princess of Wales, 1714–20. *Second Edition.* Portrait. 8vo. 10s. 6d.

CRABBE'S (Rev. George) Life, Letters, and Journals. By his Son. Portrait. Fcap. 8vo. 3s.

——————— Life and Poetical Works. Plates. 8 Vols. Fcap. 8vo. 24s.

——————— Life and Poetical Works. Plates. Royal 8vo. 7s.

CROKER'S (J. W.) Progressive Geography for Children. *Fifth Edition.* 18mo. 1s. 6d.

———— Stories for Children, Selected from the History of England. *Fifteenth Edition.* Woodcuts. 16mo. 2s. 6d.

———— Boswell's Life of Johnson. Including the Tour to the Hebrides. Portraits. Royal 8vo. 10s.

———— Essays on the Early Period of the French Revolution. 8vo. 15s.

———— Historical Essay on the Guillotine. Fcap. 8vo. 1s.

CROMWELL (OLIVER) and John Bunyan. By ROBERT SOUTHEY. Post 8vo. 2s.

CROWE'S AND CAVALCASELLE'S Notices of the Early Flemish Painters; their Lives and Works. Woodcuts. Post 8vo. 12s.

———— History of Painting in Italy, from 2nd to 16th Century. Derived from Historical Researches as well as inspection of the Works of Art in that Country. With 70 Illustrations. Vols. I. and II. 8vo. 42s.

CUNNINGHAM'S (ALLAN) Poems and Songs. Now first collected and arranged, with Biographical Notice. 24mo. 2s. 6d.

CURETON (REV. W.) Remains of a very Ancient Recension of the Four Gospels in Syriac, hitherto unknown in Europe. Discovered, Edited, and Translated. 4to. 24s.

CURTIUS' (PROFESSOR) Student's Greek Grammar, for the use of Colleges and the Upper Forms. Translated under the Author's revision. Edited by DR. WM. SMITH. Post 8vo. 7s. 6d.

———— Smaller Greek Grammar for the use of the Middle and Lower Forms, abridged from the above. 12mo. 3s. 6d.

———— First Greek Course; containing Delectus, Exercise Book, and Vocabularies. 12mo. 3s. 6d.

CURZON'S (HON. ROBERT) ARMENIA AND ERZEROUM. A Year on the Frontiers of Russia, Turkey, and Persia. *Third Edition.* Woodcuts. Post 8vo. 7s. 6d.

CUST'S (GENERAL) Annals of the Wars of the 18th & 19th Centuries. 9 Vols. Fcap. 8vo. 5s. each.

———— Lives and Characters of the Warriors of All Nations who have Commanded Fleets and Armies before the Enemy. 8vo.

DARWIN'S (CHARLES) Journal of Researches into the Natural History of the Countries visited during a Voyage round the World. Post 8vo. 9s.

———— Origin of Species by Means of Natural Selection; or, the Preservation of Favoured Races in the Struggle for Life. Post 8vo. 14s.

———— Fertilization of Orchids through Insect Agency, and as to the good of Intercrossing. Woodcuts. Post 8vo. 9s.

DAVIS'S (NATHAN) Visit to the Ruined Cities of Numidia and Carthaginia. Illustrations. 8vo. 16s.

DAVY'S (SIR HUMPHRY) Consolations in Travel; or, Last Days of a Philosopher. *Fifth Edition.* Woodcuts. Fcap. 8vo. 6s.

———— Salmonia; or, Days of Fly Fishing. *Fourth Edition.* Woodcuts. Fcap. 8vo. 6s.

DELEPIERRE'S (Octave) History of Flemish Literature. From the Twelfth Century. 8vo. 9s.

DENNIS' (George) Cities and Cemeteries of Etruria. Plates. 2 Vols. 8vo. 42s.

DERBY'S (Edward Earl of) Translation of the Iliad of Homer into English Blank Verse. 2 Vols. 8vo. 24s.

DIXON'S (Hepworth) Story of the Life of Lord Bacon. Portrait. Fcap. 8vo. 7s. 6d.

DOG-BREAKING; the Most Expeditious, Certain, and Easy Method, whether great excellence or only mediocrity be required. By Lieut.-Gen. Hutchinson. Fourth and Revised Edition. With additional Woodcuts. Crown 8vo.

DOMESTIC MODERN COOKERY. Founded on Principles of Economy and Practical Knowledge, and adapted for Private Families. New Edition. Woodcuts. Fcap. 8vo. 5s.

DOUGLAS'S (General Sir Howard) Life and Adventures; From Notes, Conversations, and Correspondence. By S. W. Fullom. Portrait. 8vo. 15s.

—————— On the Theory and Practice of Gunnery. 5th Edition. Plates. 8vo. 21s.

—————— Military Bridges, and the Passages of Rivers in Military Operations. Third Edition. Plates. 8vo. 21s.

—————— Naval Warfare with Steam. Second Edition. 8vo. 8s. 6d.

—————— Modern Systems of Fortification, with special reference to the Naval, Littoral, and Internal Defence of England. Plans. 8vo. 12s.

DRAKE'S (Sir Francis) Life, Voyages, and Exploits, by Sea and Land. By John Barrow. Third Edition. Post 8vo. 2s.

DRINKWATER'S (John) History of the Siege of Gibraltar, 1779-1783. With a Description and Account of that Garrison from the Earliest Periods. Post 8vo. 2s.

DU CHAILLU'S (Paul B.) EQUATORIAL AFRICA, with Accounts of the Gorilla, the Nest-building Ape, Chimpanzee, Crocodile, &c. Illustrations. 8vo. 21s.

DUFFERIN'S (Lord) Letters from High Latitudes, being some Account of a Yacht Voyage to Iceland, &c., in 1856. Fourth Edition. Woodcuts. Post 8vo. 9s.

DYER'S (Thomas H.) History of Modern Europe, from the taking of Constantinople by the Turks to the close of the War in the Crimea. 4 Vols. 8vo. 60s.

EASTLAKE'S (Sir Charles) Italian Schools of Painting. From the German of Kügler. Edited, with Notes. Third Edition. Illustrated from the Old Masters. 2 Vols. Post 8vo. 30s.

EASTWICK'S (E. B.) Handbook for Bombay and Madras, with Directions for Travellers, Officers, &c. Map. 2 Vols. Post 8vo. 24s.

EDWARDS' (W. H.) Voyage up the River Amazon, including a Visit to Para. Post 8vo. 2s.

ELDON'S (Lord) Public and Private Life, with Selections from his Correspondence and Diaries. By Horace Twiss. *Third Edition.* Portrait. 2 Vols. Post 8vo. 21*s.*

ELLIS (Rev. W.) Visits to Madagascar, including a Journey to the Capital, with notices of Natural History, and Present Civilisation of the People. *Fifth Thousand.* Map and Woodcuts. 8vo. 16*s.*

———— (Mrs.) Education of Character, with Hints on Moral Training. Post 8vo. 7*s.* 6*d.*

ELLESMERE'S (Lord) Two Sieges of Vienna by the Turks. Translated from the German. Post 8vo. 2*s.*

———————————— Campaign of 1812 in Russia, from the German of General Carl Von Clausewitz. Map. 8vo. 10*s.* 6*d.*

———————————— Poems. Crown 4to. 24*s.*

———————————— Essays on History, Biography, Geography, and Engineering. 8vo. 12*s.*

ELPHINSTONE'S (Hon. Mountstuart) History of India—the Hindoo and Mahomedan Periods. *Fourth Edition.* Map. 8vo. 18*s.*

ENGEL'S (Carl) Music of the Most Ancient Nations ; particularly of the Assyrians, Egyptians, and Hebrews; with Special Reference to the Discoveries in Western Asia and in Egypt. With 100 Illustrations. 8vo. 16*s.*

ENGLAND (History of) from the Peace of Utrecht to the Peace of Versailles, 1713—83. By Lord Mahon (Earl Stanhope). *Library Edition,* 7 Vols. 8vo. 93*s.*; or *Popular Edition,* 7 Vols. Post 8vo. 35*s.*

———————————— From the First Invasion by the Romans, down to the 14th year of Queen Victoria's Reign. By Mrs. Markham. 118*th Edition.* Woodcuts. 12mo. 6*s.*

———————————— (The Student's Hume). A History of England from the Earliest Times. Based on the History by David Hume. Corrected and continued to 1858. Edited by Wm. Smith, LL.D. Woodcuts. Post 8vo. 7*s.* 6*d.*

ENGLISHWOMAN IN AMERICA. Post 8vo. 10*s.* 6*d.*

ESKIMAUX and English Vocabulary, for Travellers in the Arctic Regions. 16mo. 3*s.* 6*d.*

ESSAYS FROM "THE TIMES." Being a Selection from the Literary Papers which have appeared in that Journal. *Seventh Thousand.* 2 vols. Fcap. 8vo. 8*s.*

EXETER'S (Bishop of) Letters to the late Charles Butler, on the Theological parts of his Book of the Roman Catholic Church; with Remarks on certain Works of Dr. Milner and Dr. Lingard, and on some parts of the Evidence of Dr. Doyle. *Second Edition.* 8vo. 16*s.*

FAMILY RECEIPT-BOOK. A Collection of a Thousand Valuable and Useful Receipts. Fcap. 8vo. 5*s.* 6*d.*

FARRAR'S (Rev. A. S.) Critical History of Free Thought in reference to the Christian Religion. Being the Bampton Lectures, 1862. 8vo. 16*s.*

———————————— (F. W.) Origin of Language, based on Modern Researches. Fcap. 8vo. 5*s.*

FEATHERSTONHAUGH'S (G. W.) Tour through the Slave States of North America, from the River Potomac to Texas and the Frontiers of Mexico. Plates. 2 Vols. 8vo. 26s.

FERGUSSON'S (JAMES) Palaces of Nineveh and Persepolis Restored. Woodcuts. 8vo. 16s.

———————— History of the Modern Styles of Architecture, completing the above work. With 312 Illustrations. 8vo. 31s. 6d.

FISHER'S (REV. GEORGE) Elements of Geometry, for the Use of Schools. Fifth Edition. 18mo. 1s. 6d.

———————— First Principles of Algebra, for the Use of Schools. Fifth Edition. 18mo. 1s. 6d.

FLOWER GARDEN (THE). By REV. THOS. JAMES. Fcap. 8vo. 1s.

FONNEREAU'S (T. G.) Diary of a Dutiful Son. Fcap. 8vo. 4s. 6d.

FORBES' (C. S.) Iceland; its Volcanoes, Geysers, and Glaciers. Illustrations. Post 8vo. 14s.

FORD'S (RICHARD) Handbook for Spain, Andalusia, Ronda, Valencia, Catalonia, Granada, Gallicia, Arragon, Navarre, &c. Third Edition. 2 Vols. Post 8vo. 30s.

———————— Gatherings from Spain. Post 8vo. 3s. 6d.

FORSTER'S (JOHN) Arrest of the Five Members by Charles the First. A Chapter of English History re-written. Post 8vo. 12s.

———————— Grand Remonstrance, 1641. With an Essay on English freedom under the Plantagenet and Tudor Sovereigns. Second Edition. Post 8vo. 12s.

———————— Oliver Cromwell, Daniel De Foe, Sir Richard Steele, Charles Churchill, Samuel Foote. Third Edition. Post 8vo. 12s.

FORSYTH'S (WILLIAM) Life and Times of Cicero. With Selections from his Correspondence and his Orations. Illustrations. 2 Vols. Post 8vo. 18s.

FORTUNE'S (ROBERT) Narrative of Two Visits to the Tea Countries of China, 1843-52. Third Edition. Woodcuts. 2 Vols. Post 8vo. 18s.

———————— Third Visit to China. 1853-6. Woodcuts. 8vo. 16s.

———————— Yedo and Peking. With Notices of the Agriculture and Trade of Japan and China. Illustrations. 8vo. 16s.

FOSS' (Edward) Judges of England. With Sketches of their Lives, and Notices of the Courts at Westminster, from the Conquest to the Present Time. 9 Vols. 8vo. 114s.

FRANCE (HISTORY OF). From the Conquest by the Gauls to the Death of Louis Philippe. By Mrs. MARKHAM. 56th Thousand. Woodcuts. 12mo. 6s.

———————— (THE STUDENT'S HISTORY OF). From the Earliest Times to the Establishment of the Second Empire, 1852. By W. H. PEARSON. Edited by WM. SMITH, LL.D. Woodcuts. Post 8vo. 7s. 6d.

FRENCH (THE) in Algiers; The Soldier of the Foreign Legion— and the Prisoners of Abd-el-Kadir. Translated by Lady DUFF GORDON. Post 8vo. 2s.

GALTON'S (FRANCIS) Art of Travel ; or, Hints on the Shifts and
Contrivances available in Wild Countries. *Third Edition.* Woodcuts. Post 8vo. 7s. 6d.

GEOGRAPHY (THE STUDENT'S MANUAL OF ANCIENT). By Rev.
W. L. BEVAN. Edited by WM. SMITH, LL.D. Woodcuts. Post 8vo.
7s. 6d.

———————— Journal of the Royal Geographical Society of
London. 8vo.

GERMANY (HISTORY OF). From the Invasion by Marius, to the present time. By Mrs. MARKHAM. *Fifteenth Thousand.* Woodcuts. 12mo. 6s.

GIBBON'S (EDWARD) History of the Decline and Fall of the
Roman Empire. *A New Edition.* Preceded by his Autobiography.
Edited, with Notes, by Dr. WM. SMITH. Maps. 8 Vols. 8vo. 60s.

———————— (The Student's Gibbon) ; Being an Epitome of the
above work, incorporating the Researches of Recent Commentators. By
Dr. WM. SMITH. *Ninth Thousand.* Woodcuts. Post 8vo. 7s. 6d.

GIFFARD'S (EDWARD) Deeds of Naval Daring ; or, Anecdotes of
the British Navy. New Edition. Fcap. 8vo. 3s. 6d.

GOLDSMITH'S (OLIVER) Works. A New Edition. Printed from
the last editions revised by the Author. Edited by PETER CUNNING-
HAM. Vignettes. 4 Vols. 8vo. 30s. (Murray's British Classics.)

GLADSTONE'S (RIGHT HON. W. E.) Financial Statements of 1853,
60, 63, and 64 ; also his Speeches on Tax-Bills, 1861, and on Charities,
1863. *Second Edition.* 8vo. 12s.

———————— Wedgwood : an Address delivered at Burslem.
Woodcuts. Post 8vo. 2s.

GLEIG'S (REV. G. R.) Campaigns of the British Army at Washington and New Orleans. Post 8vo. 2s.

———— Story of the Battle of Waterloo. Post 8vo. 3s. 6d.

———— Narrative of Sale's Brigade in Affghanistan. Post 8vo. 2s.

———— Life of Robert Lord Clive. Post 8vo. 3s. 6d.

———— Life and Letters of Sir Thomas Munro. Post 8vo 3s. 6d.

GORDON'S (SIR ALEX. DUFF) Sketches of German Life, and Scenes
from the War of Liberation. From the German. Post 8vo. 3s. 6d.

———————— (LADY DUFF) Amber-Witch : A Trial for Witchcraft. From the German. Post 8vo. 2s.

———————— French in Algiers. 1. The Soldier of the Foreign
Legion. 2. The Prisoners of Abd-el-Kadir. From the French.
Post 8vo. 2s.

GOUGER'S (HENRY) Personal Narrative of Two Years' Imprisonment in Burmah. *Second Edition.* Woodcuts. Post 8vo. 12s.

GRAMMAR (THE STUDENT'S GREEK.) For Colleges, and the
Upper Forms. By PROFESSOR CURTIUS. Translated under the Revision
of the Author. Edited by WM. SMITH, LL.D. Post 8vo. 7s. 6d.

———————— (THE STUDENT'S LATIN). For Colleges and the
Upper Forms. By WM. SMITH, LL.D, Post 8vo. 7s. 6d.

GREECE (THE STUDENT'S HISTORY OF). From the Earliest
Times to the Roman Conquest. By WM. SMITH, LL.D. Woodcuts. Post 8vo. 7s. 6d.

GRENVILLE (THE) PAPERS. Being the Public and Private
Correspondence of George Grenville, including his PRIVATE DIARY.
Edited by W. J. SMITH. 4 Vols. 8vo. 16s. each.

GREY (EARL) on Parliamentary Government and Reform. A New
Edition, containing Suggestions for the Improvement of our Representative System, and an Examination of the Reform Bills of 1859—61.
8vo. 9s.

GREY'S (SIR GEORGE) Polynesian Mythology, and Ancient
Traditional History of the New Zealand Race. Woodcuts. Post
8vo. 10s. 6d.

GROTE'S (GEORGE) History of Greece. From the Earliest Times
to the close of the generation contemporary with the death of Alexander
the Great. Fourth Edition. Maps. 8 vols. 8vo. 112s.

———— PLATO, and the other Companions of Socrates. 3
Vols. 8vo.

———— (MRS.) Memoir of Ary Scheffer. Post 8vo. 8s. 6d.

———— Collected Papers. 8vo. 10s. 6d.

GUIZOT'S (M.) Meditations on Christianity. Containing 1.
NATURAL PROBLEMS. 2. CHRISTIAN DOGMAS. 3. THE SUPERNATURAL.
4. LIMITS OF SCIENCE. 5. REVELATION. 6. INSPIRATION OF HOLY
SCRIPTURE. 7. GOD ACCORDING TO THE BIBLE. 8. JESUS CHRIST
ACCORDING TO THE GOSPELS. Post 8vo. 9s. 6d.

HALLAM'S (HENRY) Constitutional History of England, from the
Accession of Henry the Seventh to the Death of George the Second.
Seventh Edition. 3 Vols. 8vo. 30s.

———— History of Europe during the Middle Ages.
Tenth Edition. 3 Vols. 8vo. 30s.

———— Literary History of Europe, during the 15th, 16th and
17th Centuries. Fourth Edition. 3 Vols. 8vo. 36s.

———— Literary Essays and Characters. Fcap. 8vo. 2s.

———— Historical Works. Containing History of England,
—Middle Ages of Europe,—Literary History of Europe. 10 Vols.
Post 8vo. 6s each.

———— (ARTHUR) Remains; in Verse and Prose. With Preface, Memoir, and Portrait. Fcap. 8vo. 7s. 6d.

HAMILTON'S (JAMES) Wanderings in North Africa. Post 8vo. 12s.

HART'S ARMY LIST. (Quarterly and Annually.) 8vo. 10s. 6d.
and 21s each.

HANNAH'S (Rev. Dr.) Bampton Lectures for 1863; the Divine
and Human Elements in Holy Scripture. 8vo. 10s. 6d.

HAY'S (J. H. DRUMMOND) Western Barbary, its wild Tribes and
savage Animals. Post 8vo. 2s.

HEAD'S (SIR FRANCIS) Horse and his Rider. Woodcuts. Post 8vo. 5s.

———— Rapid Journeys across the Pampas. Post 8vo. 2s.

———— Bubbles from the Brunnen of Nassau. 16mo. 5s.

———— Emigrant. Fcap. 8vo. 2s. 6d.

———— Stokers and Pokers; or, N.-Western Railway. Post
8vo. 2s.

———— Fortnight in Ireland. Map. 8vo. 12s.

———— (SIR EDMUND) Shall and Will; or, Future Auxiliary
Verbs. Fcap. 8vo. 4s.

HAND-BOOK—TRAVEL-TALK. English, German, French, and Italian. 18mo. 3s. 6d.

———————— NORTH GERMANY, HOLLAND, BELGIUM, and the Rhine to Switzerland. Map. Post 8vo. 10s.

———————— KNAPSACK GUIDE TO BELGIUM AND THE RHINE. Post 8vo. (In the Press.)

———————— SOUTH GERMANY, Bavaria, Austria, Styria, Salzberg, the Austrian and Bavarian Alps, the Tyrol, Hungary, and the Danube, from Ulm to the Black Sea. Map. Post 8vo. 10s.

———————— KNAPSACK GUIDE TO THE TYROL. Post 8vo. (In the Press.)

———————— PAINTING. German, Flemish, and Dutch Schools. Edited by DR. WAAGEN. Woodcuts. 2 Vols. Post 8vo. 24s.

———————— LIVES OF THE EARLY FLEMISH PAINTERS, with Notices of their Works. By CROWE and CAVALCASELLE. Illustrations. Post 8vo. 12s.

———————— SWITZERLAND, Alps of Savoy, and Piedmont. Maps. Post 8vo. 9s.

———————— KNAPSACK GUIDE TO SWITZERLAND. Post 8vo. 5s.

———————— FRANCE, Normandy, Brittany, the French Alps, the Rivers Loire, Seine, Rhone, and Garonne, Dauphiné, Provence, and the Pyrenees. Maps. Post 8vo. 10s.

———————— KNAPSACK GUIDE TO FRANCE. Post 8vo. (In the Press.)

———————— PARIS AND ITS ENVIRONS. Map. Post 8vo. 5s.

———————— SPAIN, Andalusia, Ronda, Granada, Valencia, Catalonia, Gallicia, Arragon, and Navarre. Maps. 2 Vols. Post 8vo. 30s.

———————— PORTUGAL, LISBON, &c. Map. Post 8vo.

———————— NORTH ITALY, Piedmont, Liguria, Venetia, Lombardy, Parma, Modena, and Romagna. Map. Post 8vo. 12s.

———————— CENTRAL ITALY, Lucca, Tuscany, Florence, The Marches, Umbria, and the Patrimony of St. Peter's. Map. Post 8vo. 10s.

———————— ROME AND ITS ENVIRONS. Map. Post 8vo. 9s.

———————— SOUTH ITALY, Two Sicilies, Naples, Pompeii, Herculaneum, and Vesuvius. Map. Post 8vo. 10s.

———————— KNAPSACK GUIDE TO ITALY. Post 8vo. 6s.

———————— SICILY, Palermo, Messina, Catania, Syracuse, Etna, and the Ruins of the Greek Temples. Map. Post 8vo. 12s.

———————— PAINTING. The Italian Schools. From the German of KUGLER. Edited by Sir CHARLES EASTLAKE, R.A. Woodcuts. 2 Vols. Post 8vo. 30s.

———————— LIVES OF THE EARLY ITALIAN PAINTERS, AND PROGRESS OF PAINTING IN ITALY, from CIMABUE to BASSANO. By Mrs. JAMESON. Woodcuts. Post 8vo. 12s.

HAND-BOOK—DICTIONARY OF ITALIAN PAINTERS. By A LADY. Edited by RALPH WORNUM. With a Chart. Post 8vo. 6s. 6d.

———————— GREECE, the Ionian Islands, Albania, Thessaly, and Macedonia. Maps. Post 8vo. 15s.

———————— TURKEY, Malta, Asia Minor, Constantinople, Armenia, Mesopotamia, &c. Maps. Post 8vo. (*In the Press.*)

———————— EGYPT, Thebes, the Nile, Alexandria, Cairo, the Pyramids, Mount Sinai, &c. Map. Post 8vo. 15s.

———————— SYRIA & PALESTINE, Peninsula of Sinai, Edom, and Syrian Desert. Maps. 2 Vols. Post 8vo. 24s.

———————— BOMBAY AND MADRAS. Map. 2 Vols. Post 8vo. 24s.

———————— NORWAY. Map. Post 8vo. 5s.

———————— DENMARK, SWEDEN and NORWAY. Maps. Post 8vo. 15s.

———————— RUSSIA, THE BALTIC AND FINLAND. Maps. Post 8vo. 12s.

———————— MODERN LONDON. A Complete Guide to all the Sights and Objects of Interest in the Metropolis. Map. 16mo. 3s. 6d.

———————— WESTMINSTER ABBEY. Woodcuts. 16mo. 1s.

———————— KENT AND SUSSEX, Canterbury, Dover, Ramsgate, Sheerness, Rochester, Chatham, Woolwich, Brighton, Chichester, Worthing, Hastings, Lewes, Arundel, &c. Map. Post 8vo. 10s.

———————— SURREY, HANTS, Kingston, Croydon, Reigate, Guildford, Winchester, Southampton, Portsmouth, and Isle of Wight. Maps. Post 8vo. 7s. 6d.

———————— BERKS, BUCKS, AND OXON, Windsor, Eton, Reading, Aylesbury, Uxbridge, Wycombe, Henley, the City and University of Oxford, and the Descent of the Thames to Maidenhead and Windsor. Map. Post 8vo. 7s. 6d.

———————— WILTS, DORSET, AND SOMERSET, Salisbury, Chippenham, Weymouth, Sherborne, Wells, Bath, Bristol, Taunton, &c. Map. Post 8vo. 7s. 6d.

———————— DEVON AND CORNWALL, Exeter, Ilfracombe, Linton, Sidmouth, Dawlish, Teignmouth, Plymouth, Devonport, Torquay, Launceston, Truro, Penzance, Falmouth, &c. Maps. Post 8vo. 7s. 6d.

———————— NORTH AND SOUTH WALES, Bangor, Carnarvon, Beaumaris, Snowdon. Conway, Menai Straits, Carmarthen, Pembroke, Tenby, Swansea, The Wye, &c. Maps. 2 Vols. Post 8vo. 12s.

———————— CATHEDRALS OF ENGLAND—Southern Division, Winchester, Salisbury, Exeter, Wells, Chichester, Rochester, Canterbury. With 110 Illustrations. 2 Vols. Crown 8vo. 24s.

———————— CATHEDRALS OF ENGLAND—Eastern Division, Oxford, Peterborough, Norwich, Ely, and Lincoln. With 90 Illustrations. Crown 8vo. 18s.

———————— CATHEDRALS OF ENGLAND—Western Division, Bristol, Gloucester, Hereford, Worcester, and Lichfield. With 50 Illustrations. Crown 8vo. 16s.

———————— FAMILIAR QUOTATIONS. From English Authors. *Third Edition.* Fcap. 8vo. 5s.

HEBER'S (BISHOP) Journey through India. *Twelfth Edition.* 2 Vols. Post 8vo. 7s.

———— Poetical Works. *Sixth Edition.* Portrait. Fcap. 8vo. 6s.

HERODOTUS. A New English Version. Edited, with Notes and Essays, historical, ethnographical, and geographical. By Rev. G. RAWLINSON, assisted by SIR HENRY RAWLINSON and SIR J. G. WILKINSON. *Second Edition.* Maps and Woodcuts. 4 Vols. 8vo. 48s.

HESSEY (REV. DR.). Sunday—Its Origin, History, and Present Obligations. Being the Bampton Lectures for 1860. *Second Edition.* 8vo. 16s.

HICKMAN'S (WM.) Treatise on the Law and Practice of Naval Courts-Martial. 8vo. 10s. 6d.

HILLARD'S (G. S.) Six Months in Italy. 2 Vols. Post 8vo. 16s.

HOLLWAY'S (J. G.) Month in Norway. Fcap. 8vo. 2s.

HONEY BEE (THE). An Essay. By REV. THOMAS JAMES. Reprinted from the "Quarterly Review." Fcap. 8vo. 1s.

HOOK'S (DEAN) Church Dictionary. *Ninth Edition.* 8vo. 16s.

———— (THEODORE)Life. By J. G. LOCKHART. Reprinted from the "Quarterly Review." Fcap. 8vo. 1s.

HOOKER'S (Dr. J. D.) Himalayan Journals; or, Notes of an Oriental Naturalist in Bengal, the Sikkim and Nepal Himalayas, the Khasia Mountains, &c. *Second Edition.* Woodcuts. 2 Vols. Post 8vo. 18s.

HOPE'S (A. J. BERESFORD) English Cathedral of the Nineteenth Century. With Illustrations. 8vo. 12s.

HORACE (Works of). Edited by DEAN MILMAN. With 300 Woodcuts. Crown 8vo. 21s.

———— (Life of). By DEAN MILMAN. Woodcuts, and coloured Borders. 8vo. 9s.

HUME'S (THE STUDENT'S) History of England, from the Invasion of Julius Cæsar to the Revolution of 1688. Corrected and continued to 1858. Edited by Dr. Wm. Smith. Woodcuts. Post 8vo. 7s. 6d.

HUTCHINSON (GEN.) on the most expeditious, certain, and easy Method of Dog-Breaking. *Fourth Edition.* Enlarged and revised, with additional Illustrations. Crown 8vo.

HUTTON'S (H. E.) Principia Græca; an Introduction to the Study of Greek. Comprehending Grammar, Delectus, and Exercise-book, with Vocabularies. *Third Edition.* 12mo. 3s. 6d.

c

HOME AND COLONIAL LIBRARY. A Series of Works adapted for all circles and classes of Readers, having been selected for their acknowledged interest and ability of the Authors. Post 8vo. Published at 2s. and 3s. 6d. each, and arranged under two distinctive heads as follows :—

CLASS A.

HISTORY, BIOGRAPHY, AND HISTORIC TALES.

1. SIEGE OF GIBRALTAR. By JOHN DRINKWATER. 2s.

2. THE AMBER-WITCH. By LADY DUFF GORDON. 2s.

3. CROMWELL AND BUNYAN. By ROBERT SOUTHEY. 2s.

4. LIFE OF SIR FRANCIS DRAKE. By JOHN BARROW. 2s.

5. CAMPAIGNS AT WASHINGTON. By REV. G. R. GLEIG. 2s.

6. THE FRENCH IN ALGIERS. By LADY DUFF GORDON. 2s.

7. THE FALL OF THE JESUITS. 2s.

8. LIVONIAN TALES. 2s.

9. LIFE OF CONDE. By LORD MAHON. 3s. 6d.

10. SALE'S BRIGADE. By REV. G. R. GLEIG. 2s.

11. THE SIEGES OF VIENNA. By LORD ELLESMERE. 2s.

12. THE WAYSIDE CROSS. By CAPT. MILMAN. 2s.

13. SKETCHES OF GERMAN LIFE. By SIR A. GORDON. 3s. 6d.

14. THE BATTLE OF WATERLOO. By REV. G. R. GLEIG. 3s. 6d.

15. AUTOBIOGRAPHY OF STEFFENS. 2s.

16. THE BRITISH POETS. By THOMAS CAMPBELL. 3s. 6d.

17. HISTORICAL ESSAYS. By LORD MAHON. 3s. 6d.

18. LIFE OF LORD CLIVE. By REV. G. R. GLEIG. 3s. 6d.

19. NORTH - WESTERN RAILWAY. By SIR F. B. HEAD. 2s.

20. LIFE OF MUNRO. By REV. G. R. GLEIG. 3s. 6d.

CLASS B.

VOYAGES, TRAVELS, AND ADVENTURES.

1. BIBLE IN SPAIN. By GEORGE BORROW. 3s. 6d.

2. GIPSIES OF SPAIN. By GEORGE BORROW. 3s. 6d.

3 & 4. JOURNALS IN INDIA. By BISHOP HEBER. 2 Vols. 7s.

5. TRAVELS IN THE HOLY LAND. By IRBY and MANGLES. 2s.

6. MOROCCO AND THE MOORS. By J. DRUMMOND HAY. 2s.

7. LETTERS FROM THE BALTIC. By a LADY. 2s.

8. NEW SOUTH WALES. By MRS. MEREDITH. 2s.

9. THE WEST INDIES. By M. G. LEWIS. 2s.

10. SKETCHES OF PERSIA. By SIR JOHN MALCOLM. 3s. 6d.

11. MEMOIRS OF FATHER RIPA. 2s.

12. 13. TYPEE AND OMOO. By HERMANN MELVILLE. 2 Vols. 7s.

14. MISSIONARY LIFE IN CANADA. By REV. J. ABBOTT. 2s.

15. LETTERS FROM MADRAS. By a LADY. 2s.

16. HIGHLAND SPORTS. By CHARLES ST. JOHN. 3s. 6d.

17. PAMPAS JOURNEYS. By SIR F. B. HEAD. 2s.

18. GATHERINGS FROM SPAIN. By RICHARD FORD. 3s. 6d.

19. THE RIVER AMAZON. By W. H. EDWARDS. 2s.

20. MANNERS & CUSTOMS OF INDIA. By REV. C. ACLAND. 2s.

21. ADVENTURES IN MEXICO. By G. F. RUXTON. 3s. 6d.

22. PORTUGAL AND GALLICIA. By LORD CARNARVON. 3s. 6d.

23. BUSH LIFE IN AUSTRALIA. By Rev. H. W. HAYGARTH. 2s.

24. THE LIBYAN DESERT. By BAYLE ST. JOHN. 2s.

25. SIERRA LEONE. By a LADY. 3s. 6d.

*** Each work may be had separately.

IRBY AND MANGLES' Travels in Egypt, Nubia, Syria, and the Holy Land. Post 8vo. 2s.

JAMES' (Rev. Thomas) Fables of Æsop. A New Translation, with Historical Preface. With 100 Woodcuts by Tenniel and Wolf. *Thirty-eighth Thousand.* Post 8vo. 2s. 6d.

JAMESON'S (Mrs.) Lives of the Early Italian Painters, from Cimabue to Bassano, and the Progress of Painting in Italy. *New Edition.* With Woodcuts. Post 8vo. 12s.

JESSE'S (Edward) Gleanings in Natural History. *Eighth Edition.* Fcp. 8vo. 6s.

JOHNSON'S (Dr. Samuel) Life. By James Boswell. Including the Tour to the Hebrides. Edited by the late Mr. Croker. Portraits. Royal 8vo. 10s.

———— Lives of the most eminent English Poets. Edited by Peter Cunningham. 3 vols. 8vo. 22s. 6d. (Murray's British Classics.)

JOURNAL OF A NATURALIST. Woodcuts. Post 8vo. 9s. 6d.

KEN'S (Bishop) Life. By A Layman. *Second Edition.* Portrait. 2 Vols. 8vo. 18s.

———— Exposition of the Apostles' Creed. Extracted from his "Practice of Divine Love." Fcap. 1s. 6d.

———— Approach to the Holy Altar. Extracted from his "Manual of Prayer" and "Practice of Divine Love." Fcap. 8vo. 1s. 6d.

KING'S (Rev. S. W.) Italian Valleys of the Alps; a Tour through all the Romantic and less-frequented "Vals" of Northern Piedmont. Illustrations. Crown 8vo. 18s.

———— (Rev. C. W.) Antique Gems; their Origin, Use, and Value, as Interpreters of Ancient History, and as illustrative of Ancient Art. Illustrations. 8vo. 42s.

KING EDWARD VIth's Latin Grammar; or, an Introduction to the Latin Tongue, for the Use of Schools. *Sixteenth Edition.* 12mo. 3s. 6d.

———————————— First Latin Book; or, the Accidence, Syntax, and Prosody, with an English Translation for the Use of Junior Classes. *Fourth Edition.* 12mo. 2s. 6d.

KIRK'S (J. Foster) History of Charles the Bold, Duke of Burgundy. Portrait. 2 Vols. 8vo. 30s.

KERR'S (Robert) GENTLEMAN'S HOUSE; or, How to Plan English Residences, from the Parsonage to the Palace. With Tables of Accommodation and Cost, and a Series of Selected Views and Plans. 8vo. 21s.

c 2

KUGLER'S Italian Schools of Painting. Edited, with Notes, by Sir Charles Eastlake. *Third Edition.* Woodcuts. 2 Vols. Post 8vo. 30s.

———— German, Dutch, and Flemish Schools of Painting. Edited, with Notes, by Dr. Waagen. *Second Edition.* Woodcuts. 2 Vols. Post 8vo. 24s.

LANGUAGE (The English). A Series of Lectures. By George P. Marsh. Edited, with additional Chapters and Notes, by Wm. Smith, LL.D. Post 8vo. 7s. 6d.

LATIN GRAMMAR (King Edward VIth's). For the Use of Schools. *Sixteenth Edition.* 12mo. 3s. 6d.

———— First Book (King Edward VIth's); or, the Accidence, Syntax, and Prosody, with English Translation for Junior Classes. *Fourth Edition.* 12mo. 2s. 6d.

LAYARD'S (A. H.) Nineveh and its Remains. Being a Narrative of Researches and Discoveries amidst the Ruins of Assyria. With an Account of the Chaldean Christians of Kurdistan; the Yezedis, or Devil-worshippers; and an Enquiry into the Manners and Arts of the Ancient Assyrians. *Sixth Edition.* Plates and Woodcuts. 2 Vols. 8vo. 36s.

———————— Nineveh and Babylon; being the Result of a Second Expedition to Assyria. *Fourteenth Thousand.* Plates 8vo. 21s. Or *Fine Paper,* 2 Vols. 8vo. 30s.

———— Popular Account of Nineveh. 15th *Edition.* With Woodcuts. Post 8vo. 5s.

LEAKE'S (Col.) Topography of Athens, with Remarks on its Antiquities. *Second Edition.* Plates. 2 Vols. 8vo. 30s.

———— Travels in Northern Greece. Maps. 4 Vols. 8vo. 60s.

———— Disputed Questions of Ancient Geography. Map. 8vo. 6s. 6d.

———— Numismata Hellenica, and Supplement. Completing descriptive Catalogue of Twelve Thousand Greek Coins, with Notes Geographical and Historical. With Map and Appendix. 4to. 63s.

———— Peloponnesiaca. 8vo. 15s.

———— Degradation of Science in England. 8vo. 3s. 6d.

LESLIE'S (C. R.) Handbook for Young Painters. With Illustrations. Post 8vo. 10s. 6d.

———————— Autobiographical Recollections, with Selections from his Correspondence. Edited by Tom Taylor. Portrait. 2 Vols. Post 8vo. 18s.

———————— Life of Sir Joshua Reynolds. With an Account of his Works, and a Sketch of his Cotemporaries. By Tom Taylor. Illustrations. 2 Vols. 8vo.

LETTERS FROM THE SHORES OF THE BALTIC. By a Lady. Post 8vo. 2s.

———————— Madras. By a Lady. Post 8vo. 2s.

———————— Sierra Leone. By a Lady. Edited by the Honourable Mrs. Norton. Post 8vo. 3s. 6d.

LEWIS' (Sir G. C.) Essay on the Government of Dependencies. 8vo. 12s.

———— Glossary of Provincial Words used in Herefordshire and some of the adjoining Counties. 12mo. 4s. 6d.

———— (M. G.) Journal of a Residence among the Negroes in the West Indies. Post 8vo. 2s.

LIDDELL'S (Dean) History of Rome. From the Earliest Times to the Establishment of the Empire. With the History of Literature and Art. 2 Vols. 8vo. 28s.

———— Student's History of Rome. Abridged from the above Work. 25th Thousand. With Woodcuts. Post 8vo. 7s. 6d.

LINDSAY'S (Lord) Lives of the Lindsays; or, a Memoir of the Houses of Crawfurd and Balcarres. With Extracts from Official Papers and Personal Narratives. Second Edition. 3 Vols. 8vo. 24s.

————Report of the Claim of James, Earl of Crawfurd and Balcarres, to the Original Dukedom of Montrose, created in 1488 Folio. 15s.

———— Scepticism; a Retrogressive Movement in Theology and Philosophy. 8vo. 9s.

LISPINGS from LOW LATITUDES; or, the Journal of the Hon. Impulsia Gushington. Edited by Lord Dufferin. With 24 Plates, 4to. 21s.

LITERATURE ⅂ (English). A Manual for Students. By T. B. Shaw. Edited, with Notes and Illustrations, by Wm. Smith, LL.D. Post 8vo. 7s. 6d.

————(Choice Specimens of). Selected from the Chief English Writers. By Thos. 'B. Shaw, M.A. Edited by Wm. Smith, LL.D. Post 8vo. 7s. 6d.

LITTLE ARTHUR'S HISTORY OF ENGLAND. By Lady Callcott. 120th Thousand. With 20 Woodcuts. Fcap. 8vo. 2s. 6d.

LIVINGSTONE'S (Rev. Dr.) Popular Account of his Missionary Travels in South Africa. Illustrations. Post 8vo. 6s.

———— Narrative of an Expedition to the Zambezi and its Tributaries; and of the Discovery of Lakes Shirwa and Nyassa. 1858-64. By David and Charles Livingstone. Map and Illustrations. 8vo.

LIVONIAN TALES. By the Author of "Letters from the Baltic." Post 8vo. 2s.

LOCKHART'S (J. G.) Ancient Spanish Ballads. Historical and Romantic. Translated, with Notes. Illustrated Edition. 4to. 21s. Or, Popular Edition, Post 8vo. 2s. 6d.

———— Life of Robert Burns. Fifth Edition. Fcap. 8vo. 3s.

LONDON'S (Bishop of) Dangers and Safeguards of Modern Theology. Containing Suggestions to the Theological Student under present difficulties. Second Edition. 8vo. 9s.

LOUDON'S (Mrs.) Instructions in Gardening for Ladies. With Directions and Calendar of Operations for Every Month. Eighth Edition. Woodcuts. Fcap. 8vo. 5s.

LUCAS' (SAMUEL) Secularia; or, Surveys on the Main Stream of History. 8vo. 12s.

LUCKNOW : a Lady's Diary of the Siege. *Fourth Thousand.* Fcap. 8vo. 4s. 6d.

LYELL'S (SIR CHARLES) Elements of Geology; or, the Ancient Changes of the Earth and its Inhabitants considered as illustrative of Geology. *Sixth Edition.* Woodcuts. 8vo. 18s.

———— Geological Evidences of the Antiquity of Man. *Third Edition.* Illustrations. 8vo. 14s.

LYTTELTON'S (LORD) Ephemera. Post 8vo. 10s. 6d.

LYTTON'S (SIR EDWARD BULWER) Poems. *New Edition.* Revised. Post 8vo. 10s. 6d.

MAHON'S (LORD) History of England, from the Peace of Utrecht to the Peace of Versailles, 1713—83. *Library Edition.* 7 Vols. 8vo. 93s. *Popular Edition,* 7 Vols. Post 8vo. 35s.

———— " Forty-Five ; " a Narrative of the Rebellion in Scotland. Post 8vo. 3s.

———— History of British India from its Origin till the Peace of 1783. Post 8vo. 3s. 6d.

———— Spain under Charles the Second; 1690 to 1700. *Second Edition.* Post 8vo. 6s. 6d.

———— Life of William Pitt, with Extracts from his MS. Papers. *Second Edition.* Portraits. 4 Vols. Post 8vo. 42s.

———— Condé, surnamed the Great. Post 8vo. 3s. 6d.

———— Belisarius. *Second Edition.* Post 8vo. 10s. 6d.

———— Historical and Critical Essays. Post 8vo. 3s. 6d.

———— Miscellanies. *Second Edition.* Post 8vo. 5s. 6d.

———— Story of Joan of Arc. Fcap. 8vo. 1s.

———— Addresses. Fcap. 8vo. 1s.

M<sup>c</sup>CLINTOCK'S (CAPT. SIR F. L.) Narrative of the Discovery of the Fate of Sir John Franklin and his Companions in the Arctic Seas. *Twelfth Thousand.* Illustrations. 8vo. 16s.

M<sup>c</sup>CULLOCH'S (J. R.) Collected Edition of RICARDO's Political Works. With Notes and Memoir. *Second Edition.* 8vo. 16s.

MACDOUGALL (COL.) On Modern Warfare as Influenced by Modern Artillery. With Plans. Post 8vo. 12s.

MAINE (H. SUMNER) On Ancient Law : its Connection with the Early History of Society, and its Relation to Modern Ideas. *Second Edition.* 8vo. 12s.

MALCOLM'S (SIR JOHN) Sketches of Persia. *Third Edition.* Post 8vo. 3s. 6d.

MANSEL (REV. H. L.) Limits of Religious Thought Examined. Being the Bampton Lectures for 1858. *Fourth Edition.* Post 8vo. 7s. 6d.

MANSFIELD (SIR WILLIAM) On the Introduction of a Gold Currency into India : a Contribution to the Literature of Political Economy. 8vo. 3s. 6d.

MANTELL'S (GIDEON A.) Thoughts on Animalcules; or, the Invisible World, as revealed by the Microscope. *Second Edition.* Plates. 16mo. 6s.

MANUAL OF SCIENTIFIC ENQUIRY, Prepared for the Use of Officers and Travellers. By various Writers. Edited by Sir J. F. HERSCHEL and Rev. R. MAIN. *Third Edition.* Maps. Post 8vo. 9s. *(Published by order of the Lords of the Admiralty.)*

MARKHAM'S (MRS.) History of England. From the First Invasion by the Romans, down to the fourteenth year of Queen Victoria's Reign. 156th *Edition.* Woodcuts. 12mo. 6s.

———— History of France. From the Conquest by the Gauls, to the Death of Louis Philippe. *Sixtieth Edition.* Woodcuts. 12mo. 6s.

———— History of Germany. From the Invasion by Marius, to the present time. *Fifteenth Edition.* Woodcuts. 12mo. 6s.

———— History of Greece. From the Earliest Times to the Roman Conquest. By Dr. WM. SMITH. Woodcuts. 16mo. 3s. 6d.

———— History of Rome. From the Earliest Times to the Establishment of the Empire. By DR. WM. SMITH. Woodcuts. 16mo. 3s. 6d.

———— (CLEMENTS, R.) Travels in Peru and India, for the purpose of collecting Cinchona Plants, and introducing Bark into India. Maps and Illustrations. 8vo. 16s.

MARKLAND'S (J. H.) Reverence due to Holy Places. *Third Edition.* Fcap. 8vo. 2s.

MARRYAT'S (JOSEPH) History of Modern and Mediæval Pottery and Porcelain. With a Description of the Manufacture. *Second Edition.* Plates and Woodcuts. 8vo. 31s. 6d.

———— (HORACE) Jutland, the Danish Isles, and Copenhagen. Illustrations. 2 Vols. Post 8vo. 24s.

———— Sweden and Isle of Gothland. Illustrations. 2 Vols. Post 8vo. 28s.

MATTHIÆ'S (AUGUSTUS) Greek Grammar for Schools. Abridged from the Larger Grammar. By Blomfield. *Ninth Edition.* Revised by EDWARDS. 12mo. 3s.

MAUREL'S (JULES) Essay on the Character, Actions, and Writings of the Duke of Wellington. *Second Edition.* Fcap. 8vo. 1s. 6d.

MAXIMS AND HINTS on Angling and Chess. By RICHARD PENN. Woodcuts. 12mo. 1s.

MAYNE'S (R. C.) Four Years in British Columbia and Vancouver Island. Its Forests, Rivers, Coasts, and Gold Fields, and Resources for Colonisation. Illustrations. 8vo. 16s.

MELVILLE'S (HERMANN) Typee and Omoo; or, Adventures amongst the Marquesas and South Sea Islands. 2 Vols. Post 8vo. 7s.

MEREDITH'S (MRS. CHARLES) Notes and Sketches of New South Wales. Post 8vo. 2s.

MESSIAH (THE): A Narrative of the Life, Travels, Death, Resurrection, and Ascension of our Blessed Lord. By a Layman. Author of the " Life of Bishop Ken." Map. 8vo. 18s.

MICHIE'S (Alexander) Siberian Overland Route from Peking to Petersburg, through the Deserts and Steppes of Mongolia, Tartary, &c. Maps and Illustrations. 8vo. 16s.

MILLS' (Arthur) India in 1858 ; A Summary of the Existing Administration. Second Edition. Map. 8vo. 10s. 6d.

———— (Rev. John) Three Months' Residence at Nablus, with an Account of the Modern Samaritans. Illustrations. Post 8vo. 10s. 6d.

MILMAN'S (Dean) History of the Jews, from the Earliest Period, brought down to Modern Times. New Edition. 3 Vols. 8vo. 36s.

———— Christianity, from the Birth of Christ to the Abolition of Paganism in the Roman Empire. New Edition. 3 Vols. 8vo. 36s.

———— Latin Christianity; including that of the Popes to the Pontificate of Nicholas V. New Edition. 9 Vols. 8vo 84s.

———— Character and Conduct of the Apostles considered as an Evidence of Christianity. 8vo. 10s. 6d.

———— Life and Works of Horace. With 300 Woodcuts. 2 Vols. Crown 8vo. 30s.

———— Poetical Works. Plates. 3 Vols. Fcap. 8vo. 18s.

———— Fall of Jerusalem. Fcap. 8vo. 1s.

———— (Capt. E. A.) Wayside Cross. A Tale of the Carlist War. Post 8vo. 2s.

MILNES' (R. Monckton, Lord Houghton) Poetical Works. Fcap. 8vo. 6s.

MODERN DOMESTIC COOKERY. Founded on Principles of Economy and Practical Knowledge and adapted for Private Families. New Edition. Woodcuts. Fcap. 8vo. 5s.

MOORE'S (Thomas) Life and Letters of Lord Byron. Plates. 6 Vols. Fcap: 8vo. 18s.

———— Life and Letters of Lord Byron. Portraits. Royal 8vo. 9s.

MOTLEY'S (J. L.) History of the United Netherlands : from the Death of William the Silent to the Synod of Dort. Embracing the English-Dutch struggle against Spain; and a detailed Account of the Spanish Armada. Portraits. 2 Vols. 8vo. 30s.

MOUHOT'S (Henri) Siam, Cambojia, and Lao ; a Narrative of Travels and Discoveries. Illustrations. 2 vols. 8vo. 32s.

MOZLEY'S (Rev. J. B.) Treatise on Predestination. 8vo. 14s.

———— Primitive Doctrine of Baptismal Regeneration. 8vo. 7s. 6d.

MUNDY'S (GENERAL) Pen and Pencil Sketches in India. *Third Edition.* Plates. Post 8vo. 7s. 6d.

——————— (ADMIRAL) Account of the Italian Revolution, with Notices of Garibaldi, Francis II., and Victor Emmanuel. Post 8vo. 12s.

MUNRO'S (GENERAL SIR THOMAS) Life and Letters. By the REV. G. R. GLEIG. Post 8vo. 3s. 6d.

MURCHISON'S (SIR RODERICK) Russia in Europe and the Ural Mountains. With Coloured Maps, Plates, Sections, &c. 2 Vols. Royal 4to.

——————— Siluria ; or, a History of the Oldest Rocks containing Organic Remains. *Third Edition.* Map and Plates. 8vo. 42s.

MURRAY'S RAILWAY READING. Containing :—

WELLINGTON. By LORD ELLESMERE. 6d.	HALLAM'S LITERARY ESSAYS. 2s.
NIMROD ON THE CHASE. 1s.	MAHON'S JOAN OF ARC. 1s.
ESSAYS FROM "THE TIMES." 2 Vols. 8s.	HEAD'S EMIGRANT. 2s. 6d.
MUSIC AND DRESS. 1s.	NIMROD ON THE ROAD. 1s.
LAYARD'S ACCOUNT OF NINEVEH. 5s.	CROKER ON THE GUILLOTINE. 1s.
MILMAN'S FALL OF JERUSALEM. 1s.	HOLLWAY'S NORWAY. 2s.
MAHON'S "FORTY-FIVE." 3s.	MAUREL'S WELLINGTON. 1s. 6d.
LIFE OF THEODORE HOOK. 1s.	CAMPBELL'S LIFE OF BACON. 2s. 6d.
DEEDS OF NAVAL DARING. 3s. 6d.	THE FLOWER GARDEN. 1s.
THE HONEY BEE. 1s.	LOCKHART'S SPANISH BALLADS. 2s. 6d.
JAMES' ÆSOP'S FABLES. 2s. 6d.	TAYLOR'S NOTES FROM LIFE. 2s.
NIMROD ON THE TURF. 1s. 6d.	REJECTED ADDRESSES. 1s.
ART OF DINING. 1s. 6d.	PENN'S HINTS ON ANGLING. 1s.

MUSIC AND DRESS. By a LADY. Reprinted from the " Quarterly Review." Fcap. 8vo. 1s.

NAPIER'S (SIR WM.) English Battles and Sieges of the Peninsular War. *Third Edition.* Portrait. Post 8vo. 10s. 6d.

——————— Life and Letters. Edited by H. A. BRUCE, M.P. Portraits. 2 Vols. Crown 8vo. 28s.

——————— Life of General Sir Charles Napier; chiefly derived from his Journals and Letters. *Second Edition.* Portraits. 4 Vols. Post 8vo. 48s.

NAUTICAL ALMANACK. Royal 8vo. 2s. 6d. (*By Authority.*)

NAVY LIST. (*Published Quarterly, by Authority.*) 16mo. 2s. 6d.

NEW TESTAMENT (THE) Illustrated by a Plain Explanatory Commentary, and authentic Views of Sacred Places, from Sketches and Photographs. Edited by ARCHDEACON CHURTON and REV. BASIL JONES. With 110 Illustrations. 2 Vols. Crown 8vo.

NEWDEGATE'S (C. N.) Customs' Tariffs of all Nations; collected and arranged up to the year 1855. 4to. 30s.

NICHOLLS' (SIR GEORGE) History of the English, Irish and Scotch Poor Laws. 4 Vols. 8vo.

——————— (Rev. H. G.) Historical Account of the Forest of Dean. Woodcuts, &c. Post 8vo. 10s. 6d.

——————— Personalities of the Forest of Dean, its successive Officials, Gentry, and Commonalty. Post 8vo. 3s. 6d.

NICOLAS' (Sir Harris) Historic Peerage of England. Exhibiting the Origin, Descent, and Present State of every Title of Peerage which has existed in this Country since the Conquest. By WILLIAM COURTHOPE. 8vo. 30s.

NIMROD On the Chace—The Turf—and The Road. Reprinted from the "Quarterly Review." Woodcuts. Fcap. 8vo. 3s. 6d.

O'CONNOR'S (R.) Field Sports of France; or, Hunting, Shooting, and Fishing on the Continent. Woodcuts. 12mo. 7s. 6d.

OXENHAM'S (Rev. W.) English Notes for Latin Elegiacs; designed for early Proficients in the Art of Latin Versification, with Prefatory Rules of Composition in Elegiac Metre. Fourth Edition. 12mo. 3s. 6d.

PARIS' (Dr.) Philosophy in Sport made Science in Earnest; or, the First Principles of Natural Philosophy inculcated by aid of the Toys and Sports of Youth. Ninth Edition. Woodcuts. Post 8vo. 7s. 6d.

PEEL'S (Sir Robert) Memoirs. Edited by Earl Stanhope and Mr. Cardwell. 2 Vols. Post 8vo. 7s. 6d. each.

PENN'S (Richard) Maxims and Hints for an Angler and Chessplayer. New Edition. Woodcuts. Fcap. 8vo. 1s.

PENROSE'S (F. C.) Principles of Athenian Architecture, and the Optical Refinements exhibited in the Construction of the Ancient Buildings at Athens, from a Survey. With 40 Plates. Folio. 5l. 5s.

PERCY'S (John, M.D.) Metallurgy of Iron and Steel; or, the Art of Extracting Metals from their Ores and adapting them to various purposes of Manufacture. Illustrations. 8vo. 42s.

PHILLIPP (Charles Spencer March) On Jurisprudence. 8vo. 12s.

PHILLIPS' (John) Memoirs of William Smith, the Geologist. Portrait. 8vo. 7s. 6d.

———— Geology of Yorkshire, The Coast, and Limestone District. Plates. 4to. Part I., 20s.—Part II., 30s.

———— Rivers, Mountains, and Sea Coast of Yorkshire. With Essays on the Climate, Scenery, and Ancient Inhabitants. Second Edition, Plates. 8vo. 15s.

PHILPOTT'S (Bishop) Letters to the late Charles Butler, on the Theological parts of his "Book of the Roman Catholic Church;" with Remarks on certain Works of Dr. Milner and Dr. Lingard, and on some parts of the Evidence of Dr. Doyle. Second Edition. 8vo. 16s.

POPE'S (Alexander) Life and Works. A New Edition. Containing nearly 500 unpublished Letters. Edited with a New Life, Introductions and Notes. By Rev. Whitwell Elwin. Portraits. 8vo. (In the Press.)

PORTER'S (Rev. J. L.) Five Years in Damascus. With Travels to Palmyra, Lebanon and other Scripture Sites. Map and Woodcuts. 2 Vols. Post 8vo. 21s.

———— Handbook for Syria and Palestine: including an Account of the Geography, History, Antiquities, and Inhabitants of these Countries, the Peninsula of Sinai, Edom, and the Syrian Desert. Maps. 2 Vols. Post 8vo. 24s.

PRAYER-BOOK (The Illustrated), with 1000 Illustrations of Borders, Initials, Vignettes, &c. Medium 8vo. 18s. cloth; 31s. 6d. calf; 36s. morrocco.

PRECEPTS FOR THE CONDUCT OF LIFE. Extracted from the Scriptures. *Second Edition.* Fcap. 8vo. 1s.

PUSS IN BOOTS. With 12 Illustrations. By OTTO SPECKTER. Coloured, 16mo. 2s. 6d.

QUARTERLY REVIEW (THE). 8vo. 6s.

RAMBLES in Syria among the Turkomans and Bedaweens. Post 8vo. 10s. 6d.

RAWLINSON'S (REV. GEORGE) Herodotus. A New English Version. Edited with Notes and Essays. Assisted by SIR HENRY RAWLINSON and SIR J. G. WILKINSON. *Second Edition.* Maps and Woodcut. 4 Vols. 8vo. 48s.

———————— Historical Evidences of the truth of the Scripture Records stated anew. *Second Edition.* 8vo. 14s.

———————— Five Great Monarchies of the Ancient World. Illustrations. 4 Vols. 8vo. 16s. each.

Vols. I.—II., Chaldæa and Assyria. Vols. III.—IV., Babylon, Media, and Persia.

REJECTED ADDRESSES (THE). By JAMES AND HORACE SMITH. Fcap. 8vo. 1s., or *Fine Paper*, Portrait, fcap. 8vo. 5s.

RENNIE'S (D. F.) British Arms in Peking, 1860; Kagosima, 1862. Post 8vo. 12s.

———————— Pekin and the Pekinese : Narrative of a Residence at the British Embassy. Illustrations. 2 Vols. Post 8vo.

REYNOLDS' (SIR JOSHUA) His Life and Times. Commenced by C. R. LESLIE, R.A., and continued by TOM TAYLOR. Portraits and Illustrations. 2 Vols. 8vo.

RICARDO'S (DAVID) Political Works. With a Notice of his Life and Writings. By J. R. M'CULLOCH. *New Edition.* 8vo. 16s.

RIPA'S (FATHER) Memoirs during Thirteen Years' Residence at the Court of Peking. From the Italian. Post 8vo. 2s.

ROBERTSON'S (CANON) History of the Christian Church, from the Apostolic Age to the Concordat of Worms, A.D. 1123. *Second Edition.* 3 Vols. 8vo. 38s.

ROBINSON'S (REV. DR.) Biblical Researches in the Holy Land. Being a Journal of Travels in 1838 and 1852. Maps. 3 Vols. 8vo. 45s.

———————— Physical Geography of the Holy Land. Post 8vo. 10s. 6d.

ROME (THE STUDENT'S HISTORY OF). FROM THE EARLIEST TIMES TO THE ESTABLISHMENT OF THE EMPIRE. By DEAN LIDDELL. Woodcuts. Post 8vo. 7s. 6d.

ROWLAND'S (DAVID) Manual of the English Constitution; Its Rise, Growth, and Present State. Post 8vo. 10s. 6d.

———————— Laws of Nature the Foundation of Morals. Post 8vo

RUNDELL'S (MRS.) Domestic Cookery, adapted for Private Families. *New Edition.* Woodcuts. Fcap. 8vo. 5s.

RUSSELL'S (J. RUTHERFURD, M.D.) Art of Medicine—Its History and its Heroes. Portraits. 8vo. 14s.

RUXTON'S (GEORGE F.) Travels in Mexico; with Adventures among the Wild Tribes and Animals of the Prairies and Rocky Mountains. Post 8vo. 3s. 6d.

SALE'S (SIR ROBERT) Brigade in Affghanistan. With an Account of the Defence of Jellalabad. By REV. G. R. GLEIG. Post 8vo. 2s.

SANDWITH'S (HUMPHRY) Siege of Kars. Post 8vo. 3s. 6d.

SCOTT'S (G. GILBERT) Secular and Domestic Architecture, Present and Future. Second Edition. 8vo. 9s.

———— (Master of Baliol) University Sermons Post 8vo. 8s. 6d.

SCROPE'S (G. P.) Geology and Extinct Volcanoes of Central France. Second Edition. Illustrations. Medium 8vo. 30s.

SELF-HELP. With Illustrations of Character and Conduct. By SAMUEL SMILES. 50th Thousand. Post 8vo. 6s.

SENIOR'S (N. W.) Suggestions on Popular Education. 8vo. 9s.

SHAFTESBURY (LORD CHANCELLOR); Memoirs of his Early Life. With his Letters, &c. By W. D. CHRISTIE. Portrait. 8vo. 10s. 6d.

SHAW'S (T. B.) Student's Manual of English Literature. Edited, with Notes and Illustrations, by DR. WM. SMITH. Post 8vo. 7s. 6d.

———— Choice Specimens of English Literature. Selected from the Chief English Writers. Edited by WM. SMITH, LL.D. Post 8vo. 7s. 6d.

SIERRA LEONE; Described in Letters to Friends at Home. By A LADY. Post 8vo. 3s. 6d.

SIMMONS on Courts-Martial. 5th Edition. 8vo. 14s.

SMILES' (SAMUEL) Lives of British Engineers; from the Earliest Period to the Death of Robert Stephenson; with an account of their Principal Works, and a History of Inland Communication in Britain. Portraits and Illustrations. 3 Vols. 8vo. 63s.

———— George and Robert Stephenson; the Story of their Lives. With Portraits and 70 Woodcuts. Post 8vo. 6s.

———— James Brindley and the Early Engineers. With Portrait and 50 Woodcuts. Post 8vo. 6s.

———— Self-Help. With Illustrations of Character and Conduct. Post 8vo. 6s.

———— Industrial Biography: Iron-Workers and Tool Makers. A companion volume to "Self-Help." Post 8vo. 6s.

———— Workmen's Earnings—Savings—and Strikes. Fcap. 8vo. 1s. 6d.

SOMERVILLE'S (MARY) Physical Geography. Fifth Edition. Portrait. Post 8vo. 9s.

———————— Connexion of the Physical Sciences. Ninth Edition. Woodcuts. Post 8vo. 9s.

SOUTH'S (JOHN F.) Household Surgery; or, Hints on Emergencies. Seventeenth Thousand. Woodcuts. Fcp. 8vo. 4s. 6d.

SMITH'S (DR. WM.) Dictionary of the Bible; its Antiquities, Biography, Geography, and Natural History. Illustrations. 3 Vols. 8vo. 105s.

———— Greek and Roman Antiquities. 2nd Edition. Woodcuts. 8vo. 42s.

———————— Biography and Mythology. Woodcuts. 3 Vols. 8vo. 5l. 15s. 6d.

———————— Geography. Woodcuts. 2 Vols. 8vo. 80s.

———— Classical Dictionary of Mythology, Biography, and Geography, compiled from the above. With 750 Woodcuts. 8vo. 18s.

———— Latin-English Dictionary. 3rd Edition. Revised. 8vo. 21s.

———— Smaller Classical Dictionary. Woodcuts. Crown 8vo. 7s. 6d.

————————Dictionary of Antiquities. Woodcuts. Crown 8vo. 7s. 6d.

———————— Latin-English Dictionary. 12mo. 7s. 6d.

———— Latin-English Vocabulary; for Phædrus, Cornelius Nepos, and Cæsar. 2nd Edition. 12mo. 3s. 6d.

———— Principia Latina—Part I. A Grammar, Delectus, and Exercise Book, with Vocabularies. 6th Edition. 12mo. 3s. 6d.

———————— Part II. A Reading-book of Mythology, Geography, Roman Antiquities, and History. With Notes and Dictionary. 3rd Edition. 12mo. 3s. 6d.

———————— Part III. A Latin Poetry Book. Hexameters and Pentameters; Eclogæ Ovidianæ; Latin Prosody, &c. 2nd Edition. 12mo. 3s. 6d.

———————— Part IV. Latin Prose Composition. Rules of Syntax, with Examples, Explanations of Synonyms, and Exercises on the Syntax. Second Edition. 12mo. 3s. 6d.

———— Student's Greek Grammar. By Professor CURTIUS. Post 8vo. 7s. 6d.

———————— Latin Grammar. Post 8vo. 7s. 6d.

———————— Latin Grammar. Abridged from the above. 12mo. 3s. 6d.

———— Smaller Greek Grammar. Abridged from Curtius. 12mo. 3s. 6d.

STANLEY'S (DEAN) Sinai and Palestine, in Connexion with their History. Map. 8vo. 16s.

———————— Bible in the Holy Land. Woodcuts. Fcap. 8vo. 2s. 6d.

———— St. Paul's Epistles to the Corinthians. 8vo. 18s.

———— Eastern Church. Plans. 8vo. 12s.

———— Jewish Church. Vol. 1. ABRAHAM TO SAMUEL. Plans. 8vo. 16s.

———————— Vol. 2. SAMUEL TO THE CAPTIVITY. 8vo. 16s.

———— Historical Memorials of Canterbury. Woodcuts. Post 8vo. 7s. 6d.

———— Sermons in the East, with Notices of the Places Visited. 8vo. 9s.

————Sermons on Evangelical and Apostolical Teaching. Post 8vo. 7s. 6d.

———— ADDRESSES AND CHARGES OF BISHOP STANLEY. With Memoir. 8vo. 10s. 6d.

SOUTHEY'S (ROBERT) Book of the Church. *Seventh Edition.* Post 8vo. 7s. 6d.

———— Lives of Bunyan and Cromwell. Post 8vo. 2s.

SPECKTER'S (OTTO) Puss in Boots. With 12 Woodcuts. Square 12mo. 1s. 6d. plain, or 2s. 6d. coloured.

———— Charmed Roe; or, the Story of the Little Brother and Sister. Illustrated. 16mo.

ST. JOHN'S (CHARLES) Wild Sports and Natural History of the Highlands. Post 8vo. 3s. 6d.

———— (BAYLE) Adventures in the Libyan Desert and the Oasis of Jupiter Ammon. Woodcuts. Post 8vo. 2s.

STANHOPE'S (EARL) Life of William Pitt. With Extracts from his M.S. Papers. *Second Edition.* Portraits. 4 Vols. Post 8vo. 42s.

———— Miscellanies. *Second Edition.* Post 8vo. 5s. 6d.

STEPHENSON (GEORGE and ROBERT). The Story of their Lives. By SAMUEL SMILES. With Portraits and 70 Illustrations. Post 8vo. 6s.

STUDENT'S HUME. A History of England from the Invasion of Julius Cæsar to the Revolution of 1688. By DAVID HUME, and continued to 1858. Woodcuts. Post 8vo. 7s. 6d.
*** A Smaller History of England. 12mo. 3s. 6d.

———— HISTORY OF FRANCE; from the Earliest Times to the Establishment of the Second Empire, 1852. By W. H. PEARSON, M.A. Woodcuts. Post 8vo. 7s. 6d.

———— HISTORY OF GREECE; from the Earliest Times to the Roman Conquest. With the History of Literature and Art. By WM. SMITH, LL.D. Woodcuts. Crown 8vo. 7s. 6d. (Questions. 2s.)
*** A SMALLER HISTORY OF GREECE. 12mo. 3s. 6d.

———— HISTORY OF ROME; from the Earliest Times to the Establishment of the Empire. With the History of Literature and Art. By Dean LIDDELL. Woodcuts. Crown 8vo. 7s. 6d.
*** A SMALLER HISTORY OF ROME. 12mo. 3s. 6d.

———— GIBBON; an Epitome of the History of the Decline and Fall of the Roman Empire. By EDWARD GIBBON. Incorporating the Researches of Recent Commentators. Woodcuts. Post 8vo. 7s. 6d.

———— MANUAL OF ANCIENT GEOGRAPHY. By Rev. W. L. BEVAN, M.A. Woodcuts. Post 8vo. 7s. 6d.

———— ENGLISH LANGUAGE. By GEORGE P. MARSH. Post 8vo. 7s. 6d.

———— ENGLISH LITERATURE. By T. B. SHAW, M.A. Post 8vo. 7s. 6d.

———— SPECIMENS OF ENGLISH LITERATURE. Selected from the Chief Writers. By THOMAS B. SHAW, M.A. Post 8vo. 7s. 6d.

STOTHARD'S (Thos.) Life. With Personal Reminiscences.
By Mrs. Bray. With Portrait and 60 Woodcuts. 4to. 21s.

STREET'S (G. E.) Gothic Architecture in Spain. From Personal
Observations during several journeys through that country. Illustrations. Medium 8vo.

————— Brick and Marble Architecture of Italy in the
Middle Ages. Plates. 8vo. 21s.

SWIFT'S (Jonathan) Life, Letters, Journals, and Works. By
John Forster. 8vo. (In Preparation.)

SYME'S (Professor) Principles of Surgery. 5th Edition. 8vo. 12s.

TAIT'S (Bishop) Dangers and Safeguards of Modern Theology.
8vo. 9s.

TAYLOR'S (Henry) Notes from Life. Fcap. 8vo. 2s.

THOMSON'S (Archbishop) Lincoln's Inn Sermons. 8vo. 10s. 6d.

THREE-LEAVED MANUAL OF FAMILY PRAYER; arranged
so as to save the trouble of turning the Pages backwards and forwards.
Royal 8vo. 2s.

TRANSACTIONS OF THE ETHNOLOGICAL SOCIETY OF
LONDON. New Series. Vols. I. and II. 8vo.

TREMENHEERE'S (H. S.) Political Experience of the Ancients,
in its bearing on Modern Times. Fcap. 8vo. 2s. 6d.

TRISTRAM (H. B.). The Great Sahara. Wanderings South of the
Atlas Mountains. Map and Illustrations. Post 8vo. 15s.

TWISS' (Horace) Public and Private Life of Lord Chancellor Eldon,
with Selections from his Correspondence. Portrait. Third Edition.
2 Vols. Post 8vo. 21s.

TYLOR'S (E. B.) Researches into the Early History of Mankind,
and the Development of Civilization. Illustrations. 8vo.

TYNDALL'S (John) Glaciers of the Alps. With an account of
Three Years' Observations and Experiments on their General Phe-
nomena. Woodcuts. Post 8vo. 14s.

TYTLER'S (Patrick Fraser) Memoirs. By Rev. J. W. Burgon,
M.A. 8vo. 9s.

VAUGHAN'S (Rev. Dr.) Sermons preached in Harrow School.
8vo. 10s. 6d.

VENABLES' (Rev. R. L.) Domestic Scenes in Russia. Post 8vo. 5s.

WAAGEN'S (Dr.) Treasures of Art in Great Britain. Being an
Account of the Chief Collections of Paintings, Sculpture, Manuscripts,
Miniatures, &c. &c., in this Country. Obtained from Personal Inspec-
tion during Visits to England. 4 Vols. 8vo.

WALSH'S (Sir John) Practical Results of the Reform Bill of
1832. 8vo. 5s. 6d.

VAMBERY'S (Arminius) Travels in Central Asia, from Teheran
across the Turkoman Desert, on the Eastern Shore of the Caspian to
Khiva, Bokhara, and Samarcand in 1863. Map and Illustrations. 8vo. 21s.

WELLINGTON'S (The Duke of) Despatches during his various Campaigns. Compiled from Official and other Authentic Documents. By Col. Gurwood, C.B. 8 Vols. 8vo. 21s. each.

——————————— Supplementary Despatches, and other Papers. Edited by his Son. Vols. I. to XII. 8vo. 20s. each.

——————————— Selections from his Despatches and General Orders. By Colonel Gurwood. 8vo. 18s.

——————————— Speeches in Parliament. 2 Vols. 8vo. 42s.

WILKINSON'S (Sir J. G.) Popular Account of the Private Life, Manners, and Customs of the Ancient Egyptians. *New Edition.* Revised and Condensed. With 500 Woodcuts. 2 Vols. Post 8vo. 12s.

——————————— Handbook for Egypt.—Thebes, the Nile, Alexandria, Cairo, the Pyramids, Mount Sinai, &c. Map. Post 8vo. 15s.

——————————— (G. B.) Working Man's Handbook to South Australia; with Advice to the Farmer, and Detailed Information for the several Classes of Labourers and Artisans. Map. 18mo. 1s. 6d.

WILSON'S (Bishop Daniel) Life, with Extracts from his Letters and Journals. By Rev. Josiah Bateman. *Second Edition.* Illustrations. Post 8vo. 9s.

——————————— (Genl. Sir Robert) Secret History of the French Invasion of Russia, and Retreat of the French Army, 1812. *Second Edition.* 8vo. 15s.

——————————— Private Diary of Travels, Personal Services, and Public Events, during Missions and Employments in Spain, Sicily, Turkey, Russia, Poland, Germany, &c. 1812-14. 2 Vols. 8vo. 26s.

——————————— Autobiographical Memoirs. Containing an Account of his Early Life down to the Peace of Tilsit. Portrait. 2 Vols. 8vo. 26s.

WORDSWORTH'S (Canon) Journal of a Tour in Athens and Attica. *Third Edition.* Plates. Post 8vo. 8s. 6d.

——————————— Pictorial, Descriptive, and Historical Account of Greece, with a History of Greek Art, by G. Scharf, F.S.A. *New Edition.* With 600 Woodcuts. Royal 8vo. 28s.

WORNUM (Ralph). A Biographical Dictionary of Italian Painters : with a Table of the Contemporary Schools of Italy. By a Lady. Post 8vo. 6s. 6d.